X-MEN

PRELUDE TO ONSLAUGHT

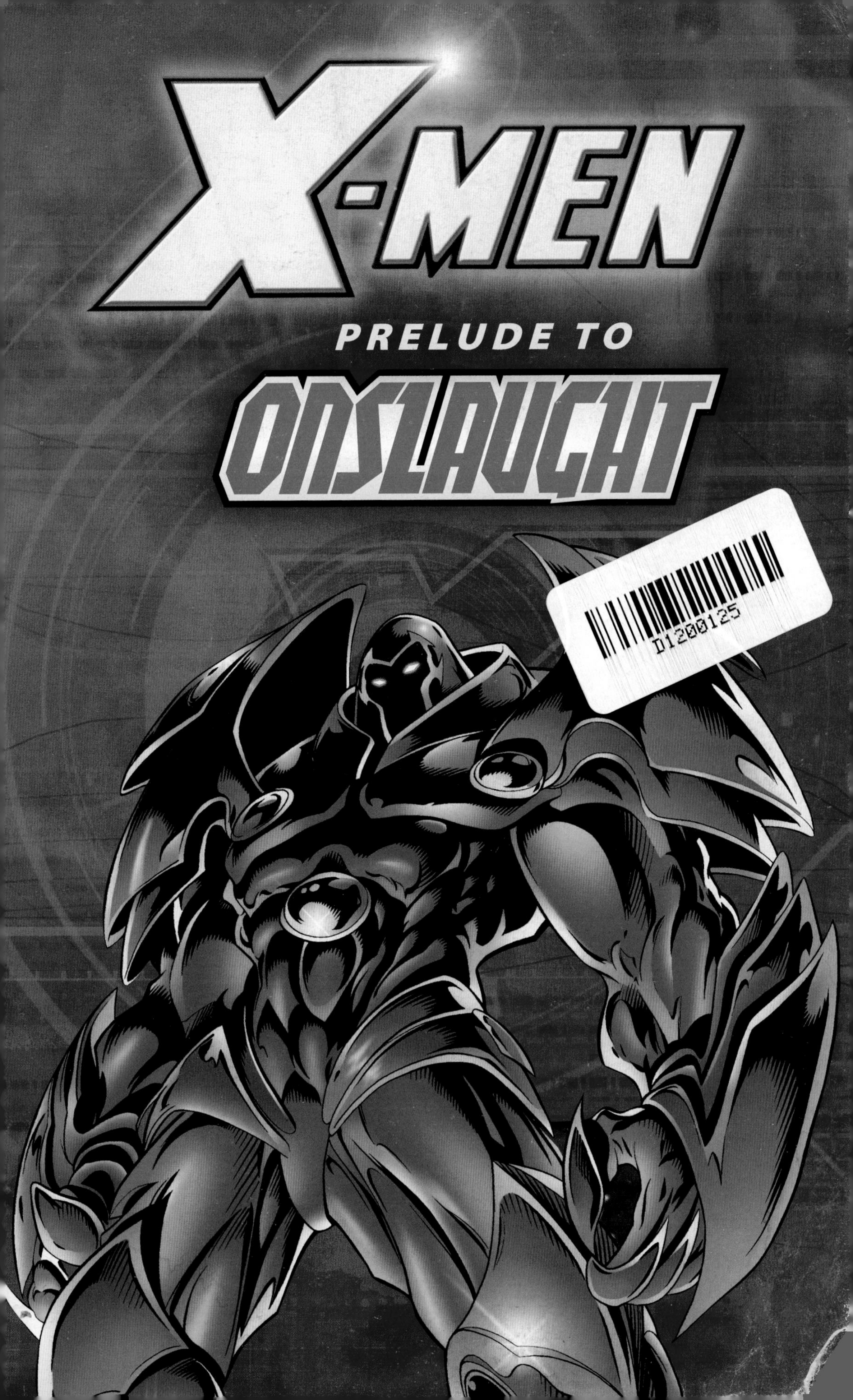

X-MEN

PRELUDE TO

ONSLAUGHT

Writers:
Scott Lobdell, Jeph Loeb & Terry Kavanagh
with John Ostrander, Jim Lee, Fabian Nicieza, Larry Hama,
Mark Waid, Todd Dezago & Warren Ellis

Pencilers:
Andy Kubert, Ian Churchill, Pasqual Ferry, Steve Skroce, Val Semeiks
& Rick Leonardi with John Romita Jr., Tom Grummett, Adam Kubert,
Jeff Matsuda, Adam Pollina, Nick Gnazzo, Bryan Hitch, Mike S. Miller,
Steve Epting & Casey Jones

Inkers:
Cam Smith, Scott Hanna, Tim Townsend, Rob Hunter, Mark Morales,
David Hunt & Bud LaRosa with Scott Williams, Chris Ivy,
Bill Sienkiewicz, Dan Panosian, Bob Wiacek, Matt Ryan, Ian Akin,
Dan Green, Mark Pennington, Al Milgrom, Art Thibert, Paul Neary,
Mike Sellers, Scott Koblish, Harry Candelario & Tom Simmons

Colorists:
Joe Rosas & Electric Crayon, Steve Buccellato & Team Bucce, and
Mike Thomas & Graphic Color Works and Malibu with Gina Going,
Matt Webb, Kevin Somers, Marie Javins, Christie Scheele,
Ariane Lenshoek & Digital Chameleon

Letterers:
Richard Starkings & Comicraft with Tom Orzechowski & Bill Oakley

Editors:
Bob Harras, Mark Powers & Jaye Gardner
with Lisa Patrick, Kelly Corvese & Suzanne Gaffney

Cover Art: Andy Kubert
Cover Colors: John Kalisz

Collection Editor: Jeph York
Assistant Editor: Alex Starbuck
Editors, Special Projects: Mark D. Beazley & Jennifer Grünwald
Senior Editor, Special Projects: Jeff Youngquist
Senior Vice President of Sales: David Gabriel
Book Designer: Michael Chatham
Production: ColorTek & Ryan Devall
Editor in Chief: Joe Quesada
Publisher: Dan Buckley
Executive Producer: Alan Fine

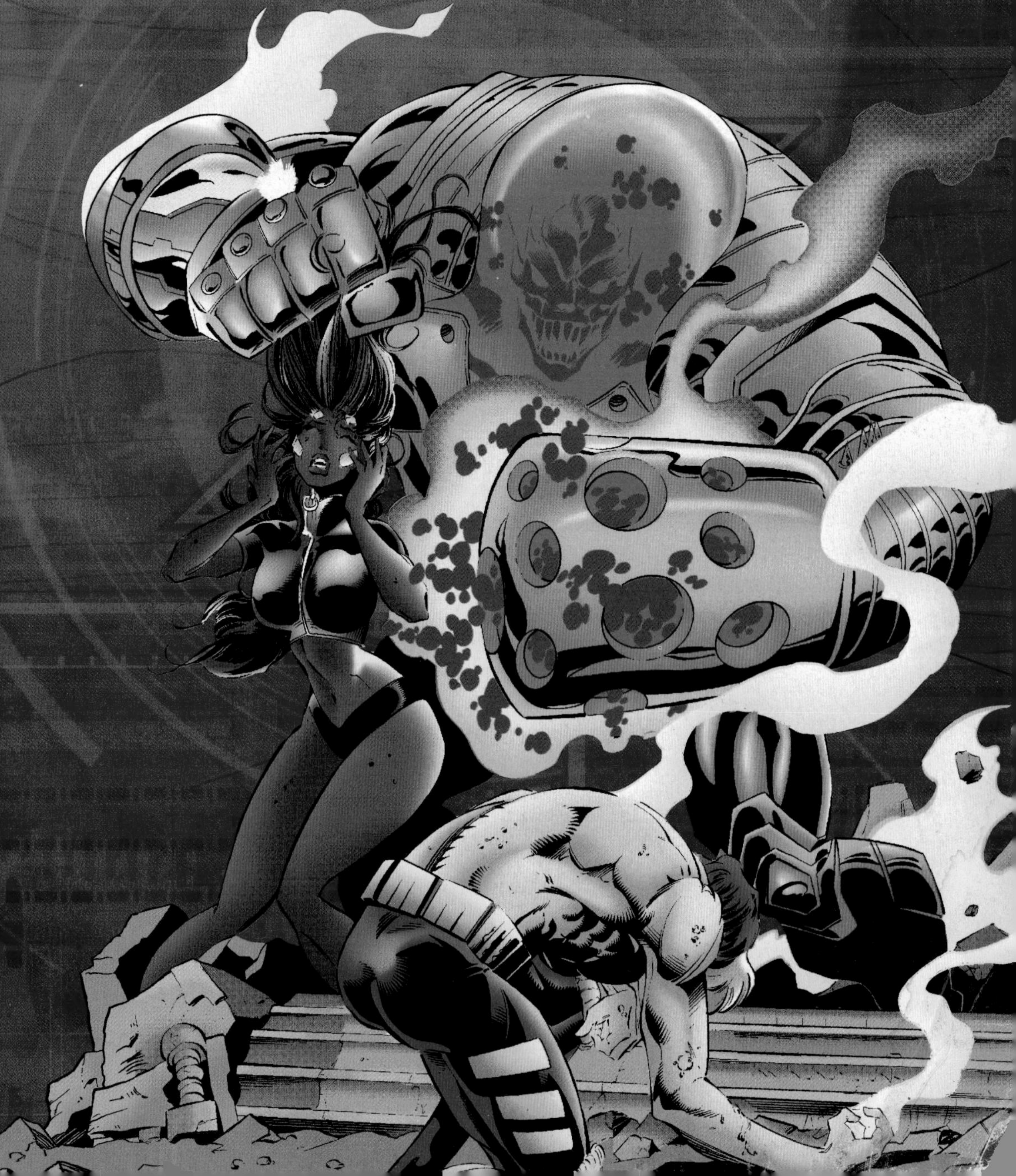

MARVEL COMICS
THE UNCANNY
X-MEN
$1.25 US
$1.50 CAN/UK 70p
287
APR
...AND TWO MUST FALL!

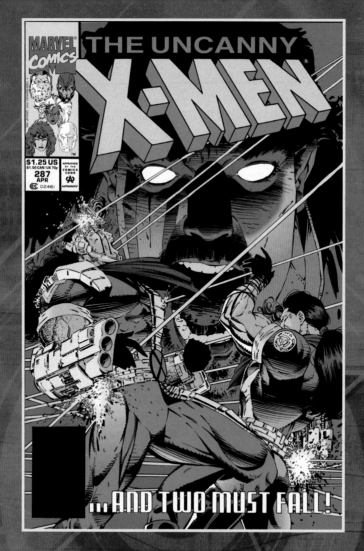

ONSLAUGHT!

Onslaught! The villainous name reverberated loudly across the landscape of the Marvel Universe in the 1990s. Onslaught was everywhere – and before he was defeated, he decimated New York City, inflicted the deepest wounds that the X-Men had suffered in years – and was responsible for the seeming deaths of the Avengers and the Fantastic Four!

The X-Men had heard Onslaught's name whispered, known of his dark threat for months before his arrival. They tried vainly to plan for Onslaught's inevitable strike, suffering attacks from his minions as he watched from the shadows – but they knew nothing of their mysterious foe.

How did Onslaught come to be? What were his dark origins – and how did he plot his rise to power? The riddle of Onslaught's past begins in the future: approximately eighty years from now, when Bishop, a mutant policeman in a dystopian world, pursued a fugitive with his partners – and stumbled across a disturbing recording...

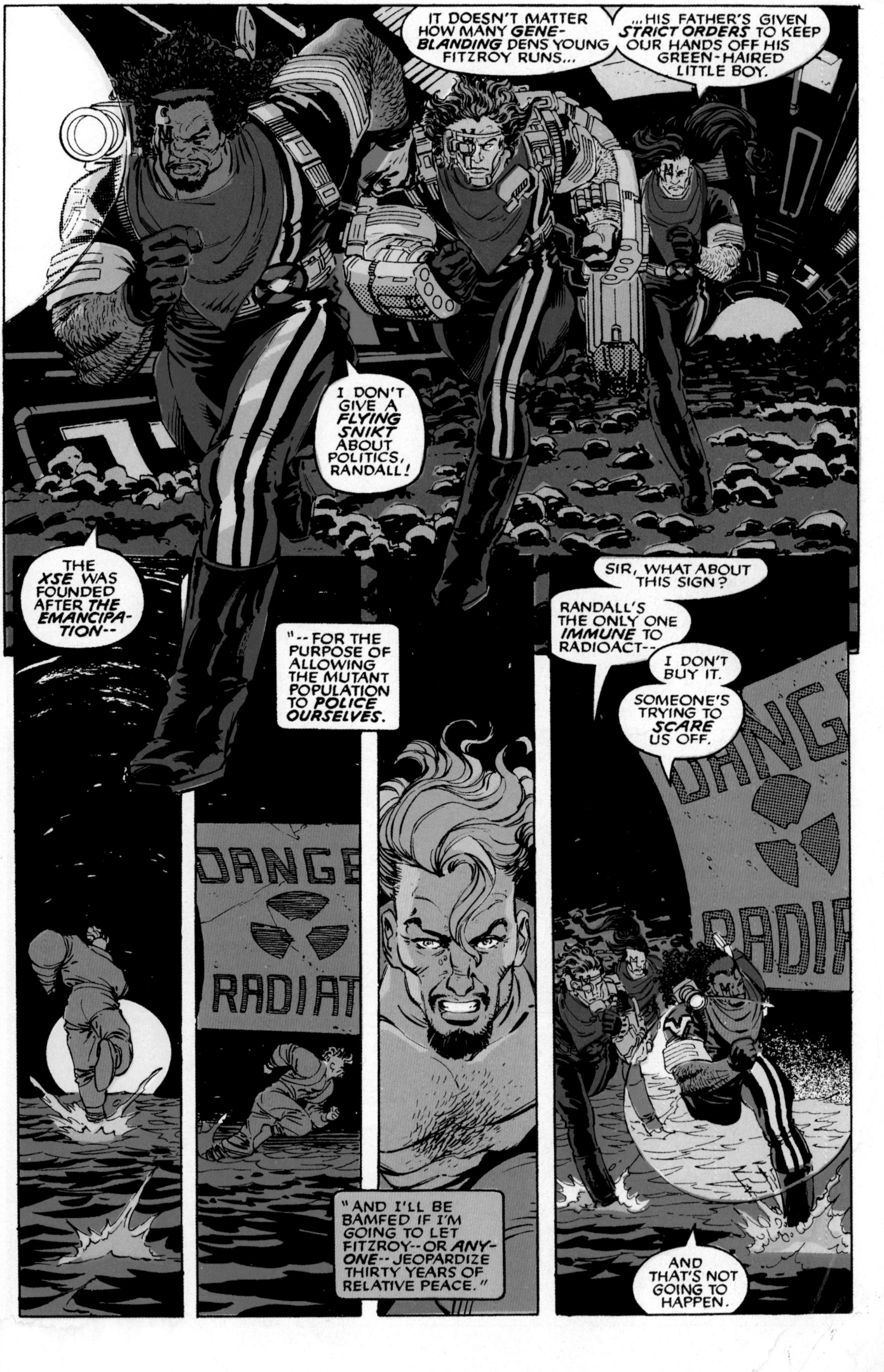
IT DOESN'T MATTER HOW MANY GENE-BLANDING DENS YOUNG FITZROY RUNS...
...HIS FATHER'S GIVEN STRICT ORDERS TO KEEP OUR HANDS OFF HIS GREEN-HAIRED LITTLE BOY.
I DON'T GIVE A FLYING SNIKT ABOUT POLITICS, RANDALL!
THE XSE WAS FOUNDED AFTER THE EMANCIPATION--
"--FOR THE PURPOSE OF ALLOWING THE MUTANT POPULATION TO POLICE OURSELVES.
DANGE
RADIAT
"AND I'LL BE BAMFED IF I'M GOING TO LET FITZROY--OR ANYONE--JEOPARDIZE THIRTY YEARS OF RELATIVE PEACE."
SIR, WHAT ABOUT THIS SIGN?
RANDALL'S THE ONLY ONE IMMUNE TO RADIOACT--
I DON'T BUY IT.
SOMEONE'S TRYING TO SCARE US OFF.
DANG
RADIA
AND THAT'S NOT GOING TO HAPPEN.

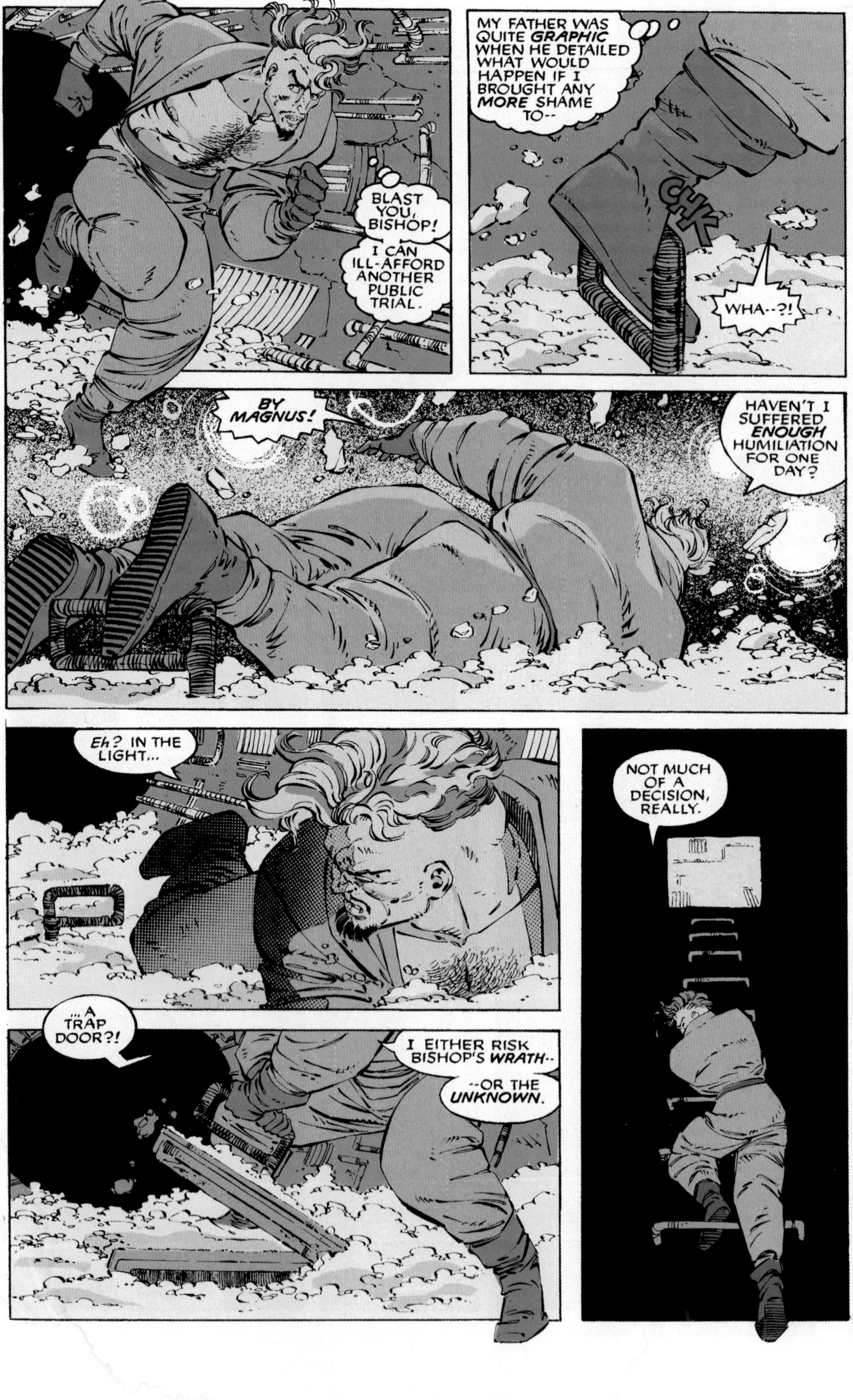
BLAST YOU, BISHOP!
I CAN ILL-AFFORD ANOTHER PUBLIC TRIAL.
MY FATHER WAS QUITE GRAPHIC WHEN HE DETAILED WHAT WOULD HAPPEN IF I BROUGHT ANY MORE SHAME TO--
CHK
WHA--?!
BY MAGNUS!
HAVEN'T I SUFFERED ENOUGH HUMILIATION FOR ONE DAY?
Eh? IN THE LIGHT...
...A TRAP DOOR?!
I EITHER RISK BISHOP'S WRATH--
--OR THE UNKNOWN.
NOT MUCH OF A DECISION, REALLY.

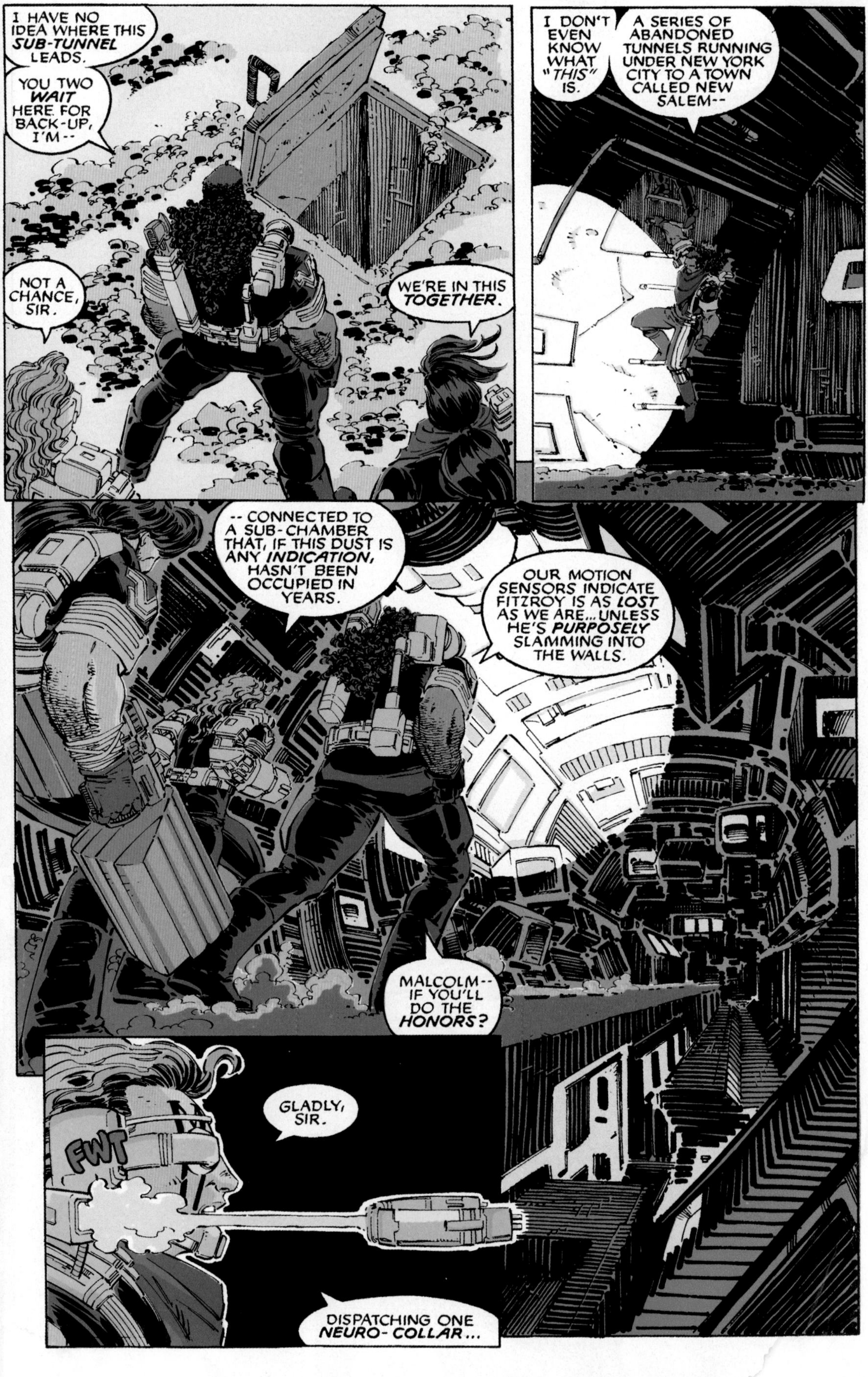

I HAVE NO IDEA WHERE THIS SUB-TUNNEL LEADS.
YOU TWO WAIT HERE FOR BACK-UP, I'M --
NOT A CHANCE, SIR.
WE'RE IN THIS TOGETHER.
I DON'T EVEN KNOW WHAT "THIS" IS.
A SERIES OF ABANDONED TUNNELS RUNNING UNDER NEW YORK CITY TO A TOWN CALLED NEW SALEM--
-- CONNECTED TO A SUB-CHAMBER THAT, IF THIS DUST IS ANY INDICATION, HASN'T BEEN OCCUPIED IN YEARS.
OUR MOTION SENSORS INDICATE FITZROY IS AS LOST AS WE ARE... UNLESS HE'S PURPOSELY SLAMMING INTO THE WALLS.
MALCOLM-- IF YOU'LL DO THE HONORS?
GLADLY, SIR.
FWT
DISPATCHING ONE NEURO-COLLAR...

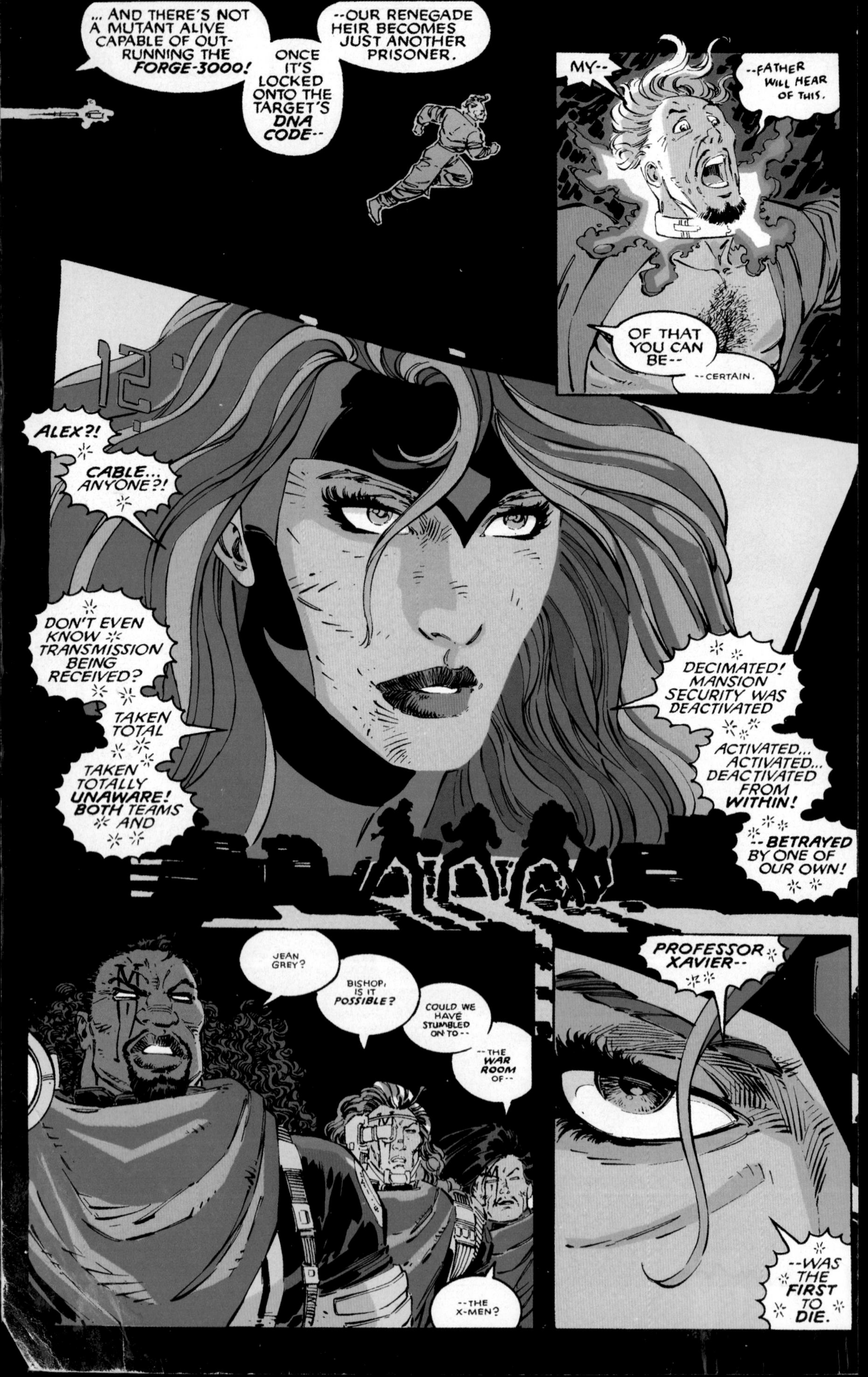

... AND THERE'S NOT A MUTANT ALIVE CAPABLE OF OUT-RUNNING THE FORGE-3000!
--OUR RENEGADE HEIR BECOMES JUST ANOTHER PRISONER.
ONCE IT'S LOCKED ONTO THE TARGET'S DNA CODE--
MY--
--FATHER WILL HEAR OF THIS.
OF THAT YOU CAN BE--
--CERTAIN.
ALEX?!
CABLE... ANYONE?!
DON'T EVEN KNOW TRANSMISSION BEING RECEIVED?
TAKEN TOTAL
TAKEN TOTALLY UNAWARE! BOTH TEAMS AND
DECIMATED! MANSION SECURITY WAS DEACTIVATED
ACTIVATED... ACTIVATED... DEACTIVATED FROM WITHIN!
--BETRAYED BY ONE OF OUR OWN!
JEAN GREY?
BISHOP, IS IT POSSIBLE?
COULD WE HAVE STUMBLED ON TO--
--THE WAR ROOM OF--
--THE X-MEN?
PROFESSOR XAVIER--
--WAS THE FIRST TO DIE.

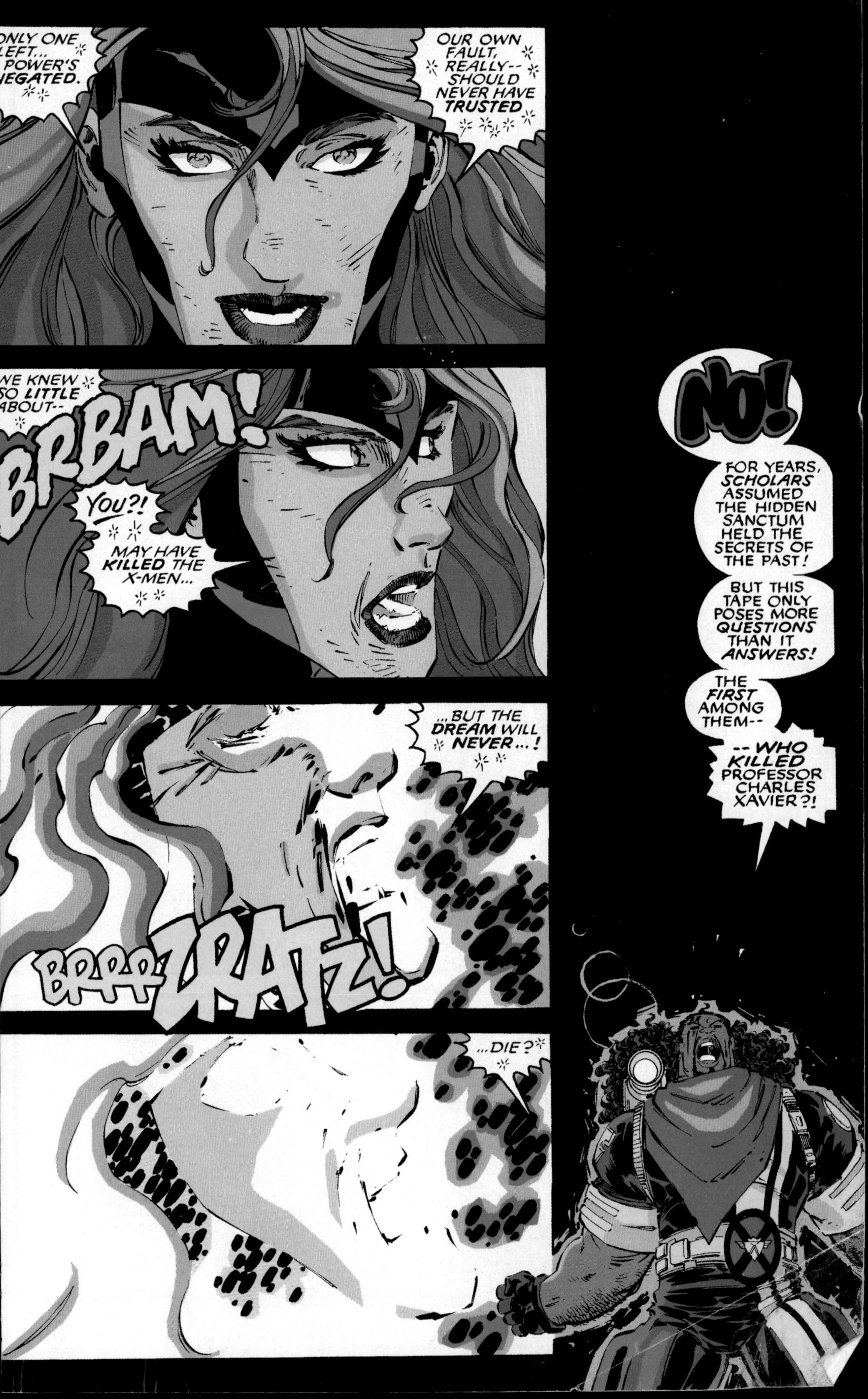

ONLY ONE LEFT... POWER'S NEGATED.
OUR OWN FAULT, REALLY-- SHOULD NEVER HAVE TRUSTED
WE KNEW SO LITTLE ABOUT--
BRBAM!
YOU?!
MAY HAVE KILLED THE X-MEN...
...BUT THE DREAM WILL NEVER...!
BRRRZRATZ!
...DIE?
NO!
FOR YEARS, SCHOLARS ASSUMED THE HIDDEN SANCTUM HELD THE SECRETS OF THE PAST!
BUT THIS TAPE ONLY POSES MORE QUESTIONS THAN IT ANSWERS!
THE FIRST AMONG THEM--
--WHO KILLED PROFESSOR CHARLES XAVIER?!

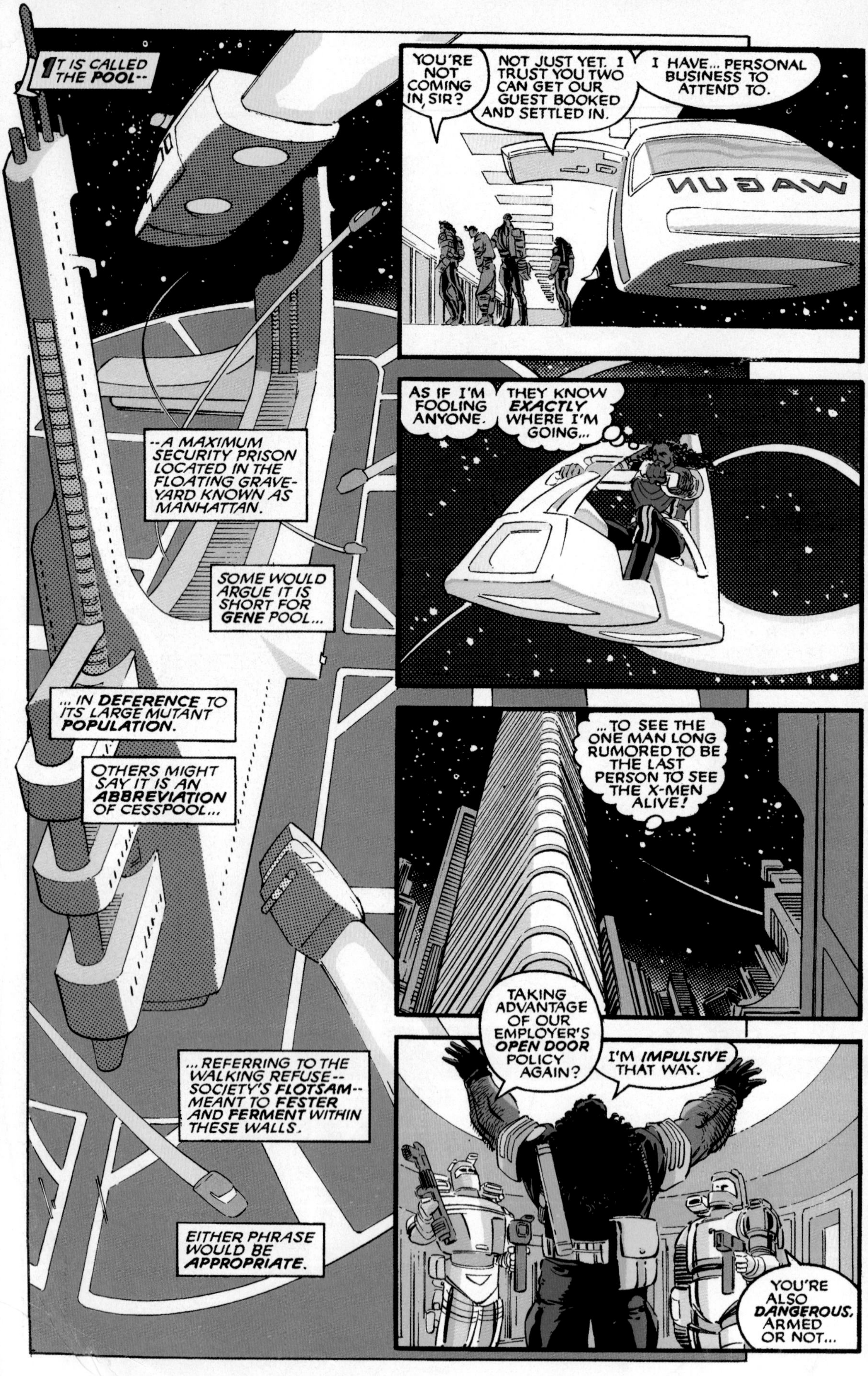
IT IS CALLED THE POOL--
YOU'RE NOT COMING IN, SIR?
NOT JUST YET. I TRUST YOU TWO CAN GET OUR GUEST BOOKED AND SETTLED IN.
I HAVE... PERSONAL BUSINESS TO ATTEND TO.
--A MAXIMUM SECURITY PRISON LOCATED IN THE FLOATING GRAVE-YARD KNOWN AS MANHATTAN.
AS IF I'M FOOLING ANYONE.
THEY KNOW EXACTLY WHERE I'M GOING...
SOME WOULD ARGUE IT IS SHORT FOR GENE POOL...
...IN DEFERENCE TO ITS LARGE MUTANT POPULATION.
OTHERS MIGHT SAY IT IS AN ABBREVIATION OF CESSPOOL...
...TO SEE THE ONE MAN LONG RUMORED TO BE THE LAST PERSON TO SEE THE X-MEN ALIVE!
...REFERRING TO THE WALKING REFUSE-- SOCIETY'S FLOTSAM-- MEANT TO FESTER AND FERMENT WITHIN THESE WALLS.
TAKING ADVANTAGE OF OUR EMPLOYER'S OPEN DOOR POLICY AGAIN?
I'M IMPULSIVE THAT WAY.
EITHER PHRASE WOULD BE APPROPRIATE.
YOU'RE ALSO DANGEROUS. ARMED OR NOT...

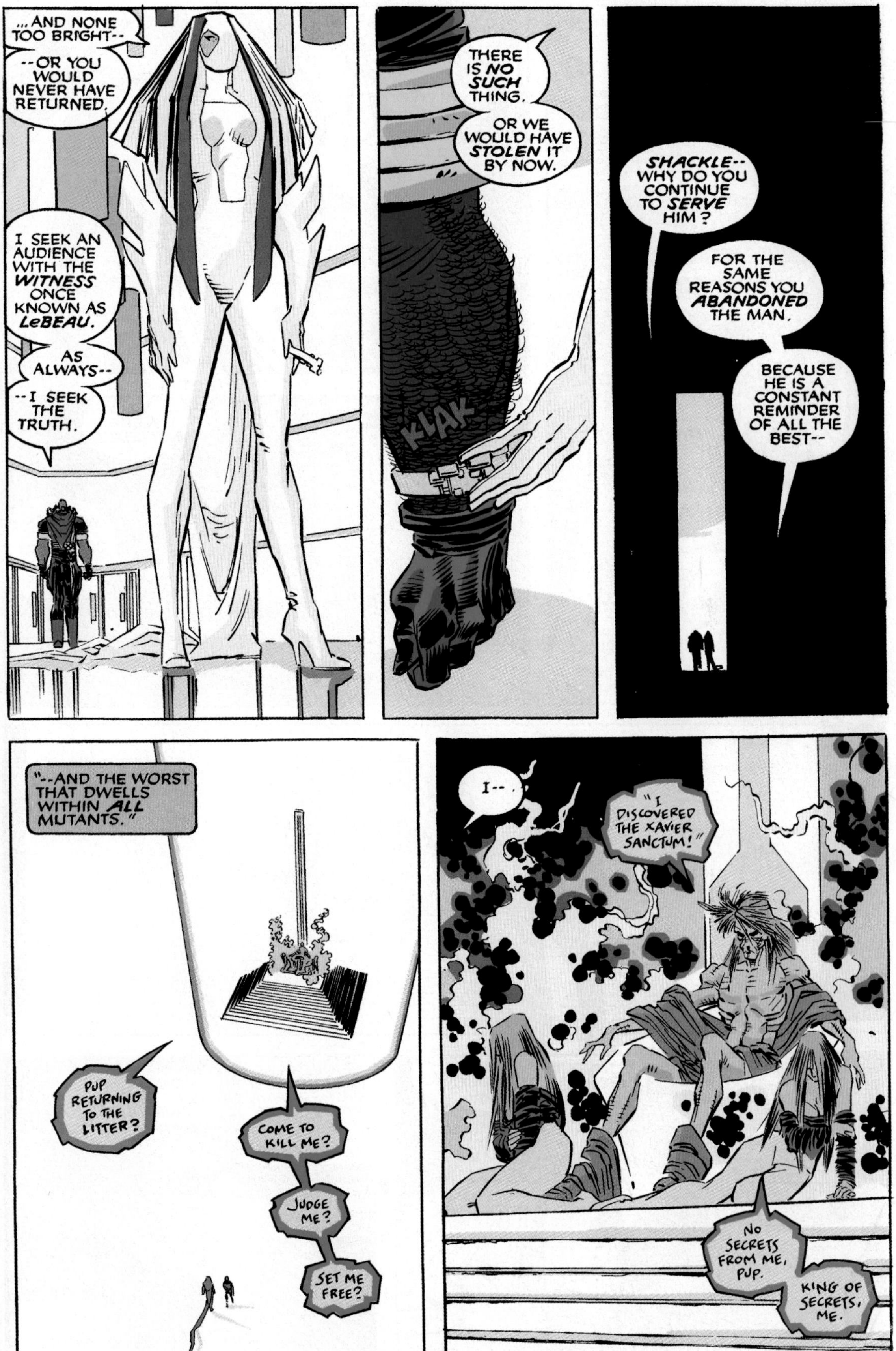
...AND NONE TOO BRIGHT--
--OR YOU WOULD NEVER HAVE RETURNED.
I SEEK AN AUDIENCE WITH THE WITNESS ONCE KNOWN AS LeBEAU.
AS ALWAYS--
--I SEEK THE TRUTH.
THERE IS NO SUCH THING.
OR WE WOULD HAVE STOLEN IT BY NOW.
KLAK
SHACKLE-- WHY DO YOU CONTINUE TO SERVE HIM?
FOR THE SAME REASONS YOU ABANDONED THE MAN.
BECAUSE HE IS A CONSTANT REMINDER OF ALL THE BEST--
"--AND THE WORST THAT DWELLS WITHIN ALL MUTANTS."
PUP RETURNING TO THE LITTER?
COME TO KILL ME?
JUDGE ME?
SET ME FREE?
I--
"I DISCOVERED THE XAVIER SANCTUM!"
NO SECRETS FROM ME, PUP.
KING OF SECRETS, ME.

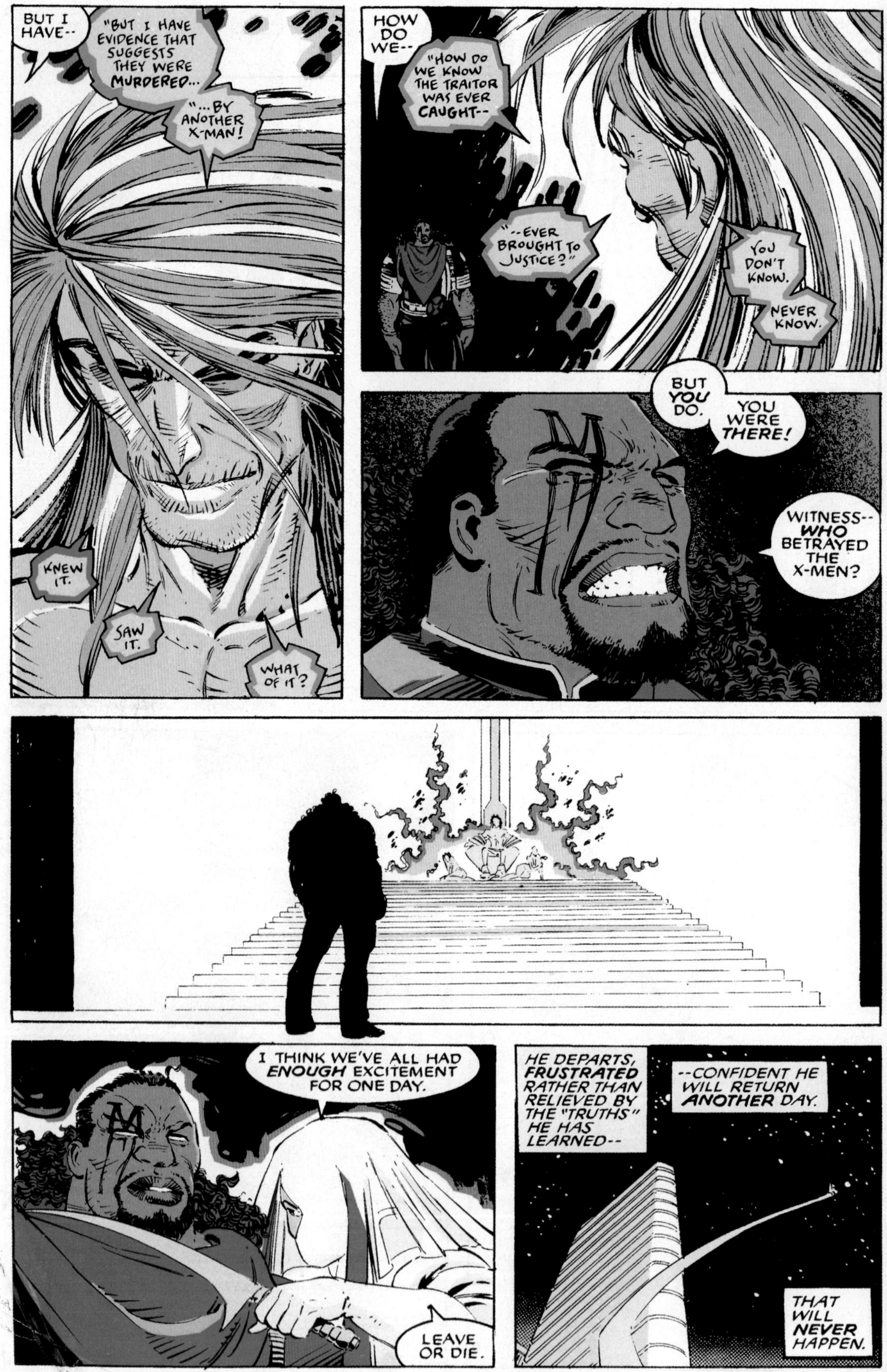
BUT I HAVE--
"BUT I HAVE EVIDENCE THAT SUGGESTS THEY WERE MURDERED...
"...BY ANOTHER X-MAN!
KNEW IT.
SAW IT.
WHAT OF IT?
HOW DO WE--
"HOW DO WE KNOW THE TRAITOR WAS EVER CAUGHT--
"--EVER BROUGHT TO JUSTICE?"
YOU DON'T KNOW.
NEVER KNOW.
BUT YOU DO.
YOU WERE THERE!
WITNESS-- WHO BETRAYED THE X-MEN?
I THINK WE'VE ALL HAD ENOUGH EXCITEMENT FOR ONE DAY.
LEAVE OR DIE.
HE DEPARTS, FRUSTRATED RATHER THAN RELIEVED BY THE "TRUTHS" HE HAS LEARNED--
--CONFIDENT HE WILL RETURN ANOTHER DAY.
THAT WILL NEVER HAPPEN.

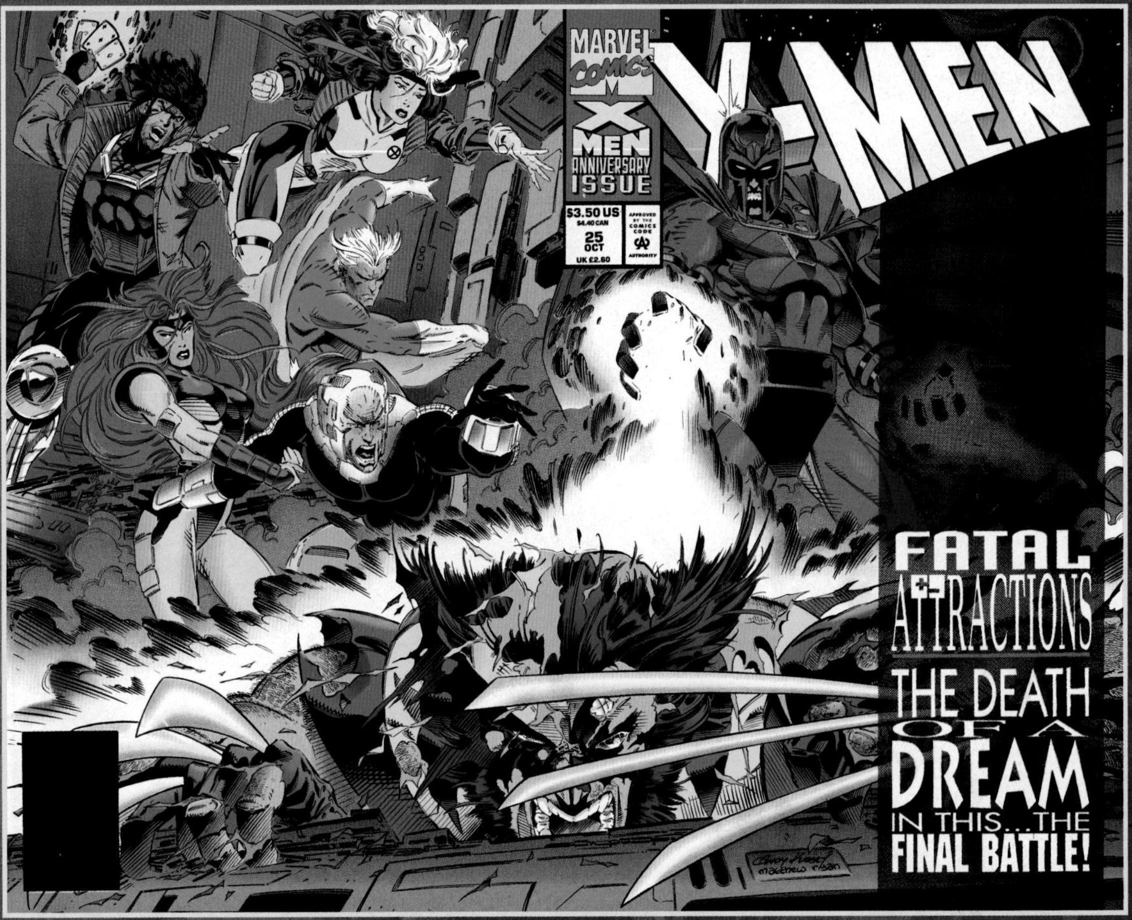
MARVEL COMICS
X-MEN ANNIVERSARY ISSUE
$3.50 US
$4.40 CAN
25 OCT
UK £2.60
APPROVED BY THE COMICS CODE AUTHORITY
X-MEN
FATAL ATTRACTIONS
THE DEATH OF A DREAM
IN THIS...THE FINAL BATTLE!

Fitzroy soon time-traveled to the present, and Bishop followed. Fitzroy clashed with the energy vampire Selene, and was defeated by the paramilitary mutant Cable and his team, X-Force. Bishop joined the X-Men, where he suspected Gambit of being the so-called "X-Traitor" because of his similarities to the Witness. But the truth was far darker than any of the X-Men could suspect – Onslaught was an evil entity of pure psionic energy, a split persona sprung from the mutant mind of the X-Men's founder, Professor Charles Xavier!

Onslaught's creation had its genesis in two seemingly unrelated events. The first came during a battle aboard Magneto's space station, when an injured and desperate master of magnetism grievously wounded Wolverine – and Professor X lashed out, switching off Magneto's mind. Unbeknownst to anyone, this act left a small sliver of Magneto's evil essence inside Xavier's psyche.

Much later, Nate Grey arrived on our Earth – a younger, much more powerful version of Cable, hailing from a dimension where Xavier had perished, the evil Apocalypse ruled supreme and Magneto led the X-Men. Sensing Grey and believing him to be Stryfe, the evil clone of Cable who created the mutant-killing Legacy Virus, Xavier decided to investigate...

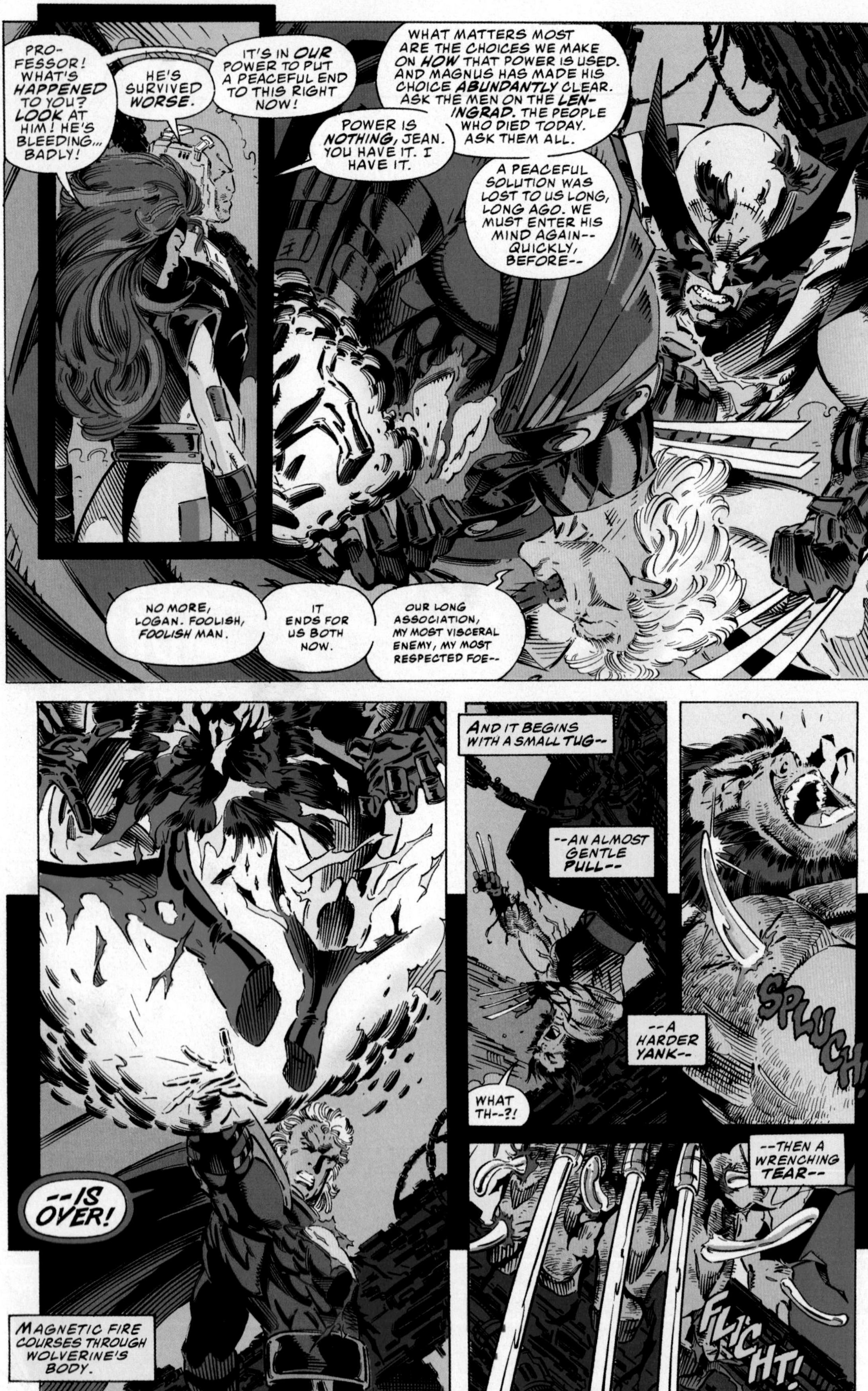
PRO-FESSOR! WHAT'S HAPPENED TO YOU? LOOK AT HIM! HE'S BLEEDING... BADLY!
HE'S SURVIVED WORSE.
IT'S IN OUR POWER TO PUT A PEACEFUL END TO THIS RIGHT NOW!
POWER IS NOTHING, JEAN. YOU HAVE IT. I HAVE IT.
WHAT MATTERS MOST ARE THE CHOICES WE MAKE ON HOW THAT POWER IS USED. AND MAGNUS HAS MADE HIS CHOICE ABUNDANTLY CLEAR. ASK THE MEN ON THE LENINGRAD. THE PEOPLE WHO DIED TODAY. ASK THEM ALL.
A PEACEFUL SOLUTION WAS LOST TO US LONG, LONG AGO. WE MUST ENTER HIS MIND AGAIN--QUICKLY, BEFORE--
NO MORE, LOGAN. FOOLISH, FOOLISH MAN.
IT ENDS FOR US BOTH NOW.
OUR LONG ASSOCIATION, MY MOST VISCERAL ENEMY, MY MOST RESPECTED FOE--
--IS OVER!
MAGNETIC FIRE COURSES THROUGH WOLVERINE'S BODY.
AND IT BEGINS WITH A SMALL TUG--
--AN ALMOST GENTLE PULL--
--A HARDER YANK--
WHAT TH--?!
SPLUCH!
--THEN A WRENCHING TEAR--
FLITCHT!

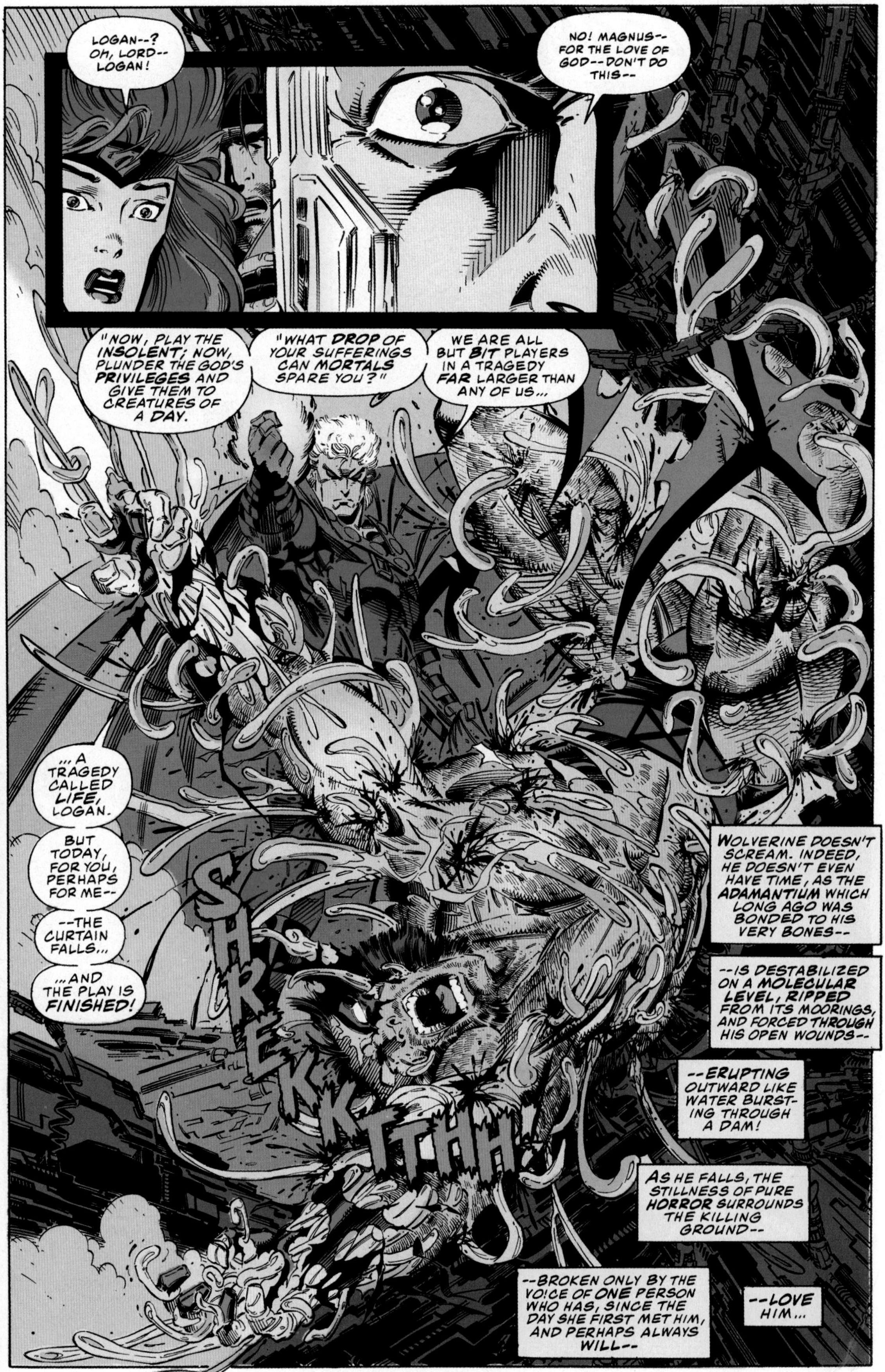
LOGAN--? OH, LORD-- LOGAN!
NO! MAGNUS-- FOR THE LOVE OF GOD--DON'T DO THIS--
"NOW, PLAY THE INSOLENT; NOW, PLUNDER THE GOD'S PRIVILEGES AND GIVE THEM TO CREATURES OF A DAY.
"WHAT DROP OF YOUR SUFFERINGS CAN MORTALS SPARE YOU?"
WE ARE ALL BUT BIT PLAYERS IN A TRAGEDY FAR LARGER THAN ANY OF US...
...A TRAGEDY CALLED LIFE, LOGAN.
BUT TODAY, FOR YOU, PERHAPS FOR ME--
--THE CURTAIN FALLS...
...AND THE PLAY IS FINISHED!
WOLVERINE DOESN'T SCREAM. INDEED, HE DOESN'T EVEN HAVE TIME, AS THE ADAMANTIUM WHICH LONG AGO WAS BONDED TO HIS VERY BONES--
--IS DESTABILIZED ON A MOLECULAR LEVEL, RIPPED FROM ITS MOORINGS, AND FORCED THROUGH HIS OPEN WOUNDS--
SHREKKTTHH!
--ERUPTING OUTWARD LIKE WATER BURSTING THROUGH A DAM!
AS HE FALLS, THE STILLNESS OF PURE HORROR SURROUNDS THE KILLING GROUND--
--BROKEN ONLY BY THE VOICE OF ONE PERSON WHO HAS, SINCE THE DAY SHE FIRST MET HIM, AND PERHAPS ALWAYS WILL--
--LOVE HIM...

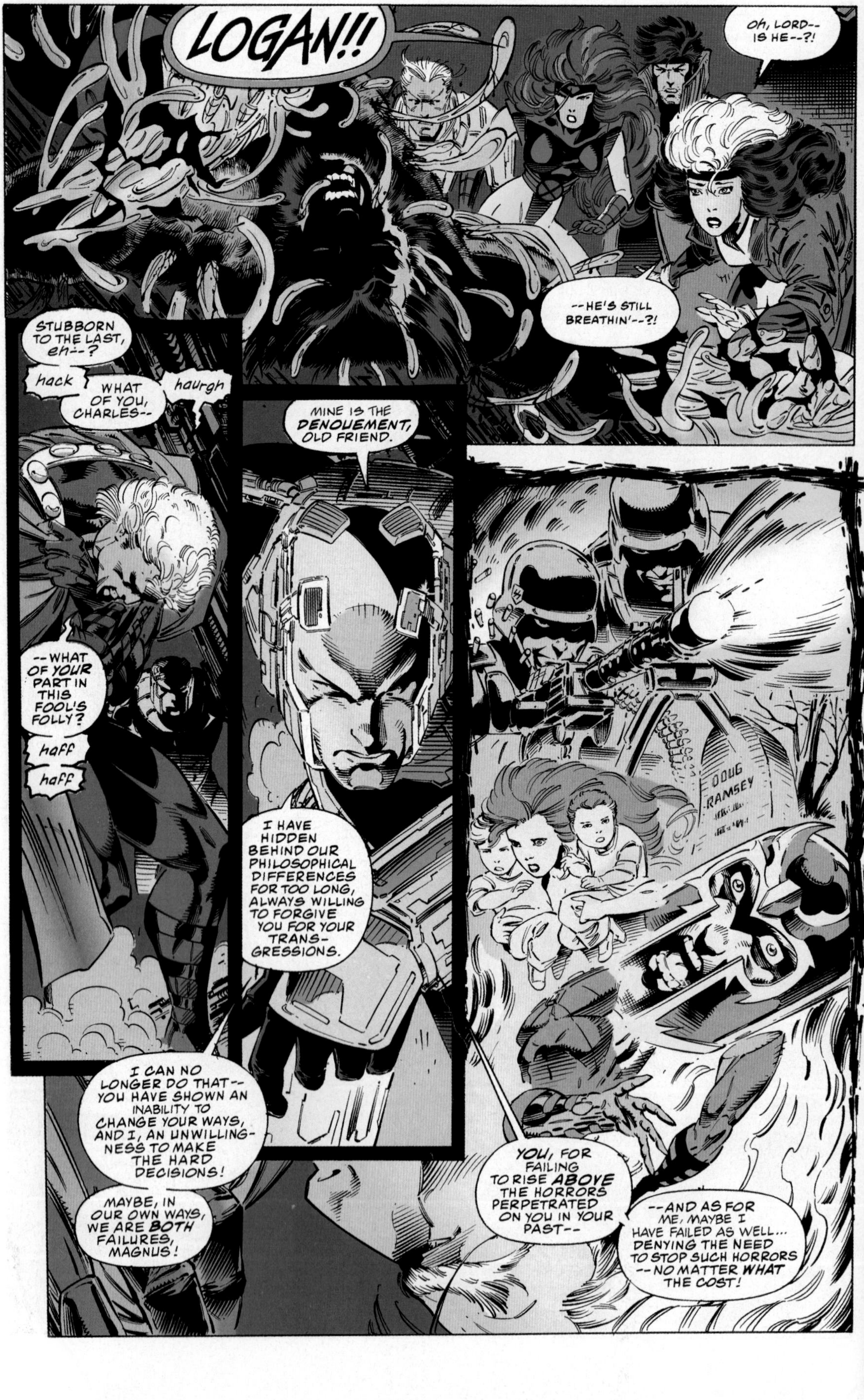
LOGAN!!
Oh, LORD-- IS HE--?!
--HE'S STILL BREATHIN'--?!
STUBBORN TO THE LAST, eh--?
hack
WHAT OF YOU, CHARLES--
haurgh
--WHAT OF YOUR PART IN THIS FOOL'S FOLLY?
haff
haff
MINE IS THE DENOUEMENT, OLD FRIEND.
I HAVE HIDDEN BEHIND OUR PHILOSOPHICAL DIFFERENCES FOR TOO LONG, ALWAYS WILLING TO FORGIVE YOU FOR YOUR TRANS-GRESSIONS.
I CAN NO LONGER DO THAT--YOU HAVE SHOWN AN INABILITY TO CHANGE YOUR WAYS, AND I, AN UNWILLING-NESS TO MAKE THE HARD DECISIONS!
MAYBE, IN OUR OWN WAYS, WE ARE BOTH FAILURES, MAGNUS!
DOUG RAMSEY
YOU, FOR FAILING TO RISE ABOVE THE HORRORS PERPETRATED ON YOU IN YOUR PAST--
--AND AS FOR ME, MAYBE I HAVE FAILED AS WELL... DENYING THE NEED TO STOP SUCH HORRORS --NO MATTER WHAT THE COST!

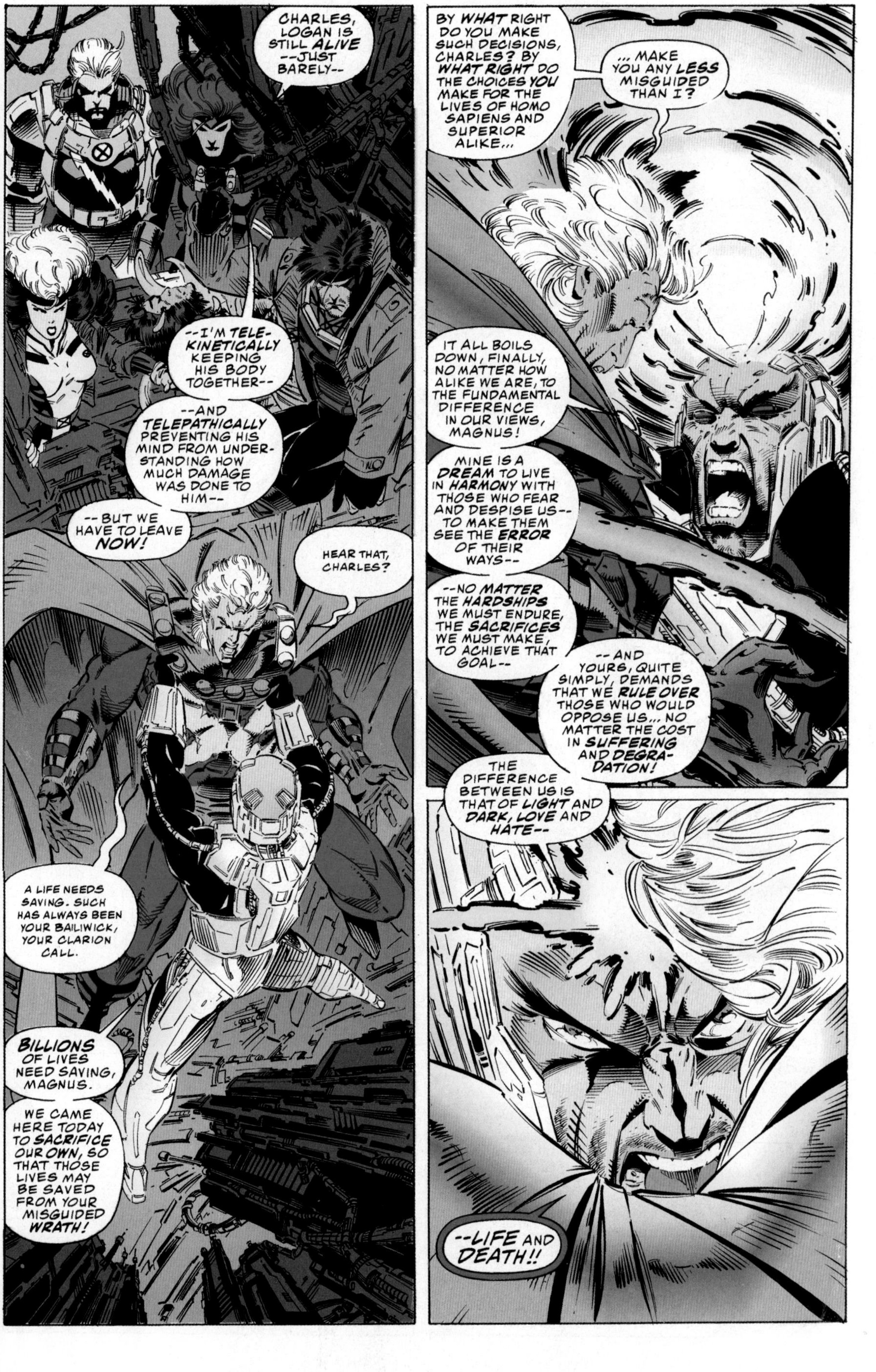
CHARLES, LOGAN IS STILL ALIVE --JUST BARELY--
--I'M TELE-KINETICALLY KEEPING HIS BODY TOGETHER--
--AND TELEPATHICALLY PREVENTING HIS MIND FROM UNDER-STANDING HOW MUCH DAMAGE WAS DONE TO HIM--
--BUT WE HAVE TO LEAVE NOW!
HEAR THAT, CHARLES?
A LIFE NEEDS SAVING. SUCH HAS ALWAYS BEEN YOUR BAILIWICK, YOUR CLARION CALL.
BILLIONS OF LIVES NEED SAVING, MAGNUS.
WE CAME HERE TODAY TO SACRIFICE OUR OWN, SO THAT THOSE LIVES MAY BE SAVED FROM YOUR MISGUIDED WRATH!
BY WHAT RIGHT DO YOU MAKE SUCH DECISIONS, CHARLES? BY WHAT RIGHT DO THE CHOICES YOU MAKE FOR THE LIVES OF HOMO SAPIENS AND SUPERIOR ALIKE...
... MAKE YOU ANY LESS MISGUIDED THAN I?
IT ALL BOILS DOWN, FINALLY, NO MATTER HOW ALIKE WE ARE, TO THE FUNDAMENTAL DIFFERENCE IN OUR VIEWS, MAGNUS!
MINE IS A DREAM TO LIVE IN HARMONY WITH THOSE WHO FEAR AND DESPISE US--TO MAKE THEM SEE THE ERROR OF THEIR WAYS--
--NO MATTER THE HARDSHIPS WE MUST ENDURE, THE SACRIFICES WE MUST MAKE, TO ACHIEVE THAT GOAL--
--AND YOURS, QUITE SIMPLY, DEMANDS THAT WE RULE OVER THOSE WHO WOULD OPPOSE US... NO MATTER THE COST IN SUFFERING AND DEGRA-DATION!
THE DIFFERENCE BETWEEN US IS THAT OF LIGHT AND DARK, LOVE AND HATE--
--LIFE AND DEATH!!

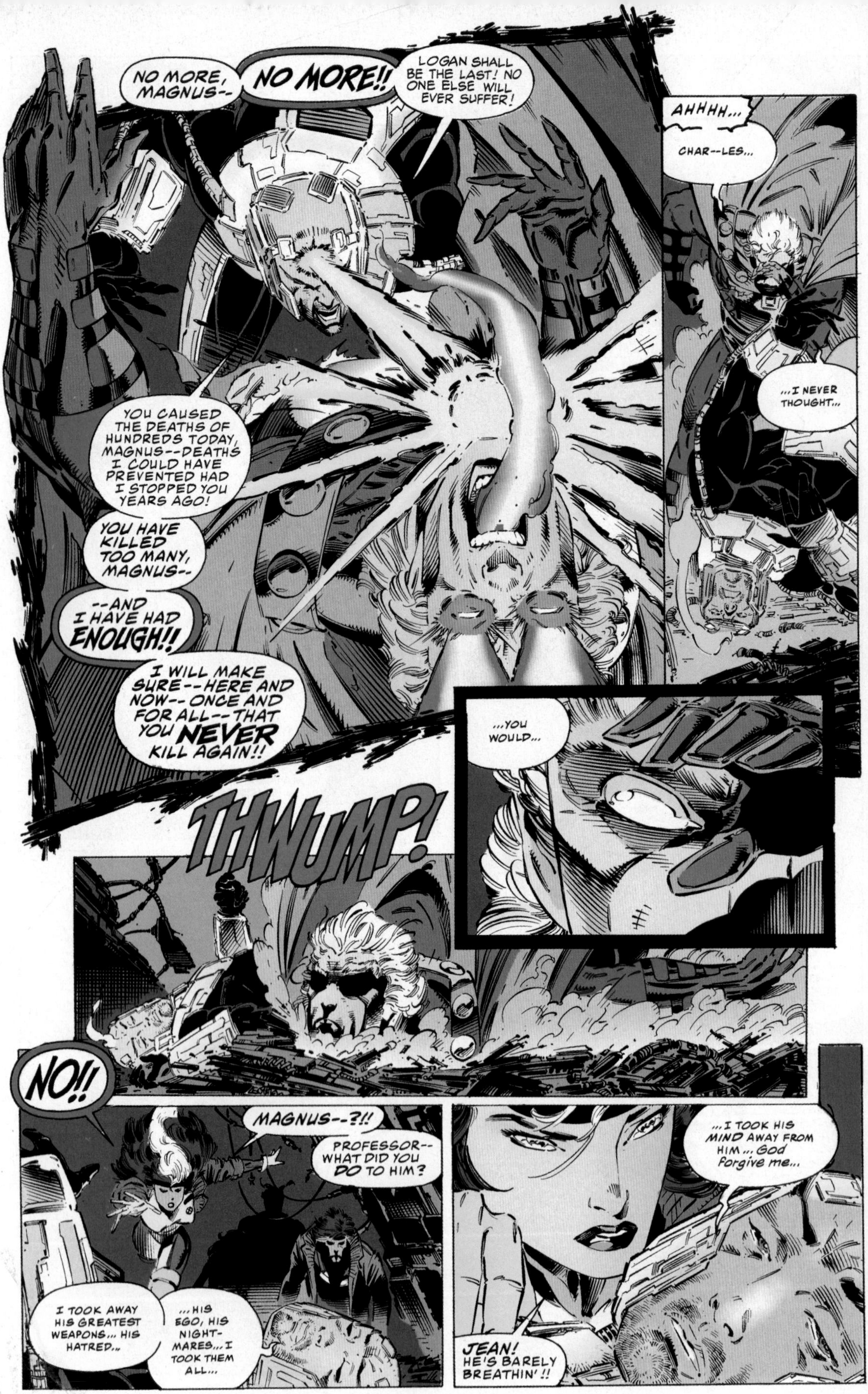
NO MORE, MAGNUS--
NO MORE!!
LOGAN SHALL BE THE LAST! NO ONE ELSE WILL EVER SUFFER!
YOU CAUSED THE DEATHS OF HUNDREDS TODAY, MAGNUS--DEATHS I COULD HAVE PREVENTED HAD I STOPPED YOU YEARS AGO!
YOU HAVE KILLED TOO MANY, MAGNUS--
--AND I HAVE HAD ENOUGH!!
I WILL MAKE SURE--HERE AND NOW-- ONCE AND FOR ALL--THAT YOU NEVER KILL AGAIN!!
AHHHH...
CHAR--LES...
...I NEVER THOUGHT...
...YOU WOULD...
THWUMP!
NO!!
MAGNUS--?!!
PROFESSOR--WHAT DID YOU DO TO HIM?
I TOOK AWAY HIS GREATEST WEAPONS... HIS HATRED...
...HIS EGO, HIS NIGHT-MARES... I TOOK THEM ALL...
...I TOOK HIS MIND AWAY FROM HIM... God forgive me...
JEAN! HE'S BARELY BREATHIN'!!

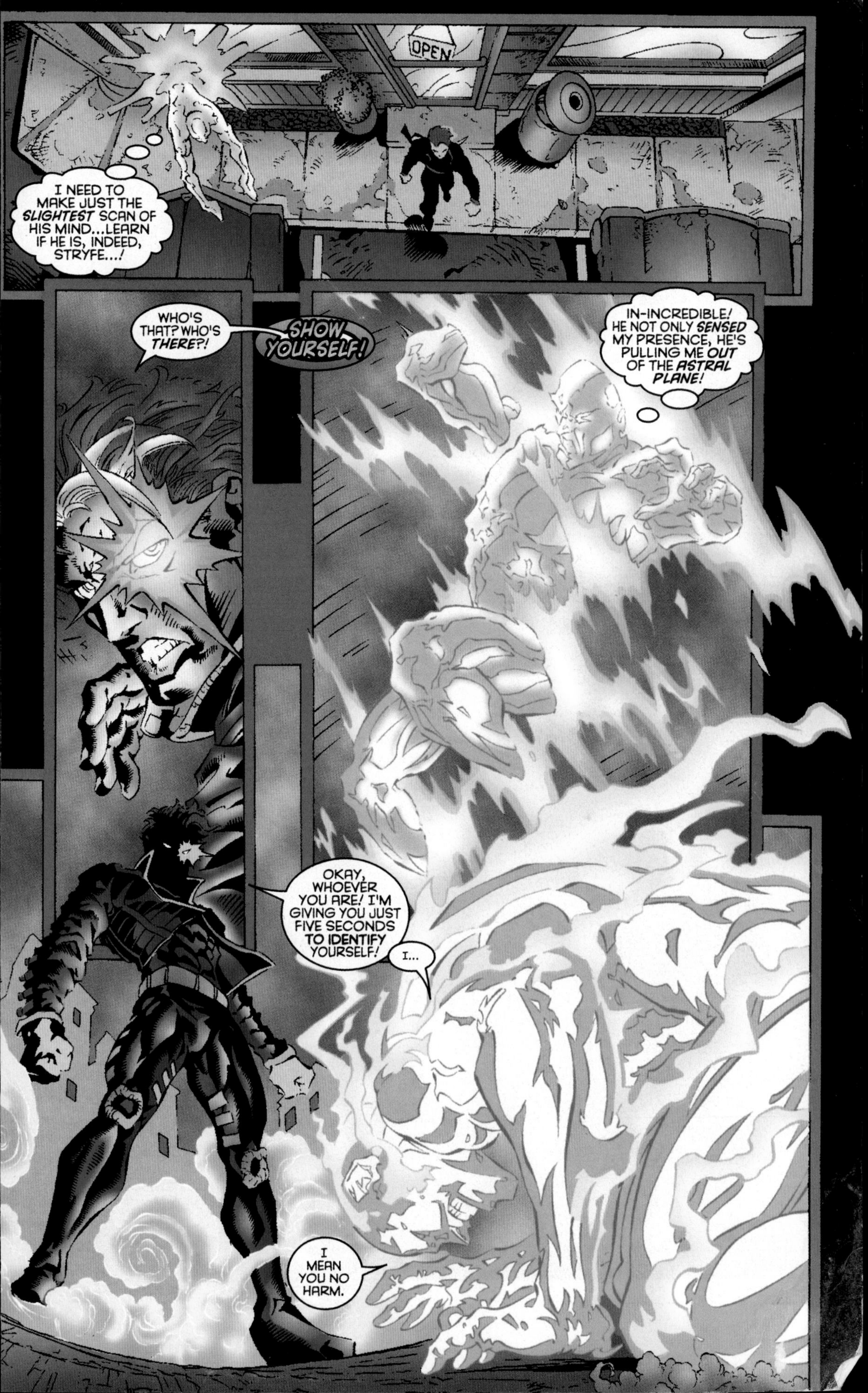
OPEN
I NEED TO MAKE JUST THE SLIGHTEST SCAN OF HIS MIND...LEARN IF HE IS, INDEED, STRYFE...!
WHO'S THAT? WHO'S THERE?!
SHOW YOURSELF!
IN-INCREDIBLE! HE NOT ONLY SENSED MY PRESENCE, HE'S PULLING ME OUT OF THE ASTRAL PLANE!
OKAY, WHOEVER YOU ARE! I'M GIVING YOU JUST FIVE SECONDS TO IDENTIFY YOURSELF!
I...
I MEAN YOU NO HARM.

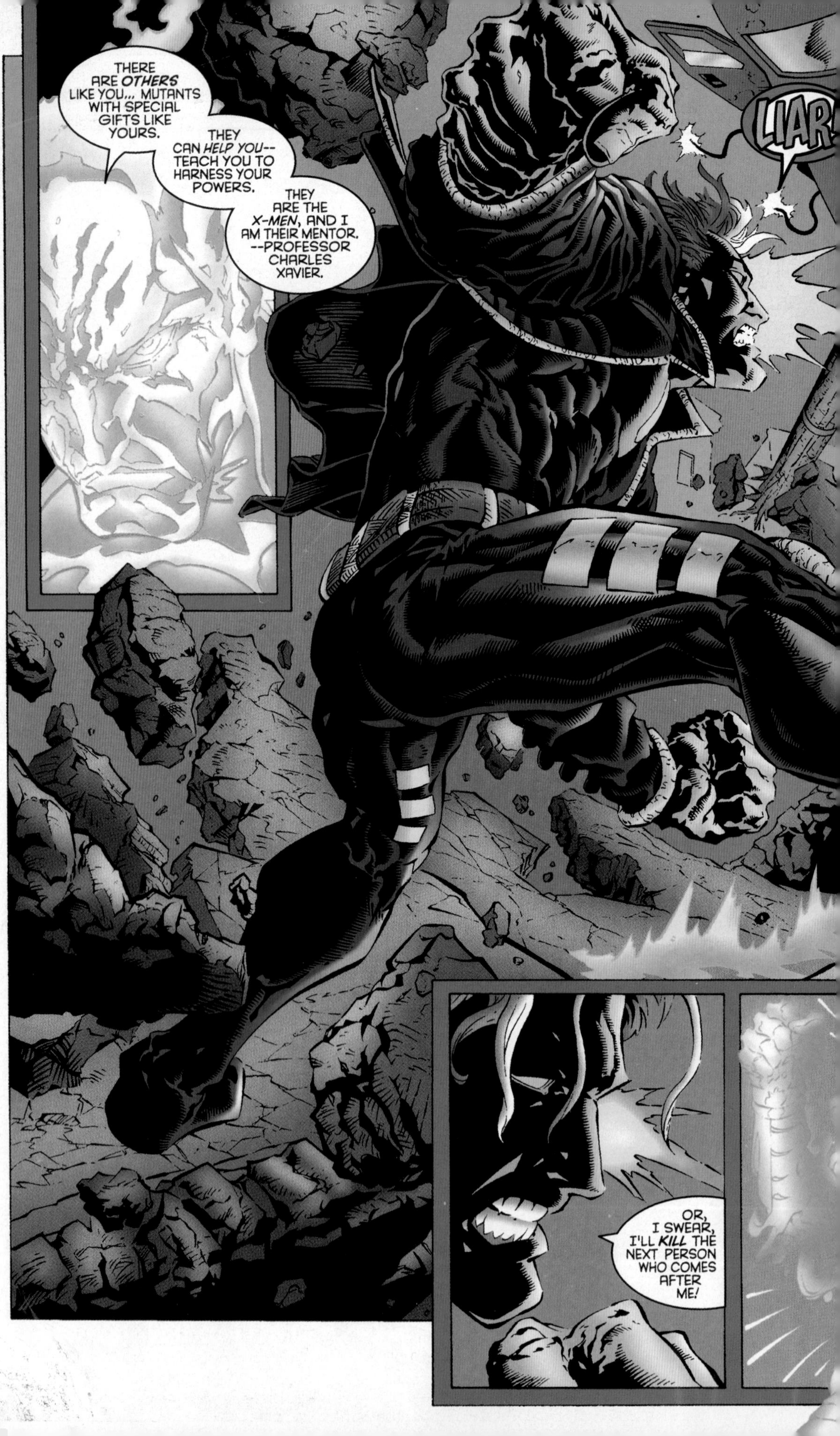

THERE ARE OTHERS LIKE YOU... MUTANTS WITH SPECIAL GIFTS LIKE YOURS.
THEY CAN HELP YOU-- TEACH YOU TO HARNESS YOUR POWERS.
THEY ARE THE X-MEN, AND I AM THEIR MENTOR. --PROFESSOR CHARLES XAVIER.
LIAR
OR, I SWEAR, I'LL KILL THE NEXT PERSON WHO COMES AFTER ME!

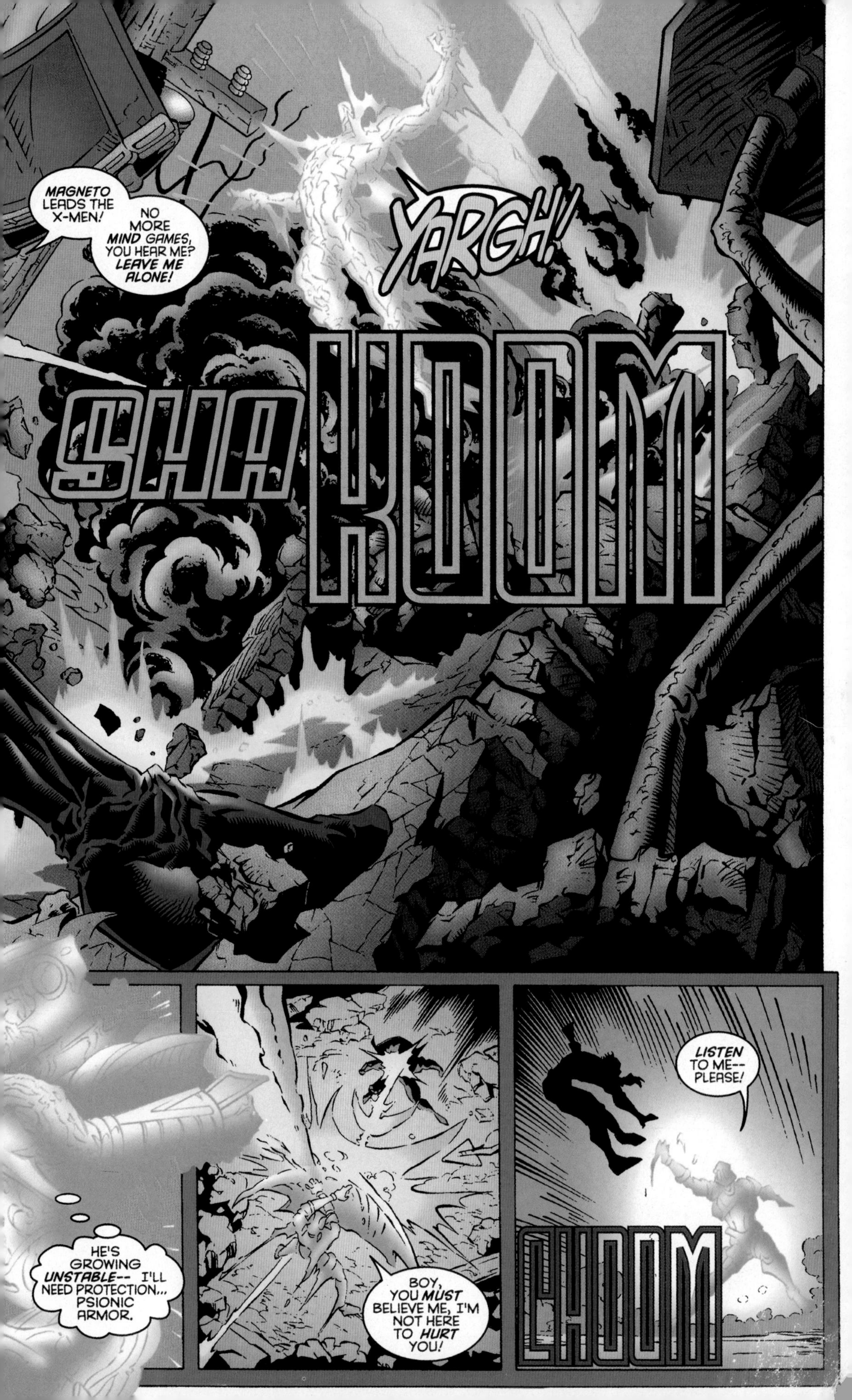
MAGNETO LEADS THE X-MEN!
NO MORE MIND GAMES, YOU HEAR ME? LEAVE ME ALONE!
YARGH!
SHA KOOM
HE'S GROWING UNSTABLE-- I'LL NEED PROTECTION,.. PSIONIC ARMOR.
BOY, YOU MUST BELIEVE ME, I'M NOT HERE TO HURT YOU!
LISTEN TO ME-- PLEASE!
CHOOM

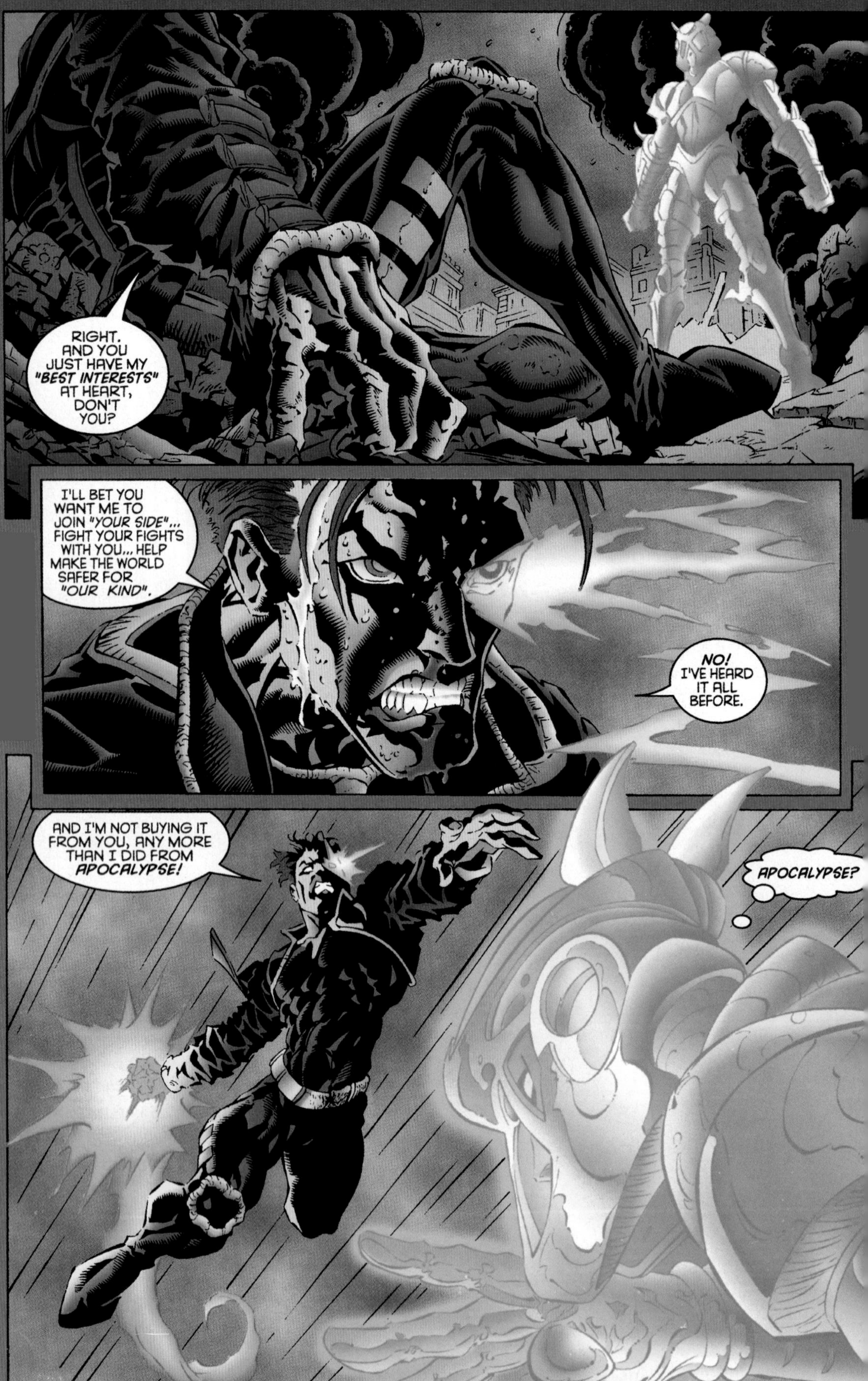
RIGHT. AND YOU JUST HAVE MY "BEST INTERESTS" AT HEART, DON'T YOU?
I'LL BET YOU WANT ME TO JOIN "YOUR SIDE"... FIGHT YOUR FIGHTS WITH YOU... HELP MAKE THE WORLD SAFER FOR "OUR KIND".
NO! I'VE HEARD IT ALL BEFORE.
AND I'M NOT BUYING IT FROM YOU, ANY MORE THAN I DID FROM APOCALYPSE!
APOCALYPSE?

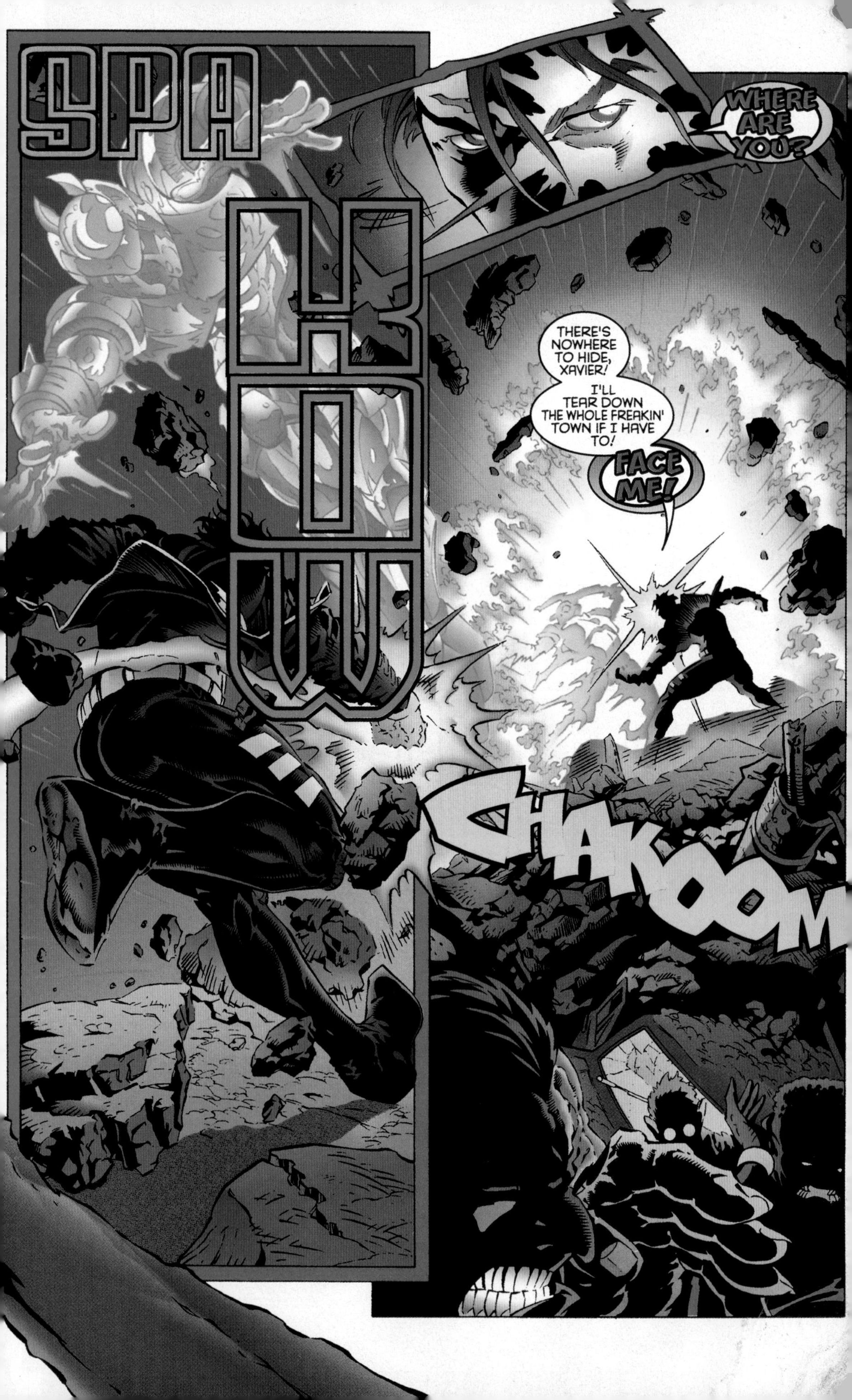
SPA
WHERE ARE YOU?
THERE'S NOWHERE TO HIDE, XAVIER!
I'LL TEAR DOWN THE WHOLE FREAKIN' TOWN IF I HAVE TO!
FACE ME!
CHAKOOM

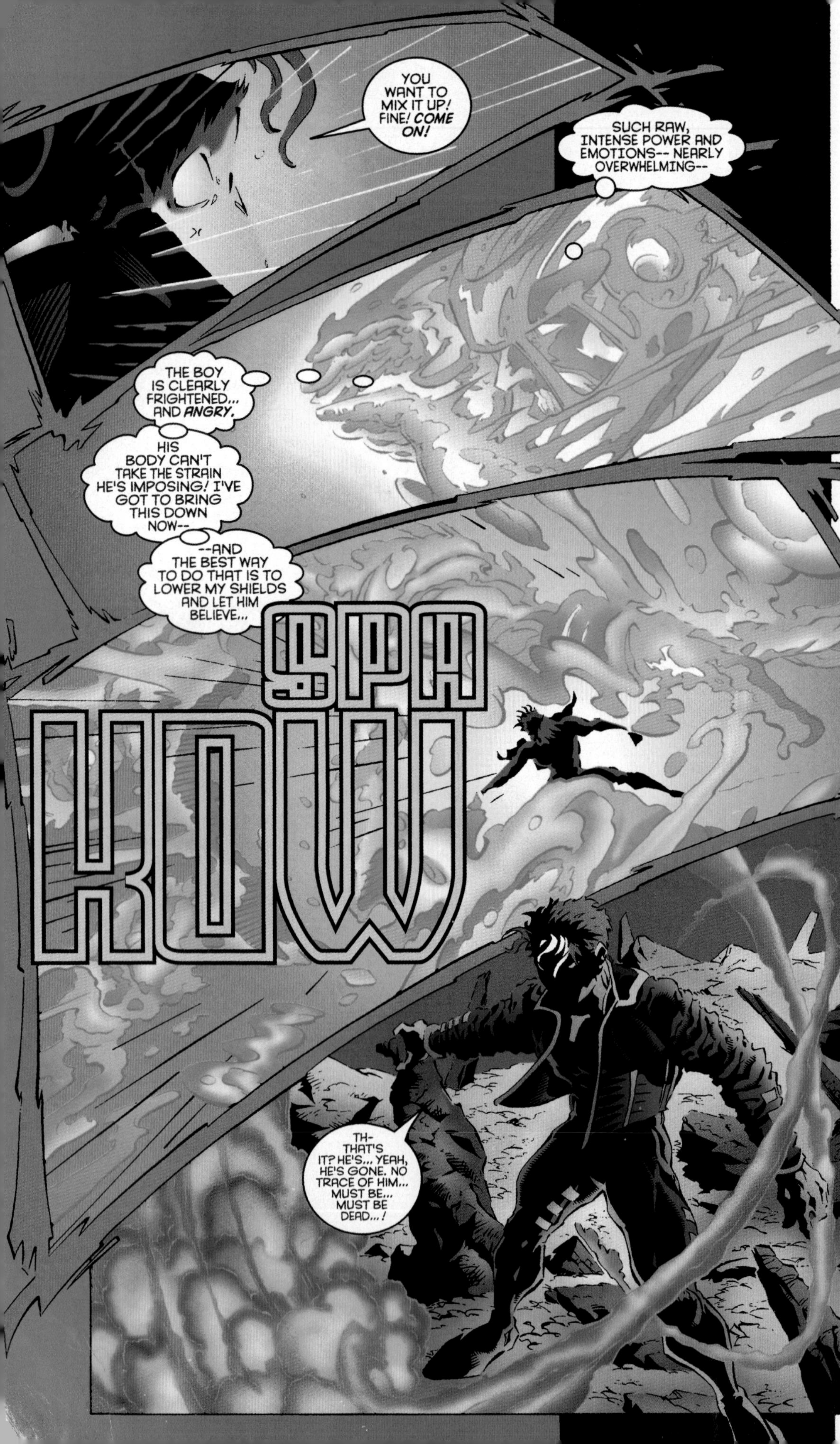
YOU WANT TO MIX IT UP! FINE! COME ON!
SUCH RAW, INTENSE POWER AND EMOTIONS-- NEARLY OVERWHELMING--
THE BOY IS CLEARLY FRIGHTENED... AND ANGRY.
HIS BODY CAN'T TAKE THE STRAIN HE'S IMPOSING! I'VE GOT TO BRING THIS DOWN NOW--
--AND THE BEST WAY TO DO THAT IS TO LOWER MY SHIELDS AND LET HIM BELIEVE...
SPA KOW
TH- THAT'S IT? HE'S... YEAH, HE'S GONE. NO TRACE OF HIM... MUST BE... MUST BE DEAD...!

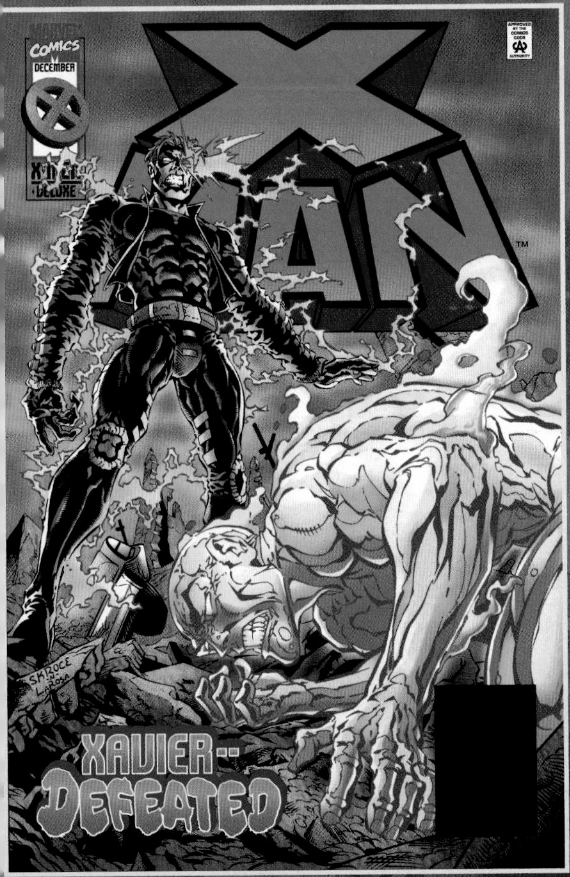
MARVEL COMICS
DECEMBER
X-MAN
X-MEN DELUXE
XAVIER--
DEFEATED

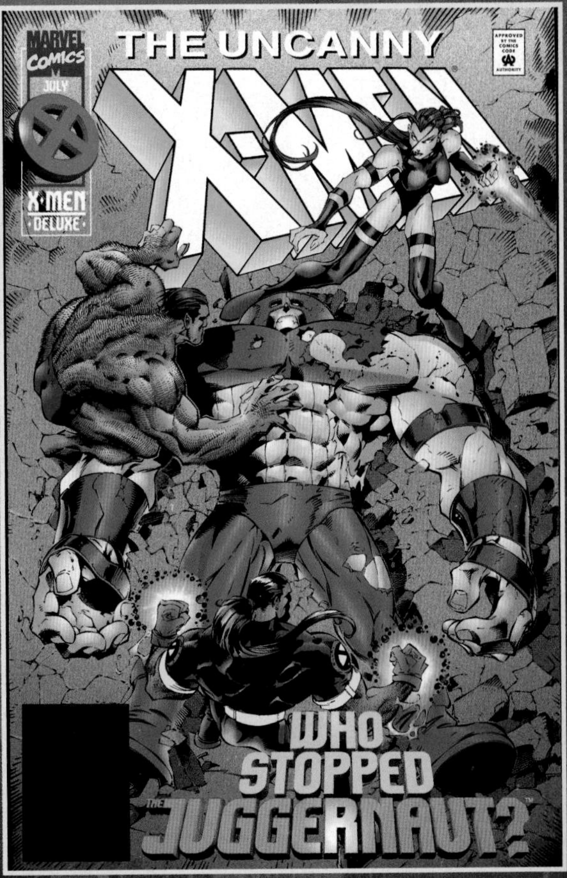
MARVEL COMICS
JULY
THE UNCANNY
X-MEN
X-MEN DELUXE
WHO STOPPED THE JUGGERNAUT?

Wolverine was shocked to learn that he had claws of bone underneath the Adamantium – but the growing evil in Xavier's psyche had witnessed an even greater revelation. Nate Grey had unwittingly shown Xavier how to bring his astral form to the physical world – an act that gave this evil an opportunity to manifest itself in the flesh.

Dubbing itself Onslaught, the entity fed on Xavier's pent-up frustrations and grew strong. With Xavier completely unaware of its existence, Onslaught devised plans of a grand power base for itself, and vengeance upon the humans that had stymied the dreams of its two "fathers."

But first, Onslaught decided to indulge in a little payback – against a foe who had bullied Xavier for years...

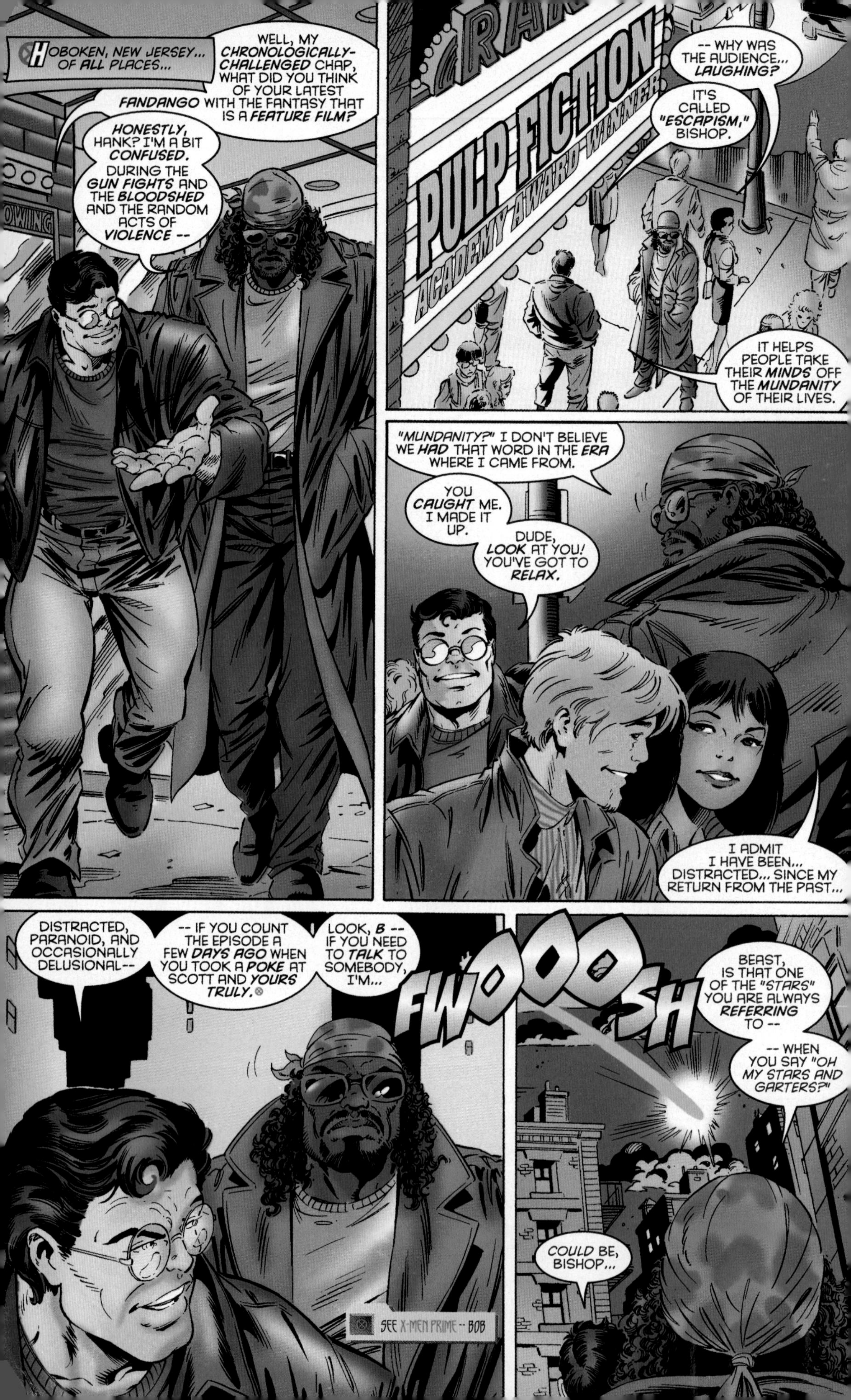
HOBOKEN, NEW JERSEY... OF ALL PLACES...
WELL, MY CHRONOLOGICALLY-CHALLENGED CHAP, WHAT DID YOU THINK OF YOUR LATEST FANDANGO WITH THE FANTASY THAT IS A FEATURE FILM?
HONESTLY, HANK? I'M A BIT CONFUSED. DURING THE GUN FIGHTS AND THE BLOODSHED AND THE RANDOM ACTS OF VIOLENCE --
PULP FICTION
ACADEMY AWARD WINNER
-- WHY WAS THE AUDIENCE... LAUGHING?
IT'S CALLED "ESCAPISM," BISHOP.
IT HELPS PEOPLE TAKE THEIR MINDS OFF THE MUNDANITY OF THEIR LIVES.
"MUNDANITY?" I DON'T BELIEVE WE HAD THAT WORD IN THE ERA WHERE I CAME FROM.
YOU CAUGHT ME. I MADE IT UP.
DUDE, LOOK AT YOU! YOU'VE GOT TO RELAX.
I ADMIT I HAVE BEEN... DISTRACTED... SINCE MY RETURN FROM THE PAST...
DISTRACTED, PARANOID, AND OCCASIONALLY DELUSIONAL--
-- IF YOU COUNT THE EPISODE A FEW DAYS AGO WHEN YOU TOOK A POKE AT SCOTT AND YOURS TRULY.
LOOK, B -- IF YOU NEED TO TALK TO SOMEBODY, I'M...
FWOOOSH
BEAST, IS THAT ONE OF THE "STARS" YOU ARE ALWAYS REFERRING TO --
-- WHEN YOU SAY "OH MY STARS AND GARTERS?"
COULD BE, BISHOP...
SEE X-MEN PRIME -- BOB

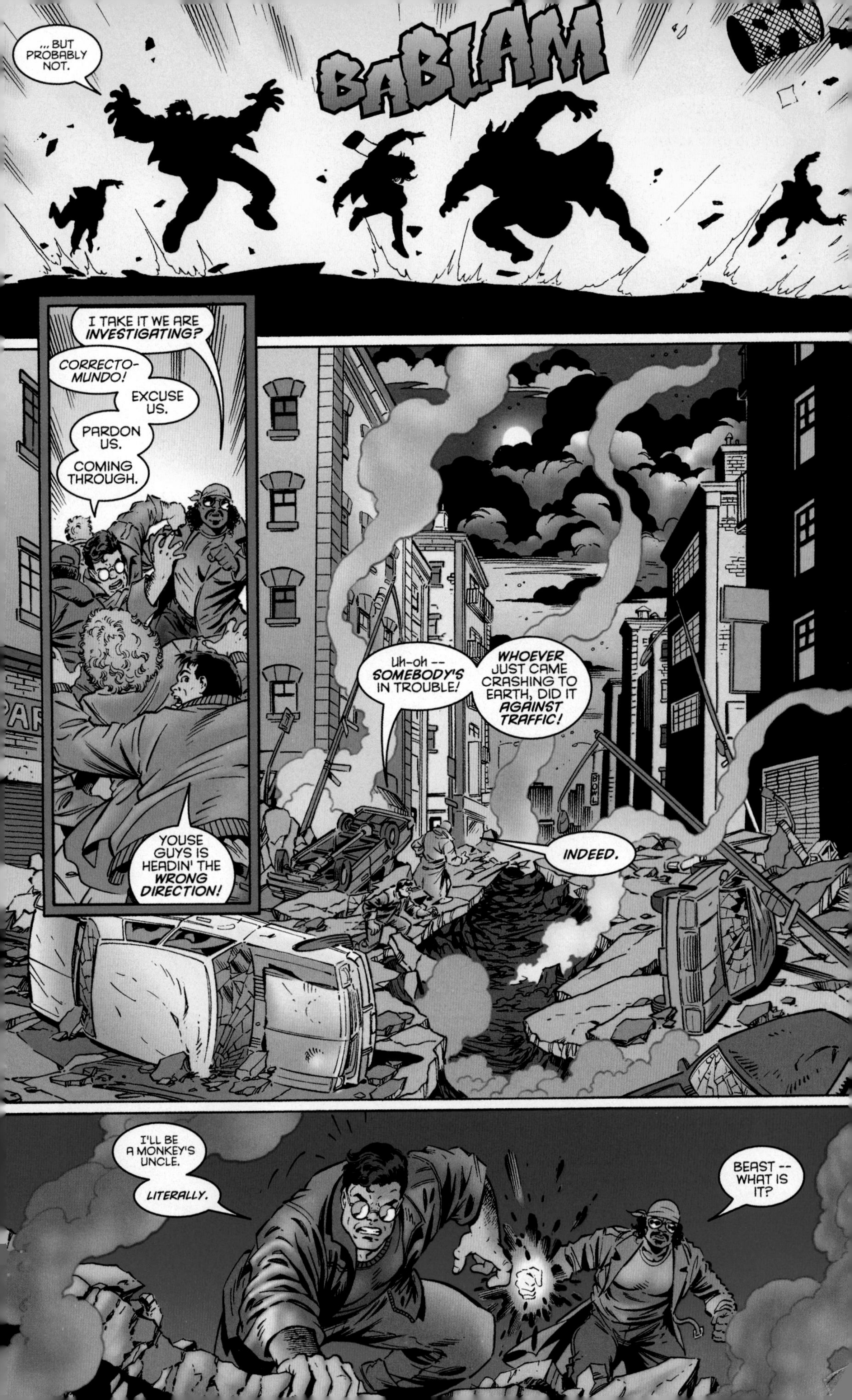

... BUT PROBABLY NOT.
BABLAM
I TAKE IT WE ARE INVESTIGATING?
CORRECTO-MUNDO!
EXCUSE US.
PARDON US.
COMING THROUGH.
YOUSE GUYS IS HEADIN' THE WRONG DIRECTION!
Uh-oh -- SOMEBODY'S IN TROUBLE!
WHOEVER JUST CAME CRASHING TO EARTH, DID IT AGAINST TRAFFIC!
INDEED.
I'LL BE A MONKEY'S UNCLE.
LITERALLY.
BEAST -- WHAT IS IT?

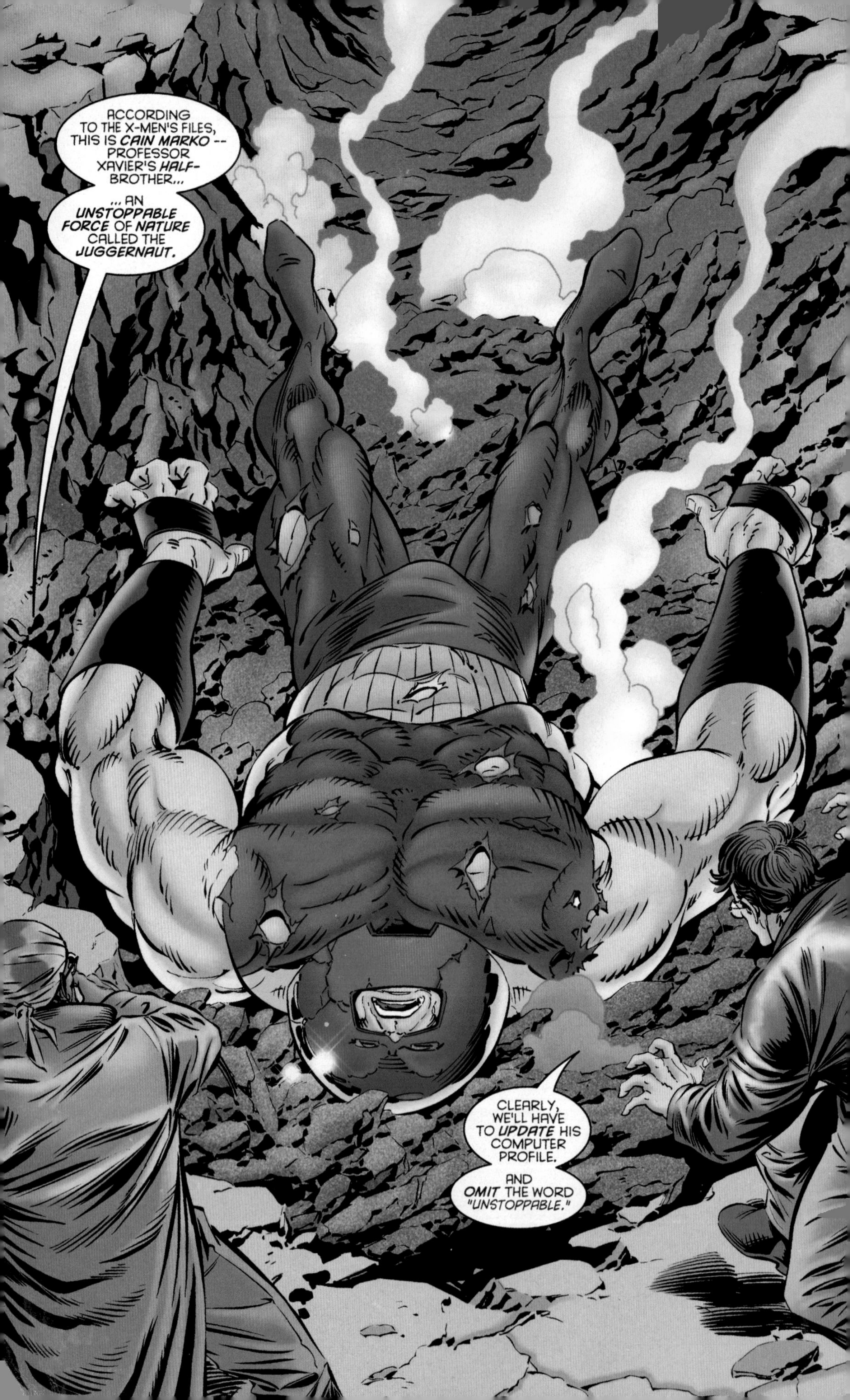

ACCORDING TO THE X-MEN'S FILES, THIS IS CAIN MARKO -- PROFESSOR XAVIER'S HALF-BROTHER...
... AN UNSTOPPABLE FORCE OF NATURE CALLED THE JUGGERNAUT.
CLEARLY, WE'LL HAVE TO UPDATE HIS COMPUTER PROFILE.
AND OMIT THE WORD "UNSTOPPABLE."

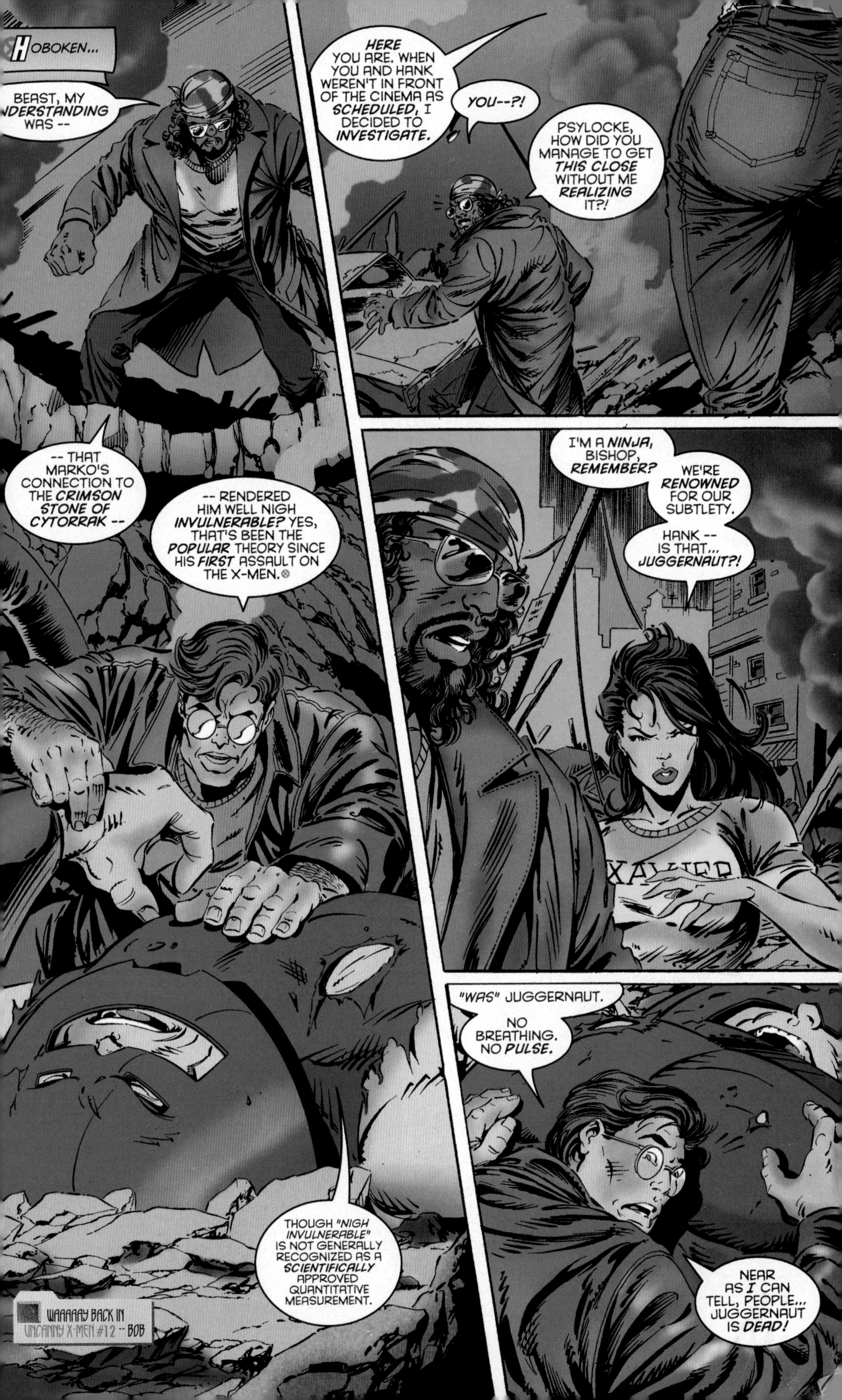

HOBOKEN...
BEAST, MY UNDERSTANDING WAS --
HERE YOU ARE. WHEN YOU AND HANK WEREN'T IN FRONT OF THE CINEMA AS SCHEDULED, I DECIDED TO INVESTIGATE.
YOU--?!
PSYLOCKE, HOW DID YOU MANAGE TO GET THIS CLOSE WITHOUT ME REALIZING IT?!
-- THAT MARKO'S CONNECTION TO THE CRIMSON STONE OF CYTORRAK --
-- RENDERED HIM WELL NIGH INVULNERABLE? YES, THAT'S BEEN THE POPULAR THEORY SINCE HIS FIRST ASSAULT ON THE X-MEN.
I'M A NINJA, BISHOP, REMEMBER?
WE'RE RENOWNED FOR OUR SUBTLETY.
HANK -- IS THAT... JUGGERNAUT?!
"WAS" JUGGERNAUT.
NO BREATHING. NO PULSE.
THOUGH "NIGH INVULNERABLE" IS NOT GENERALLY RECOGNIZED AS A SCIENTIFICALLY APPROVED QUANTITATIVE MEASUREMENT.
NEAR AS I CAN TELL, PEOPLE... JUGGERNAUT IS DEAD!
WAAAAAY BACK IN UNCANNY X-MEN #12 -- BOB

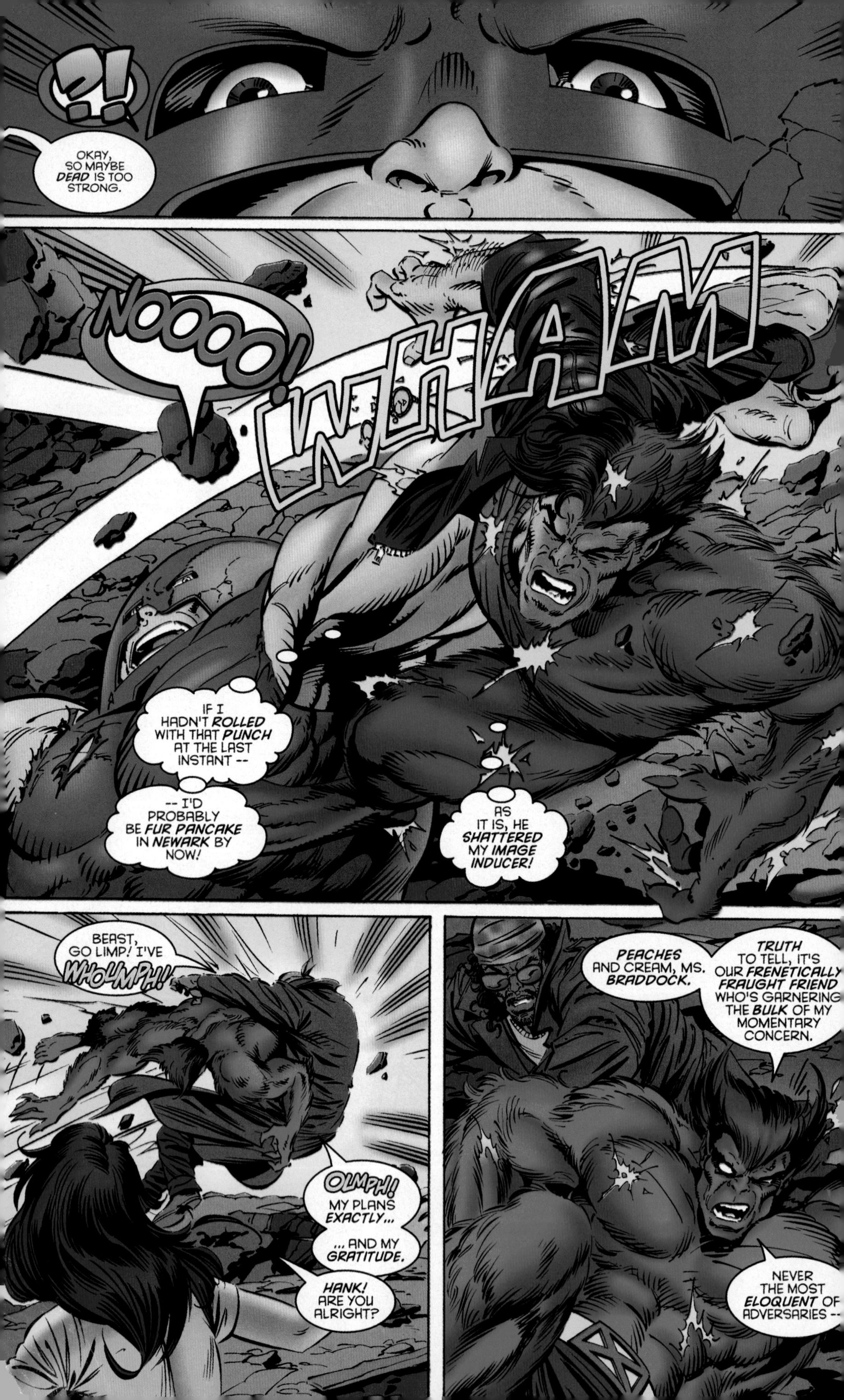
?!
OKAY, SO MAYBE DEAD IS TOO STRONG.
NOOOO!
WHAM
IF I HADN'T ROLLED WITH THAT PUNCH AT THE LAST INSTANT --
-- I'D PROBABLY BE FUR PANCAKE IN NEWARK BY NOW!
AS IT IS, HE SHATTERED MY IMAGE INDUCER!
BEAST, GO LIMP! I'VE
WHOUMPH!
OLMPH! MY PLANS EXACTLY...
... AND MY GRATITUDE.
HANK! ARE YOU ALRIGHT?
PEACHES AND CREAM, MS. BRADDOCK.
TRUTH TO TELL, IT'S OUR FRENETICALLY FRAUGHT FRIEND WHO'S GARNERING THE BULK OF MY MOMENTARY CONCERN.
NEVER THE MOST ELOQUENT OF ADVERSARIES --

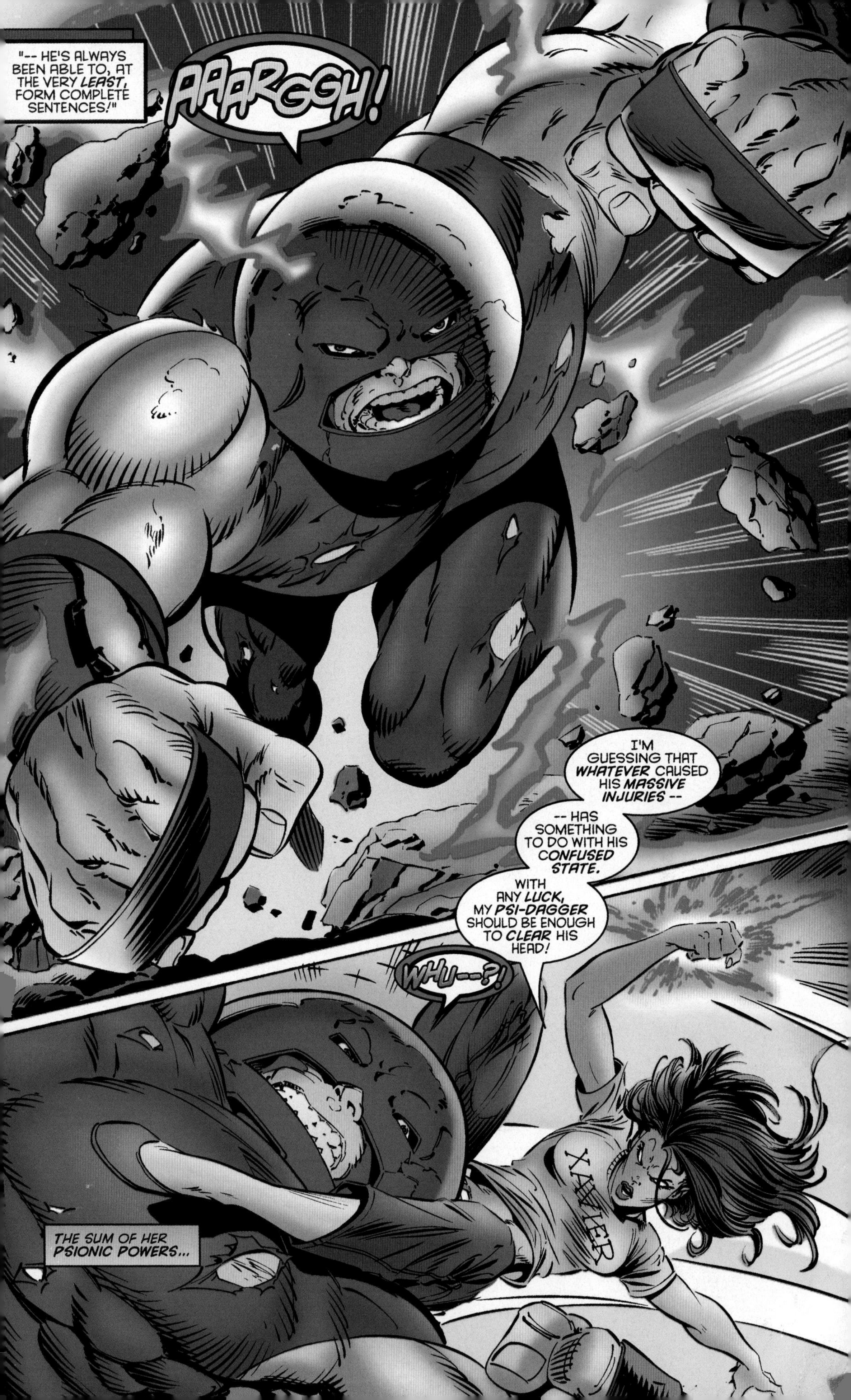
"-- HE'S ALWAYS BEEN ABLE TO, AT THE VERY LEAST, FORM COMPLETE SENTENCES!"
AAARGGH!
I'M GUESSING THAT WHATEVER CAUSED HIS MASSIVE INJURIES --
-- HAS SOMETHING TO DO WITH HIS CONFUSED STATE.
WITH ANY LUCK, MY PSI-DAGGER SHOULD BE ENOUGH TO CLEAR HIS HEAD!
WHU--?!
XAVIER
THE SUM OF HER PSIONIC POWERS...

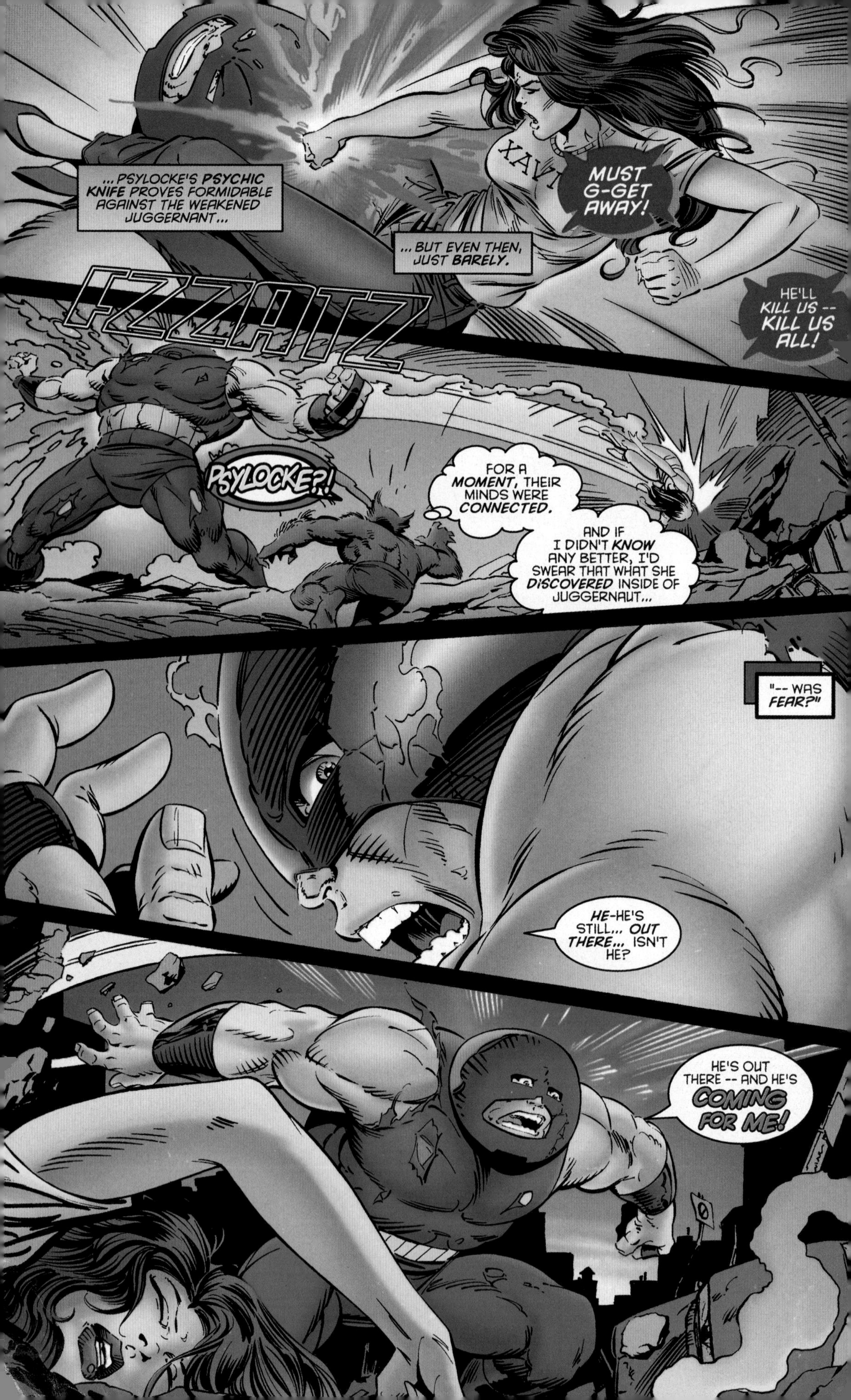
...PSYLOCKE'S PSYCHIC KNIFE PROVES FORMIDABLE AGAINST THE WEAKENED JUGGERNAUT...
MUST G-GET AWAY!
...BUT EVEN THEN, JUST BARELY.
HE'LL KILL US -- KILL US ALL!
FZZZATZ
PSYLOCKE?!
FOR A MOMENT, THEIR MINDS WERE CONNECTED.
AND IF I DIDN'T KNOW ANY BETTER, I'D SWEAR THAT WHAT SHE DISCOVERED INSIDE OF JUGGERNAUT...
"-- WAS FEAR?"
HE-HE'S STILL... OUT THERE... ISN'T HE?
HE'S OUT THERE -- AND HE'S COMING FOR ME!

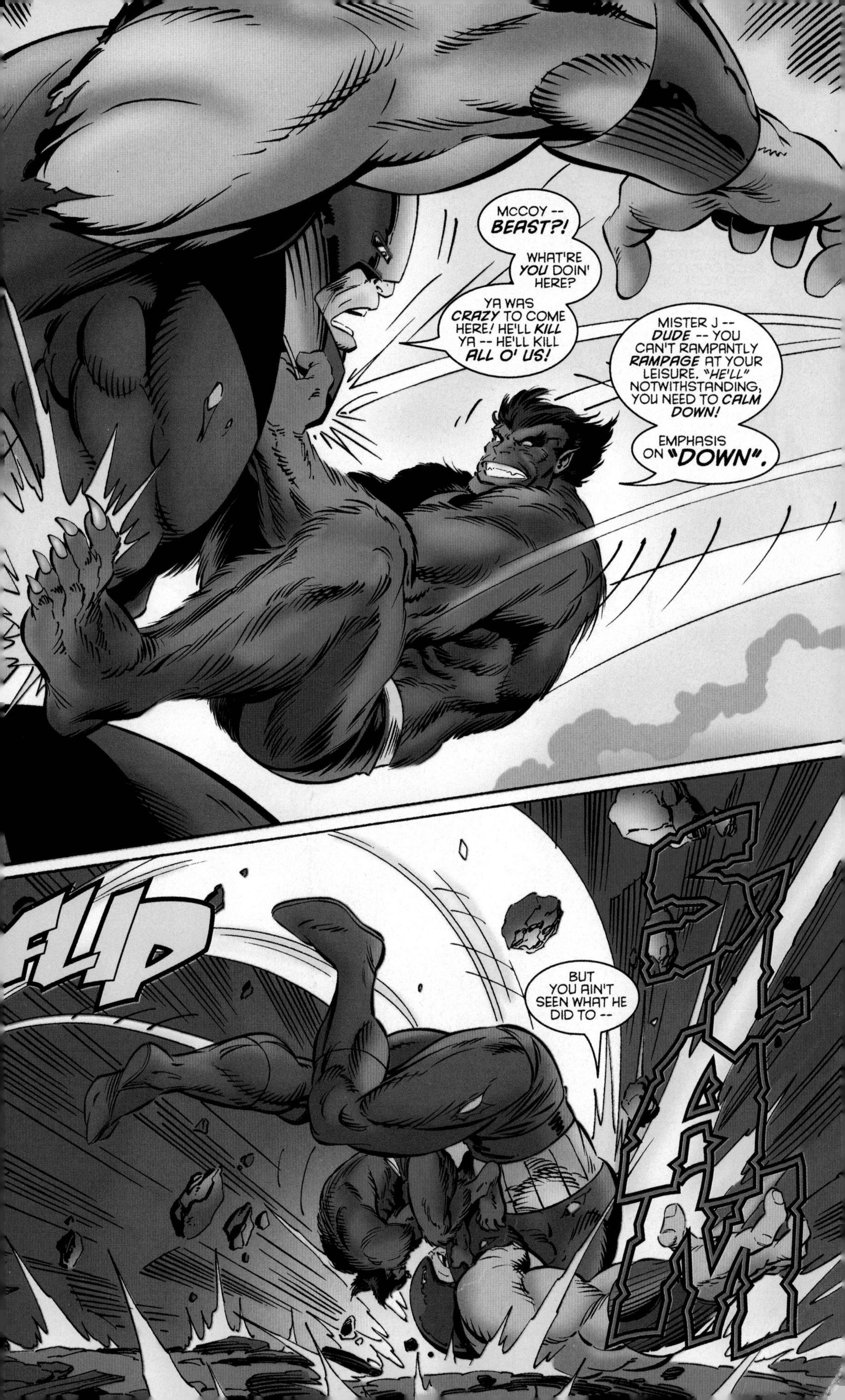
McCOY -- BEAST?!
WHAT'RE YOU DOIN' HERE?
YA WAS CRAZY TO COME HERE! HE'LL KILL YA -- HE'LL KILL ALL O' US!
MISTER J -- DUDE -- YOU CAN'T RAMPANTLY RAMPAGE AT YOUR LEISURE. "HE'LL" NOTWITHSTANDING, YOU NEED TO CALM DOWN!
EMPHASIS ON "DOWN".
BUT YOU AIN'T SEEN WHAT HE DID TO --

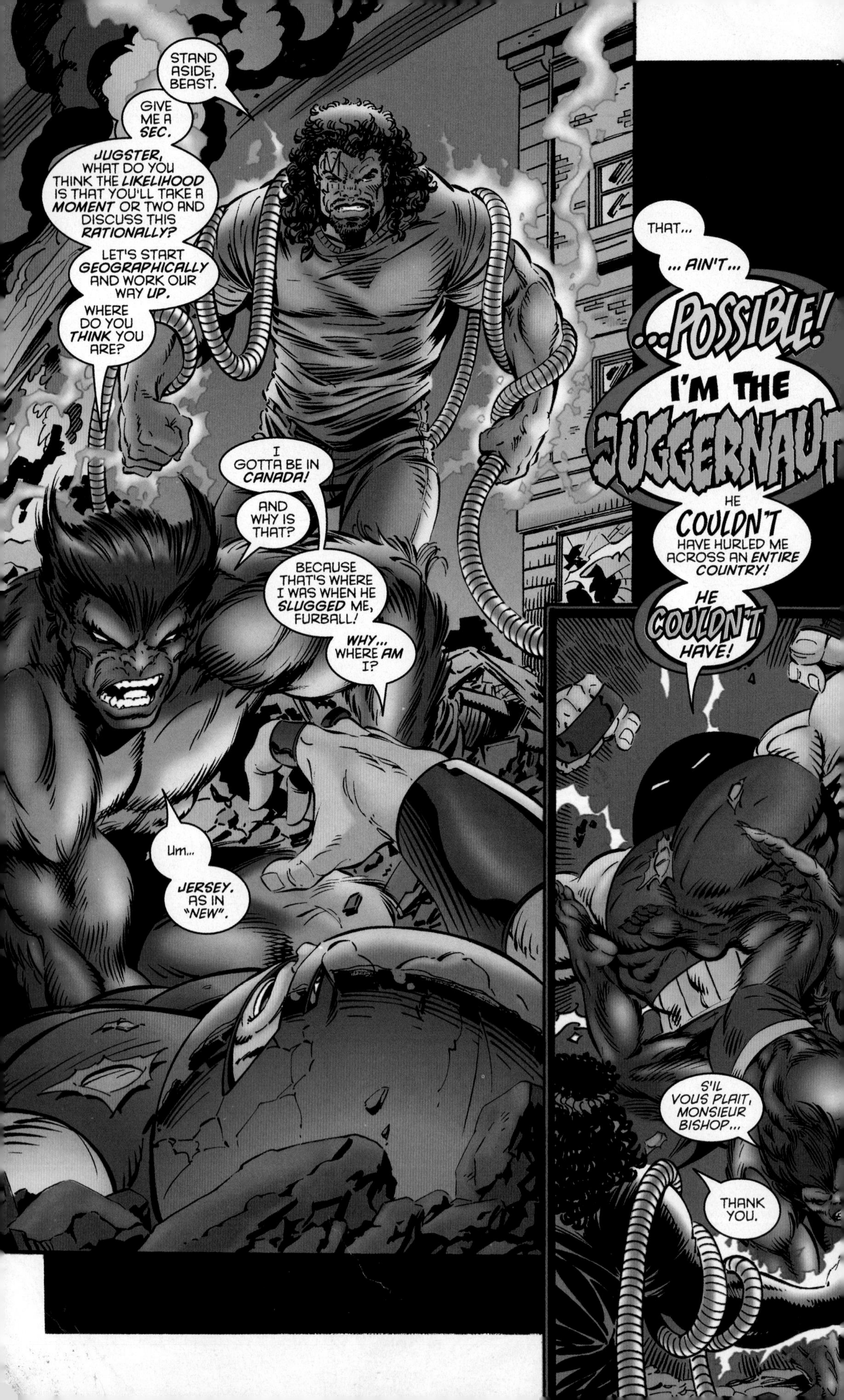
STAND ASIDE, BEAST.
GIVE ME A SEC.
JUGSTER, WHAT DO YOU THINK THE LIKELIHOOD IS THAT YOU'LL TAKE A MOMENT OR TWO AND DISCUSS THIS RATIONALLY?
LET'S START GEOGRAPHICALLY AND WORK OUR WAY UP.
WHERE DO YOU THINK YOU ARE?
I GOTTA BE IN CANADA!
AND WHY IS THAT?
BECAUSE THAT'S WHERE I WAS WHEN HE SLUGGED ME, FURBALL!
WHY... WHERE AM I?
Um...
JERSEY. AS IN "NEW".
THAT...
... AIN'T...
...POSSIBLE!
I'M THE JUGGERNAUT
HE COULDN'T HAVE HURLED ME ACROSS AN ENTIRE COUNTRY!
HE COULDN'T HAVE!
S'IL VOUS PLAIT, MONSIEUR BISHOP...
THANK YOU.

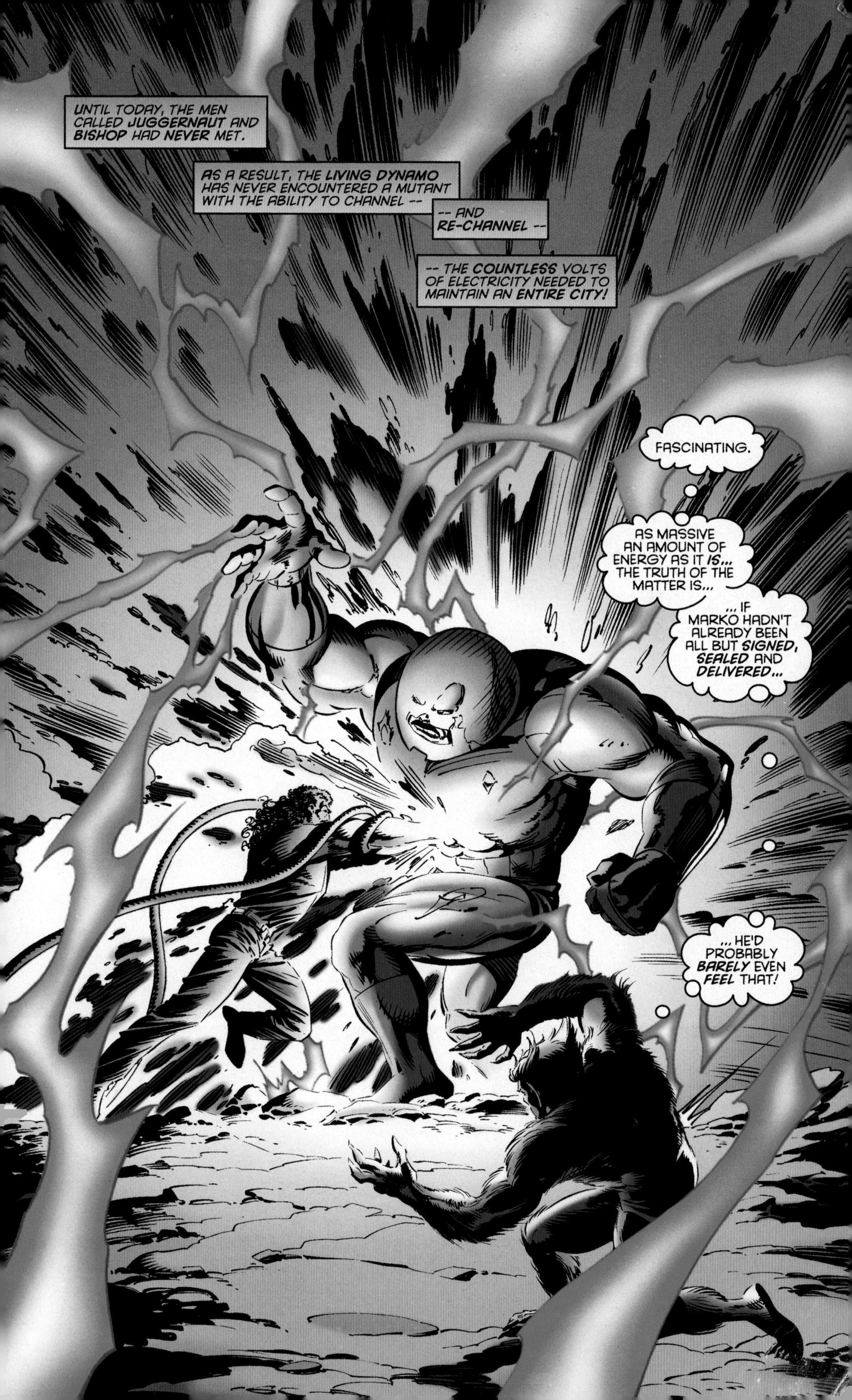
UNTIL TODAY, THE MEN CALLED JUGGERNAUT AND BISHOP HAD NEVER MET.
AS A RESULT, THE LIVING DYNAMO HAS NEVER ENCOUNTERED A MUTANT WITH THE ABILITY TO CHANNEL --
-- AND RE-CHANNEL --
-- THE COUNTLESS VOLTS OF ELECTRICITY NEEDED TO MAINTAIN AN ENTIRE CITY!
FASCINATING.
AS MASSIVE AN AMOUNT OF ENERGY AS IT IS... THE TRUTH OF THE MATTER IS...
... IF MARKO HADN'T ALREADY BEEN ALL BUT SIGNED, SEALED AND DELIVERED...
... HE'D PROBABLY BARELY EVEN FEEL THAT!

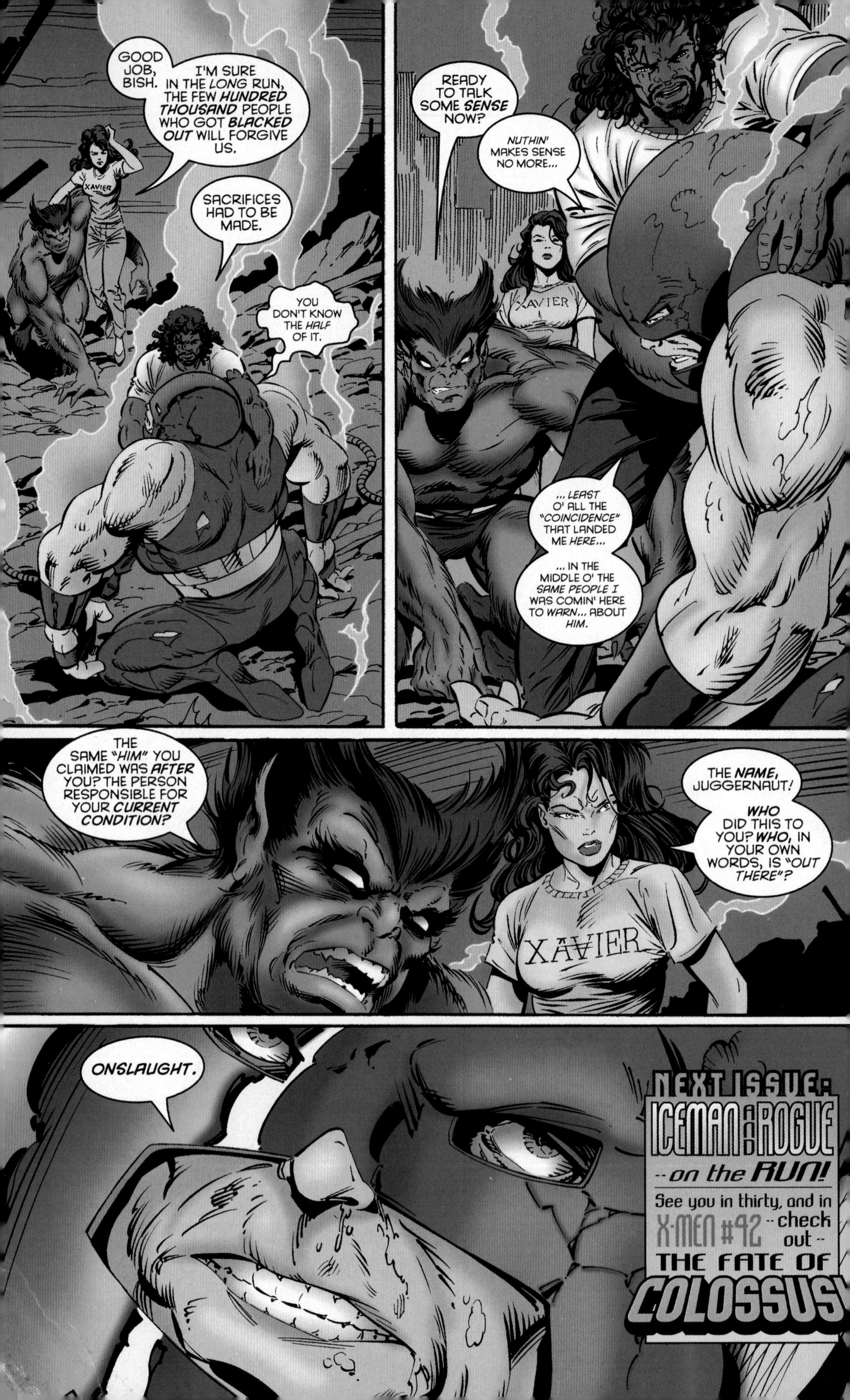
GOOD JOB, BISH.
I'M SURE IN THE LONG RUN, THE FEW HUNDRED THOUSAND PEOPLE WHO GOT BLACKED OUT WILL FORGIVE US.
SACRIFICES HAD TO BE MADE.
YOU DON'T KNOW THE HALF OF IT.
READY TO TALK SOME SENSE NOW?
NUTHIN' MAKES SENSE NO MORE...
XAVIER
...LEAST O' ALL THE "COINCIDENCE" THAT LANDED ME HERE...
...IN THE MIDDLE O' THE SAME PEOPLE I WAS COMIN' HERE TO WARN... ABOUT HIM.
THE SAME "HIM" YOU CLAIMED WAS AFTER YOU? THE PERSON RESPONSIBLE FOR YOUR CURRENT CONDITION?
THE NAME, JUGGERNAUT!
WHO DID THIS TO YOU? WHO, IN YOUR OWN WORDS, IS "OUT THERE"?
XAVIER
ONSLAUGHT.
NEXT ISSUE:
ICEMAN AND ROGUE
--on the RUN!
See you in thirty, and in X-MEN #42 --check out-- THE FATE OF COLOSSUS!

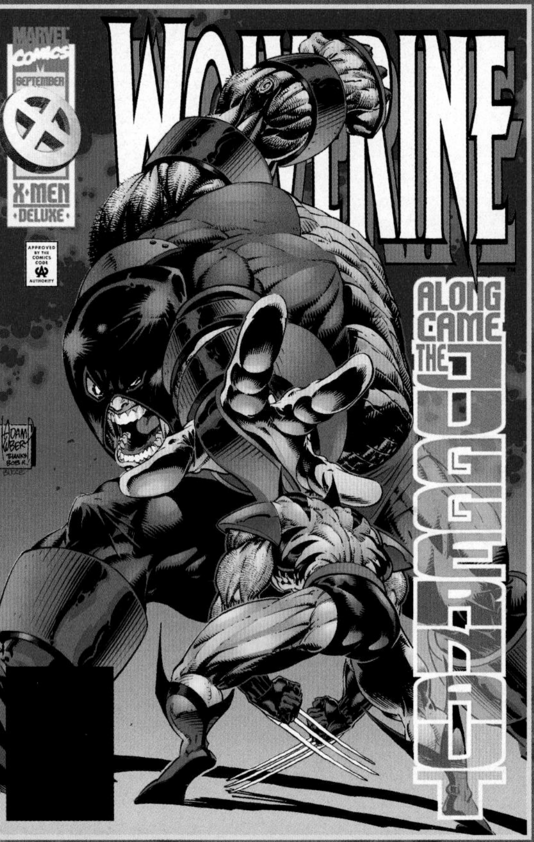
MARVEL COMICS
SEPTEMBER
X-MEN DELUXE
ALONG CAME THE JUGGERNAUT

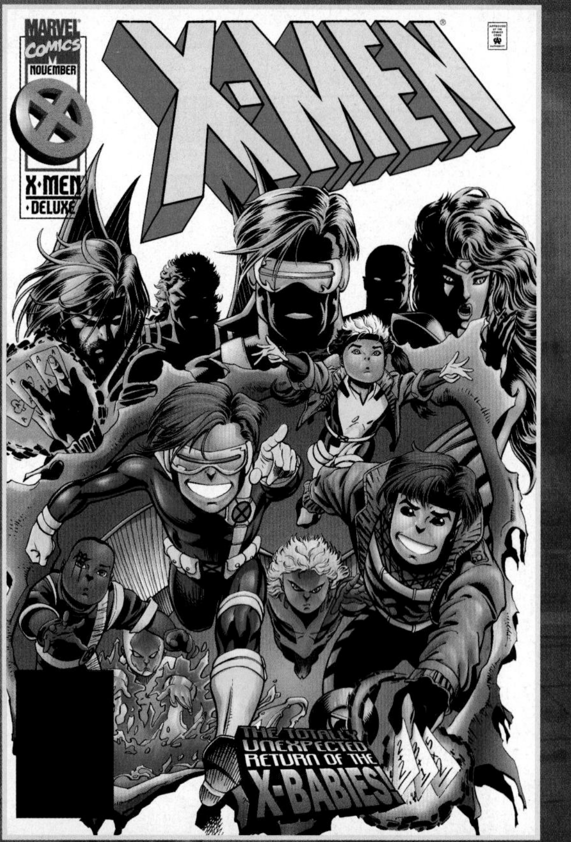
MARVEL COMICS
NOVEMBER
X-MEN
X-MEN DELUXE
THE TOTALLY UNEXPECTED RETURN OF THE X-BABIES!

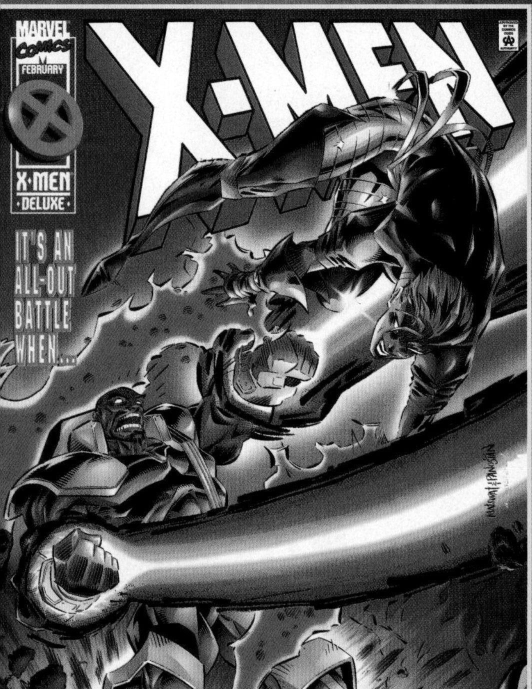
MARVEL COMICS
FEBRUARY
X-MEN
X-MEN DELUXE
IT'S AN ALL-OUT BATTLE WHEN...
BISHOP
GOES WILD!

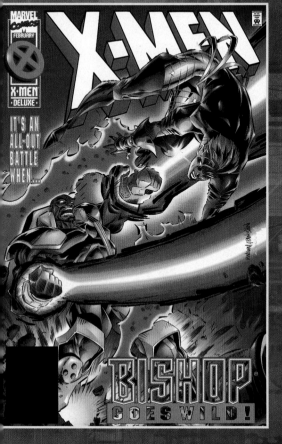

And so it was that the X-Men became aware of the force called Onslaught. Juggernaut, who saw Onslaught's face but could not consciously recall it, was targeted by shadowy figures who banished him to another dimension because he "knew too much."

Soon, however, Onslaught would make his presence known in other ways – raiding the U.S. government's Sentinel-producing facilities, and coercing the teleporter Gateway into kidnapping one of the members of Generation X, the X-Men's students – the young psychic called Chamber.

Onslaught was laying the groundwork for his grand agenda – but first, he needed to take the measure of his foes...

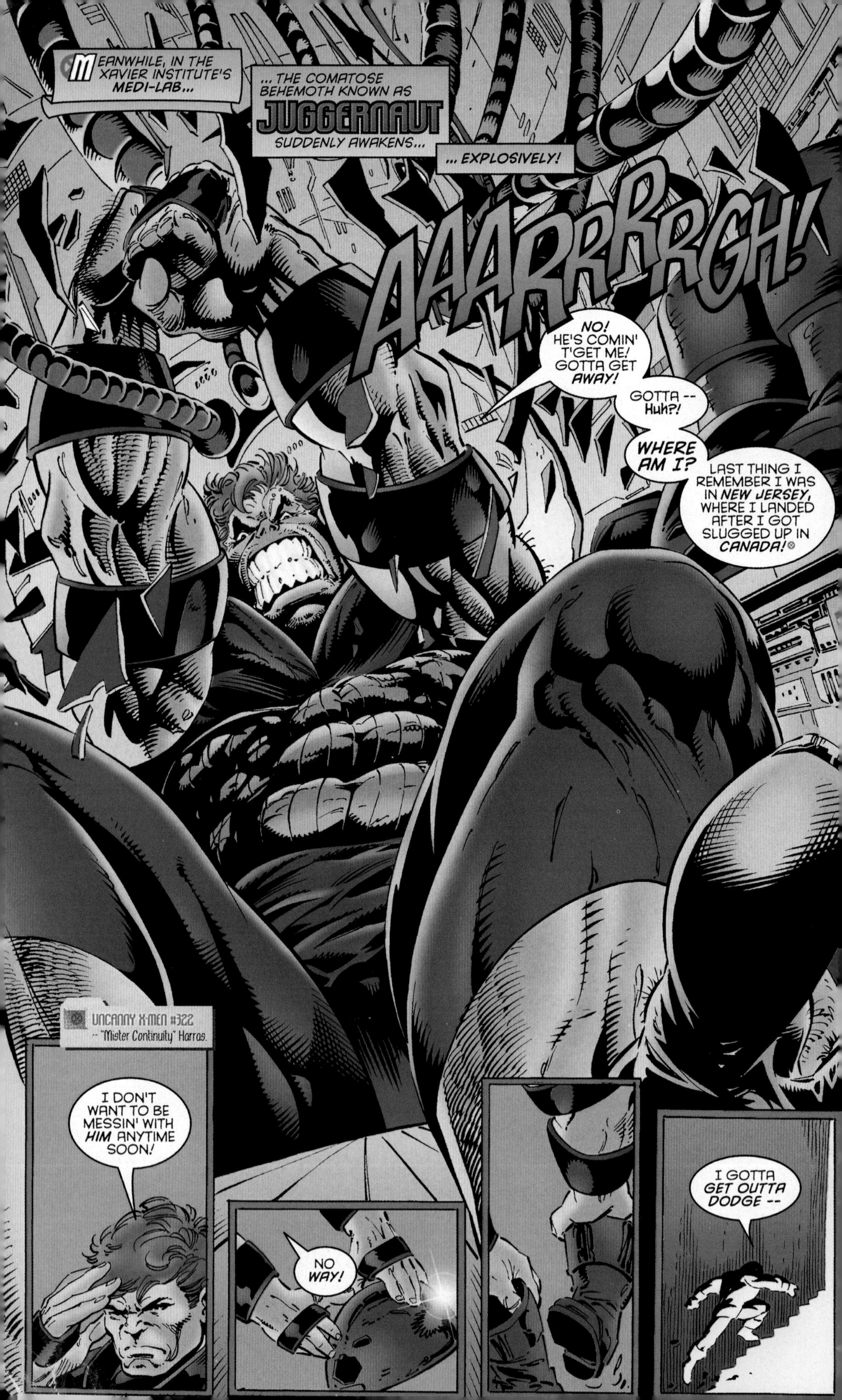

MEANWHILE, IN THE XAVIER INSTITUTE'S MEDI-LAB...
...THE COMATOSE BEHEMOTH KNOWN AS JUGGERNAUT SUDDENLY AWAKENS...
...EXPLOSIVELY!
AAARRRRGH!
NO! HE'S COMIN' T'GET ME! GOTTA GET AWAY!
GOTTA -- Huh?!
WHERE AM I?
LAST THING I REMEMBER I WAS IN NEW JERSEY, WHERE I LANDED AFTER I GOT SLUGGED UP IN CANADA!
UNCANNY X-MEN #322 -- "Mister Continuity" Harras.
I DON'T WANT TO BE MESSIN' WITH HIM ANYTIME SOON!
NO WAY!
I GOTTA GET OUTTA DODGE --

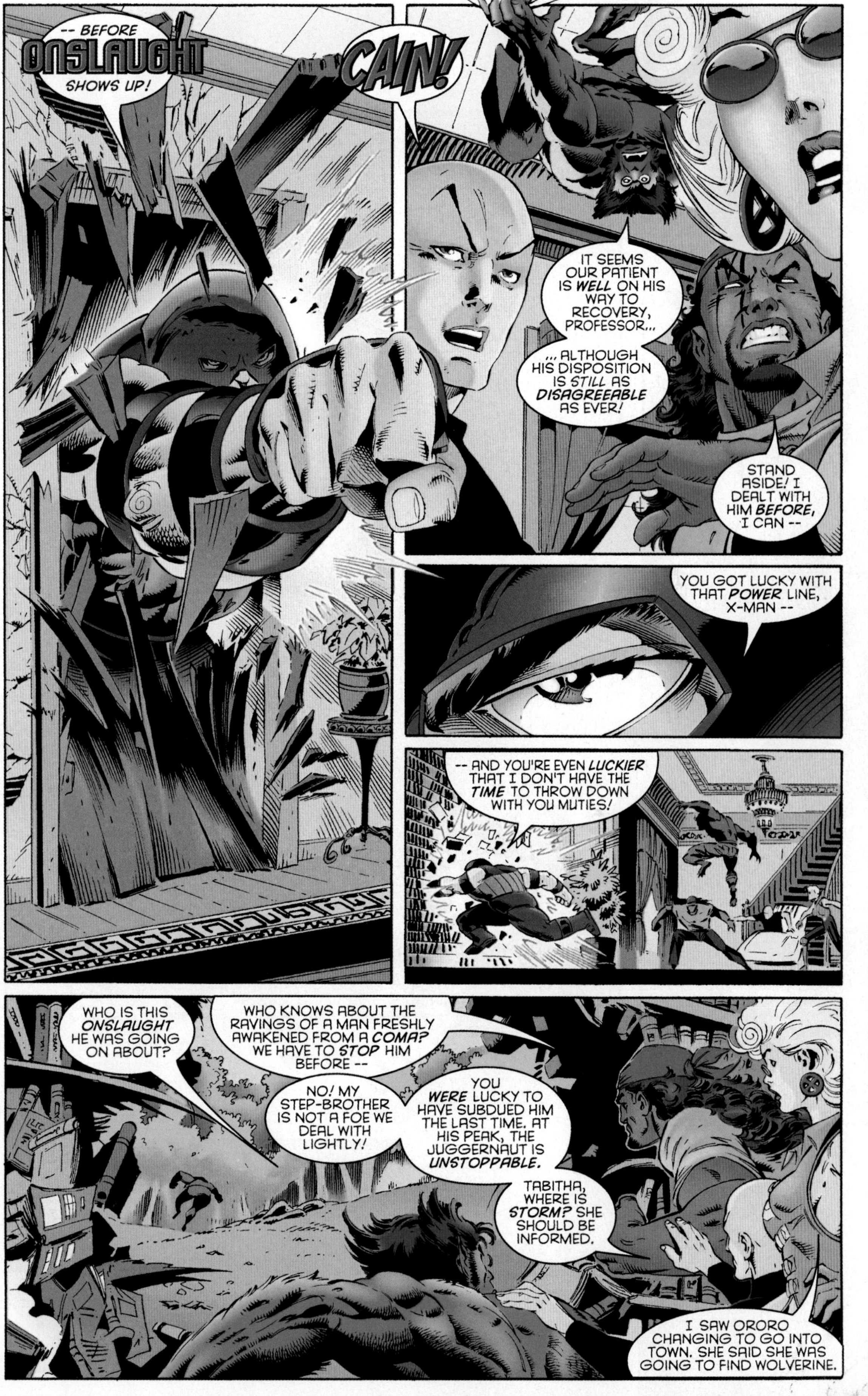
-- BEFORE ONSLAUGHT SHOWS UP!
CAIN!
IT SEEMS OUR PATIENT IS WELL ON HIS WAY TO RECOVERY, PROFESSOR...
... ALTHOUGH HIS DISPOSITION IS STILL AS DISAGREEABLE AS EVER!
STAND ASIDE! I DEALT WITH HIM BEFORE, I CAN --
YOU GOT LUCKY WITH THAT POWER LINE, X-MAN --
-- AND YOU'RE EVEN LUCKIER THAT I DON'T HAVE THE TIME TO THROW DOWN WITH YOU MUTIES!
WHO IS THIS ONSLAUGHT HE WAS GOING ON ABOUT?
WHO KNOWS ABOUT THE RAVINGS OF A MAN FRESHLY AWAKENED FROM A COMA? WE HAVE TO STOP HIM BEFORE --
NO! MY STEP-BROTHER IS NOT A FOE WE DEAL WITH LIGHTLY!
YOU WERE LUCKY TO HAVE SUBDUED HIM THE LAST TIME. AT HIS PEAK, THE JUGGERNAUT IS UNSTOPPABLE.
TABITHA, WHERE IS STORM? SHE SHOULD BE INFORMED.
I SAW ORORO CHANGING TO GO INTO TOWN. SHE SAID SHE WAS GOING TO FIND WOLVERINE.

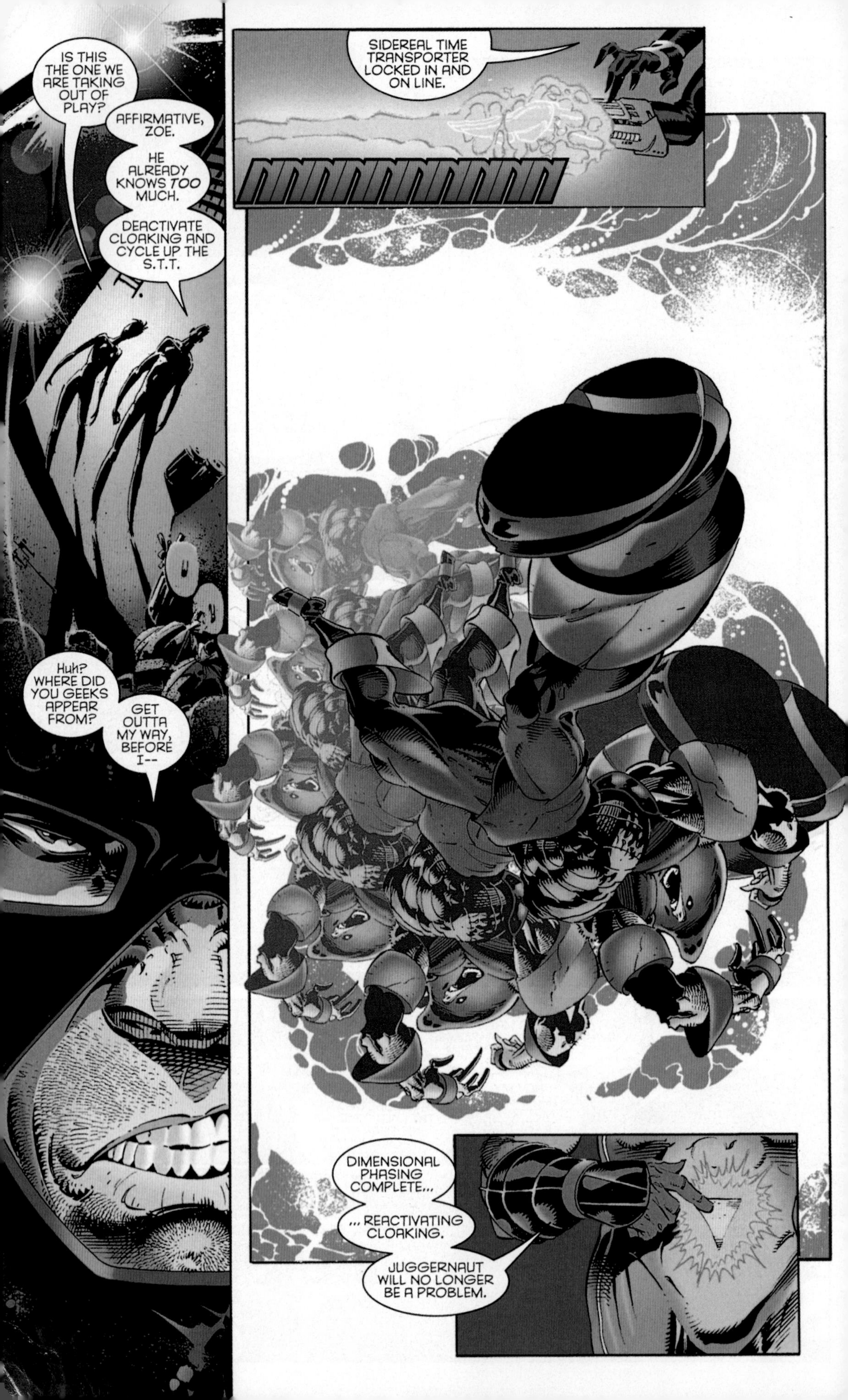
IS THIS THE ONE WE ARE TAKING OUT OF PLAY?
AFFIRMATIVE, ZOE.
HE ALREADY KNOWS TOO MUCH.
DEACTIVATE CLOAKING AND CYCLE UP THE S.T.T.
Huh? WHERE DID YOU GEEKS APPEAR FROM?
GET OUTTA MY WAY, BEFORE I--
SIDEREAL TIME TRANSPORTER LOCKED IN AND ON LINE.
NNNNNNNNNNNN
DIMENSIONAL PHASING COMPLETE...
...REACTIVATING CLOAKING.
JUGGERNAUT WILL NO LONGER BE A PROBLEM.

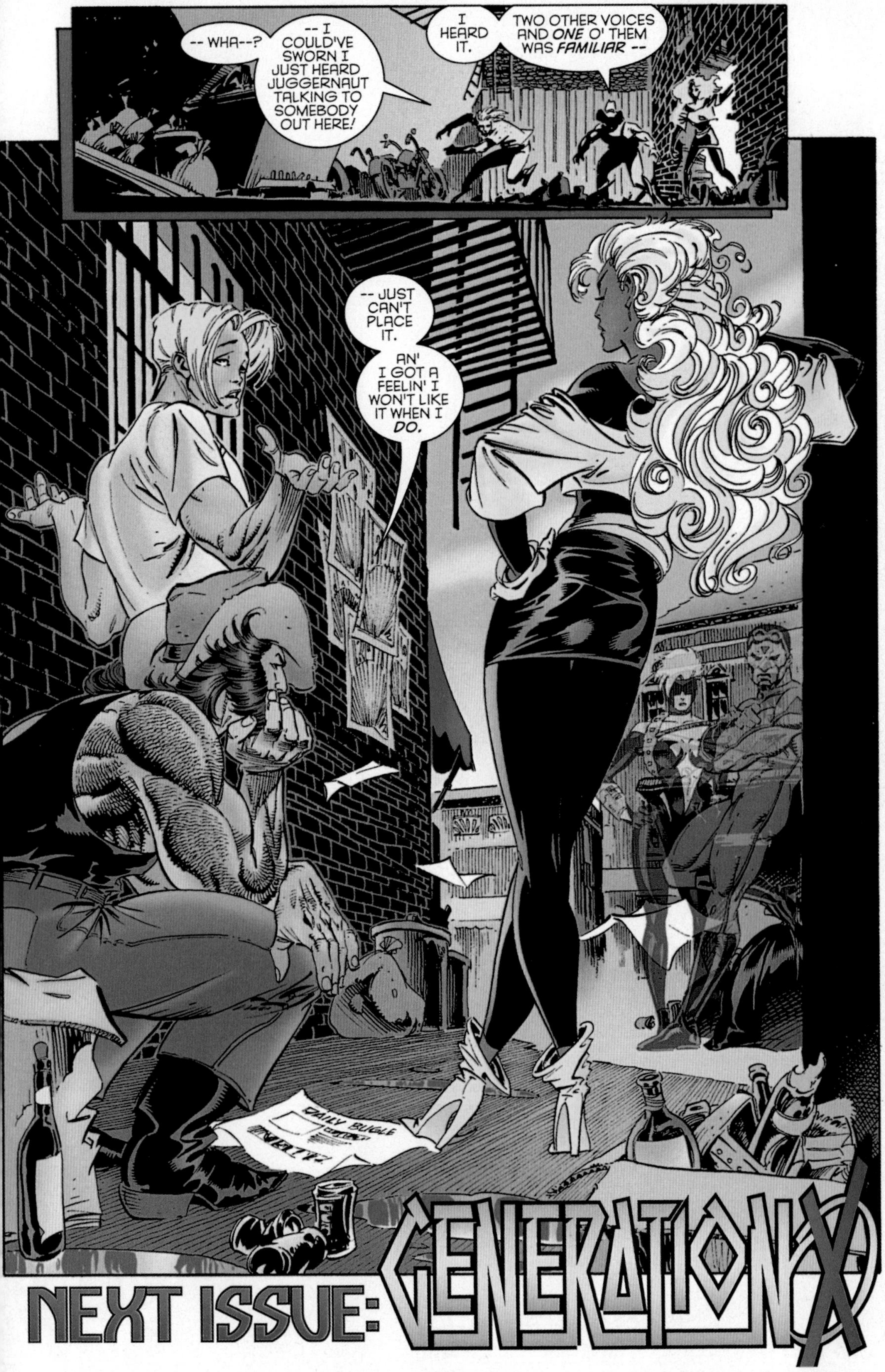
-- WHA--?
-- I COULD'VE SWORN I JUST HEARD JUGGERNAUT TALKING TO SOMEBODY OUT HERE!
I HEARD IT.
TWO OTHER VOICES AND *ONE* O' THEM WAS *FAMILIAR* --
-- JUST CAN'T PLACE IT.
AN' I GOT A FEELIN' I WON'T LIKE IT WHEN I *DO.*
DAILY BUGLE
NEXT ISSUE: GENERATION X

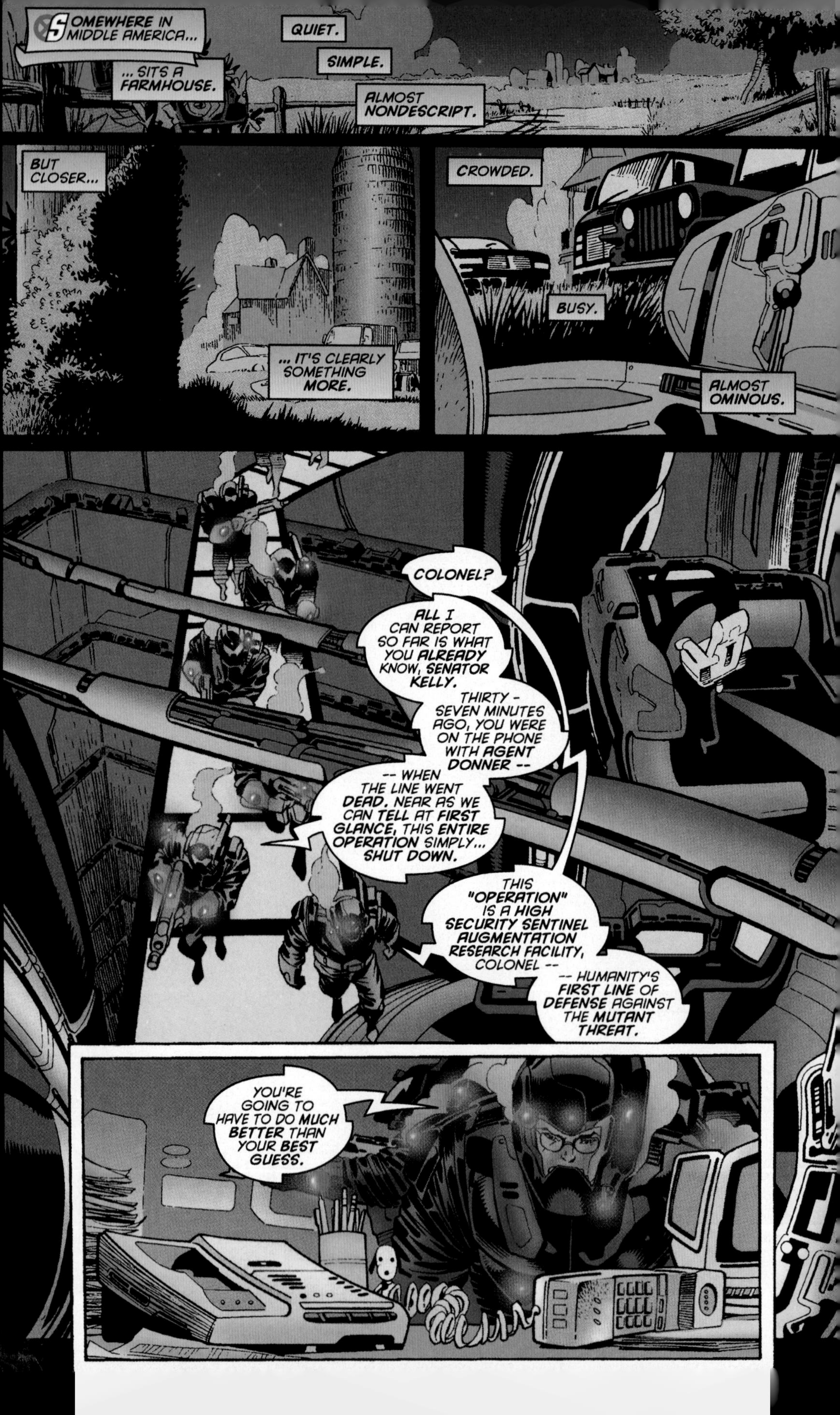
SOMEWHERE IN MIDDLE AMERICA...
... SITS A FARMHOUSE.
QUIET.
SIMPLE.
ALMOST NONDESCRIPT.
BUT CLOSER...
... IT'S CLEARLY SOMETHING MORE.
CROWDED.
BUSY.
ALMOST OMINOUS.
COLONEL?
ALL I CAN REPORT SO FAR IS WHAT YOU ALREADY KNOW, SENATOR KELLY.
THIRTY - SEVEN MINUTES AGO, YOU WERE ON THE PHONE WITH AGENT DONNER --
-- WHEN THE LINE WENT DEAD. NEAR AS WE CAN TELL AT FIRST GLANCE, THIS ENTIRE OPERATION SIMPLY... SHUT DOWN.
THIS "OPERATION" IS A HIGH SECURITY SENTINEL AUGMENTATION RESEARCH FACILITY, COLONEL --
-- HUMANITY'S FIRST LINE OF DEFENSE AGAINST THE MUTANT THREAT.
YOU'RE GOING TO HAVE TO DO MUCH BETTER THAN YOUR BEST GUESS.

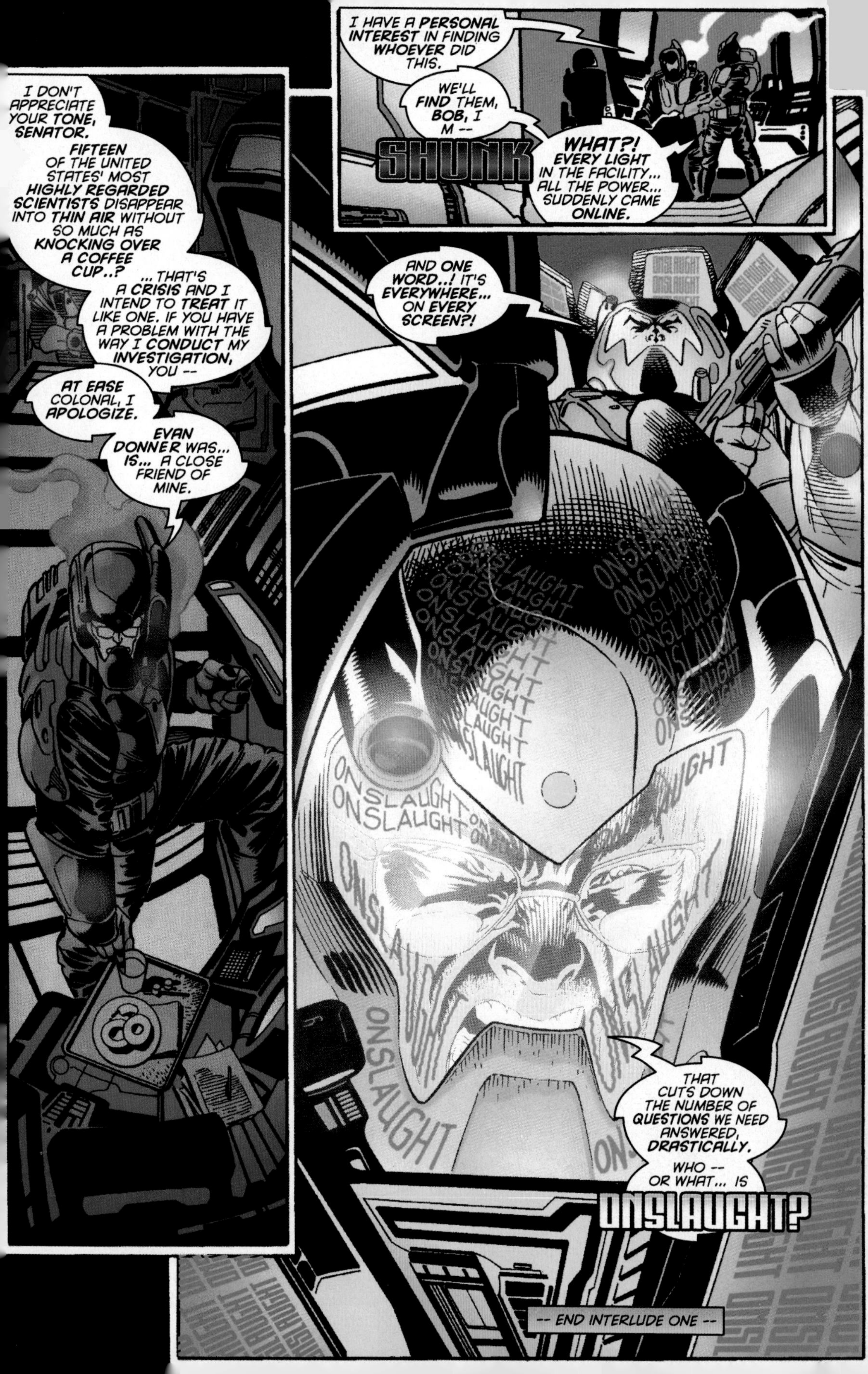
I DON'T APPRECIATE YOUR TONE, SENATOR.
FIFTEEN OF THE UNITED STATES' MOST HIGHLY REGARDED SCIENTISTS DISAPPEAR INTO THIN AIR WITHOUT SO MUCH AS KNOCKING OVER A COFFEE CUP..?
...THAT'S A CRISIS AND I INTEND TO TREAT IT LIKE ONE. IF YOU HAVE A PROBLEM WITH THE WAY I CONDUCT MY INVESTIGATION, YOU --
AT EASE COLONAL, I APOLOGIZE.
EVAN DONNER WAS... IS... A CLOSE FRIEND OF MINE.
I HAVE A PERSONAL INTEREST IN FINDING WHOEVER DID THIS.
WE'LL FIND THEM, BOB, I M --
SHUNK
WHAT?! EVERY LIGHT IN THE FACILITY... ALL THE POWER... SUDDENLY CAME ONLINE.
AND ONE WORD..! IT'S EVERYWHERE... ON EVERY SCREEN?!
THAT CUTS DOWN THE NUMBER OF QUESTIONS WE NEED ANSWERED, DRASTICALLY.
WHO -- OR WHAT... IS ONSLAUGHT?
-- END INTERLUDE ONE --

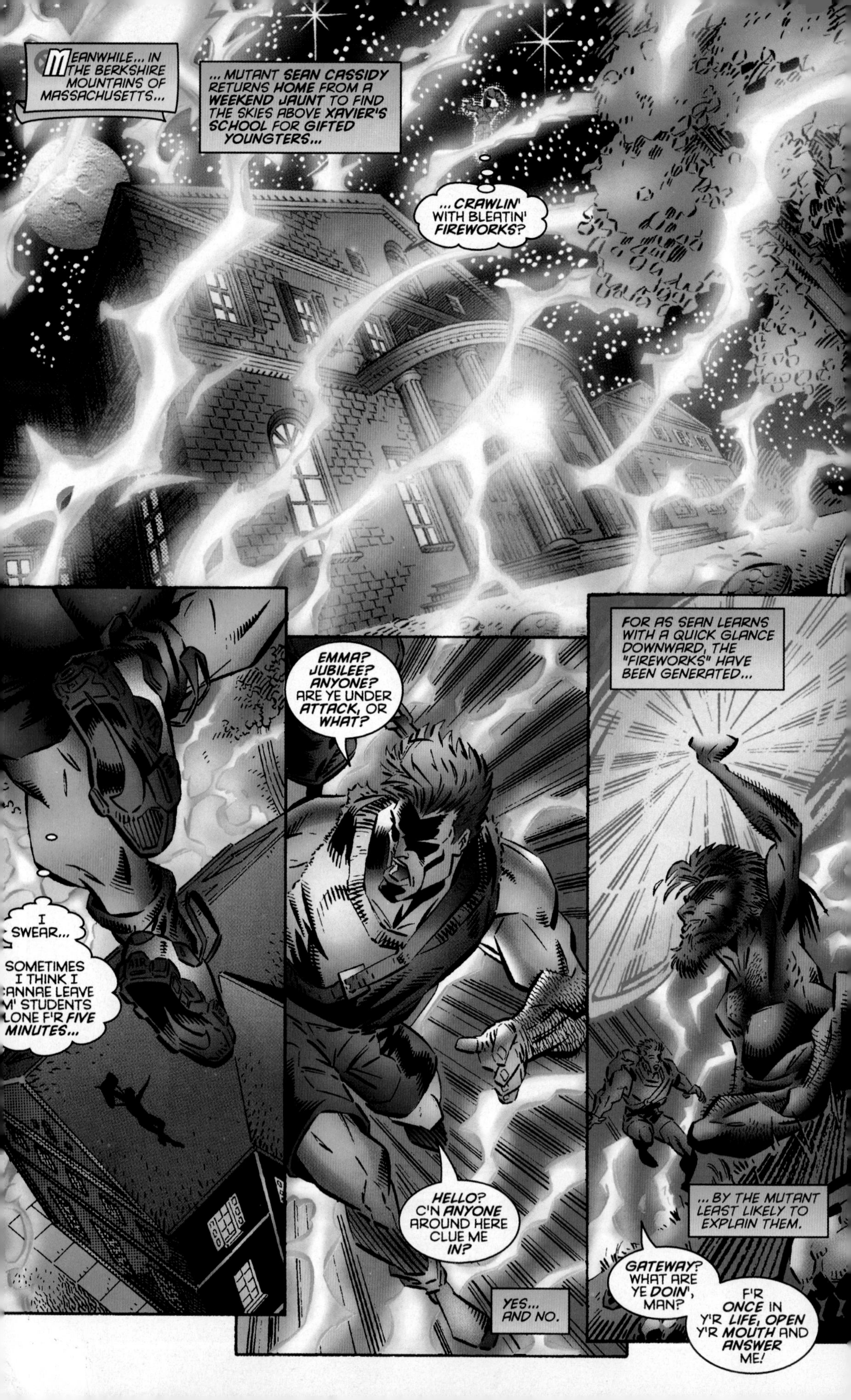
MEANWHILE... IN THE BERKSHIRE MOUNTAINS OF MASSACHUSETTS...
...MUTANT SEAN CASSIDY RETURNS HOME FROM A WEEKEND JAUNT TO FIND THE SKIES ABOVE XAVIER'S SCHOOL FOR GIFTED YOUNGTERS...
...CRAWLIN' WITH BLEATIN' FIREWORKS?
I SWEAR...
SOMETIMES I THINK I CANNAE LEAVE M' STUDENTS ALONE F'R FIVE MINUTES...
EMMA? JUBILEE? ANYONE? ARE YE UNDER ATTACK, OR WHAT?
HELLO? C'N ANYONE AROUND HERE CLUE ME IN?
YES... AND NO.
FOR AS SEAN LEARNS WITH A QUICK GLANCE DOWNWARD, THE "FIREWORKS" HAVE BEEN GENERATED...
...BY THE MUTANT LEAST LIKELY TO EXPLAIN THEM.
GATEWAY? WHAT ARE YE DOIN', MAN?
F'R ONCE IN Y'R LIFE, OPEN Y'R MOUTH AND ANSWER ME!

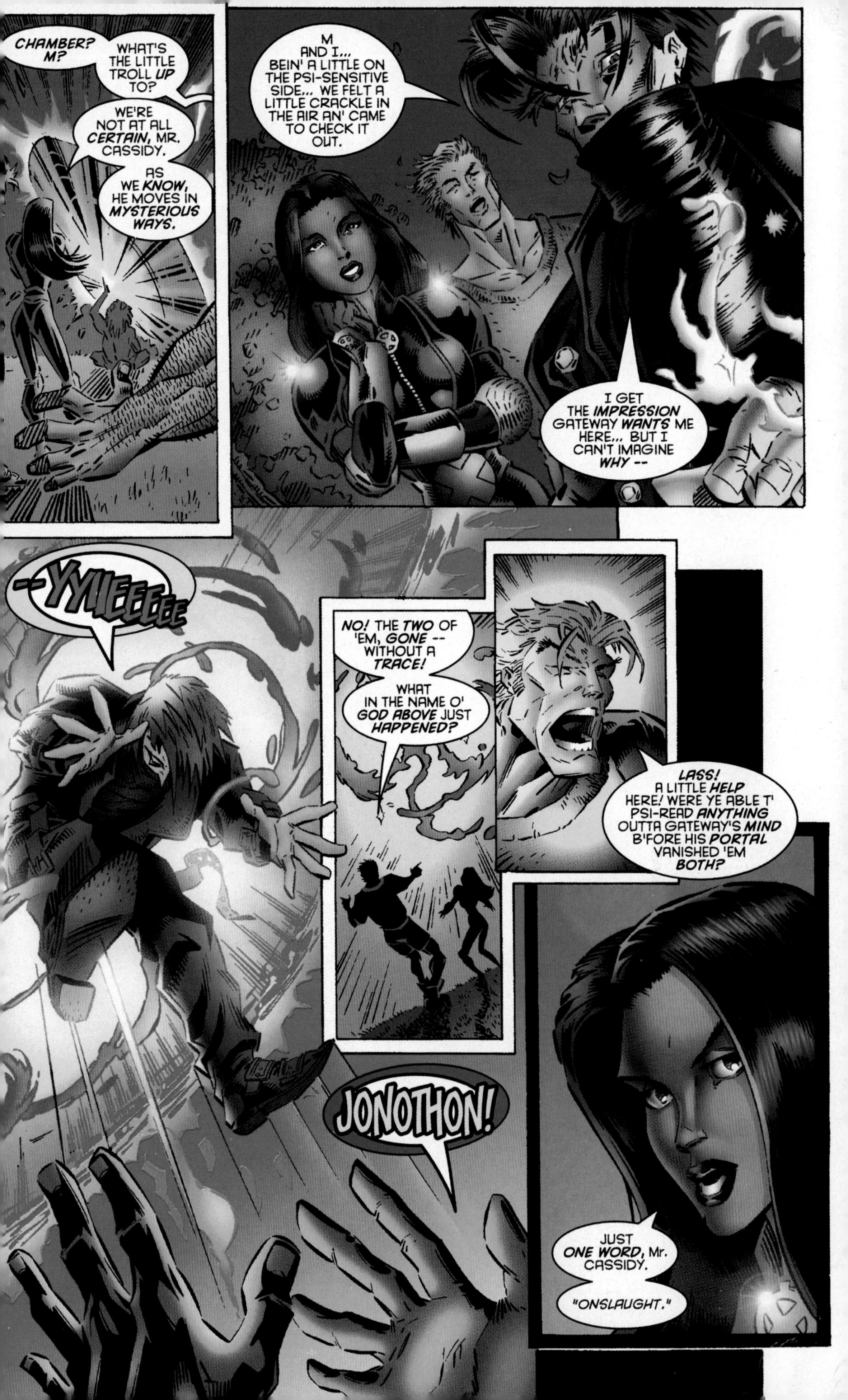
CHAMBER? M?
WHAT'S THE LITTLE TROLL UP TO?
WE'RE NOT AT ALL CERTAIN, MR. CASSIDY.
AS WE KNOW, HE MOVES IN MYSTERIOUS WAYS.
M AND I... BEIN' A LITTLE ON THE PSI-SENSITIVE SIDE... WE FELT A LITTLE CRACKLE IN THE AIR AN' CAME TO CHECK IT OUT.
I GET THE IMPRESSION GATEWAY WANTS ME HERE... BUT I CAN'T IMAGINE WHY --
--YYIIEEEEEE
NO! THE TWO OF 'EM, GONE -- WITHOUT A TRACE!
WHAT IN THE NAME O' GOD ABOVE JUST HAPPENED?
LASS! A LITTLE HELP HERE! WERE YE ABLE T' PSI-READ ANYTHING OUTTA GATEWAY'S MIND B'FORE HIS PORTAL VANISHED 'EM BOTH?
JONOTHON!
JUST ONE WORD, Mr. CASSIDY.
"ONSLAUGHT."

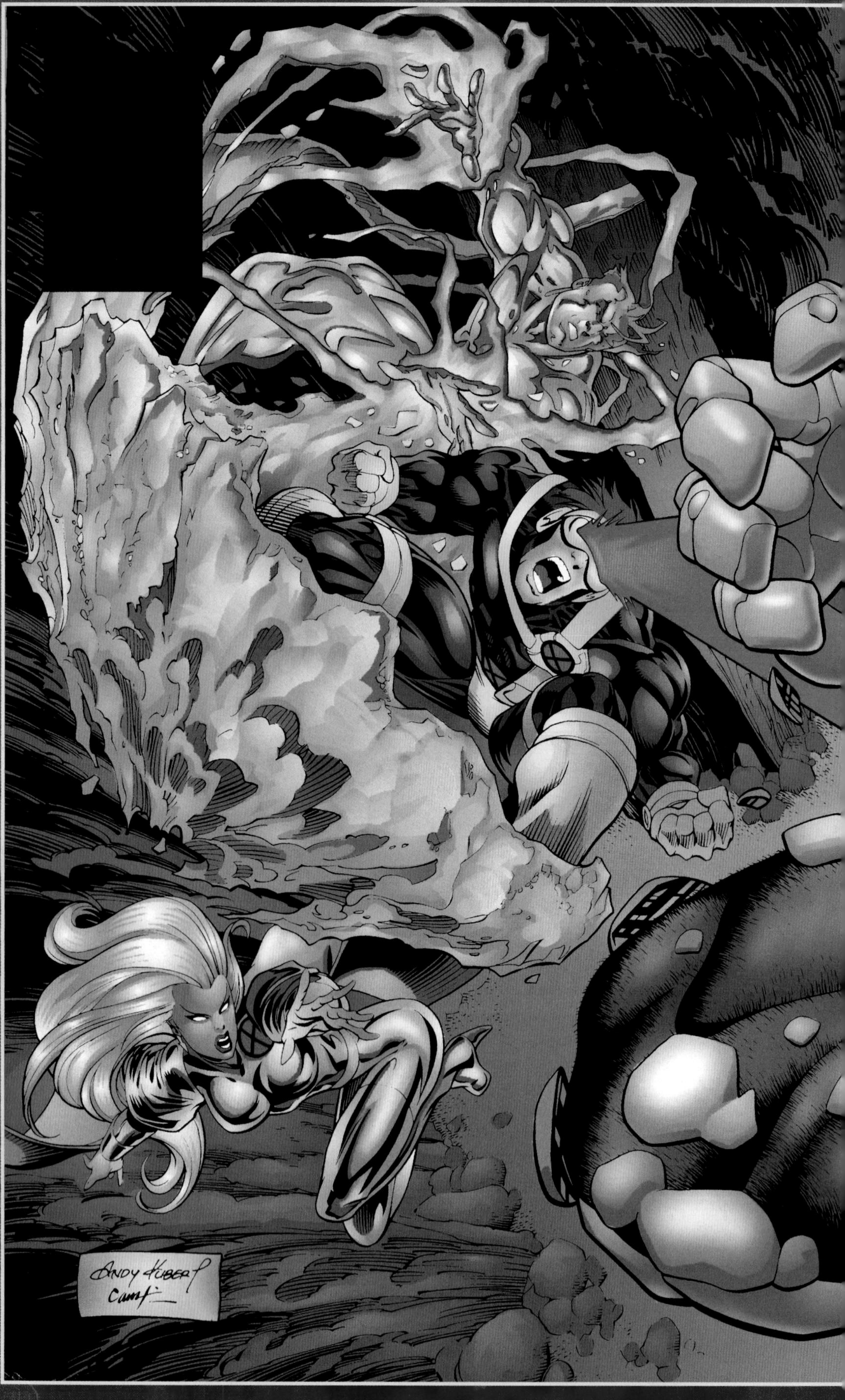
ANDY KUBERT

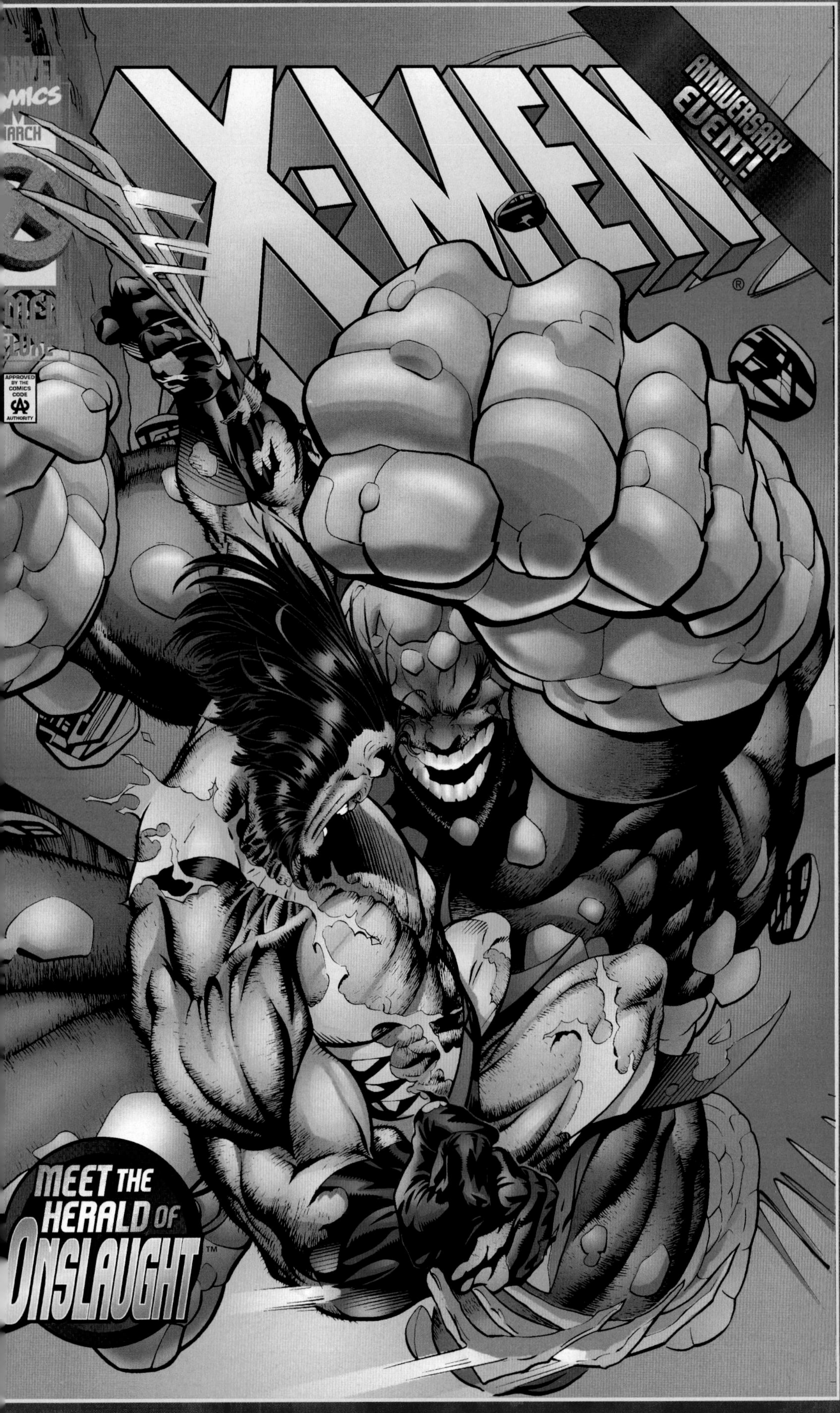

X-MEN
ANNIVERSARY EVENT!
MEET THE HERALD OF ONSLAUGHT
APPROVED BY THE COMICS CODE AUTHORITY

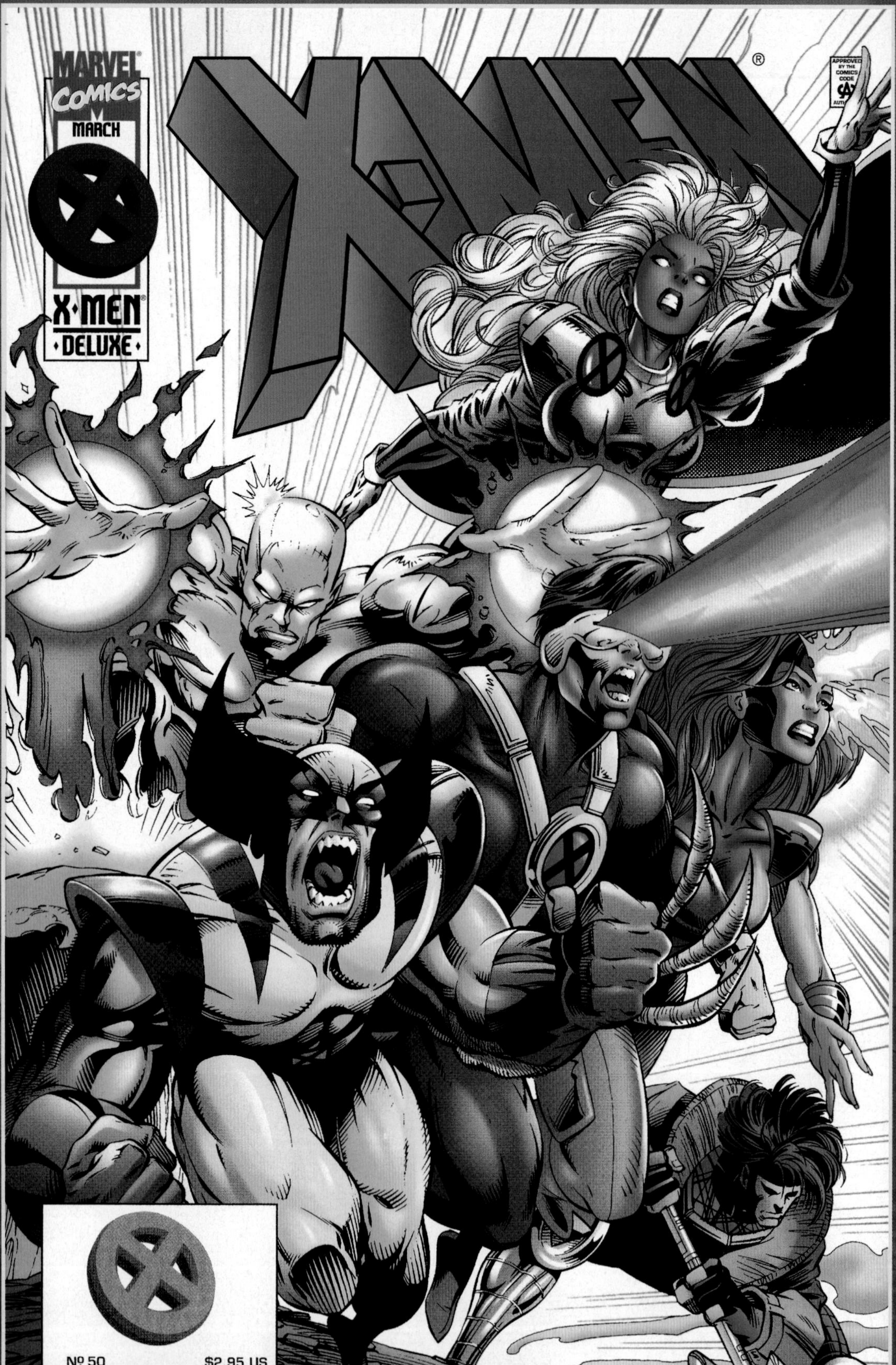
MARVEL COMICS
MARCH
X-MEN
DELUXE
X-MEN
APPROVED BY THE COMICS CODE
Nº 50
$2.95 US
American Entertainment variant cover

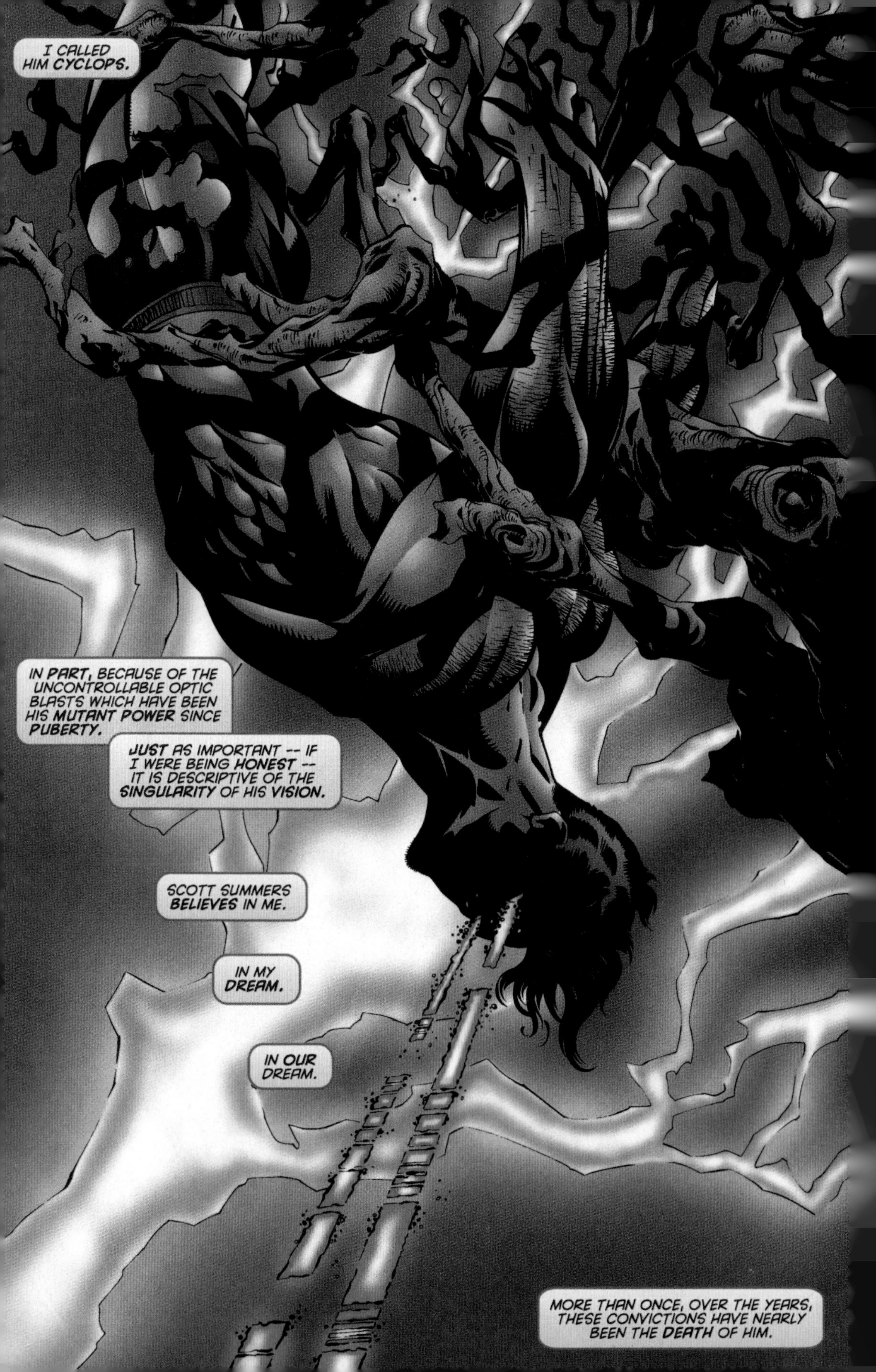
I CALLED HIM CYCLOPS.
IN PART, BECAUSE OF THE UNCONTROLLABLE OPTIC BLASTS WHICH HAVE BEEN HIS MUTANT POWER SINCE PUBERTY.
JUST AS IMPORTANT -- IF I WERE BEING HONEST -- IT IS DESCRIPTIVE OF THE SINGULARITY OF HIS VISION.
SCOTT SUMMERS BELIEVES IN ME.
IN MY DREAM.
IN OUR DREAM.
MORE THAN ONCE, OVER THE YEARS, THESE CONVICTIONS HAVE NEARLY BEEN THE DEATH OF HIM.

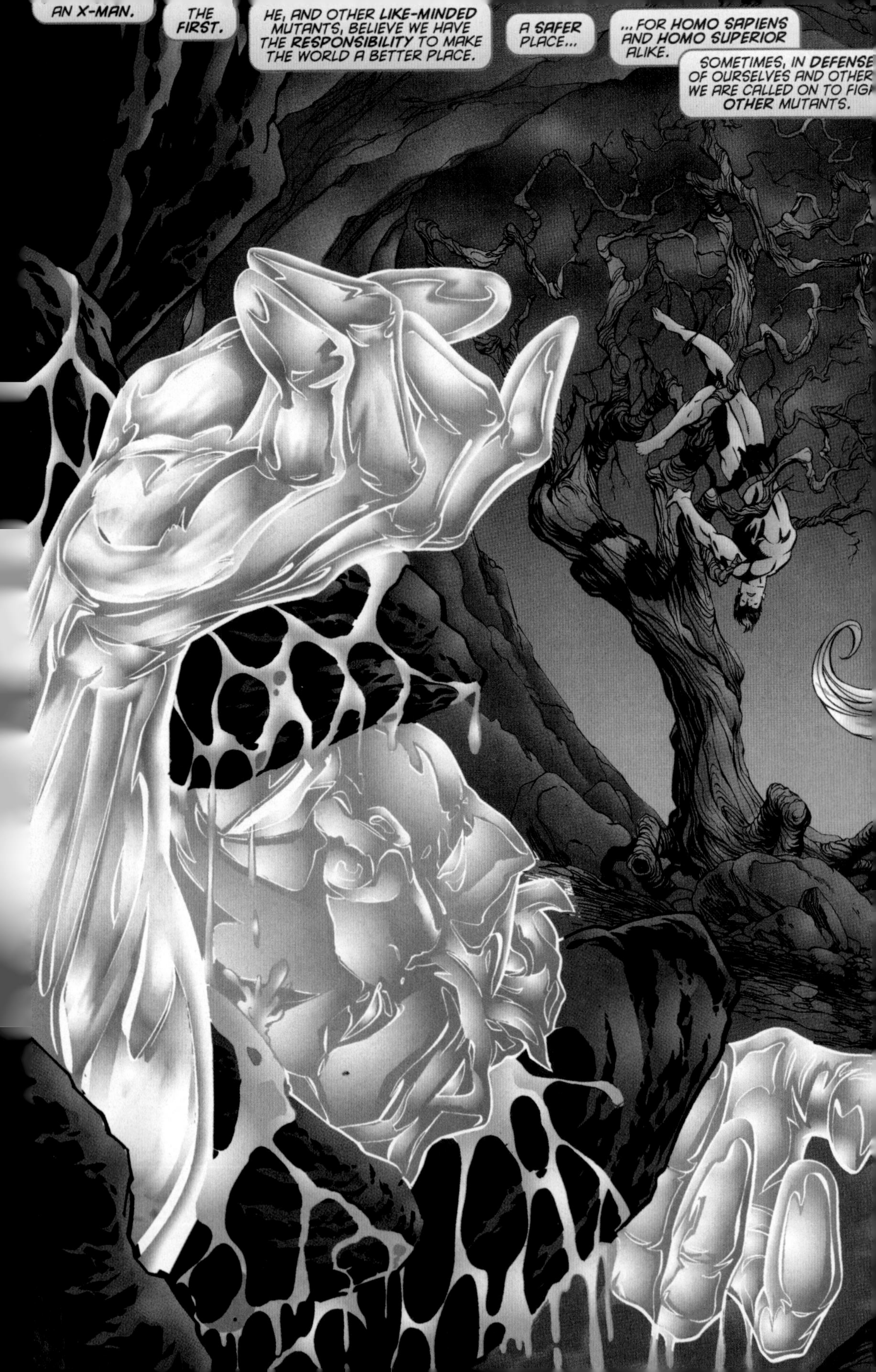
AN X-MAN.
THE FIRST.
HE, AND OTHER LIKE-MINDED MUTANTS, BELIEVE WE HAVE THE RESPONSIBILITY TO MAKE THE WORLD A BETTER PLACE.
A SAFER PLACE...
...FOR HOMO SAPIENS AND HOMO SUPERIOR ALIKE.
SOMETIMES, IN DEFENSE OF OURSELVES AND OTHER WE ARE CALLED ON TO FIG OTHER MUTANTS.

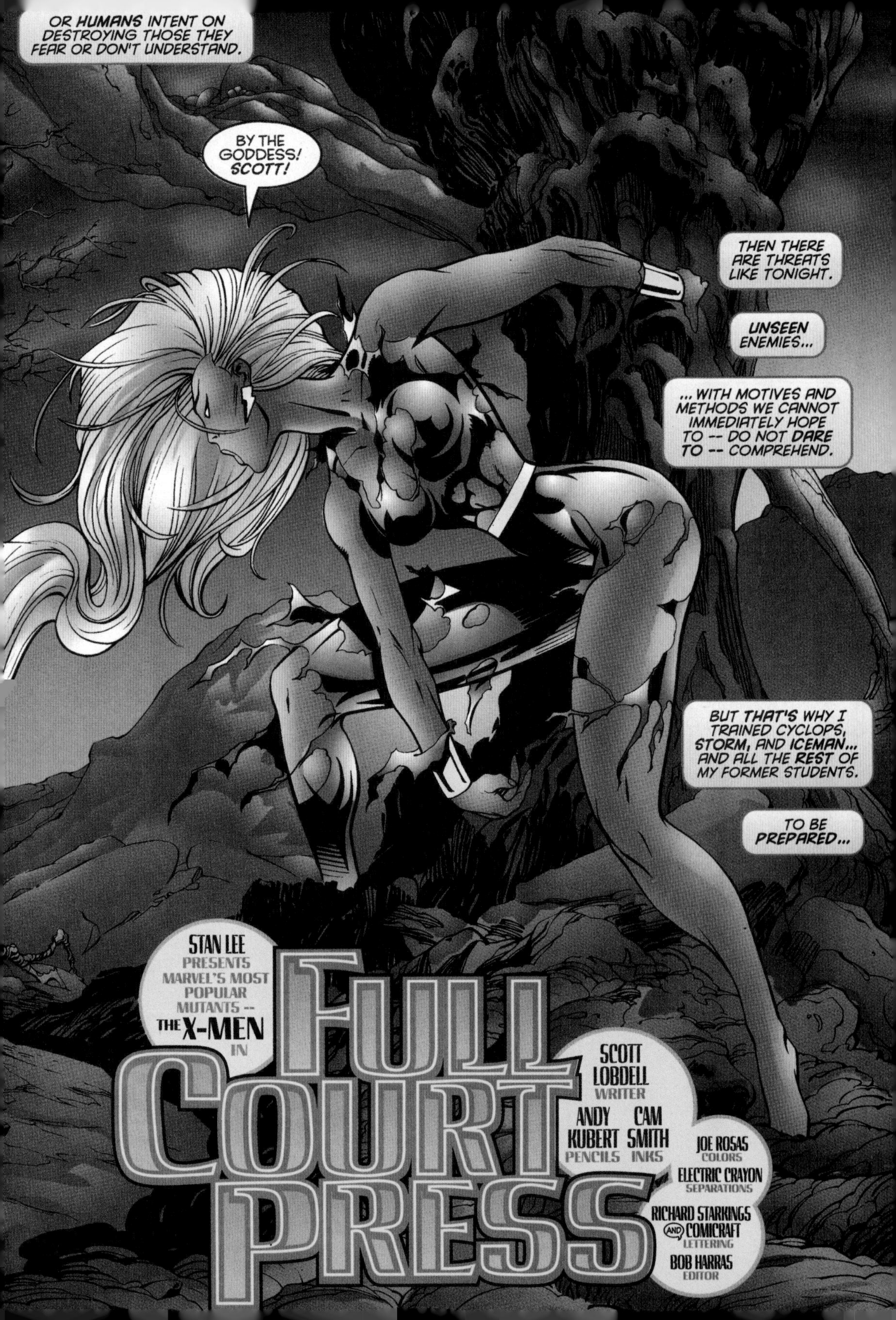
OR HUMANS INTENT ON DESTROYING THOSE THEY FEAR OR DON'T UNDERSTAND.
BY THE GODDESS! SCOTT!
THEN THERE ARE THREATS LIKE TONIGHT.
UNSEEN ENEMIES...
...WITH MOTIVES AND METHODS WE CANNOT IMMEDIATELY HOPE TO -- DO NOT DARE TO -- COMPREHEND.
BUT THAT'S WHY I TRAINED CYCLOPS, STORM, AND ICEMAN... AND ALL THE REST OF MY FORMER STUDENTS.
TO BE PREPARED...
STAN LEE PRESENTS MARVEL'S MOST POPULAR MUTANTS -- THE X-MEN IN
FULL COURT PRESS
SCOTT LOBDELL WRITER
ANDY KUBERT PENCILS
CAM SMITH INKS
JOE ROSAS COLORS
ELECTRIC CRAYON SEPARATIONS
RICHARD STARKINGS AND COMICRAFT LETTERING
BOB HARRAS EDITOR

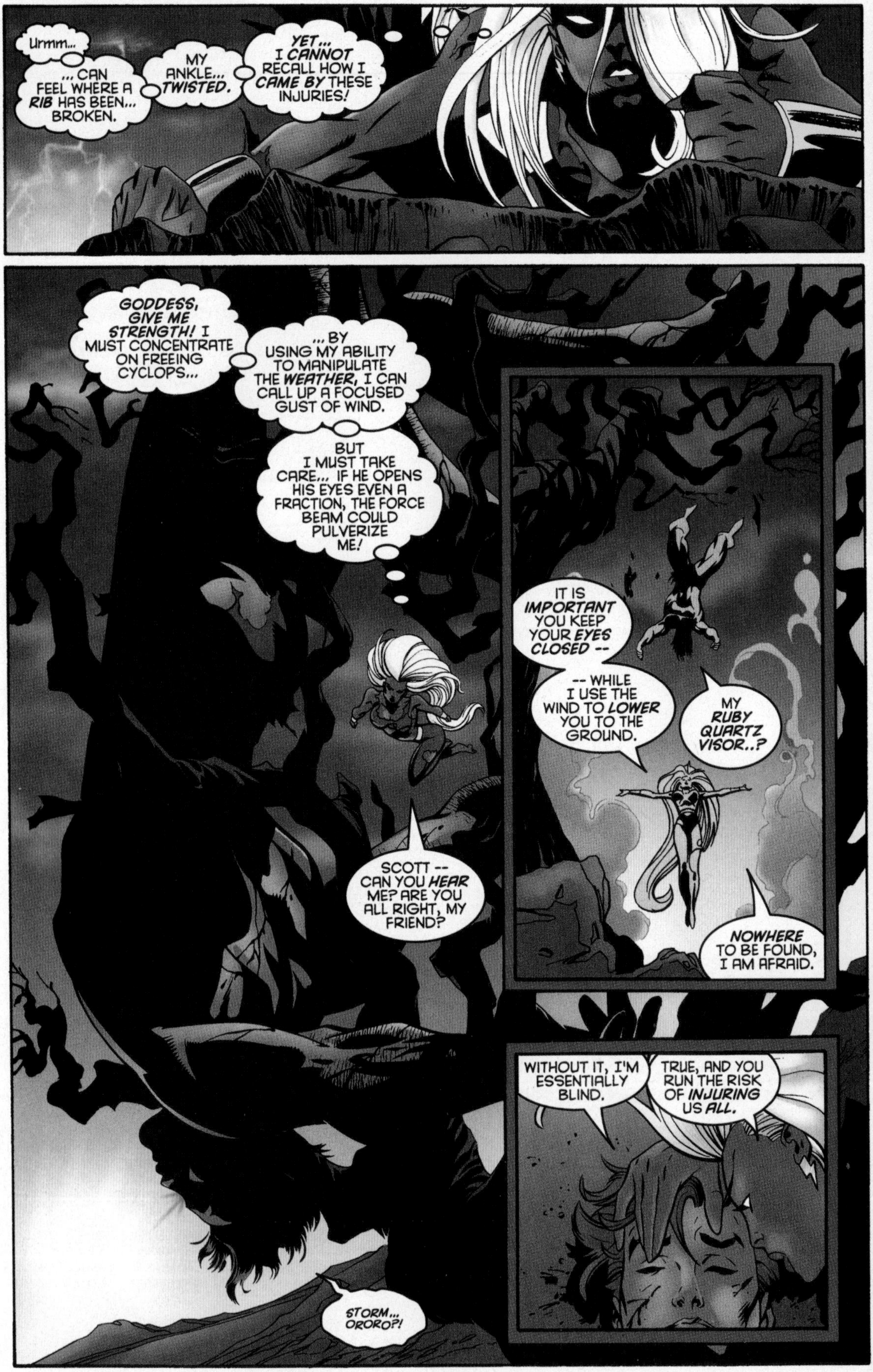
Urmm...
... CAN FEEL WHERE A RIB HAS BEEN... BROKEN.
MY ANKLE... TWISTED.
YET... I CANNOT RECALL HOW I CAME BY THESE INJURIES!
GODDESS, GIVE ME STRENGTH! I MUST CONCENTRATE ON FREEING CYCLOPS...
... BY USING MY ABILITY TO MANIPULATE THE WEATHER, I CAN CALL UP A FOCUSED GUST OF WIND.
BUT I MUST TAKE CARE... IF HE OPENS HIS EYES EVEN A FRACTION, THE FORCE BEAM COULD PULVERIZE ME!
SCOTT -- CAN YOU HEAR ME? ARE YOU ALL RIGHT, MY FRIEND?
STORM... ORORO?!
IT IS IMPORTANT YOU KEEP YOUR EYES CLOSED --
-- WHILE I USE THE WIND TO LOWER YOU TO THE GROUND.
MY RUBY QUARTZ VISOR..?
NOWHERE TO BE FOUND, I AM AFRAID.
WITHOUT IT, I'M ESSENTIALLY BLIND.
TRUE, AND YOU RUN THE RISK OF INJURING US ALL.

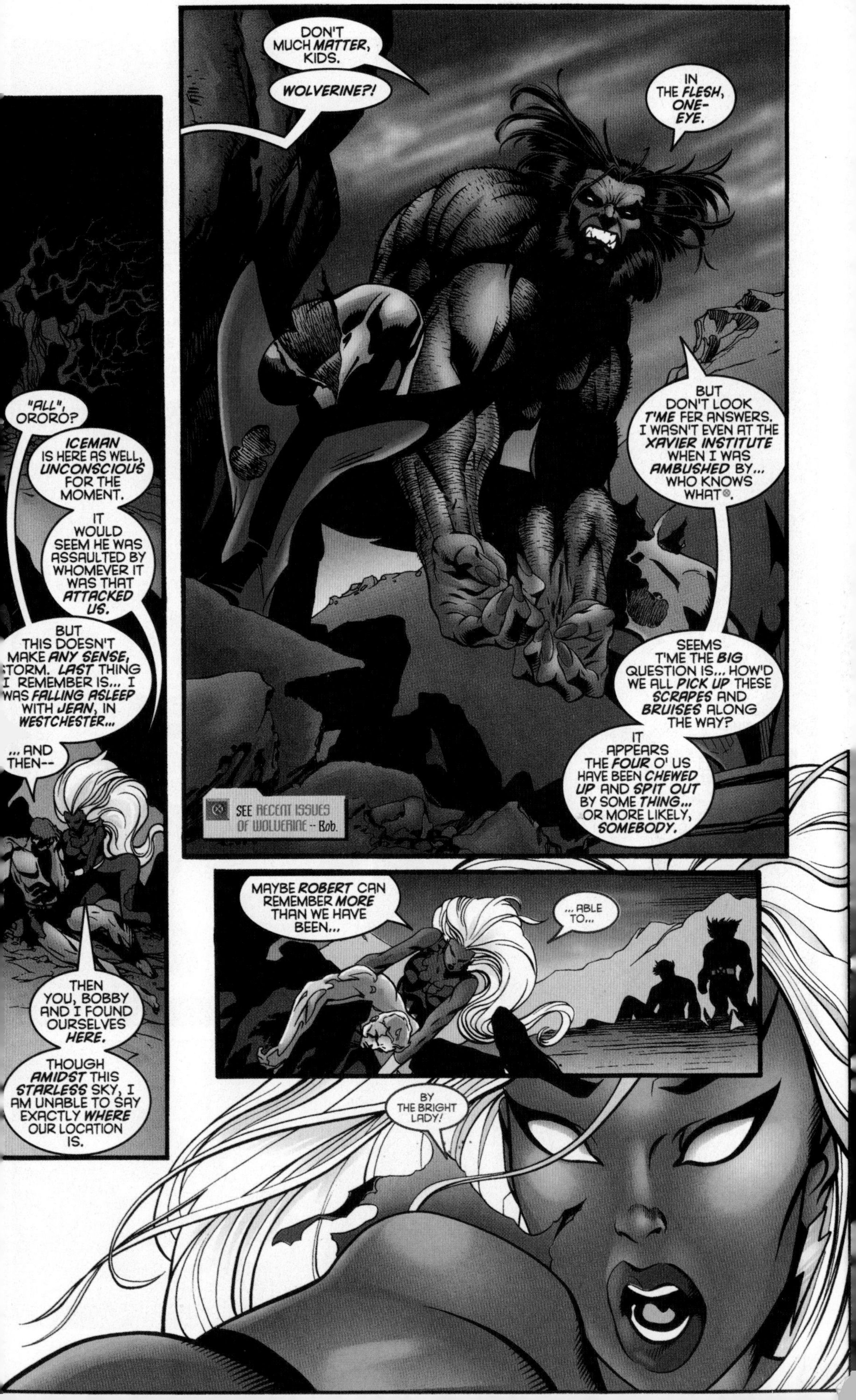

DON'T MUCH MATTER, KIDS.
WOLVERINE?!
IN THE FLESH, ONE-EYE.
BUT DON'T LOOK T'ME FER ANSWERS. I WASN'T EVEN AT THE XAVIER INSTITUTE WHEN I WAS AMBUSHED BY... WHO KNOWS WHAT.
SEE RECENT ISSUES OF WOLVERINE -- Bob.
SEEMS T'ME THE BIG QUESTION IS... HOW'D WE ALL PICK UP THESE SCRAPES AND BRUISES ALONG THE WAY?
IT APPEARS THE FOUR O' US HAVE BEEN CHEWED UP AND SPIT OUT BY SOME THING... OR MORE LIKELY, SOMEBODY.
"ALL", ORORO?
ICEMAN IS HERE AS WELL, UNCONSCIOUS FOR THE MOMENT.
IT WOULD SEEM HE WAS ASSAULTED BY WHOMEVER IT WAS THAT ATTACKED US.
BUT THIS DOESN'T MAKE ANY SENSE, STORM. LAST THING I REMEMBER IS... I WAS FALLING ASLEEP WITH JEAN, IN WESTCHESTER...
...AND THEN--
THEN YOU, BOBBY AND I FOUND OURSELVES HERE.
THOUGH AMIDST THIS STARLESS SKY, I AM UNABLE TO SAY EXACTLY WHERE OUR LOCATION IS.
MAYBE ROBERT CAN REMEMBER MORE THAN WE HAVE BEEN...
...ABLE TO...
BY THE BRIGHT LADY!

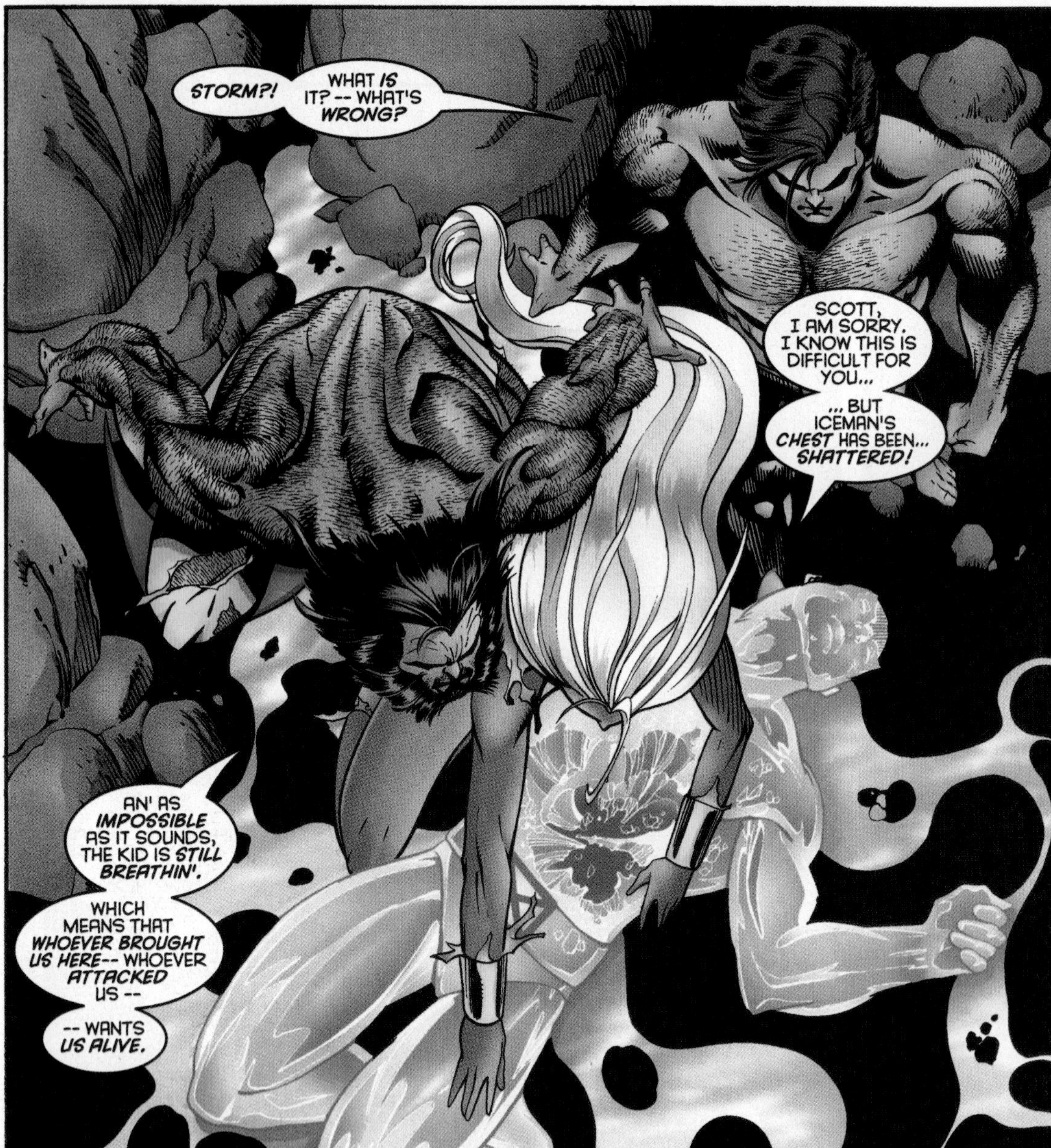
STORM?!
WHAT IS IT? -- WHAT'S WRONG?
SCOTT, I AM SORRY. I KNOW THIS IS DIFFICULT FOR YOU...
... BUT ICEMAN'S CHEST HAS BEEN... SHATTERED!
AN' AS IMPOSSIBLE AS IT SOUNDS, THE KID IS STILL BREATHIN'.
WHICH MEANS THAT WHOEVER BROUGHT US HERE-- WHOEVER ATTACKED US --
-- WANTS US ALIVE.

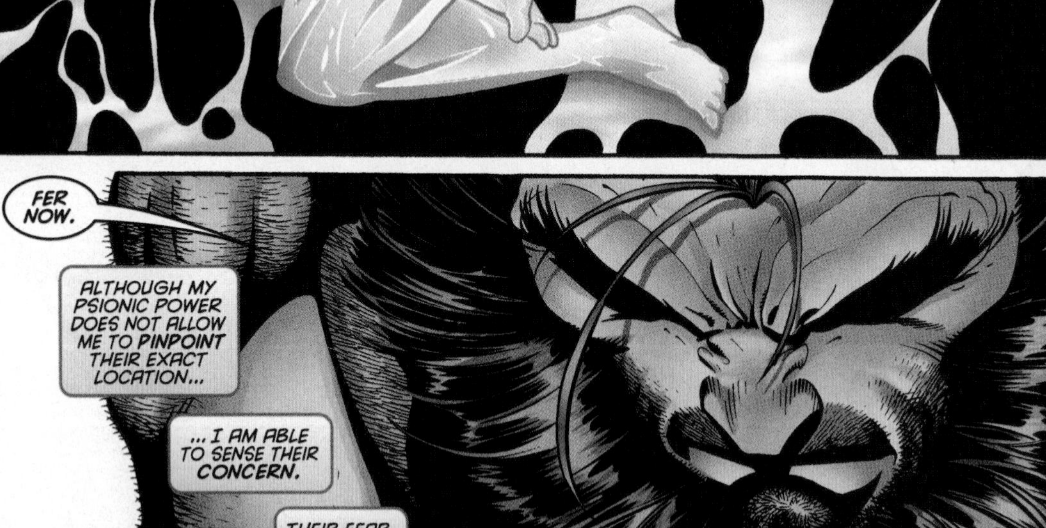
FER NOW.
ALTHOUGH MY PSIONIC POWER DOES NOT ALLOW ME TO PINPOINT THEIR EXACT LOCATION...
... I AM ABLE TO SENSE THEIR CONCERN.
THEIR FEAR.

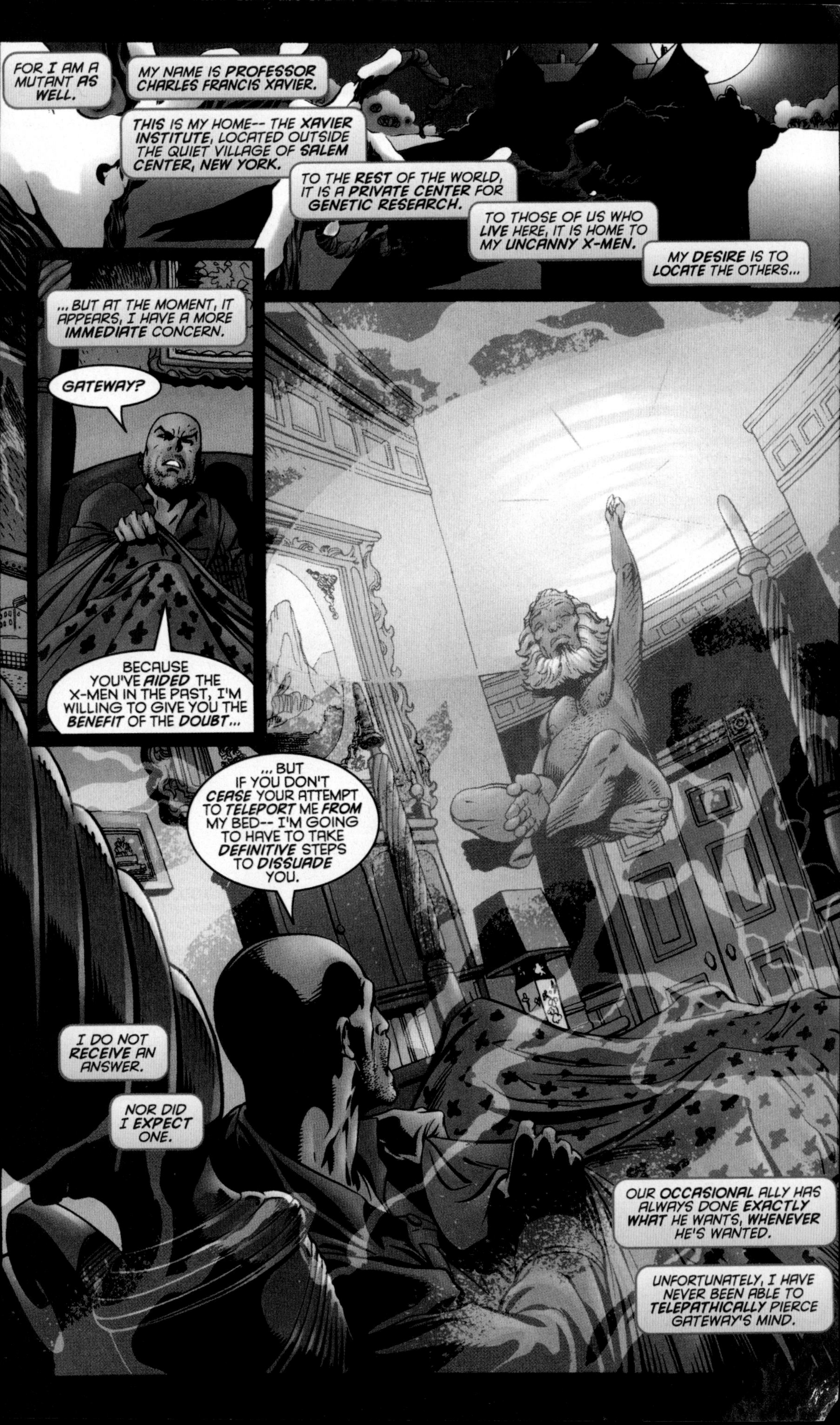
FOR I AM A MUTANT AS WELL.
MY NAME IS PROFESSOR CHARLES FRANCIS XAVIER.
THIS IS MY HOME-- THE XAVIER INSTITUTE, LOCATED OUTSIDE THE QUIET VILLAGE OF SALEM CENTER, NEW YORK.
TO THE REST OF THE WORLD, IT IS A PRIVATE CENTER FOR GENETIC RESEARCH.
TO THOSE OF US WHO LIVE HERE, IT IS HOME TO MY UNCANNY X-MEN.
MY DESIRE IS TO LOCATE THE OTHERS...
...BUT AT THE MOMENT, IT APPEARS, I HAVE A MORE IMMEDIATE CONCERN.
GATEWAY?
BECAUSE YOU'VE AIDED THE X-MEN IN THE PAST, I'M WILLING TO GIVE YOU THE BENEFIT OF THE DOUBT...
...BUT IF YOU DON'T CEASE YOUR ATTEMPT TO TELEPORT ME FROM MY BED-- I'M GOING TO HAVE TO TAKE DEFINITIVE STEPS TO DISSUADE YOU.
I DO NOT RECEIVE AN ANSWER.
NOR DID I EXPECT ONE.
OUR OCCASIONAL ALLY HAS ALWAYS DONE EXACTLY WHAT HE WANTS, WHENEVER HE'S WANTED.
UNFORTUNATELY, I HAVE NEVER BEEN ABLE TO TELEPATHICALLY PIERCE GATEWAY'S MIND.

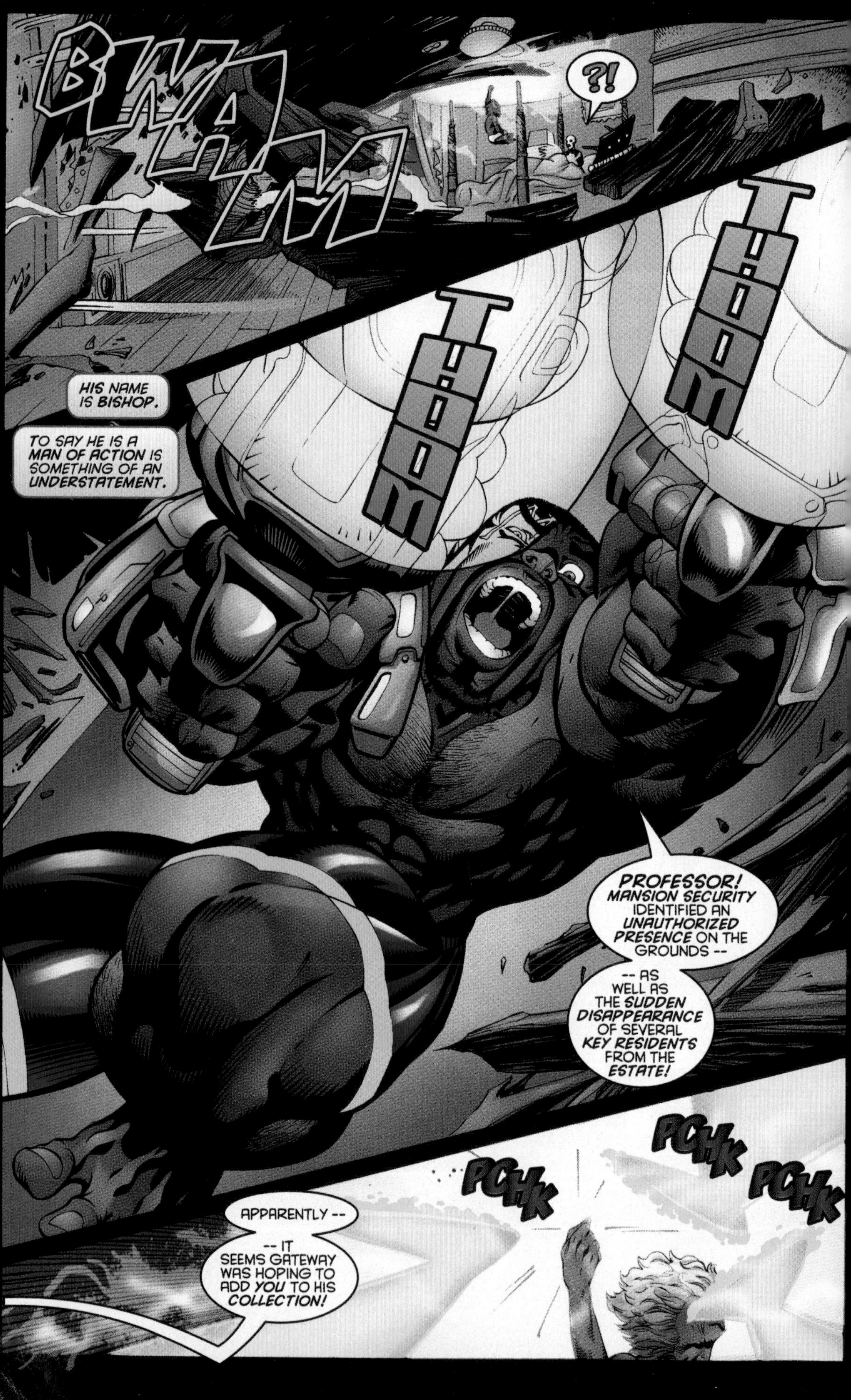
BWAM
?!
THOOM
THOOM
HIS NAME IS BISHOP.
TO SAY HE IS A MAN OF ACTION IS SOMETHING OF AN UNDERSTATEMENT.
PROFESSOR! MANSION SECURITY IDENTIFIED AN UNAUTHORIZED PRESENCE ON THE GROUNDS --
-- AS WELL AS THE SUDDEN DISAPPEARANCE OF SEVERAL KEY RESIDENTS FROM THE ESTATE!
PCHK
PCHK
PCHK
APPARENTLY --
-- IT SEEMS GATEWAY WAS HOPING TO ADD YOU TO HIS COLLECTION!

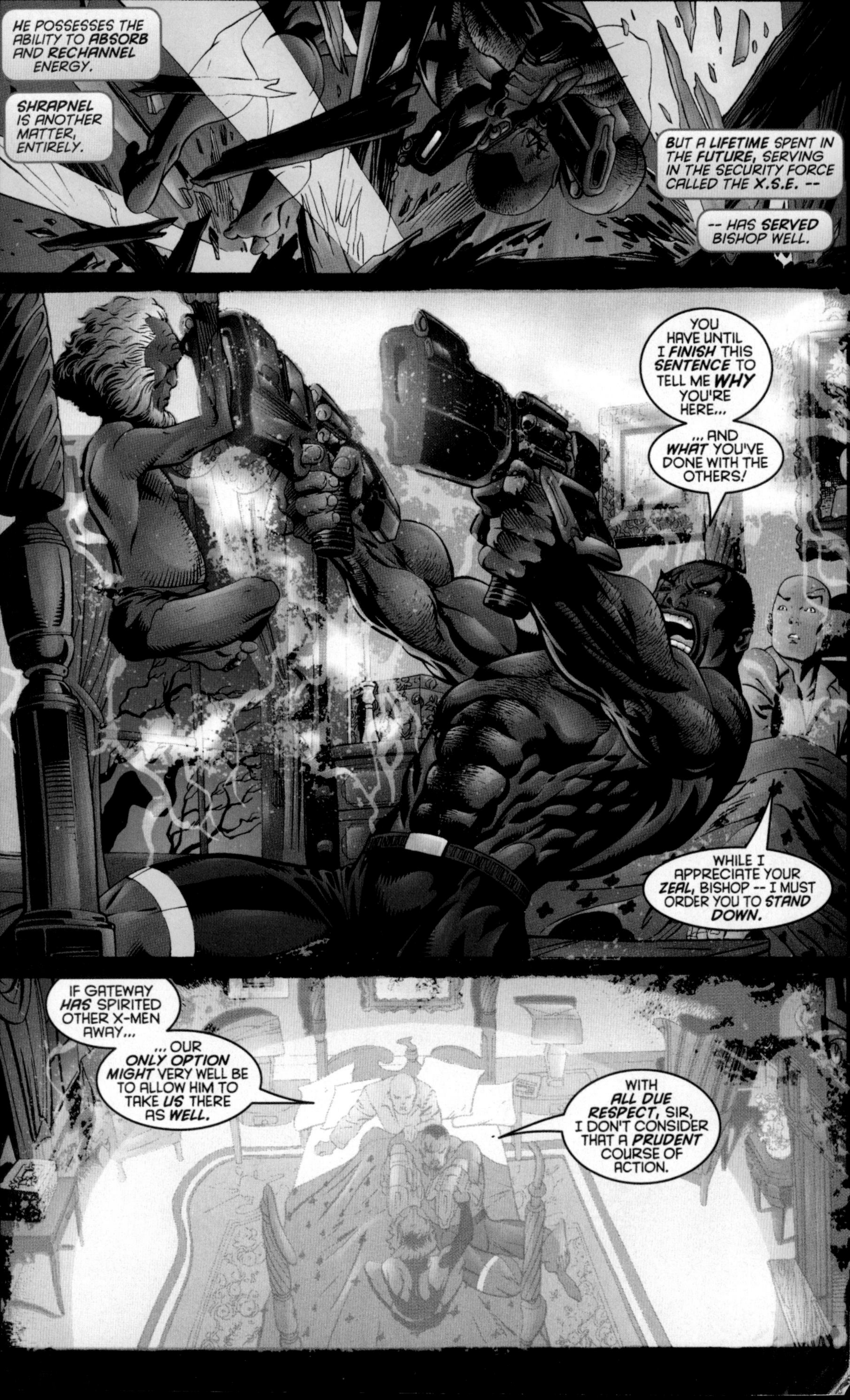
HE POSSESSES THE ABILITY TO ABSORB AND RECHANNEL ENERGY.
SHRAPNEL IS ANOTHER MATTER, ENTIRELY.
BUT A LIFETIME SPENT IN THE FUTURE, SERVING IN THE SECURITY FORCE CALLED THE X.S.E. --
-- HAS SERVED BISHOP WELL.
YOU HAVE UNTIL I FINISH THIS SENTENCE TO TELL ME WHY YOU'RE HERE...
... AND WHAT YOU'VE DONE WITH THE OTHERS!
WHILE I APPRECIATE YOUR ZEAL, BISHOP -- I MUST ORDER YOU TO STAND DOWN.
IF GATEWAY HAS SPIRITED OTHER X-MEN AWAY...
... OUR ONLY OPTION MIGHT VERY WELL BE TO ALLOW HIM TO TAKE US THERE AS WELL.
WITH ALL DUE RESPECT, SIR, I DON'T CONSIDER THAT A PRUDENT COURSE OF ACTION.

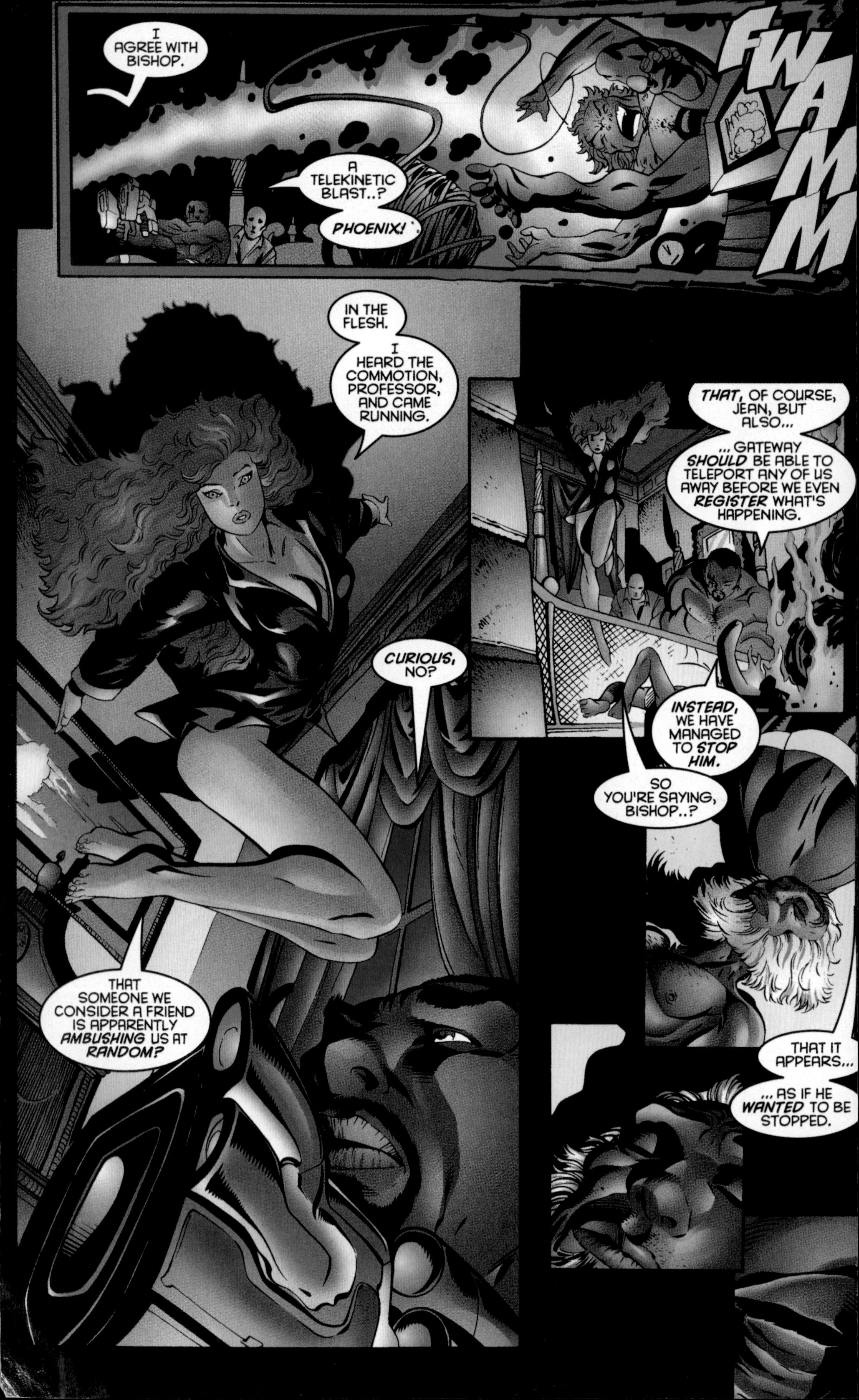

I AGREE WITH BISHOP.
FWAMM
A TELEKINETIC BLAST..?
PHOENIX!
IN THE FLESH.
I HEARD THE COMMOTION, PROFESSOR, AND CAME RUNNING.
THAT, OF COURSE, JEAN, BUT ALSO...
... GATEWAY SHOULD BE ABLE TO TELEPORT ANY OF US AWAY BEFORE WE EVEN REGISTER WHAT'S HAPPENING.
CURIOUS, NO?
INSTEAD, WE HAVE MANAGED TO STOP HIM.
SO YOU'RE SAYING, BISHOP..?
THAT SOMEONE WE CONSIDER A FRIEND IS APPARENTLY AMBUSHING US AT RANDOM?
THAT IT APPEARS...
... AS IF HE WANTED TO BE STOPPED.

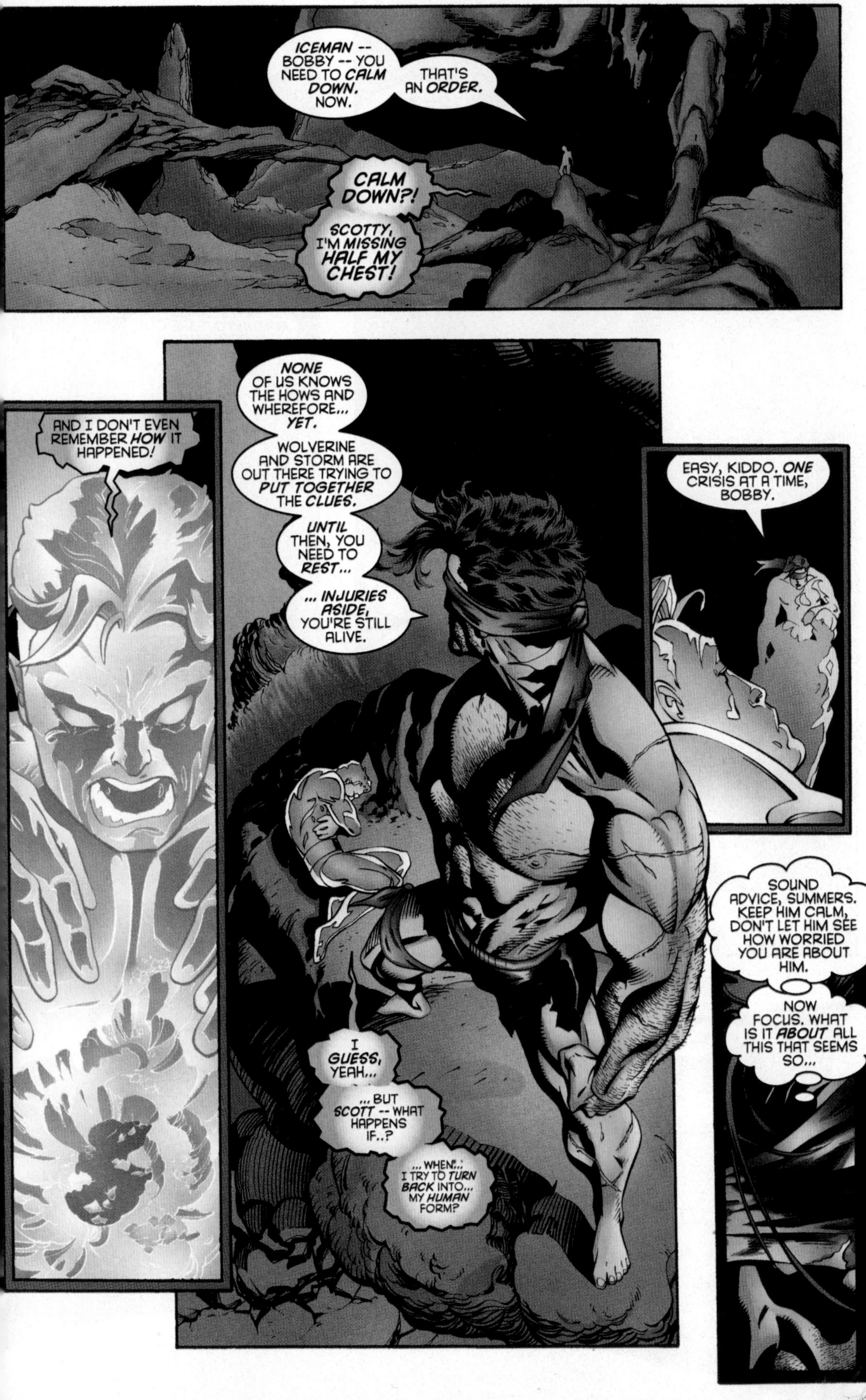
ICEMAN -- BOBBY -- YOU NEED TO CALM DOWN. NOW.
THAT'S AN ORDER.
CALM DOWN?!
SCOTTY, I'M MISSING HALF MY CHEST!
AND I DON'T EVEN REMEMBER HOW IT HAPPENED!
NONE OF US KNOWS THE HOWS AND WHEREFORE... YET.
WOLVERINE AND STORM ARE OUT THERE TRYING TO PUT TOGETHER THE CLUES.
UNTIL THEN, YOU NEED TO REST...
... INJURIES ASIDE, YOU'RE STILL ALIVE.
EASY, KIDDO. ONE CRISIS AT A TIME, BOBBY.
I GUESS, YEAH...
... BUT SCOTT -- WHAT HAPPENS IF..?
... WHEN... I TRY TO TURN BACK INTO... MY HUMAN FORM?
SOUND ADVICE, SUMMERS. KEEP HIM CALM, DON'T LET HIM SEE HOW WORRIED YOU ARE ABOUT HIM.
NOW FOCUS. WHAT IS IT ABOUT ALL THIS THAT SEEMS SO...

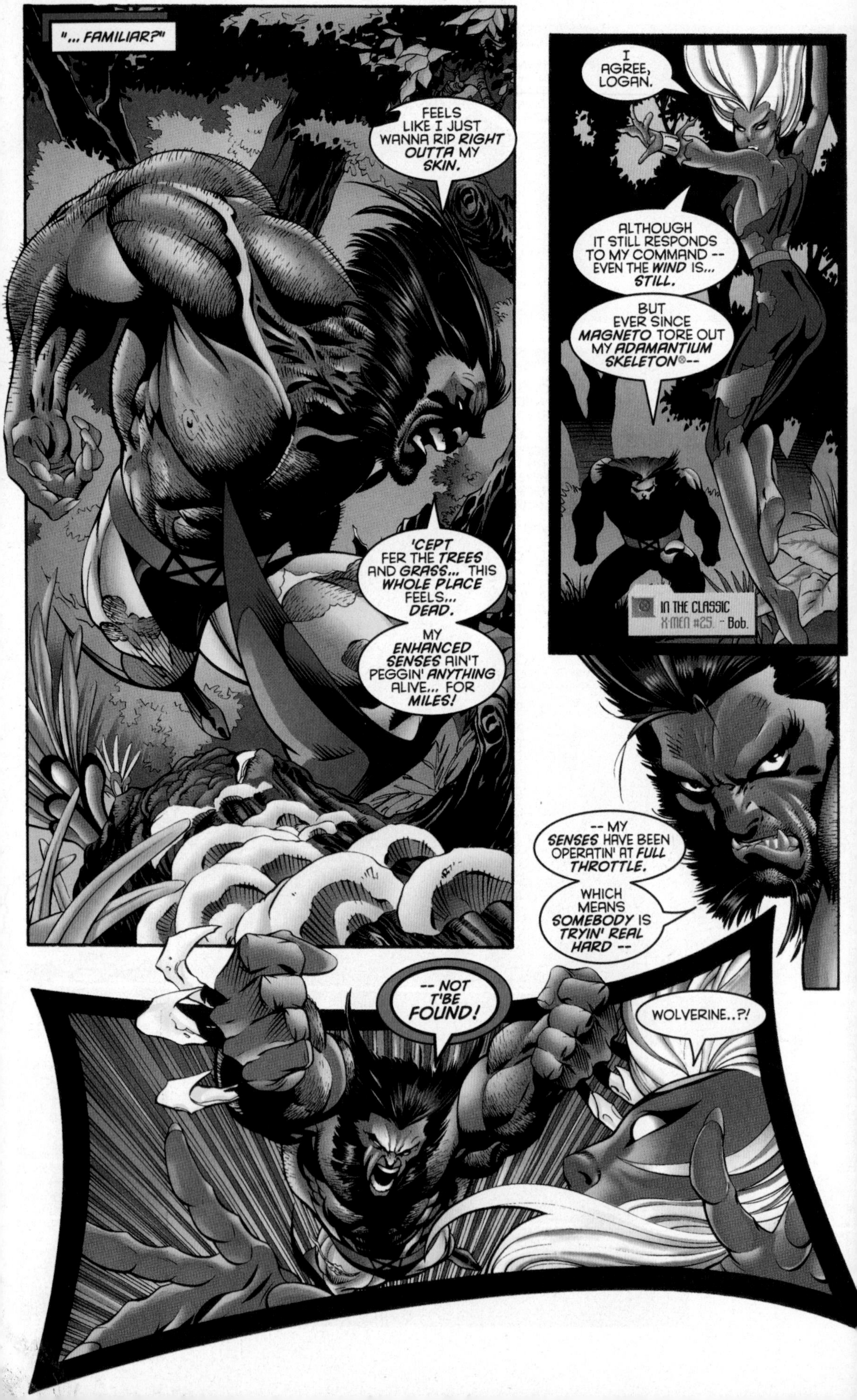

"... FAMILIAR?"
FEELS LIKE I JUST WANNA RIP RIGHT OUTTA MY SKIN.
'CEPT FER THE TREES AND GRASS... THIS WHOLE PLACE FEELS... DEAD.
MY ENHANCED SENSES AIN'T PEGGIN' ANYTHING ALIVE... FOR MILES!
I AGREE, LOGAN.
ALTHOUGH IT STILL RESPONDS TO MY COMMAND -- EVEN THE WIND IS... STILL.
BUT EVER SINCE MAGNETO TORE OUT MY ADAMANTIUM SKELETON®--
IN THE CLASSIC X-MEN #25. -- Bob.
-- MY SENSES HAVE BEEN OPERATIN' AT FULL THROTTLE.
WHICH MEANS SOMEBODY IS TRYIN' REAL HARD --
-- NOT T'BE FOUND!
WOLVERINE..?!

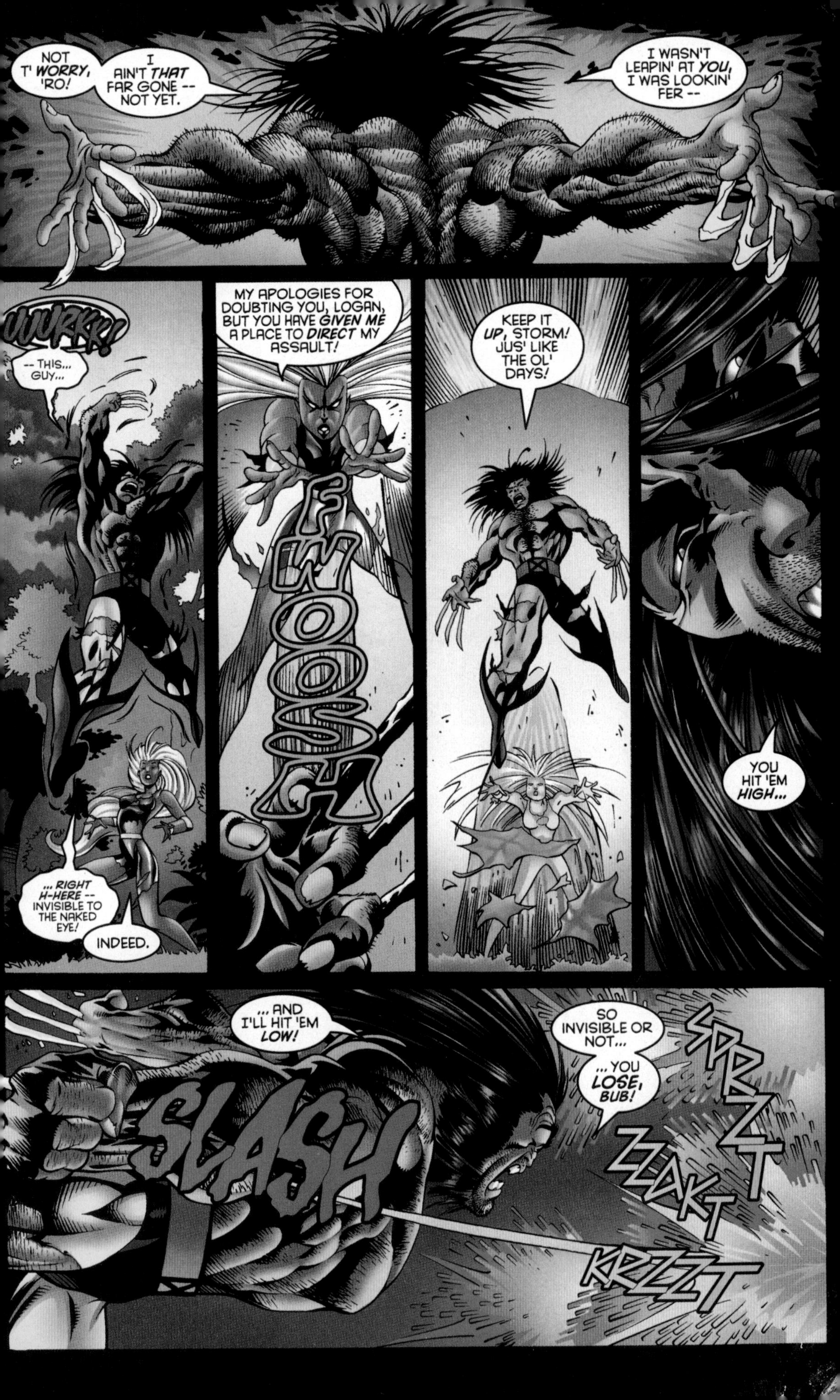
NOT T' WORRY, 'RO!
I AIN'T THAT FAR GONE -- NOT YET.
I WASN'T LEAPIN' AT YOU, I WAS LOOKIN' FER --
UUURKK!
-- THIS... GUY...
... RIGHT H-HERE -- INVISIBLE TO THE NAKED EYE!
INDEED.
MY APOLOGIES FOR DOUBTING YOU, LOGAN, BUT YOU HAVE GIVEN ME A PLACE TO DIRECT MY ASSAULT!
FWOOOSH
KEEP IT UP, STORM! JUS' LIKE THE OL' DAYS!
YOU HIT 'EM HIGH...
... AND I'LL HIT 'EM LOW!
SLASH
SO INVISIBLE OR NOT...
... YOU LOSE, BUB!
SPRZZT
ZZZAKT
KRZZZT

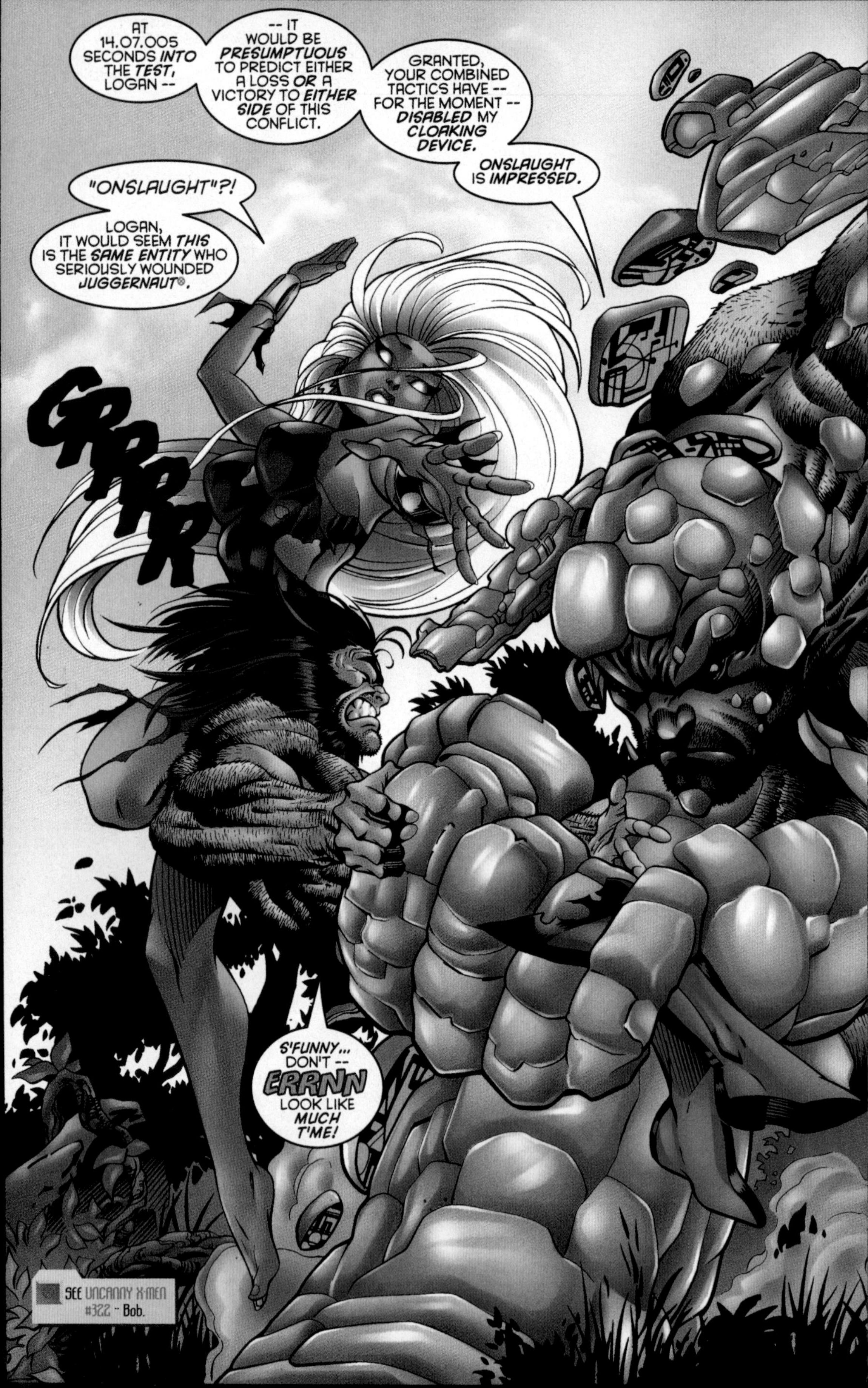
AT 14.07.005 SECONDS *INTO* THE *TEST*, LOGAN --
-- IT WOULD BE *PRESUMPTUOUS* TO PREDICT EITHER A LOSS *OR* A VICTORY TO *EITHER SIDE* OF THIS CONFLICT.
GRANTED, YOUR COMBINED TACTICS HAVE -- FOR THE MOMENT -- *DISABLED* MY *CLOAKING DEVICE.*
ONSLAUGHT IS *IMPRESSED.*
"ONSLAUGHT"?!
LOGAN, IT WOULD SEEM *THIS* IS THE *SAME ENTITY* WHO SERIOUSLY WOUNDED *JUGGERNAUT*®.
GRRRR
S'FUNNY... DON'T -- ERRNN LOOK LIKE *MUCH* T'ME!
SEE UNCANNY X-MEN #322 -- Bob.

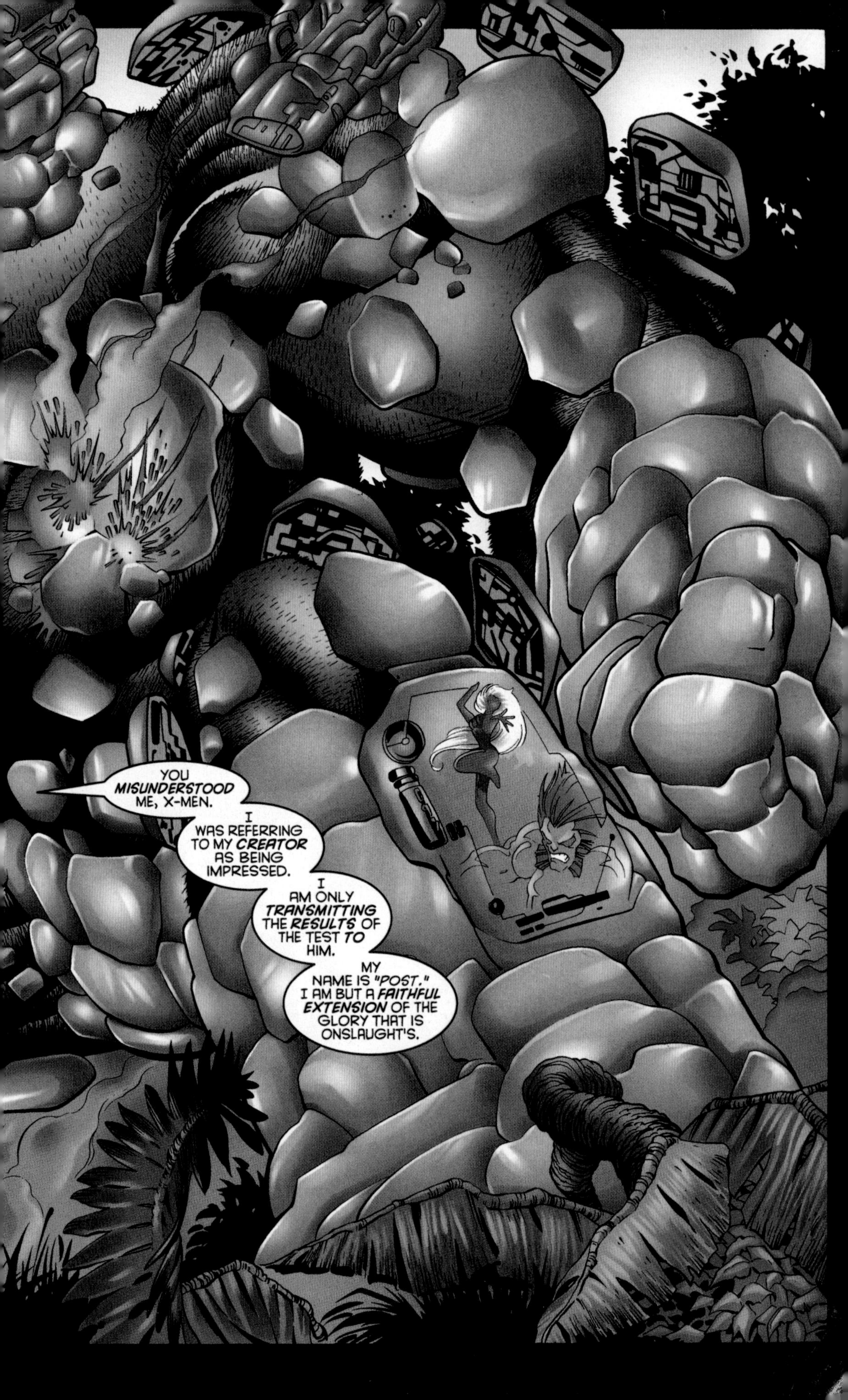
YOU *MISUNDERSTOOD* ME, X-MEN.
I WAS REFERRING TO MY *CREATOR* AS BEING IMPRESSED.
I AM ONLY *TRANSMITTING* THE *RESULTS* OF THE TEST *TO* HIM.
MY NAME IS *"POST."* I AM BUT A *FAITHFUL EXTENSION* OF THE GLORY THAT IS ONSLAUGHT'S.

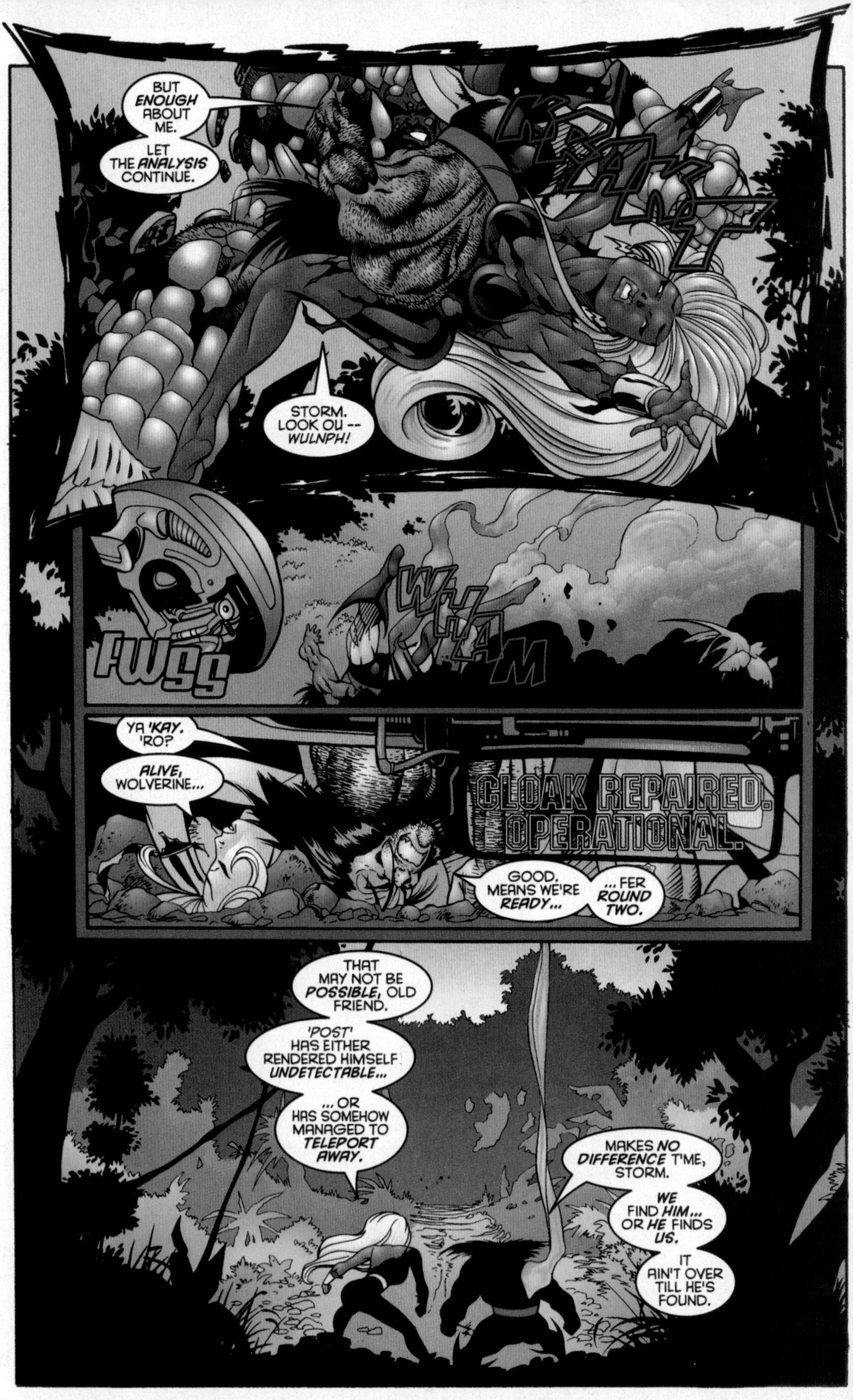
BUT ENOUGH ABOUT ME.
LET THE ANALYSIS CONTINUE.
STORM. LOOK OU -- WULNPH!
FWSS
WHAM
YA 'KAY. 'RO?
ALIVE, WOLVERINE...
CLOAK REPAIRED. OPERATIONAL.
GOOD. MEANS WE'RE READY...
...FER ROUND TWO.
THAT MAY NOT BE POSSIBLE, OLD FRIEND.
'POST' HAS EITHER RENDERED HIMSELF UNDETECTABLE...
...OR HAS SOMEHOW MANAGED TO TELEPORT AWAY.
MAKES NO DIFFERENCE T'ME, STORM.
WE FIND HIM... OR HE FINDS US.
IT AIN'T OVER TILL HE'S FOUND.

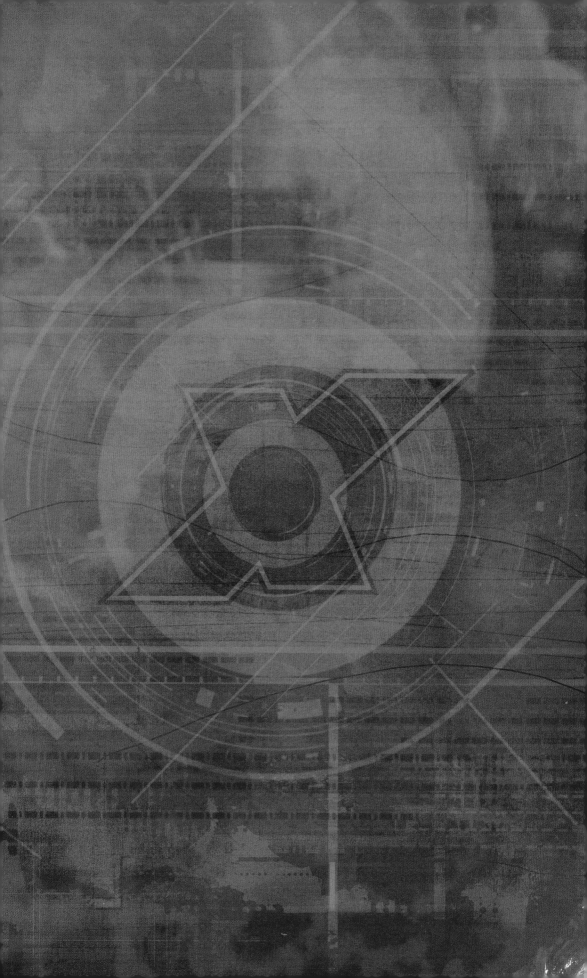

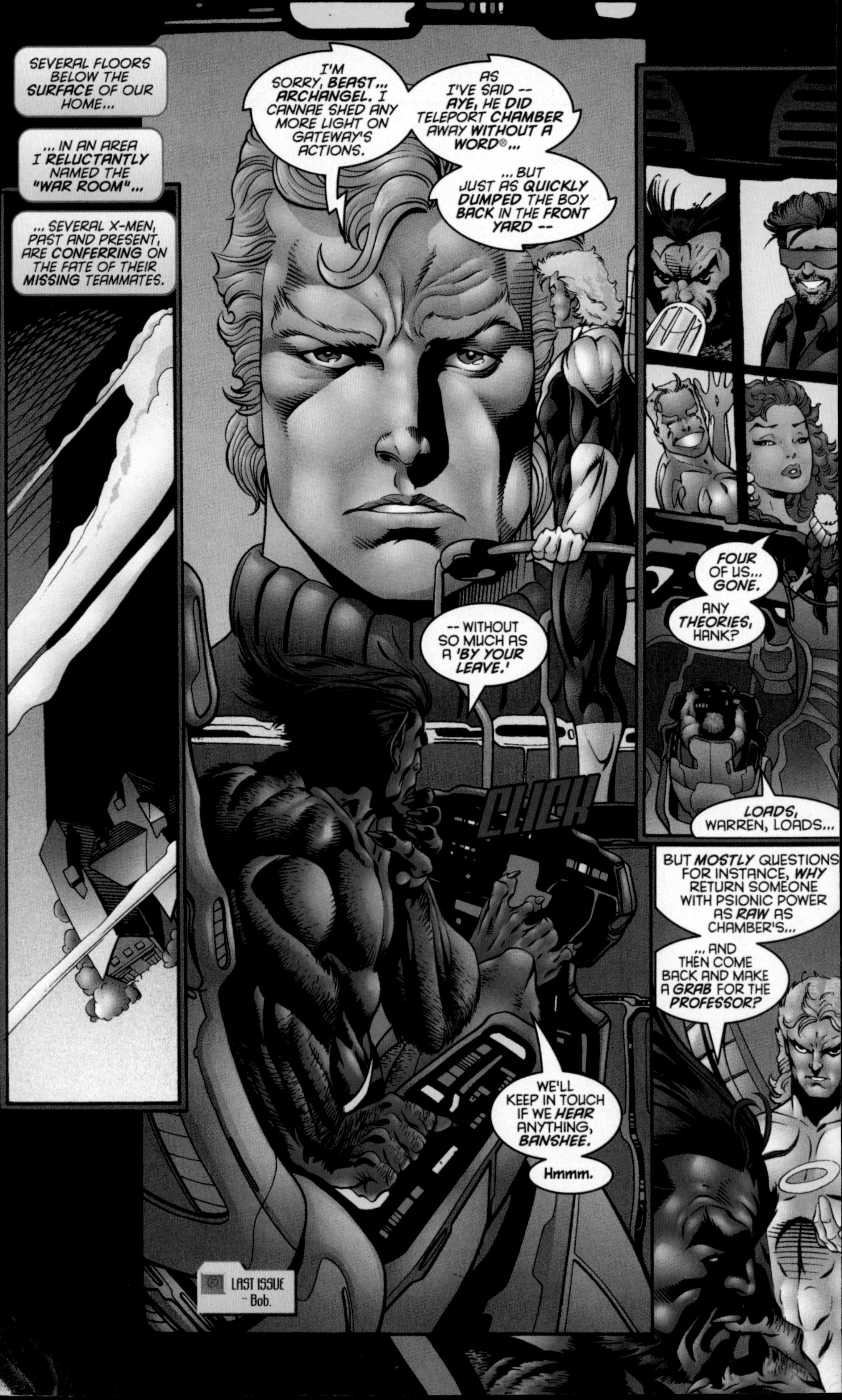

SEVERAL FLOORS BELOW THE SURFACE OF OUR HOME...
...IN AN AREA I RELUCTANTLY NAMED THE "WAR ROOM"...
...SEVERAL X-MEN, PAST AND PRESENT, ARE CONFERRING ON THE FATE OF THEIR MISSING TEAMMATES.
I'M SORRY, BEAST... ARCHANGEL. I CANNAE SHED ANY MORE LIGHT ON GATEWAY'S ACTIONS.
AS I'VE SAID -- AYE, HE DID TELEPORT CHAMBER AWAY WITHOUT A WORD®...
...BUT JUST AS QUICKLY DUMPED THE BOY BACK IN THE FRONT YARD --
-- WITHOUT SO MUCH AS A 'BY YOUR LEAVE.'
CLICK
WE'LL KEEP IN TOUCH IF WE HEAR ANYTHING, BANSHEE.
Hmmm.
® LAST ISSUE -- Bob.
FOUR OF US... GONE.
ANY THEORIES, HANK?
LOADS, WARREN, LOADS...
BUT MOSTLY QUESTIONS FOR INSTANCE, WHY RETURN SOMEONE WITH PSIONIC POWER AS RAW AS CHAMBER'S...
...AND THEN COME BACK AND MAKE A GRAB FOR THE PROFESSOR?

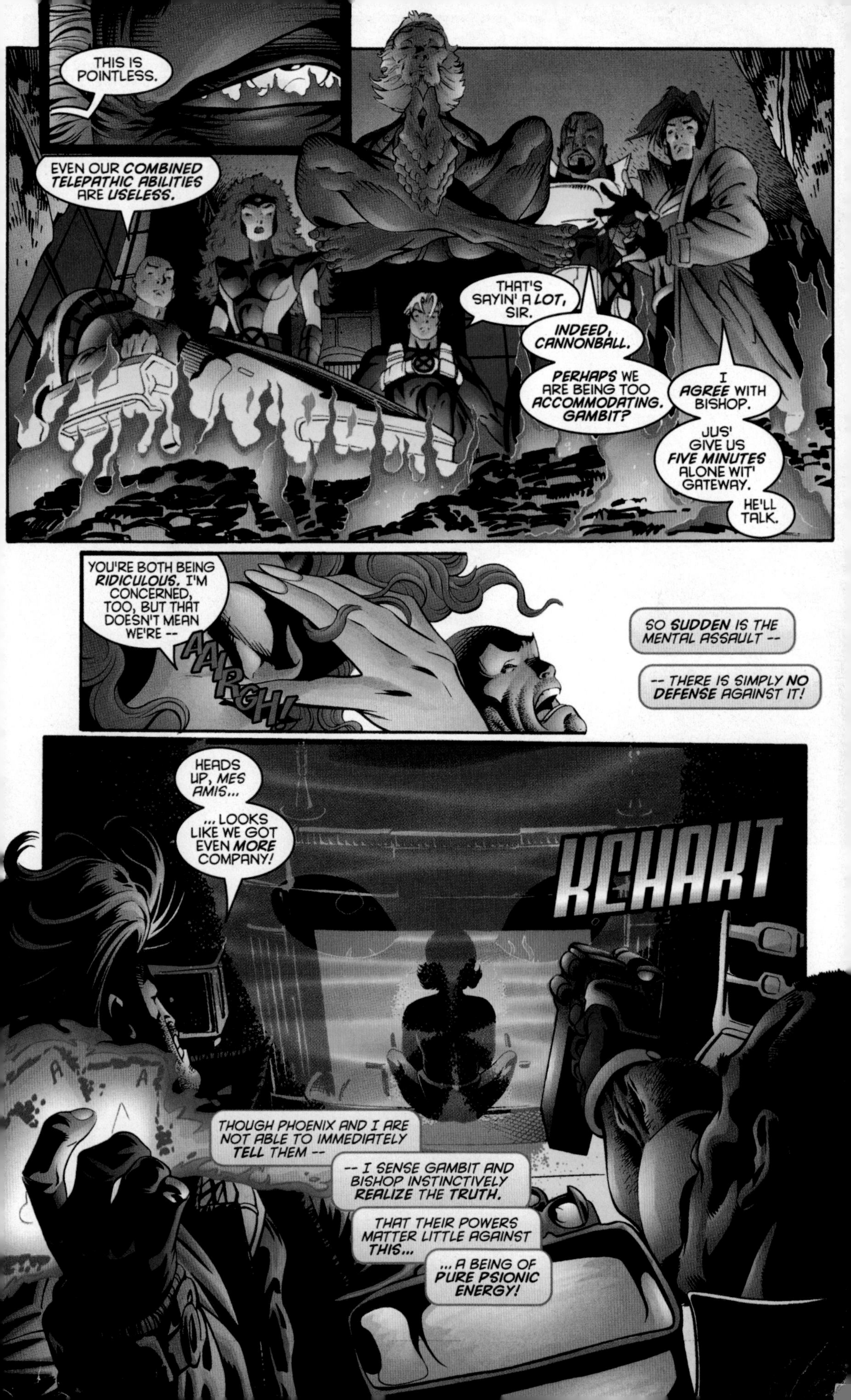
THIS IS POINTLESS.
EVEN OUR COMBINED TELEPATHIC ABILITIES ARE USELESS.
THAT'S SAYIN' A LOT, SIR.
INDEED, CANNONBALL.
PERHAPS WE ARE BEING TOO ACCOMMODATING. GAMBIT?
I AGREE WITH BISHOP.
JUS' GIVE US FIVE MINUTES ALONE WIT' GATEWAY.
HE'LL TALK.
YOU'RE BOTH BEING RIDICULOUS. I'M CONCERNED, TOO, BUT THAT DOESN'T MEAN WE'RE --
AAARGH!
SO SUDDEN IS THE MENTAL ASSAULT --
-- THERE IS SIMPLY NO DEFENSE AGAINST IT!
HEADS UP, MES AMIS...
...LOOKS LIKE WE GOT EVEN MORE COMPANY!
KCHAKT
THOUGH PHOENIX AND I ARE NOT ABLE TO IMMEDIATELY TELL THEM --
-- I SENSE GAMBIT AND BISHOP INSTINCTIVELY REALIZE THE TRUTH.
THAT THEIR POWERS MATTER LITTLE AGAINST THIS...
...A BEING OF PURE PSIONIC ENERGY!

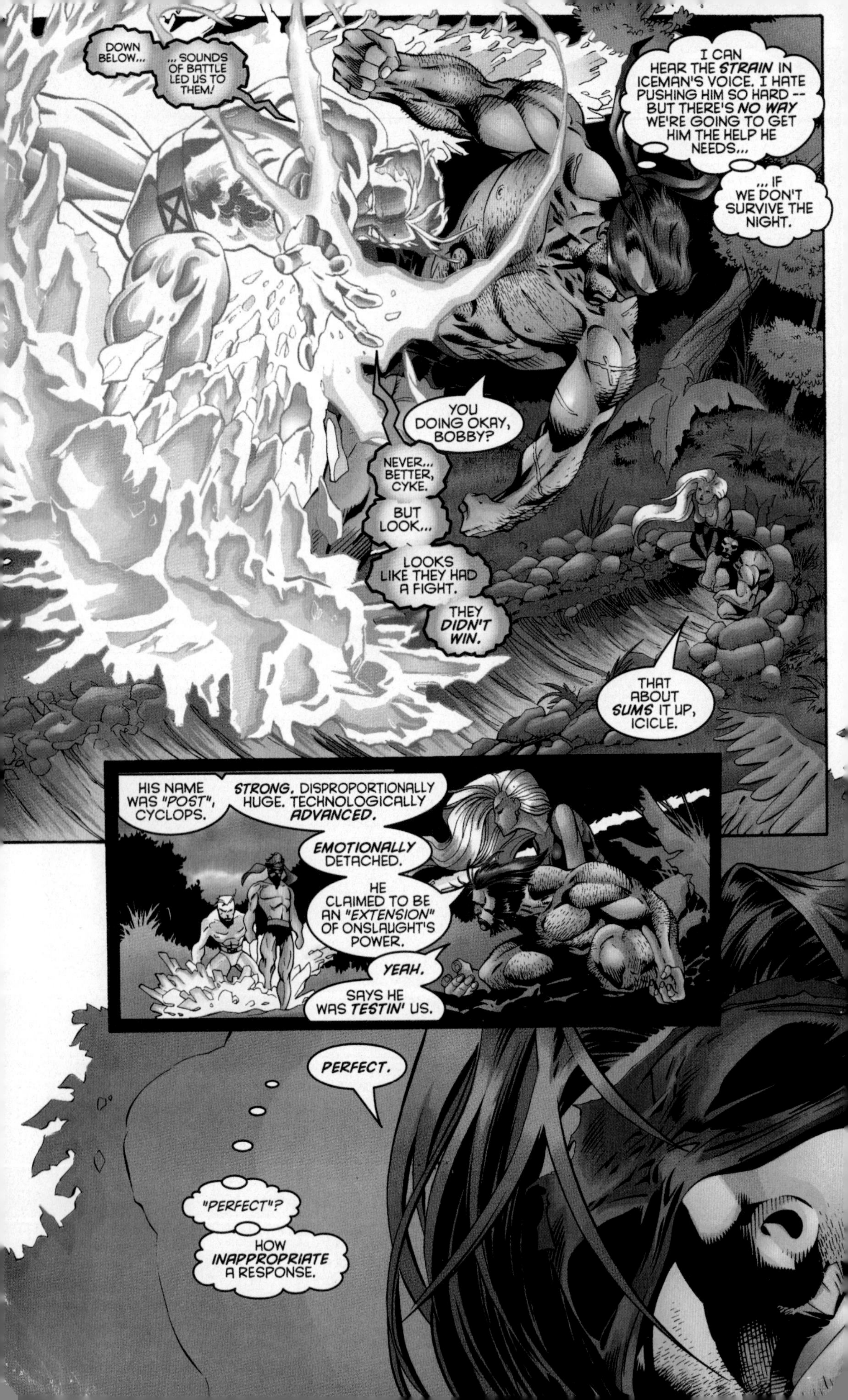
DOWN BELOW...
...SOUNDS OF BATTLE LED US TO THEM!
I CAN HEAR THE STRAIN IN ICEMAN'S VOICE. I HATE PUSHING HIM SO HARD -- BUT THERE'S NO WAY WE'RE GOING TO GET HIM THE HELP HE NEEDS...
...IF WE DON'T SURVIVE THE NIGHT.
YOU DOING OKAY, BOBBY?
NEVER... BETTER, CYKE.
BUT LOOK...
LOOKS LIKE THEY HAD A FIGHT.
THEY DIDN'T WIN.
THAT ABOUT SUMS IT UP, ICICLE.
HIS NAME WAS "POST", CYCLOPS.
STRONG. DISPROPORTIONALLY HUGE. TECHNOLOGICALLY ADVANCED.
EMOTIONALLY DETACHED.
HE CLAIMED TO BE AN "EXTENSION" OF ONSLAUGHT'S POWER.
YEAH.
SAYS HE WAS TESTIN' US.
PERFECT.
"PERFECT"?
HOW INAPPROPRIATE A RESPONSE.

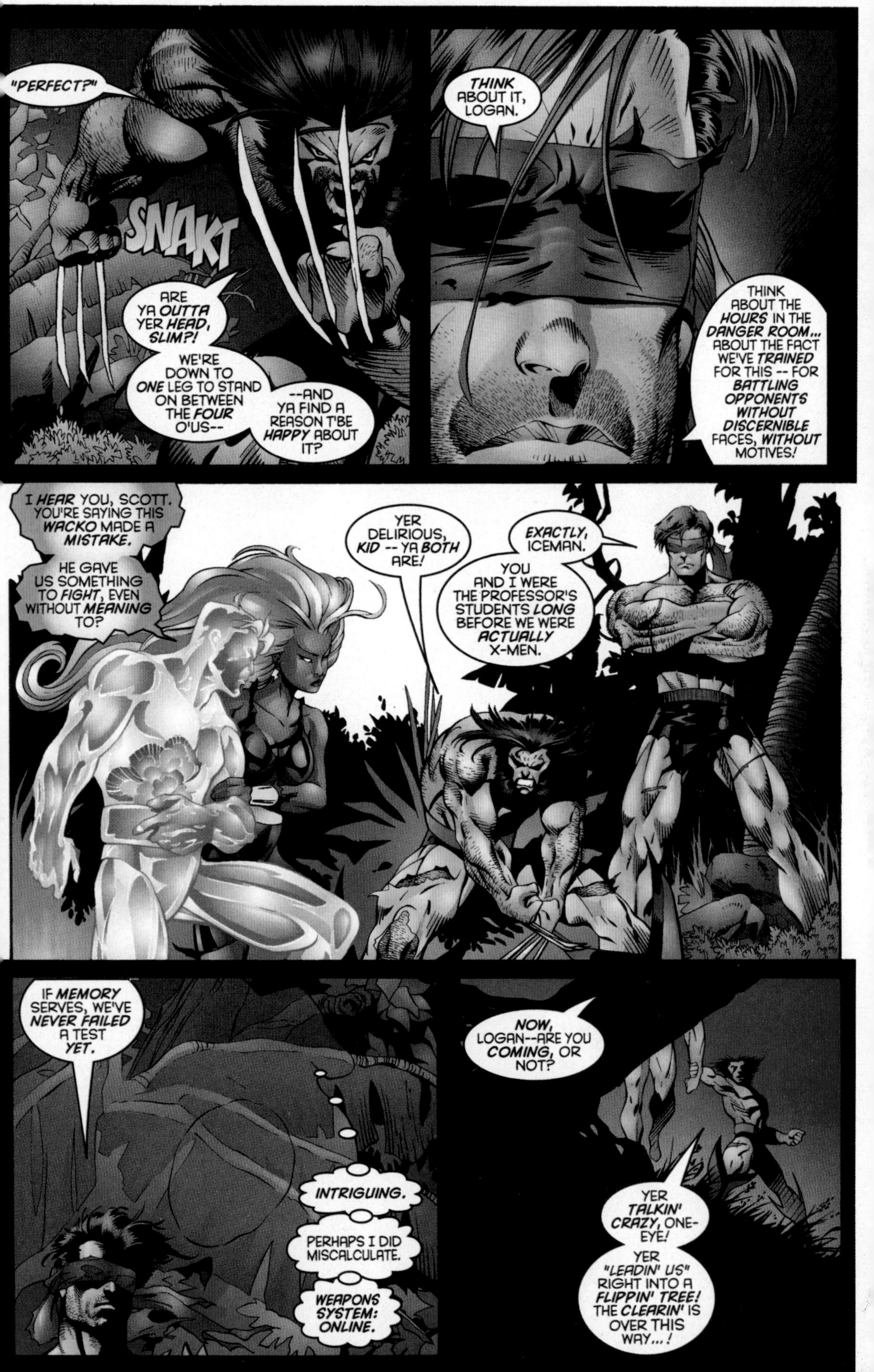
"PERFECT?"
SNAKT
ARE YA OUTTA YER HEAD, SLIM?!
WE'RE DOWN TO ONE LEG TO STAND ON BETWEEN THE FOUR O'US--
--AND YA FIND A REASON T'BE HAPPY ABOUT IT?
THINK ABOUT IT, LOGAN.
THINK ABOUT THE HOURS IN THE DANGER ROOM... ABOUT THE FACT WE'VE TRAINED FOR THIS -- FOR BATTLING OPPONENTS WITHOUT DISCERNIBLE FACES, WITHOUT MOTIVES!
I HEAR YOU, SCOTT. YOU'RE SAYING THIS WACKO MADE A MISTAKE.
HE GAVE US SOMETHING TO FIGHT, EVEN WITHOUT MEANING TO?
YER DELIRIOUS, KID -- YA BOTH ARE!
EXACTLY, ICEMAN.
YOU AND I WERE THE PROFESSOR'S STUDENTS LONG BEFORE WE WERE ACTUALLY X-MEN.
IF MEMORY SERVES, WE'VE NEVER FAILED A TEST YET.
INTRIGUING.
PERHAPS I DID MISCALCULATE.
WEAPONS SYSTEM: ONLINE.
NOW, LOGAN--ARE YOU COMING, OR NOT?
YER TALKIN' CRAZY, ONE-EYE!
YER "LEADIN' US" RIGHT INTO A FLIPPIN' TREE! THE CLEARIN' IS OVER THIS WAY...!

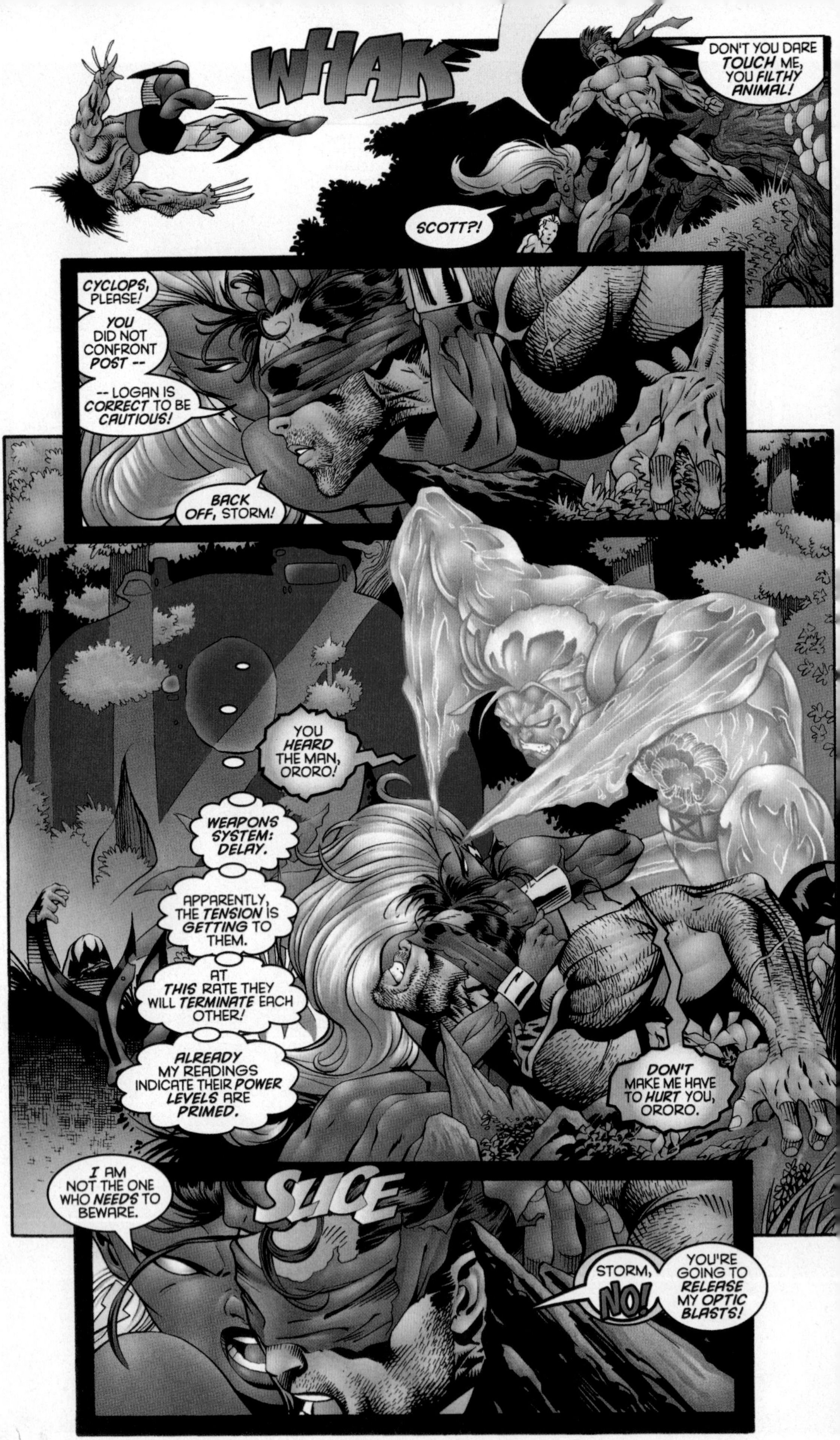
WHAK
DON'T YOU DARE TOUCH ME, YOU FILTHY ANIMAL!
SCOTT?!
CYCLOPS, PLEASE!
YOU DID NOT CONFRONT POST --
-- LOGAN IS CORRECT TO BE CAUTIOUS!
BACK OFF, STORM!
YOU HEARD THE MAN, ORORO!
WEAPONS SYSTEM: DELAY.
APPARENTLY, THE TENSION IS GETTING TO THEM.
AT THIS RATE THEY WILL TERMINATE EACH OTHER!
ALREADY MY READINGS INDICATE THEIR POWER LEVELS ARE PRIMED.
DON'T MAKE ME HAVE TO HURT YOU, ORORO.
I AM NOT THE ONE WHO NEEDS TO BEWARE.
SLICE
STORM, NO!
YOU'RE GOING TO RELEASE MY OPTIC BLASTS!

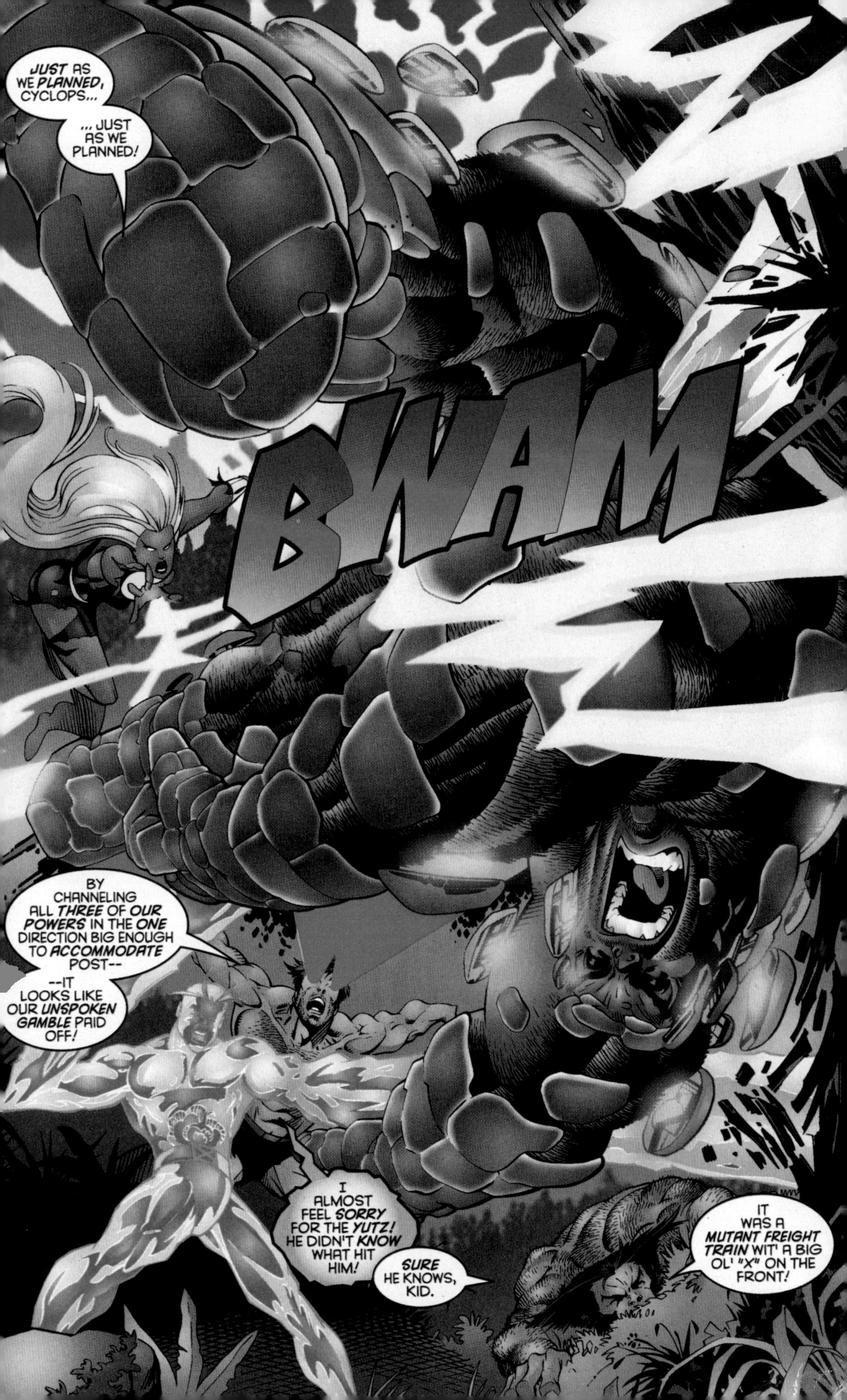
JUST AS WE PLANNED, CYCLOPS...
...JUST AS WE PLANNED!
BWAM
BY CHANNELING ALL THREE OF OUR POWERS IN THE ONE DIRECTION BIG ENOUGH TO ACCOMMODATE POST--
--IT LOOKS LIKE OUR UNSPOKEN GAMBLE PAID OFF!
I ALMOST FEEL SORRY FOR THE YUTZ! HE DIDN'T KNOW WHAT HIT HIM!
SURE HE KNOWS, KID.
IT WAS A MUTANT FREIGHT TRAIN WIT' A BIG OL' "X" ON THE FRONT!

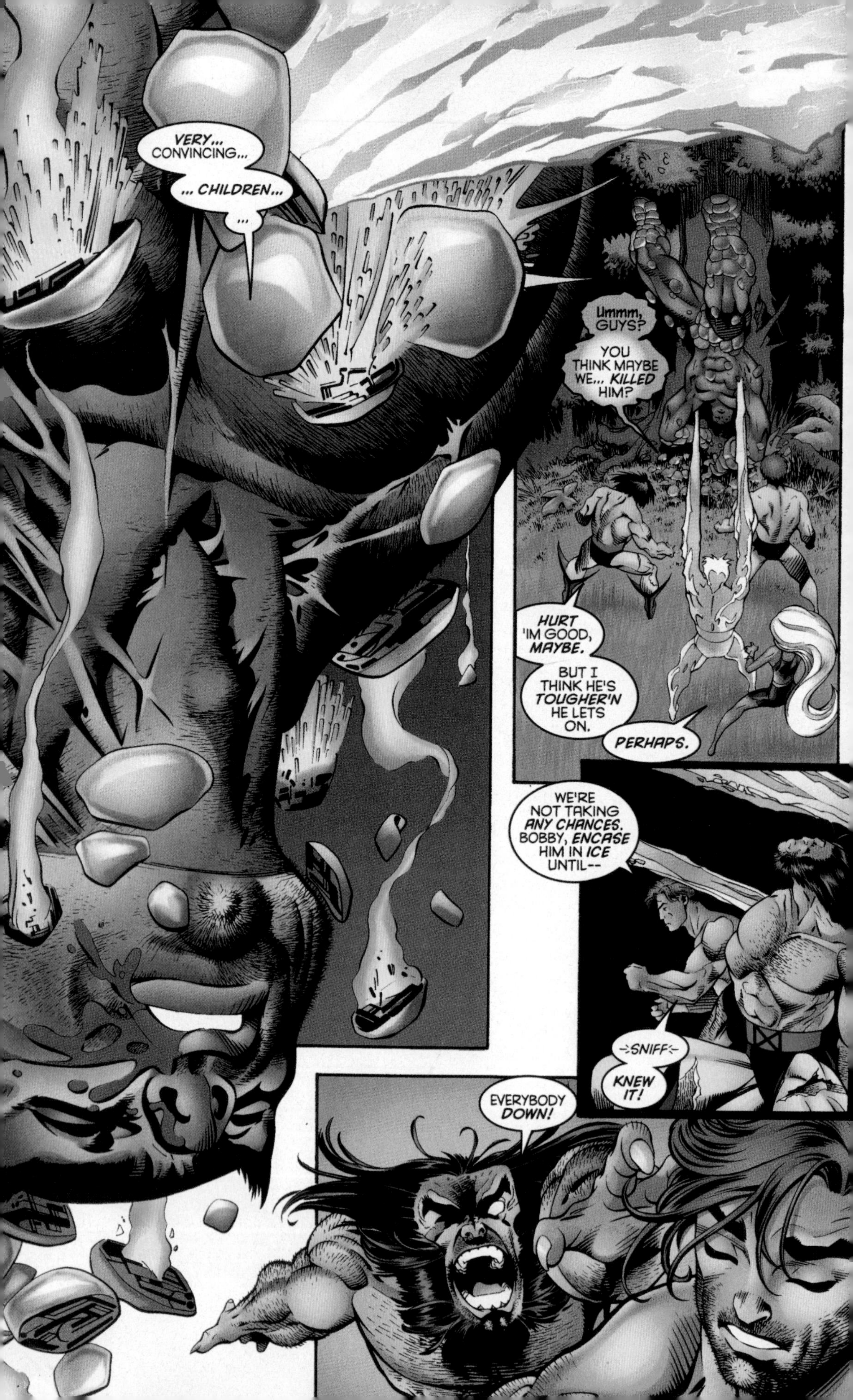
VERY... CONVINCING...
... CHILDREN...
...
Ummm, GUYS?
YOU THINK MAYBE WE... KILLED HIM?
HURT 'IM GOOD, MAYBE.
BUT I THINK HE'S TOUGHER'N HE LETS ON.
PERHAPS.
WE'RE NOT TAKING ANY CHANCES. BOBBY, ENCASE HIM IN ICE UNTIL--
-SNIFF-
KNEW IT!
EVERYBODY DOWN!

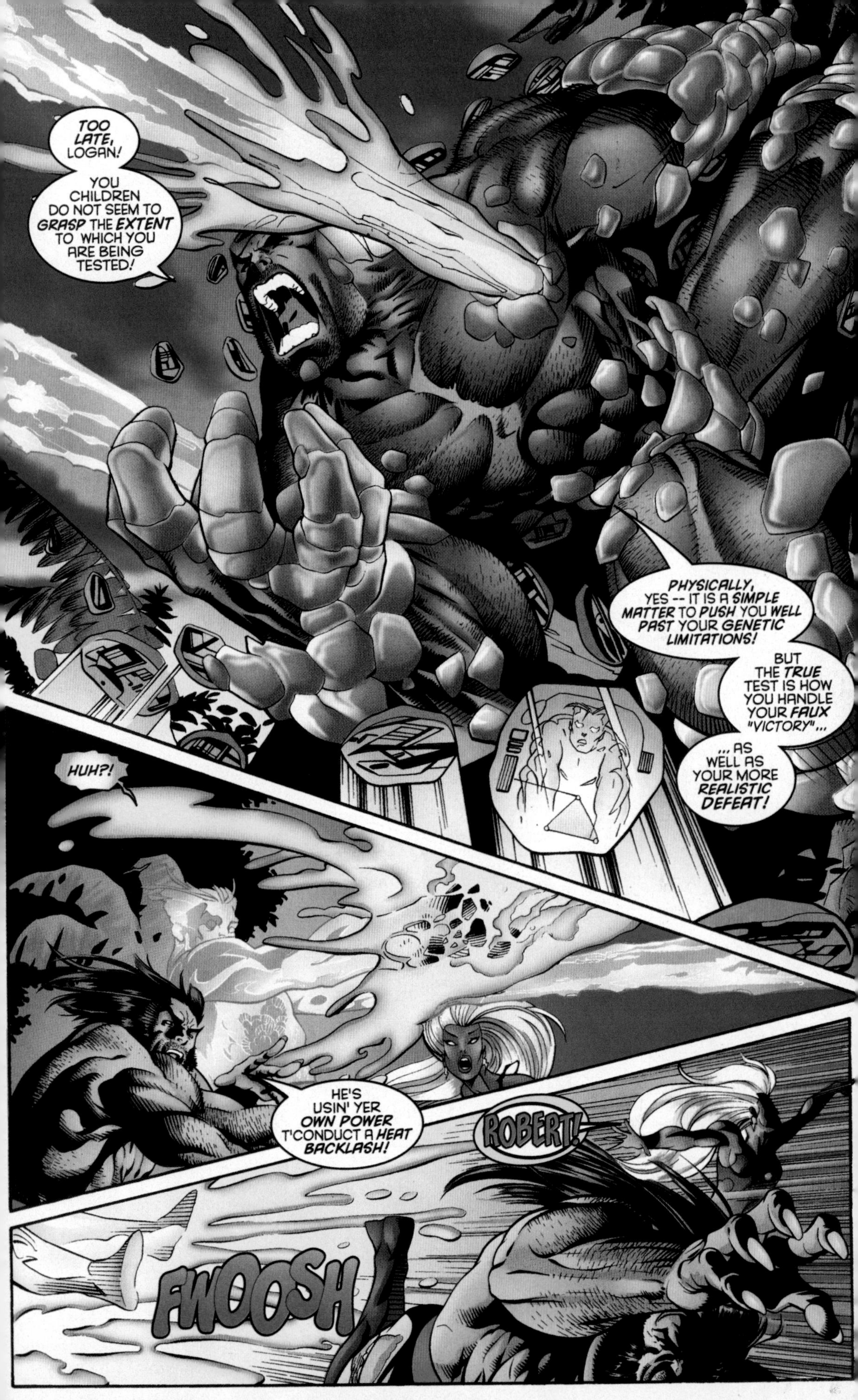
TOO LATE, LOGAN!
YOU CHILDREN DO NOT SEEM TO GRASP THE EXTENT TO WHICH YOU ARE BEING TESTED!
PHYSICALLY, YES -- IT IS A SIMPLE MATTER TO PUSH YOU WELL PAST YOUR GENETIC LIMITATIONS!
BUT THE TRUE TEST IS HOW YOU HANDLE YOUR FAUX "VICTORY"...
...AS WELL AS YOUR MORE REALISTIC DEFEAT!
HUH?!
HE'S USIN' YER OWN POWER T'CONDUCT A HEAT BACKLASH!
ROBERT!
FWOOSH

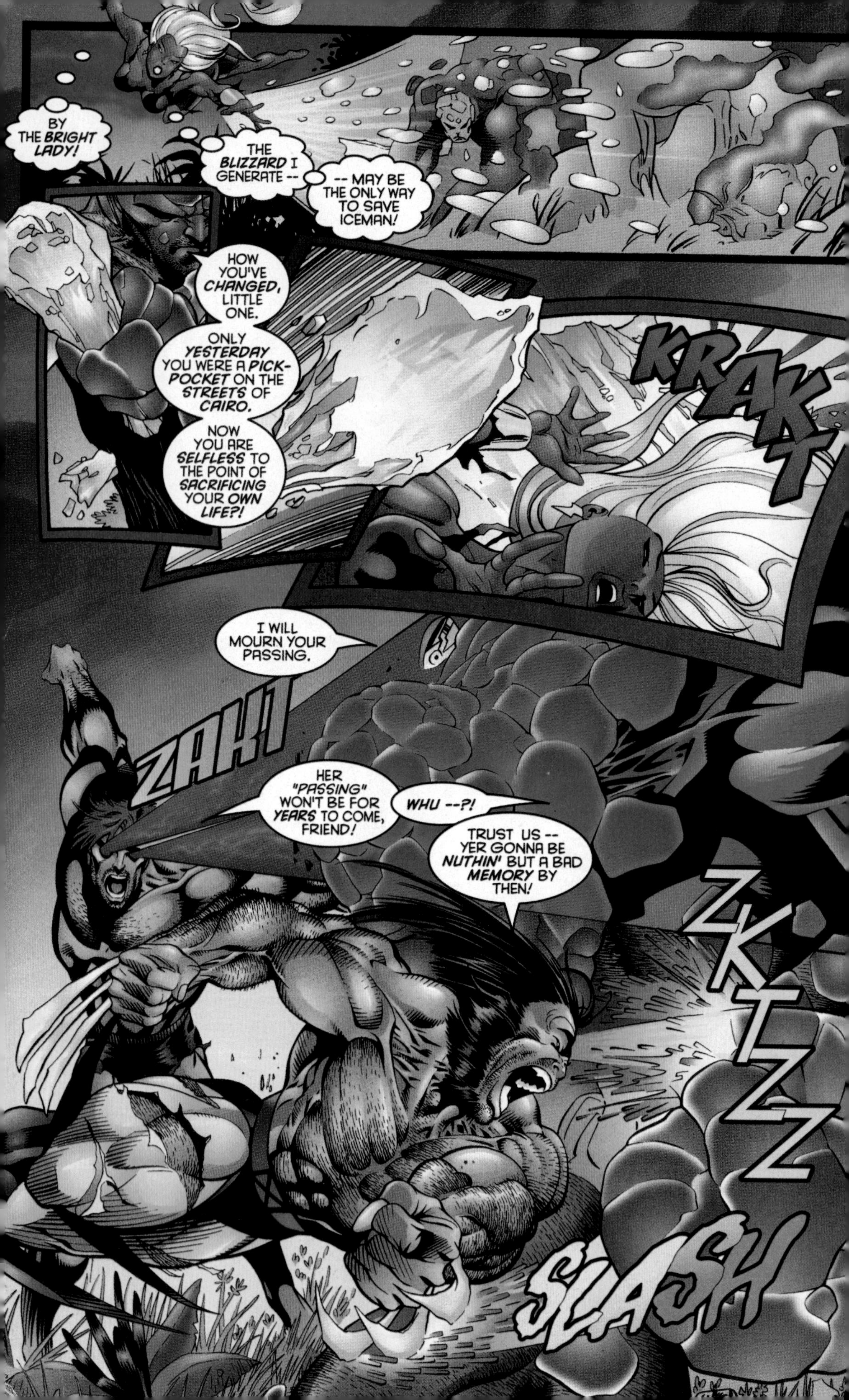

BY THE BRIGHT LADY!
THE BLIZZARD I GENERATE --
-- MAY BE THE ONLY WAY TO SAVE ICEMAN!
HOW YOU'VE CHANGED, LITTLE ONE.
ONLY YESTERDAY YOU WERE A PICK-POCKET ON THE STREETS OF CAIRO.
NOW YOU ARE SELFLESS TO THE POINT OF SACRIFICING YOUR OWN LIFE?!
KRAKT
I WILL MOURN YOUR PASSING.
ZAK!
HER "PASSING" WON'T BE FOR YEARS TO COME, FRIEND!
WHU --?!
TRUST US -- YER GONNA BE NUTHIN' BUT A BAD MEMORY BY THEN!
ZKTZZ
SLASH

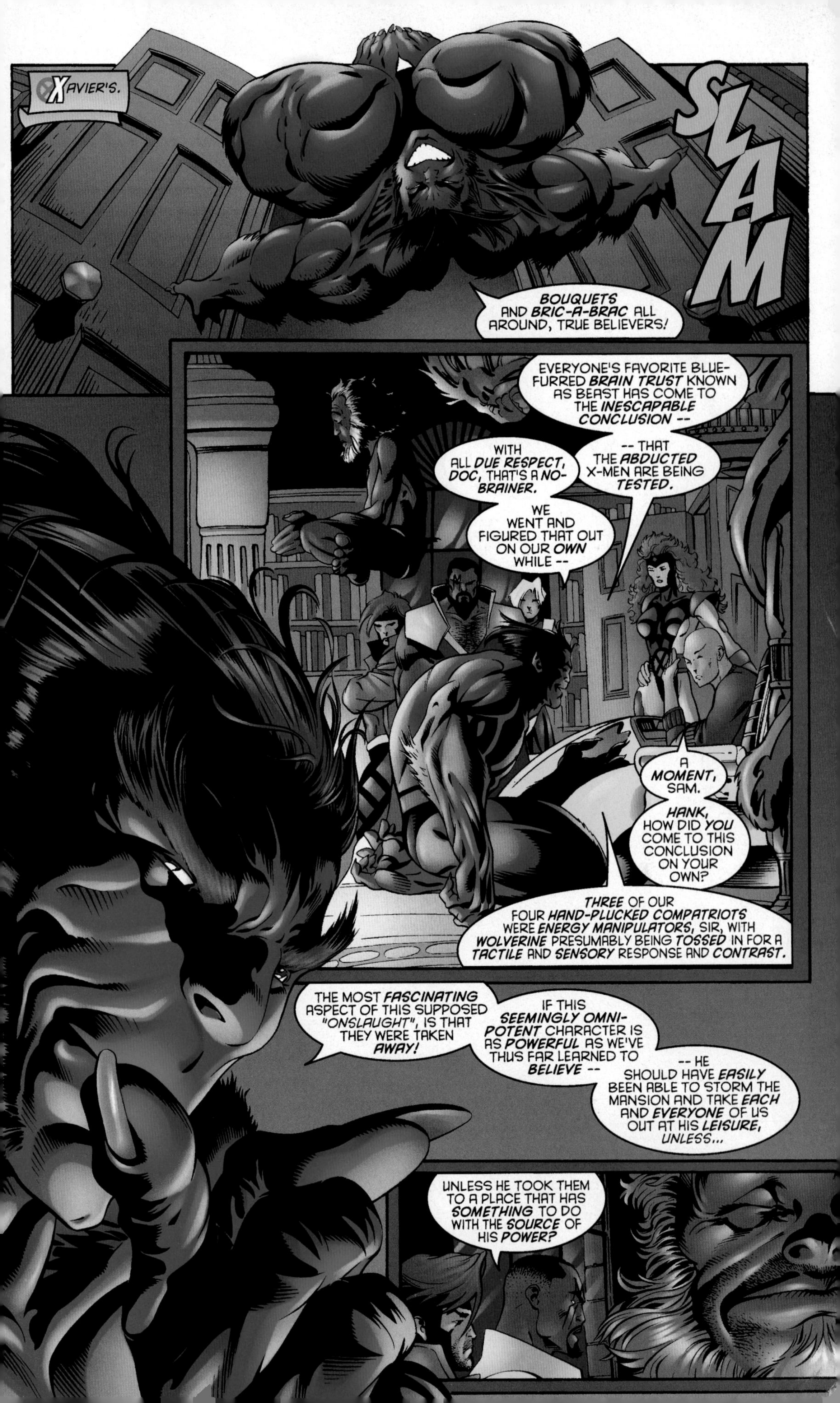
XAVIER'S.
SLAM
BOUQUETS AND BRIC-A-BRAC ALL AROUND, TRUE BELIEVERS!
EVERYONE'S FAVORITE BLUE-FURRED BRAIN TRUST KNOWN AS BEAST HAS COME TO THE INESCAPABLE CONCLUSION --
-- THAT THE ABDUCTED X-MEN ARE BEING TESTED.
WITH ALL DUE RESPECT, DOC, THAT'S A NO-BRAINER.
WE WENT AND FIGURED THAT OUT ON OUR OWN WHILE --
A MOMENT, SAM.
HANK, HOW DID YOU COME TO THIS CONCLUSION ON YOUR OWN?
THREE OF OUR FOUR HAND-PLUCKED COMPATRIOTS WERE ENERGY MANIPULATORS, SIR, WITH WOLVERINE PRESUMABLY BEING TOSSED IN FOR A TACTILE AND SENSORY RESPONSE AND CONTRAST.
THE MOST FASCINATING ASPECT OF THIS SUPPOSED "ONSLAUGHT", IS THAT THEY WERE TAKEN AWAY!
IF THIS SEEMINGLY OMNI-POTENT CHARACTER IS AS POWERFUL AS WE'VE THUS FAR LEARNED TO BELIEVE --
-- HE SHOULD HAVE EASILY BEEN ABLE TO STORM THE MANSION AND TAKE EACH AND EVERYONE OF US OUT AT HIS LEISURE, UNLESS...
UNLESS HE TOOK THEM TO A PLACE THAT HAS SOMETHING TO DO WITH THE SOURCE OF HIS POWER?

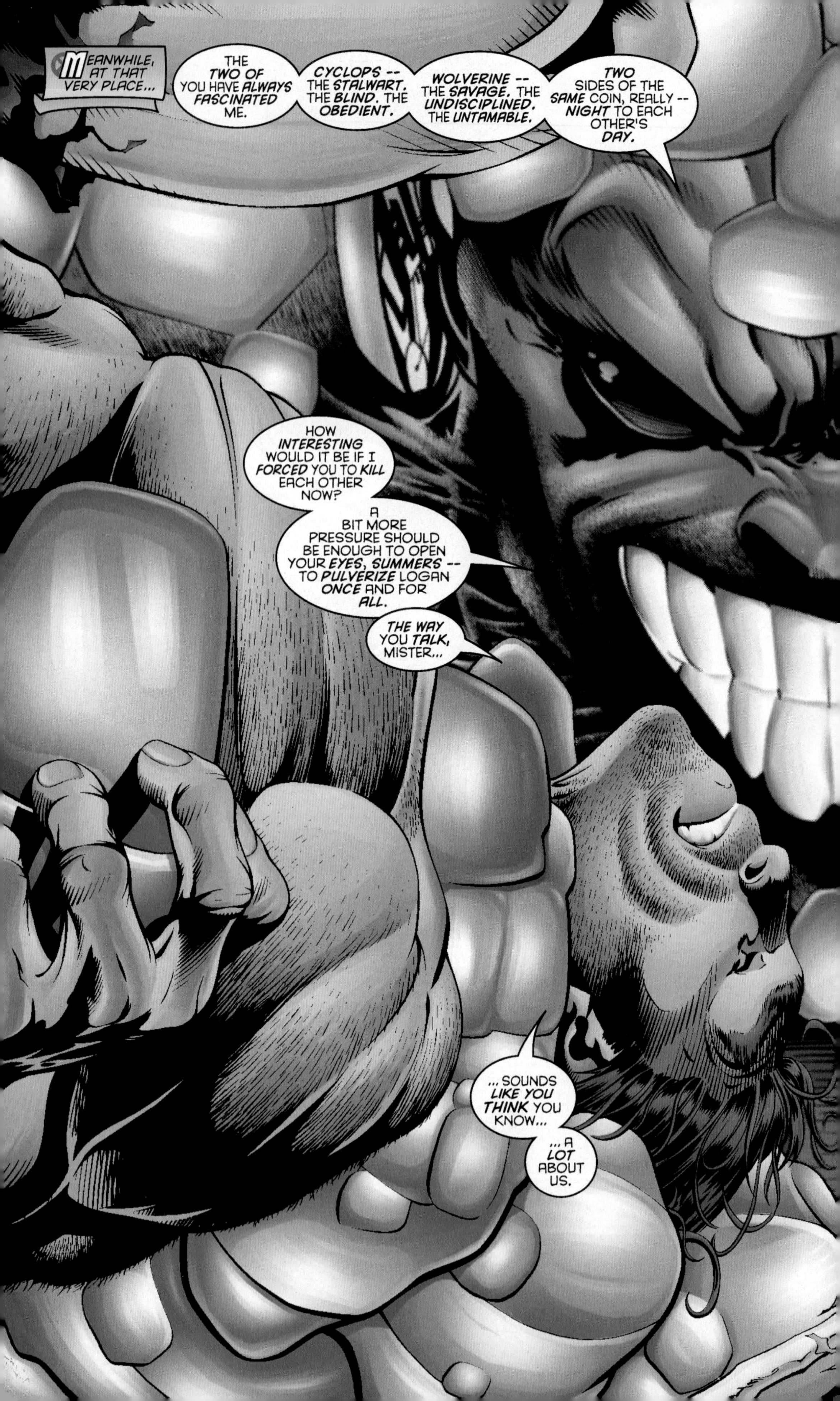
MEANWHILE, AT THAT VERY PLACE...
THE TWO OF YOU HAVE ALWAYS FASCINATED ME.
CYCLOPS -- THE STALWART. THE BLIND. THE OBEDIENT.
WOLVERINE -- THE SAVAGE. THE UNDISCIPLINED. THE UNTAMABLE.
TWO SIDES OF THE SAME COIN, REALLY -- NIGHT TO EACH OTHER'S DAY.
HOW INTERESTING WOULD IT BE IF I FORCED YOU TO KILL EACH OTHER NOW?
A BIT MORE PRESSURE SHOULD BE ENOUGH TO OPEN YOUR EYES, SUMMERS -- TO PULVERIZE LOGAN ONCE AND FOR ALL.
THE WAY YOU TALK, MISTER...
...SOUNDS LIKE YOU THINK YOU KNOW...
...A LOT ABOUT US.

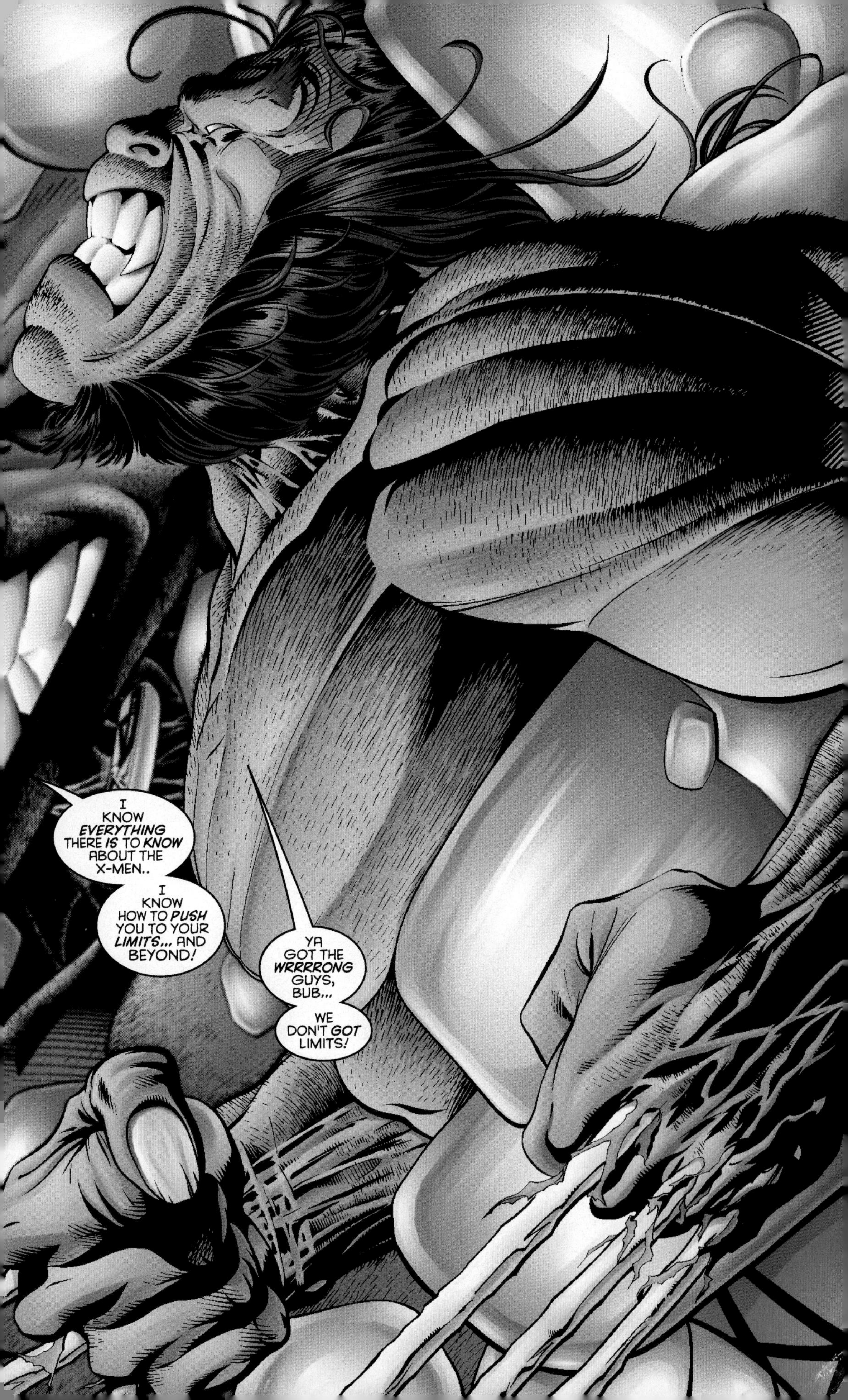
I KNOW EVERYTHING THERE IS TO KNOW ABOUT THE X-MEN..
I KNOW HOW TO PUSH YOU TO YOUR LIMITS... AND BEYOND!
YA GOT THE WRRRRONG GUYS, BUB...
WE DON'T GOT LIMITS!

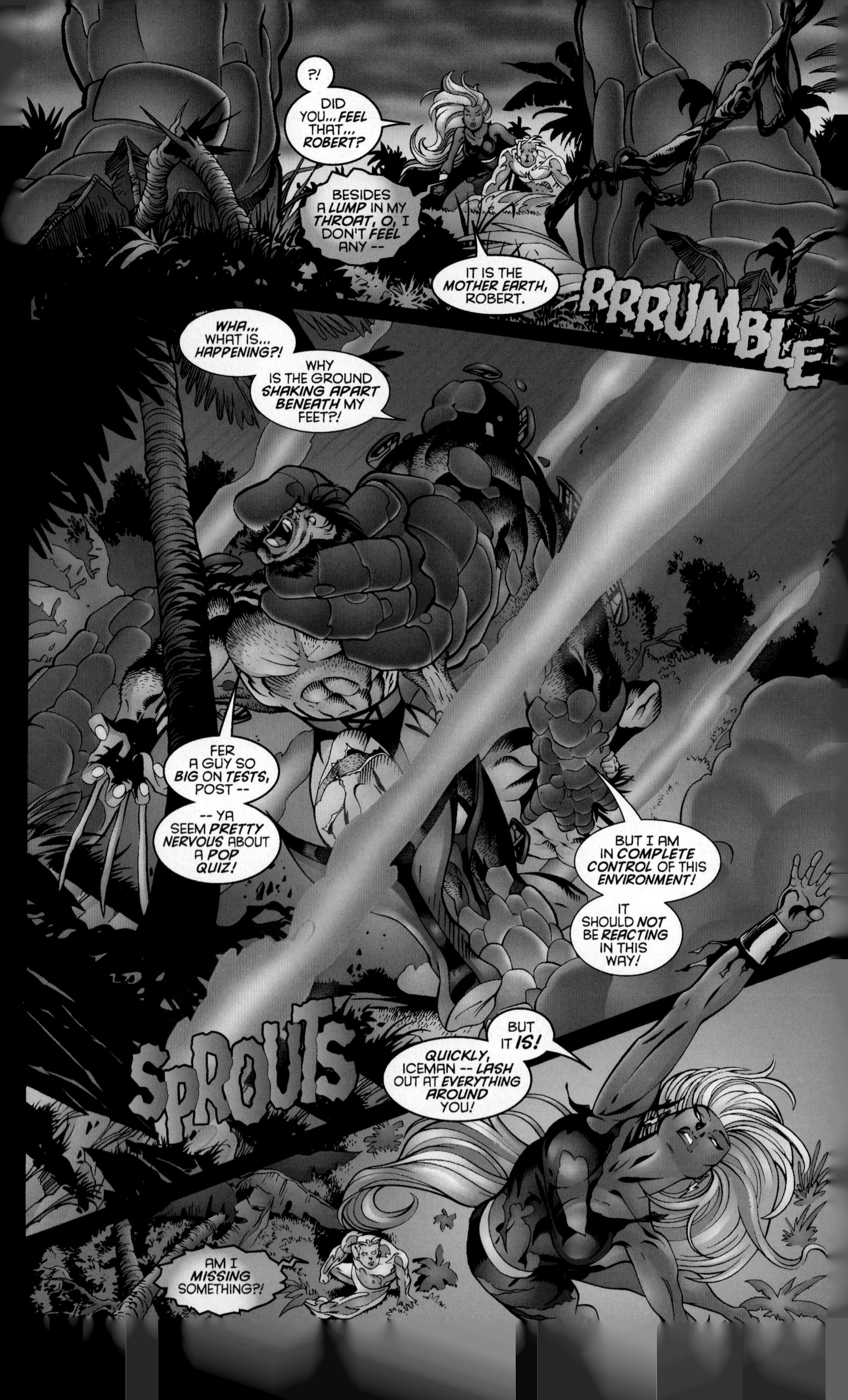
?!
DID YOU... FEEL THAT... ROBERT?
BESIDES A LUMP IN MY THROAT, O, I DON'T FEEL ANY --
IT IS THE MOTHER EARTH, ROBERT.
RRRUMBLE
WHA... WHAT IS... HAPPENING?!
WHY IS THE GROUND SHAKING APART BENEATH MY FEET?!
FER A GUY SO BIG ON TESTS, POST --
-- YA SEEM PRETTY NERVOUS ABOUT A POP QUIZ!
BUT I AM IN COMPLETE CONTROL OF THIS ENVIRONMENT!
IT SHOULD NOT BE REACTING IN THIS WAY!
SPROUTS
BUT IT IS!
QUICKLY, ICEMAN -- LASH OUT AT EVERYTHING AROUND YOU!
AM I MISSING SOMETHING?!

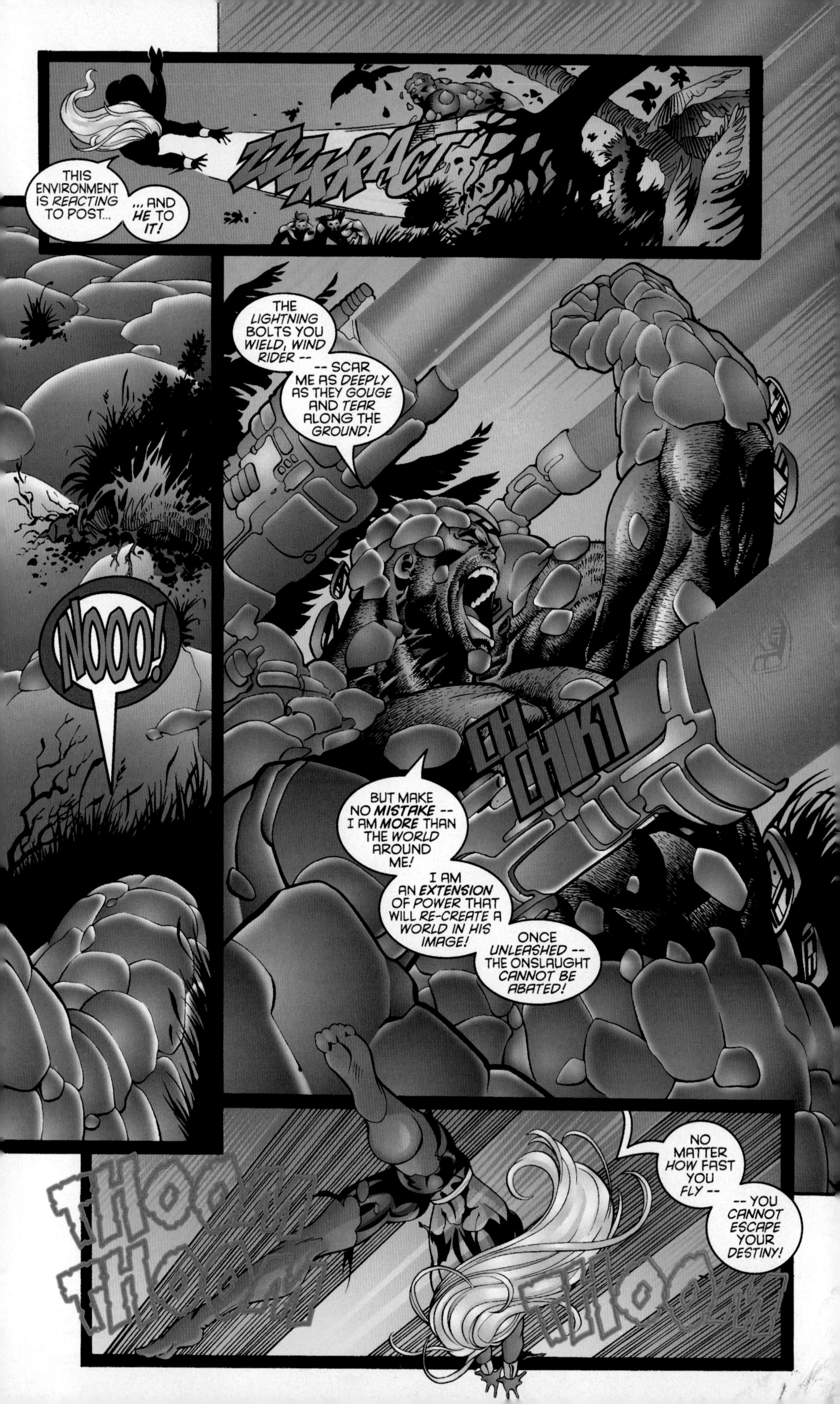

THIS ENVIRONMENT IS REACTING TO POST...
...AND HE TO IT!
ZZZKRACT!!
THE LIGHTNING BOLTS YOU WIELD, WIND RIDER --
-- SCAR ME AS DEEPLY AS THEY GOUGE AND TEAR ALONG THE GROUND!
NOOO!
CH CHIKT
BUT MAKE NO MISTAKE -- I AM MORE THAN THE WORLD AROUND ME!
I AM AN EXTENSION OF POWER THAT WILL RE-CREATE A WORLD IN HIS IMAGE!
ONCE UNLEASHED -- THE ONSLAUGHT CANNOT BE ABATED!
NO MATTER HOW FAST YOU FLY --
-- YOU CANNOT ESCAPE YOUR DESTINY!

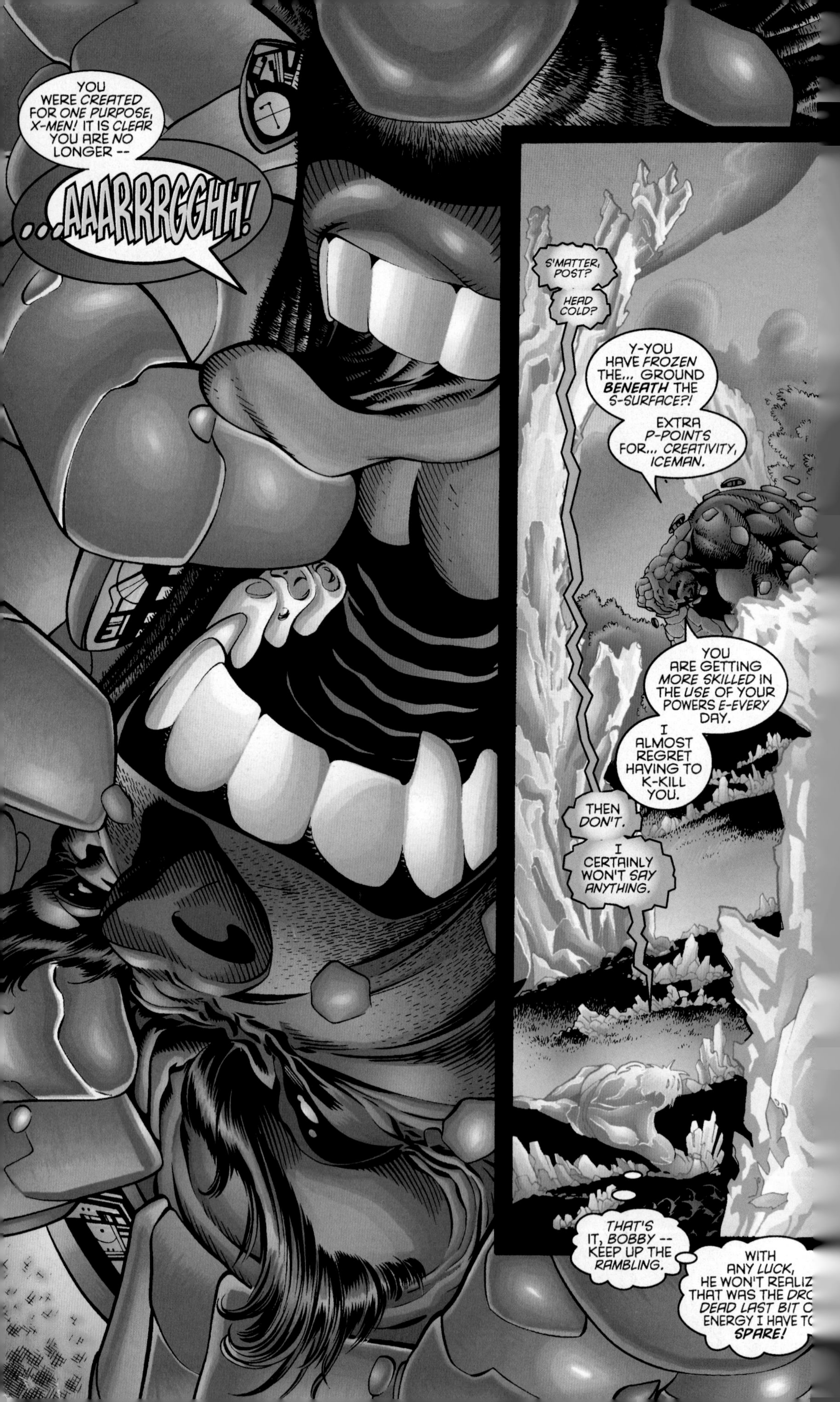

YOU WERE CREATED FOR ONE PURPOSE, X-MEN! IT IS CLEAR YOU ARE NO LONGER --
...AAARRRGGHH!
S'MATTER, POST?
HEAD COLD?
Y-YOU HAVE FROZEN THE... GROUND BENEATH THE S-SURFACE?!
EXTRA P-POINTS FOR... CREATIVITY, ICEMAN.
YOU ARE GETTING MORE SKILLED IN THE USE OF YOUR POWERS E-EVERY DAY.
I ALMOST REGRET HAVING TO K-KILL YOU.
THEN DON'T.
I CERTAINLY WON'T SAY ANYTHING.
THAT'S IT, BOBBY -- KEEP UP THE RAMBLING.

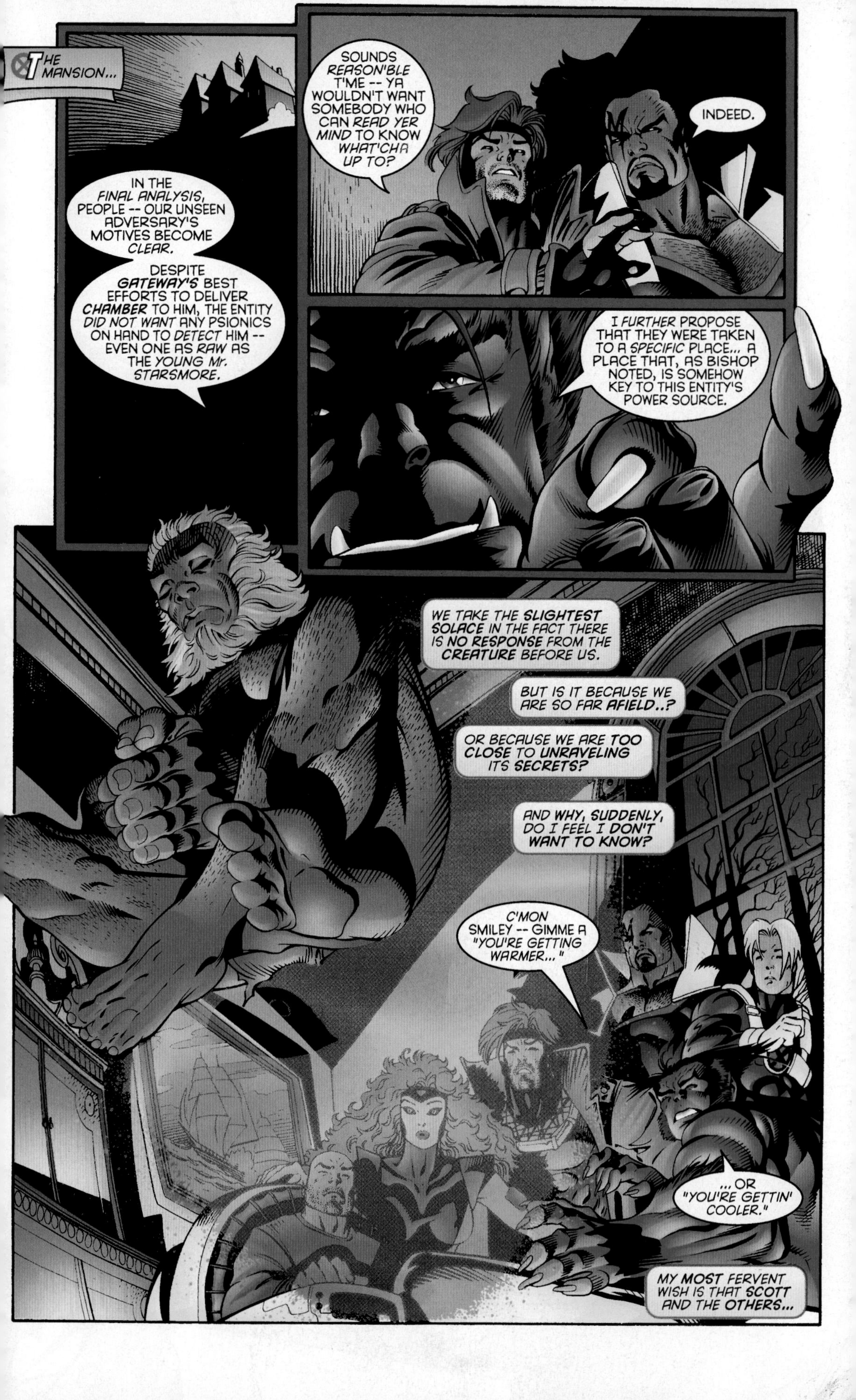

THE MANSION...
SOUNDS REASON'BLE T'ME -- YA WOULDN'T WANT SOMEBODY WHO CAN READ YER MIND TO KNOW WHAT'CHA UP TO?
INDEED.
IN THE FINAL ANALYSIS, PEOPLE -- OUR UNSEEN ADVERSARY'S MOTIVES BECOME CLEAR.
DESPITE GATEWAY'S BEST EFFORTS TO DELIVER CHAMBER TO HIM, THE ENTITY DID NOT WANT ANY PSIONICS ON HAND TO DETECT HIM -- EVEN ONE AS RAW AS THE YOUNG Mr. STARSMORE.
I FURTHER PROPOSE THAT THEY WERE TAKEN TO A SPECIFIC PLACE... A PLACE THAT, AS BISHOP NOTED, IS SOMEHOW KEY TO THIS ENTITY'S POWER SOURCE.
WE TAKE THE SLIGHTEST SOLACE IN THE FACT THERE IS NO RESPONSE FROM THE CREATURE BEFORE US.
BUT IS IT BECAUSE WE ARE SO FAR AFIELD..?
OR BECAUSE WE ARE TOO CLOSE TO UNRAVELING ITS SECRETS?
AND WHY, SUDDENLY, DO I FEEL I DON'T WANT TO KNOW?
C'MON SMILEY -- GIMME A "YOU'RE GETTING WARMER..."
...OR "YOU'RE GETTIN' COOLER."
MY MOST FERVENT WISH IS THAT SCOTT AND THE OTHERS...

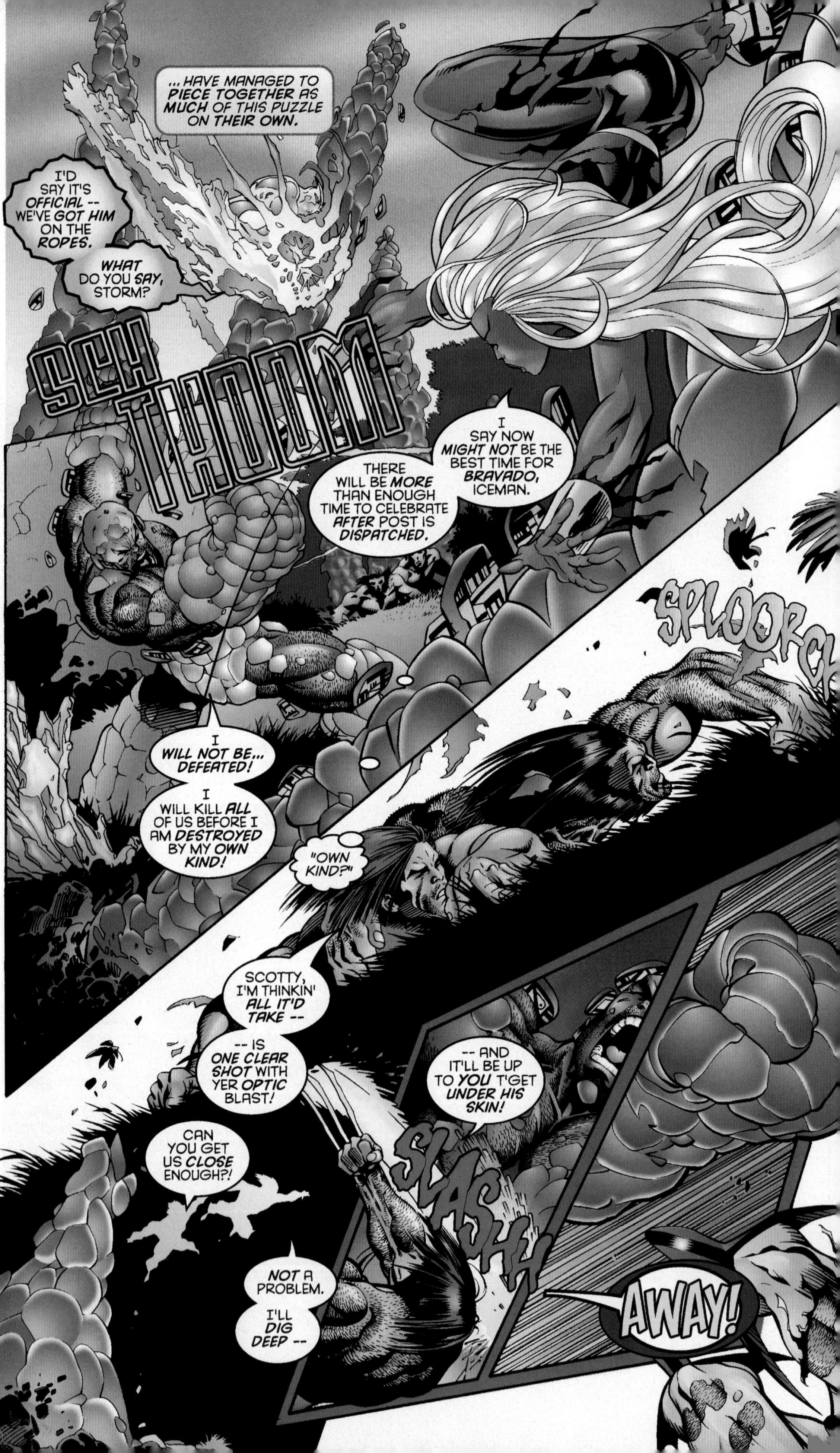
...HAVE MANAGED TO PIECE TOGETHER AS MUCH OF THIS PUZZLE ON THEIR OWN.
I'D SAY IT'S OFFICIAL -- WE'VE GOT HIM ON THE ROPES.
WHAT DO YOU SAY, STORM?
SCH THOOM
I SAY NOW MIGHT NOT BE THE BEST TIME FOR BRAVADO, ICEMAN.
THERE WILL BE MORE THAN ENOUGH TIME TO CELEBRATE AFTER POST IS DISPATCHED.
I WILL NOT BE... DEFEATED!
I WILL KILL ALL OF US BEFORE I AM DESTROYED BY MY OWN KIND!
"OWN KIND?"
SPLOORCH
SCOTTY, I'M THINKIN' ALL IT'D TAKE --
-- IS ONE CLEAR SHOT WITH YER OPTIC BLAST!
-- AND IT'LL BE UP TO YOU T'GET UNDER HIS SKIN!
CAN YOU GET US CLOSE ENOUGH?!
SLASHH
NOT A PROBLEM.
I'LL DIG DEEP --
AWAY!

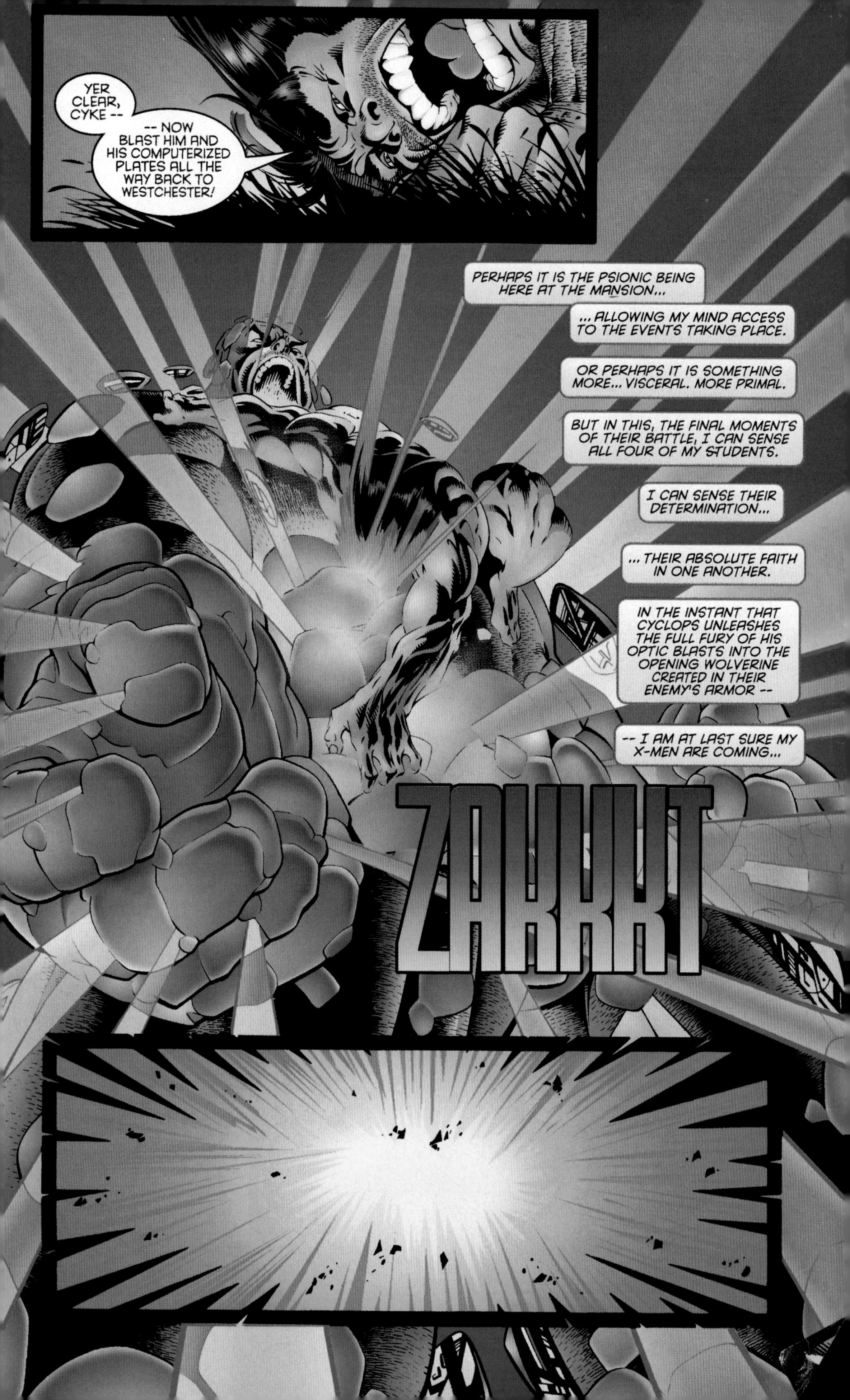
YER CLEAR, CYKE --
-- NOW BLAST HIM AND HIS COMPUTERIZED PLATES ALL THE WAY BACK TO WESTCHESTER!
PERHAPS IT IS THE PSIONIC BEING HERE AT THE MANSION...
... ALLOWING MY MIND ACCESS TO THE EVENTS TAKING PLACE.
OR PERHAPS IT IS SOMETHING MORE... VISCERAL. MORE PRIMAL.
BUT IN THIS, THE FINAL MOMENTS OF THEIR BATTLE, I CAN SENSE ALL FOUR OF MY STUDENTS.
I CAN SENSE THEIR DETERMINATION...
... THEIR ABSOLUTE FAITH IN ONE ANOTHER.
IN THE INSTANT THAT CYCLOPS UNLEASHES THE FULL FURY OF HIS OPTIC BLASTS INTO THE OPENING WOLVERINE CREATED IN THEIR ENEMY'S ARMOR --
-- I AM AT LAST SURE MY X-MEN ARE COMING...
ZAKKKT

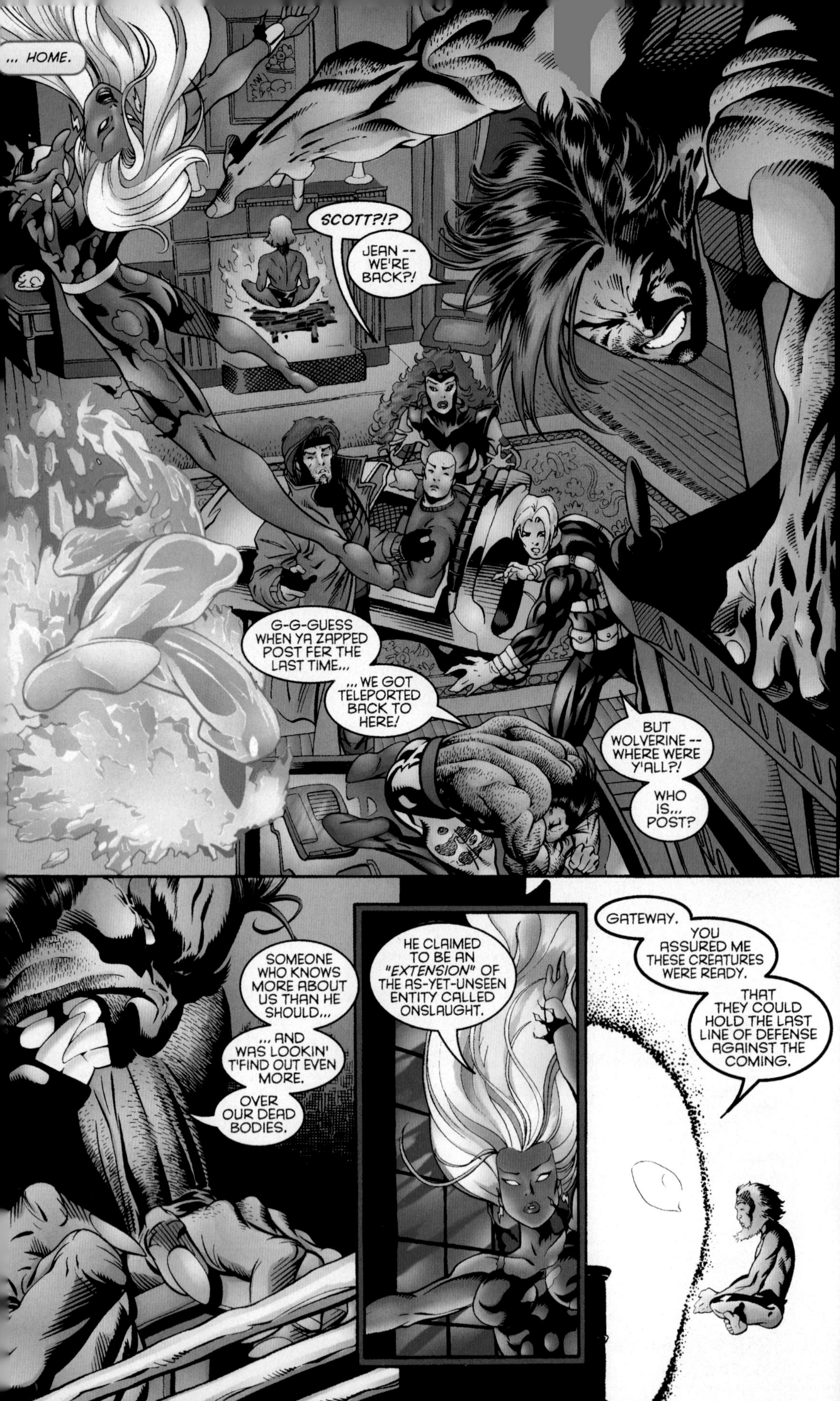
... HOME.
SCOTT?!?
JEAN -- WE'RE BACK?!
G-G-GUESS WHEN YA ZAPPED POST FER THE LAST TIME...
... WE GOT TELEPORTED BACK TO HERE!
BUT WOLVERINE -- WHERE WERE Y'ALL?!
WHO IS... POST?
SOMEONE WHO KNOWS MORE ABOUT US THAN HE SHOULD...
... AND WAS LOOKIN' T'FIND OUT EVEN MORE.
OVER OUR DEAD BODIES.
HE CLAIMED TO BE AN "EXTENSION" OF THE AS-YET-UNSEEN ENTITY CALLED ONSLAUGHT.
GATEWAY.
YOU ASSURED ME THESE CREATURES WERE READY.
THAT THEY COULD HOLD THE LAST LINE OF DEFENSE AGAINST THE COMING.

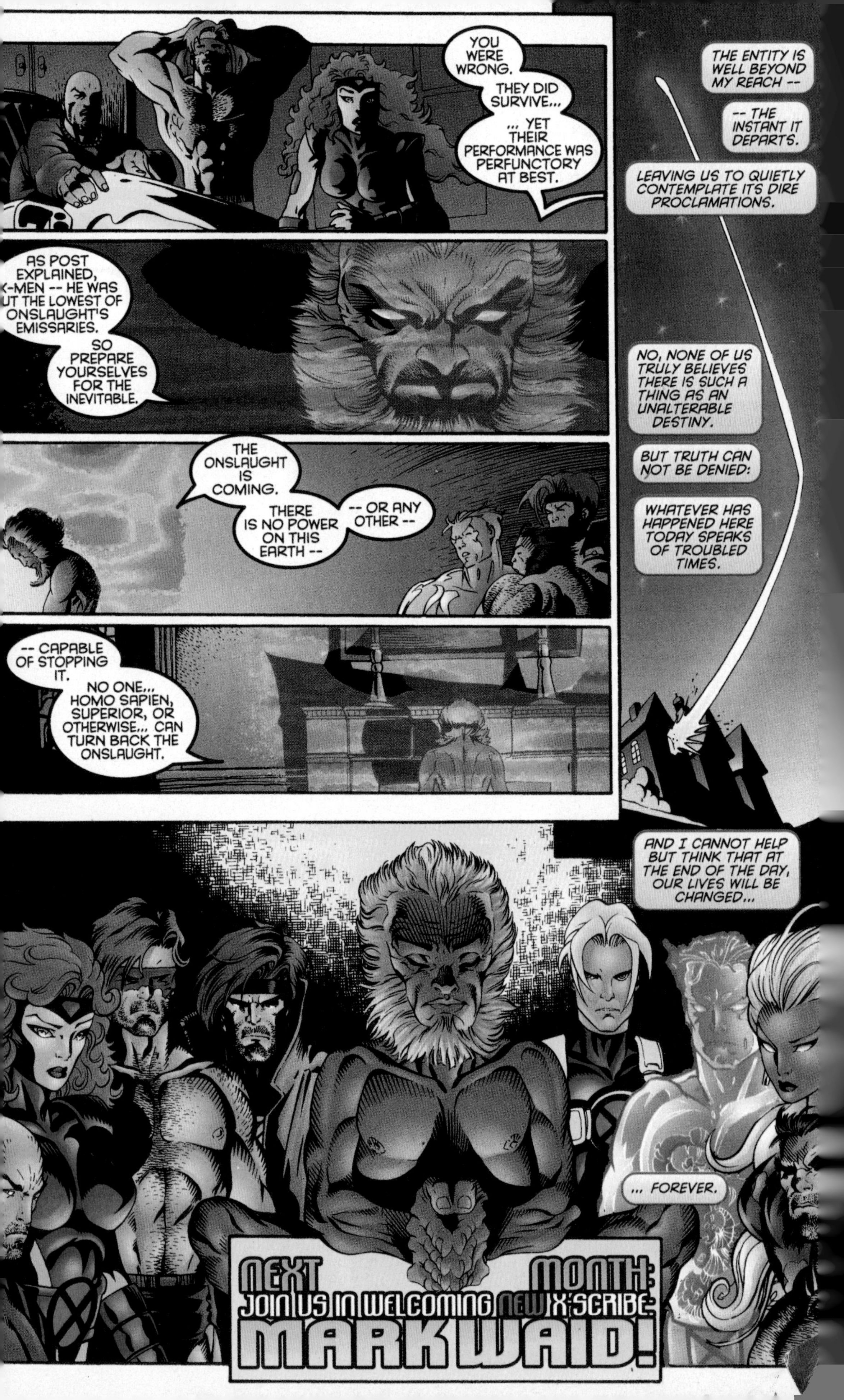

YOU WERE WRONG.
THEY DID SURVIVE...
... YET THEIR PERFORMANCE WAS PERFUNCTORY AT BEST.
AS POST EXPLAINED, -MEN -- HE WAS UT THE LOWEST OF ONSLAUGHT'S EMISSARIES.
SO PREPARE YOURSELVES FOR THE INEVITABLE.
THE ONSLAUGHT IS COMING.
THERE IS NO POWER ON THIS EARTH --
-- OR ANY OTHER --
-- CAPABLE OF STOPPING IT.
NO ONE... HOMO SAPIEN, SUPERIOR, OR OTHERWISE... CAN TURN BACK THE ONSLAUGHT.
THE ENTITY IS WELL BEYOND MY REACH --
-- THE INSTANT IT DEPARTS.
LEAVING US TO QUIETLY CONTEMPLATE IT'S DIRE PROCLAMATIONS.
NO, NONE OF US TRULY BELIEVES THERE IS SUCH A THING AS AN UNALTERABLE DESTINY.
BUT TRUTH CAN NOT BE DENIED:
WHATEVER HAS HAPPENED HERE TODAY SPEAKS OF TROUBLED TIMES.
AND I CANNOT HELP BUT THINK THAT AT THE END OF THE DAY, OUR LIVES WILL BE CHANGED...
... FOREVER.
NEXT MONTH:
JOIN US IN WELCOMING NEW X-SCRIBE:
MARK WAID!

MEANWHILE

The X-Men had their hands full with other villains. Genesis, Cable's insane stepson Tyler who believed he was Apocalypse's heir, ravaged the mind of Grizzly, Cable's former ally, sending him on a rampage and forcing X-Force's Domino to kill him. X-Force then encountered the Blob when Cable sent them to a Nimrod Sentinel plant – a plant that, unknown to X-Force, Onslaught had recently ransacked.

COMICS
MARCH
X-MEN
STILL ONLY $1.50

The "Dark Beast," an evil version of the Beast from Nate Grey's home dimension, imprisoned and took the place of the real Beast in order to hide from the mad geneticist Mr. Sinister. Elsewhere, while the X-Men searched for the site of their battle with Post, Iceman hoped to heal his injuries with the aid of Generation X's headmistress Emma Frost, who had once possessed his body and used his ice powers much more accurately than he could.

Genesis then decided to resurrect Apocalypse. He abducted Wolverine and tried to turn the feral mutant into his henchman by re-grafting Adamantium to his skeleton. But Wolverine's healing factor rejected the bonding, and when his teammate Cannonball came to the rescue, he found that something had gone terribly wrong...

MARVEL COMICS
THE UNCANNY
X-MEN
X-MEN DELUXE
ICEMAN
VS. GENERATION X's
WHITE QUEEN
--'NUFF SAID!

MARVEL COMICS
X-MEN DELUXE
MARCH
X
MEN
BEAST VS BEAST!
MEET THE REAL McCOY

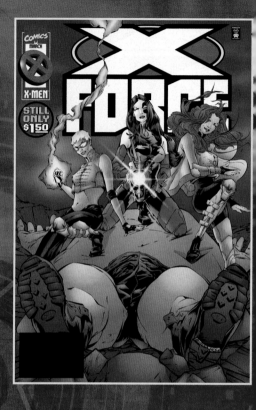

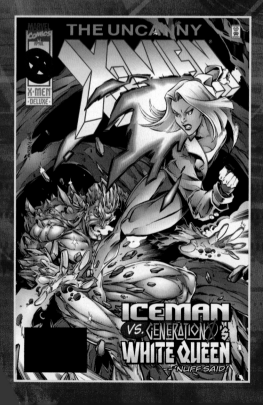

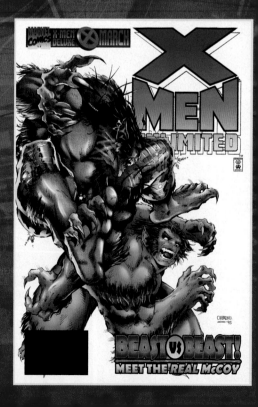

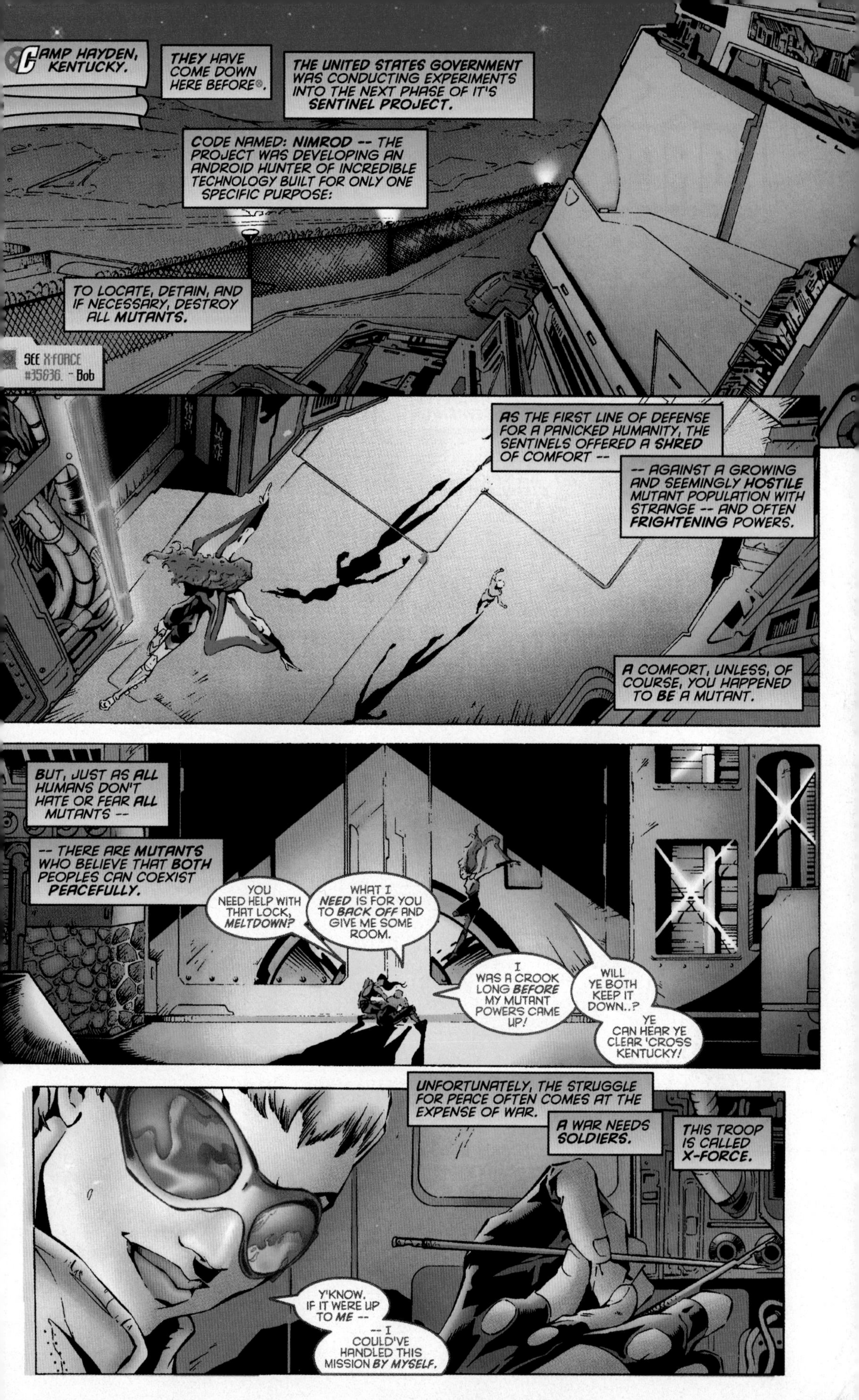

CAMP HAYDEN, KENTUCKY.
THEY HAVE COME DOWN HERE BEFORE®.
THE UNITED STATES GOVERNMENT WAS CONDUCTING EXPERIMENTS INTO THE NEXT PHASE OF IT'S SENTINEL PROJECT.
CODE NAMED: NIMROD -- THE PROJECT WAS DEVELOPING AN ANDROID HUNTER OF INCREDIBLE TECHNOLOGY BUILT FOR ONLY ONE SPECIFIC PURPOSE:
TO LOCATE, DETAIN, AND IF NECESSARY, DESTROY ALL MUTANTS.
SEE X-FORCE #35&36. -- Bob
AS THE FIRST LINE OF DEFENSE FOR A PANICKED HUMANITY, THE SENTINELS OFFERED A SHRED OF COMFORT --
-- AGAINST A GROWING AND SEEMINGLY HOSTILE MUTANT POPULATION WITH STRANGE -- AND OFTEN FRIGHTENING POWERS.
A COMFORT, UNLESS, OF COURSE, YOU HAPPENED TO BE A MUTANT.
BUT, JUST AS ALL HUMANS DON'T HATE OR FEAR ALL MUTANTS --
-- THERE ARE MUTANTS WHO BELIEVE THAT BOTH PEOPLES CAN COEXIST PEACEFULLY.
YOU NEED HELP WITH THAT LOCK, MELTDOWN?
WHAT I NEED IS FOR YOU TO BACK OFF AND GIVE ME SOME ROOM.
I WAS A CROOK LONG BEFORE MY MUTANT POWERS CAME UP!
WILL YE BOTH KEEP IT DOWN..?
YE CAN HEAR YE CLEAR 'CROSS KENTUCKY!
UNFORTUNATELY, THE STRUGGLE FOR PEACE OFTEN COMES AT THE EXPENSE OF WAR.
A WAR NEEDS SOLDIERS.
THIS TROOP IS CALLED X-FORCE.
Y'KNOW. IF IT WERE UP TO ME --
-- I COULD'VE HANDLED THIS MISSION BY MYSELF.

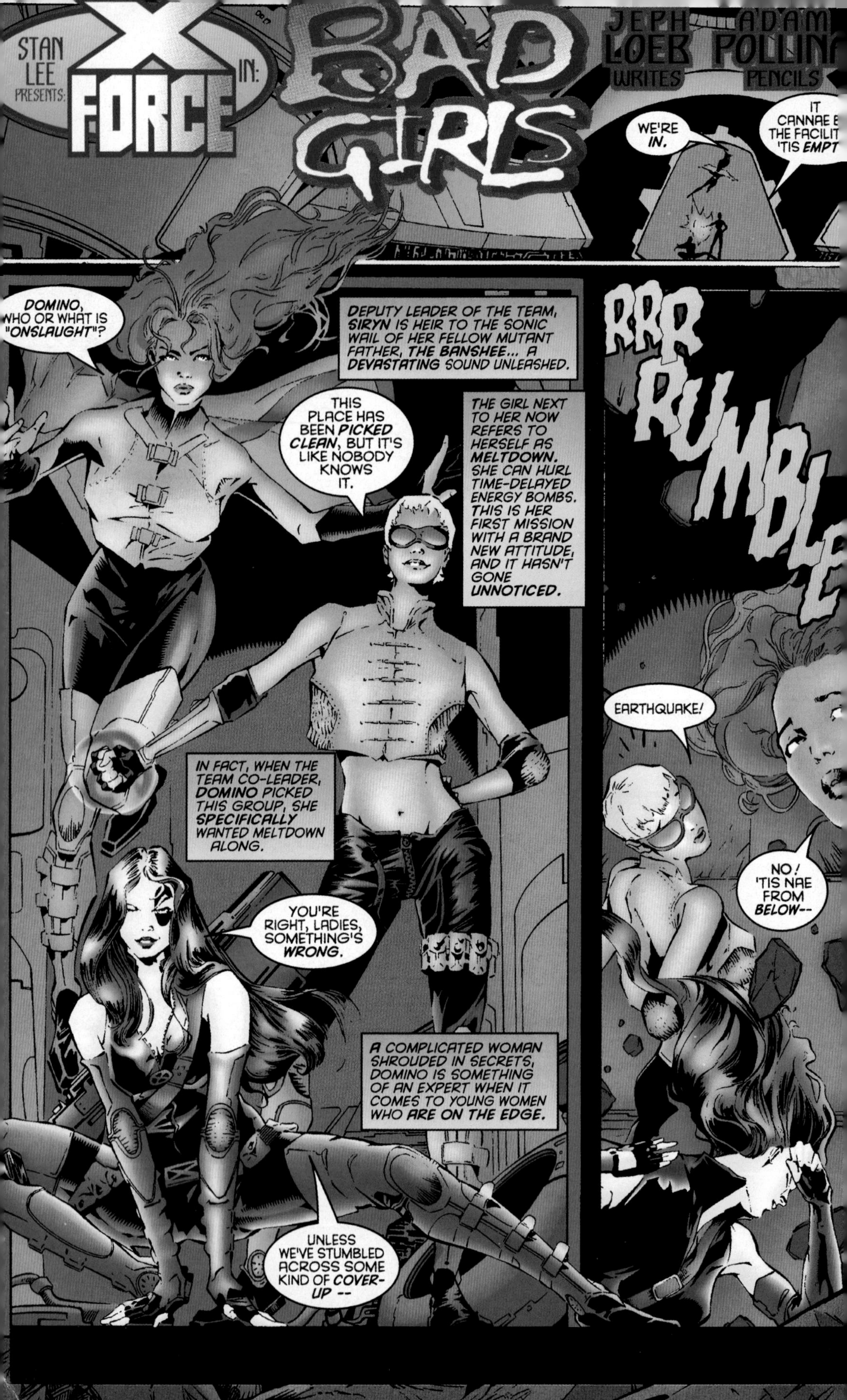
STAN LEE PRESENTS:
X-FORCE IN:
BAD GIRLS
JEPH LOEB WRITES
ADAM POLLINA PENCILS
WE'RE IN.
IT CANNAE B
THE FACILIT
'TIS EMPT
DOMINO, WHO OR WHAT IS "ONSLAUGHT"?
DEPUTY LEADER OF THE TEAM, SIRYN IS HEIR TO THE SONIC WAIL OF HER FELLOW MUTANT FATHER, THE BANSHEE... A DEVASTATING SOUND UNLEASHED.
THIS PLACE HAS BEEN PICKED CLEAN, BUT IT'S LIKE NOBODY KNOWS IT.
THE GIRL NEXT TO HER NOW REFERS TO HERSELF AS MELTDOWN. SHE CAN HURL TIME-DELAYED ENERGY BOMBS. THIS IS HER FIRST MISSION WITH A BRAND NEW ATTITUDE, AND IT HASN'T GONE UNNOTICED.
IN FACT, WHEN THE TEAM CO-LEADER, DOMINO PICKED THIS GROUP, SHE SPECIFICALLY WANTED MELTDOWN ALONG.
YOU'RE RIGHT, LADIES, SOMETHING'S WRONG.
A COMPLICATED WOMAN SHROUDED IN SECRETS, DOMINO IS SOMETHING OF AN EXPERT WHEN IT COMES TO YOUNG WOMEN WHO ARE ON THE EDGE.
UNLESS WE'VE STUMBLED ACROSS SOME KIND OF COVER-UP --
RRR RUMBLE
EARTHQUAKE!
NO! 'TIS NAE FROM BELOW--

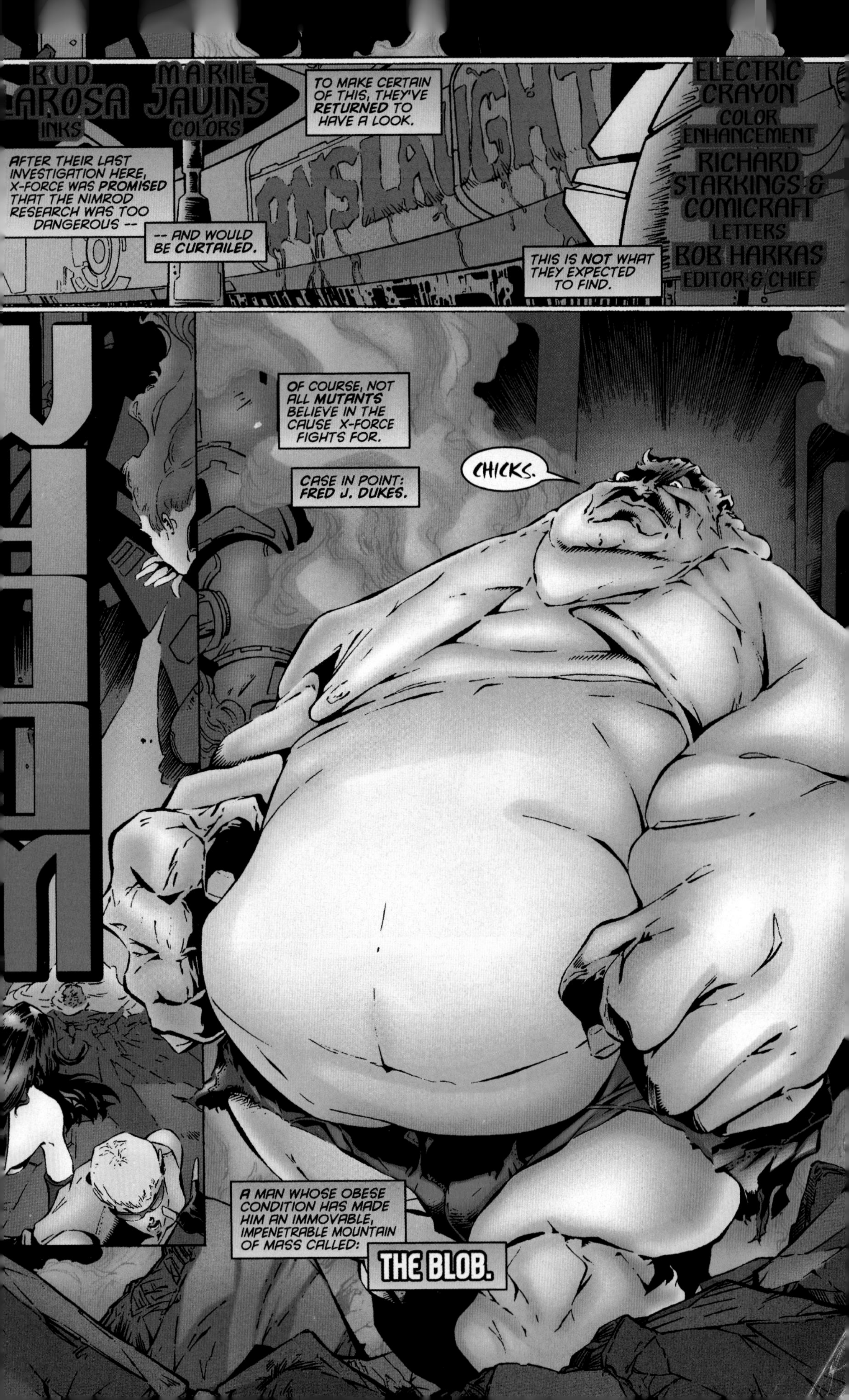
BUD LAROSA INKS
MARIE JAVINS COLORS
AFTER THEIR LAST INVESTIGATION HERE, X-FORCE WAS PROMISED THAT THE NIMROD RESEARCH WAS TOO DANGEROUS --
-- AND WOULD BE CURTAILED.
TO MAKE CERTAIN OF THIS, THEY'VE RETURNED TO HAVE A LOOK.
ONSLAUGHT
THIS IS NOT WHAT THEY EXPECTED TO FIND.
ELECTRIC CRAYON COLOR ENHANCEMENT
RICHARD STARKINGS & COMICRAFT LETTERS
BOB HARRAS EDITOR & CHIEF
OF COURSE, NOT ALL MUTANTS BELIEVE IN THE CAUSE X-FORCE FIGHTS FOR.
CASE IN POINT: FRED J. DUKES.
CHICKS.
A MAN WHOSE OBESE CONDITION HAS MADE HIM AN IMMOVABLE, IMPENETRABLE MOUNTAIN OF MASS CALLED:
THE BLOB.

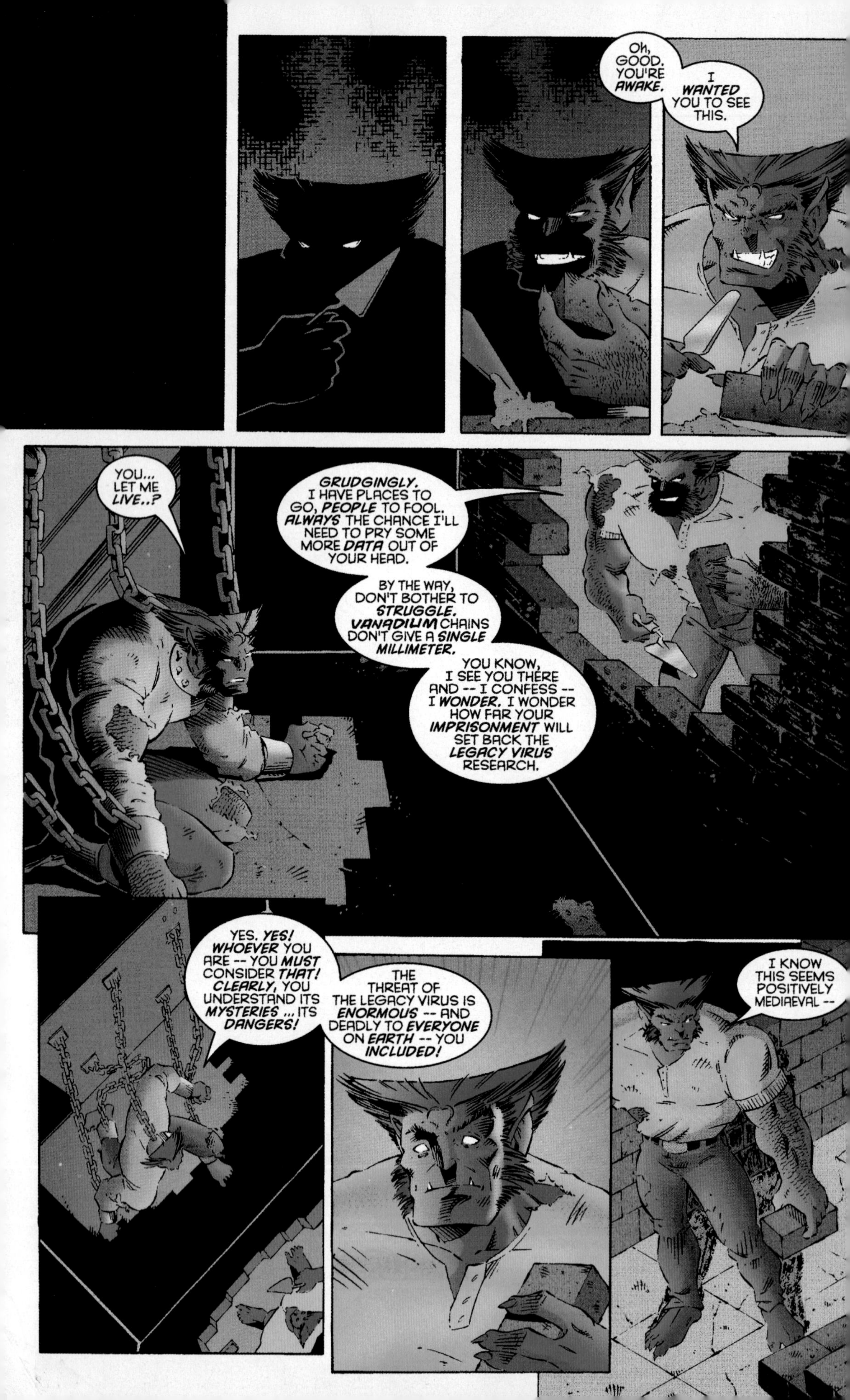
Oh, GOOD. YOU'RE AWAKE.
I WANTED YOU TO SEE THIS.
YOU... LET ME LIVE..?
GRUDGINGLY. I HAVE PLACES TO GO, PEOPLE TO FOOL. ALWAYS THE CHANCE I'LL NEED TO PRY SOME MORE DATA OUT OF YOUR HEAD.
BY THE WAY, DON'T BOTHER TO STRUGGLE. VANADIUM CHAINS DON'T GIVE A SINGLE MILLIMETER.
YOU KNOW, I SEE YOU THERE AND -- I CONFESS -- I WONDER. I WONDER HOW FAR YOUR IMPRISONMENT WILL SET BACK THE LEGACY VIRUS RESEARCH.
YES. YES! WHOEVER YOU ARE -- YOU MUST CONSIDER THAT! CLEARLY, YOU UNDERSTAND ITS MYSTERIES ... ITS DANGERS!
THE THREAT OF THE LEGACY VIRUS IS ENORMOUS -- AND DEADLY TO EVERYONE ON EARTH -- YOU INCLUDED!
I KNOW THIS SEEMS POSITIVELY MEDIAEVAL --

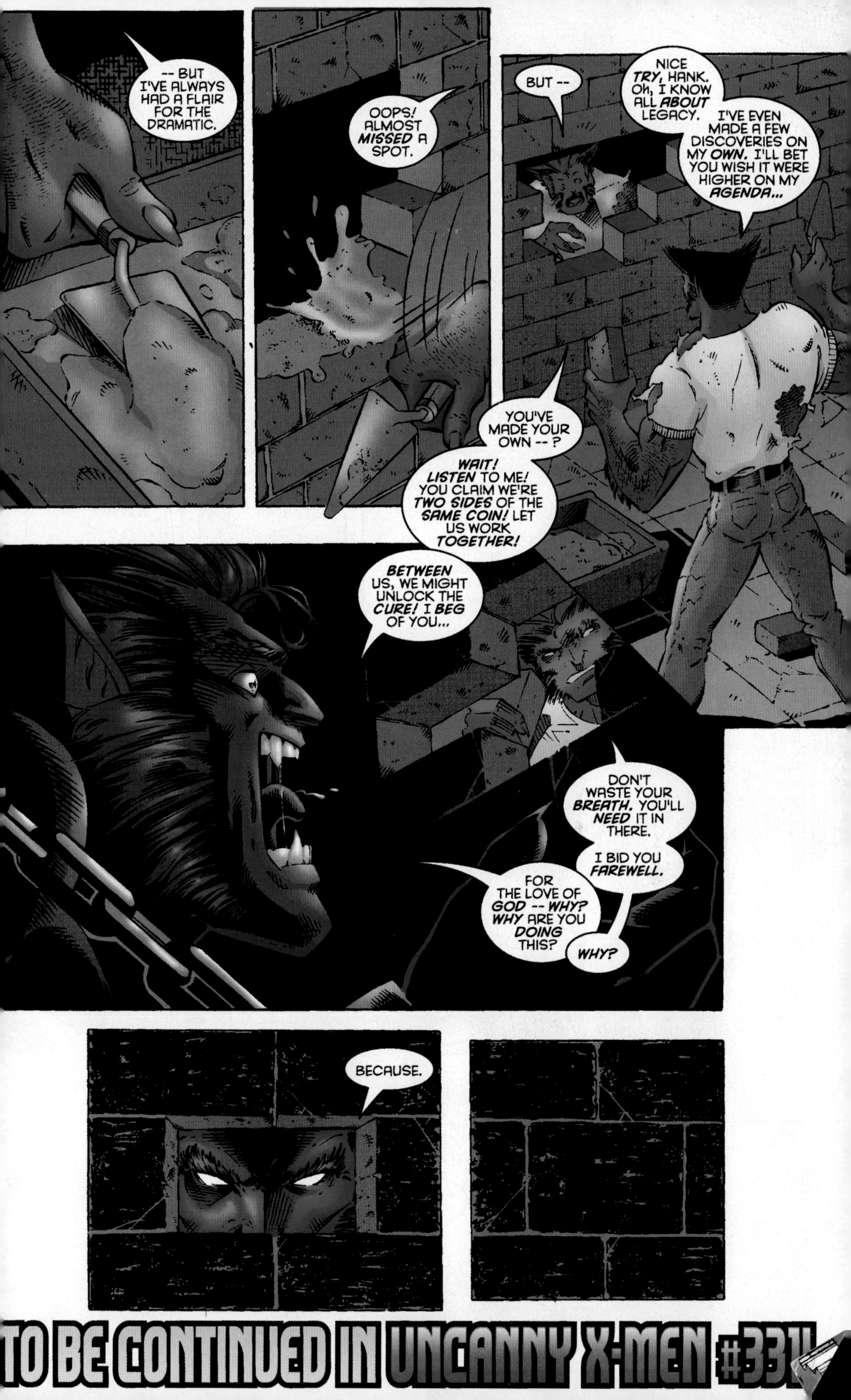

-- BUT I'VE ALWAYS HAD A FLAIR FOR THE DRAMATIC.
OOPS! ALMOST MISSED A SPOT.
BUT --
NICE TRY, HANK. OH, I KNOW ALL ABOUT LEGACY.
I'VE EVEN MADE A FEW DISCOVERIES ON MY OWN. I'LL BET YOU WISH IT WERE HIGHER ON MY AGENDA...
YOU'VE MADE YOUR OWN -- ?
WAIT! LISTEN TO ME! YOU CLAIM WE'RE TWO SIDES OF THE SAME COIN! LET US WORK TOGETHER!
BETWEEN US, WE MIGHT UNLOCK THE CURE! I BEG OF YOU...
DON'T WASTE YOUR BREATH. YOU'LL NEED IT IN THERE.
I BID YOU FAREWELL.
FOR THE LOVE OF GOD -- WHY? WHY ARE YOU DOING THIS?
WHY?
BECAUSE.
TO BE CONTINUED IN UNCANNY X-MEN #331!

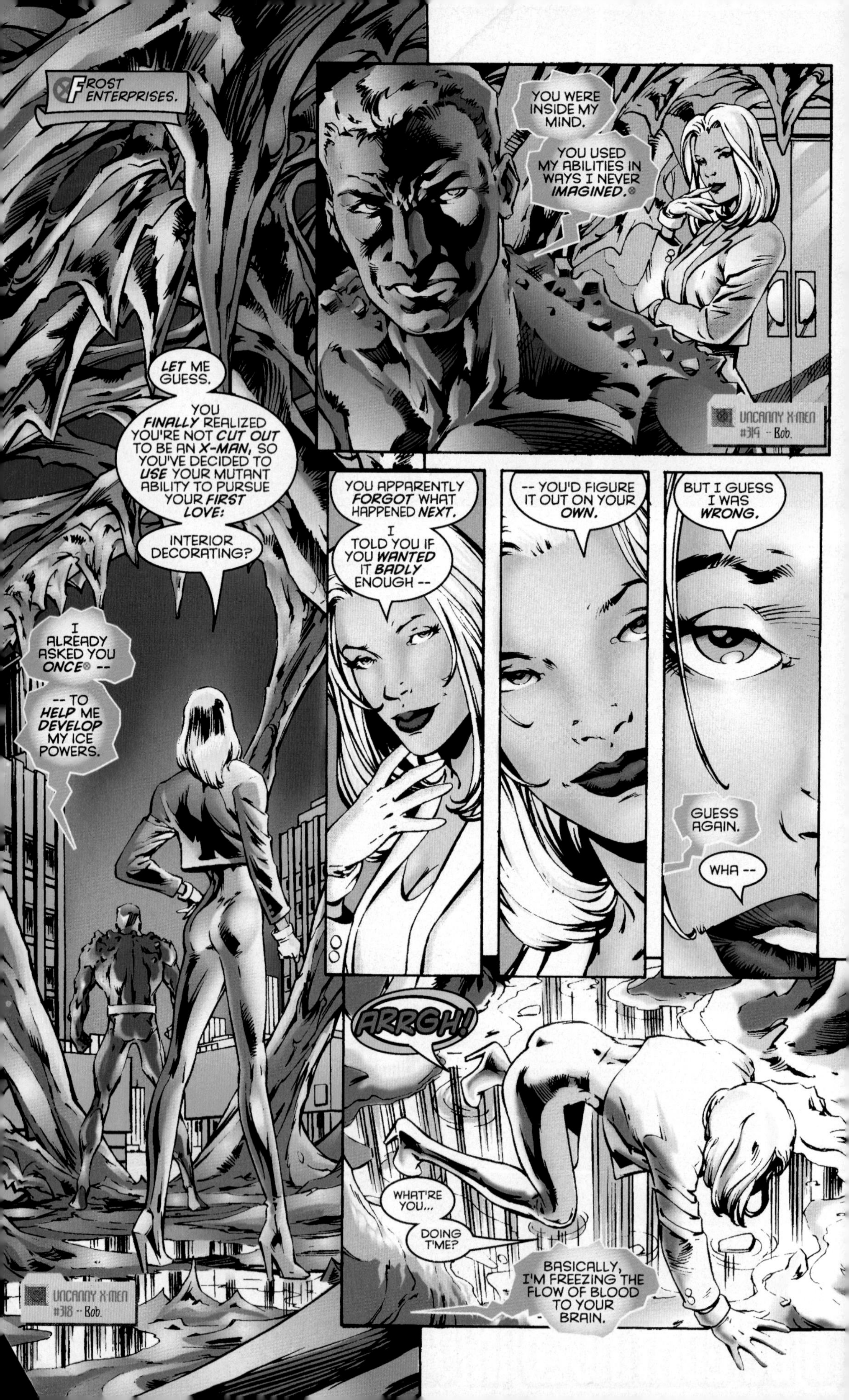
FROST ENTERPRISES.
YOU WERE INSIDE MY MIND.
YOU USED MY ABILITIES IN WAYS I NEVER IMAGINED.
UNCANNY X-MEN #314 -- Bob.
LET ME GUESS.
YOU FINALLY REALIZED YOU'RE NOT CUT OUT TO BE AN X-MAN, SO YOU'VE DECIDED TO USE YOUR MUTANT ABILITY TO PURSUE YOUR FIRST LOVE:
INTERIOR DECORATING?
I ALREADY ASKED YOU ONCE --
-- TO HELP ME DEVELOP MY ICE POWERS.
UNCANNY X-MEN #318 -- Bob.
YOU APPARENTLY FORGOT WHAT HAPPENED NEXT.
I TOLD YOU IF YOU WANTED IT BADLY ENOUGH --
-- YOU'D FIGURE IT OUT ON YOUR OWN.
BUT I GUESS I WAS WRONG.
GUESS AGAIN.
WHA --
ARRGH!
WHAT'RE YOU...
DOING T'ME?
BASICALLY, I'M FREEZING THE FLOW OF BLOOD TO YOUR BRAIN.

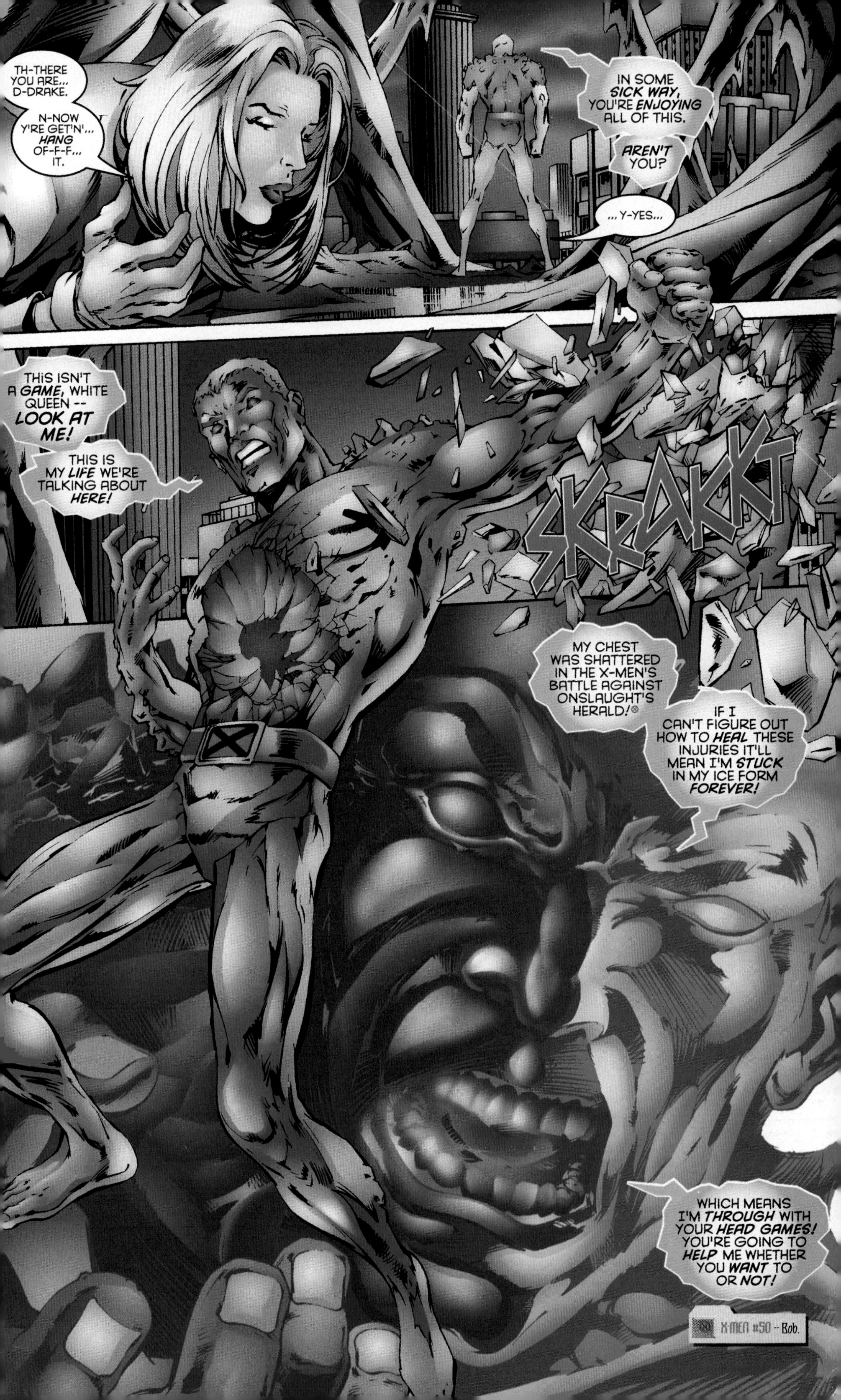
TH-THERE YOU ARE,.. D-DRAKE.
N-NOW Y'RE GET'N'... HANG OF-F-F... IT.
IN SOME SICK WAY, YOU'RE ENJOYING ALL OF THIS.
AREN'T YOU?
...Y-YES...
THIS ISN'T A GAME, WHITE QUEEN -- LOOK AT ME!
THIS IS MY LIFE WE'RE TALKING ABOUT HERE!
SKRAKKT
MY CHEST WAS SHATTERED IN THE X-MEN'S BATTLE AGAINST ONSLAUGHT'S HERALD!
IF I CAN'T FIGURE OUT HOW TO HEAL THESE INJURIES IT'LL MEAN I'M STUCK IN MY ICE FORM FOREVER!
WHICH MEANS I'M THROUGH WITH YOUR HEAD GAMES! YOU'RE GOING TO HELP ME WHETHER YOU WANT TO OR NOT!
X-MEN #50 -- Bob.

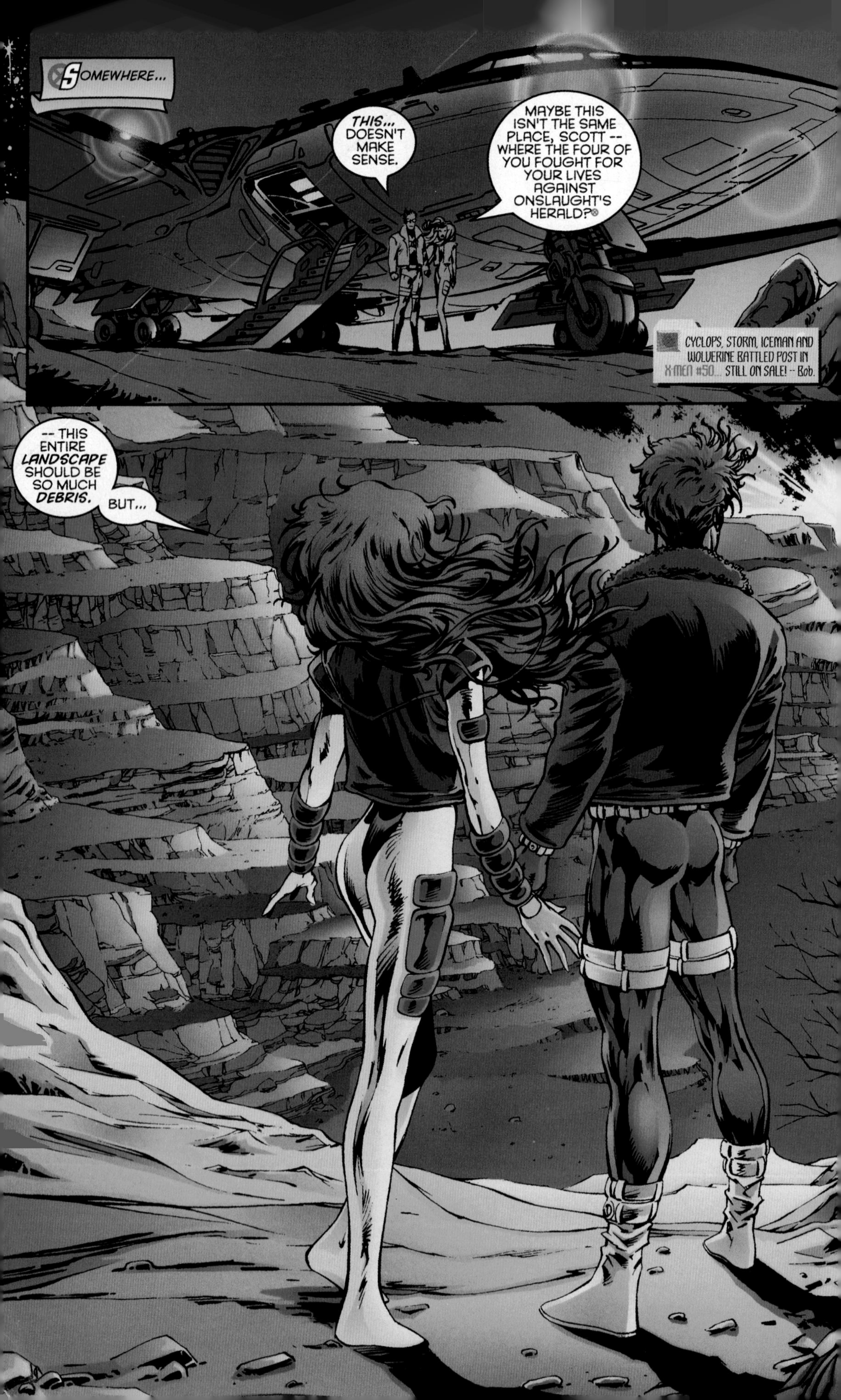
SOMEWHERE...
THIS... DOESN'T MAKE SENSE.
MAYBE THIS ISN'T THE SAME PLACE, SCOTT -- WHERE THE FOUR OF YOU FOUGHT FOR YOUR LIVES AGAINST ONSLAUGHT'S HERALD?
CYCLOPS, STORM, ICEMAN AND WOLVERINE BATTLED POST IN X-MEN #50... STILL ON SALE! -- Bob.
-- THIS ENTIRE LANDSCAPE SHOULD BE SO MUCH DEBRIS. BUT...

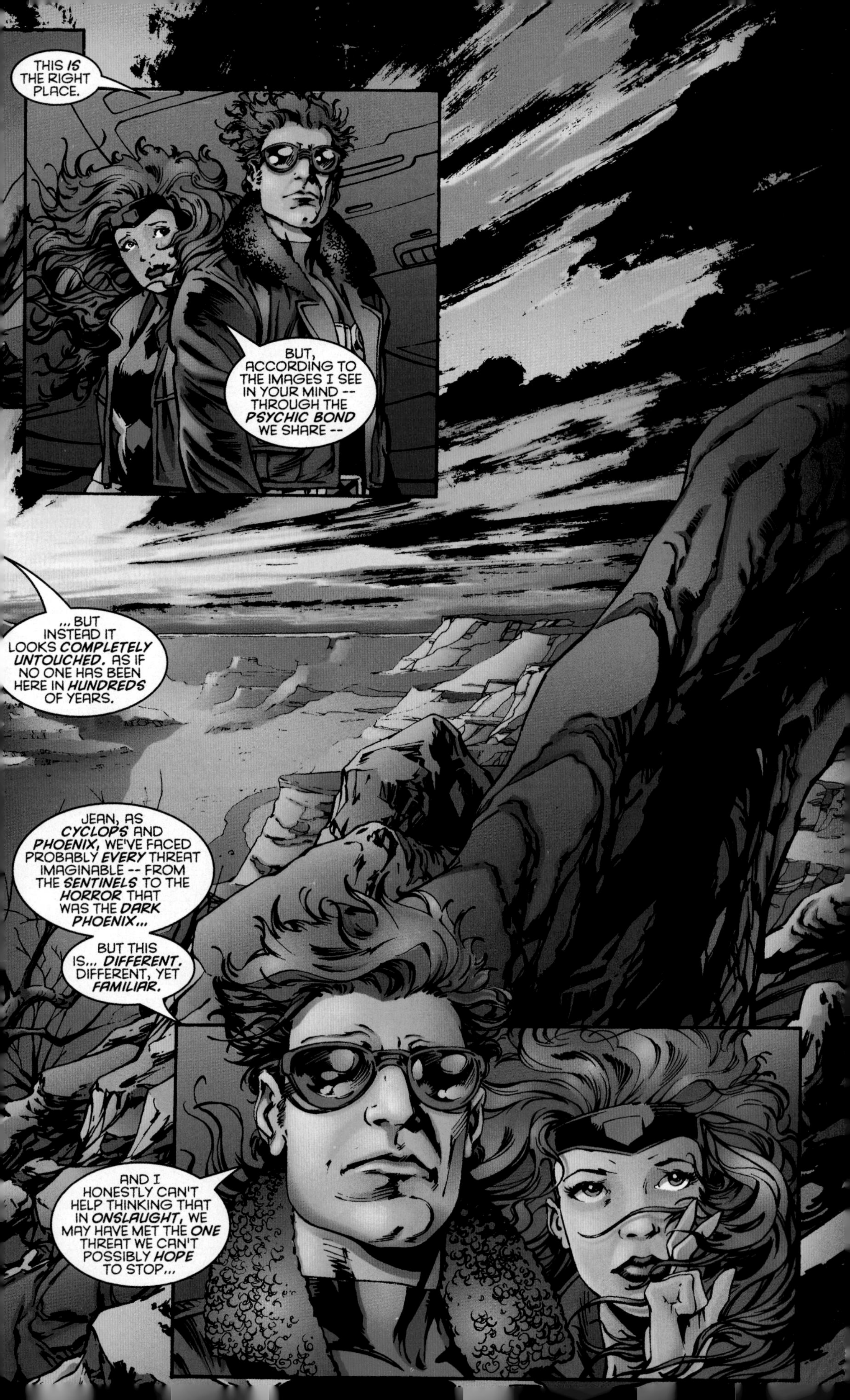

THIS *IS* THE RIGHT PLACE.
BUT, ACCORDING TO THE IMAGES I SEE IN YOUR MIND -- THROUGH THE *PSYCHIC BOND* WE SHARE --
... BUT INSTEAD IT LOOKS *COMPLETELY UNTOUCHED*. AS IF NO ONE HAS BEEN HERE IN *HUNDREDS* OF YEARS.
JEAN, AS *CYCLOPS* AND *PHOENIX*, WE'VE FACED PROBABLY *EVERY* THREAT IMAGINABLE -- FROM THE *SENTINELS* TO THE *HORROR* THAT WAS THE *DARK PHOENIX*...
BUT THIS IS... *DIFFERENT*. DIFFERENT, YET *FAMILIAR*.
AND I HONESTLY CAN'T HELP THINKING THAT IN *ONSLAUGHT*, WE MAY HAVE MET THE *ONE* THREAT WE CAN'T POSSIBLY *HOPE* TO STOP...

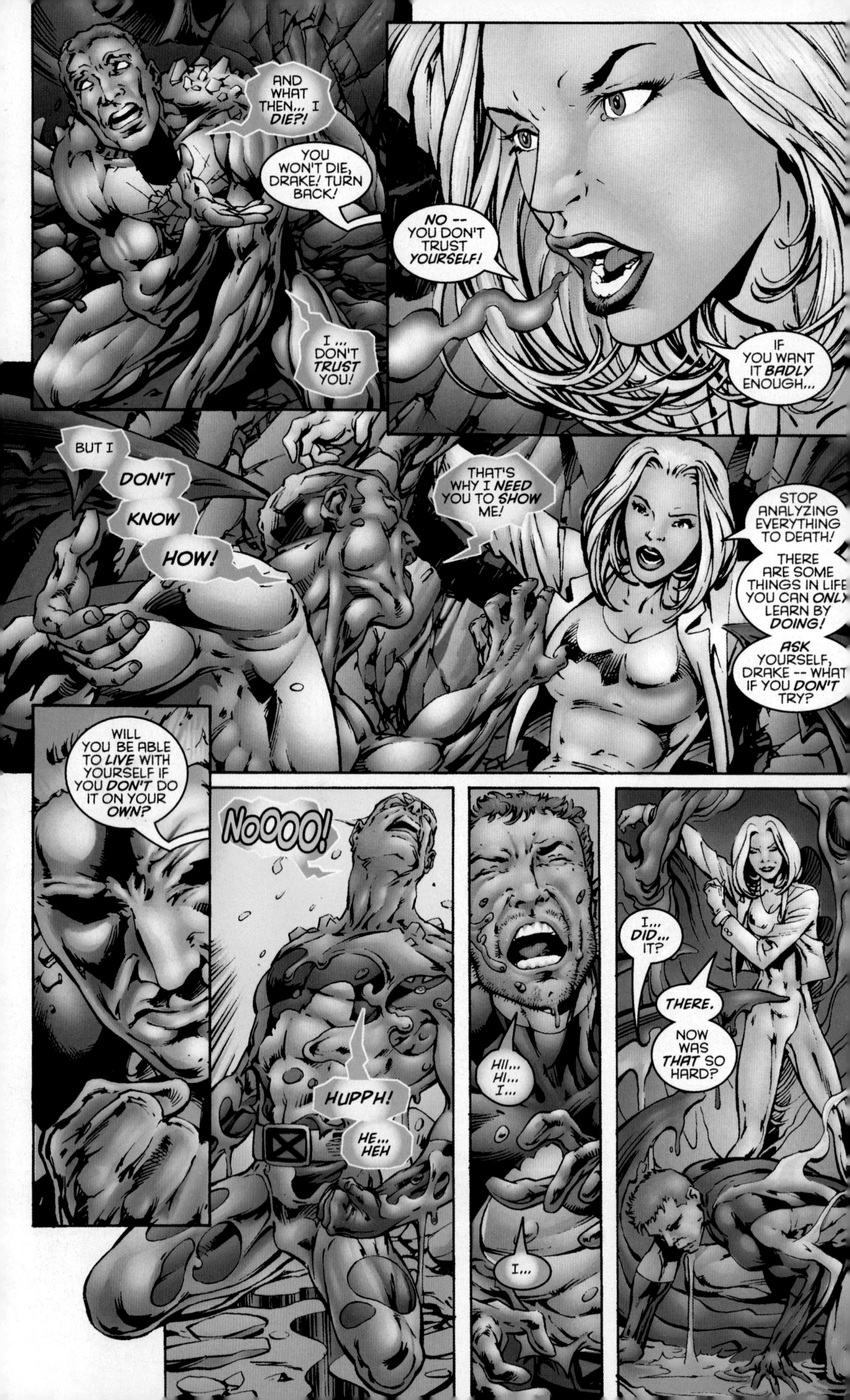
AND WHAT THEN... I DIE?!
YOU WON'T DIE, DRAKE! TURN BACK!
I... DON'T TRUST YOU!
NO -- YOU DON'T TRUST YOURSELF!
IF YOU WANT IT BADLY ENOUGH...
BUT I DON'T KNOW HOW!
THAT'S WHY I NEED YOU TO SHOW ME!
STOP ANALYZING EVERYTHING TO DEATH!
THERE ARE SOME THINGS IN LIFE YOU CAN ONLY LEARN BY DOING!
ASK YOURSELF, DRAKE -- WHAT IF YOU DON'T TRY?
WILL YOU BE ABLE TO LIVE WITH YOURSELF IF YOU DON'T DO IT ON YOUR OWN?
NoOOO!
HUPPH!
HE... HEH
HI... HI... I...
I...
I... DID... IT?
THERE.
NOW WAS THAT SO HARD?

WHERE IS YOUR FURRY-CLAWED FRIEND, STRIPLING--?
EEEEEEEEEE
WHO--?! THAT WAS GAUNTLET!
YOU'RE NEXT, CREEP..!
...WOLVERINE'S GONNA PUT A WHUPPIN' ON YOU TO WRITE HOME ABOUT!
INDEED.
HE'LL HAVE TO COME TO ME HERE, THEN...
...TO THE REVIVAL CRECHE OF APOCALYPSE!
HERE, TO THE NEXUS OF GENETIC FULFILLMENT --
-- WHEREIN ARE HARVESTED THE FRUITS OF NATURAL SELECTION!
SURVIVAL O' THE FITTEST, RIGHT?
AH DON'T THINK YOUR DARK RIDERS MADE THE CUT.
AH DON'T THINK YOU'RE GONNA MAKE THE CUT, EITHER..!
...

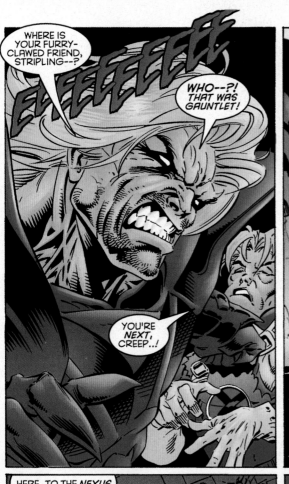

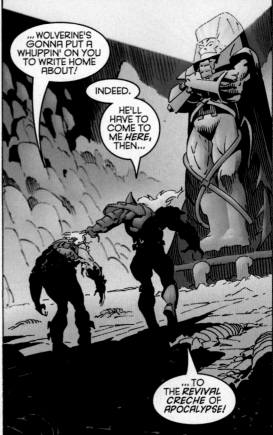

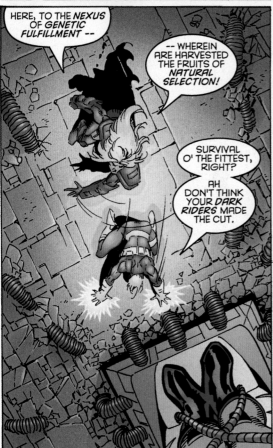

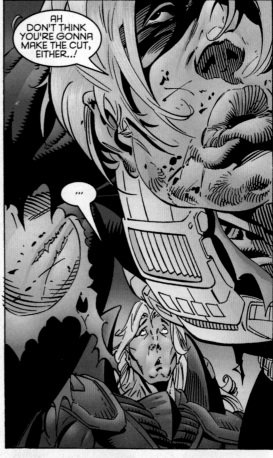

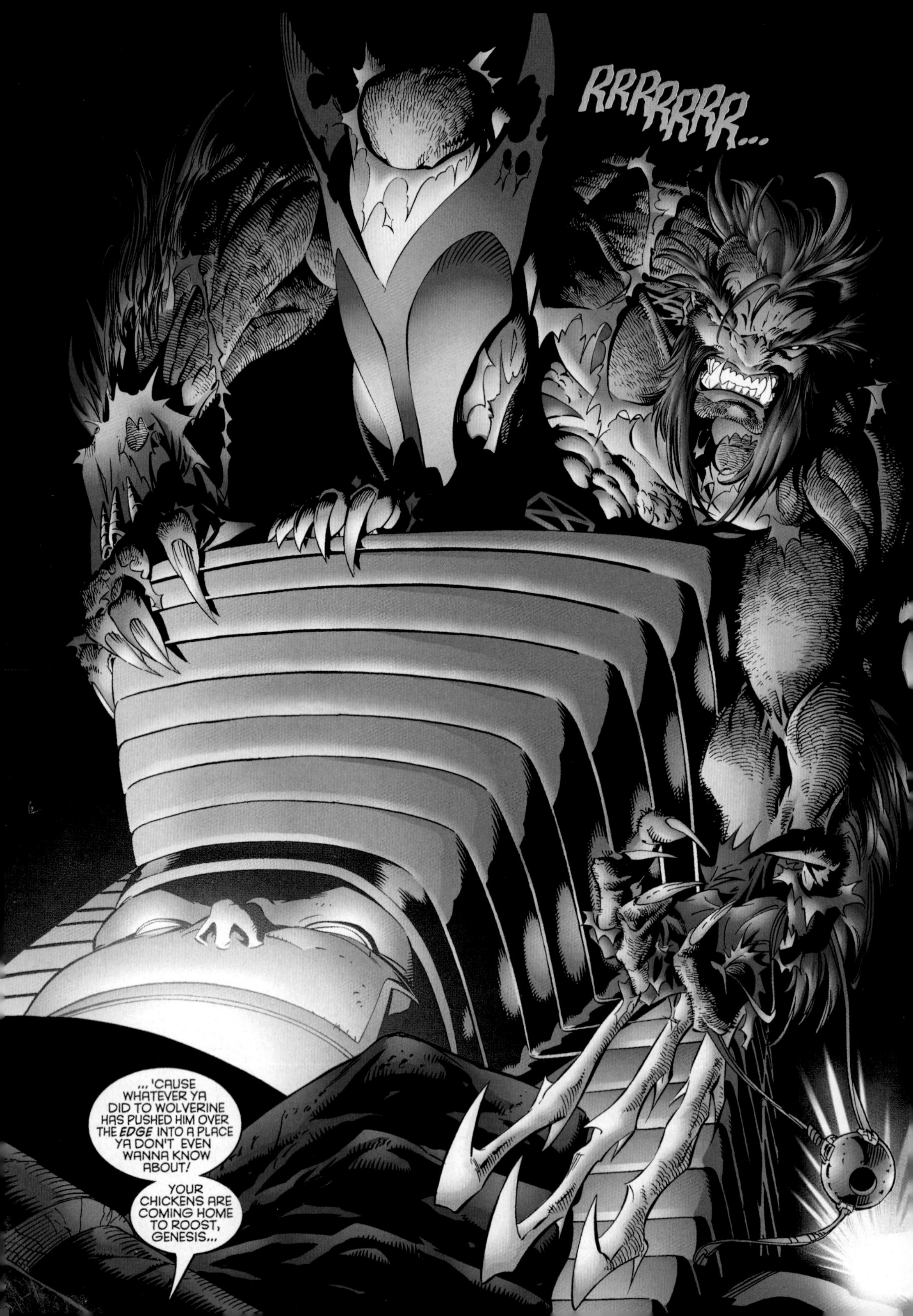
RRRRRRR...
...'CAUSE WHATEVER YA DID TO WOLVERINE HAS PUSHED HIM OVER THE EDGE INTO A PLACE YA DON'T EVEN WANNA KNOW ABOUT!
YOUR CHICKENS ARE COMING HOME TO ROOST, GENESIS...

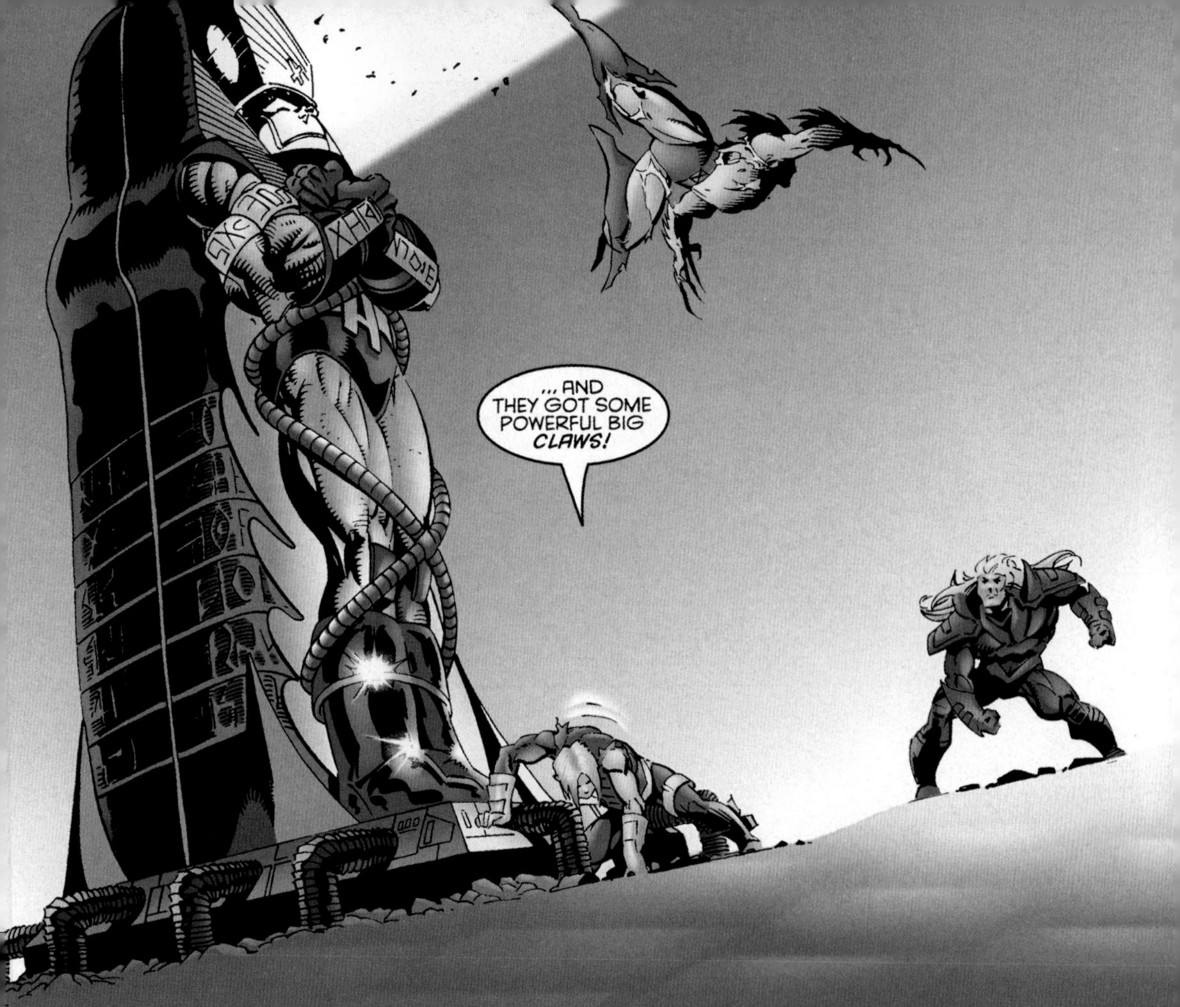
... AND THEY GOT SOME POWERFUL BIG CLAWS!

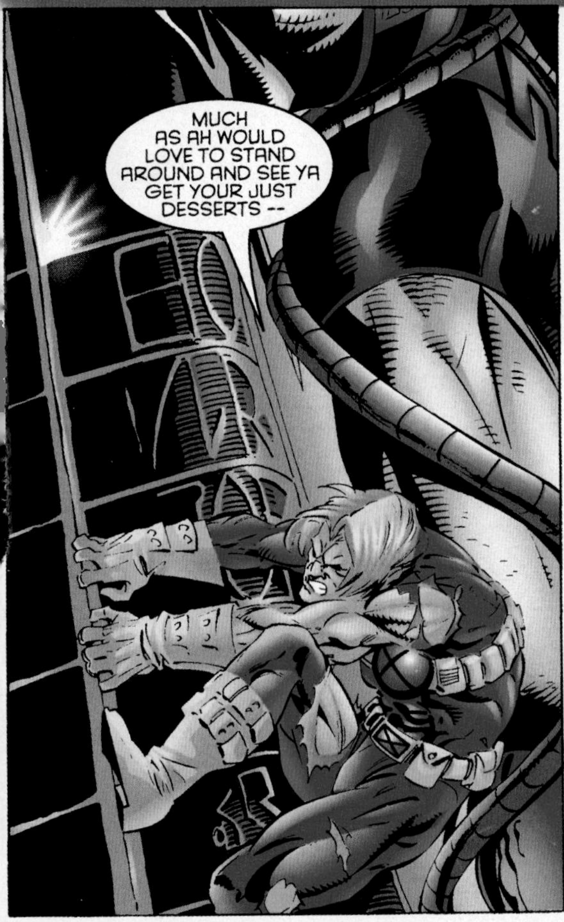
MUCH AS AH WOULD LOVE TO STAND AROUND AND SEE YA GET YOUR JUST DESSERTS --

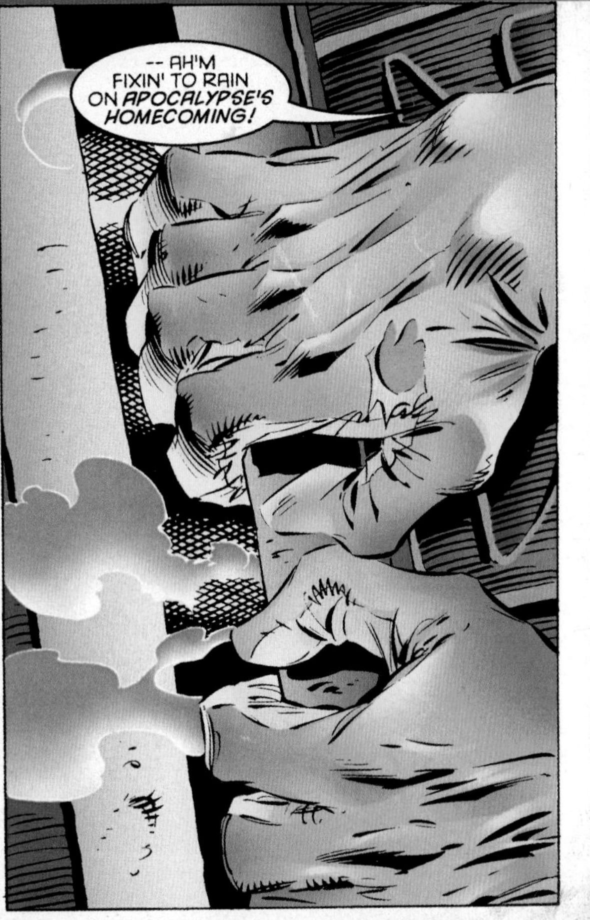
-- AH'M FIXIN' TO RAIN ON APOCALYPSE'S HOMECOMING!

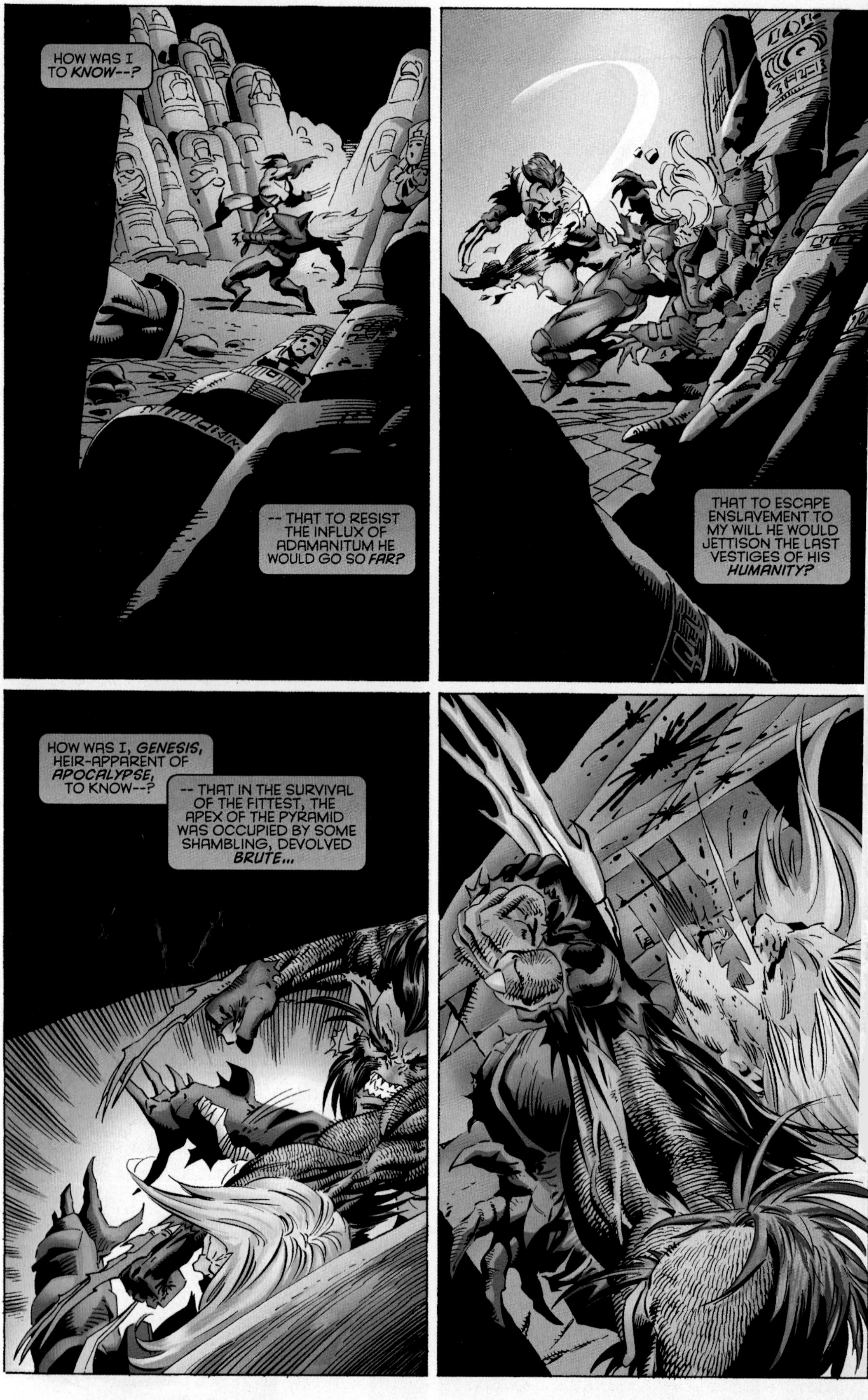
HOW WAS I TO *KNOW*--?
-- THAT TO RESIST THE INFLUX OF ADAMANITUM HE WOULD GO SO *FAR*?
THAT TO ESCAPE ENSLAVEMENT TO MY WILL HE WOULD JETTISON THE LAST VESTIGES OF HIS *HUMANITY*?
HOW WAS I, *GENESIS*, HEIR-APPARENT OF *APOCALYPSE*, TO KNOW--?
-- THAT IN THE SURVIVAL OF THE FITTEST, THE APEX OF THE PYRAMID WAS OCCUPIED BY SOME SHAMBLING, DEVOLVED *BRUTE*...

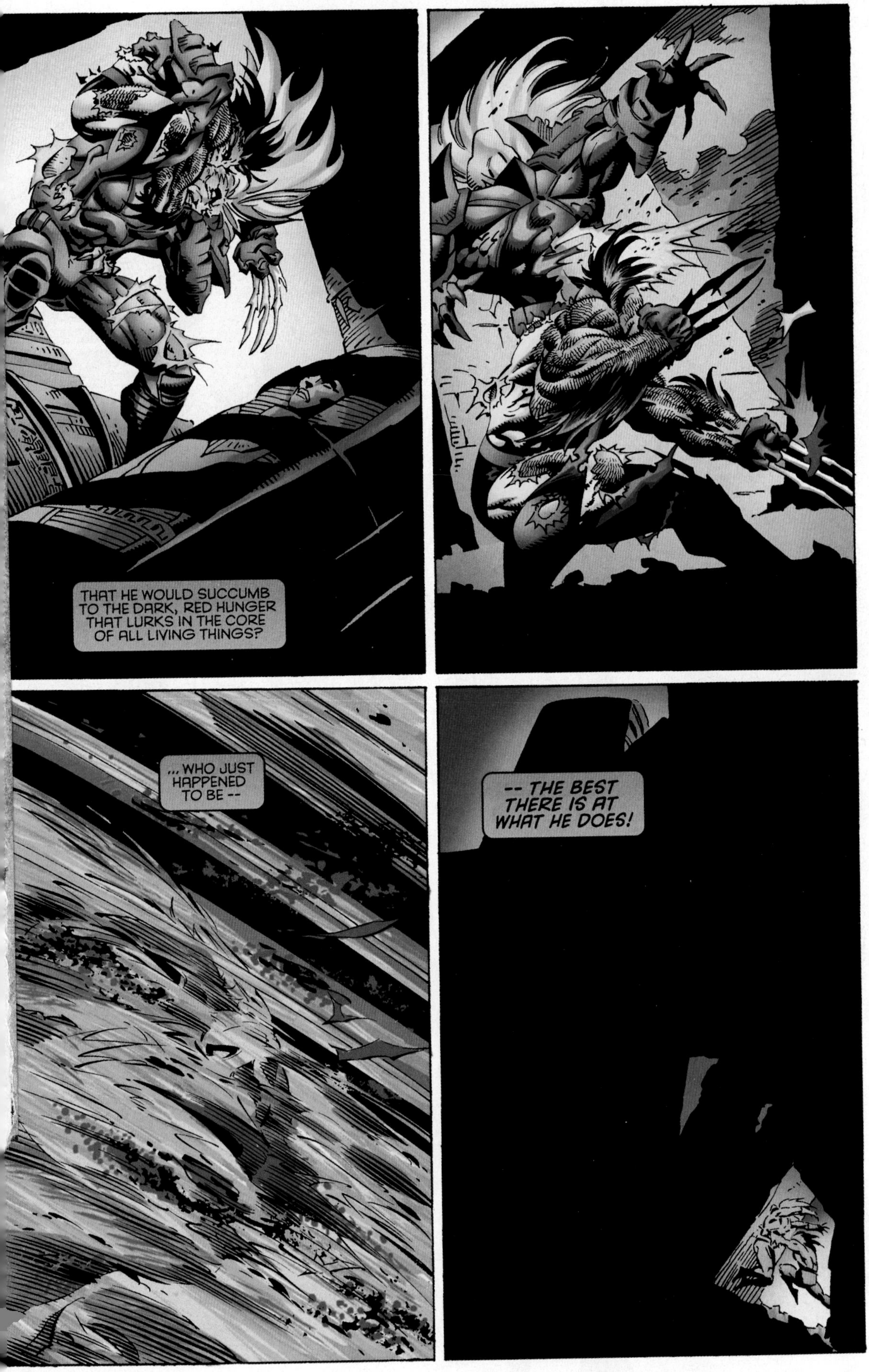
THAT HE WOULD SUCCUMB TO THE DARK, RED HUNGER THAT LURKS IN THE CORE OF ALL LIVING THINGS?
...WHO JUST HAPPENED TO BE --
-- THE BEST THERE IS AT WHAT HE DOES!

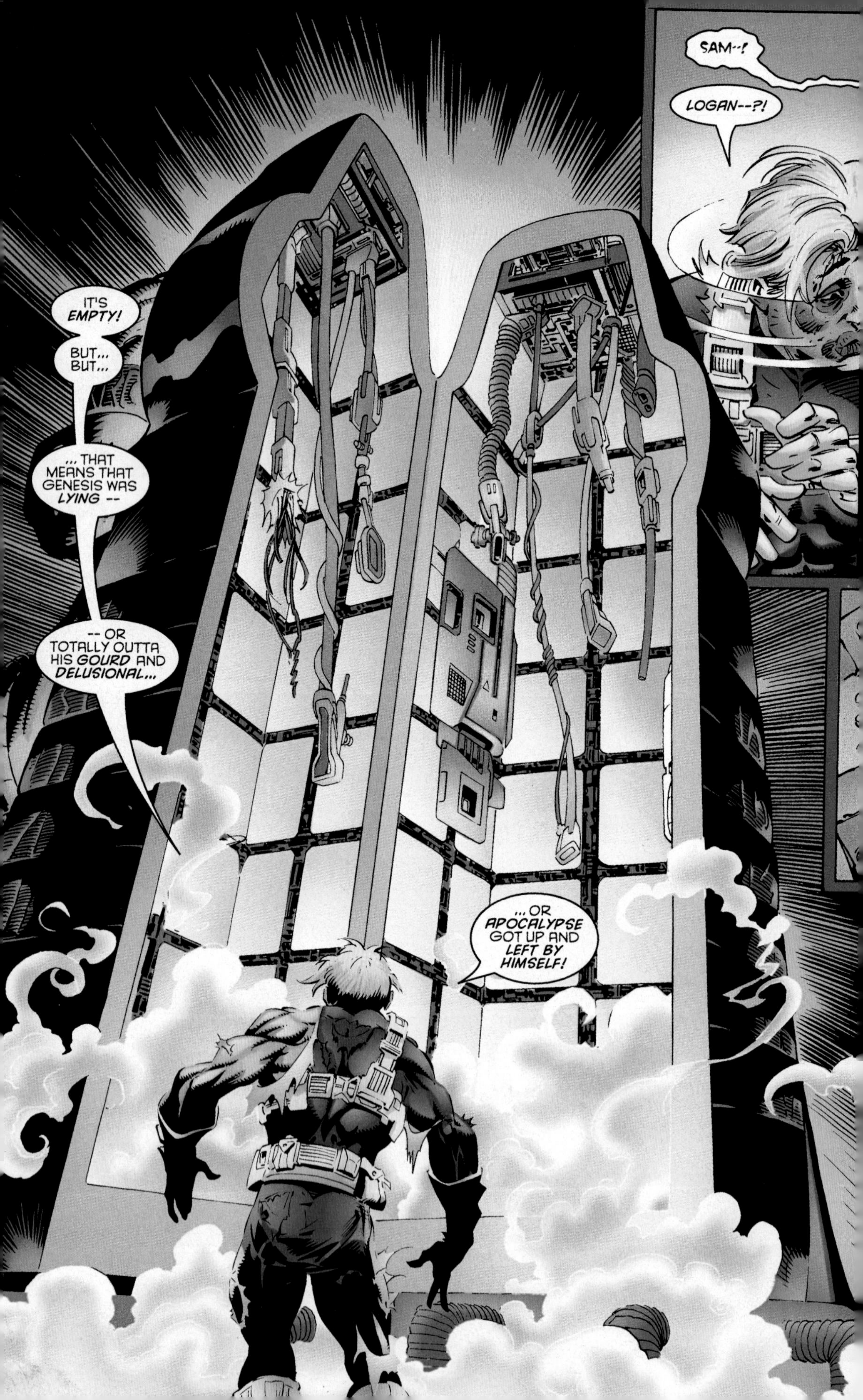
SAM--!
LOGAN--?!
IT'S EMPTY!
BUT... BUT...
...THAT MEANS THAT GENESIS WAS LYING --
-- OR TOTALLY OUTTA HIS GOURD AND DELUSIONAL...
...OR APOCALYPSE GOT UP AND LEFT BY HIMSELF!

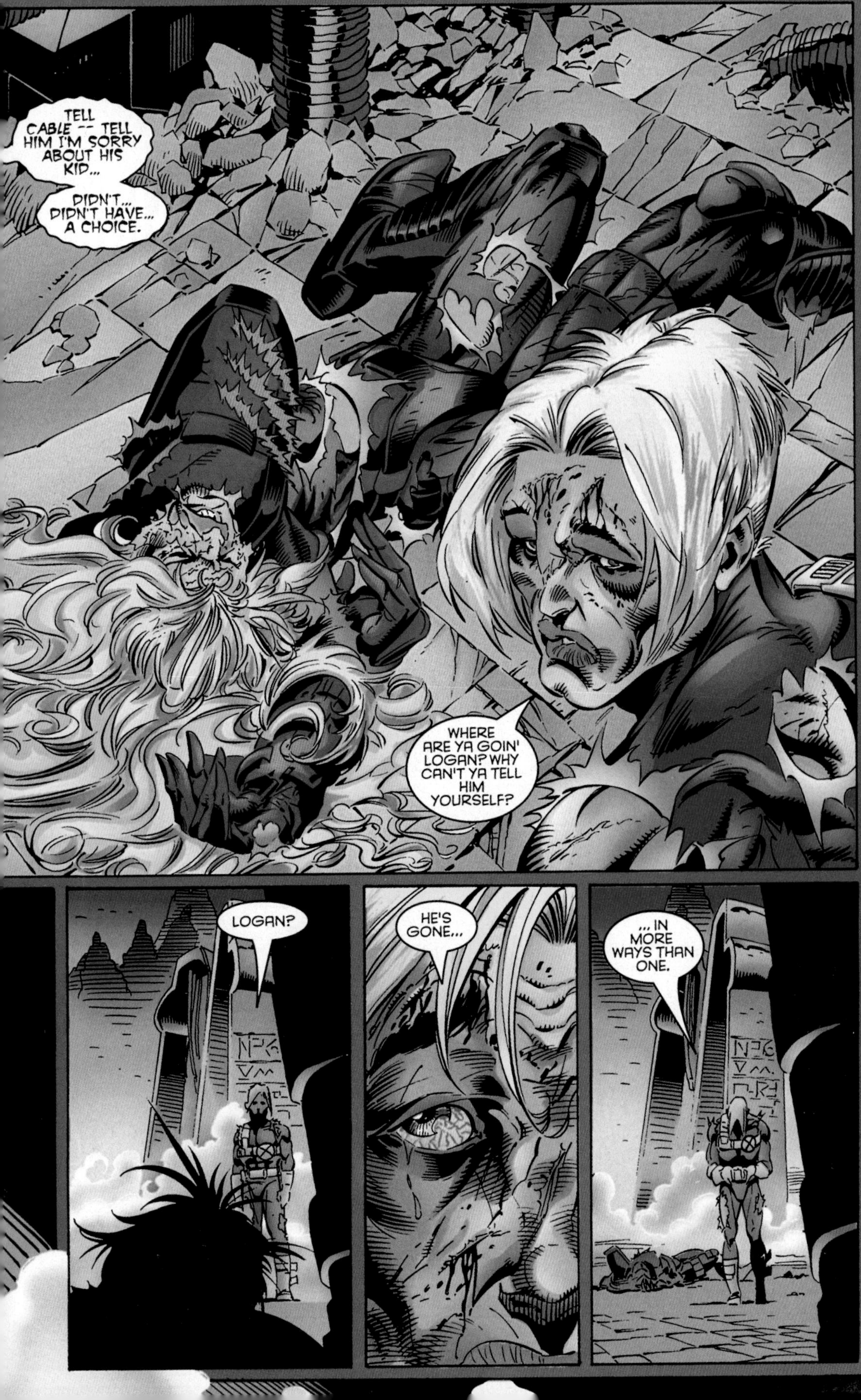
TELL CABLE -- TELL HIM I'M SORRY ABOUT HIS KID...
DIDN'T... DIDN'T HAVE... A CHOICE.
WHERE ARE YA GOIN' LOGAN? WHY CAN'T YA TELL HIM YOURSELF?
LOGAN?
HE'S GONE...
...IN MORE WAYS THAN ONE.

LATER...

At Generation X's campus, Chamber accidentally stumbled across an insight that hit closer to the truth than he knew. Meanwhile, Archangel and Psylocke left the X-Men to heal from severe injuries inflicted by the murderous Sabretooth, and cope with the fallout from Psylocke's "miracle cure" exposure to the mystic Crimson Dawn.

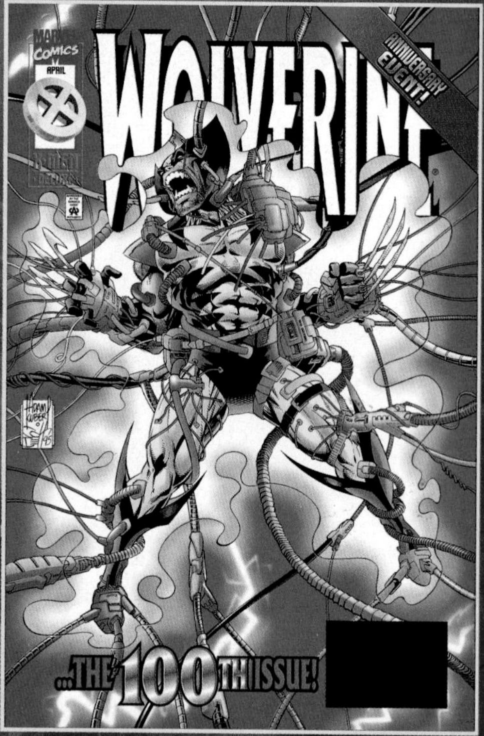
MARVEL COMICS
APRIL
WOLVERINE
ANNIVERSARY EVENT!
...THE 100TH ISSUE!

Nate Grey, who traveled to our dimension with Apocalypse's villainous son Holocaust via the reality-spanning M'Kraan Crystal, had found that his psychic abilities were far too powerful for his body to contain. His first act in our world was to seemingly resurrect Cyclops' wife Madelyne Pryor, who later fell in with Selene. Holocaust, in turn, allied with Sebastian Shaw, the Hellfire Club's Black King. Later, Nate met Threnody, a death-energy-absorbing mutant who used to work for Mr. Sinister. But when Nate battled his counterpart Cable and Magneto's acolyte Exodus, he overexerted himself and gravely injured his mind.

Cable's mentor, the diminutive Blaquesmith, advised killing Nate, believing that he was too dangerous to live. But Cable saw another way – and was determined to save him, even if it meant aggravating the techno-organic virus that had ravaged Cable's body since childhood...

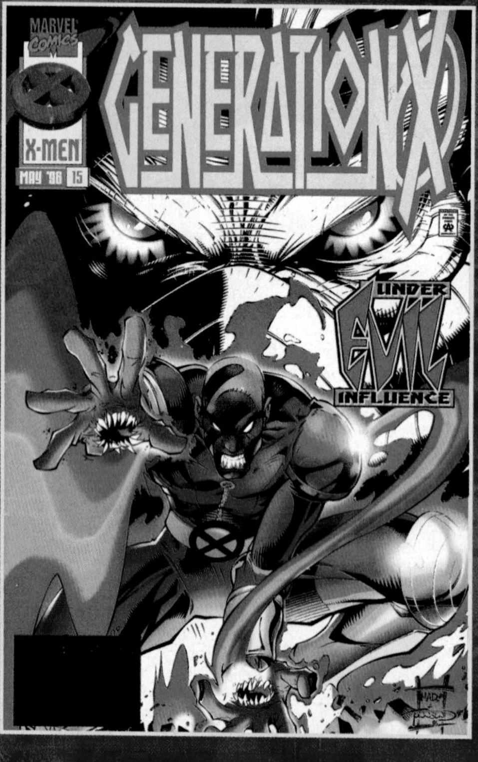
MARVEL COMICS
GENERATION X
X-MEN
MAY '96 15
UNDER EVIL INFLUENCE

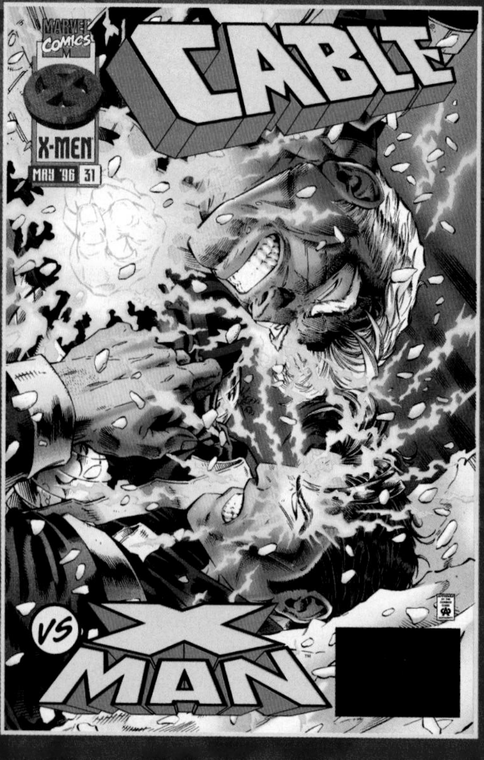
MARVEL COMICS
CABLE
X-MEN
MAY '96 31
VS
X-MAN

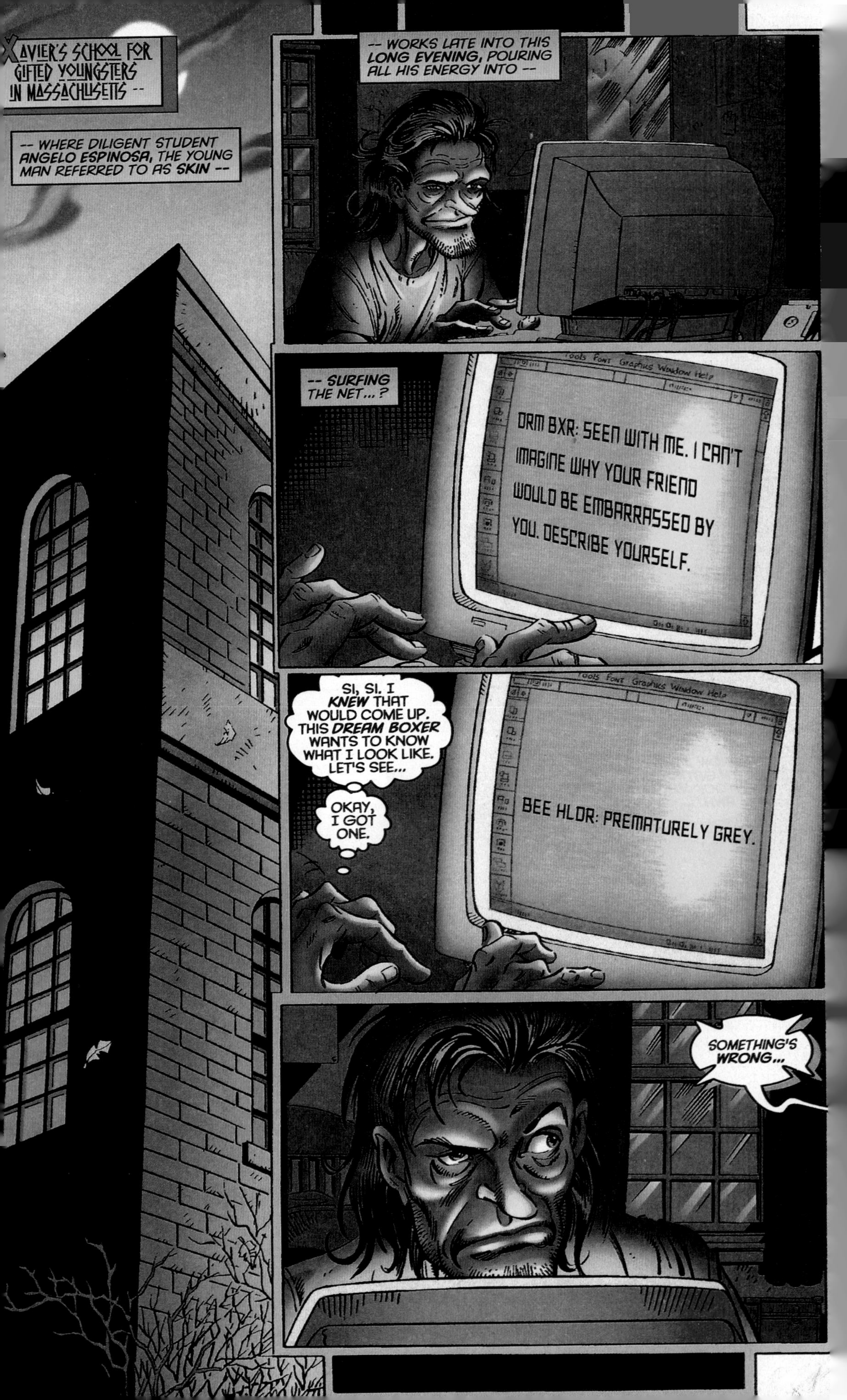
XAVIER'S SCHOOL FOR GIFTED YOUNGSTERS IN MASSACHUSETTS --
-- WHERE DILIGENT STUDENT ANGELO ESPINOSA, THE YOUNG MAN REFERRED TO AS SKIN --
-- WORKS LATE INTO THIS LONG EVENING, POURING ALL HIS ENERGY INTO --
-- SURFING THE NET...?
DRM BXR: SEEN WITH ME. I CAN'T IMAGINE WHY YOUR FRIEND WOULD BE EMBARRASSED BY YOU. DESCRIBE YOURSELF.
SI, SI. I KNEW THAT WOULD COME UP. THIS DREAM BOXER WANTS TO KNOW WHAT I LOOK LIKE. LET'S SEE...
OKAY, I GOT ONE.
BEE HLDR: PREMATURELY GREY.
SOMETHING'S WRONG...

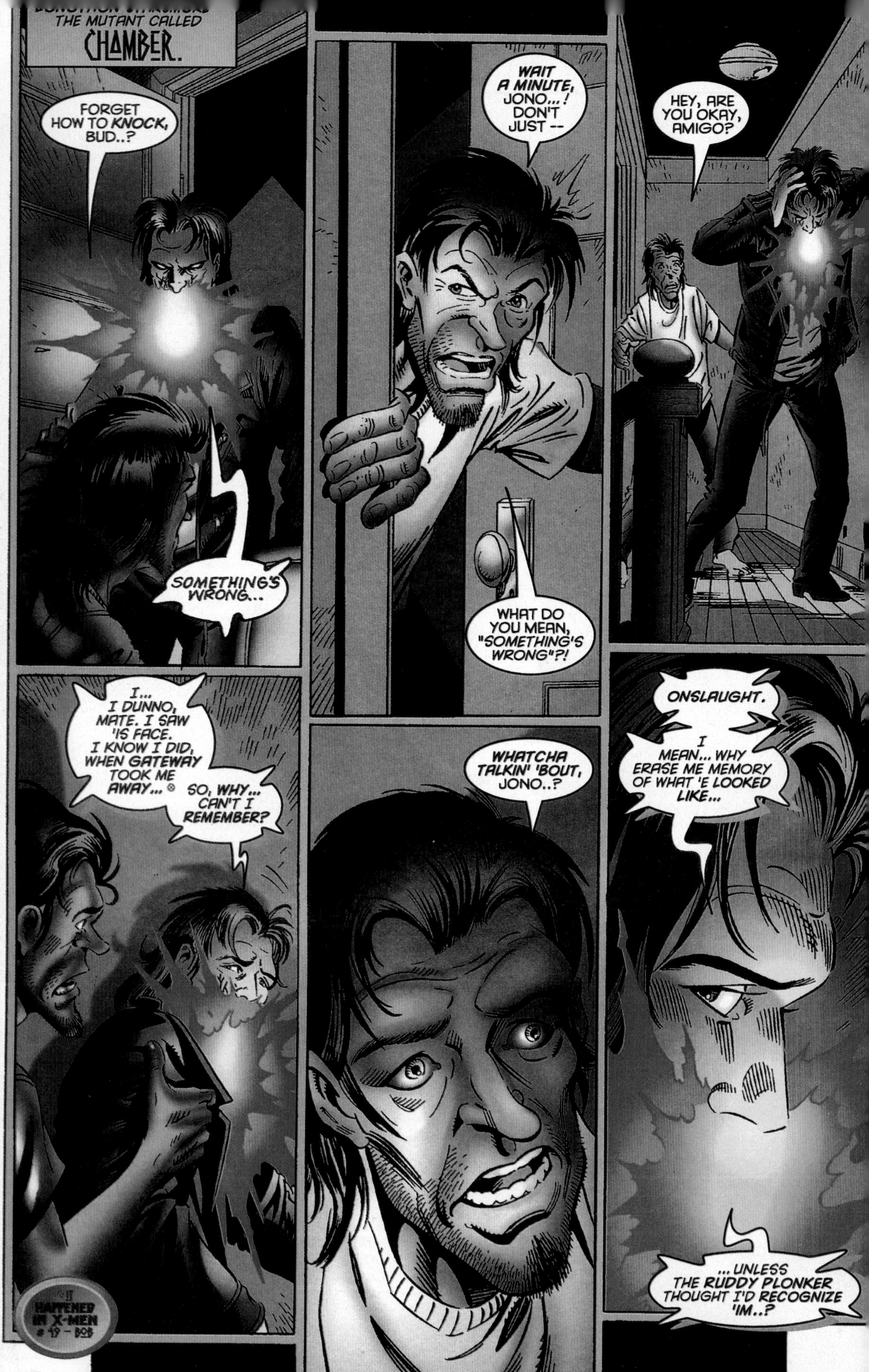
THE MUTANT CALLED
CHAMBER.
FORGET HOW TO KNOCK, BUD..?
SOMETHING'S WRONG...
WAIT A MINUTE, JONO...! DON'T JUST --
WHAT DO YOU MEAN, "SOMETHING'S WRONG"?!
HEY, ARE YOU OKAY, AMIGO?
I... I DUNNO, MATE. I SAW 'IS FACE. I KNOW I DID, WHEN GATEWAY TOOK ME AWAY...
SO, WHY... CAN'T I REMEMBER?
IT HAPPENED IN X-MEN #49 – BOB
WHATCHA TALKIN' 'BOUT, JONO..?
ONSLAUGHT.
I MEAN... WHY ERASE ME MEMORY OF WHAT 'E LOOKED LIKE...
...UNLESS THE RUDDY PLONKER THOUGHT I'D RECOGNIZE 'IM..?

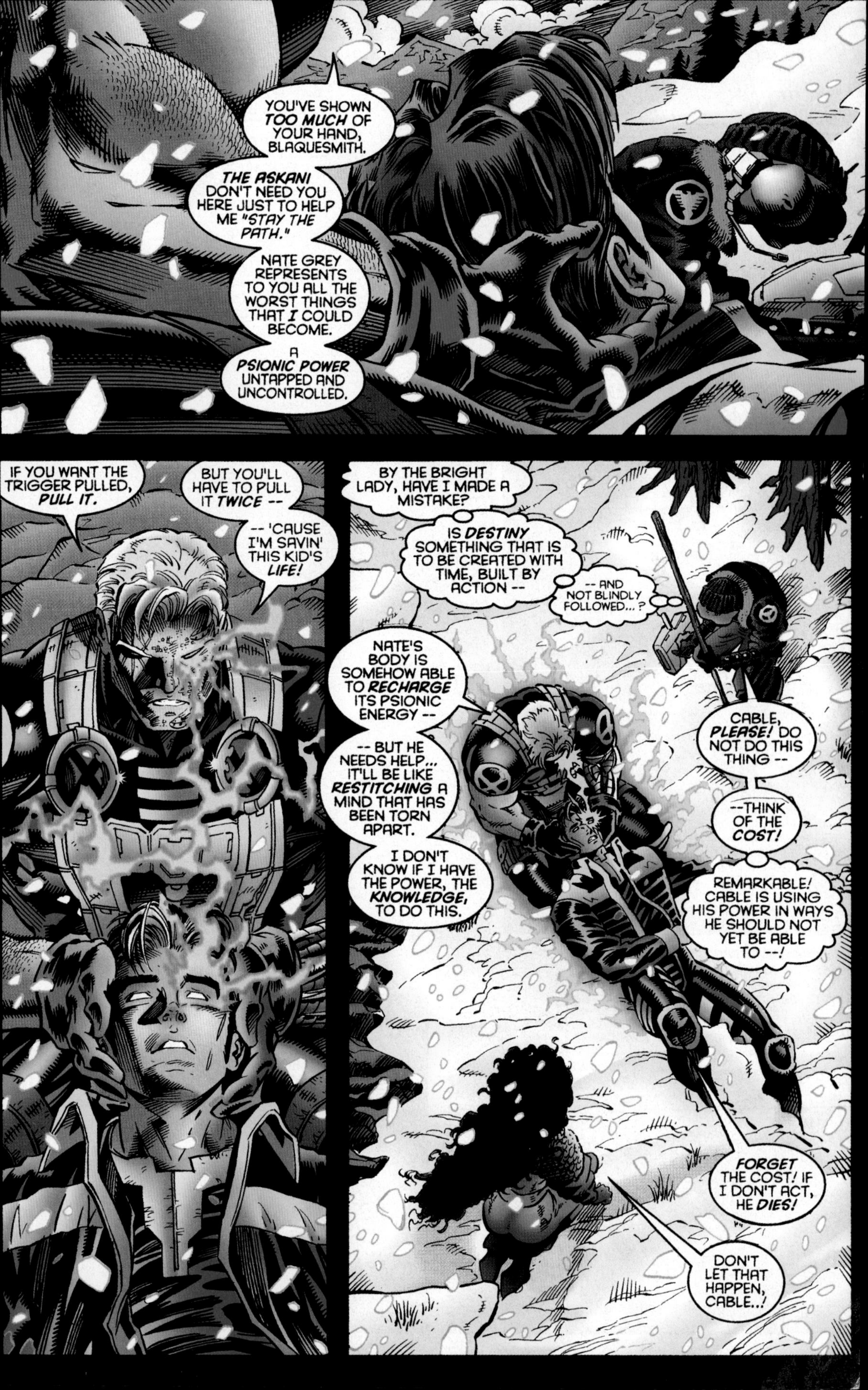
YOU'VE SHOWN TOO MUCH OF YOUR HAND, BLAQUESMITH.
THE ASKANI DON'T NEED YOU HERE JUST TO HELP ME "STAY THE PATH."
NATE GREY REPRESENTS TO YOU ALL THE WORST THINGS THAT I COULD BECOME.
A PSIONIC POWER UNTAPPED AND UNCONTROLLED.
IF YOU WANT THE TRIGGER PULLED, PULL IT.
BUT YOU'LL HAVE TO PULL IT TWICE --
-- 'CAUSE I'M SAVIN' THIS KID'S LIFE!
BY THE BRIGHT LADY, HAVE I MADE A MISTAKE?
IS DESTINY SOMETHING THAT IS TO BE CREATED WITH TIME, BUILT BY ACTION --
-- AND NOT BLINDLY FOLLOWED...?
NATE'S BODY IS SOMEHOW ABLE TO RECHARGE ITS PSIONIC ENERGY --
-- BUT HE NEEDS HELP... IT'LL BE LIKE RESTITCHING A MIND THAT HAS BEEN TORN APART.
I DON'T KNOW IF I HAVE THE POWER, THE KNOWLEDGE, TO DO THIS.
CABLE, PLEASE! DO NOT DO THIS THING --
--THINK OF THE COST!
REMARKABLE! CABLE IS USING HIS POWER IN WAYS HE SHOULD NOT YET BE ABLE TO --!
FORGET THE COST! IF I DON'T ACT, HE DIES!
DON'T LET THAT HAPPEN, CABLE..!

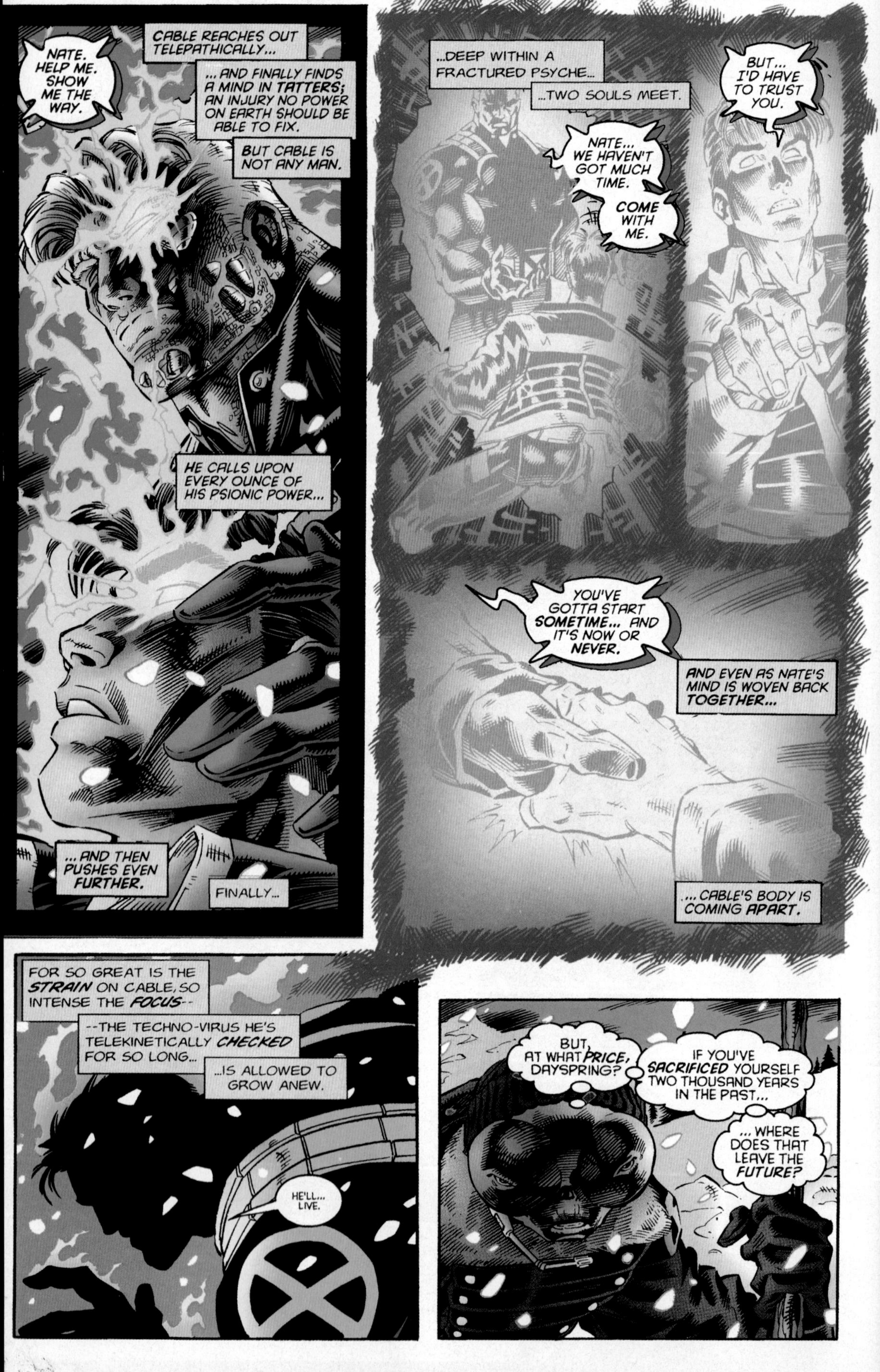
CABLE REACHES OUT TELEPATHICALLY...
NATE. HELP ME. SHOW ME THE WAY.
... AND FINALLY FINDS A MIND IN TATTERS; AN INJURY NO POWER ON EARTH SHOULD BE ABLE TO FIX.
BUT CABLE IS NOT ANY MAN.
HE CALLS UPON EVERY OUNCE OF HIS PSIONIC POWER...
... AND THEN PUSHES EVEN FURTHER.
FINALLY...
...DEEP WITHIN A FRACTURED PSYCHE...
...TWO SOULS MEET.
NATE... WE HAVEN'T GOT MUCH TIME.
COME WITH ME.
BUT... I'D HAVE TO TRUST YOU.
YOU'VE GOTTA START SOMETIME... AND IT'S NOW OR NEVER.
AND EVEN AS NATE'S MIND IS WOVEN BACK TOGETHER...
... CABLE'S BODY IS COMING APART.
FOR SO GREAT IS THE STRAIN ON CABLE, SO INTENSE THE FOCUS--
--THE TECHNO-VIRUS HE'S TELEKINETICALLY CHECKED FOR SO LONG...
...IS ALLOWED TO GROW ANEW.
HE'LL... LIVE.
BUT, AT WHAT PRICE, DAYSPRING?
IF YOU'VE SACRIFICED YOURSELF TWO THOUSAND YEARS IN THE PAST...
... WHERE DOES THAT LEAVE THE FUTURE?

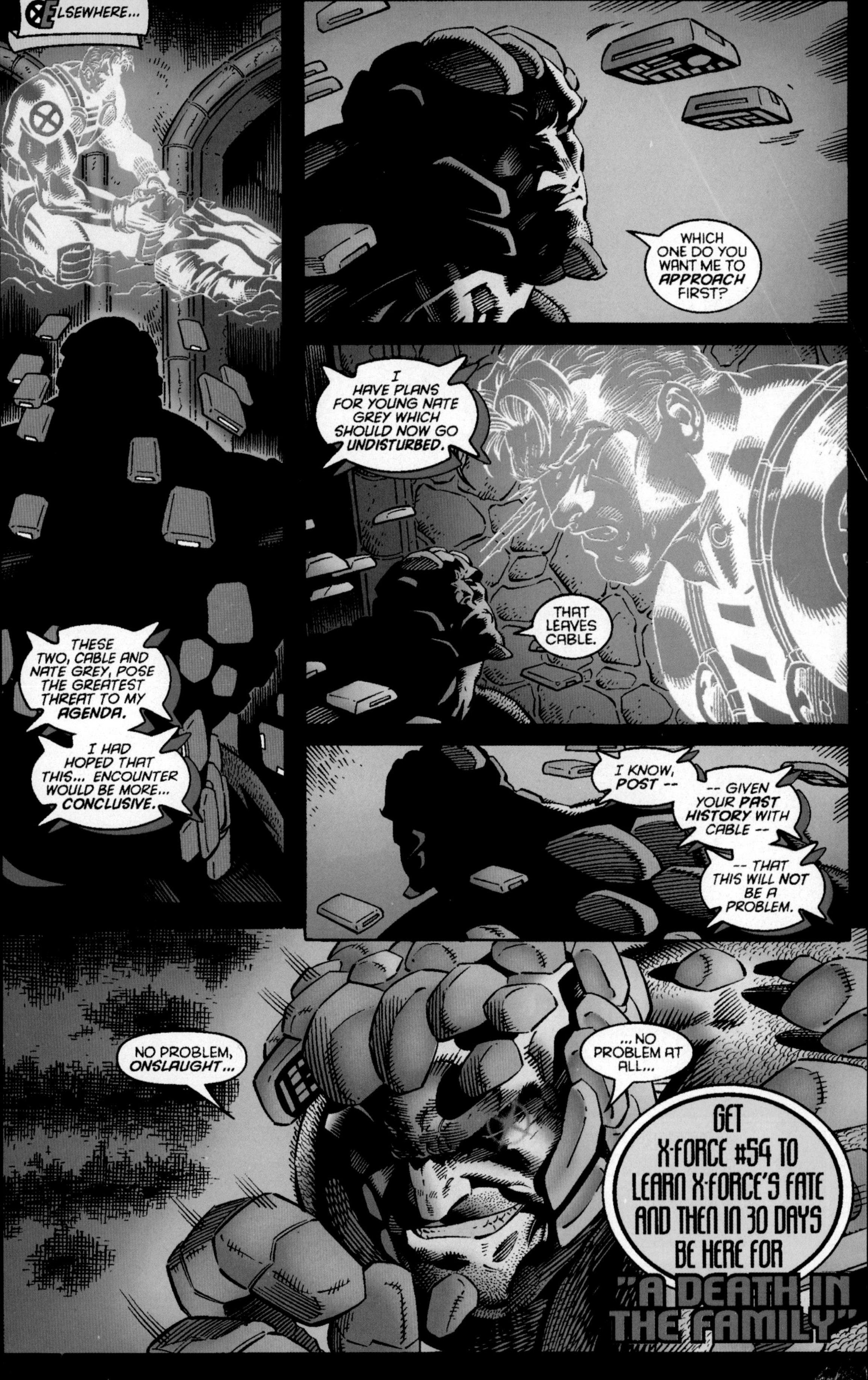
ELSEWHERE...
WHICH ONE DO YOU WANT ME TO APPROACH FIRST?
THESE TWO, CABLE AND NATE GREY, POSE THE GREATEST THREAT TO MY AGENDA.
I HAD HOPED THAT THIS... ENCOUNTER WOULD BE MORE... CONCLUSIVE.
I HAVE PLANS FOR YOUNG NATE GREY WHICH SHOULD NOW GO UNDISTURBED.
THAT LEAVES CABLE.
I KNOW, POST --
-- GIVEN YOUR PAST HISTORY WITH CABLE --
-- THAT THIS WILL NOT BE A PROBLEM.
NO PROBLEM, ONSLAUGHT...
...NO PROBLEM AT ALL...
GET X-FORCE #54 TO LEARN X-FORCE'S FATE AND THEN IN 30 DAYS BE HERE FOR
"A DEATH IN THE FAMILY"

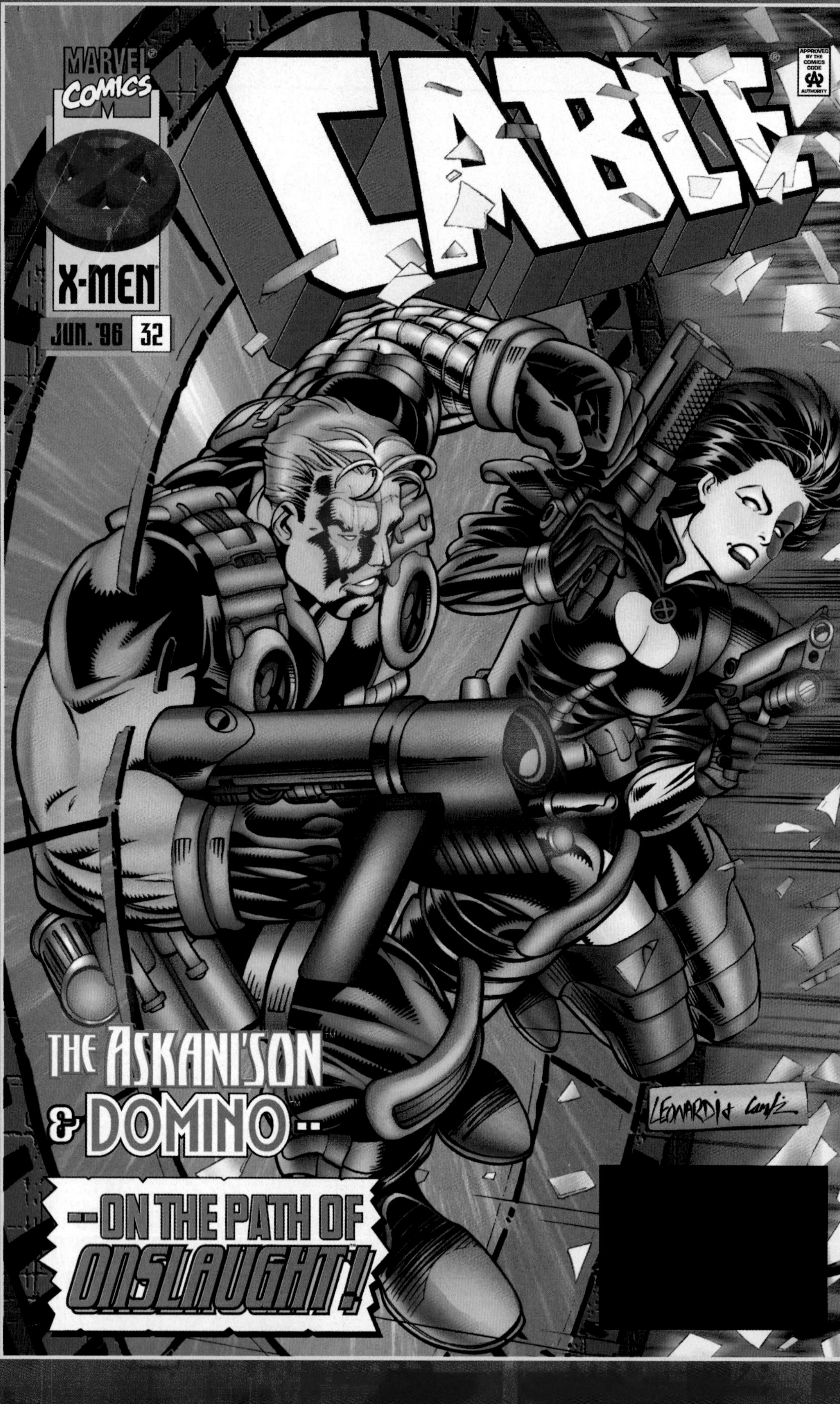
MARVEL COMICS
CABLE
APPROVED BY THE COMICS CODE AUTHORITY
X-MEN
JUN. '96
32
THE ASKANI'SON & DOMINO--
--ON THE PATH OF ONSLAUGHT!

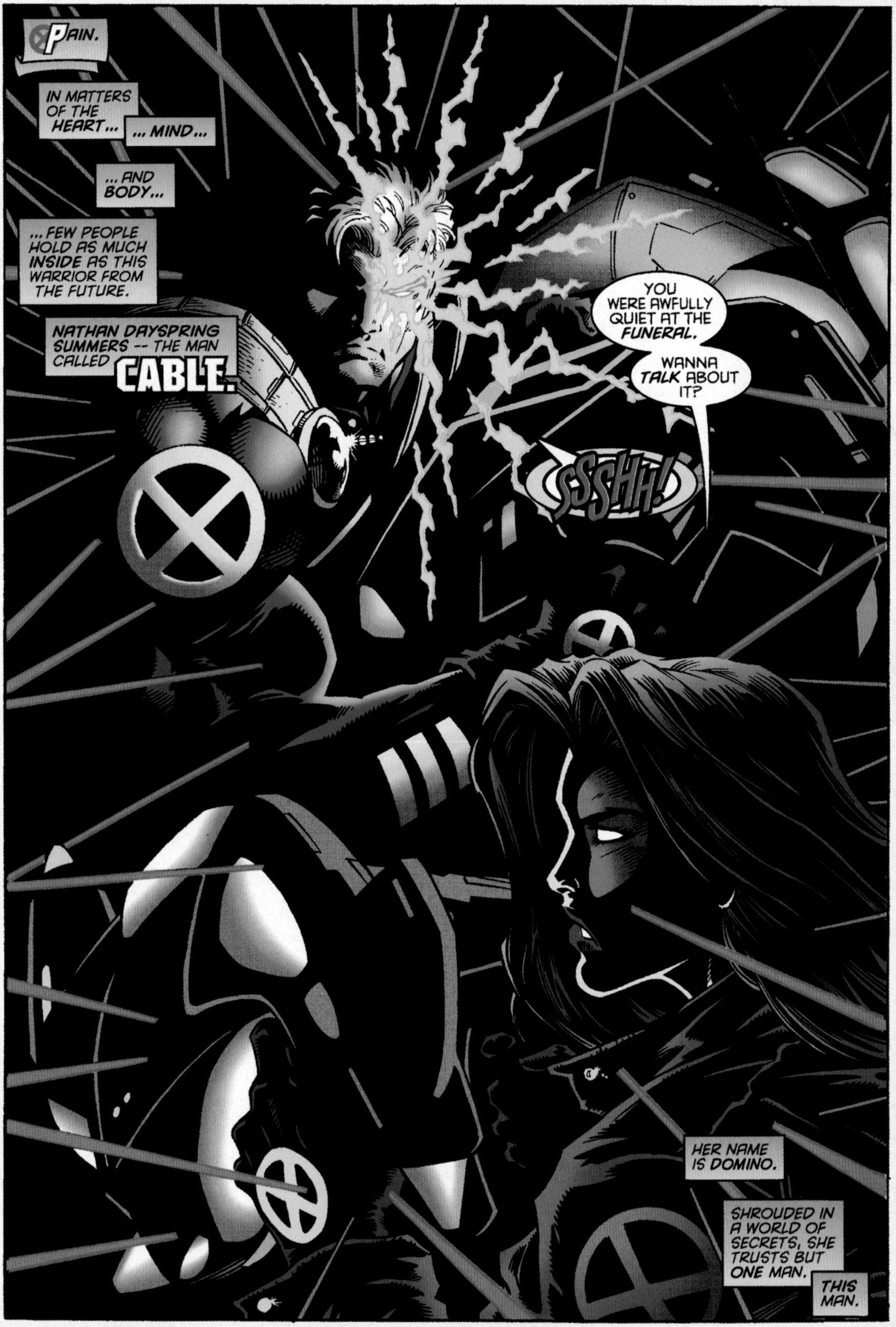
PAIN.
IN MATTERS OF THE HEART...
...MIND...
...AND BODY...
...FEW PEOPLE HOLD AS MUCH INSIDE AS THIS WARRIOR FROM THE FUTURE.
NATHAN DAYSPRING SUMMERS -- THE MAN CALLED
CABLE.
YOU WERE AWFULLY QUIET AT THE FUNERAL.
WANNA TALK ABOUT IT?
SSSHH!
HER NAME IS DOMINO.
SHROUDED IN A WORLD OF SECRETS, SHE TRUSTS BUT ONE MAN.
THIS MAN.

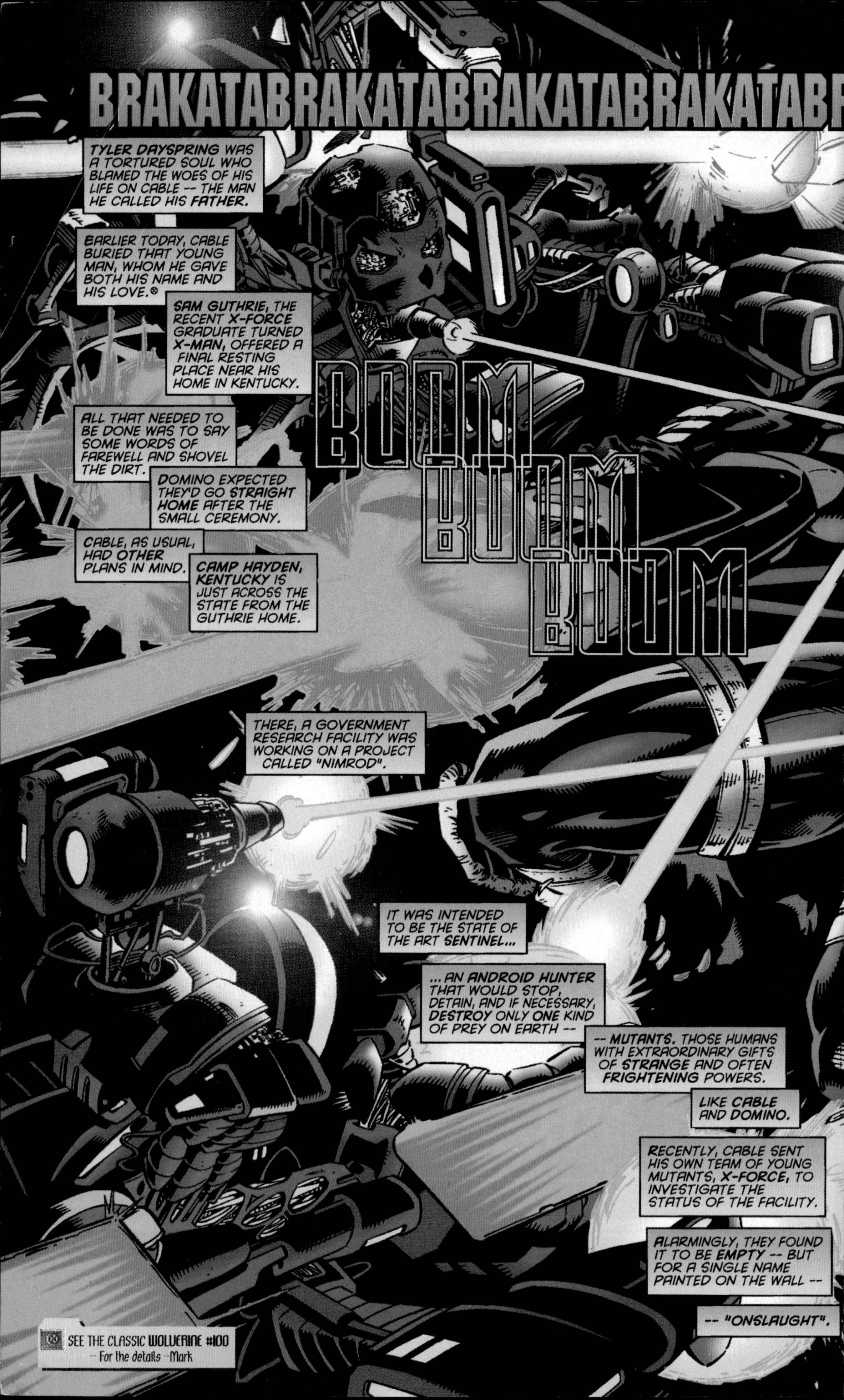
BRAKATABRAKATABRAKATABRAKATABR
TYLER DAYSPRING WAS A TORTURED SOUL WHO BLAMED THE WOES OF HIS LIFE ON CABLE -- THE MAN HE CALLED HIS FATHER.
EARLIER TODAY, CABLE BURIED THAT YOUNG MAN, WHOM HE GAVE BOTH HIS NAME AND HIS LOVE.
SAM GUTHRIE, THE RECENT X-FORCE GRADUATE TURNED X-MAN, OFFERED A FINAL RESTING PLACE NEAR HIS HOME IN KENTUCKY.
BOOM
BOOM
BOOM
ALL THAT NEEDED TO BE DONE WAS TO SAY SOME WORDS OF FAREWELL AND SHOVEL THE DIRT.
DOMINO EXPECTED THEY'D GO STRAIGHT HOME AFTER THE SMALL CEREMONY.
CABLE, AS USUAL, HAD OTHER PLANS IN MIND.
CAMP HAYDEN, KENTUCKY IS JUST ACROSS THE STATE FROM THE GUTHRIE HOME.
THERE, A GOVERNMENT RESEARCH FACILITY WAS WORKING ON A PROJECT CALLED "NIMROD".
IT WAS INTENDED TO BE THE STATE OF THE ART SENTINEL...
...AN ANDROID HUNTER THAT WOULD STOP, DETAIN, AND IF NECESSARY, DESTROY ONLY ONE KIND OF PREY ON EARTH --
-- MUTANTS. THOSE HUMANS WITH EXTRAORDINARY GIFTS OF STRANGE AND OFTEN FRIGHTENING POWERS.
LIKE CABLE AND DOMINO.
RECENTLY, CABLE SENT HIS OWN TEAM OF YOUNG MUTANTS, X-FORCE, TO INVESTIGATE THE STATUS OF THE FACILITY.
ALARMINGLY, THEY FOUND IT TO BE EMPTY -- BUT FOR A SINGLE NAME PAINTED ON THE WALL --
-- "ONSLAUGHT".
SEE THE CLASSIC WOLVERINE #100
-- For the details --Mark

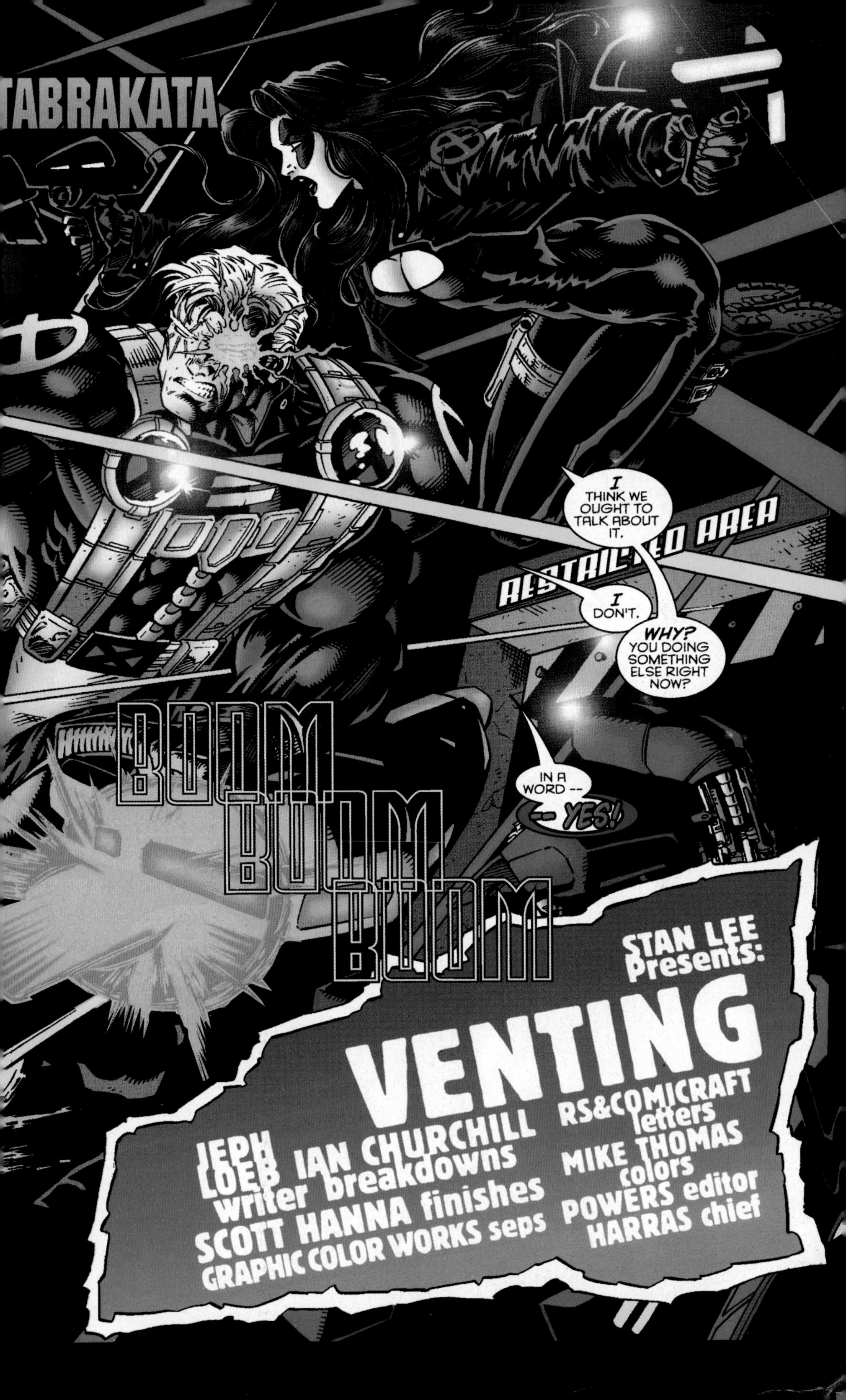
TABRAKATA
I THINK WE OUGHT TO TALK ABOUT IT.
I DON'T.
WHY? YOU DOING SOMETHING ELSE RIGHT NOW?
IN A WORD --
-- YES!
BOOM BOOM BOOM
STAN LEE Presents:
VENTING
JEPH LOEB writer
IAN CHURCHILL breakdowns
SCOTT HANNA finishes
GRAPHIC COLOR WORKS seps
RS&COMICRAFT letters
MIKE THOMAS colors
POWERS editor
HARRAS chief

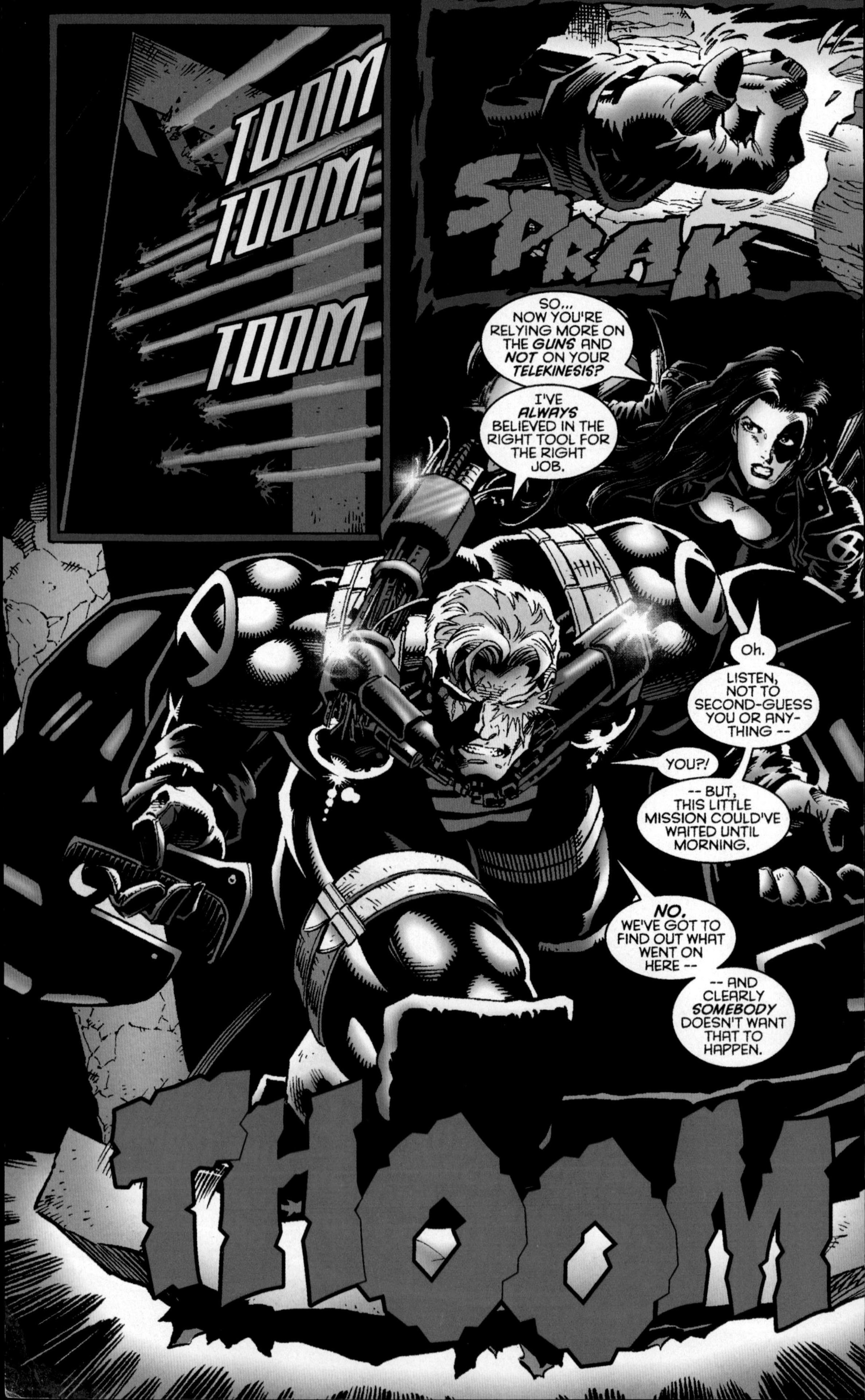
TOOM
TOOM
TOOM
SPRAK
SO... NOW YOU'RE RELYING MORE ON THE *GUNS* AND *NOT* ON YOUR *TELEKINESIS?*
I'VE *ALWAYS* BELIEVED IN THE RIGHT TOOL FOR THE RIGHT JOB.
Oh.
LISTEN, NOT TO SECOND-GUESS YOU OR ANY-THING --
YOU?!
-- BUT, THIS LITTLE MISSION COULD'VE WAITED UNTIL MORNING.
NO. WE'VE GOT TO FIND OUT WHAT WENT ON HERE --
-- AND CLEARLY *SOMEBODY* DOESN'T WANT THAT TO HAPPEN.
THOOM

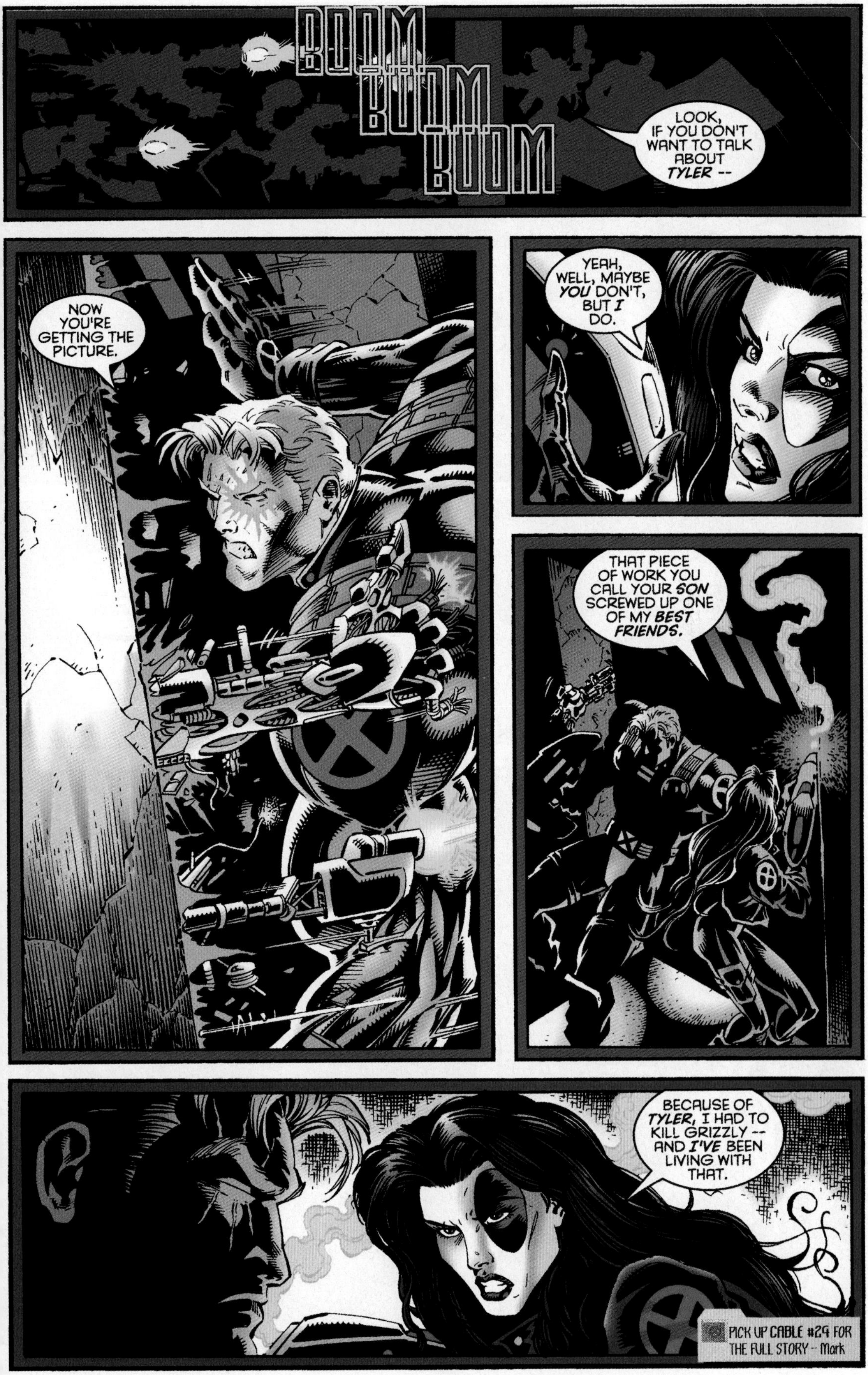
BOOM
BOOM
BOOM
LOOK, IF YOU DON'T WANT TO TALK ABOUT TYLER --
NOW YOU'RE GETTING THE PICTURE.
YEAH, WELL, MAYBE YOU DON'T, BUT I DO.
THAT PIECE OF WORK YOU CALL YOUR SON SCREWED UP ONE OF MY BEST FRIENDS.
BECAUSE OF TYLER, I HAD TO KILL GRIZZLY -- AND I'VE BEEN LIVING WITH THAT.
PICK UP CABLE #29 FOR THE FULL STORY -- Mark

WHEN I SENT THE TEAM DOWN HERE, YOU TOLD ME THIS FACILITY WAS *EMPTY.*

IT *WAS.*

WELL, IT ISN'T *NOW.*

CABLE...

DON'T *IGNORE* THIS --

LOOK, DOM, THIS *"ONSLAUGHT"* HAS EVERYONE JUMPING AT SHADOWS...

...AND NOW WE'VE GOT OUR FIRST REAL SHOT AT *TRACKING* IT.

THAT'S MY CONCERN NOW. TYLER'S *GONE...*

...AND *NOTHING* CAN EVER *CHANGE* THAT.

YOUR... ARM!

ARE YOU HAVING TROUBLE CONTROLLING THE TECHNO VIRUS?

IS THAT WHY YOU'RE NOT USING YOUR POWERS?

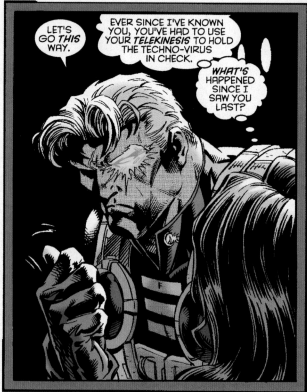

LET'S GO *THIS* WAY.

EVER SINCE I'VE KNOWN YOU, YOU'VE HAD TO USE YOUR *TELEKINESIS* TO HOLD THE TECHNO-VIRUS IN CHECK.

WHAT'S HAPPENED SINCE I SAW YOU LAST?

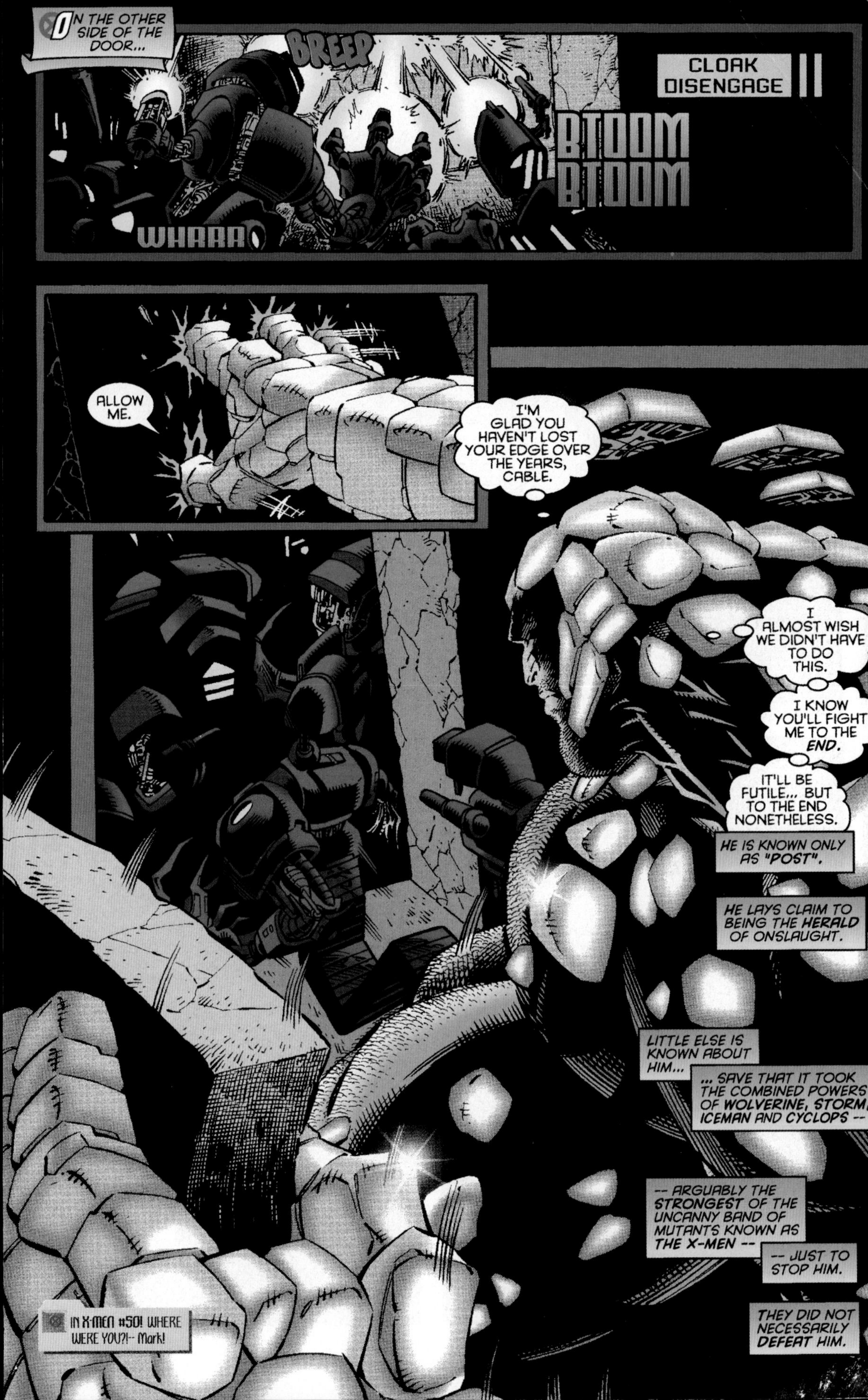
ON THE OTHER SIDE OF THE DOOR...
BREEP
CLOAK DISENGAGE
BTOOM BTOOM
WHARR
ALLOW ME.
I'M GLAD YOU HAVEN'T LOST YOUR EDGE OVER THE YEARS, CABLE.
I ALMOST WISH WE DIDN'T HAVE TO DO THIS.
I KNOW YOU'LL FIGHT ME TO THE END.
IT'LL BE FUTILE... BUT TO THE END NONETHELESS.
HE IS KNOWN ONLY AS "POST".
HE LAYS CLAIM TO BEING THE HERALD OF ONSLAUGHT.
LITTLE ELSE IS KNOWN ABOUT HIM...
... SAVE THAT IT TOOK THE COMBINED POWERS OF WOLVERINE, STORM, ICEMAN AND CYCLOPS --
-- ARGUABLY THE STRONGEST OF THE UNCANNY BAND OF MUTANTS KNOWN AS THE X-MEN --
-- JUST TO STOP HIM.
THEY DID NOT NECESSARILY DEFEAT HIM.
IN X-MEN #50! WHERE WERE YOU?!-- Mark!

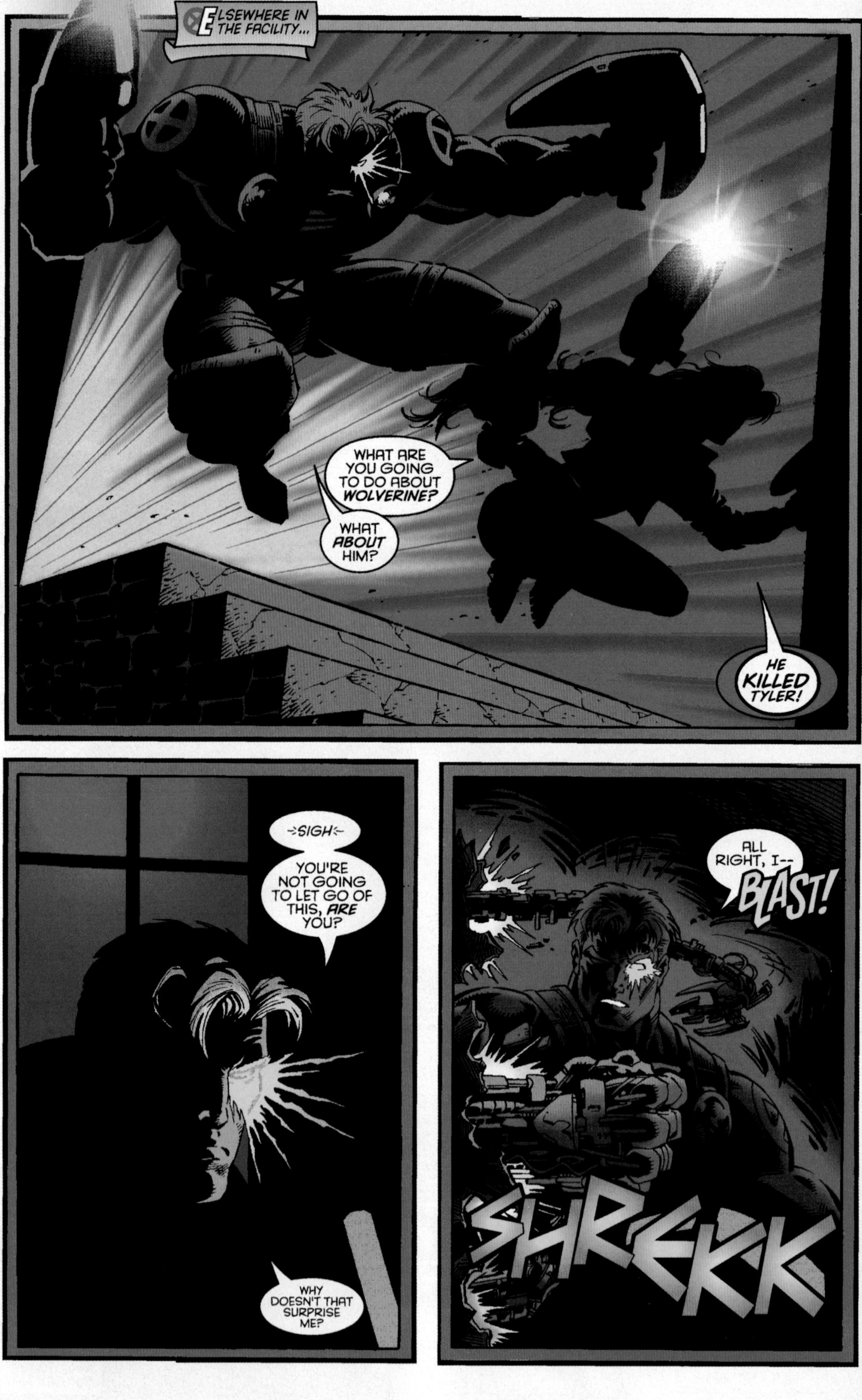
ELSEWHERE IN THE FACILITY...
WHAT ARE YOU GOING TO DO ABOUT WOLVERINE?
WHAT ABOUT HIM?
HE KILLED TYLER!
-SIGH-
YOU'RE NOT GOING TO LET GO OF THIS, ARE YOU?
WHY DOESN'T THAT SURPRISE ME?
ALL RIGHT, I--
BLAST!
SHREKK

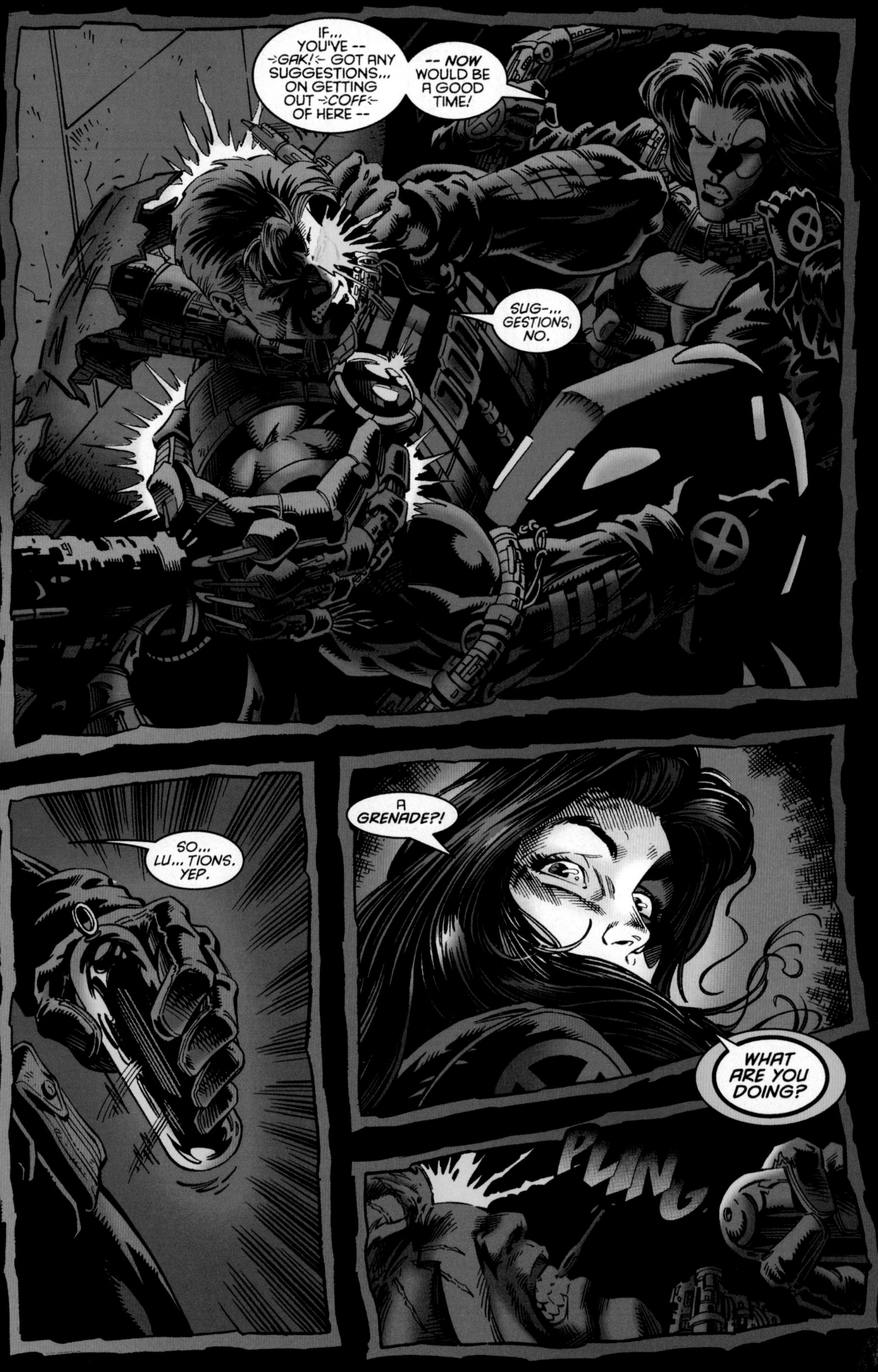
IF... YOU'VE -- ⇒GAK!⇐ GOT ANY SUGGESTIONS... ON GETTING OUT ⇒COFF⇐ OF HERE --
-- NOW WOULD BE A GOOD TIME!
SUG-... GESTIONS, NO.
SO... LU... TIONS. YEP.
A GRENADE?!
WHAT ARE YOU DOING?
PLING

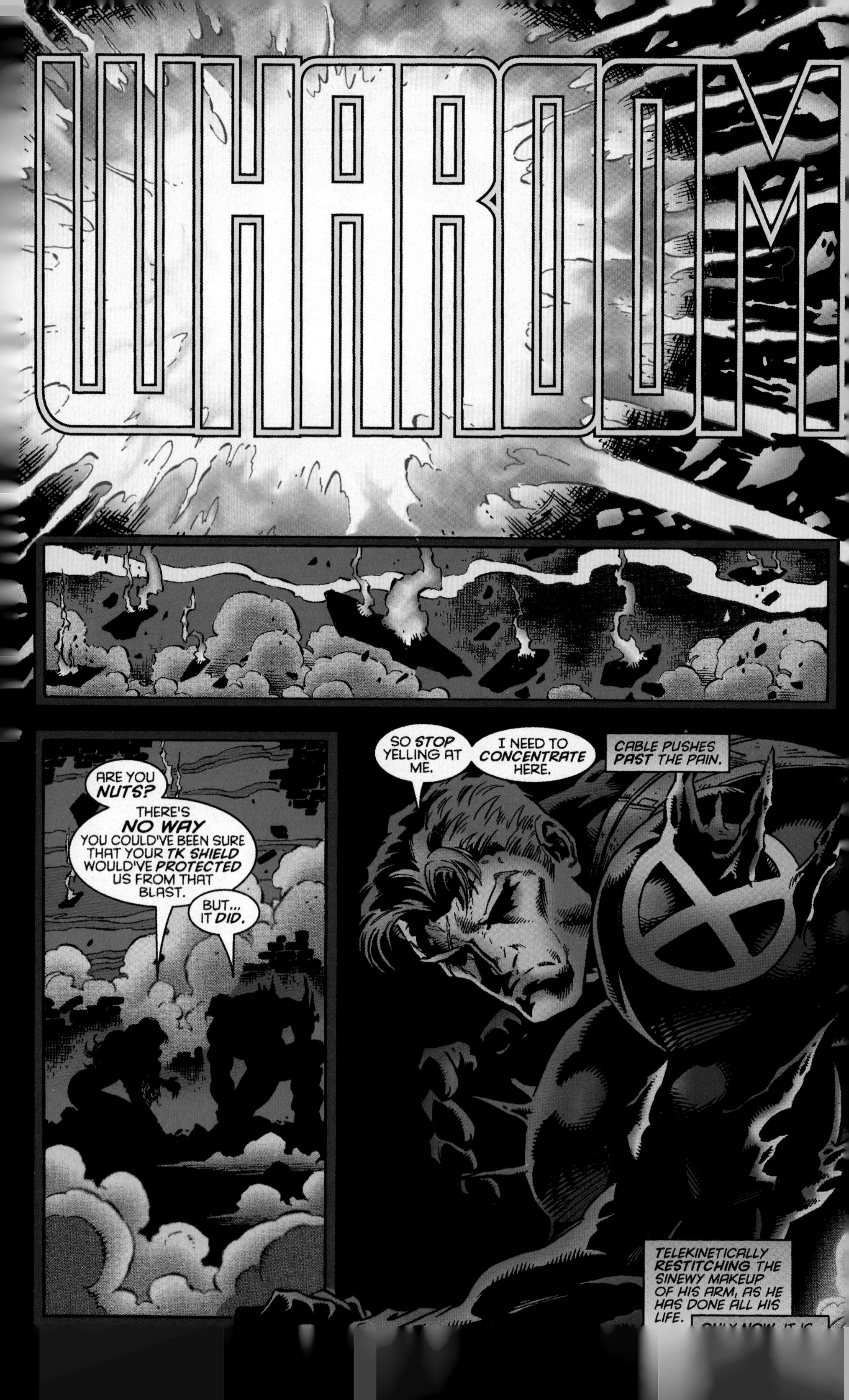
ARE YOU NUTS?
THERE'S NO WAY YOU COULD'VE BEEN SURE THAT YOUR TK SHIELD WOULD'VE PROTECTED US FROM THAT BLAST.
BUT... IT DID.
SO STOP YELLING AT ME.
I NEED TO CONCENTRATE HERE.
CABLE PUSHES PAST THE PAIN.
TELEKINETICALLY RESTITCHING THE SINEWY MAKEUP OF HIS ARM, AS HE HAS DONE ALL HIS LIFE.

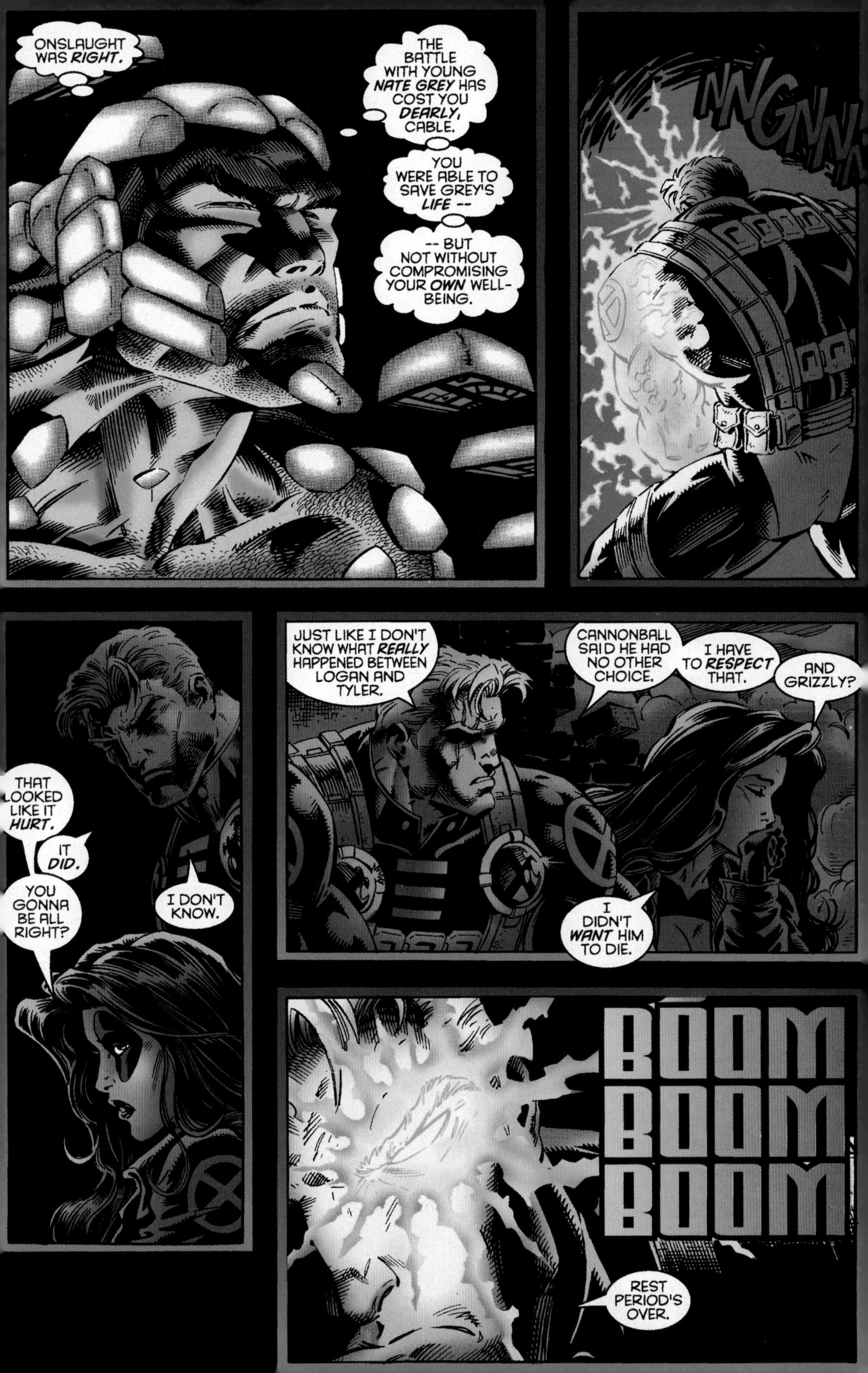

ONSLAUGHT WAS *RIGHT*.
THE BATTLE WITH YOUNG *NATE GREY* HAS COST YOU *DEARLY*, CABLE.
YOU WERE ABLE TO SAVE GREY'S *LIFE* --
-- BUT NOT WITHOUT COMPROMISING YOUR *OWN* WELL-BEING.
NNGNN
THAT LOOKED LIKE IT *HURT*.
IT *DID*.
YOU GONNA BE ALL RIGHT?
I DON'T KNOW.
JUST LIKE I DON'T KNOW WHAT *REALLY* HAPPENED BETWEEN LOGAN AND TYLER.
CANNONBALL SAID HE HAD NO OTHER CHOICE.
I HAVE TO *RESPECT* THAT.
AND GRIZZLY?
I DIDN'T *WANT* HIM TO DIE.
BOOM
BOOM
BOOM
REST PERIOD'S OVER.

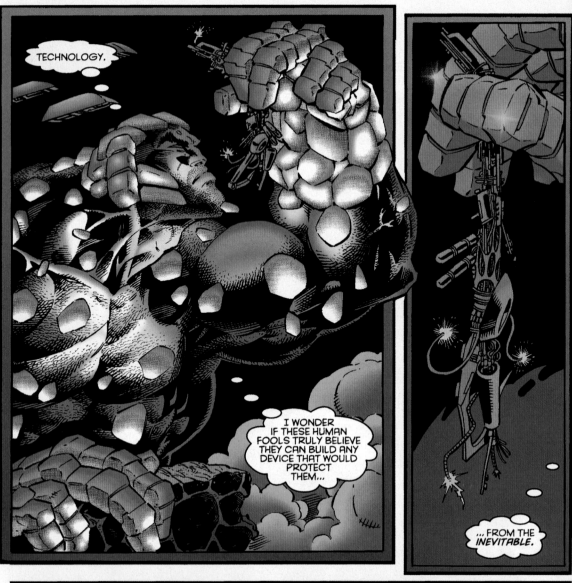

TECHNOLOGY.

I WONDER IF THESE HUMAN FOOLS TRULY BELIEVE THEY CAN BUILD ANY DEVICE THAT WOULD PROTECT THEM...

...FROM THE *INEVITABLE.*

ON THE OTHER HAND...

...CABLE'S ONE OF THE WORLD'S MOST *POWERFUL* TELEPATHS...

...AND HE'S USING HIS MUTANT ABILITIES IN NEW AND *IMPRESSIVE* WAYS.

I AM *BEGINNING* TO UNDERSTAND WHY ONSLAUGHT HAS... *CONCERNS* ABOUT MY OLD FRIEND...

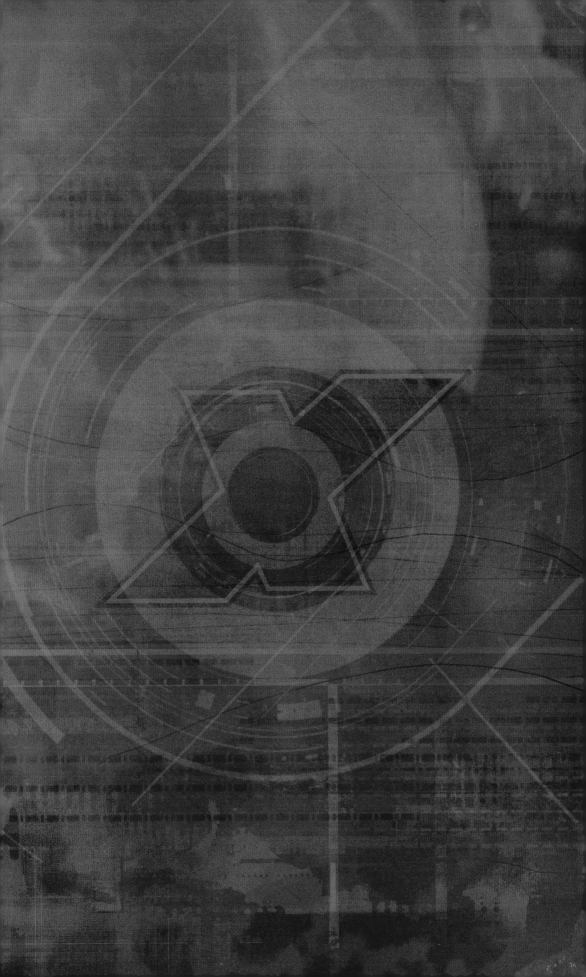

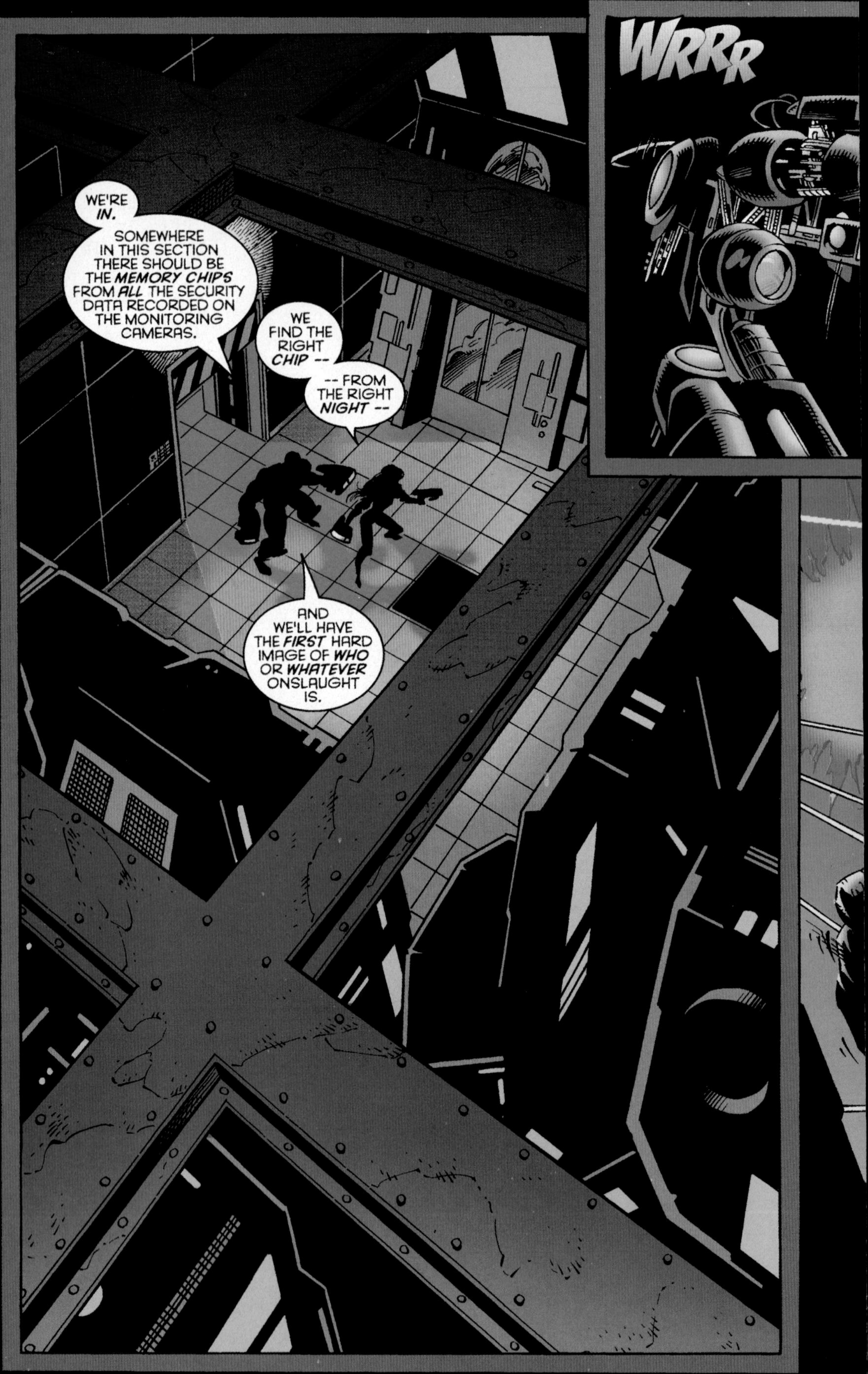
WE'RE IN.
SOMEWHERE IN THIS SECTION THERE SHOULD BE THE MEMORY CHIPS FROM ALL THE SECURITY DATA RECORDED ON THE MONITORING CAMERAS.
WE FIND THE RIGHT CHIP --
-- FROM THE RIGHT NIGHT --
AND WE'LL HAVE THE FIRST HARD IMAGE OF WHO OR WHATEVER ONSLAUGHT IS.
WRRR

RRRZZZ
BREET
CHCHUK
BRAKATABRAKATA
BRAKATABRAKATA
BOOM
BOOM
BOOM
YOU KNOW...
...WHOEVER'S TRYING TO STOP US...
...THEY'RE VERY GOOD.
I WAS JUST GOING TO SAY THAT!

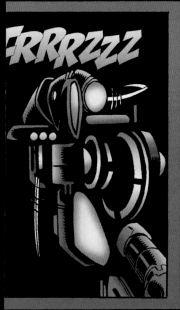

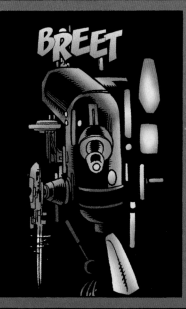

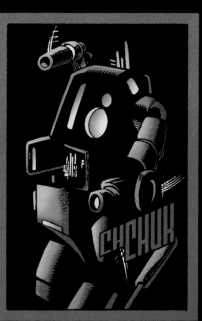

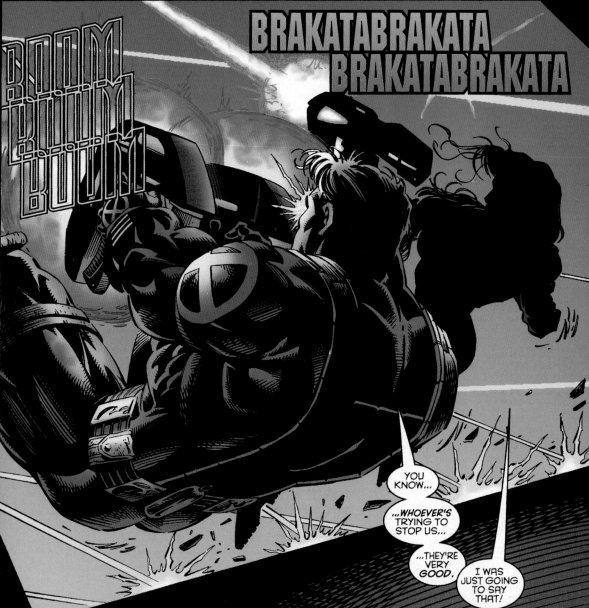

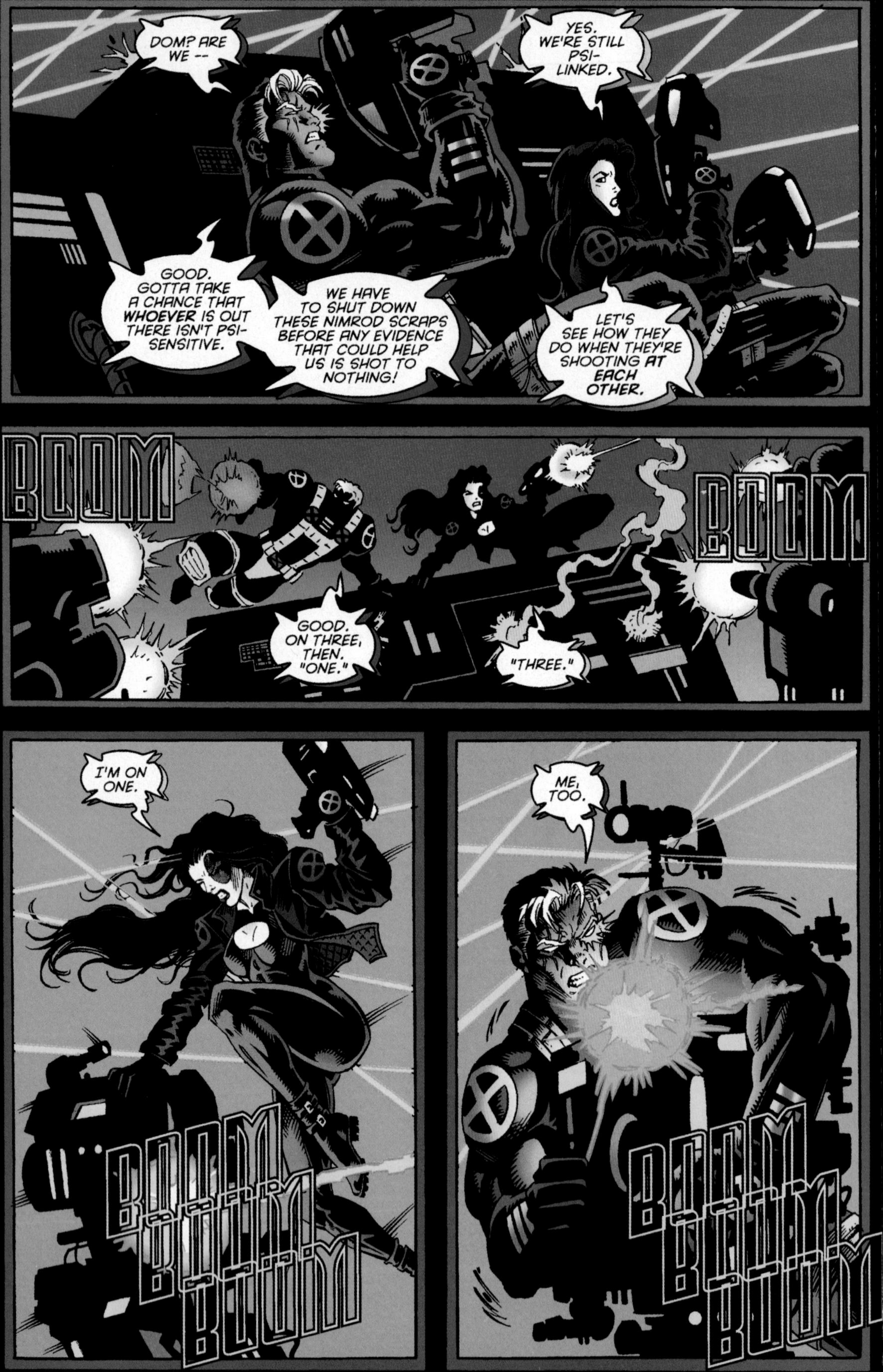
DOM? ARE WE --
YES. WE'RE STILL PSI-LINKED.
GOOD. GOTTA TAKE A CHANCE THAT **WHOEVER** IS OUT THERE ISN'T PSI-SENSITIVE.
WE HAVE TO SHUT DOWN THESE NIMROD SCRAPS BEFORE ANY EVIDENCE THAT COULD HELP US IS SHOT TO NOTHING!
LET'S SEE HOW THEY DO WHEN THEY'RE SHOOTING **AT EACH OTHER**.
BOOM
BOOM
GOOD. ON THREE, THEN. "ONE."
"THREE."
I'M ON ONE.
BOOM BOOM BOOM
ME, TOO.
BOOM BOOM BOOM

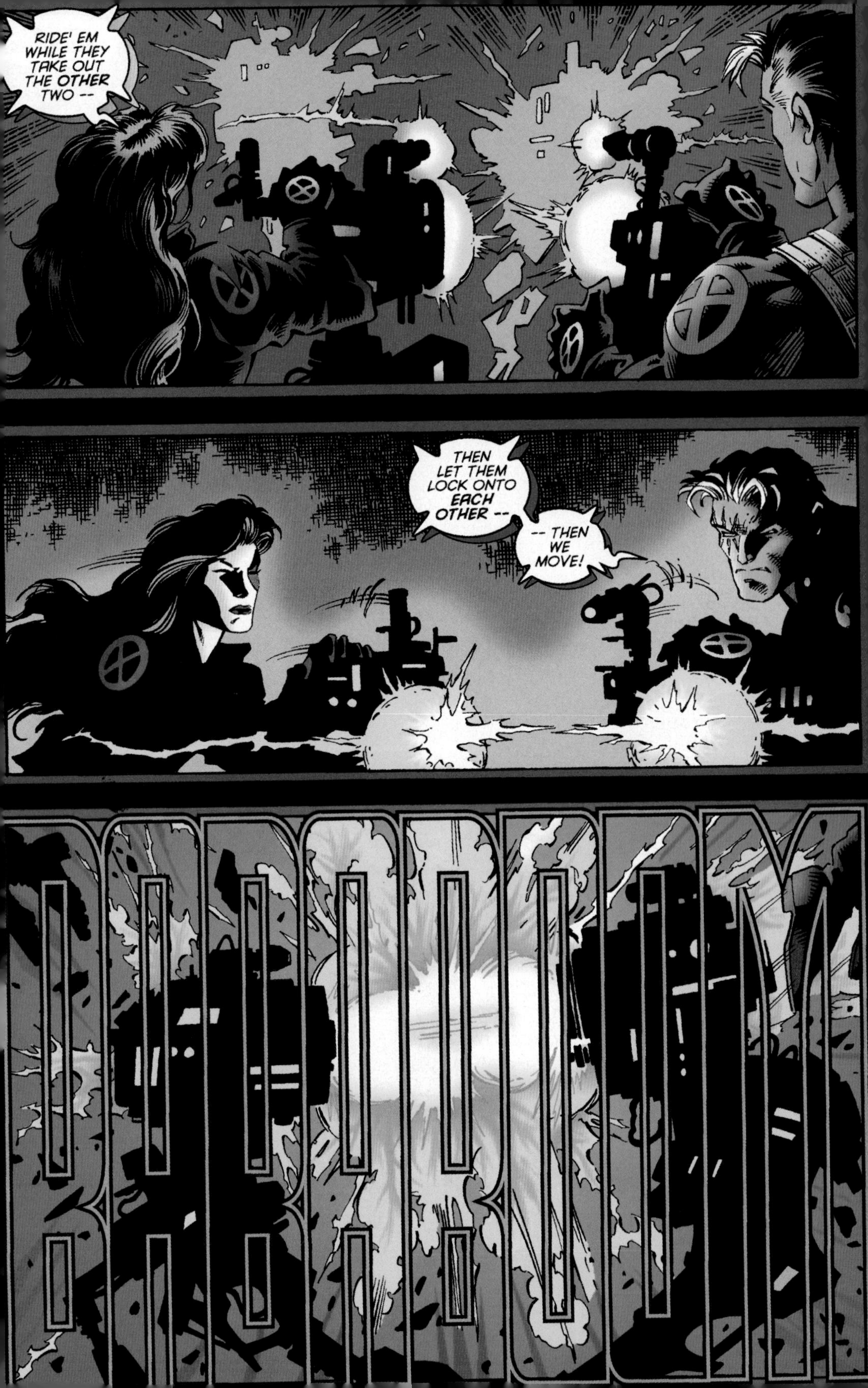
RIDE' EM WHILE THEY TAKE OUT THE OTHER TWO --
THEN LET THEM LOCK ONTO EACH OTHER --
-- THEN WE MOVE!

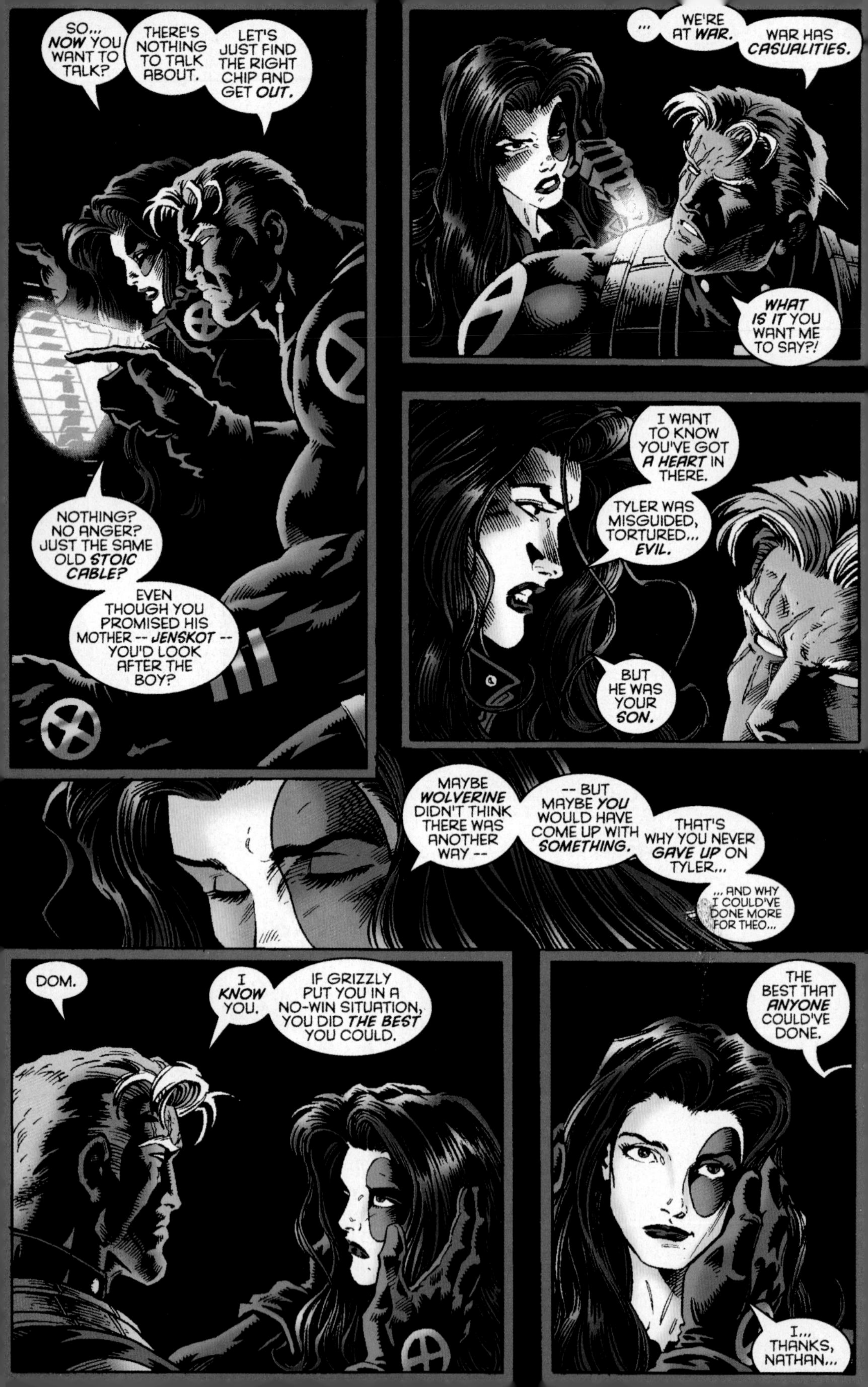
SO... NOW YOU WANT TO TALK?
THERE'S NOTHING TO TALK ABOUT.
LET'S JUST FIND THE RIGHT CHIP AND GET OUT.
NOTHING? NO ANGER? JUST THE SAME OLD STOIC CABLE?
EVEN THOUGH YOU PROMISED HIS MOTHER -- JENSKOT -- YOU'D LOOK AFTER THE BOY?
...
WE'RE AT WAR.
WAR HAS CASUALITIES.
WHAT IS IT YOU WANT ME TO SAY?!
I WANT TO KNOW YOU'VE GOT A HEART IN THERE.
TYLER WAS MISGUIDED, TORTURED... EVIL.
BUT HE WAS YOUR SON.
MAYBE WOLVERINE DIDN'T THINK THERE WAS ANOTHER WAY --
-- BUT MAYBE YOU WOULD HAVE COME UP WITH SOMETHING.
THAT'S WHY YOU NEVER GAVE UP ON TYLER...
...AND WHY I COULD'VE DONE MORE FOR THEO...
DOM.
I KNOW YOU.
IF GRIZZLY PUT YOU IN A NO-WIN SITUATION, YOU DID THE BEST YOU COULD.
THE BEST THAT ANYONE COULD'VE DONE.
I... THANKS, NATHAN...

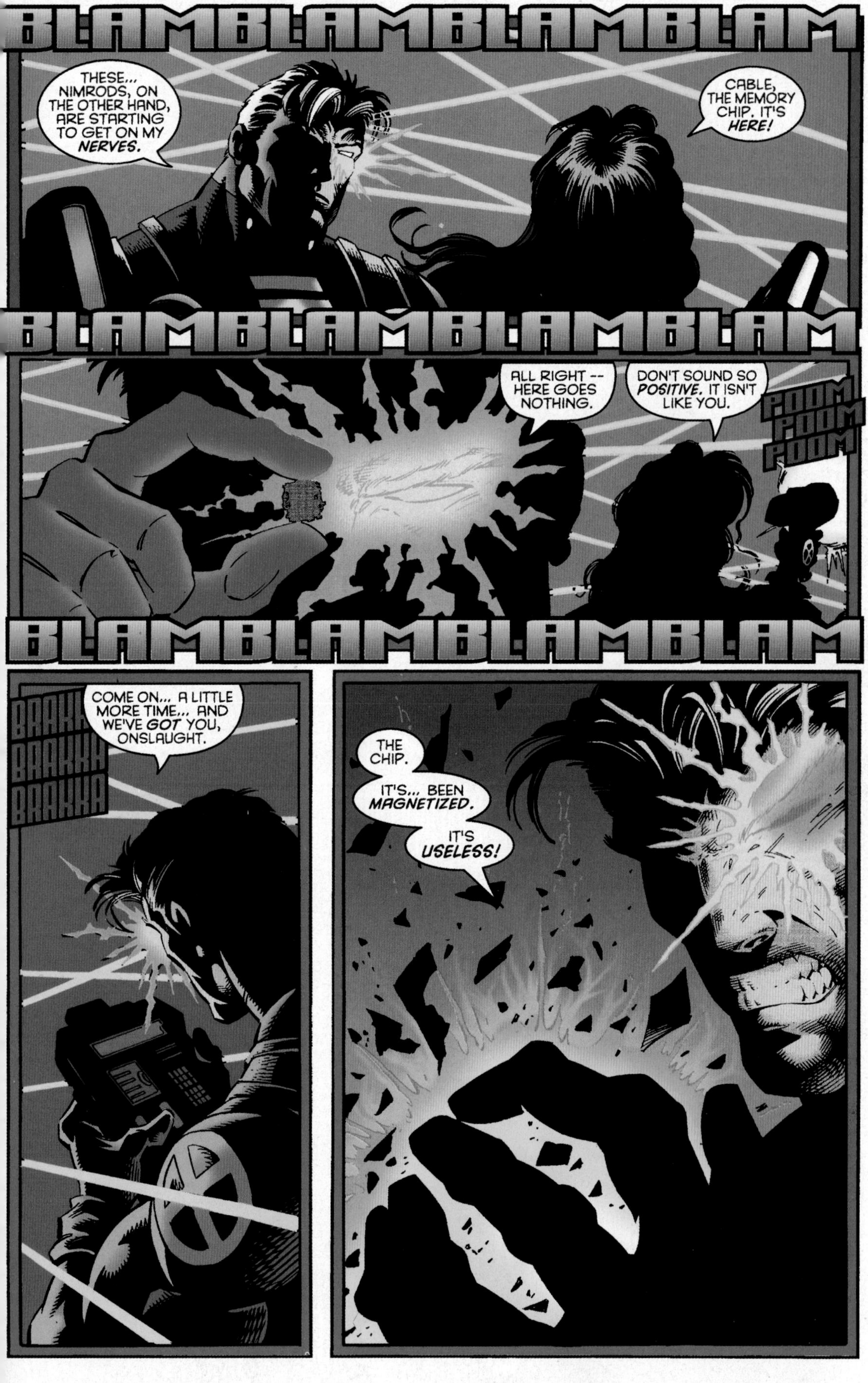
BLAMBLAMBLAMBLAM
THESE... NIMRODS, ON THE OTHER HAND, ARE STARTING TO GET ON MY NERVES.
CABLE, THE MEMORY CHIP. IT'S HERE!
BLAMBLAMBLAMBLAM
ALL RIGHT -- HERE GOES NOTHING.
DON'T SOUND SO POSITIVE. IT ISN'T LIKE YOU.
POOM POOM POOM
BLAMBLAMBLAMBLAM
BRAKKA BRAKKA BRAKKA
COME ON... A LITTLE MORE TIME... AND WE'VE GOT YOU, ONSLAUGHT.
THE CHIP.
IT'S... BEEN MAGNETIZED.
IT'S USELESS!

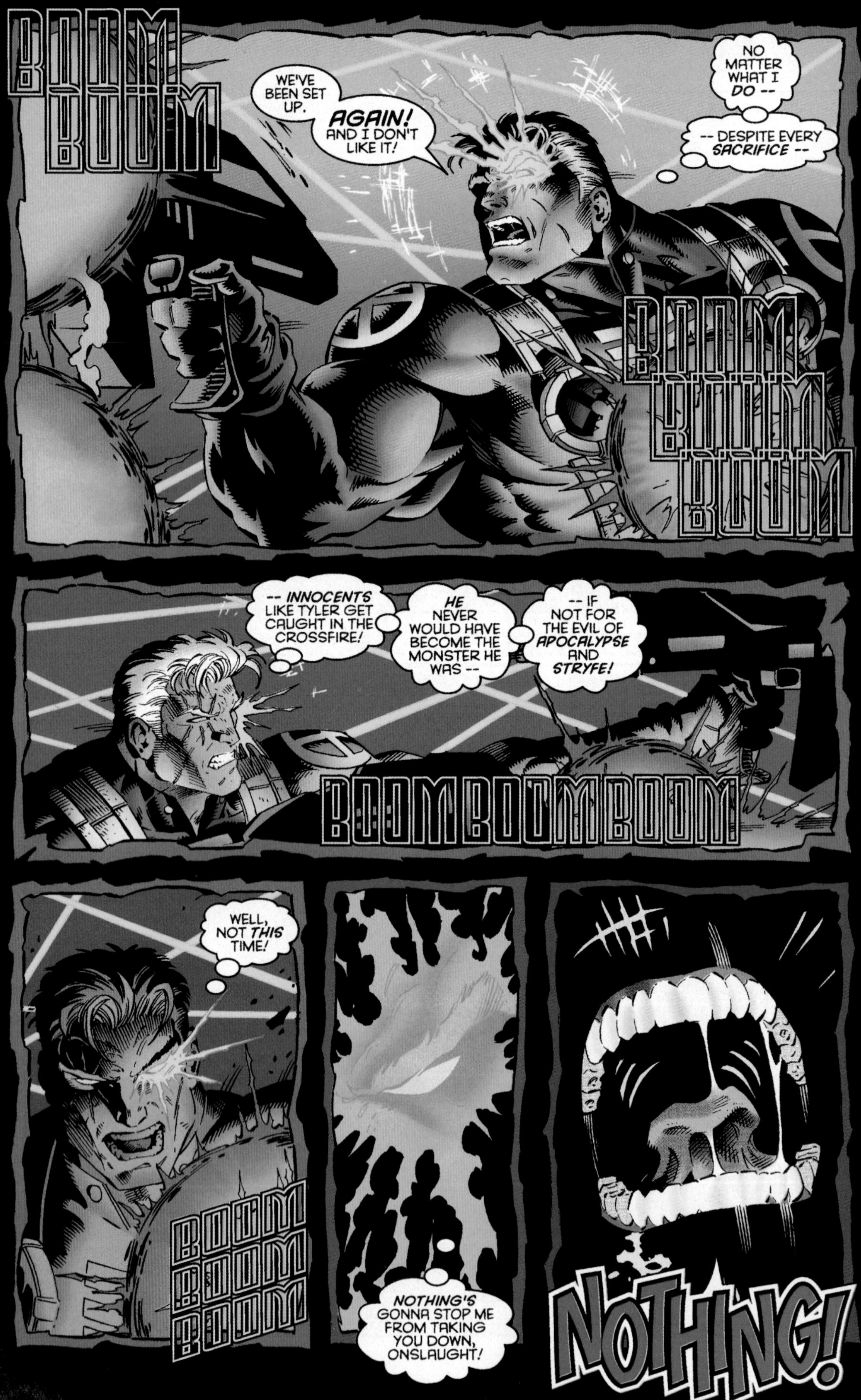
BOOM BOOM
WE'VE BEEN SET UP. AGAIN! AND I DON'T LIKE IT!
NO MATTER WHAT I DO --
-- DESPITE EVERY SACRIFICE --
BOOM BOOM BOOM
-- INNOCENTS LIKE TYLER GET CAUGHT IN THE CROSSFIRE!
HE NEVER WOULD HAVE BECOME THE MONSTER HE WAS --
-- IF NOT FOR THE EVIL OF APOCALYPSE AND STRYFE!
BOOM BOOM BOOM
WELL, NOT THIS TIME!
BOOM BOOM BOOM
NOTHING'S GONNA STOP ME FROM TAKING YOU DOWN, ONSLAUGHT!
NOTHING!

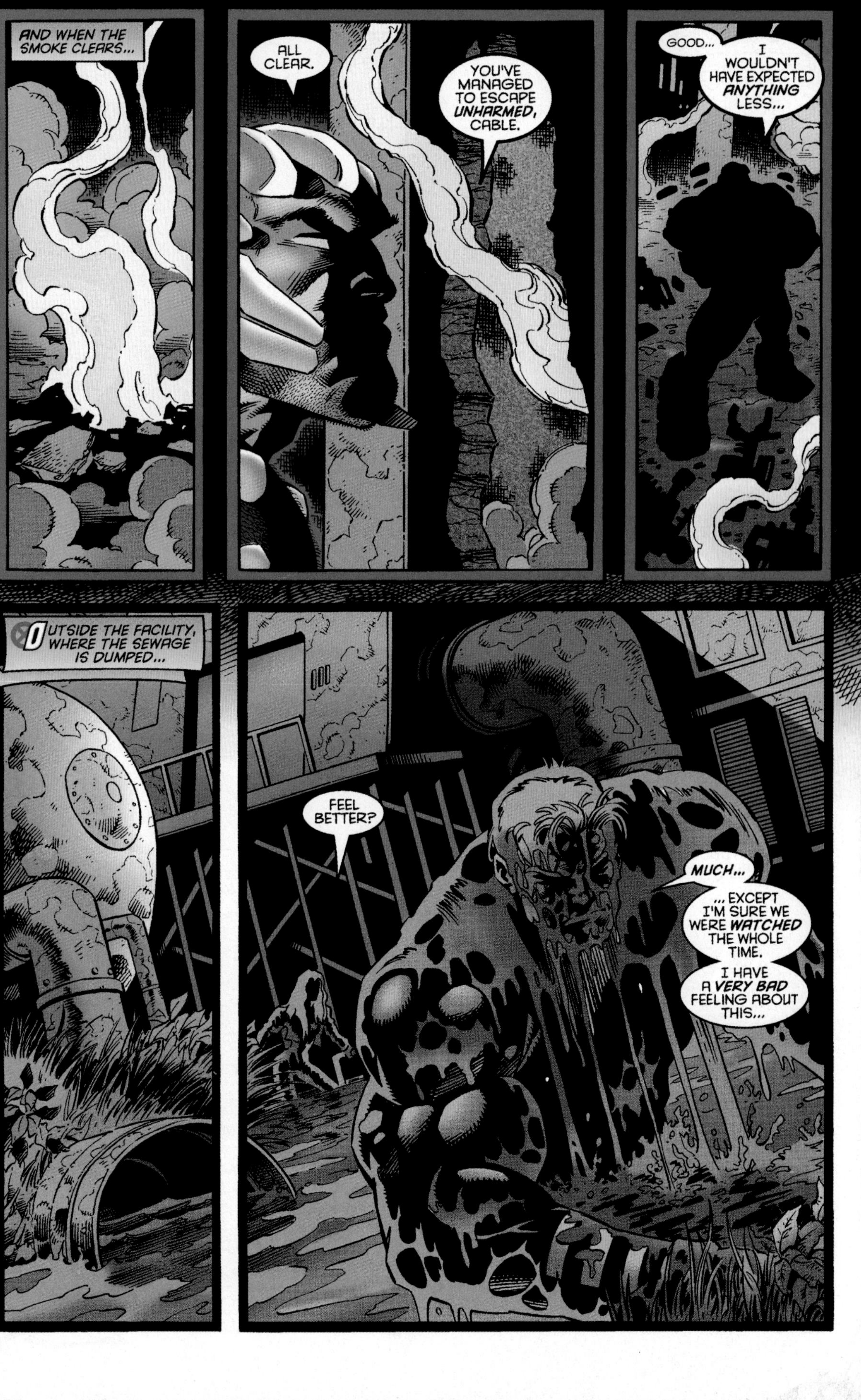
AND WHEN THE SMOKE CLEARS...
ALL CLEAR.
YOU'VE MANAGED TO ESCAPE UNHARMED, CABLE.
GOOD...
I WOULDN'T HAVE EXPECTED ANYTHING LESS...
OUTSIDE THE FACILITY, WHERE THE SEWAGE IS DUMPED...
FEEL BETTER?
MUCH...
...EXCEPT I'M SURE WE WERE WATCHED THE WHOLE TIME.
I HAVE A VERY BAD FEELING ABOUT THIS...

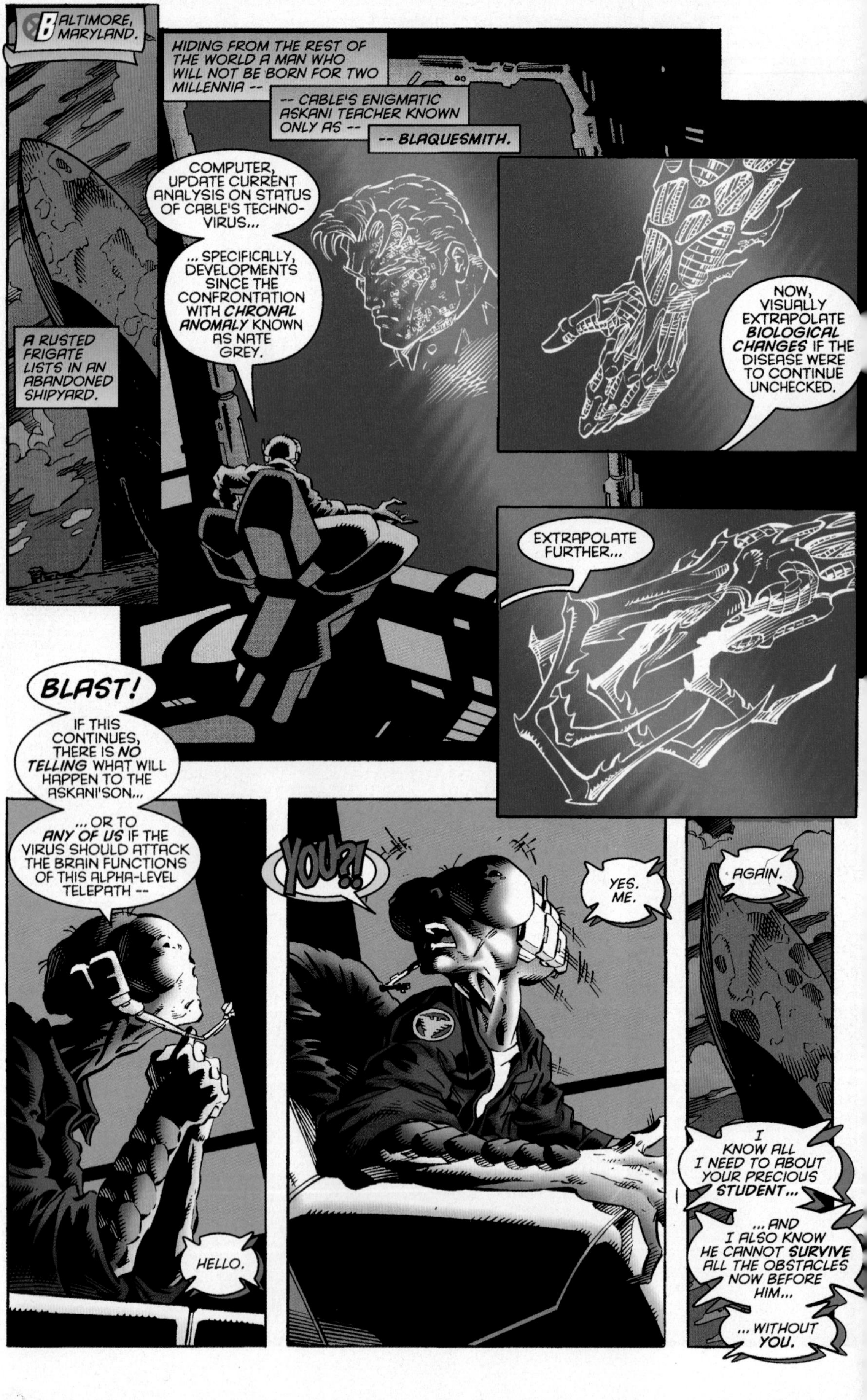
BALTIMORE, MARYLAND.
HIDING FROM THE REST OF THE WORLD A MAN WHO WILL NOT BE BORN FOR TWO MILLENNIA --
-- CABLE'S ENIGMATIC ASKANI TEACHER KNOWN ONLY AS --
-- BLAQUESMITH.
COMPUTER, UPDATE CURRENT ANALYSIS ON STATUS OF CABLE'S TECHNO-VIRUS...
... SPECIFICALLY, DEVELOPMENTS SINCE THE CONFRONTATION WITH CHRONAL ANOMALY KNOWN AS NATE GREY.
A RUSTED FRIGATE LISTS IN AN ABANDONED SHIPYARD.
NOW, VISUALLY EXTRAPOLATE BIOLOGICAL CHANGES IF THE DISEASE WERE TO CONTINUE UNCHECKED.
EXTRAPOLATE FURTHER...
BLAST!
IF THIS CONTINUES, THERE IS NO TELLING WHAT WILL HAPPEN TO THE ASKANI'SON...
... OR TO ANY OF US IF THE VIRUS SHOULD ATTACK THE BRAIN FUNCTIONS OF THIS ALPHA-LEVEL TELEPATH --
HELLO.
YOU?!
YES. ME.
AGAIN.
I KNOW ALL I NEED TO ABOUT YOUR PRECIOUS STUDENT...
... AND I ALSO KNOW HE CANNOT SURVIVE ALL THE OBSTACLES NOW BEFORE HIM...
... WITHOUT YOU.

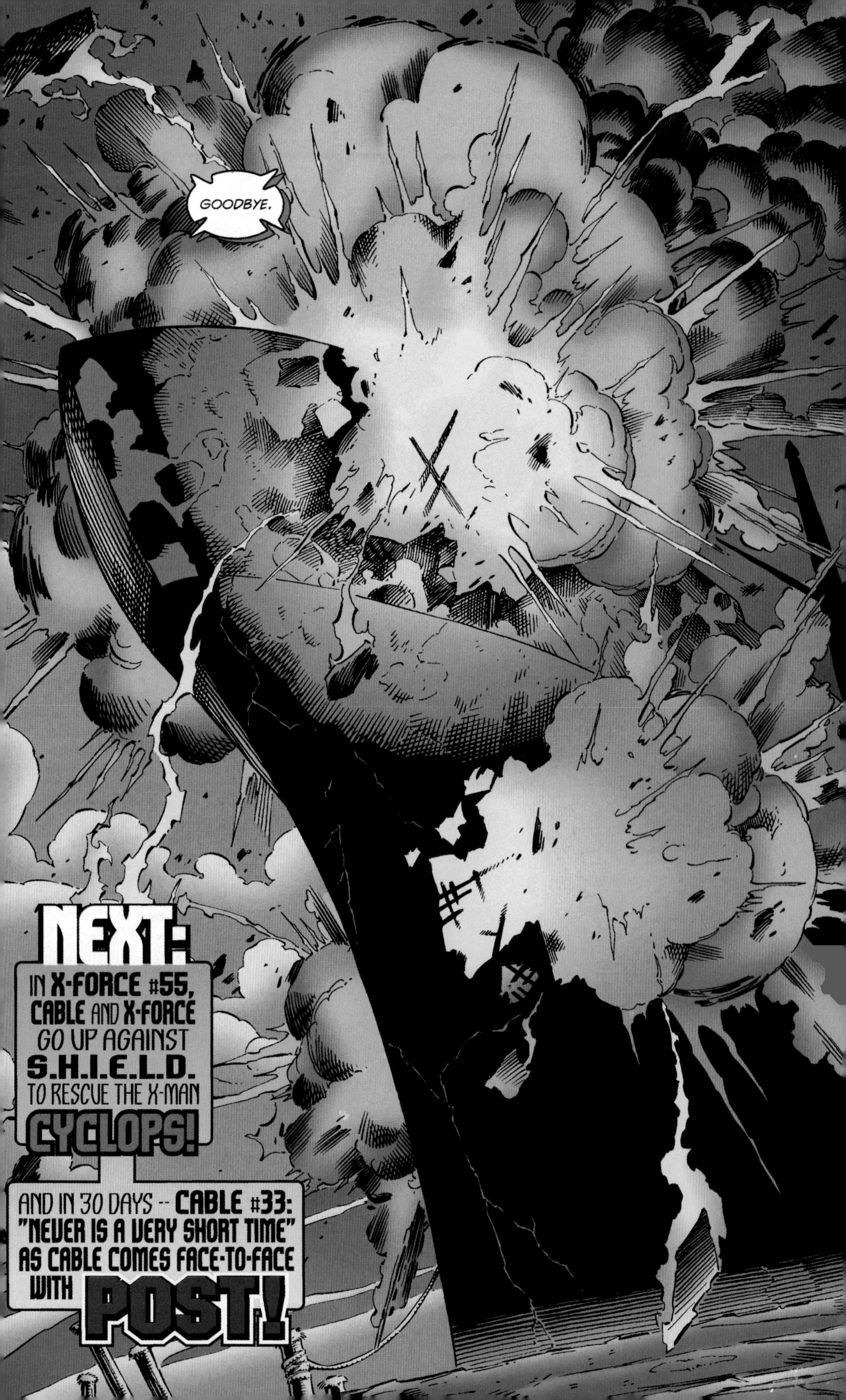
GOODBYE.
NEXT:
IN X-FORCE #55, CABLE AND X-FORCE GO UP AGAINST S.H.I.E.L.D. TO RESCUE THE X-MAN CYCLOPS!
AND IN 30 DAYS -- CABLE #33: "NEVER IS A VERY SHORT TIME" AS CABLE COMES FACE-TO-FACE WITH POST!

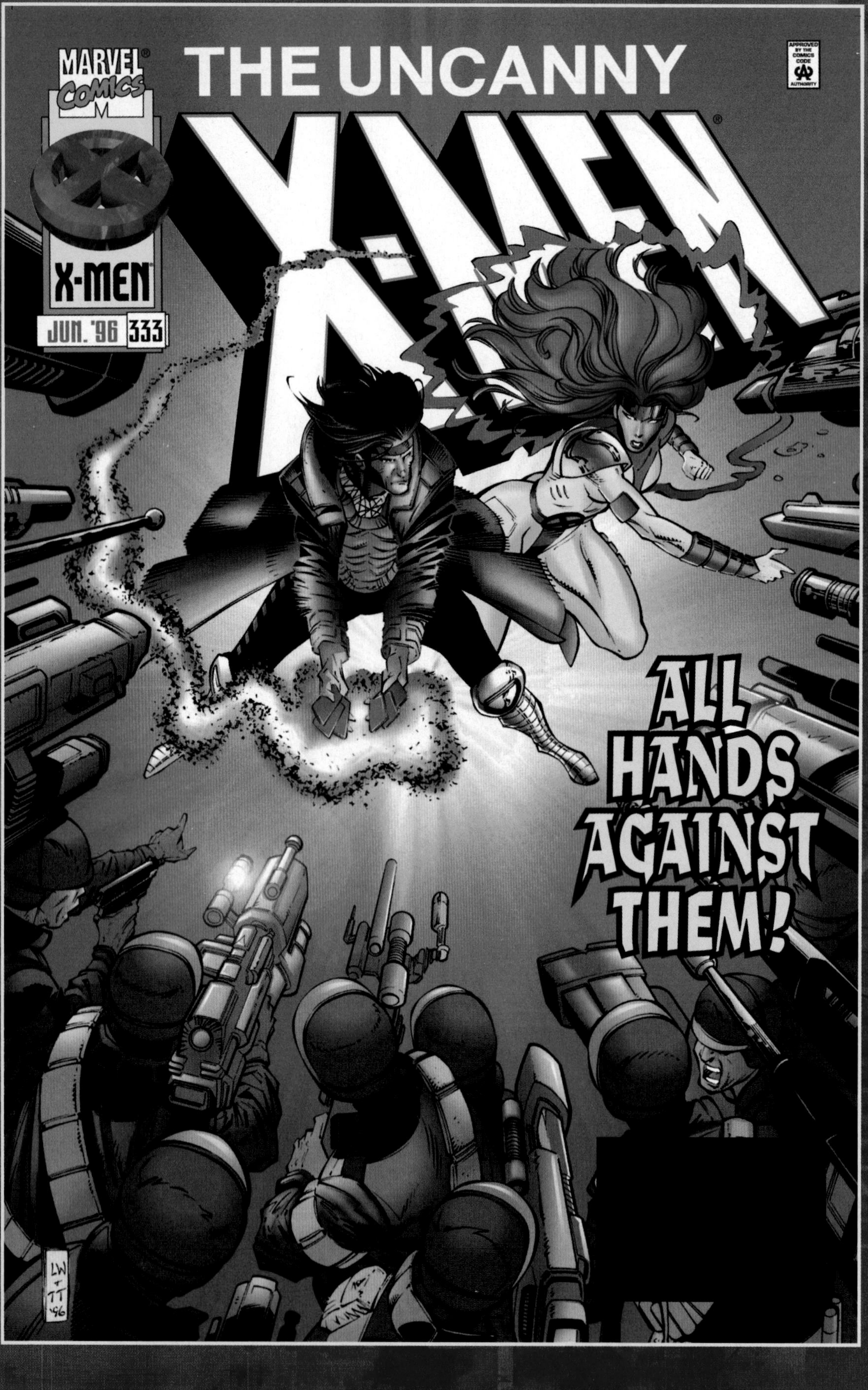
MARVEL COMICS
THE UNCANNY
X-MEN
APPROVED BY THE COMICS CODE AUTHORITY
X-MEN
JUN. '96 333
ALL HANDS AGAINST THEM!
LW + TT '96

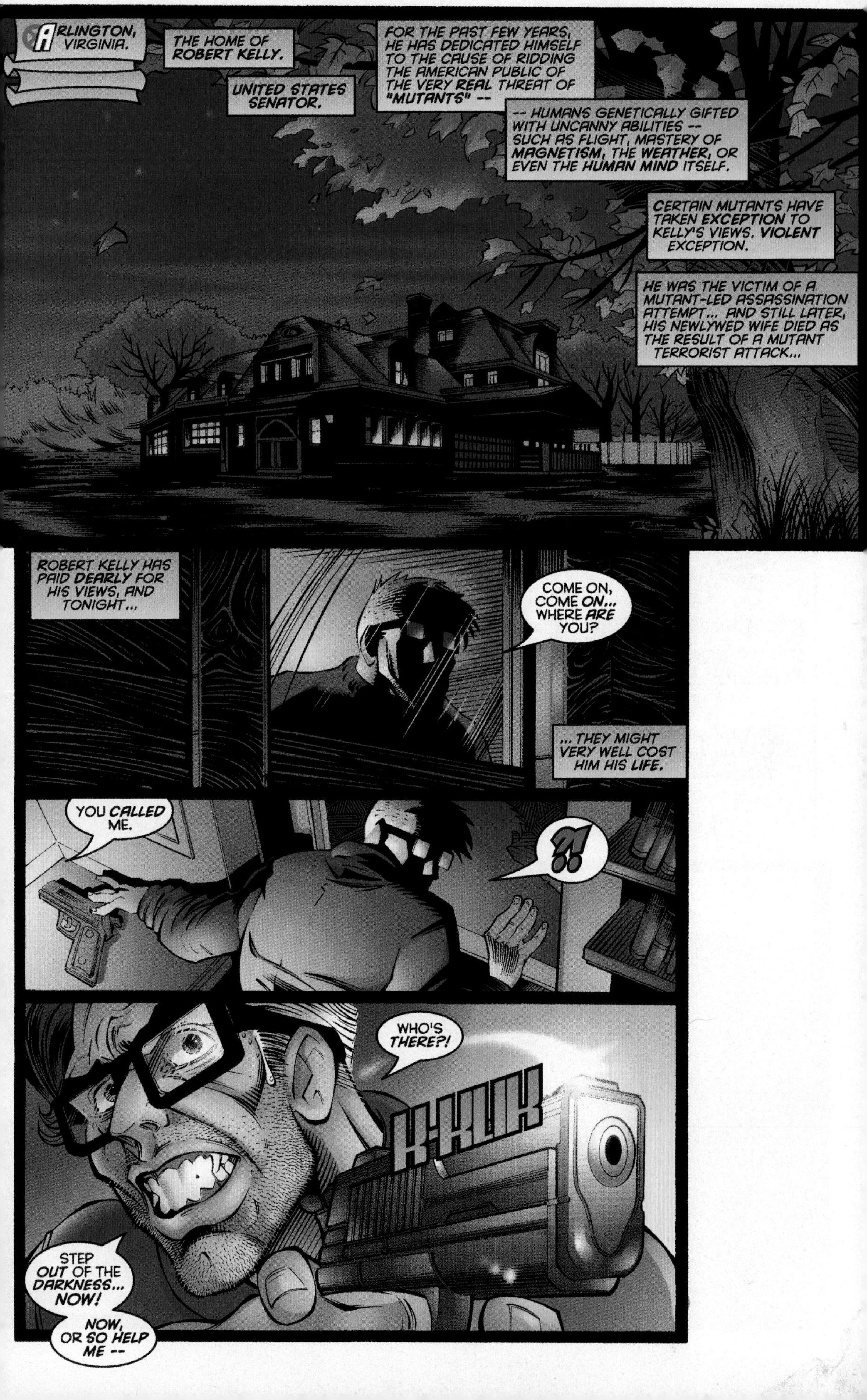
ARLINGTON, VIRGINIA.
THE HOME OF ROBERT KELLY.
UNITED STATES SENATOR.
FOR THE PAST FEW YEARS, HE HAS DEDICATED HIMSELF TO THE CAUSE OF RIDDING THE AMERICAN PUBLIC OF THE VERY REAL THREAT OF "MUTANTS" --
-- HUMANS GENETICALLY GIFTED WITH UNCANNY ABILITIES -- SUCH AS FLIGHT, MASTERY OF MAGNETISM, THE WEATHER, OR EVEN THE HUMAN MIND ITSELF.
CERTAIN MUTANTS HAVE TAKEN EXCEPTION TO KELLY'S VIEWS. VIOLENT EXCEPTION.
HE WAS THE VICTIM OF A MUTANT-LED ASSASSINATION ATTEMPT... AND STILL LATER, HIS NEWLYWED WIFE DIED AS THE RESULT OF A MUTANT TERRORIST ATTACK...
ROBERT KELLY HAS PAID DEARLY FOR HIS VIEWS, AND TONIGHT...
COME ON, COME ON... WHERE ARE YOU?
...THEY MIGHT VERY WELL COST HIM HIS LIFE.
YOU CALLED ME.
?!
WHO'S THERE?!
K-KLIK
STEP OUT OF THE DARKNESS... NOW!
NOW, OR SO HELP ME --

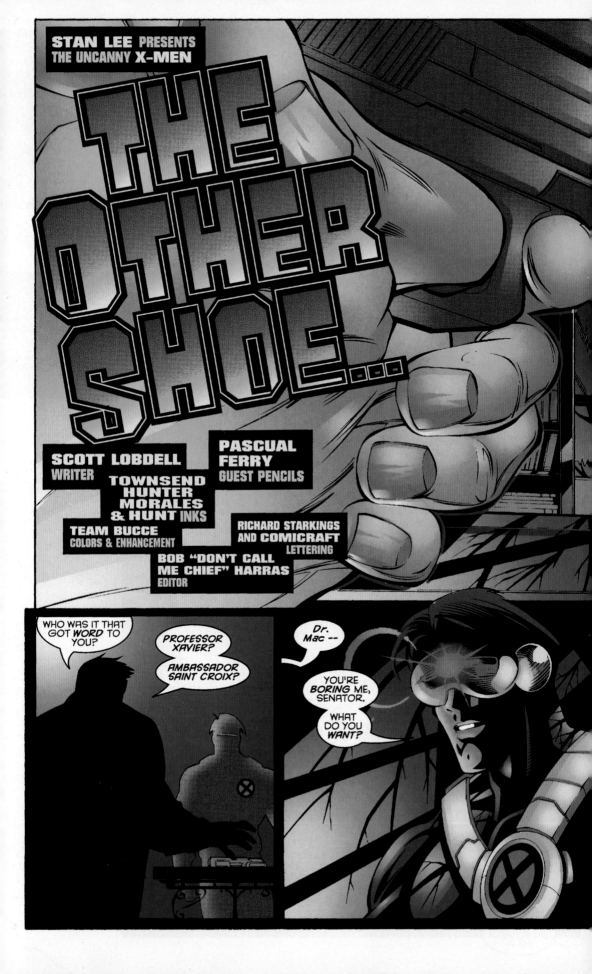

STAN LEE PRESENTS
THE UNCANNY X-MEN

THE OTHER SHOE...

SCOTT LOBDELL
WRITER

PASCUAL FERRY
GUEST PENCILS

TOWNSEND HUNTER MORALES & HUNT INKS

TEAM BUCCE
COLORS & ENHANCEMENT

RICHARD STARKINGS AND COMICRAFT
LETTERING

BOB "DON'T CALL ME CHIEF" HARRAS
EDITOR

WHO WAS IT THAT GOT *WORD* TO YOU?

PROFESSOR XAVIER?

AMBASSADOR SAINT CROIX?

Dr. Mac --

YOU'RE *BORING* ME, SENATOR.

WHAT DO YOU *WANT?*

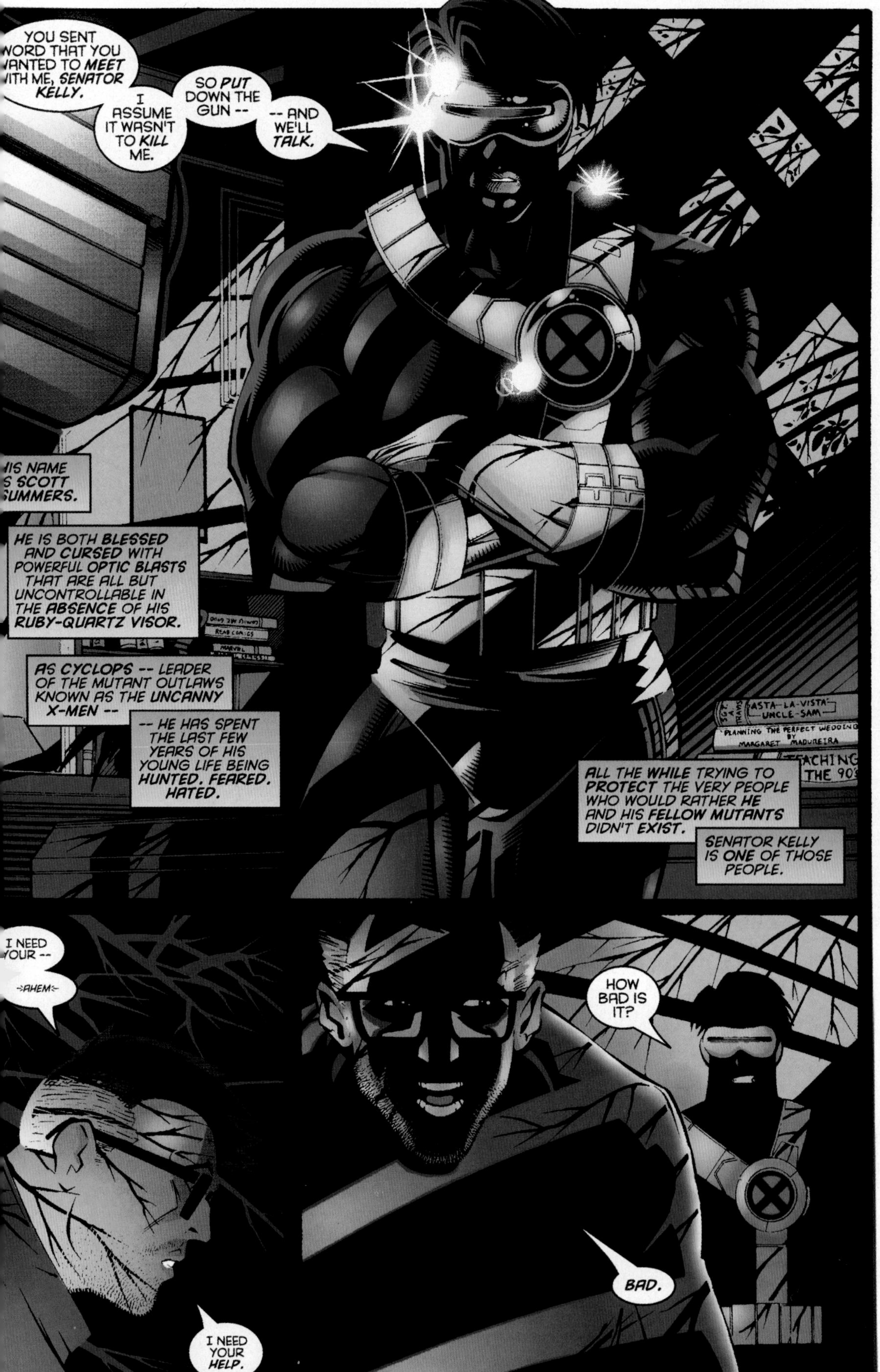

YOU SENT WORD THAT YOU WANTED TO MEET WITH ME, SENATOR KELLY.
I ASSUME IT WASN'T TO KILL ME.
SO PUT DOWN THE GUN --
-- AND WE'LL TALK.
HIS NAME IS SCOTT SUMMERS.
HE IS BOTH BLESSED AND CURSED WITH POWERFUL OPTIC BLASTS THAT ARE ALL BUT UNCONTROLLABLE IN THE ABSENCE OF HIS RUBY-QUARTZ VISOR.
AS CYCLOPS -- LEADER OF THE MUTANT OUTLAWS KNOWN AS THE UNCANNY X-MEN --
-- HE HAS SPENT THE LAST FEW YEARS OF HIS YOUNG LIFE BEING HUNTED. FEARED. HATED.
ALL THE WHILE TRYING TO PROTECT THE VERY PEOPLE WHO WOULD RATHER HE AND HIS FELLOW MUTANTS DIDN'T EXIST.
SENATOR KELLY IS ONE OF THOSE PEOPLE.
HASTA-LA-VISTA UNCLE-SAM
PLANNING THE PERFECT WEDDING BY MARGARET MADUREIRA
TEACHING THE 90'S
I NEED YOUR --
AHEM
HOW BAD IS IT?
BAD.
I NEED YOUR HELP.

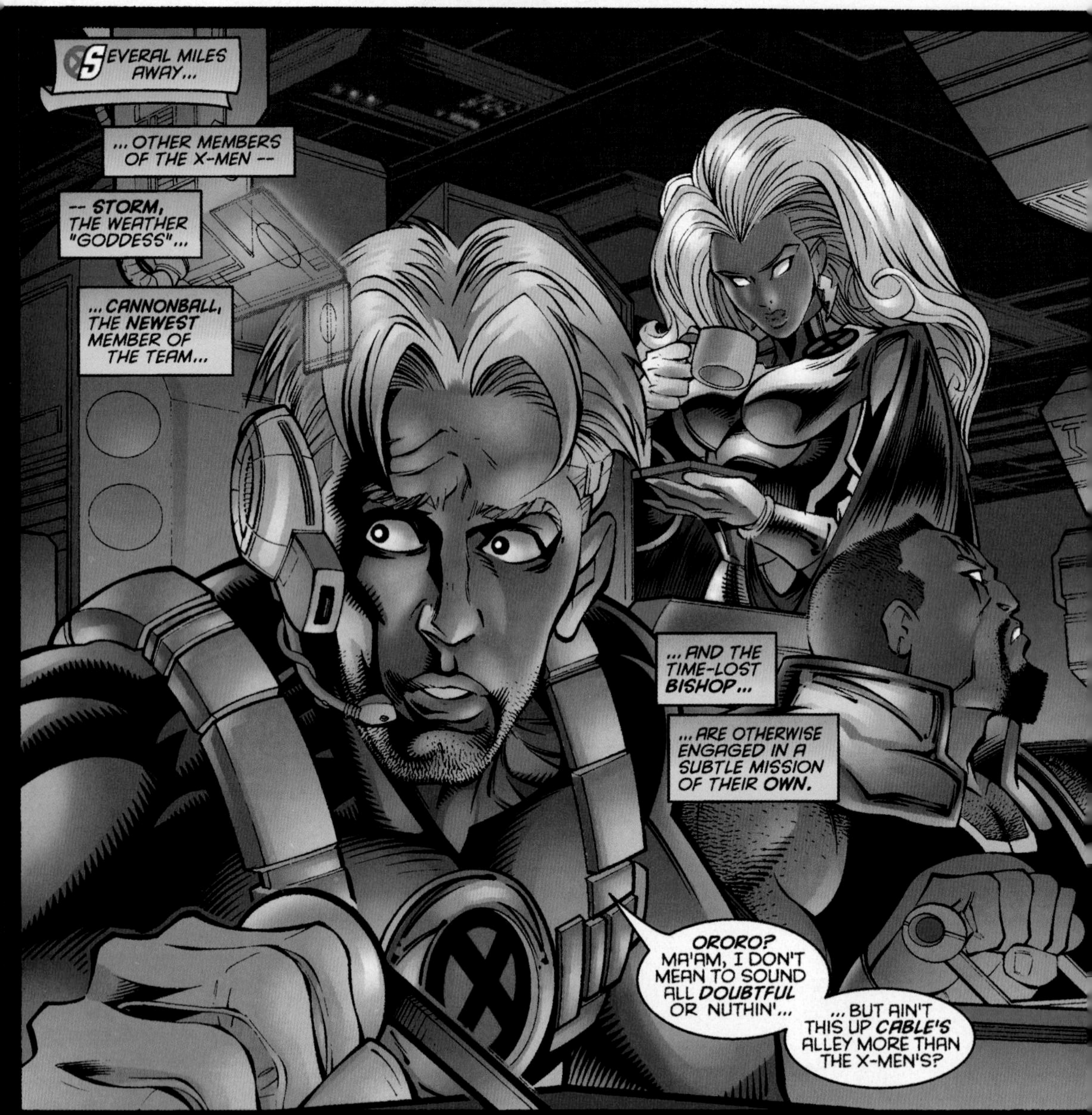
SEVERAL MILES AWAY...
...OTHER MEMBERS OF THE X-MEN --
-- STORM, THE WEATHER "GODDESS"...
...CANNONBALL, THE NEWEST MEMBER OF THE TEAM...
...AND THE TIME-LOST BISHOP...
...ARE OTHERWISE ENGAGED IN A SUBTLE MISSION OF THEIR OWN.
ORORO? MA'AM, I DON'T MEAN TO SOUND ALL DOUBTFUL OR NUTHIN'...
...BUT AIN'T THIS UP CABLE'S ALLEY MORE THAN THE X-MEN'S?

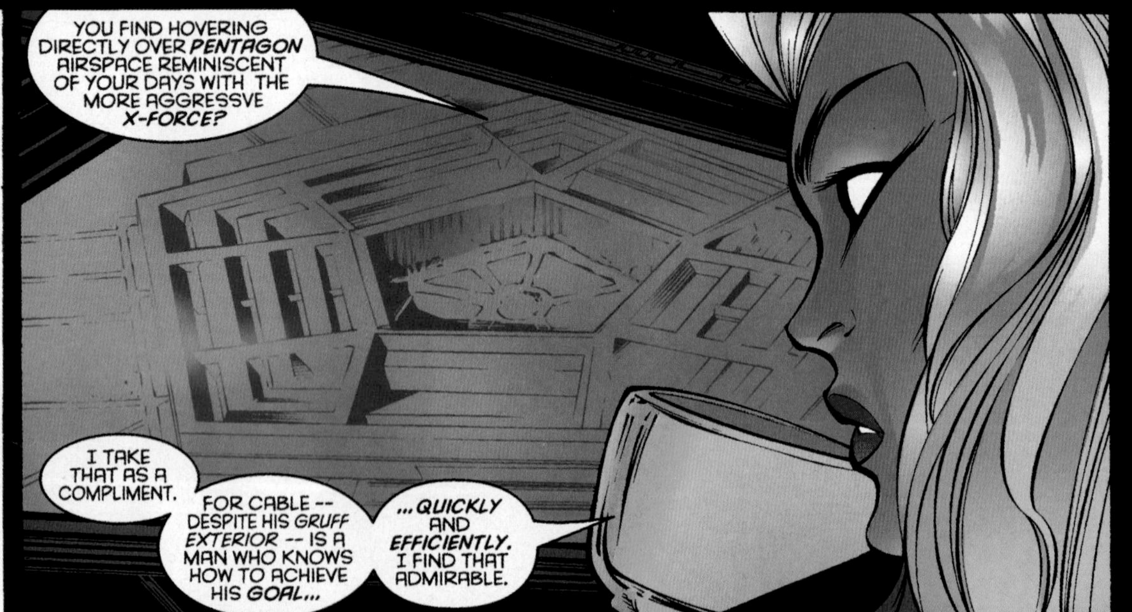
YOU FIND HOVERING DIRECTLY OVER PENTAGON AIRSPACE REMINISCENT OF YOUR DAYS WITH THE MORE AGGRESSVE X-FORCE?
I TAKE THAT AS A COMPLIMENT.
FOR CABLE -- DESPITE HIS GRUFF EXTERIOR -- IS A MAN WHO KNOWS HOW TO ACHIEVE HIS GOAL...
...QUICKLY AND EFFICIENTLY. I FIND THAT ADMIRABLE.

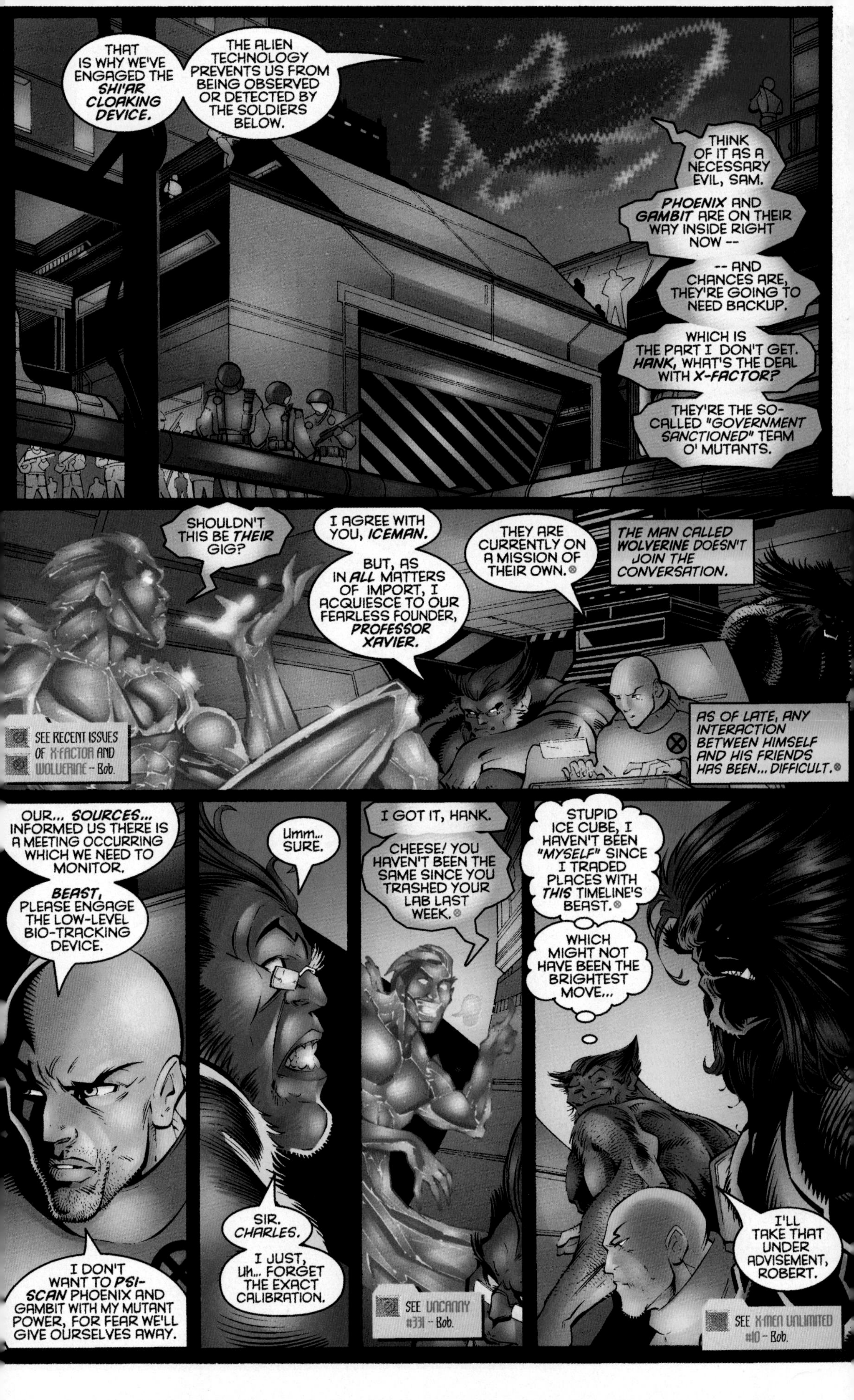
THAT IS WHY WE'VE ENGAGED THE SHI'AR CLOAKING DEVICE.
THE ALIEN TECHNOLOGY PREVENTS US FROM BEING OBSERVED OR DETECTED BY THE SOLDIERS BELOW.
THINK OF IT AS A NECESSARY EVIL, SAM.
PHOENIX AND GAMBIT ARE ON THEIR WAY INSIDE RIGHT NOW --
-- AND CHANCES ARE, THEY'RE GOING TO NEED BACKUP.
WHICH IS THE PART I DON'T GET. HANK, WHAT'S THE DEAL WITH X-FACTOR?
THEY'RE THE SO-CALLED "GOVERNMENT SANCTIONED" TEAM O' MUTANTS.
SHOULDN'T THIS BE THEIR GIG?
I AGREE WITH YOU, ICEMAN.
BUT, AS IN ALL MATTERS OF IMPORT, I ACQUIESCE TO OUR FEARLESS FOUNDER, PROFESSOR XAVIER.
THEY ARE CURRENTLY ON A MISSION OF THEIR OWN.
THE MAN CALLED WOLVERINE DOESN'T JOIN THE CONVERSATION.
AS OF LATE, ANY INTERACTION BETWEEN HIMSELF AND HIS FRIENDS HAS BEEN... DIFFICULT.
SEE RECENT ISSUES OF X-FACTOR AND WOLVERINE -- Bob.
OUR... SOURCES... INFORMED US THERE IS A MEETING OCCURRING WHICH WE NEED TO MONITOR.
BEAST, PLEASE ENGAGE THE LOW-LEVEL BIO-TRACKING DEVICE.
I DON'T WANT TO PSI-SCAN PHOENIX AND GAMBIT WITH MY MUTANT POWER, FOR FEAR WE'LL GIVE OURSELVES AWAY.
Umm... SURE.
SIR. CHARLES.
I JUST, uh... FORGET THE EXACT CALIBRATION.
I GOT IT, HANK.
CHEESE! YOU HAVEN'T BEEN THE SAME SINCE YOU TRASHED YOUR LAB LAST WEEK.
SEE UNCANNY #331 -- Bob.
STUPID ICE CUBE, I HAVEN'T BEEN "MYSELF" SINCE I TRADED PLACES WITH THIS TIMELINE'S BEAST.
WHICH MIGHT NOT HAVE BEEN THE BRIGHTEST MOVE...
I'LL TAKE THAT UNDER ADVISEMENT, ROBERT.
SEE X-MEN UNLIMITED #10 -- Bob.

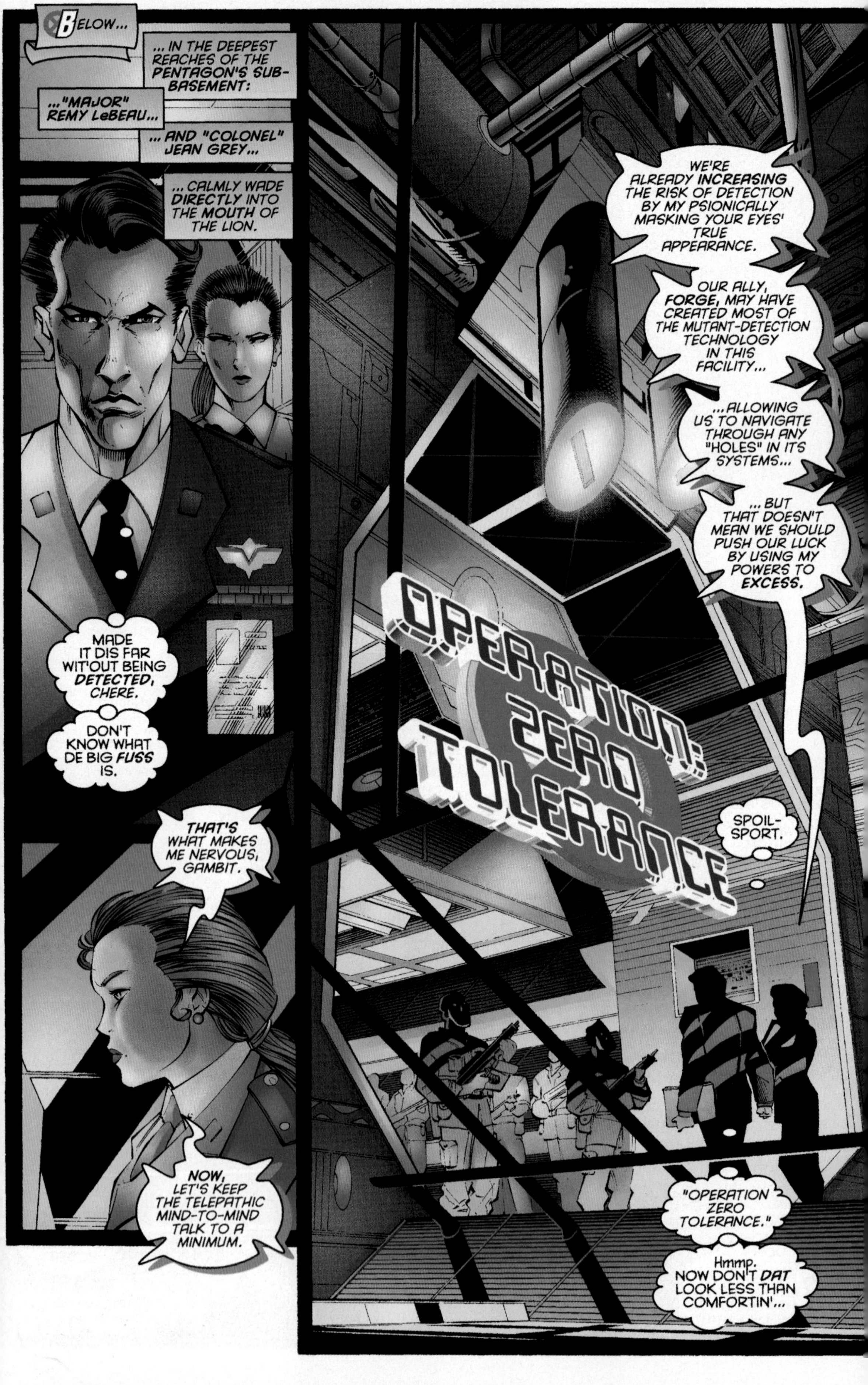
BELOW...
...IN THE DEEPEST REACHES OF THE PENTAGON'S SUB-BASEMENT:
..."MAJOR" REMY LeBEAU...
...AND "COLONEL" JEAN GREY...
...CALMLY WADE DIRECTLY INTO THE MOUTH OF THE LION.
MADE IT DIS FAR WIT'OUT BEING DETECTED, CHERE.
DON'T KNOW WHAT DE BIG FUSS IS.
THAT'S WHAT MAKES ME NERVOUS, GAMBIT.
NOW, LET'S KEEP THE TELEPATHIC MIND-TO-MIND TALK TO A MINIMUM.
WE'RE ALREADY INCREASING THE RISK OF DETECTION BY MY PSIONICALLY MASKING YOUR EYES' TRUE APPEARANCE.
OUR ALLY, FORGE, MAY HAVE CREATED MOST OF THE MUTANT-DETECTION TECHNOLOGY IN THIS FACILITY...
...ALLOWING US TO NAVIGATE THROUGH ANY "HOLES" IN ITS SYSTEMS...
...BUT THAT DOESN'T MEAN WE SHOULD PUSH OUR LUCK BY USING MY POWERS TO EXCESS.
OPERATION: ZERO TOLERANCE
SPOIL-SPORT.
"OPERATION ZERO TOLERANCE."
Hmmp. NOW DON'T DAT LOOK LESS THAN COMFORTIN'...

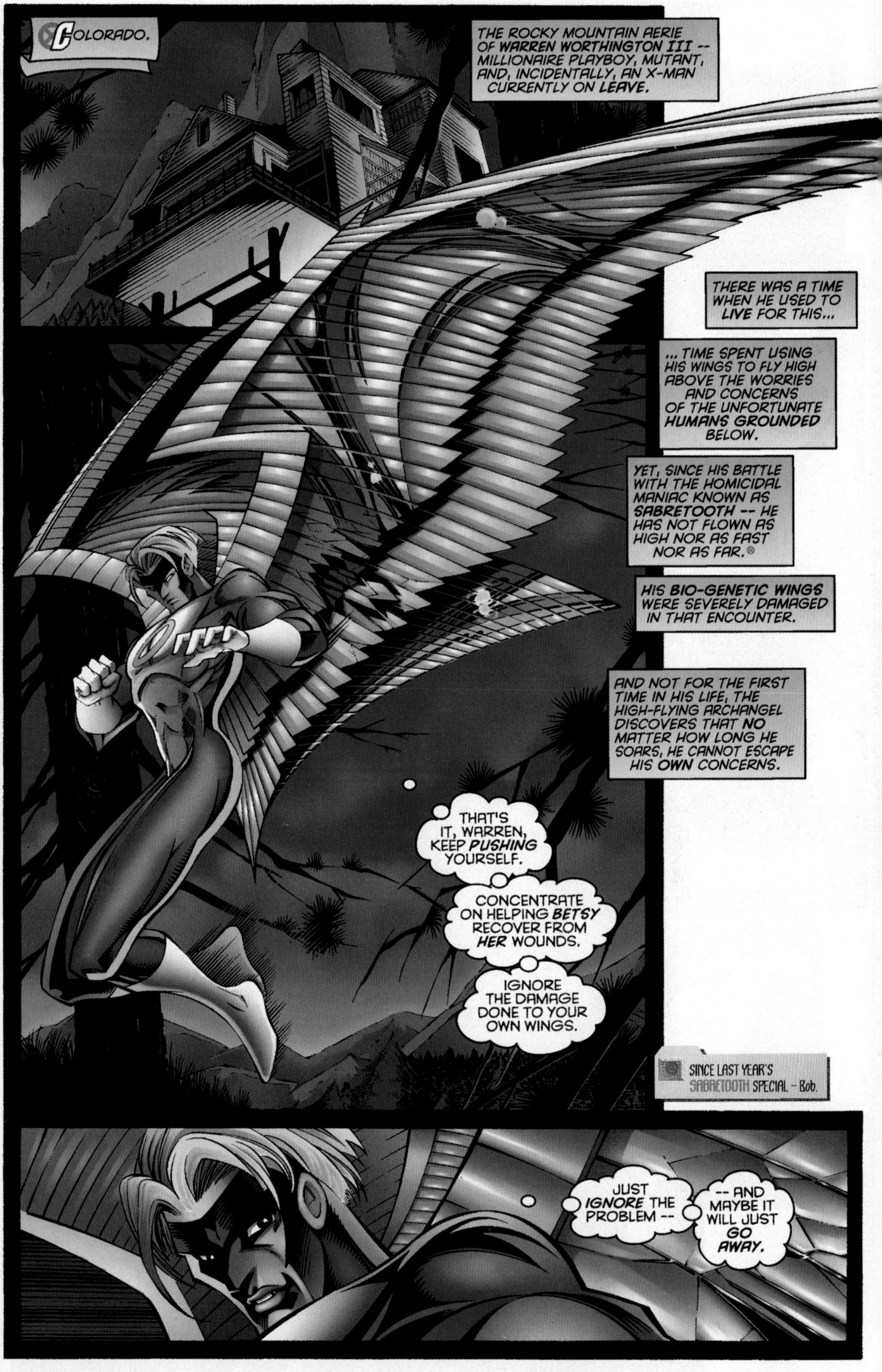
COLORADO.
THE ROCKY MOUNTAIN AERIE OF WARREN WORTHINGTON III -- MILLIONAIRE PLAYBOY, MUTANT, AND, INCIDENTALLY, AN X-MAN CURRENTLY ON LEAVE.
THERE WAS A TIME WHEN HE USED TO LIVE FOR THIS...
...TIME SPENT USING HIS WINGS TO FLY HIGH ABOVE THE WORRIES AND CONCERNS OF THE UNFORTUNATE HUMANS GROUNDED BELOW.
YET, SINCE HIS BATTLE WITH THE HOMICIDAL MANIAC KNOWN AS SABRETOOTH -- HE HAS NOT FLOWN AS HIGH NOR AS FAST NOR AS FAR.
HIS BIO-GENETIC WINGS WERE SEVERELY DAMAGED IN THAT ENCOUNTER.
AND NOT FOR THE FIRST TIME IN HIS LIFE, THE HIGH-FLYING ARCHANGEL DISCOVERS THAT NO MATTER HOW LONG HE SOARS, HE CANNOT ESCAPE HIS OWN CONCERNS.
THAT'S IT, WARREN, KEEP PUSHING YOURSELF.
CONCENTRATE ON HELPING BETSY RECOVER FROM HER WOUNDS.
IGNORE THE DAMAGE DONE TO YOUR OWN WINGS.
SINCE LAST YEAR'S SABRETOOTH SPECIAL -- Bob.
JUST IGNORE THE PROBLEM --
-- AND MAYBE IT WILL JUST GO AWAY.

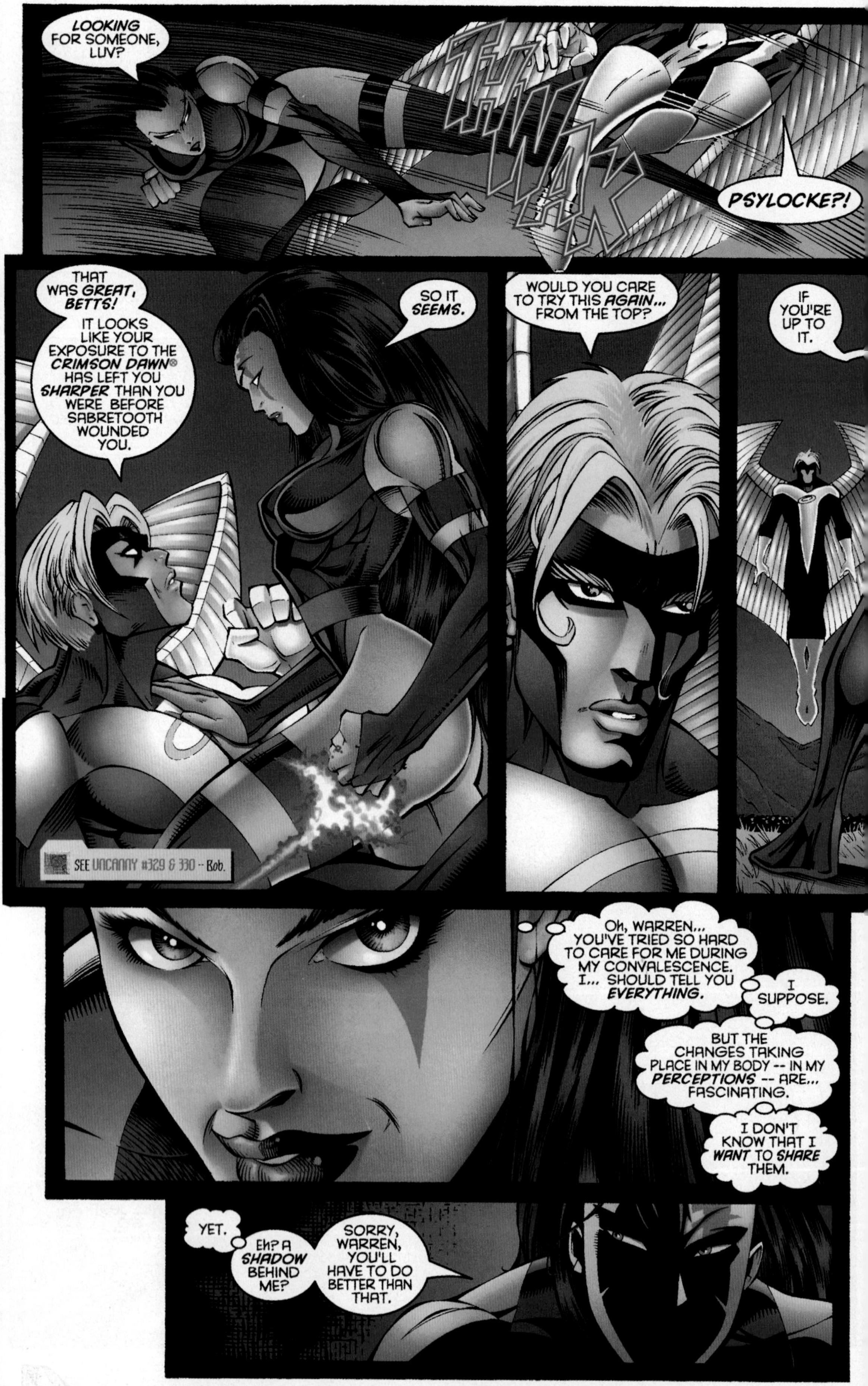
LOOKING FOR SOMEONE, LUV?
THWAK
PSYLOCKE?!
THAT WAS GREAT, BETTS!
IT LOOKS LIKE YOUR EXPOSURE TO THE CRIMSON DAWN® HAS LEFT YOU SHARPER THAN YOU WERE BEFORE SABRETOOTH WOUNDED YOU.
SO IT SEEMS.
SEE UNCANNY #329 & 330 -- Bob.
WOULD YOU CARE TO TRY THIS AGAIN... FROM THE TOP?
IF YOU'RE UP TO IT.
Oh, WARREN... YOU'VE TRIED SO HARD TO CARE FOR ME DURING MY CONVALESCENCE. I... SHOULD TELL YOU EVERYTHING.
I SUPPOSE.
BUT THE CHANGES TAKING PLACE IN MY BODY -- IN MY PERCEPTIONS -- ARE... FASCINATING.
I DON'T KNOW THAT I WANT TO SHARE THEM.
YET.
Eh? A SHADOW BEHIND ME?
SORRY, WARREN, YOU'LL HAVE TO DO BETTER THAN THAT.

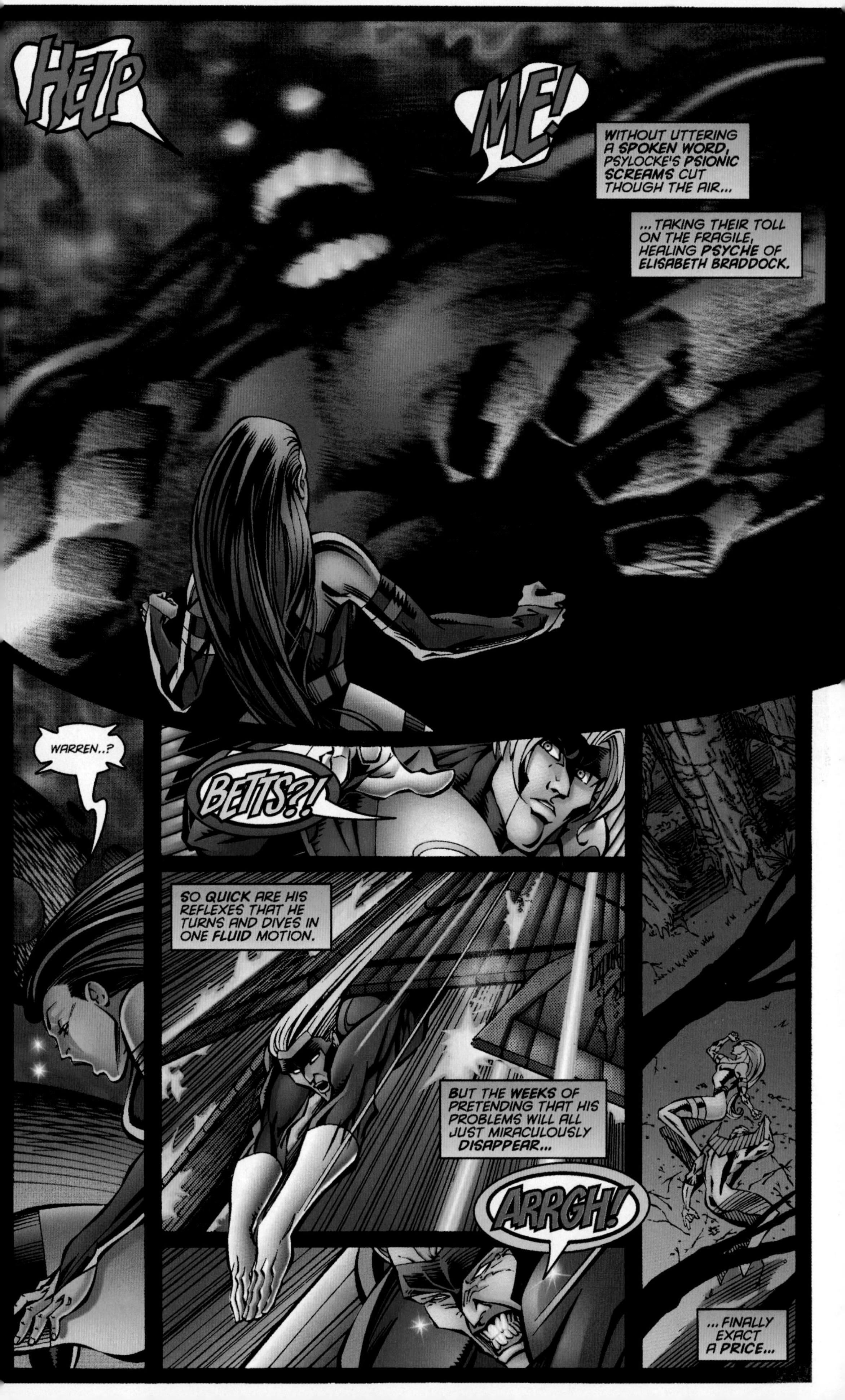
HELP
ME!
WITHOUT UTTERING A SPOKEN WORD, PSYLOCKE'S PSIONIC SCREAMS CUT THOUGH THE AIR...
...TAKING THEIR TOLL ON THE FRAGILE, HEALING PSYCHE OF ELISABETH BRADDOCK.
WARREN..?
BETTS?!
SO QUICK ARE HIS REFLEXES THAT HE TURNS AND DIVES IN ONE FLUID MOTION.
BUT THE WEEKS OF PRETENDING THAT HIS PROBLEMS WILL ALL JUST MIRACULOUSLY DISAPPEAR...
ARRGH!
...FINALLY EXACT A PRICE...

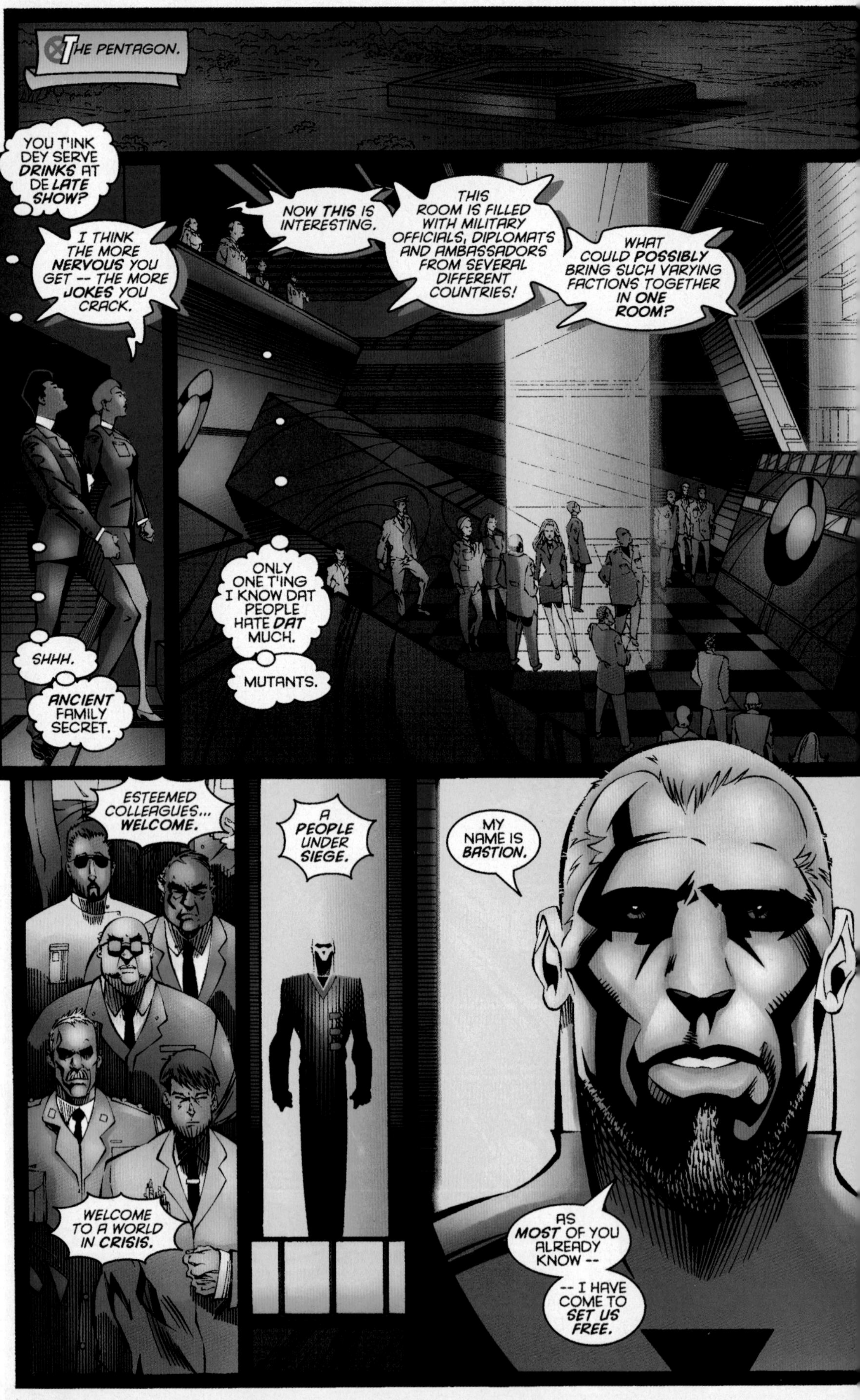
THE PENTAGON.
YOU T'INK DEY SERVE DRINKS AT DE LATE SHOW?
I THINK THE MORE NERVOUS YOU GET -- THE MORE JOKES YOU CRACK.
NOW THIS IS INTERESTING.
THIS ROOM IS FILLED WITH MILITARY OFFICIALS, DIPLOMATS AND AMBASSADORS FROM SEVERAL DIFFERENT COUNTRIES!
WHAT COULD POSSIBLY BRING SUCH VARYING FACTIONS TOGETHER IN ONE ROOM?
ONLY ONE T'ING I KNOW DAT PEOPLE HATE DAT MUCH.
MUTANTS.
SHHH.
ANCIENT FAMILY SECRET.
ESTEEMED COLLEAGUES... WELCOME.
WELCOME TO A WORLD IN CRISIS.
A PEOPLE UNDER SIEGE.
MY NAME IS BASTION.
AS MOST OF YOU ALREADY KNOW --
-- I HAVE COME TO SET US FREE.

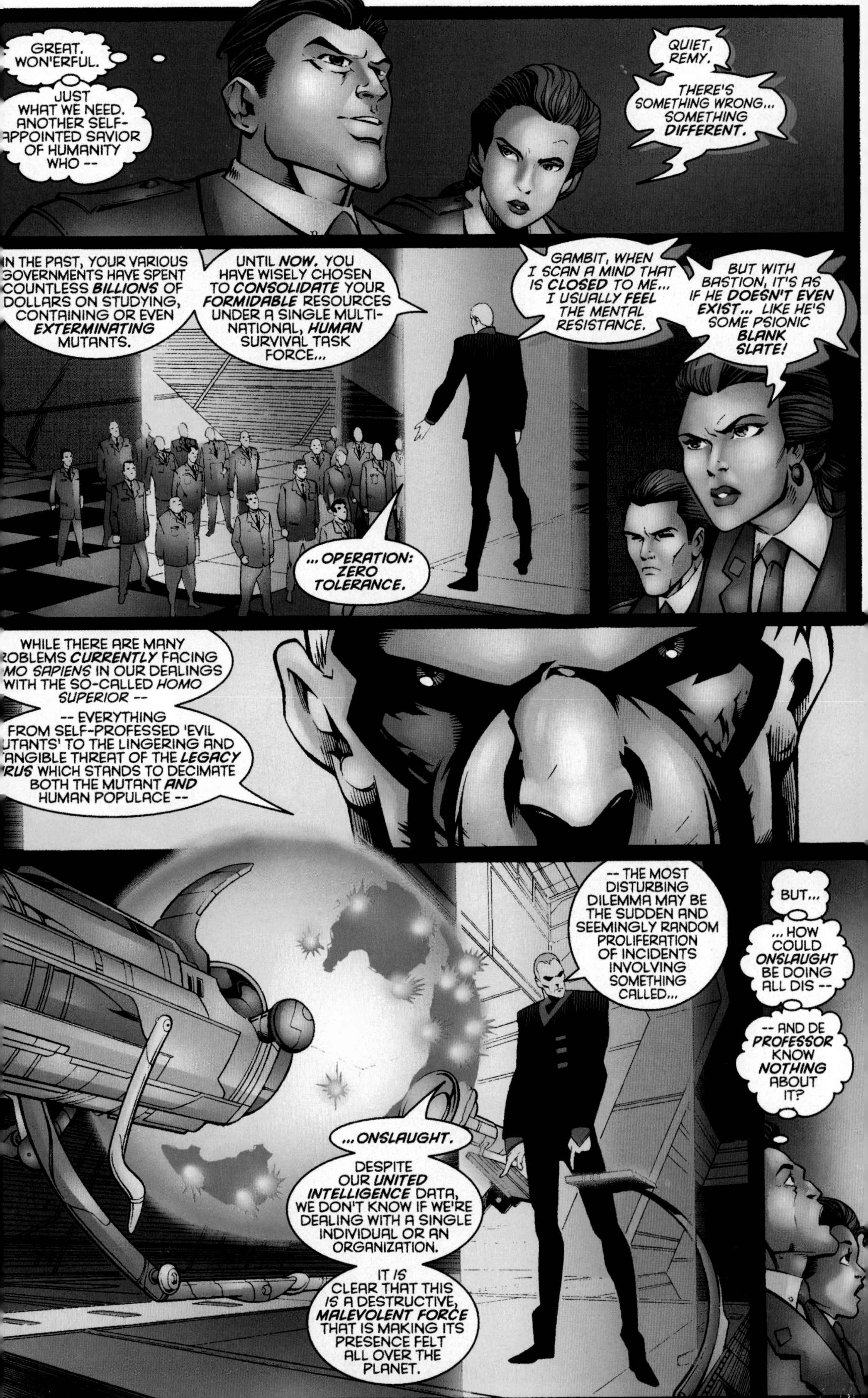

GREAT, WON'ERFUL.
JUST WHAT WE NEED. ANOTHER SELF-APPOINTED SAVIOR OF HUMANITY WHO --
QUIET, REMY.
THERE'S SOMETHING WRONG... SOMETHING DIFFERENT.
IN THE PAST, YOUR VARIOUS GOVERNMENTS HAVE SPENT COUNTLESS BILLIONS OF DOLLARS ON STUDYING, CONTAINING OR EVEN EXTERMINATING MUTANTS.
UNTIL NOW. YOU HAVE WISELY CHOSEN TO CONSOLIDATE YOUR FORMIDABLE RESOURCES UNDER A SINGLE MULTI-NATIONAL, HUMAN SURVIVAL TASK FORCE...
...OPERATION: ZERO TOLERANCE.
GAMBIT, WHEN I SCAN A MIND THAT IS CLOSED TO ME... I USUALLY FEEL THE MENTAL RESISTANCE.
BUT WITH BASTION, IT'S AS IF HE DOESN'T EVEN EXIST... LIKE HE'S SOME PSIONIC BLANK SLATE!
WHILE THERE ARE MANY PROBLEMS CURRENTLY FACING HOMO SAPIENS IN OUR DEALINGS WITH THE SO-CALLED HOMO SUPERIOR --
-- EVERYTHING FROM SELF-PROFESSED 'EVIL MUTANTS' TO THE LINGERING AND TANGIBLE THREAT OF THE LEGACY VIRUS WHICH STANDS TO DECIMATE BOTH THE MUTANT AND HUMAN POPULACE --
-- THE MOST DISTURBING DILEMMA MAY BE THE SUDDEN AND SEEMINGLY RANDOM PROLIFERATION OF INCIDENTS INVOLVING SOMETHING CALLED...
...ONSLAUGHT.
DESPITE OUR UNITED INTELLIGENCE DATA, WE DON'T KNOW IF WE'RE DEALING WITH A SINGLE INDIVIDUAL OR AN ORGANIZATION.
IT IS CLEAR THAT THIS IS A DESTRUCTIVE, MALEVOLENT FORCE THAT IS MAKING ITS PRESENCE FELT ALL OVER THE PLANET.
BUT...
...HOW COULD ONSLAUGHT BE DOING ALL DIS --
-- AND DE PROFESSOR KNOW NOTHING ABOUT IT?

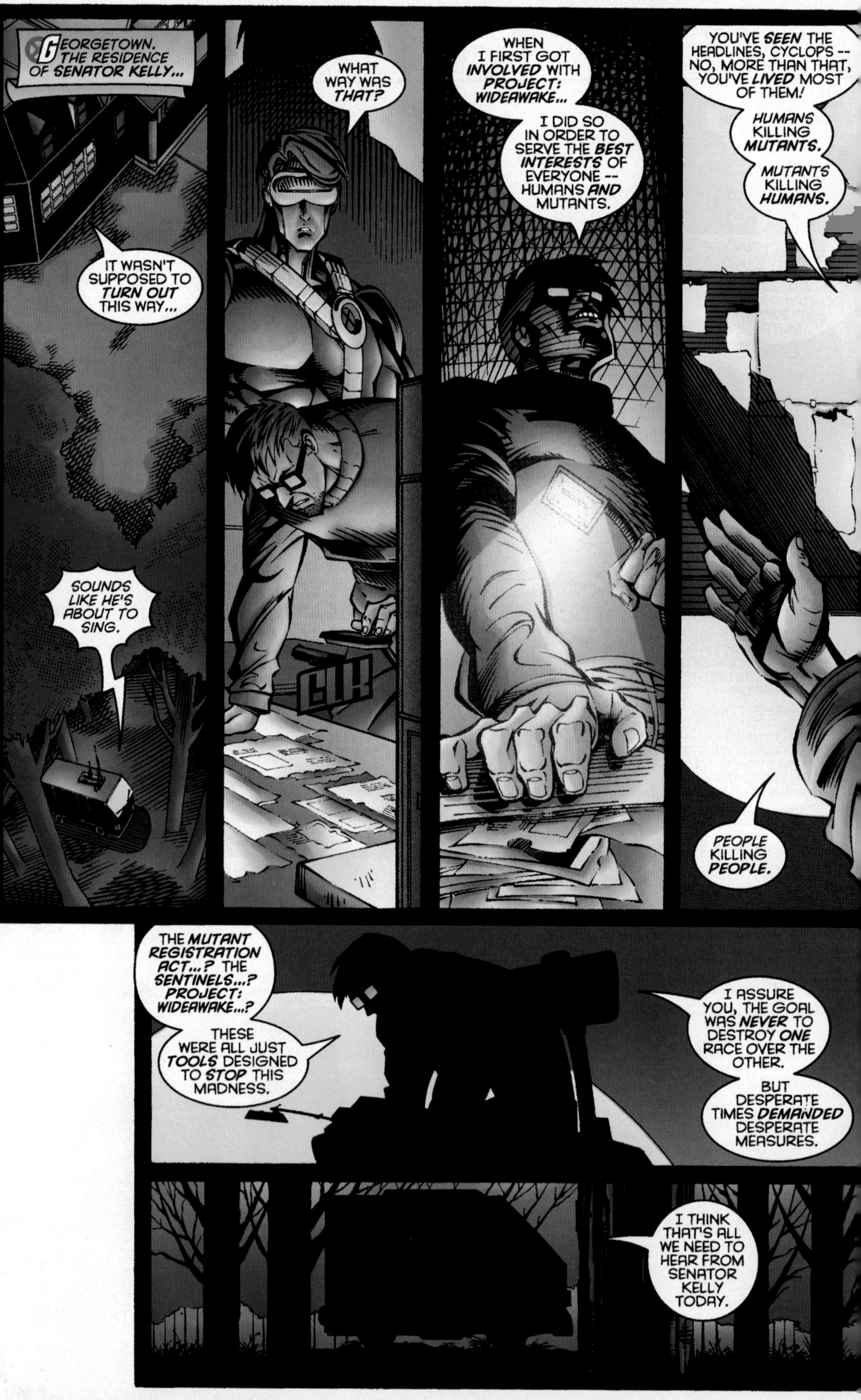
GEORGETOWN. THE RESIDENCE OF SENATOR KELLY...
IT WASN'T SUPPOSED TO TURN OUT THIS WAY...
SOUNDS LIKE HE'S ABOUT TO SING.
WHAT WAY WAS THAT?
CLIK
WHEN I FIRST GOT INVOLVED WITH PROJECT: WIDEAWAKE...
I DID SO IN ORDER TO SERVE THE BEST INTERESTS OF EVERYONE -- HUMANS AND MUTANTS.
YOU'VE SEEN THE HEADLINES, CYCLOPS -- NO, MORE THAN THAT, YOU'VE LIVED MOST OF THEM!
HUMANS KILLING MUTANTS.
MUTANTS KILLING HUMANS.
PEOPLE KILLING PEOPLE.
THE MUTANT REGISTRATION ACT...? THE SENTINELS...? PROJECT: WIDEAWAKE...?
THESE WERE ALL JUST TOOLS DESIGNED TO STOP THIS MADNESS.
I ASSURE YOU, THE GOAL WAS NEVER TO DESTROY ONE RACE OVER THE OTHER.
BUT DESPERATE TIMES DEMANDED DESPERATE MEASURES.
I THINK THAT'S ALL WE NEED TO HEAR FROM SENATOR KELLY TODAY.

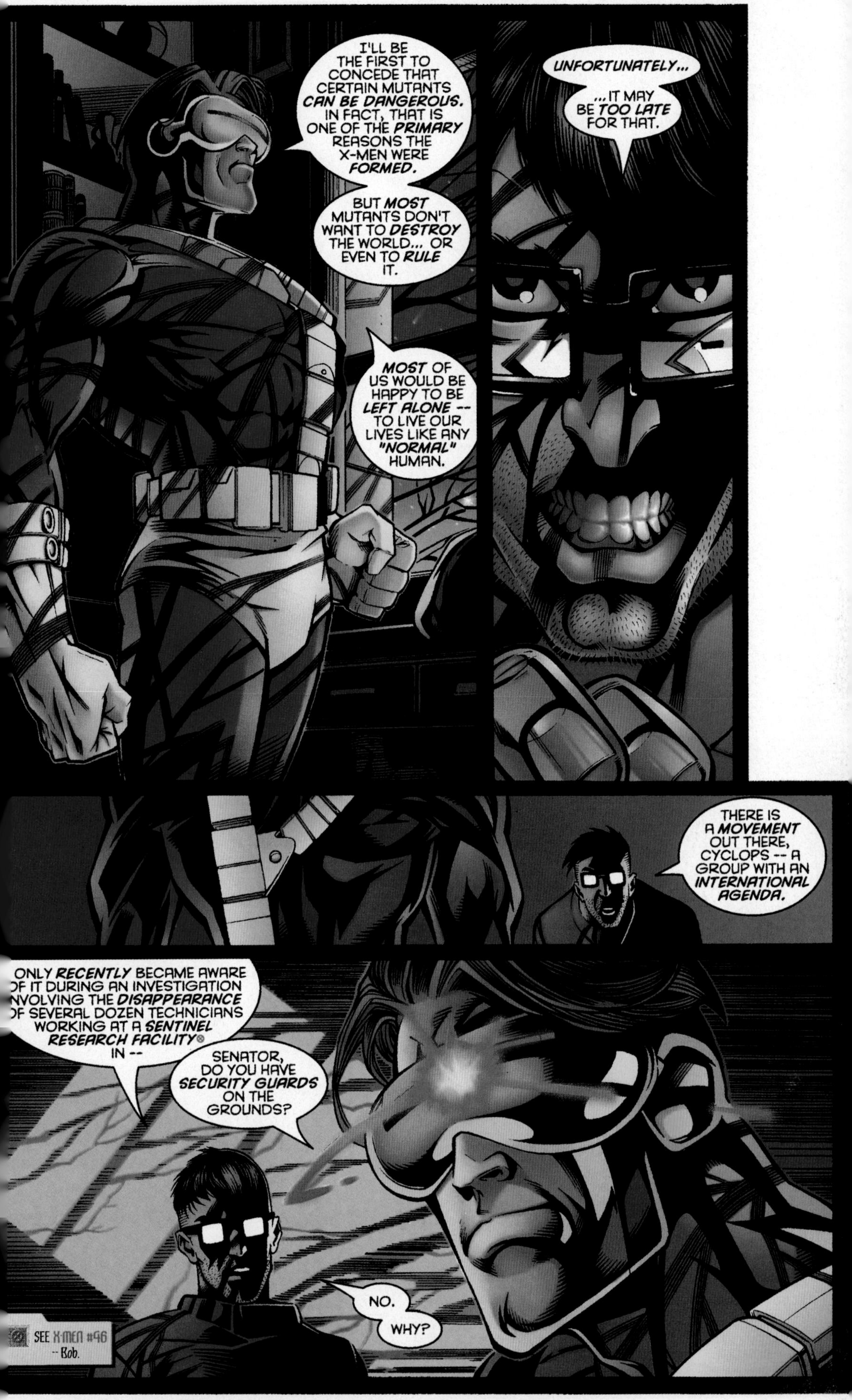

I'LL BE THE FIRST TO CONCEDE THAT CERTAIN MUTANTS CAN BE DANGEROUS. IN FACT, THAT IS ONE OF THE PRIMARY REASONS THE X-MEN WERE FORMED.
BUT MOST MUTANTS DON'T WANT TO DESTROY THE WORLD... OR EVEN TO RULE IT.
MOST OF US WOULD BE HAPPY TO BE LEFT ALONE -- TO LIVE OUR LIVES LIKE ANY "NORMAL" HUMAN.
UNFORTUNATELY...
...IT MAY BE TOO LATE FOR THAT.
THERE IS A MOVEMENT OUT THERE, CYCLOPS -- A GROUP WITH AN INTERNATIONAL AGENDA.
ONLY RECENTLY BECAME AWARE OF IT DURING AN INVESTIGATION INVOLVING THE DISAPPEARANCE OF SEVERAL DOZEN TECHNICIANS WORKING AT A SENTINEL RESEARCH FACILITY IN --
SENATOR, DO YOU HAVE SECURITY GUARDS ON THE GROUNDS?
NO.
WHY?
SEE X-MEN #46 -- Bob.

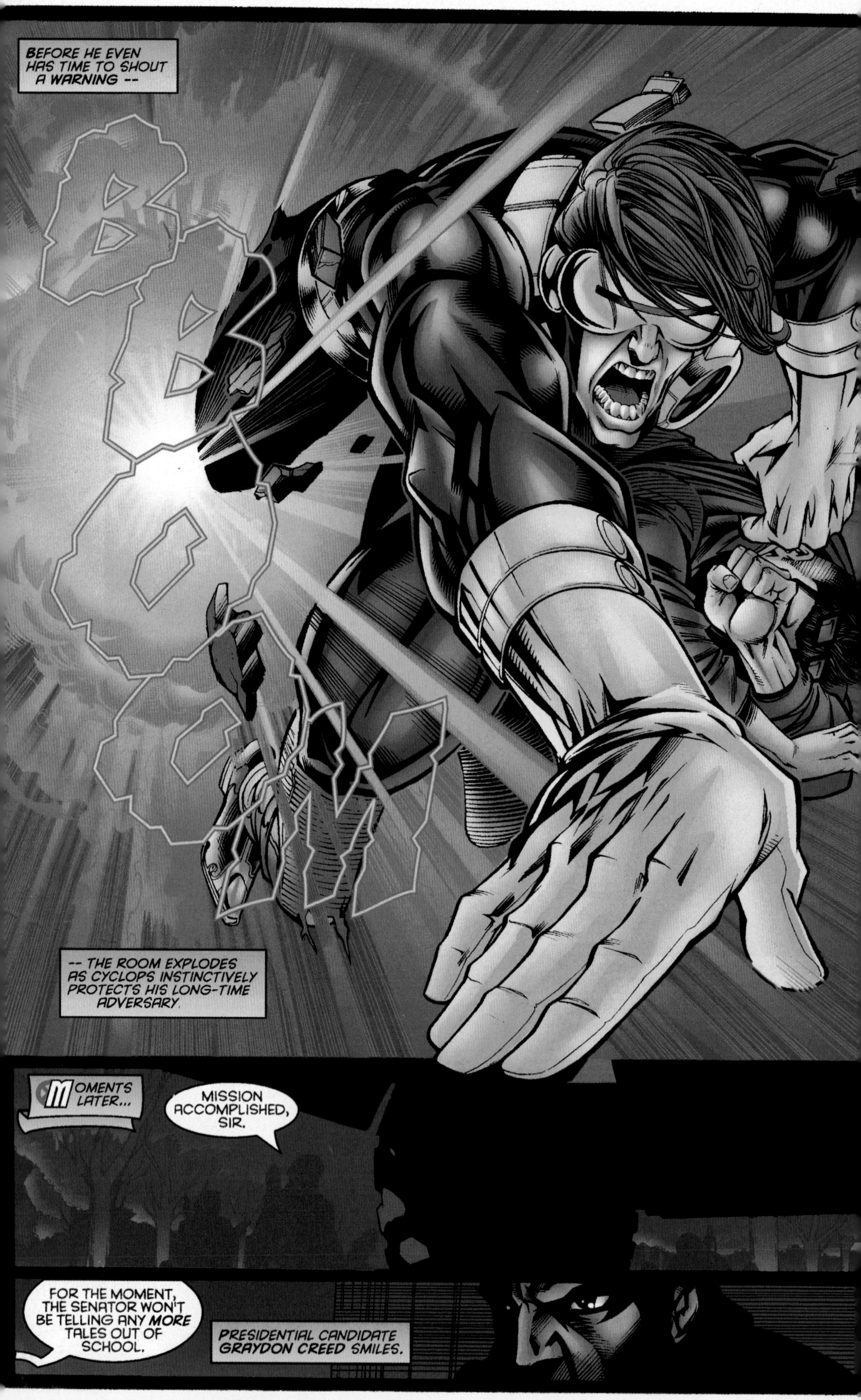
BEFORE HE EVEN HAS TIME TO SHOUT A WARNING --
BOOOM
-- THE ROOM EXPLODES AS CYCLOPS INSTINCTIVELY PROTECTS HIS LONG-TIME ADVERSARY.
MOMENTS LATER...
MISSION ACCOMPLISHED, SIR.
FOR THE MOMENT, THE SENATOR WON'T BE TELLING ANY MORE TALES OUT OF SCHOOL.
PRESIDENTIAL CANDIDATE GRAYDON CREED SMILES.

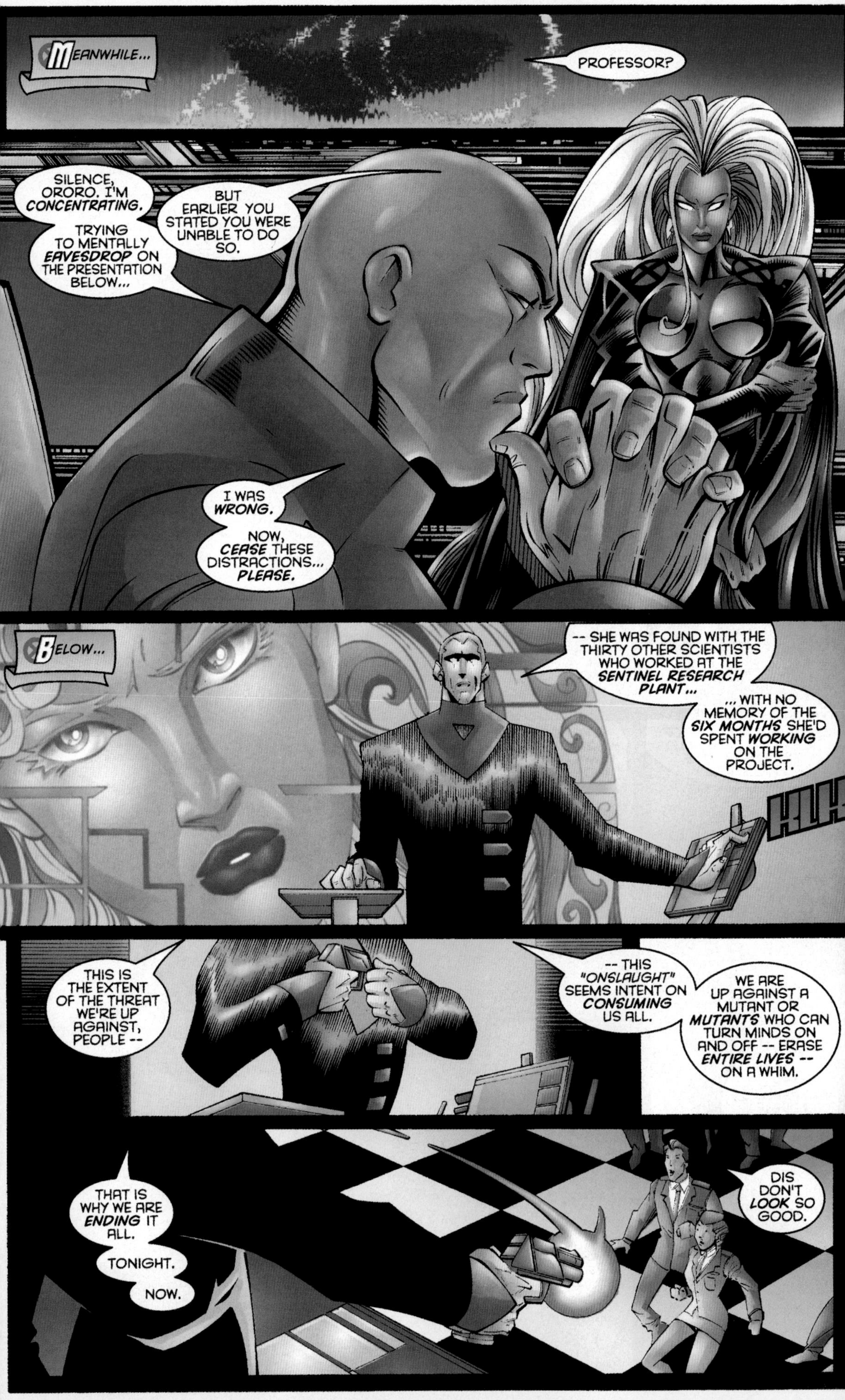
MEANWHILE...
PROFESSOR?
SILENCE, ORORO. I'M CONCENTRATING.
TRYING TO MENTALLY EAVESDROP ON THE PRESENTATION BELOW...
BUT EARLIER YOU STATED YOU WERE UNABLE TO DO SO.
I WAS WRONG.
NOW, CEASE THESE DISTRACTIONS... PLEASE.
BELOW...
-- SHE WAS FOUND WITH THE THIRTY OTHER SCIENTISTS WHO WORKED AT THE SENTINEL RESEARCH PLANT...
... WITH NO MEMORY OF THE SIX MONTHS SHE'D SPENT WORKING ON THE PROJECT.
THIS IS THE EXTENT OF THE THREAT WE'RE UP AGAINST, PEOPLE --
-- THIS "ONSLAUGHT" SEEMS INTENT ON CONSUMING US ALL.
WE ARE UP AGAINST A MUTANT OR MUTANTS WHO CAN TURN MINDS ON AND OFF -- ERASE ENTIRE LIVES -- ON A WHIM.
THAT IS WHY WE ARE ENDING IT ALL.
TONIGHT.
NOW.
DIS DON'T LOOK SO GOOD.

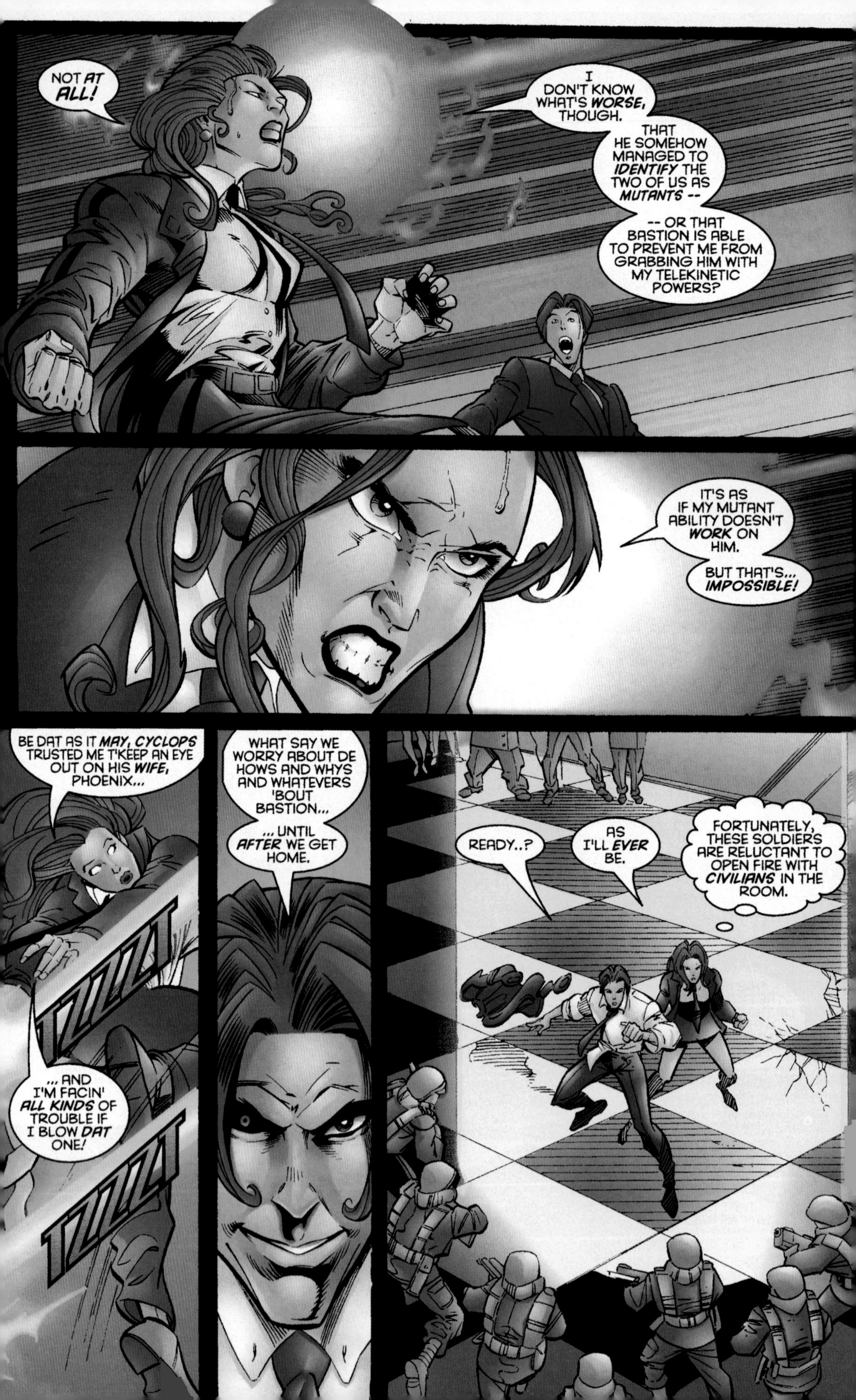
NOT AT ALL!
I DON'T KNOW WHAT'S WORSE, THOUGH.
THAT HE SOMEHOW MANAGED TO IDENTIFY THE TWO OF US AS MUTANTS --
-- OR THAT BASTION IS ABLE TO PREVENT ME FROM GRABBING HIM WITH MY TELEKINETIC POWERS?
IT'S AS IF MY MUTANT ABILITY DOESN'T WORK ON HIM.
BUT THAT'S... IMPOSSIBLE!
BE DAT AS IT MAY, CYCLOPS TRUSTED ME T'KEEP AN EYE OUT ON HIS WIFE, PHOENIX...
TZZZT
... AND I'M FACIN' ALL KINDS OF TROUBLE IF I BLOW DAT ONE!
TZZZT
WHAT SAY WE WORRY ABOUT DE HOWS AND WHYS AND WHATEVERS 'BOUT BASTION...
... UNTIL AFTER WE GET HOME.
READY..?
AS I'LL EVER BE.
FORTUNATELY, THESE SOLDIERS ARE RELUCTANT TO OPEN FIRE WITH CIVILIANS IN THE ROOM.

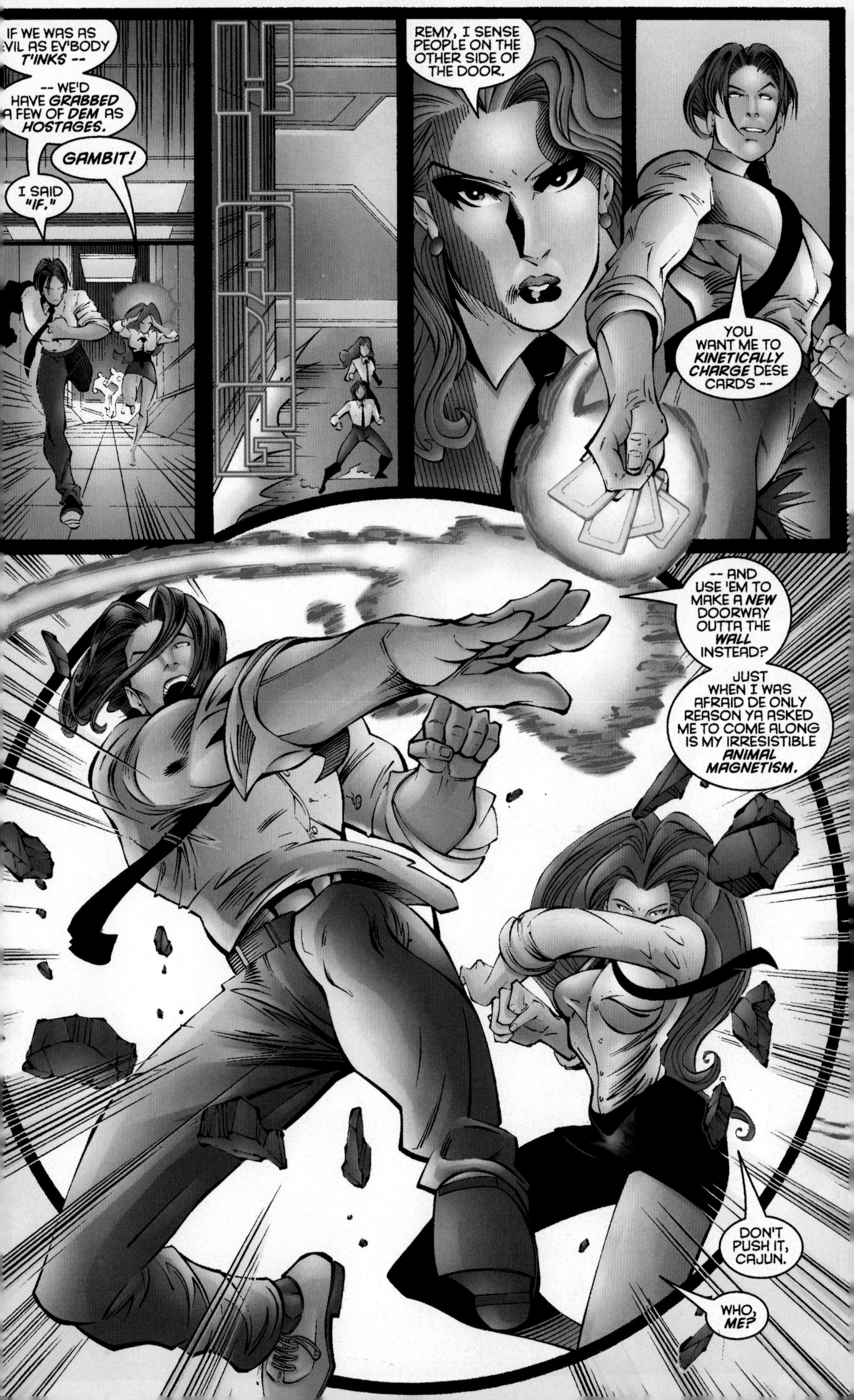
IF WE WAS AS EVIL AS EV'BODY T'INKS --
-- WE'D HAVE GRABBED A FEW OF DEM AS HOSTAGES.
GAMBIT!
I SAID "IF."
REMY, I SENSE PEOPLE ON THE OTHER SIDE OF THE DOOR.
YOU WANT ME TO KINETICALLY CHARGE DESE CARDS --
-- AND USE 'EM TO MAKE A NEW DOORWAY OUTTA THE WALL INSTEAD?
JUST WHEN I WAS AFRAID DE ONLY REASON YA ASKED ME TO COME ALONG IS MY IRRESISTIBLE ANIMAL MAGNETISM.
DON'T PUSH IT, CAJUN.
WHO, ME?

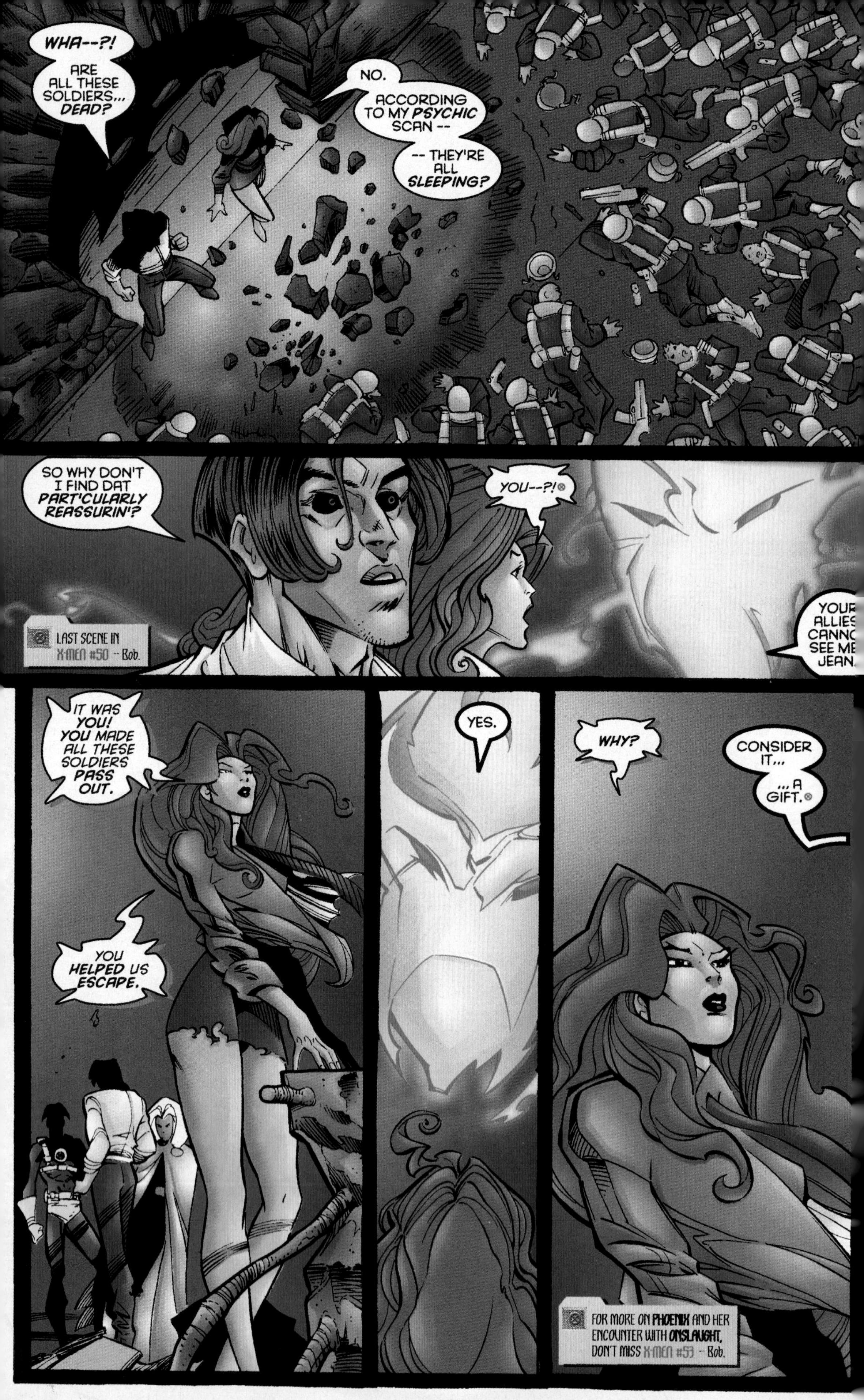
WHA--?! ARE ALL THESE SOLDIERS... DEAD?
NO. ACCORDING TO MY PSYCHIC SCAN --
-- THEY'RE ALL SLEEPING?
SO WHY DON'T I FIND DAT PART'CULARLY REASSURIN'?
YOU--?!
LAST SCENE IN X-MEN #50 -- Bob.
YOUR ALLIES CANNO SEE ME JEAN.
IT WAS YOU! YOU MADE ALL THESE SOLDIERS PASS OUT.
YOU HELPED US ESCAPE.
YES.
WHY?
CONSIDER IT... ...A GIFT.
FOR MORE ON PHOENIX AND HER ENCOUNTER WITH ONSLAUGHT, DON'T MISS X-MEN #53 -- Bob.

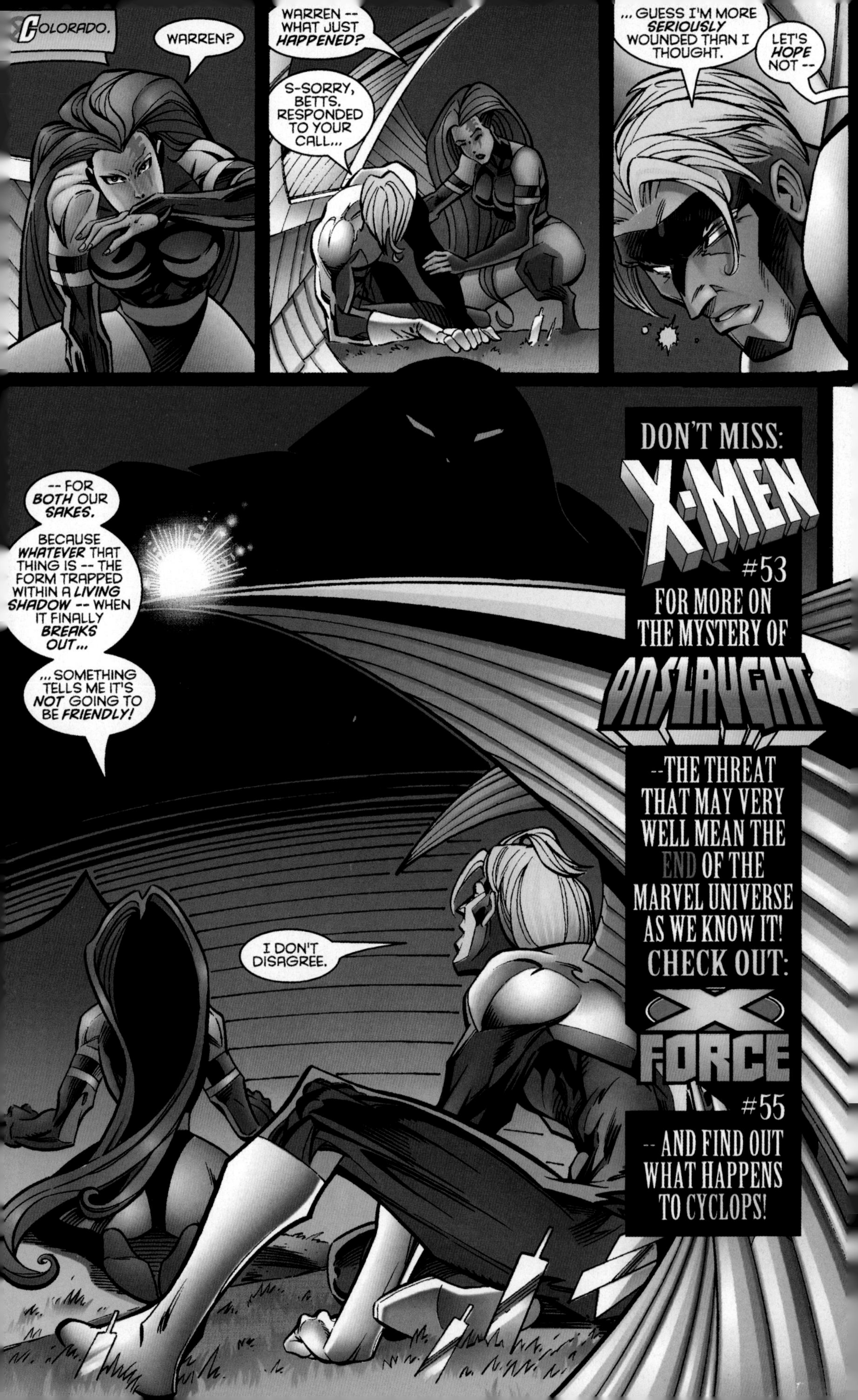

COLORADO.
WARREN?
WARREN -- WHAT JUST HAPPENED?
S-SORRY, BETTS. RESPONDED TO YOUR CALL...
...GUESS I'M MORE SERIOUSLY WOUNDED THAN I THOUGHT.
LET'S HOPE NOT --
-- FOR BOTH OUR SAKES.
BECAUSE WHATEVER THAT THING IS -- THE FORM TRAPPED WITHIN A LIVING SHADOW -- WHEN IT FINALLY BREAKS OUT...
...SOMETHING TELLS ME IT'S NOT GOING TO BE FRIENDLY!
I DON'T DISAGREE.
DON'T MISS:
X-MEN
#53
FOR MORE ON THE MYSTERY OF
ONSLAUGHT
--THE THREAT THAT MAY VERY WELL MEAN THE END OF THE MARVEL UNIVERSE AS WE KNOW IT!
CHECK OUT:
X FORCE
#55
-- AND FIND OUT WHAT HAPPENS TO CYCLOPS!

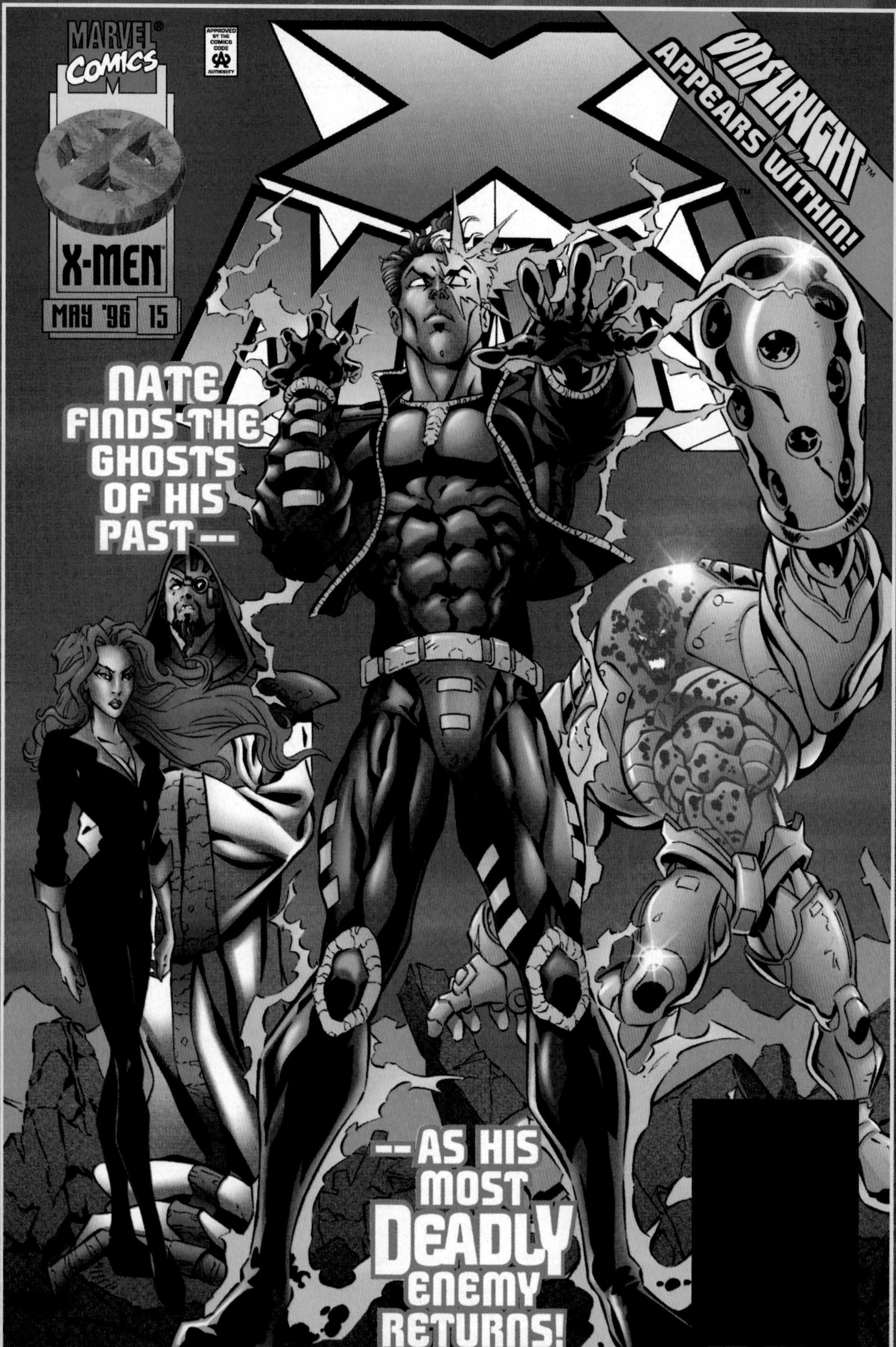
MARVEL® COMICS
APPROVED BY THE COMICS CODE AUTHORITY
X-MEN®
MAY '96 15
ONSLAUGHT™ APPEARS WITHIN!
NATE FINDS THE GHOSTS OF HIS PAST --
-- AS HIS MOST DEADLY ENEMY RETURNS!

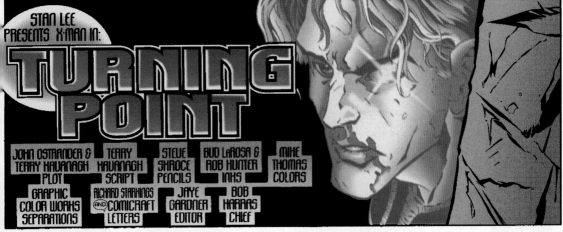

STAN LEE PRESENTS X-MAN IN:

TURNING POINT

JOHN OSTRANDER & TERRY KAVANAGH
PLOT

TERRY KAVANAGH
SCRIPT

STEVE SKROCE
PENCILS

BUD LaROSA & ROB HUNTER
INKS

MIKE THOMAS
COLORS

GRAPHIC COLOR WORKS SEPARATIONS

RICHARD STARKINGS AND COMICRAFT LETTERS

JAYE GARDNER
EDITOR

BOB HARRAS
CHIEF

FOR THE FIRST TIME IN FAR TOO MANY MONTHS...

...THE WANDERER KNOWS EXACTLY WHERE HE IS.

NATE GREY RECOGNIZES THIS WORLD WITHOUT A FUTURE --

-- THIS LAND OF LITTLE LIGHT, AND LESS COLOR.

HE REMEMBERS IT AS A PLACE OF PURPOSE AND MEANING TO HIM...

...A PLACE FAMILIAR WITH FRIENDS AND WOULD-BE FAMILY.

WELCOME *HOME*, BOY.

THE *PRODIGAL SON* FINALLY RETURNS.

ARE YOU *REALLY* --

-- CAN IT POSSIBLY BE --

BUT SOMETHING IS WRONG HERE...

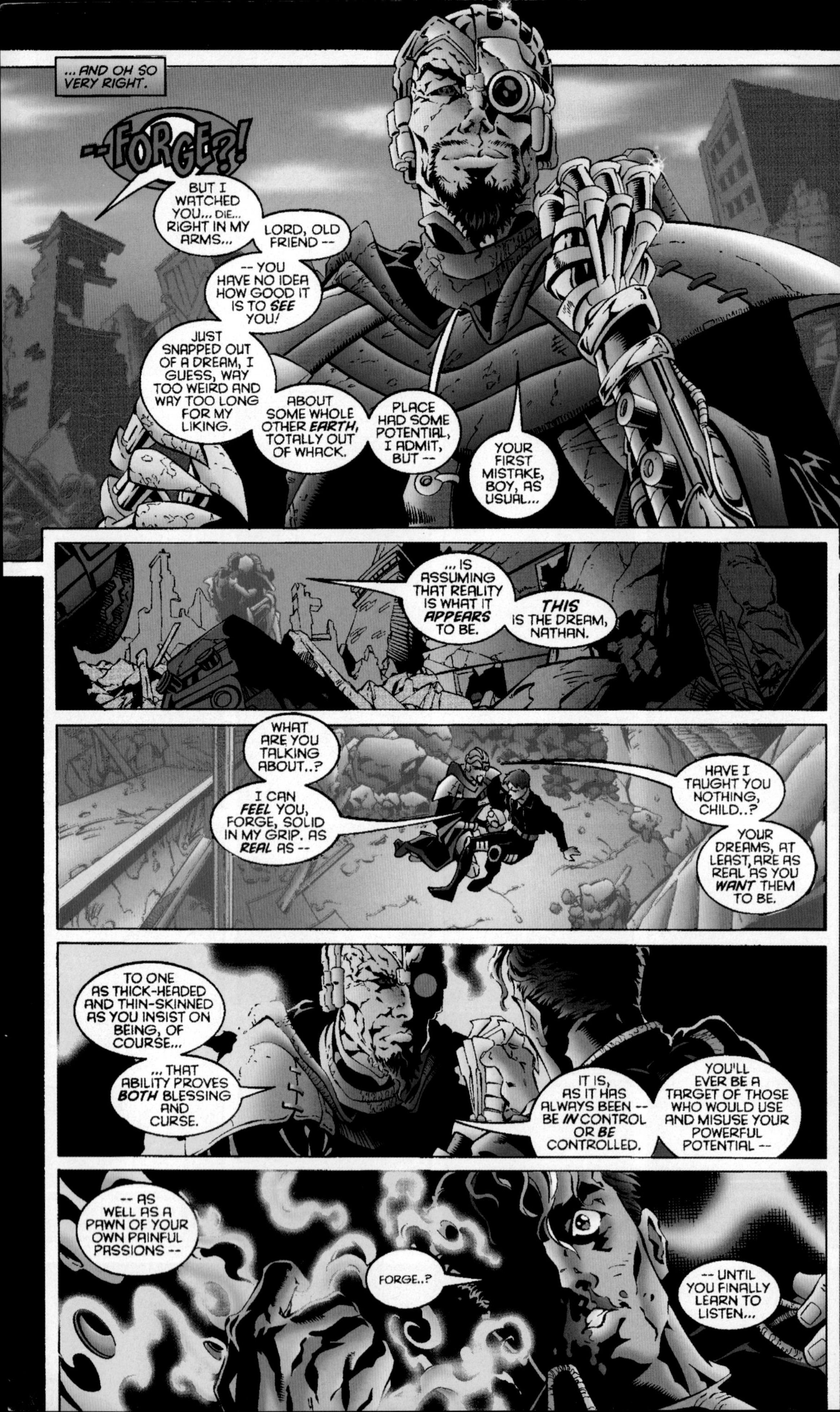
...AND OH SO VERY RIGHT.
--FORGE?!
BUT I WATCHED YOU... DIE... RIGHT IN MY ARMS...
LORD, OLD FRIEND --
-- YOU HAVE NO IDEA HOW GOOD IT IS TO SEE YOU!
JUST SNAPPED OUT OF A DREAM, I GUESS, WAY TOO WEIRD AND WAY TOO LONG FOR MY LIKING.
ABOUT SOME WHOLE OTHER EARTH, TOTALLY OUT OF WHACK.
PLACE HAD SOME POTENTIAL, I ADMIT, BUT --
YOUR FIRST MISTAKE, BOY, AS USUAL...
...IS ASSUMING THAT REALITY IS WHAT IT APPEARS TO BE.
THIS IS THE DREAM, NATHAN.
WHAT ARE YOU TALKING ABOUT..?
I CAN FEEL YOU, FORGE, SOLID IN MY GRIP. AS REAL AS --
HAVE I TAUGHT YOU NOTHING, CHILD..?
YOUR DREAMS, AT LEAST, ARE AS REAL AS YOU WANT THEM TO BE.
TO ONE AS THICK-HEADED AND THIN-SKINNED AS YOU INSIST ON BEING, OF COURSE...
...THAT ABILITY PROVES BOTH BLESSING AND CURSE.
IT IS, AS IT HAS ALWAYS BEEN -- BE IN CONTROL OR BE CONTROLLED.
YOU'LL EVER BE A TARGET OF THOSE WHO WOULD USE AND MISUSE YOUR POWERFUL POTENTIAL --
-- AS WELL AS A PAWN OF YOUR OWN PAINFUL PASSIONS --
FORGE..?
-- UNTIL YOU FINALLY LEARN TO LISTEN...

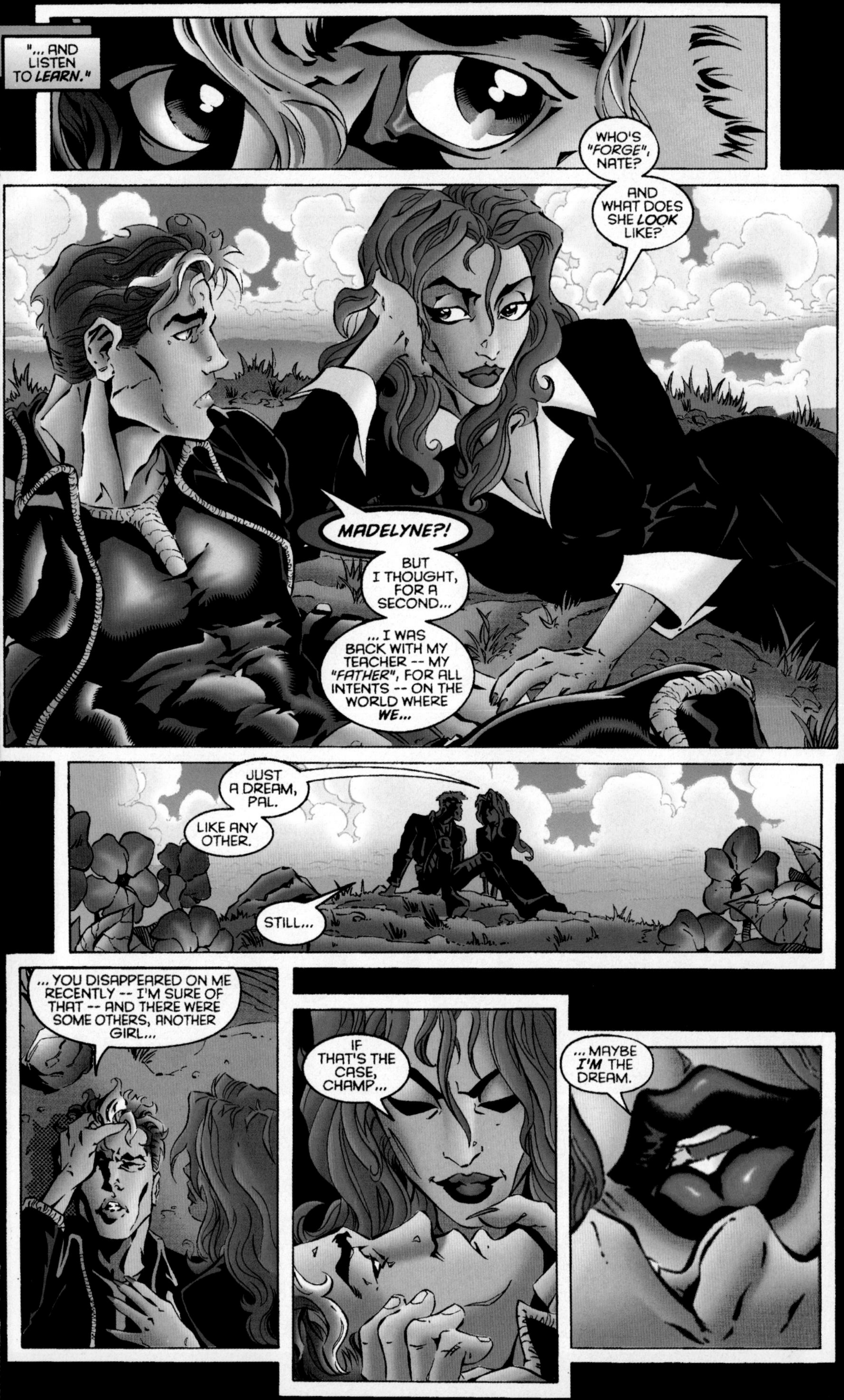
"... AND LISTEN TO *LEARN*."
WHO'S "*FORGE*", NATE?
AND WHAT DOES SHE *LOOK* LIKE?
MADELYNE?!
BUT I THOUGHT, FOR A SECOND...
... I WAS BACK WITH MY TEACHER -- MY "*FATHER*", FOR ALL INTENTS -- ON THE WORLD WHERE *WE*...
JUST A DREAM, PAL.
LIKE ANY OTHER.
STILL...
... YOU DISAPPEARED ON ME RECENTLY -- I'M SURE OF THAT -- AND THERE WERE SOME OTHERS, ANOTHER GIRL...
IF THAT'S THE CASE, CHAMP...
... MAYBE *I'M* THE DREAM.

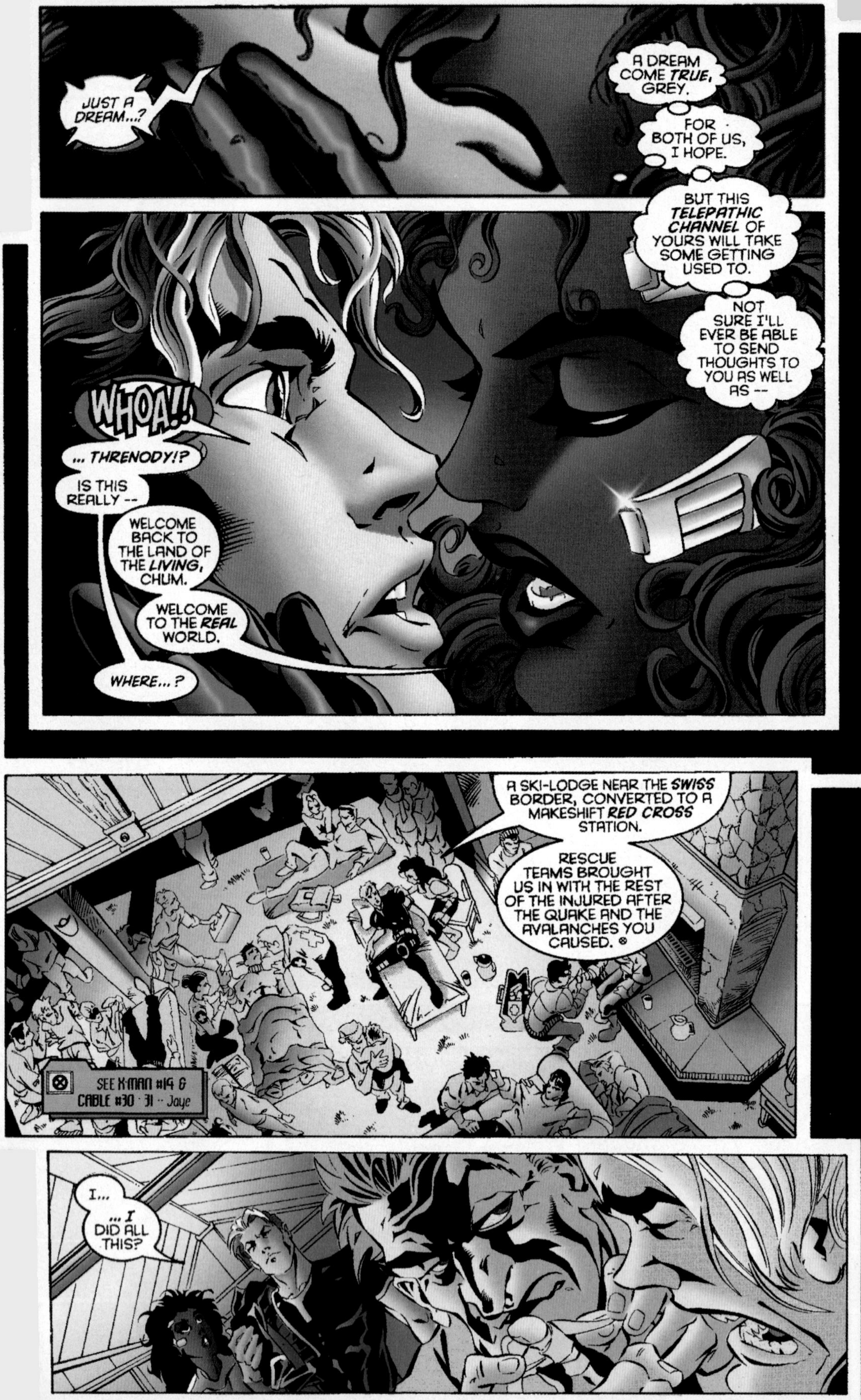
JUST A DREAM...?
A DREAM COME TRUE, GREY.
FOR BOTH OF US, I HOPE.
BUT THIS TELEPATHIC CHANNEL OF YOURS WILL TAKE SOME GETTING USED TO.
NOT SURE I'LL EVER BE ABLE TO SEND THOUGHTS TO YOU AS WELL AS --
WHOA!!
... THRENODY!?
IS THIS REALLY --
WELCOME BACK TO THE LAND OF THE LIVING, CHUM.
WELCOME TO THE REAL WORLD.
WHERE...?
A SKI-LODGE NEAR THE SWISS BORDER, CONVERTED TO A MAKESHIFT RED CROSS STATION.
RESCUE TEAMS BROUGHT US IN WITH THE REST OF THE INJURED AFTER THE QUAKE AND THE AVALANCHES YOU CAUSED.
SEE X-MAN #14 & CABLE #30 · 31 -- Jaye
I...
... I DID ALL THIS?

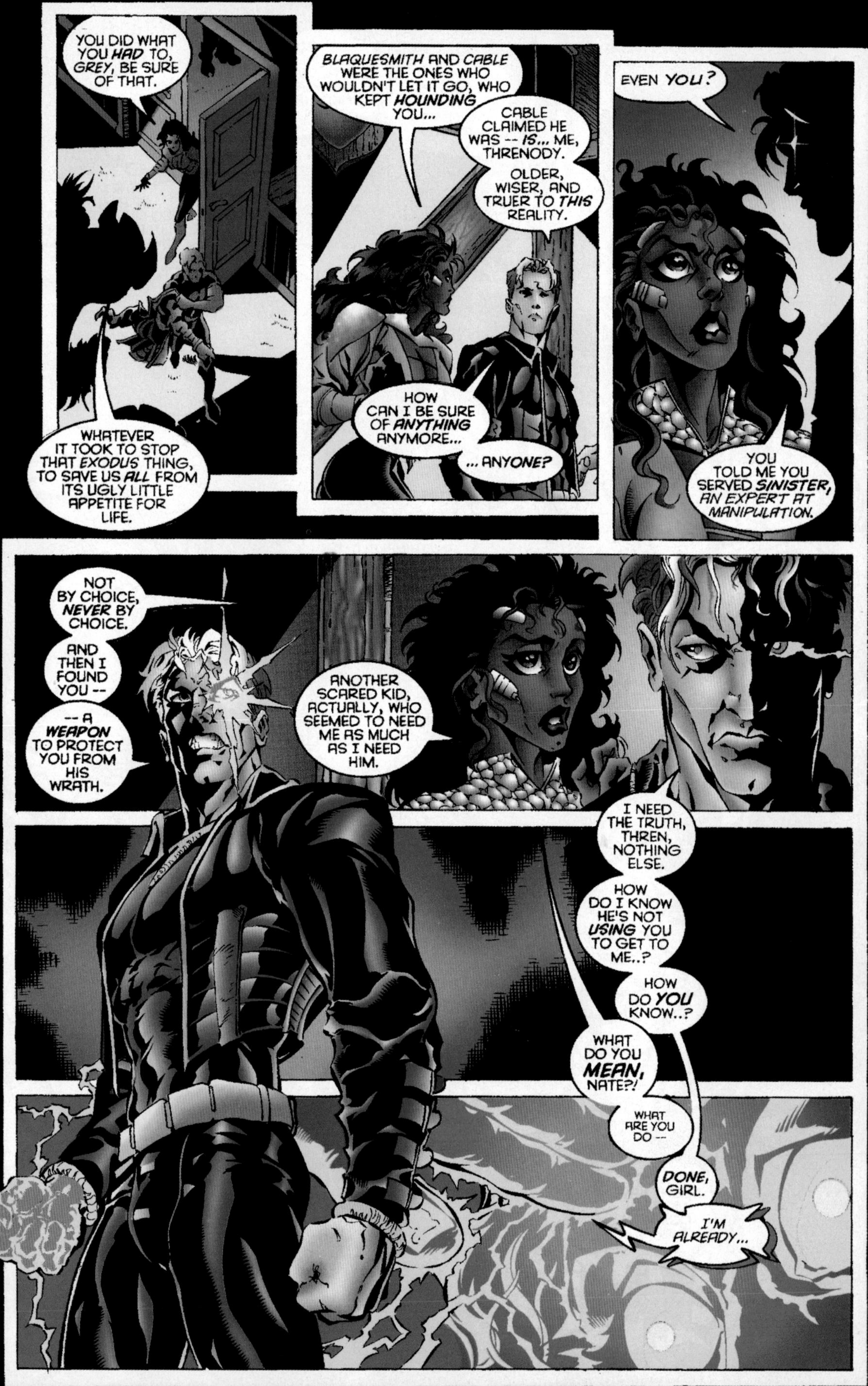
YOU DID WHAT YOU HAD TO, GREY, BE SURE OF THAT.
WHATEVER IT TOOK TO STOP THAT EXODUS THING, TO SAVE US ALL FROM ITS UGLY LITTLE APPETITE FOR LIFE.
BLAQUESMITH AND CABLE WERE THE ONES WHO WOULDN'T LET IT GO, WHO KEPT HOUNDING YOU...
CABLE CLAIMED HE WAS -- IS... ME, THRENODY.
OLDER, WISER, AND TRUER TO THIS REALITY.
HOW CAN I BE SURE OF ANYTHING ANYMORE...
... ANYONE?
EVEN YOU?
YOU TOLD ME YOU SERVED SINISTER, AN EXPERT AT MANIPULATION.
NOT BY CHOICE, NEVER BY CHOICE.
AND THEN I FOUND YOU --
-- A WEAPON TO PROTECT YOU FROM HIS WRATH.
ANOTHER SCARED KID, ACTUALLY, WHO SEEMED TO NEED ME AS MUCH AS I NEED HIM.
I NEED THE TRUTH, THREN, NOTHING ELSE.
HOW DO I KNOW HE'S NOT USING YOU TO GET TO ME..?
HOW DO YOU KNOW..?
WHAT DO YOU MEAN, NATE?!
WHAT ARE YOU DO --
DONE, GIRL.
I'M ALREADY...

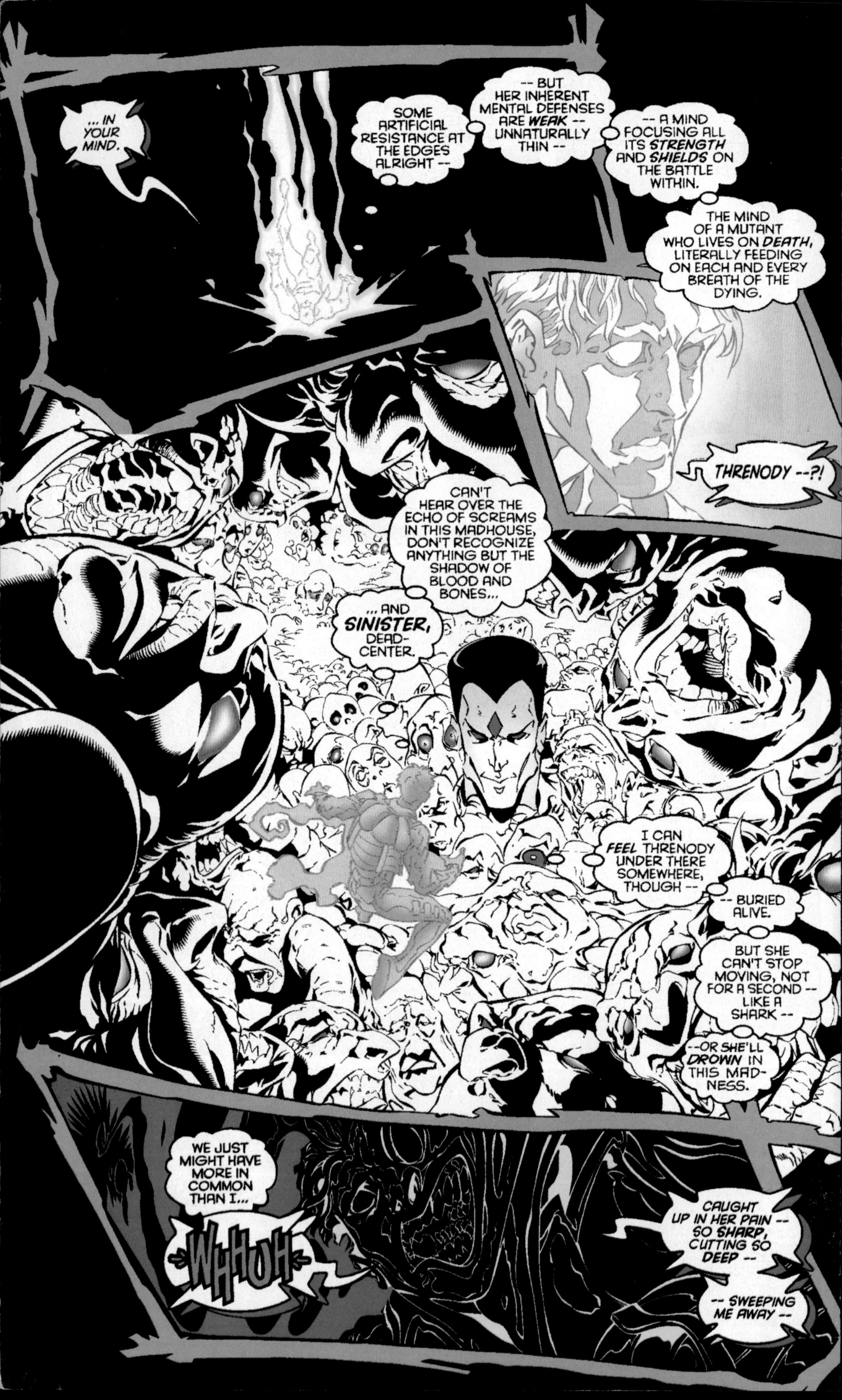
...IN YOUR MIND.
SOME ARTIFICIAL RESISTANCE AT THE EDGES ALRIGHT --
-- BUT HER INHERENT MENTAL DEFENSES ARE WEAK -- UNNATURALLY THIN --
-- A MIND FOCUSING ALL ITS STRENGTH AND SHIELDS ON THE BATTLE WITHIN.
THE MIND OF A MUTANT WHO LIVES ON DEATH, LITERALLY FEEDING ON EACH AND EVERY BREATH OF THE DYING.
THRENODY --?!
CAN'T HEAR OVER THE ECHO OF SCREAMS IN THIS MADHOUSE, DON'T RECOGNIZE ANYTHING BUT THE SHADOW OF BLOOD AND BONES...
...AND SINISTER, DEAD-CENTER.
I CAN FEEL THRENODY UNDER THERE SOMEWHERE, THOUGH --
-- BURIED ALIVE.
BUT SHE CAN'T STOP MOVING, NOT FOR A SECOND -- LIKE A SHARK --
--OR SHE'LL DROWN IN THIS MADNESS.
WE JUST MIGHT HAVE MORE IN COMMON THAN I...
WHHUH
CAUGHT UP IN HER PAIN -- SO SHARP, CUTTING SO DEEP --
-- SWEEPING ME AWAY --

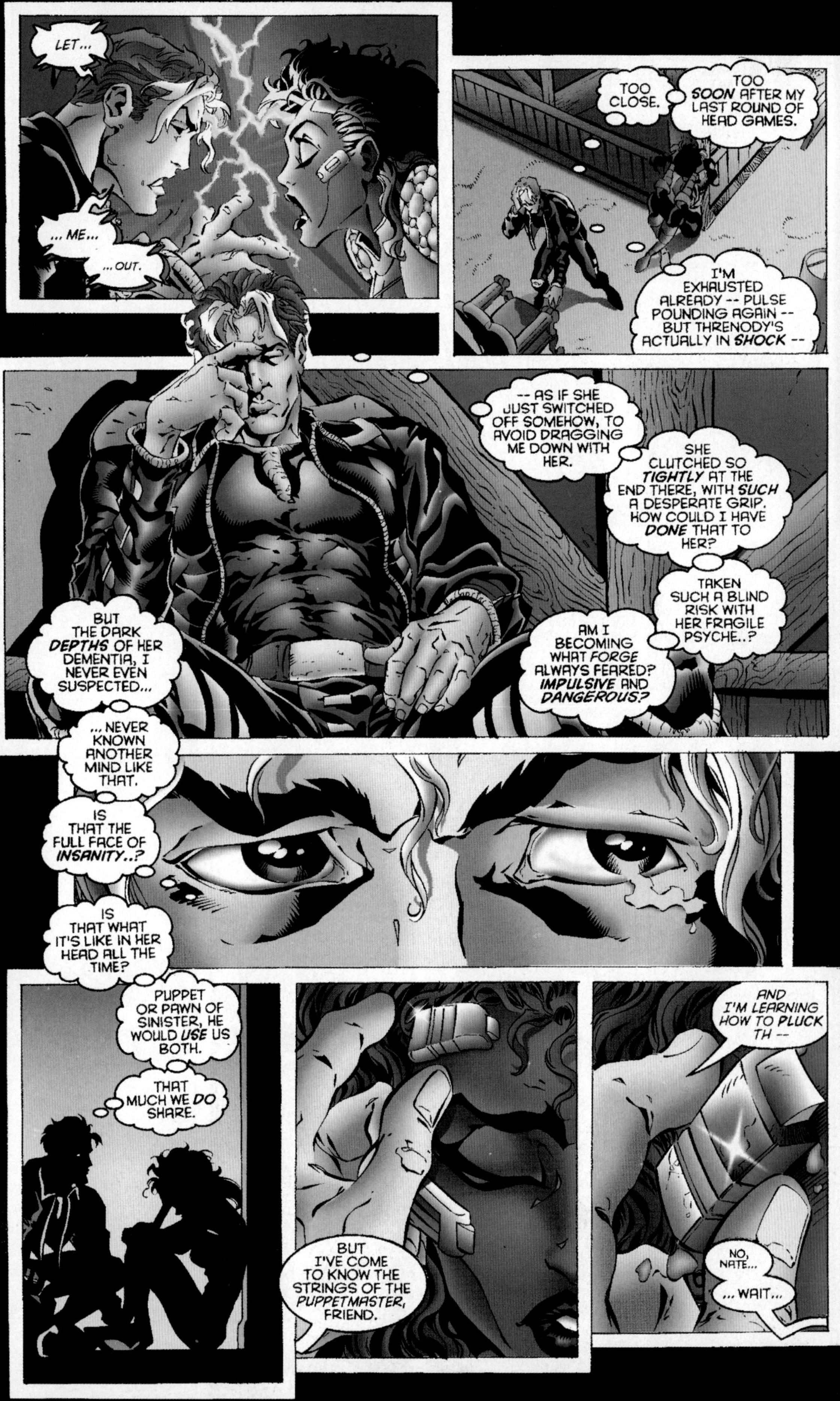
LET...
...ME...
...OUT.
TOO CLOSE.
TOO SOON AFTER MY LAST ROUND OF HEAD GAMES.
I'M EXHAUSTED ALREADY -- PULSE POUNDING AGAIN -- BUT THRENODY'S ACTUALLY IN SHOCK --
-- AS IF SHE JUST SWITCHED OFF SOMEHOW, TO AVOID DRAGGING ME DOWN WITH HER.
SHE CLUTCHED SO TIGHTLY AT THE END THERE, WITH SUCH A DESPERATE GRIP. HOW COULD I HAVE DONE THAT TO HER?
TAKEN SUCH A BLIND RISK WITH HER FRAGILE PSYCHE..?
AM I BECOMING WHAT FORGE ALWAYS FEARED? IMPULSIVE AND DANGEROUS?
BUT THE DARK DEPTHS OF HER DEMENTIA, I NEVER EVEN SUSPECTED...
...NEVER KNOWN ANOTHER MIND LIKE THAT.
IS THAT THE FULL FACE OF INSANITY..?
IS THAT WHAT IT'S LIKE IN HER HEAD ALL THE TIME?
PUPPET OR PAWN OF SINISTER, HE WOULD USE US BOTH.
THAT MUCH WE DO SHARE.
BUT I'VE COME TO KNOW THE STRINGS OF THE PUPPETMASTER, FRIEND.
AND I'M LEARNING HOW TO PLUCK TH --
NO, NATE...
...WAIT...

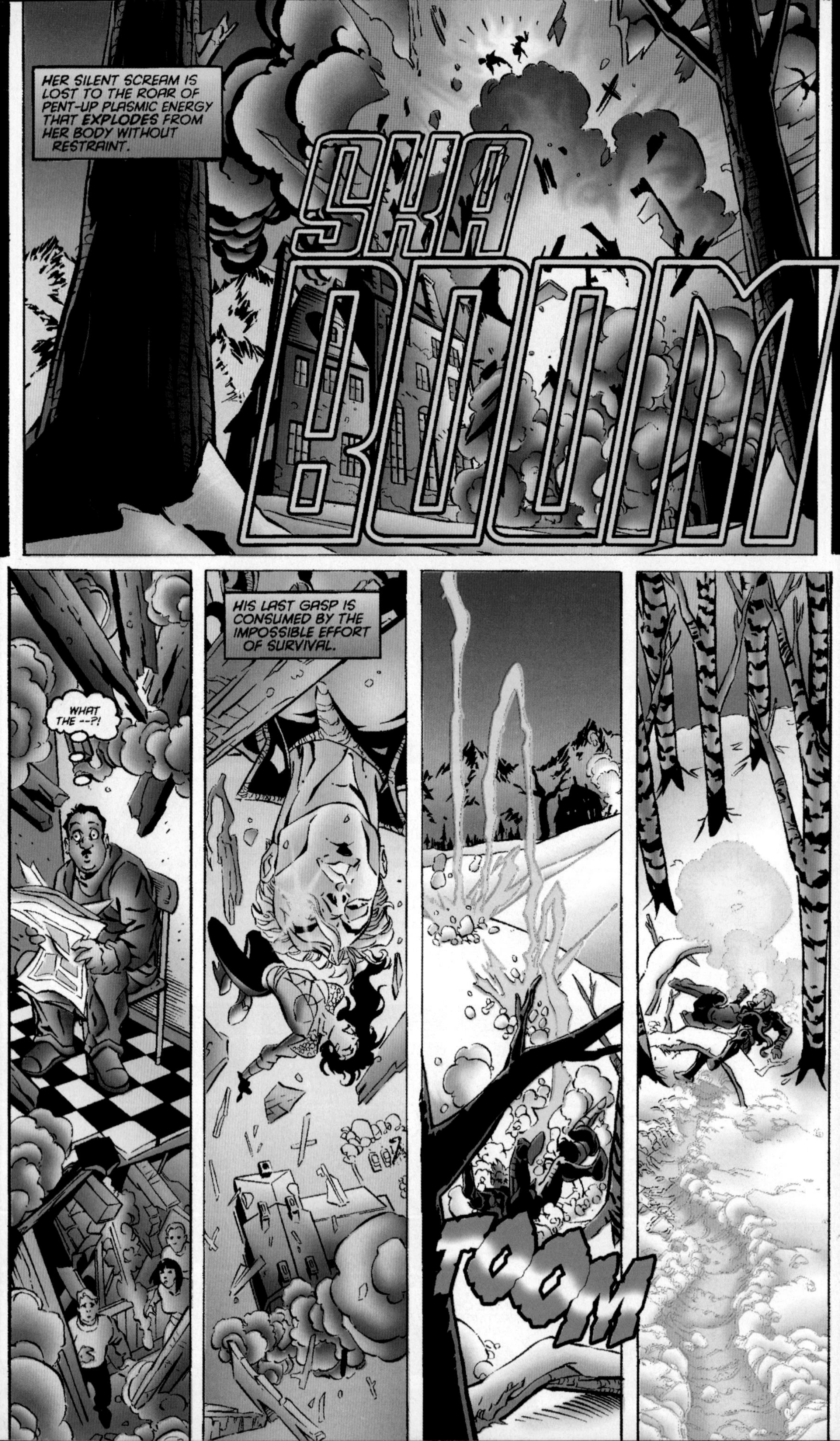
HER SILENT SCREAM IS LOST TO THE ROAR OF PENT-UP PLASMIC ENERGY THAT EXPLODES FROM HER BODY WITHOUT RESTRAINT.
SKA BOOM
WHAT THE --?!
HIS LAST GASP IS CONSUMED BY THE IMPOSSIBLE EFFORT OF SURVIVAL.
TOOM

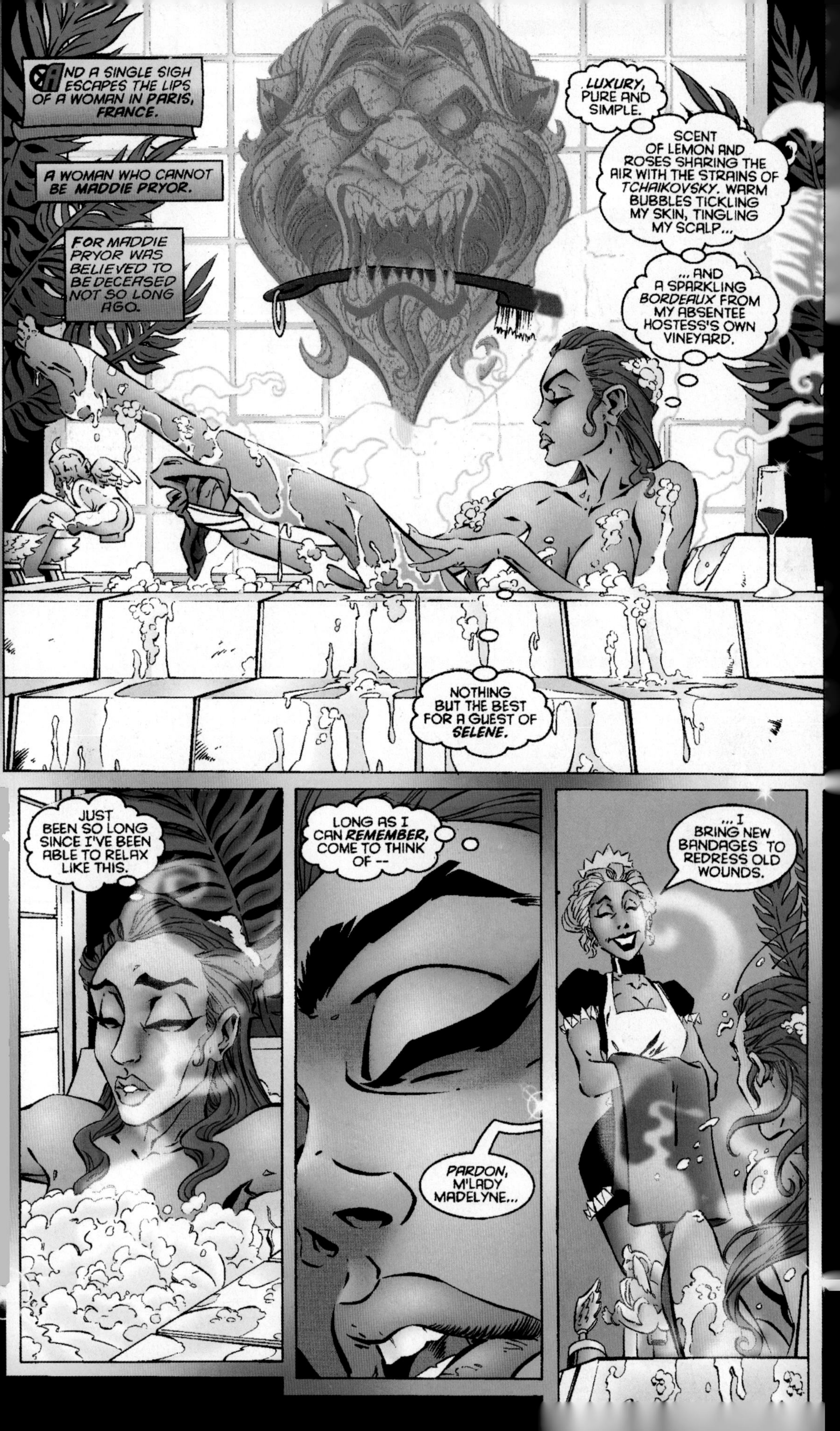
AND A SINGLE SIGH ESCAPES THE LIPS OF A WOMAN IN PARIS, FRANCE.
A WOMAN WHO CANNOT BE MADDIE PRYOR.
FOR MADDIE PRYOR WAS BELIEVED TO BE DECEASED NOT SO LONG AGO.
LUXURY, PURE AND SIMPLE.
SCENT OF LEMON AND ROSES SHARING THE AIR WITH THE STRAINS OF TCHAIKOVSKY. WARM BUBBLES TICKLING MY SKIN, TINGLING MY SCALP...
... AND A SPARKLING BORDEAUX FROM MY ABSENTEE HOSTESS'S OWN VINEYARD.
NOTHING BUT THE BEST FOR A GUEST OF SELENE.
JUST BEEN SO LONG SINCE I'VE BEEN ABLE TO RELAX LIKE THIS.
LONG AS I CAN REMEMBER, COME TO THINK OF --
PARDON, M'LADY MADELYNE...
... I BRING NEW BANDAGES TO REDRESS OLD WOUNDS.

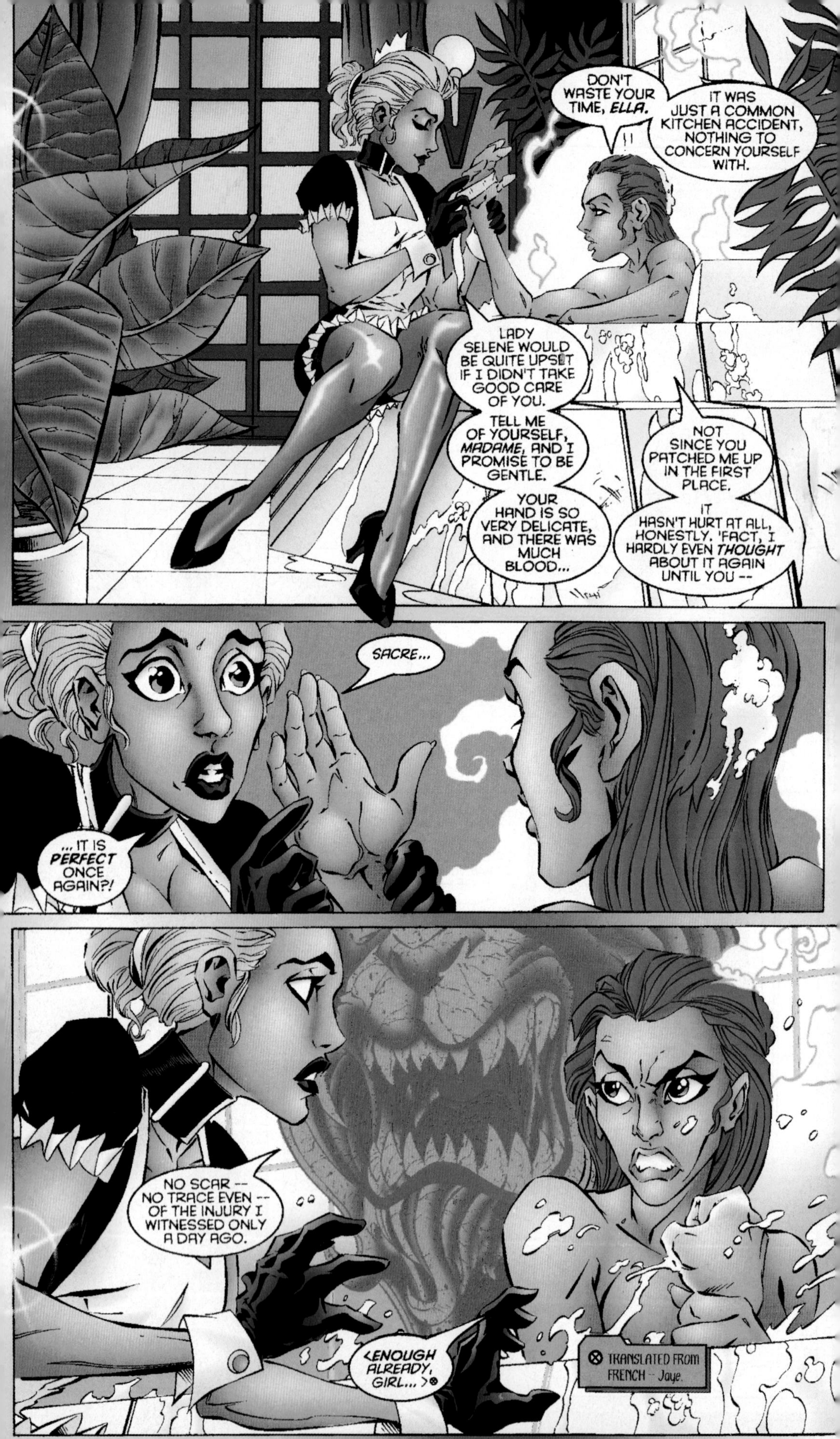

DON'T WASTE YOUR TIME, ELLA.
IT WAS JUST A COMMON KITCHEN ACCIDENT, NOTHING TO CONCERN YOURSELF WITH.
LADY SELENE WOULD BE QUITE UPSET IF I DIDN'T TAKE GOOD CARE OF YOU.
TELL ME OF YOURSELF, MADAME, AND I PROMISE TO BE GENTLE.
YOUR HAND IS SO VERY DELICATE, AND THERE WAS MUCH BLOOD...
NOT SINCE YOU PATCHED ME UP IN THE FIRST PLACE.
IT HASN'T HURT AT ALL, HONESTLY. 'FACT, I HARDLY EVEN THOUGHT ABOUT IT AGAIN UNTIL YOU --
SACRE...
...IT IS PERFECT ONCE AGAIN?!
NO SCAR -- NO TRACE EVEN -- OF THE INJURY I WITNESSED ONLY A DAY AGO.
<ENOUGH ALREADY, GIRL...>
TRANSLATED FROM FRENCH -- Jaye.

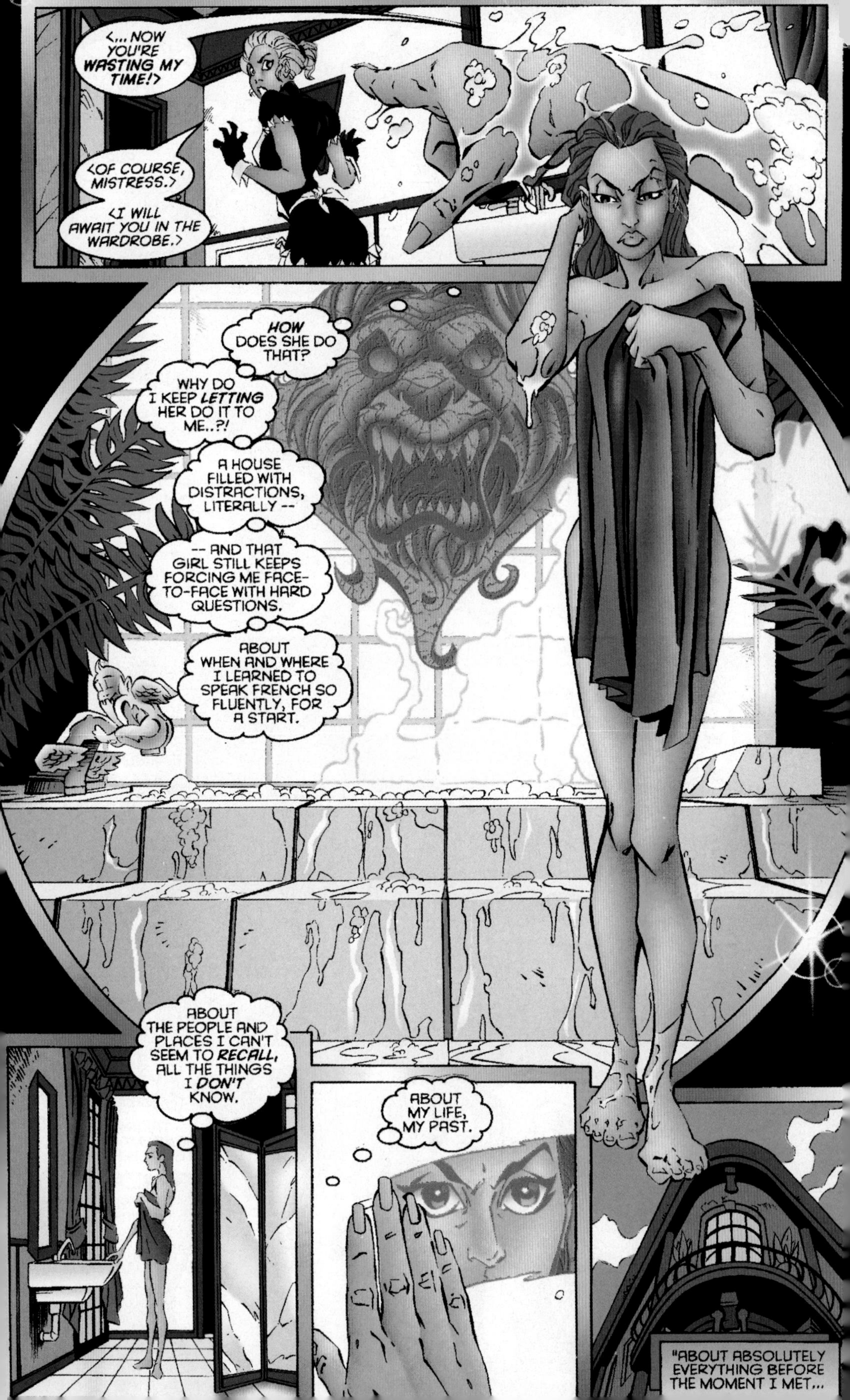

<...NOW YOU'RE WASTING MY TIME!>
<OF COURSE, MISTRESS.>
<I WILL AWAIT YOU IN THE WARDROBE.>
HOW DOES SHE DO THAT?
WHY DO I KEEP LETTING HER DO IT TO ME..?!
A HOUSE FILLED WITH DISTRACTIONS, LITERALLY --
-- AND THAT GIRL STILL KEEPS FORCING ME FACE-TO-FACE WITH HARD QUESTIONS.
ABOUT WHEN AND WHERE I LEARNED TO SPEAK FRENCH SO FLUENTLY, FOR A START.
ABOUT THE PEOPLE AND PLACES I CAN'T SEEM TO RECALL, ALL THE THINGS I DON'T KNOW.
ABOUT MY LIFE, MY PAST.
"ABOUT ABSOLUTELY EVERYTHING BEFORE THE MOMENT I MET...

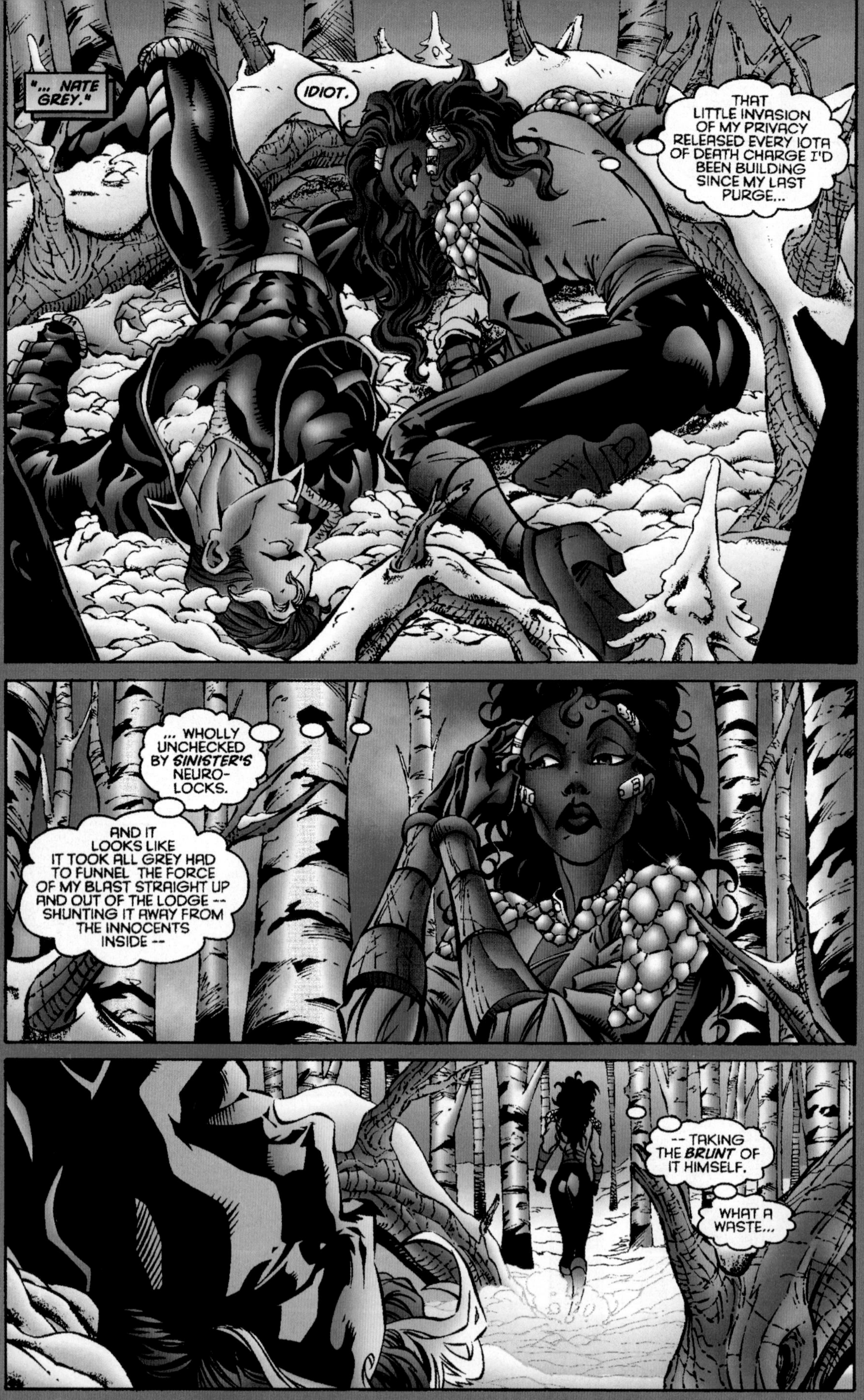
"... NATE GREY."
IDIOT.
THAT LITTLE INVASION OF MY PRIVACY RELEASED EVERY IOTA OF DEATH CHARGE I'D BEEN BUILDING SINCE MY LAST PURGE...
... WHOLLY UNCHECKED BY *SINISTER'S* NEURO-LOCKS.
AND IT LOOKS LIKE IT TOOK ALL GREY HAD TO FUNNEL THE FORCE OF MY BLAST STRAIGHT UP AND OUT OF THE LODGE -- SHUNTING IT AWAY FROM THE INNOCENTS INSIDE --
-- TAKING THE *BRUNT* OF IT HIMSELF.
WHAT A WASTE...

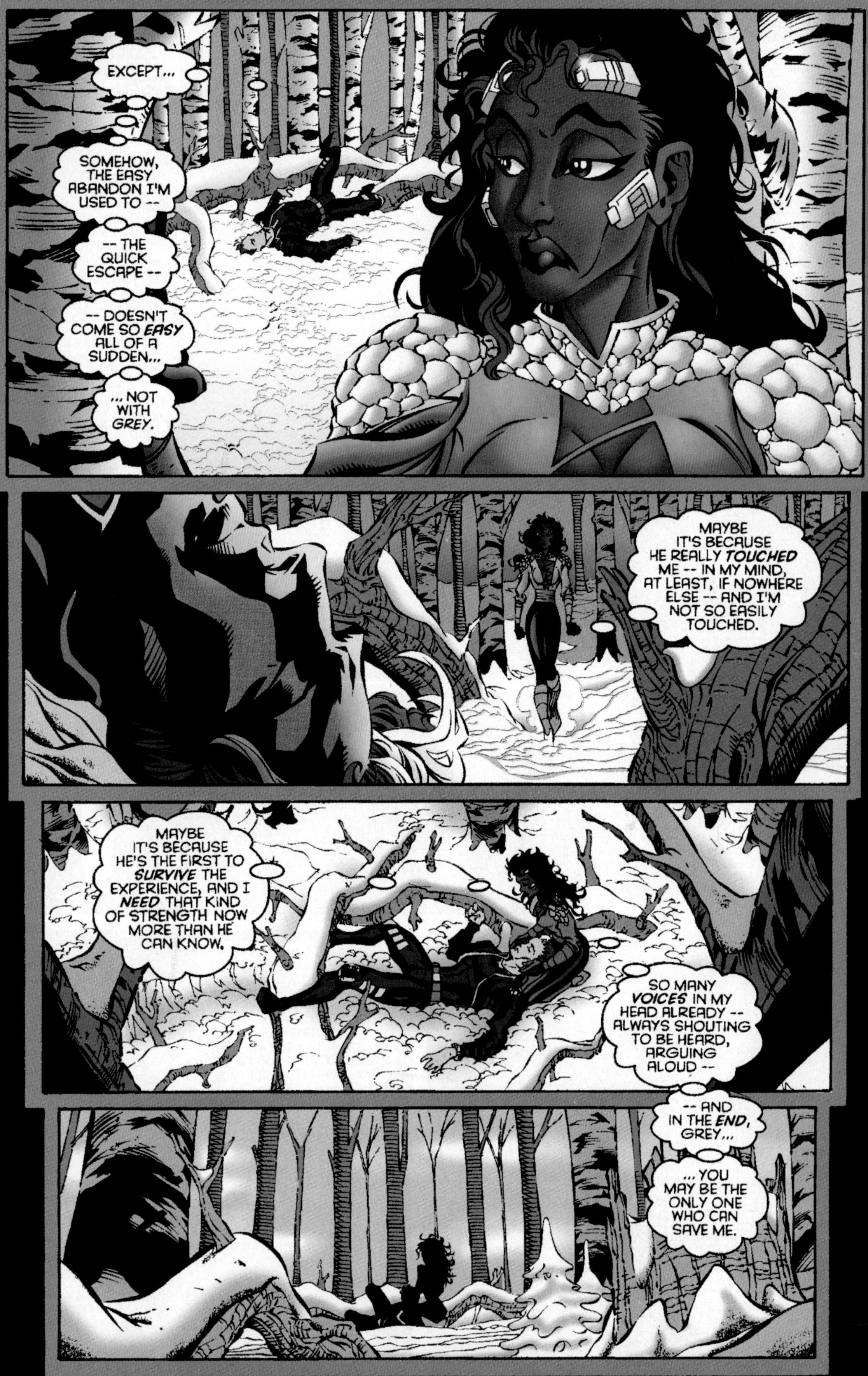
EXCEPT...
SOMEHOW, THE EASY ABANDON I'M USED TO --
-- THE QUICK ESCAPE --
-- DOESN'T COME SO *EASY* ALL OF A SUDDEN...
...NOT WITH *GREY*.
MAYBE IT'S BECAUSE HE REALLY *TOUCHED* ME -- IN MY MIND, AT LEAST, IF NOWHERE ELSE -- AND I'M NOT SO EASILY TOUCHED.
MAYBE IT'S BECAUSE HE'S THE FIRST TO *SURVIVE* THE EXPERIENCE, AND I *NEED* THAT KIND OF STRENGTH NOW MORE THAN HE CAN KNOW.
SO MANY *VOICES* IN MY HEAD ALREADY -- ALWAYS SHOUTING TO BE HEARD, ARGUING ALOUD --
-- AND IN THE *END*, GREY...
...YOU MAY BE THE ONLY ONE WHO CAN SAVE ME.

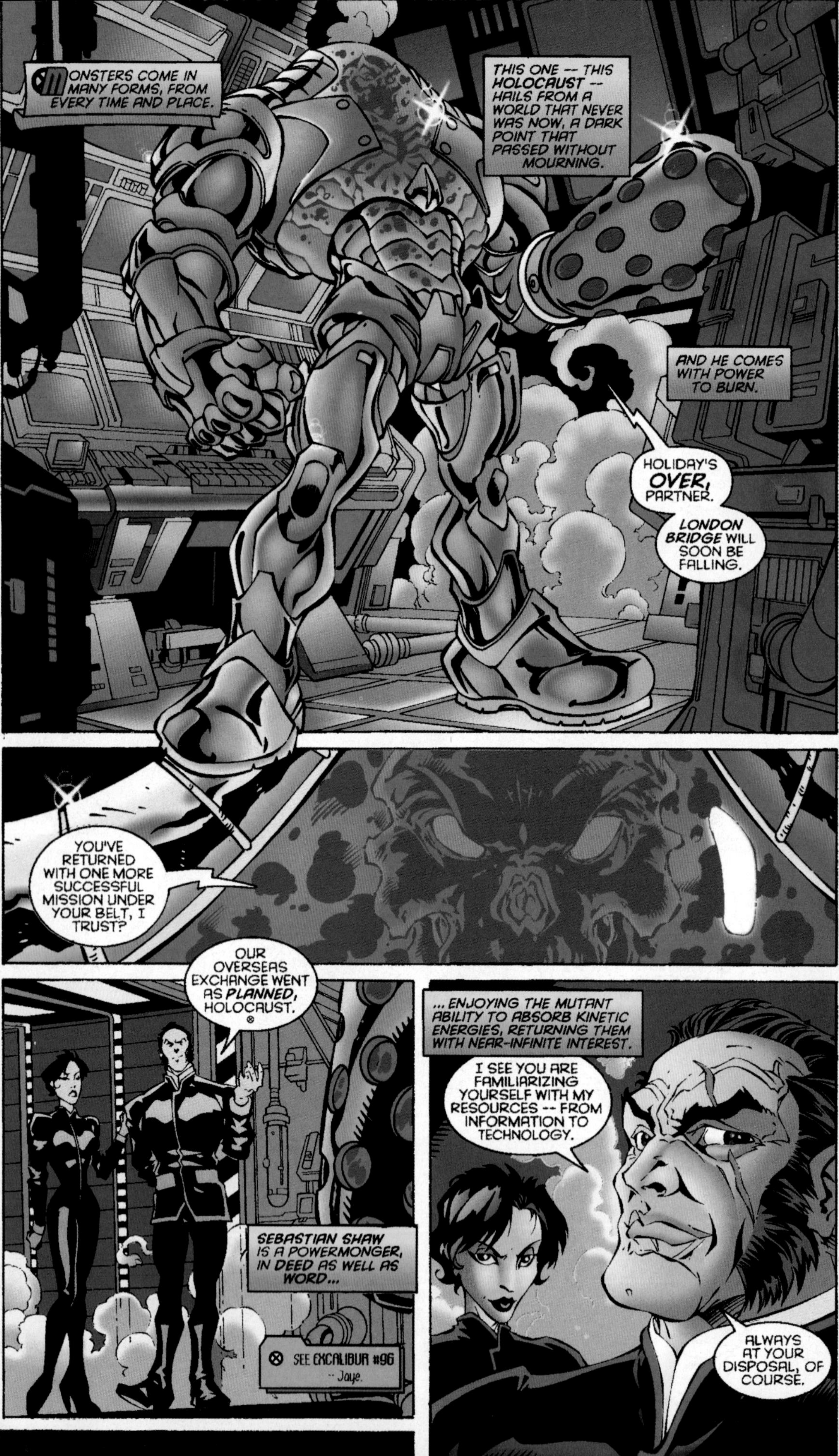
MONSTERS COME IN MANY FORMS, FROM EVERY TIME AND PLACE.
THIS ONE -- THIS HOLOCAUST -- HAILS FROM A WORLD THAT NEVER WAS NOW, A DARK POINT THAT PASSED WITHOUT MOURNING.
AND HE COMES WITH POWER TO BURN.
HOLIDAY'S OVER, PARTNER.
LONDON BRIDGE WILL SOON BE FALLING.
YOU'VE RETURNED WITH ONE MORE SUCCESSFUL MISSION UNDER YOUR BELT, I TRUST?
OUR OVERSEAS EXCHANGE WENT AS PLANNED, HOLOCAUST.
SEBASTIAN SHAW IS A POWERMONGER, IN DEED AS WELL AS WORD...
SEE EXCALIBUR #96 -- Jaye.
... ENJOYING THE MUTANT ABILITY TO ABSORB KINETIC ENERGIES, RETURNING THEM WITH NEAR-INFINITE INTEREST.
I SEE YOU ARE FAMILIARIZING YOURSELF WITH MY RESOURCES -- FROM INFORMATION TO TECHNOLOGY.
ALWAYS AT YOUR DISPOSAL, OF COURSE.

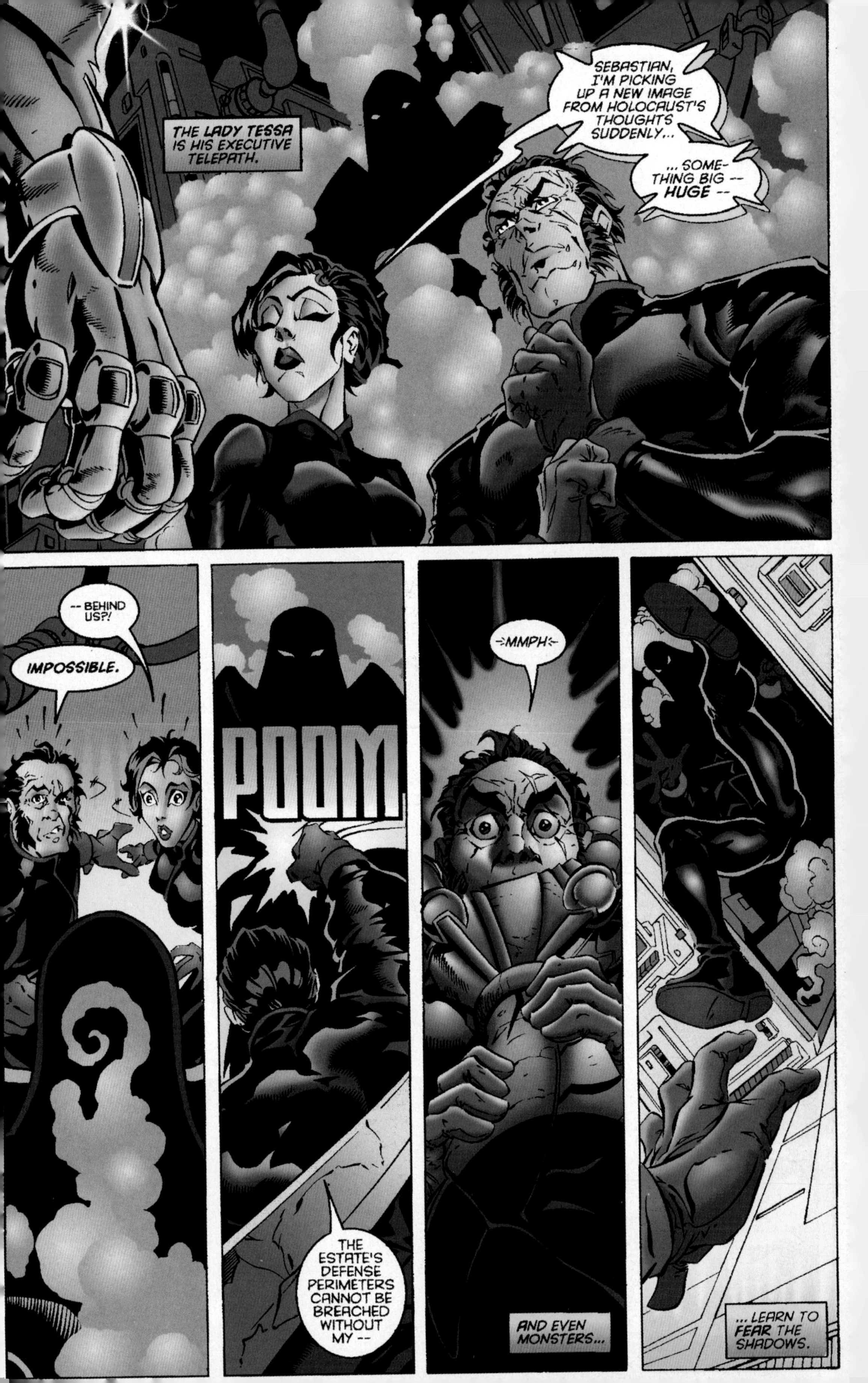
THE LADY TESSA IS HIS EXECUTIVE TELEPATH.
SEBASTIAN, I'M PICKING UP A NEW IMAGE FROM HOLOCAUST'S THOUGHTS SUDDENLY...
... SOME-THING BIG -- HUGE --
-- BEHIND US?!
IMPOSSIBLE.
POOM
THE ESTATE'S DEFENSE PERIMETERS CANNOT BE BREACHED WITHOUT MY --
-MMPH-
AND EVEN MONSTERS...
...LEARN TO FEAR THE SHADOWS.

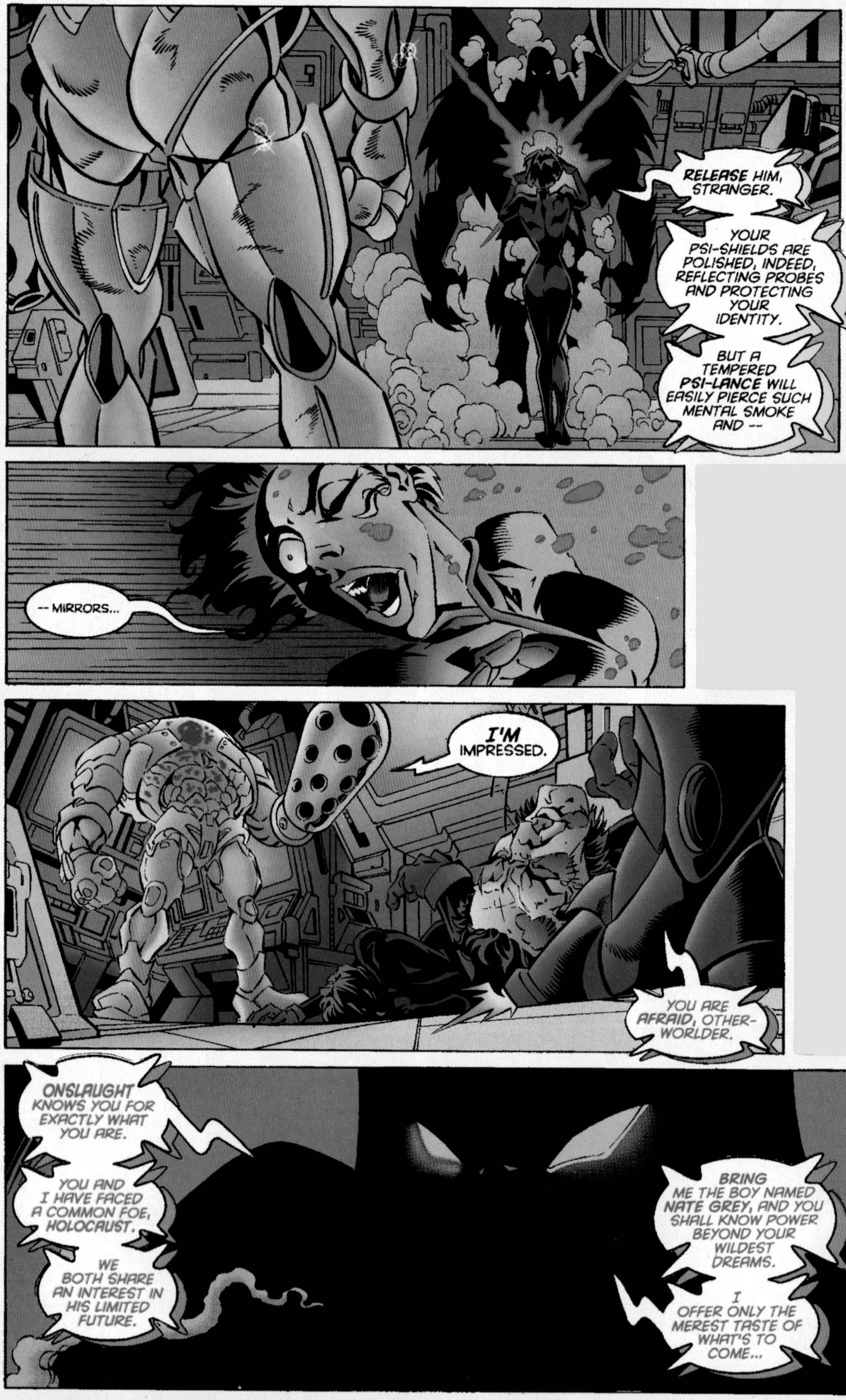
RELEASE HIM, STRANGER.
YOUR PSI-SHIELDS ARE POLISHED, INDEED, REFLECTING PROBES AND PROTECTING YOUR IDENTITY.
BUT A TEMPERED PSI-LANCE WILL EASILY PIERCE SUCH MENTAL SMOKE AND --
-- MIRRORS...
I'M IMPRESSED.
YOU ARE AFRAID, OTHER-WORLDER.
ONSLAUGHT KNOWS YOU FOR EXACTLY WHAT YOU ARE.
YOU AND I HAVE FACED A COMMON FOE, HOLOCAUST.
WE BOTH SHARE AN INTEREST IN HIS LIMITED FUTURE.
BRING ME THE BOY NAMED NATE GREY, AND YOU SHALL KNOW POWER BEYOND YOUR WILDEST DREAMS.
I OFFER ONLY THE MEREST TASTE OF WHAT'S TO COME...

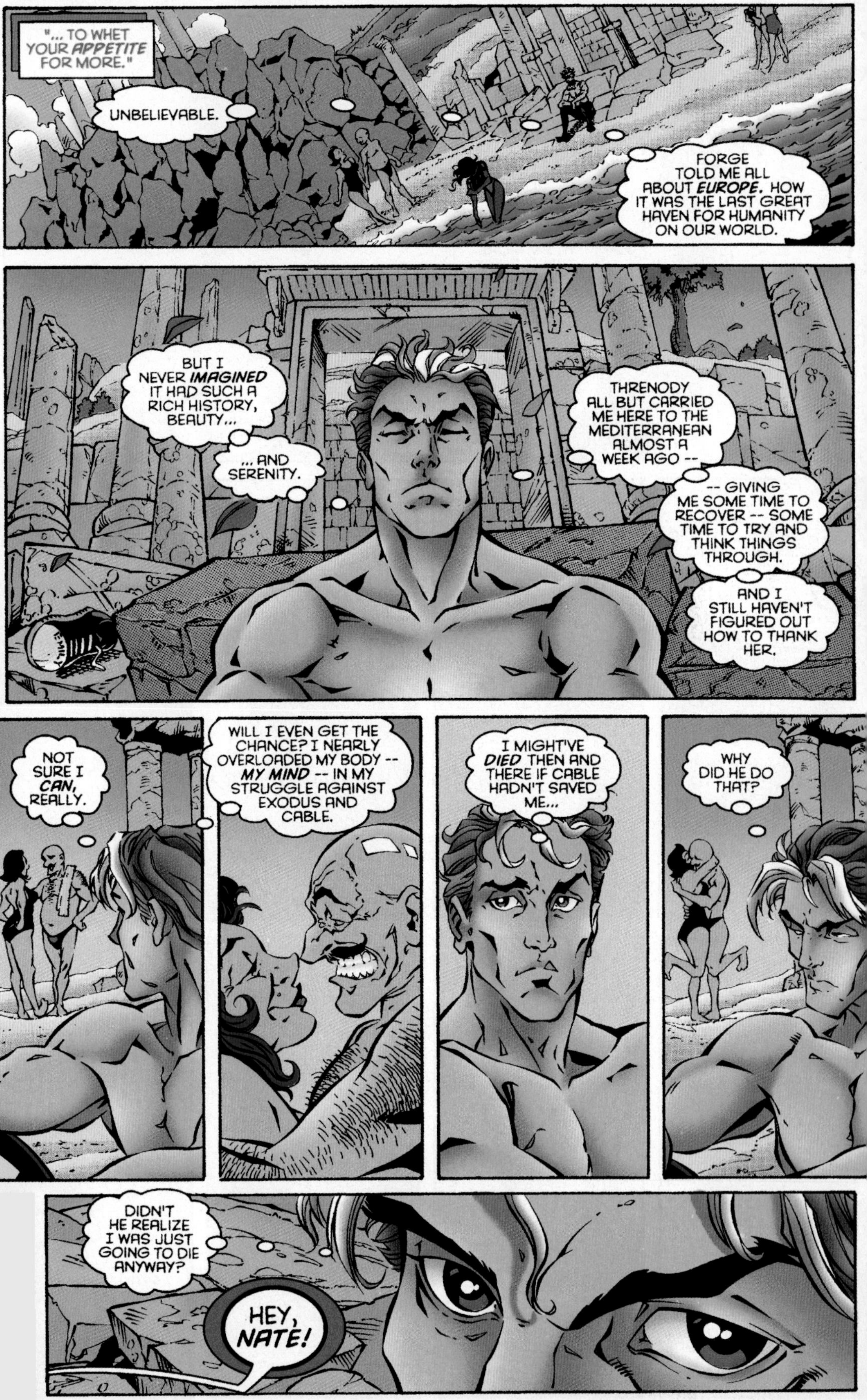
"... TO WHET YOUR APPETITE FOR MORE."
UNBELIEVABLE.
FORGE TOLD ME ALL ABOUT EUROPE. HOW IT WAS THE LAST GREAT HAVEN FOR HUMANITY ON OUR WORLD.
BUT I NEVER IMAGINED IT HAD SUCH A RICH HISTORY, BEAUTY...
... AND SERENITY.
THRENODY ALL BUT CARRIED ME HERE TO THE MEDITERRANEAN ALMOST A WEEK AGO --
-- GIVING ME SOME TIME TO RECOVER -- SOME TIME TO TRY AND THINK THINGS THROUGH.
AND I STILL HAVEN'T FIGURED OUT HOW TO THANK HER.
NOT SURE I CAN, REALLY.
WILL I EVEN GET THE CHANCE? I NEARLY OVERLOADED MY BODY -- MY MIND -- IN MY STRUGGLE AGAINST EXODUS AND CABLE.
I MIGHT'VE DIED THEN AND THERE IF CABLE HADN'T SAVED ME...
WHY DID HE DO THAT?
DIDN'T HE REALIZE I WAS JUST GOING TO DIE ANYWAY?
HEY, NATE!

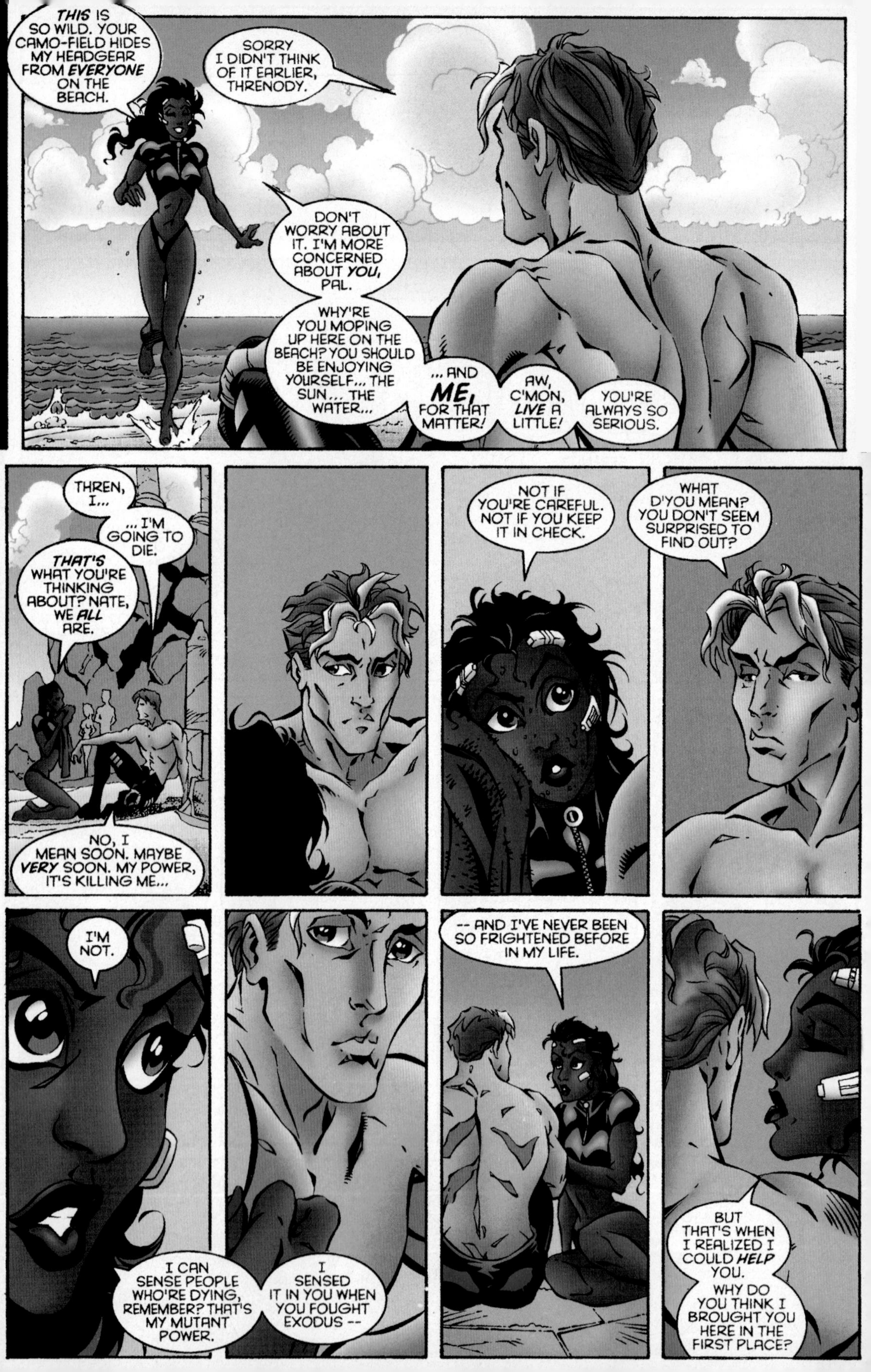

THIS IS SO WILD. YOUR CAMO-FIELD HIDES MY HEADGEAR FROM EVERYONE ON THE BEACH.
SORRY I DIDN'T THINK OF IT EARLIER, THRENODY.
DON'T WORRY ABOUT IT. I'M MORE CONCERNED ABOUT YOU, PAL.
WHY'RE YOU MOPING UP HERE ON THE BEACH? YOU SHOULD BE ENJOYING YOURSELF... THE SUN... THE WATER...
...AND ME, FOR THAT MATTER!
AW, C'MON, LIVE A LITTLE!
YOU'RE ALWAYS SO SERIOUS.
THREN, I...
...I'M GOING TO DIE.
THAT'S WHAT YOU'RE THINKING ABOUT? NATE, WE ALL ARE.
NO, I MEAN SOON. MAYBE VERY SOON. MY POWER, IT'S KILLING ME...
NOT IF YOU'RE CAREFUL. NOT IF YOU KEEP IT IN CHECK.
WHAT D'YOU MEAN? YOU DON'T SEEM SURPRISED TO FIND OUT?
I'M NOT.
I CAN SENSE PEOPLE WHO'RE DYING, REMEMBER? THAT'S MY MUTANT POWER.
I SENSED IT IN YOU WHEN YOU FOUGHT EXODUS --
-- AND I'VE NEVER BEEN SO FRIGHTENED BEFORE IN MY LIFE.
BUT THAT'S WHEN I REALIZED I COULD HELP YOU.
WHY DO YOU THINK I BROUGHT YOU HERE IN THE FIRST PLACE?

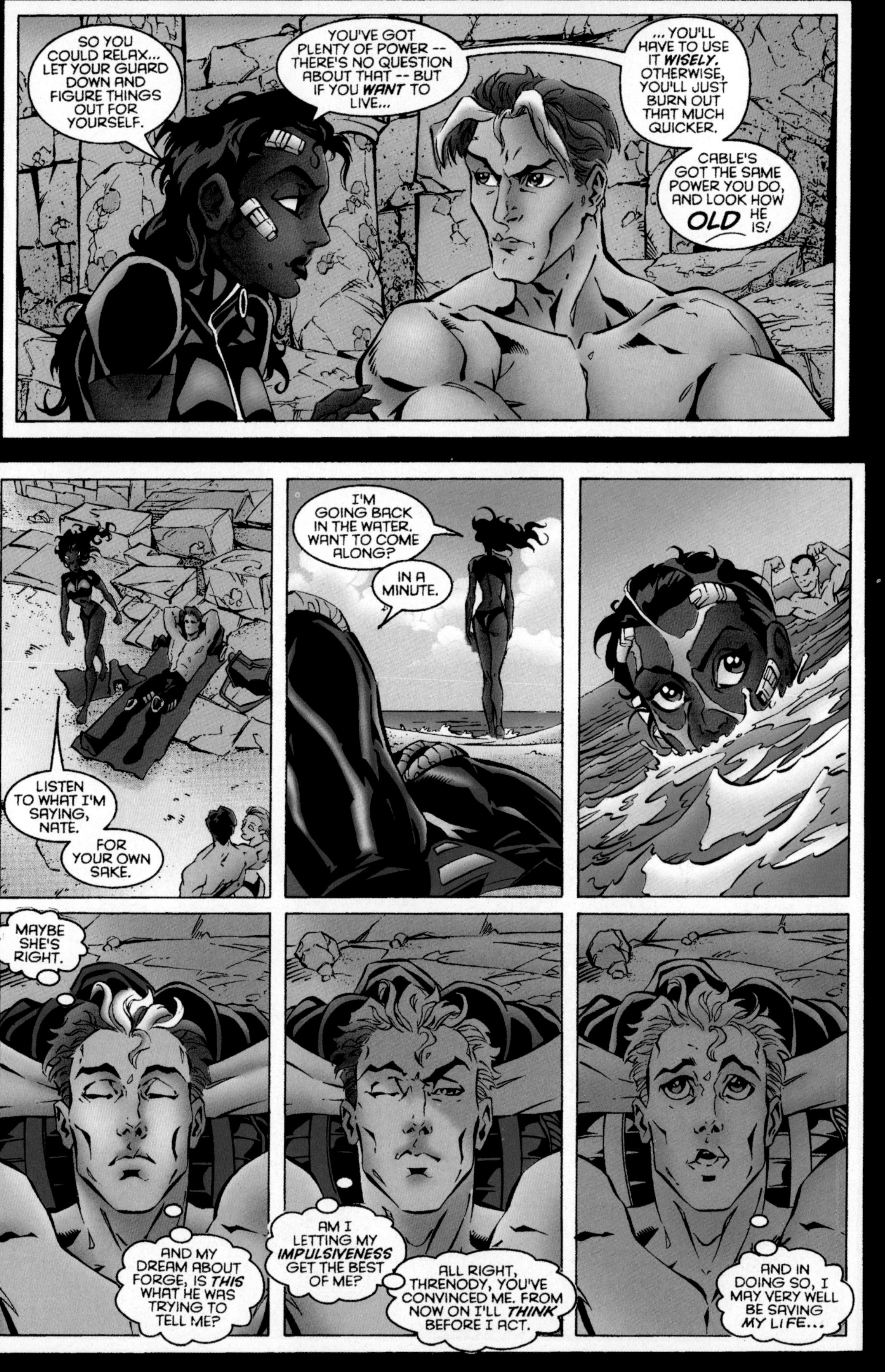
SO YOU COULD RELAX... LET YOUR GUARD DOWN AND FIGURE THINGS OUT FOR YOURSELF.
YOU'VE GOT PLENTY OF POWER -- THERE'S NO QUESTION ABOUT THAT -- BUT IF YOU WANT TO LIVE...
...YOU'LL HAVE TO USE IT WISELY. OTHERWISE, YOU'LL JUST BURN OUT THAT MUCH QUICKER.
CABLE'S GOT THE SAME POWER YOU DO, AND LOOK HOW OLD HE IS!
LISTEN TO WHAT I'M SAYING, NATE.
FOR YOUR OWN SAKE.
I'M GOING BACK IN THE WATER. WANT TO COME ALONG?
IN A MINUTE.
MAYBE SHE'S RIGHT.
AND MY DREAM ABOUT FORGE, IS THIS WHAT HE WAS TRYING TO TELL ME?
AM I LETTING MY IMPULSIVENESS GET THE BEST OF ME?
ALL RIGHT, THRENODY, YOU'VE CONVINCED ME. FROM NOW ON I'LL THINK BEFORE I ACT.
AND IN DOING SO, I MAY VERY WELL BE SAVING MY LIFE...

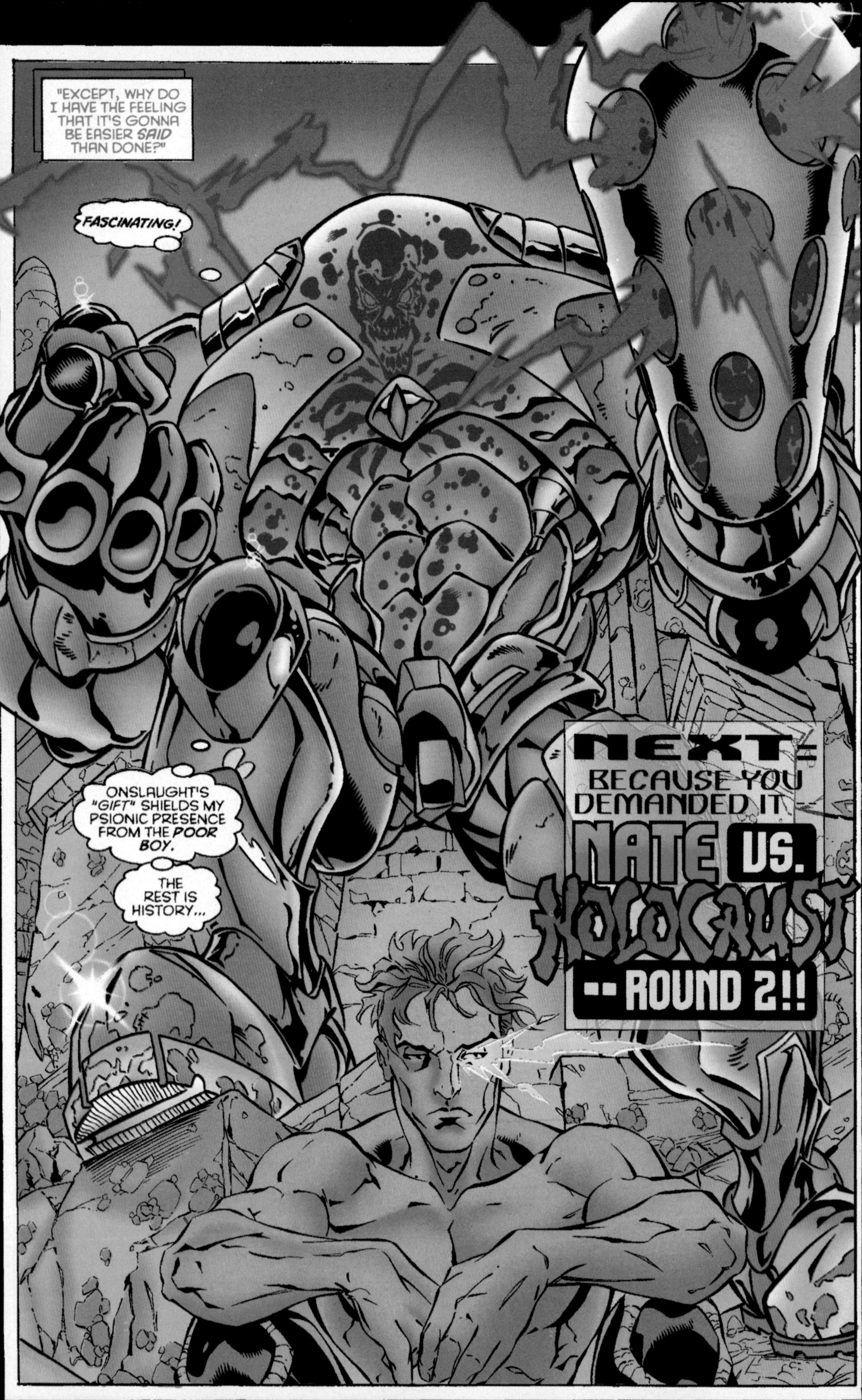
"EXCEPT, WHY DO I HAVE THE FEELING THAT IT'S GONNA BE EASIER SAID THAN DONE?"
FASCINATING!
ONSLAUGHT'S "GIFT" SHIELDS MY PSIONIC PRESENCE FROM THE POOR BOY.
THE REST IS HISTORY...
NEXT:
BECAUSE YOU DEMANDED IT
NATE VS. HOLOCAUST
-- ROUND 2!!

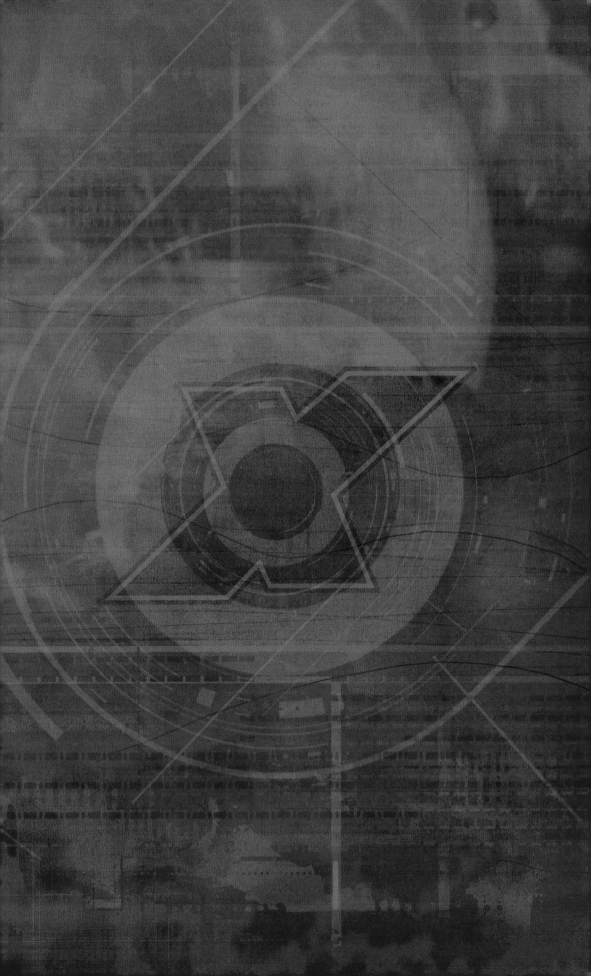

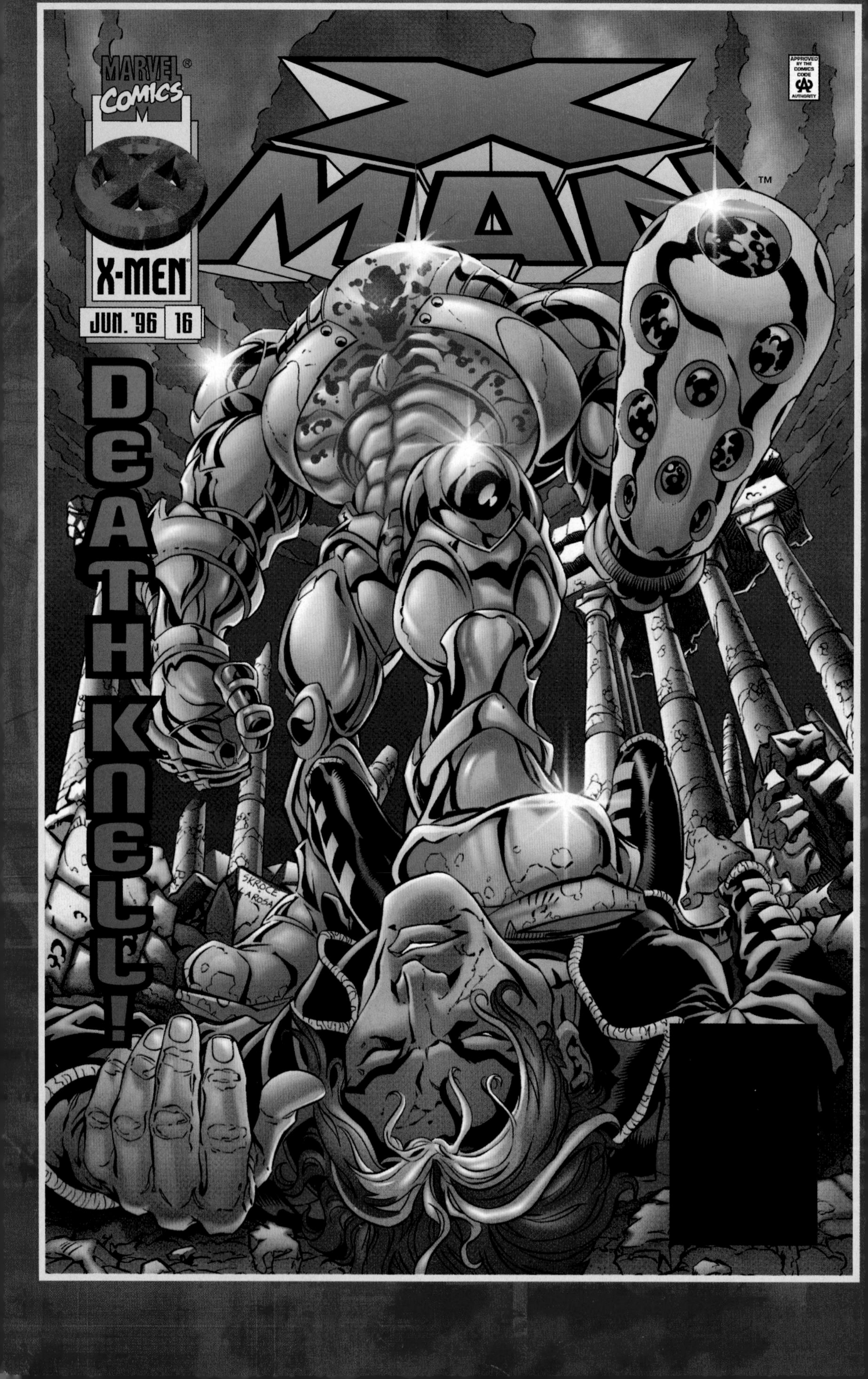
MARVEL COMICS
X-MAN
APPROVED BY THE COMICS CODE AUTHORITY
X-MEN
JUN. '96 16
DEATH KNELL!
SKROCE LAROSA

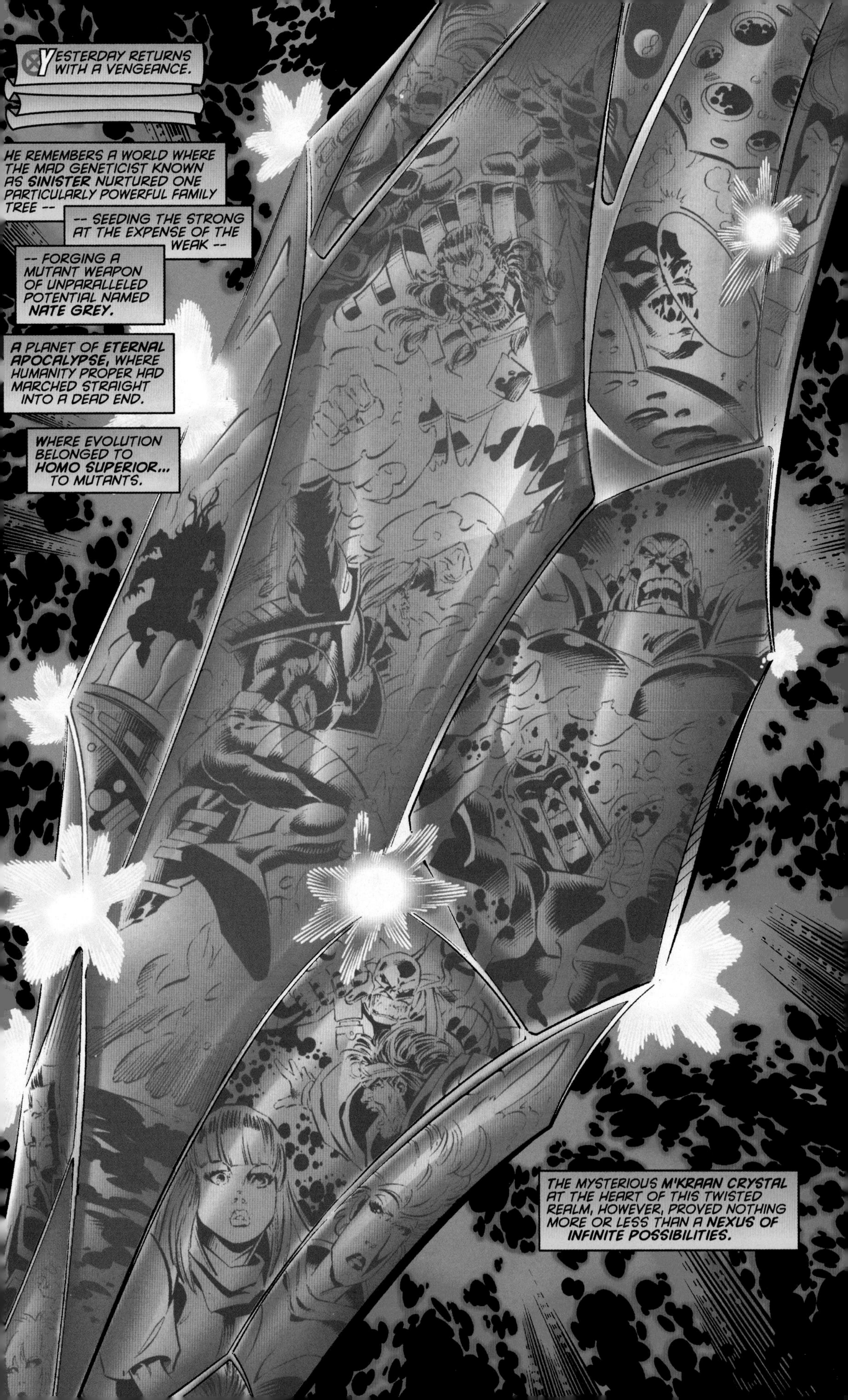
YESTERDAY RETURNS WITH A VENGEANCE.
HE REMEMBERS A WORLD WHERE THE MAD GENETICIST KNOWN AS SINISTER NURTURED ONE PARTICULARLY POWERFUL FAMILY TREE --
-- SEEDING THE STRONG AT THE EXPENSE OF THE WEAK --
-- FORGING A MUTANT WEAPON OF UNPARALLELED POTENTIAL NAMED NATE GREY.
A PLANET OF ETERNAL APOCALYPSE, WHERE HUMANITY PROPER HAD MARCHED STRAIGHT INTO A DEAD END.
WHERE EVOLUTION BELONGED TO HOMO SUPERIOR... TO MUTANTS.
THE MYSTERIOUS M'KRAAN CRYSTAL AT THE HEART OF THIS TWISTED REALM, HOWEVER, PROVED NOTHING MORE OR LESS THAN A NEXUS OF INFINITE POSSIBILITIES.

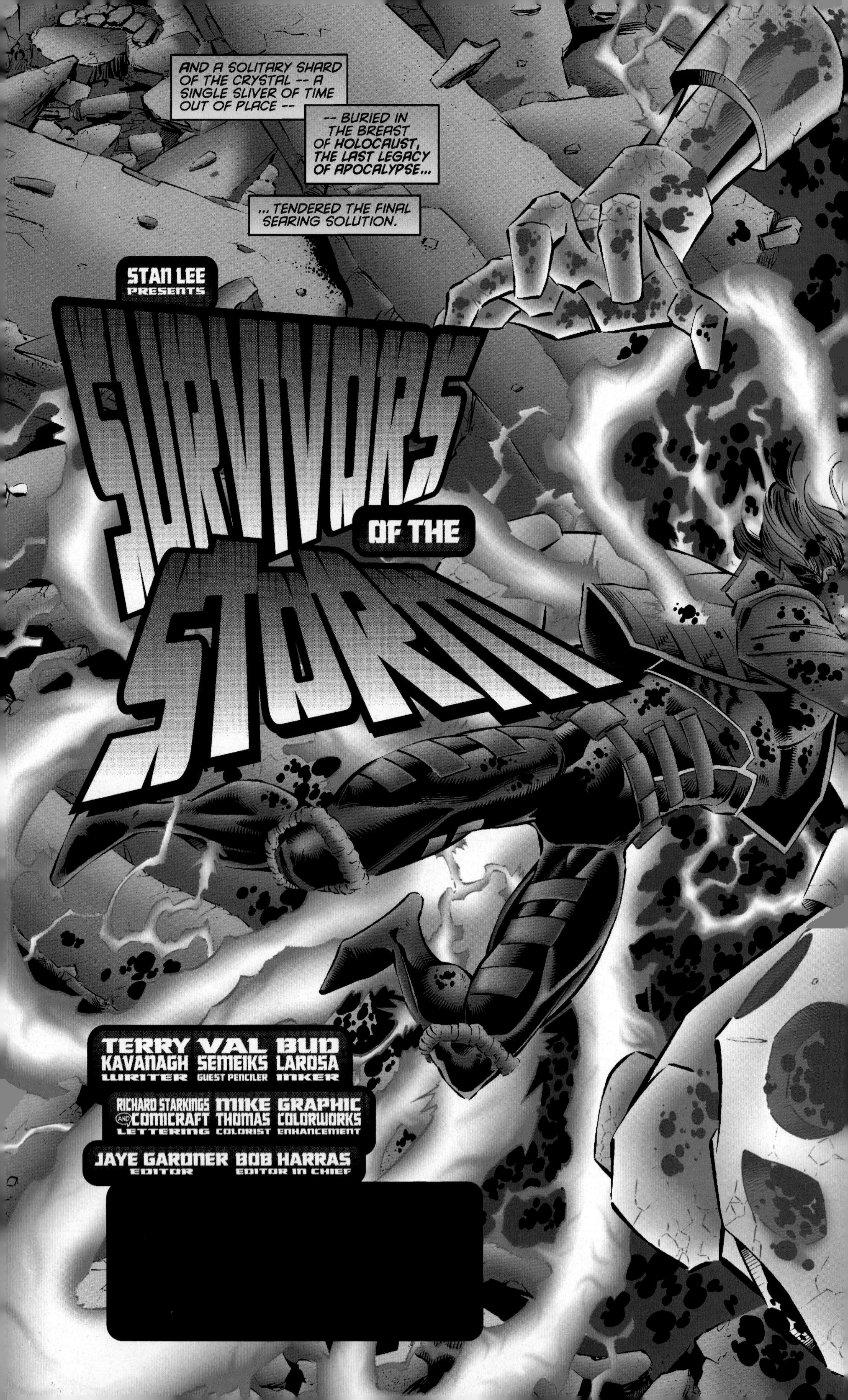
AND A SOLITARY SHARD OF THE CRYSTAL -- A SINGLE SLIVER OF TIME OUT OF PLACE --
-- BURIED IN THE BREAST OF HOLOCAUST, THE LAST LEGACY OF APOCALYPSE...
...TENDERED THE FINAL SEARING SOLUTION.
STAN LEE PRESENTS
SURVIVORS OF THE STORM
TERRY KAVANAGH WRITER
VAL SEMEIKS GUEST PENCILER
BUD LAROSA INKER
RICHARD STARKINGS AND COMICRAFT LETTERING
MIKE THOMAS COLORIST
GRAPHIC COLORWORKS ENHANCEMENT
JAYE GARDNER EDITOR
BOB HARRAS EDITOR IN CHIEF

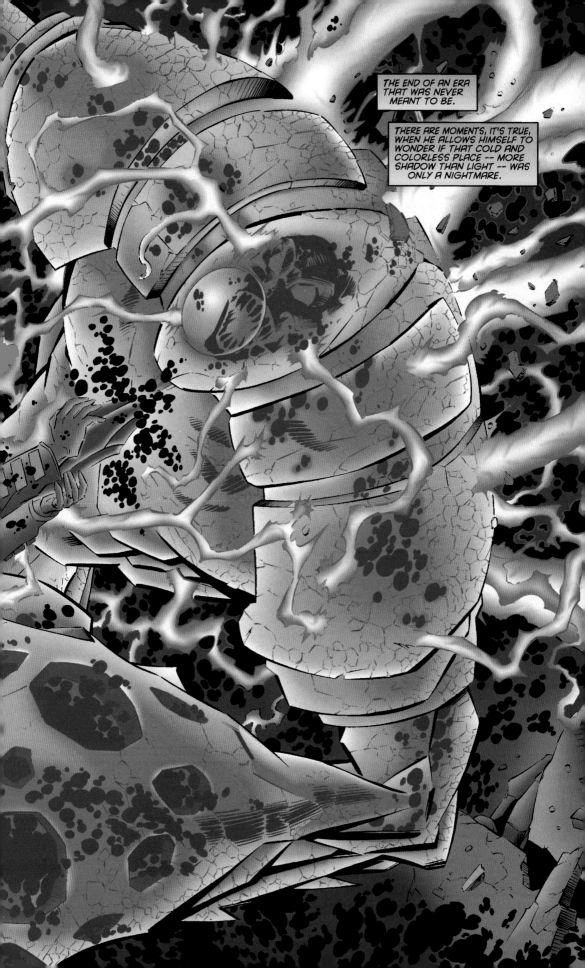

THE END OF AN ERA THAT WAS NEVER MEANT TO BE.

THERE ARE MOMENTS, IT'S TRUE, WHEN HE ALLOWS HIMSELF TO WONDER IF THAT COLD AND COLORLESS PLACE -- MORE SHADOW THAN LIGHT -- WAS ONLY A NIGHTMARE.

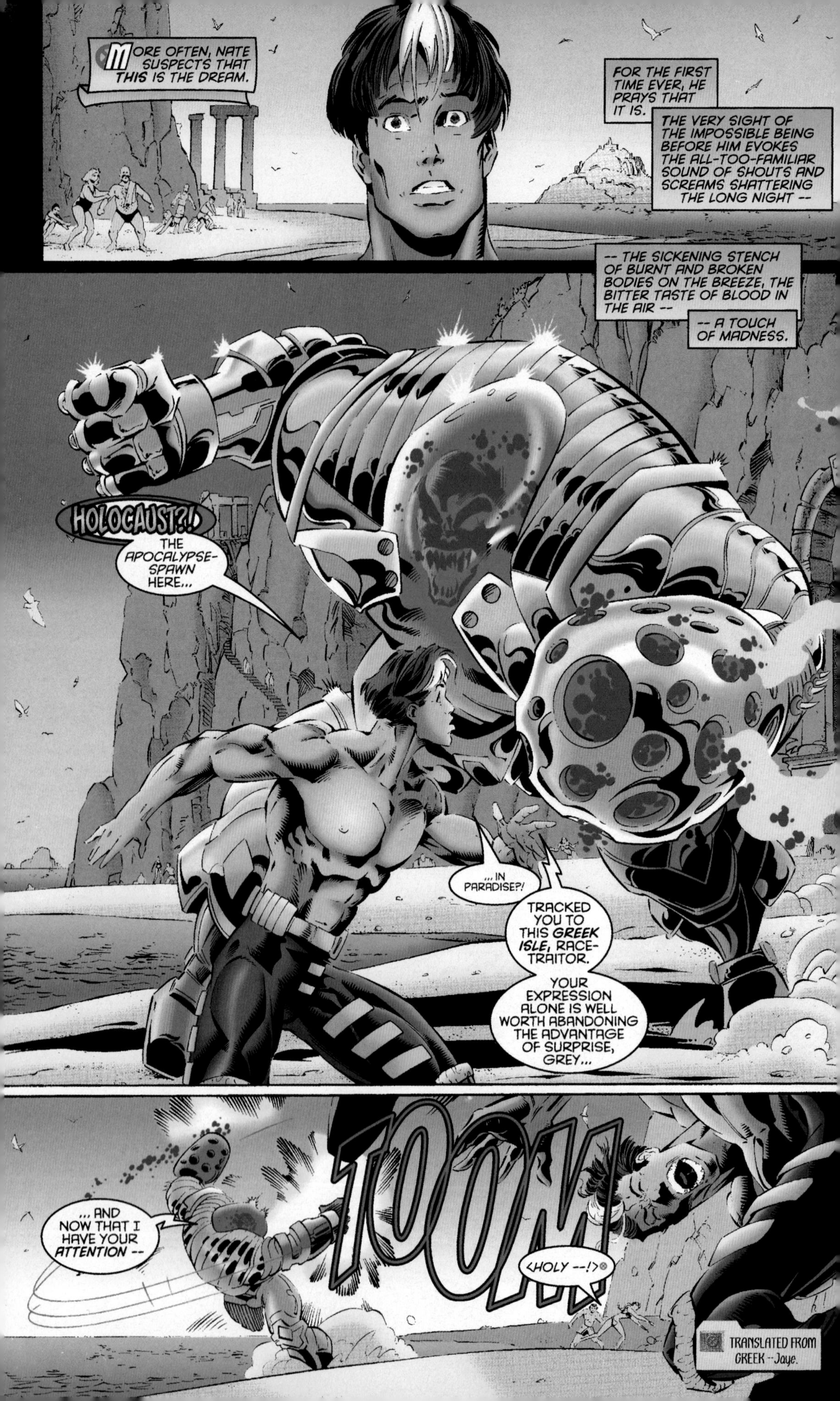
MORE OFTEN, NATE SUSPECTS THAT THIS IS THE DREAM.
FOR THE FIRST TIME EVER, HE PRAYS THAT IT IS.
THE VERY SIGHT OF THE IMPOSSIBLE BEING BEFORE HIM EVOKES THE ALL-TOO-FAMILIAR SOUND OF SHOUTS AND SCREAMS SHATTERING THE LONG NIGHT --
-- THE SICKENING STENCH OF BURNT AND BROKEN BODIES ON THE BREEZE, THE BITTER TASTE OF BLOOD IN THE AIR --
-- A TOUCH OF MADNESS.
HOLOCAUST?!
THE APOCALYPSE-SPAWN HERE...
...IN PARADISE?!
TRACKED YOU TO THIS GREEK ISLE, RACE-TRAITOR.
YOUR EXPRESSION ALONE IS WELL WORTH ABANDONING THE ADVANTAGE OF SURPRISE, GREY...
TOOOM
...AND NOW THAT I HAVE YOUR ATTENTION --
<HOLY --!>
TRANSLATED FROM GREEK --Jaye.

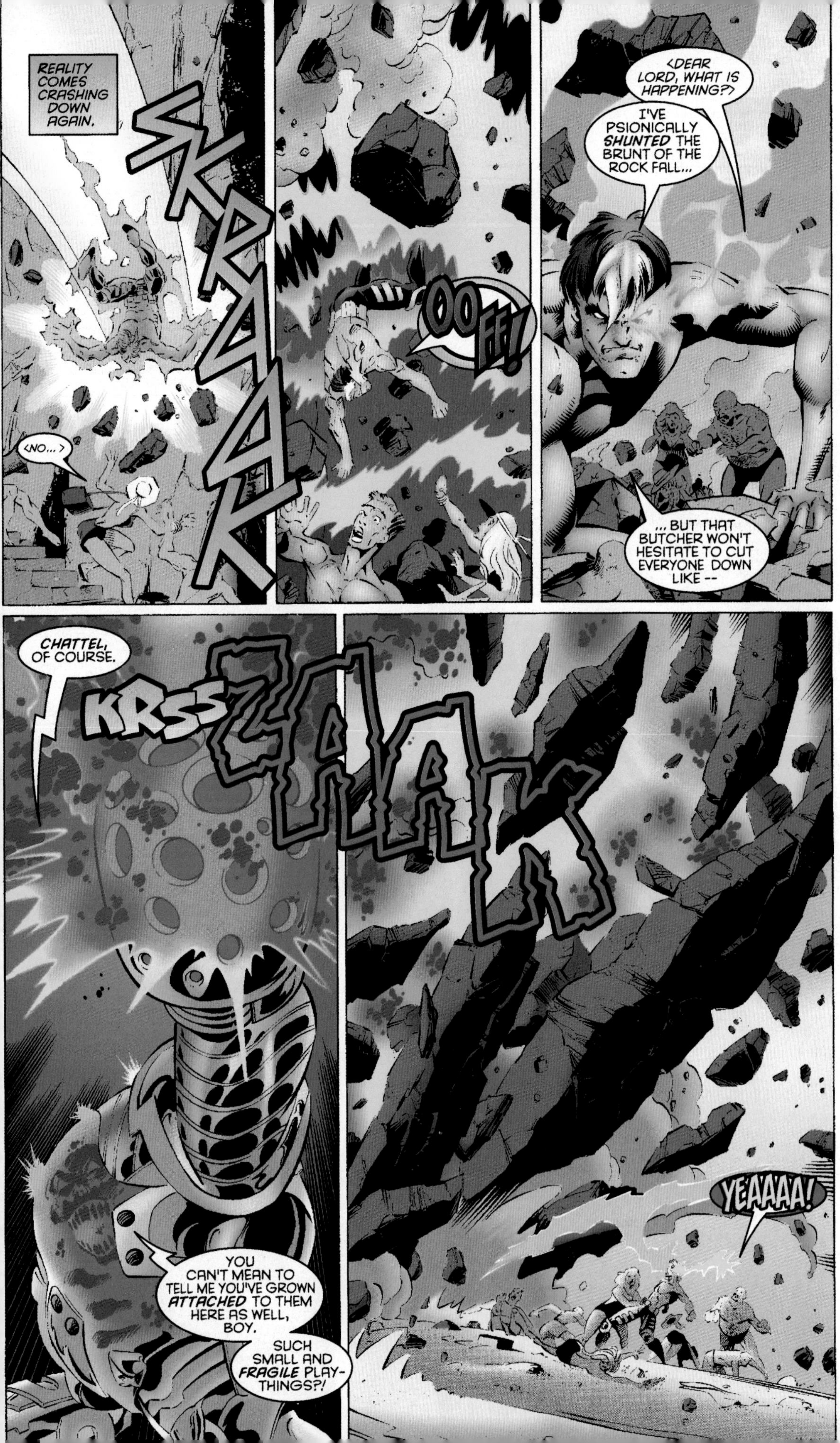

REALITY COMES CRASHING DOWN AGAIN.
SKRAAK
<NO...>
'OOFF!
<DEAR LORD, WHAT IS HAPPENING?>
I'VE PSIONICALLY SHUNTED THE BRUNT OF THE ROCK FALL...
... BUT THAT BUTCHER WON'T HESITATE TO CUT EVERYONE DOWN LIKE --
CHATTEL, OF COURSE.
KRSSZAAK
YOU CAN'T MEAN TO TELL ME YOU'VE GROWN ATTACHED TO THEM HERE AS WELL, BOY.
SUCH SMALL AND FRAGILE PLAY-THINGS?!
YEAAAA!

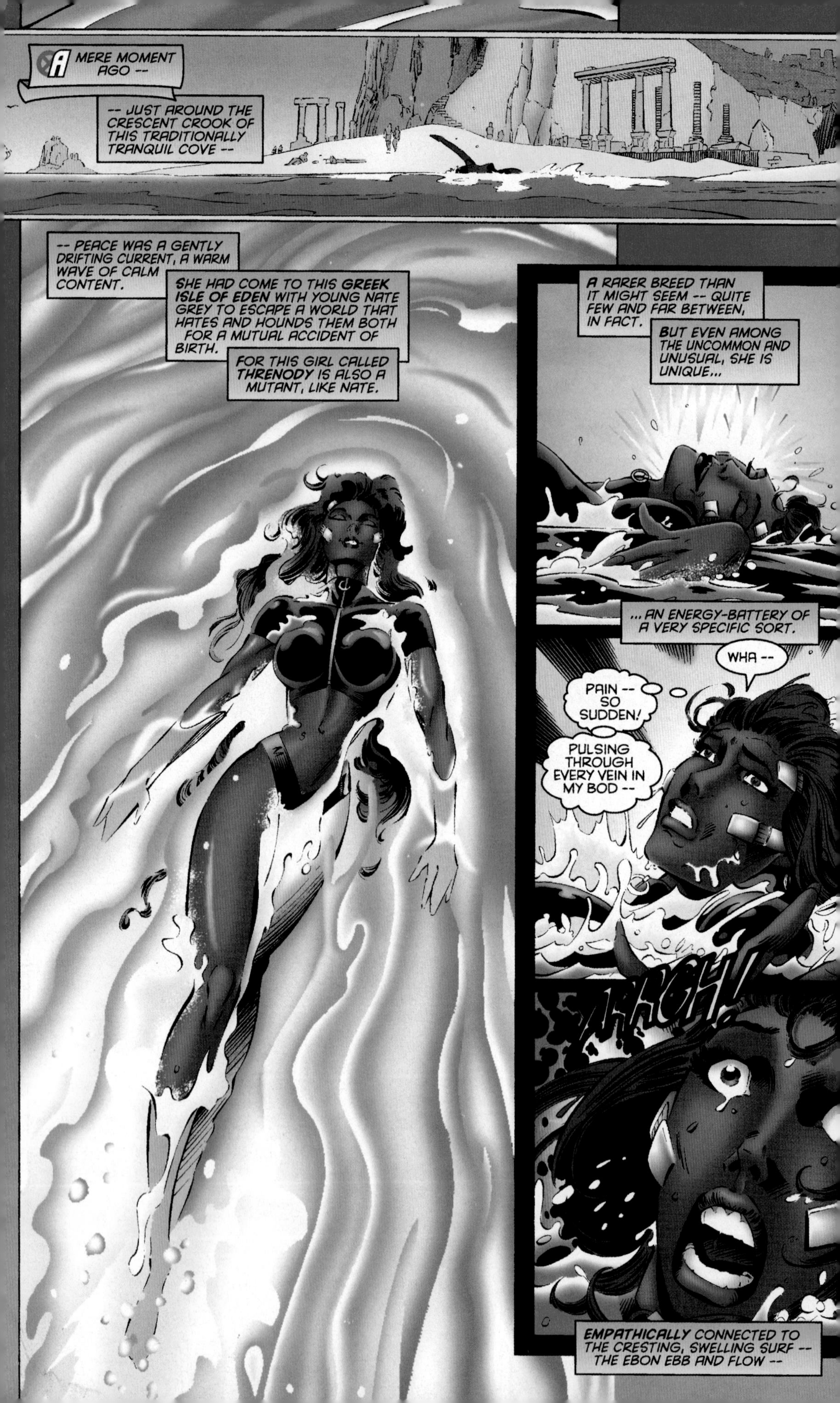
A MERE MOMENT AGO --
-- JUST AROUND THE CRESCENT CROOK OF THIS TRADITIONALLY TRANQUIL COVE --
-- PEACE WAS A GENTLY DRIFTING CURRENT, A WARM WAVE OF CALM CONTENT.
SHE HAD COME TO THIS GREEK ISLE OF EDEN WITH YOUNG NATE GREY TO ESCAPE A WORLD THAT HATES AND HOUNDS THEM BOTH FOR A MUTUAL ACCIDENT OF BIRTH.
FOR THIS GIRL CALLED THRENODY IS ALSO A MUTANT, LIKE NATE.
A RARER BREED THAN IT MIGHT SEEM -- QUITE FEW AND FAR BETWEEN, IN FACT.
BUT EVEN AMONG THE UNCOMMON AND UNUSUAL, SHE IS UNIQUE...
...AN ENERGY-BATTERY OF A VERY SPECIFIC SORT.
WHA --
PAIN -- SO SUDDEN!
PULSING THROUGH EVERY VEIN IN MY BOD --
AAARGH!
EMPATHICALLY CONNECTED TO THE CRESTING, SWELLING SURF -- THE EBON EBB AND FLOW --

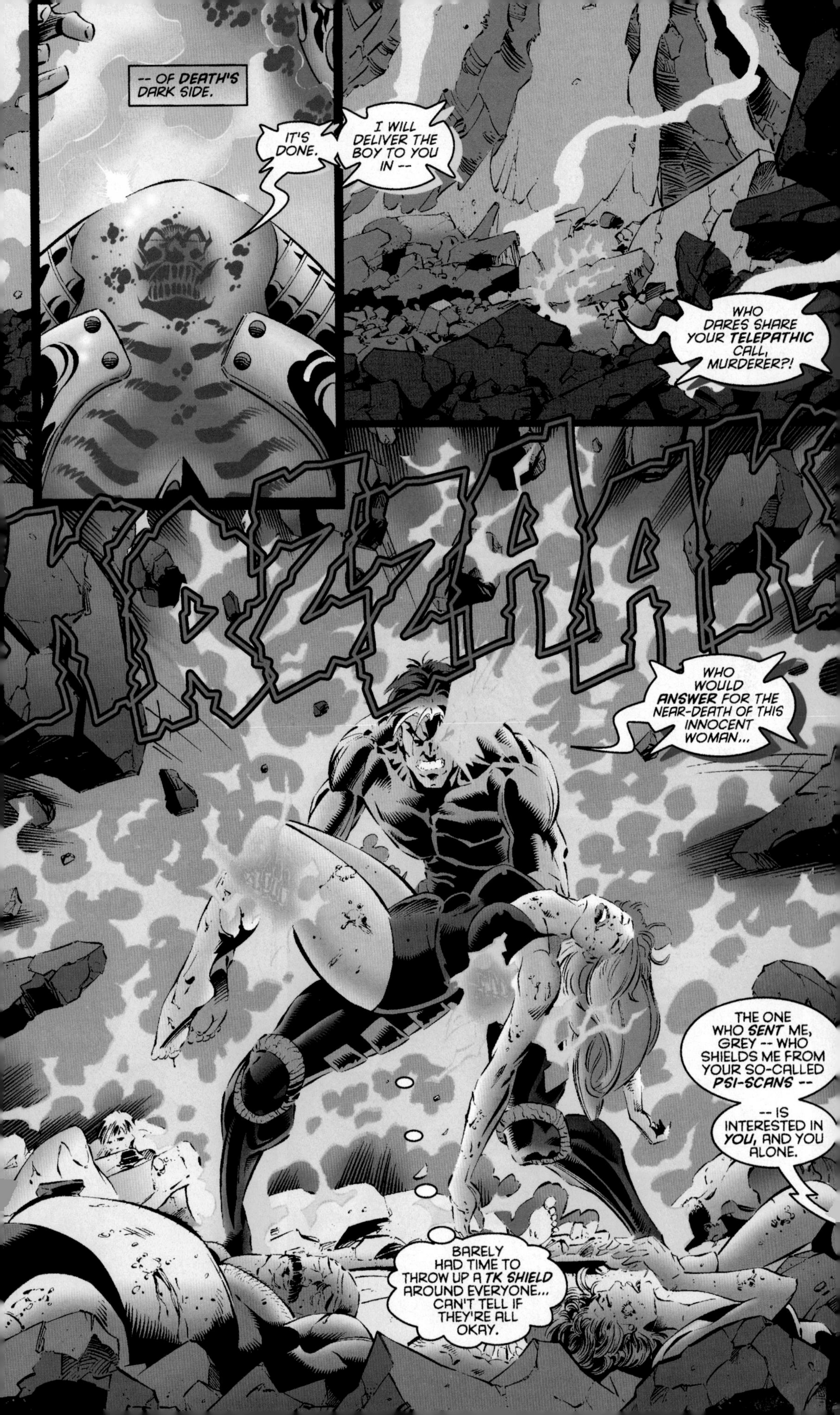
-- OF DEATH'S DARK SIDE.
IT'S DONE.
I WILL DELIVER THE BOY TO YOU IN --
WHO DARES SHARE YOUR TELEPATHIC CALL, MURDERER?!
WHO WOULD ANSWER FOR THE NEAR-DEATH OF THIS INNOCENT WOMAN...
THE ONE WHO SENT ME, GREY -- WHO SHIELDS ME FROM YOUR SO-CALLED PSI-SCANS --
-- IS INTERESTED IN YOU, AND YOU ALONE.
BARELY HAD TIME TO THROW UP A TK SHIELD AROUND EVERYONE... CAN'T TELL IF THEY'RE ALL OKAY.

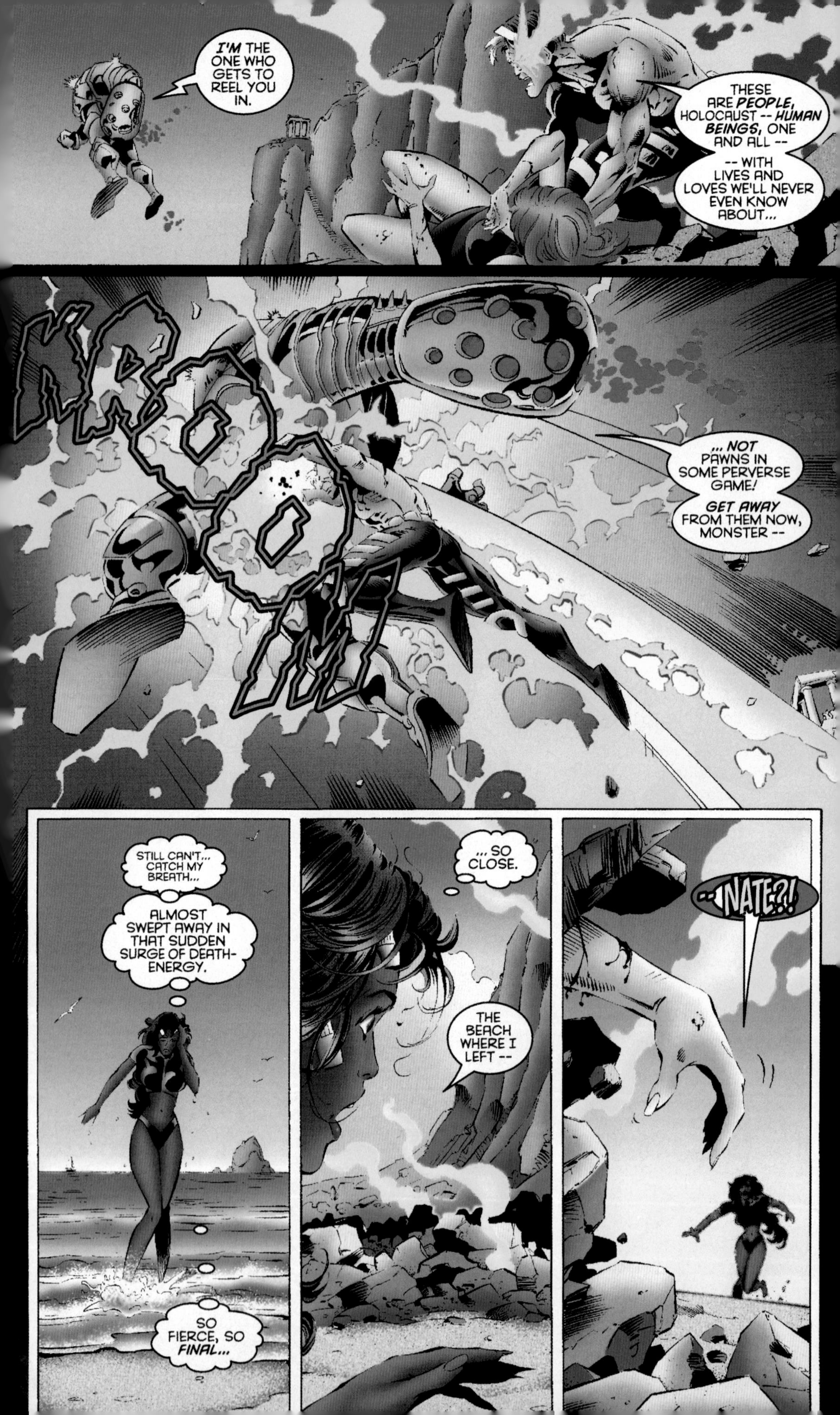
I'M THE ONE WHO GETS TO REEL YOU IN.
THESE ARE PEOPLE, HOLOCAUST -- HUMAN BEINGS, ONE AND ALL --
-- WITH LIVES AND LOVES WE'LL NEVER EVEN KNOW ABOUT...
KROOOM
... NOT PAWNS IN SOME PERVERSE GAME!
GET AWAY FROM THEM NOW, MONSTER --
STILL CAN'T... CATCH MY BREATH...
ALMOST SWEPT AWAY IN THAT SUDDEN SURGE OF DEATH-ENERGY.
SO FIERCE, SO FINAL...
... SO CLOSE.
THE BEACH WHERE I LEFT --
-- NATE?!

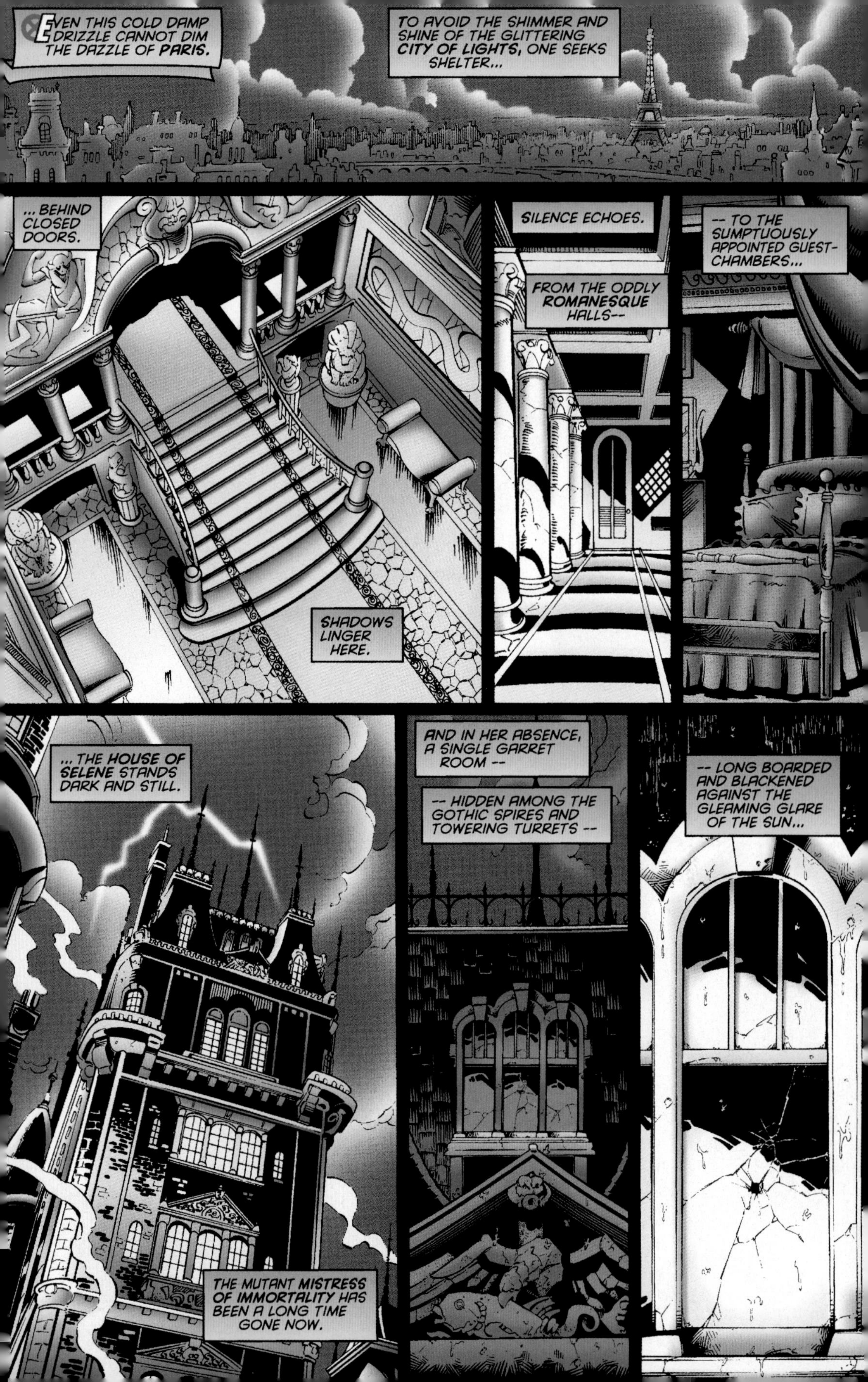
EVEN THIS COLD DAMP DRIZZLE CANNOT DIM THE DAZZLE OF PARIS.
TO AVOID THE SHIMMER AND SHINE OF THE GLITTERING CITY OF LIGHTS, ONE SEEKS SHELTER...
...BEHIND CLOSED DOORS.
SHADOWS LINGER HERE.
SILENCE ECHOES.
FROM THE ODDLY ROMANESQUE HALLS--
-- TO THE SUMPTUOUSLY APPOINTED GUEST-CHAMBERS...
...THE HOUSE OF SELENE STANDS DARK AND STILL.
THE MUTANT MISTRESS OF IMMORTALITY HAS BEEN A LONG TIME GONE NOW.
AND IN HER ABSENCE, A SINGLE GARRET ROOM --
-- HIDDEN AMONG THE GOTHIC SPIRES AND TOWERING TURRETS --
-- LONG BOARDED AND BLACKENED AGAINST THE GLEAMING GLARE OF THE SUN...

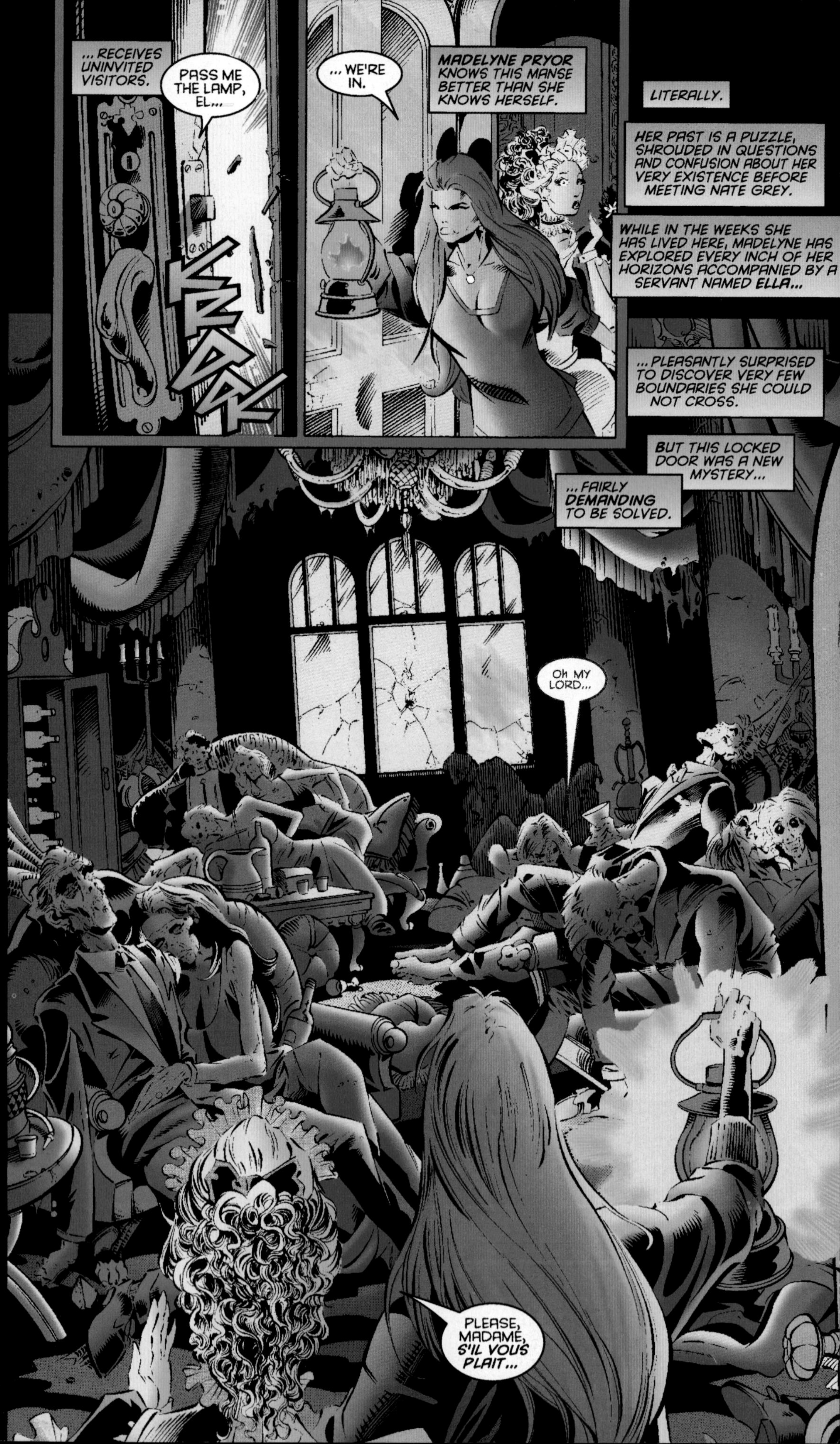
...RECEIVES UNINVITED VISITORS.
PASS ME THE LAMP, EL...
KRAACK
...WE'RE IN.
MADELYNE PRYOR KNOWS THIS MANSE BETTER THAN SHE KNOWS HERSELF.
LITERALLY.
HER PAST IS A PUZZLE, SHROUDED IN QUESTIONS AND CONFUSION ABOUT HER VERY EXISTENCE BEFORE MEETING NATE GREY.
WHILE IN THE WEEKS SHE HAS LIVED HERE, MADELYNE HAS EXPLORED EVERY INCH OF HER HORIZONS ACCOMPANIED BY A SERVANT NAMED ELLA...
...PLEASANTLY SURPRISED TO DISCOVER VERY FEW BOUNDARIES SHE COULD NOT CROSS.
BUT THIS LOCKED DOOR WAS A NEW MYSTERY...
...FAIRLY DEMANDING TO BE SOLVED.
Oh MY LORD...
PLEASE, MADAME, S'IL VOUS PLAIT...

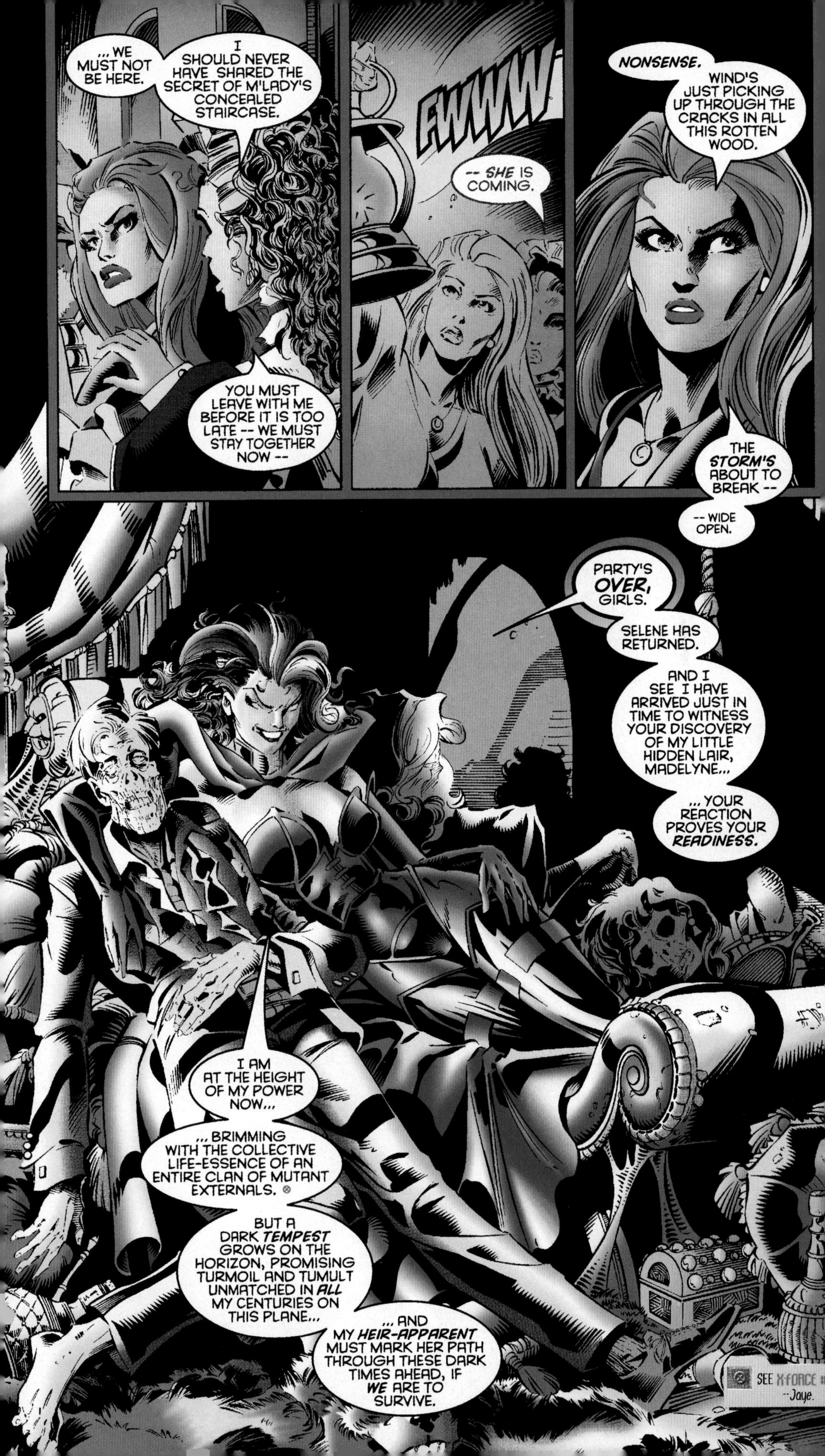

...WE MUST NOT BE HERE.
I SHOULD NEVER HAVE SHARED THE SECRET OF M'LADY'S CONCEALED STAIRCASE.
YOU MUST LEAVE WITH ME BEFORE IT IS TOO LATE -- WE MUST STAY TOGETHER NOW --
FWWW
-- SHE IS COMING.
NONSENSE. WIND'S JUST PICKING UP THROUGH THE CRACKS IN ALL THIS ROTTEN WOOD.
THE STORM'S ABOUT TO BREAK --
-- WIDE OPEN.
PARTY'S OVER, GIRLS.
SELENE HAS RETURNED.
AND I SEE I HAVE ARRIVED JUST IN TIME TO WITNESS YOUR DISCOVERY OF MY LITTLE HIDDEN LAIR, MADELYNE...
...YOUR REACTION PROVES YOUR READINESS.
I AM AT THE HEIGHT OF MY POWER NOW...
...BRIMMING WITH THE COLLECTIVE LIFE-ESSENCE OF AN ENTIRE CLAN OF MUTANT EXTERNALS.
BUT A DARK TEMPEST GROWS ON THE HORIZON, PROMISING TURMOIL AND TUMULT UNMATCHED IN ALL MY CENTURIES ON THIS PLANE...
...AND MY HEIR-APPARENT MUST MARK HER PATH THROUGH THESE DARK TIMES AHEAD, IF WE ARE TO SURVIVE.
SEE X-FORCE
--Jaye.

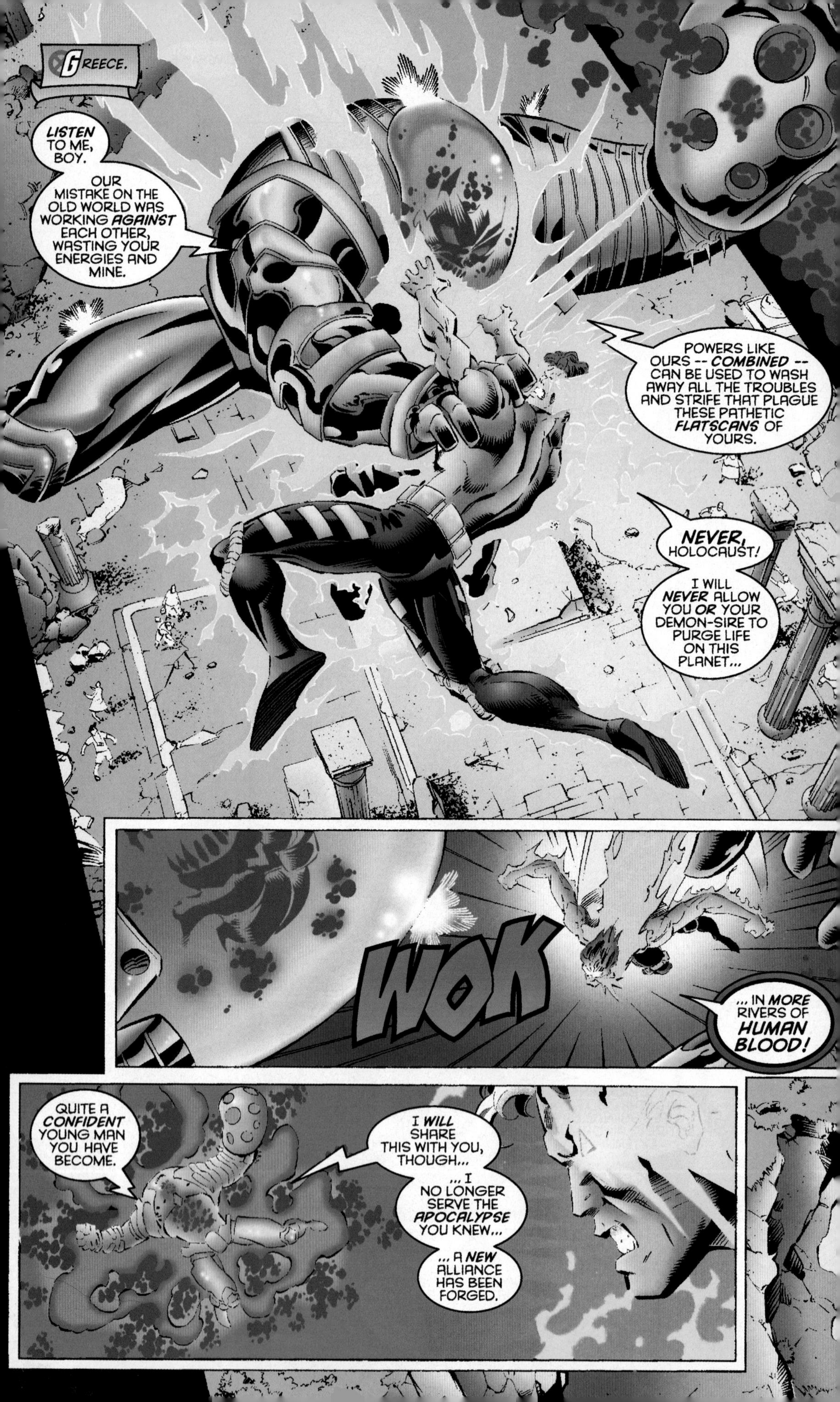

GREECE.
LISTEN TO ME, BOY.
OUR MISTAKE ON THE OLD WORLD WAS WORKING AGAINST EACH OTHER, WASTING YOUR ENERGIES AND MINE.
POWERS LIKE OURS -- COMBINED -- CAN BE USED TO WASH AWAY ALL THE TROUBLES AND STRIFE THAT PLAGUE THESE PATHETIC FLATSCANS OF YOURS.
NEVER, HOLOCAUST!
I WILL NEVER ALLOW YOU OR YOUR DEMON-SIRE TO PURGE LIFE ON THIS PLANET...
WOK
... IN MORE RIVERS OF HUMAN BLOOD!
QUITE A CONFIDENT YOUNG MAN YOU HAVE BECOME.
I WILL SHARE THIS WITH YOU, THOUGH...
... I NO LONGER SERVE THE APOCALYPSE YOU KNEW...
... A NEW ALLIANCE HAS BEEN FORGED.

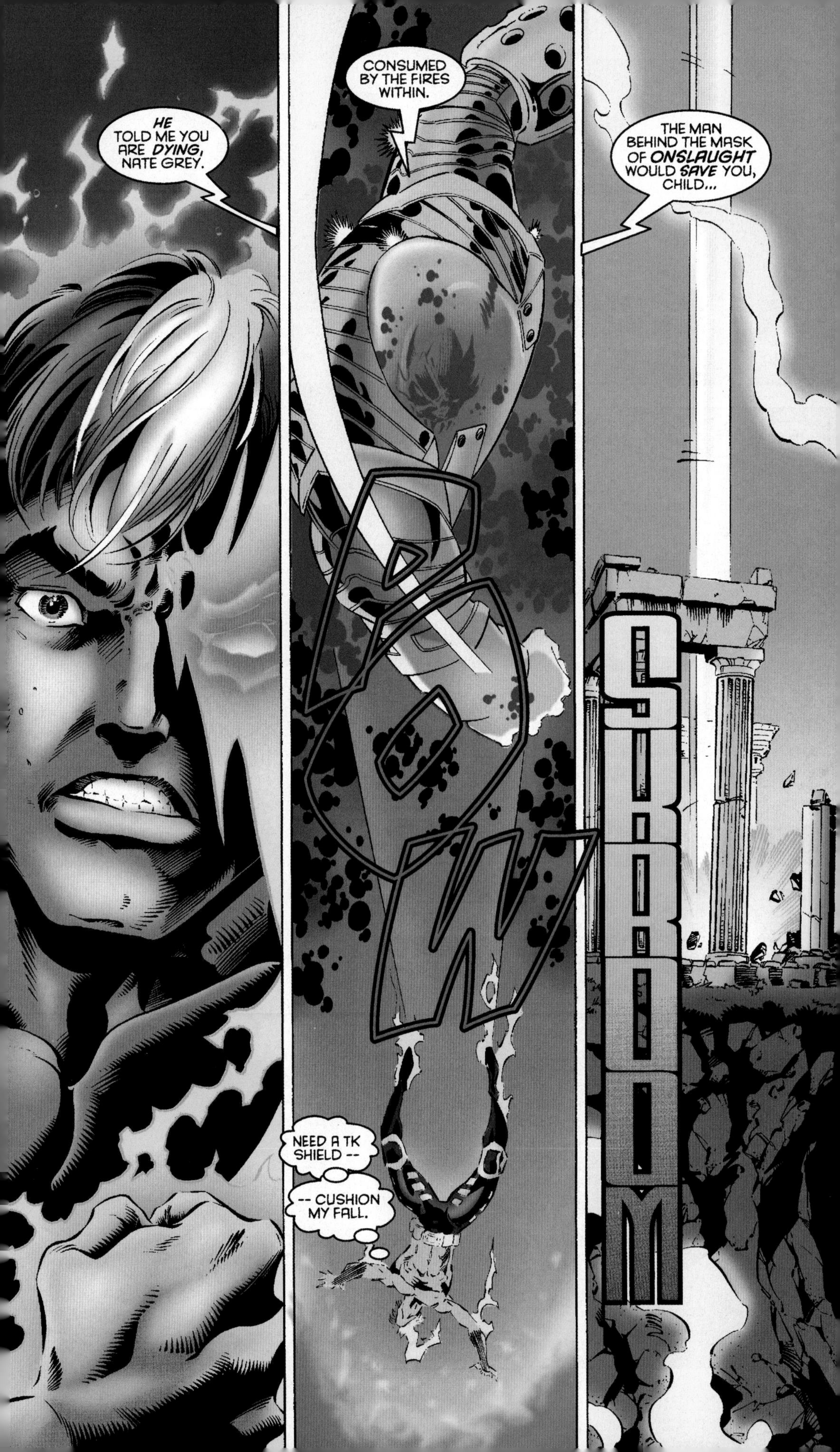
HE TOLD ME YOU ARE DYING, NATE GREY.
CONSUMED BY THE FIRES WITHIN.
THE MAN BEHIND THE MASK OF ONSLAUGHT WOULD SAVE YOU, CHILD...
BOOM
NEED A TK SHIELD --
-- CUSHION MY FALL.
SHROOOM

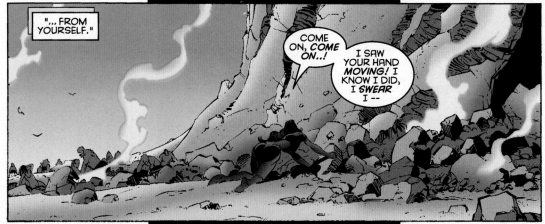

"...FROM YOURSELF."

COME ON, *COME ON*..!

I SAW YOUR HAND *MOVING!* I KNOW I DID, I *SWEAR* I --

>hkk<
>hkk<

YES...

TAKE IT EASY NOW, *HON.*

LOOKS LIKE A COUPLE OF FRACTURED RIBS, AT LEAST, MAYBE EVEN A BROKEN ARM.

YOU NEED TO GET TO A HOSPITAL AS SOON AS--

N-NO...

PLEASE...

MY *HUSBAND*--

-- YOU'VE *GOT* TO *HELP* MY HUSBAND!

ARRR!

I'LL.... TRY.

BUT THE DAMAGE IS ALREADY *DONE.*

HE *REEKS* OF DEATH, ASSAULTING MY SENSES ON AN ALMOST PHYSICAL LEVEL THE CLOSER I COME.

AND IT SOUNDS LIKE HE'S IN UNIMAGINABLE --

-- PAIN..?!

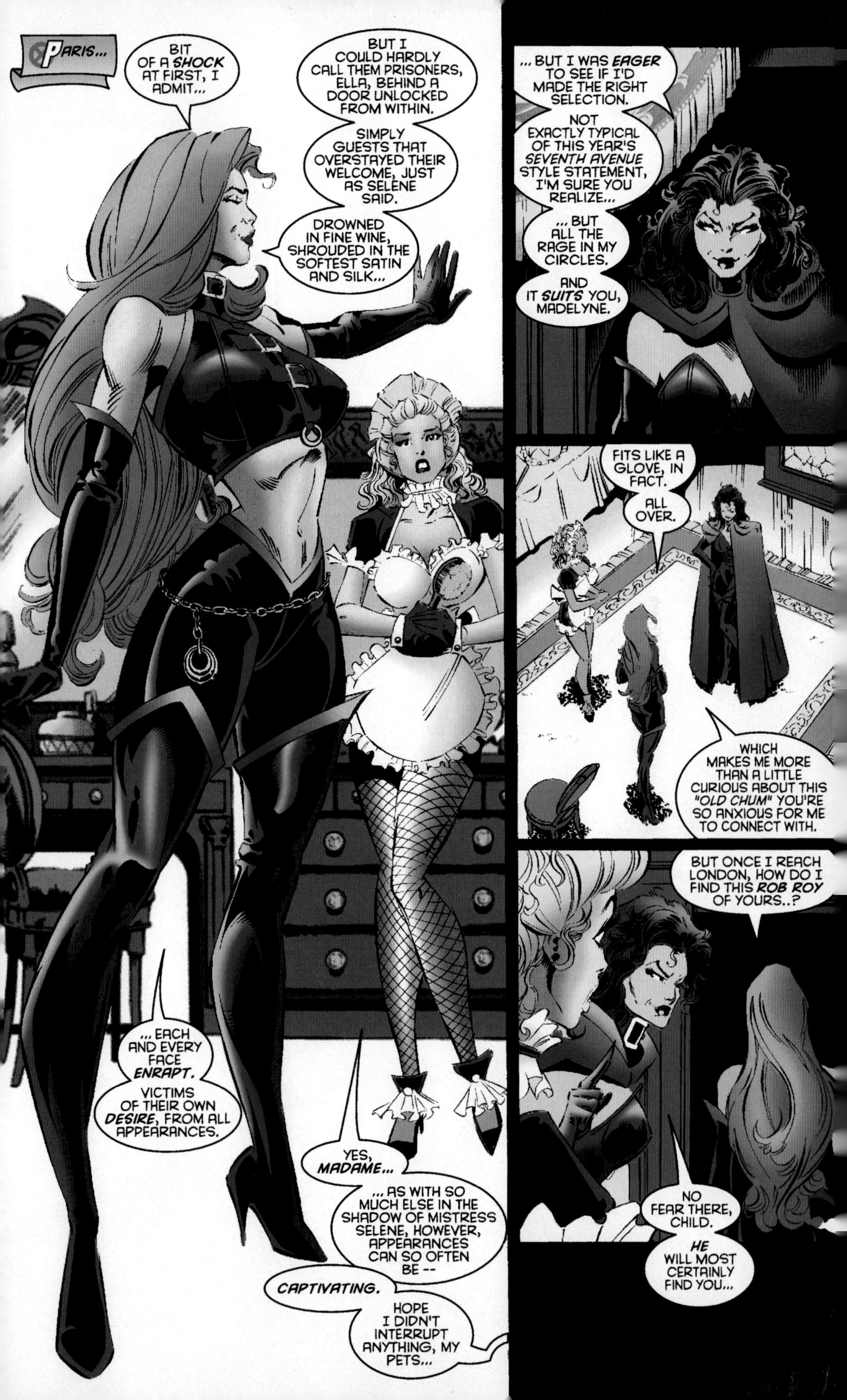
PARIS...
BIT OF A SHOCK AT FIRST, I ADMIT...
BUT I COULD HARDLY CALL THEM PRISONERS, ELLA, BEHIND A DOOR UNLOCKED FROM WITHIN.
SIMPLY GUESTS THAT OVERSTAYED THEIR WELCOME, JUST AS SELENE SAID.
DROWNED IN FINE WINE, SHROUDED IN THE SOFTEST SATIN AND SILK...
... EACH AND EVERY FACE ENRAPT.
VICTIMS OF THEIR OWN DESIRE, FROM ALL APPEARANCES.
YES, MADAME...
... AS WITH SO MUCH ELSE IN THE SHADOW OF MISTRESS SELENE, HOWEVER, APPEARANCES CAN SO OFTEN BE --
CAPTIVATING.
HOPE I DIDN'T INTERRUPT ANYTHING, MY PETS...
... BUT I WAS EAGER TO SEE IF I'D MADE THE RIGHT SELECTION.
NOT EXACTLY TYPICAL OF THIS YEAR'S SEVENTH AVENUE STYLE STATEMENT, I'M SURE YOU REALIZE...
... BUT ALL THE RAGE IN MY CIRCLES.
AND IT SUITS YOU, MADELYNE.
FITS LIKE A GLOVE, IN FACT.
ALL OVER.
WHICH MAKES ME MORE THAN A LITTLE CURIOUS ABOUT THIS "OLD CHUM" YOU'RE SO ANXIOUS FOR ME TO CONNECT WITH.
BUT ONCE I REACH LONDON, HOW DO I FIND THIS ROB ROY OF YOURS..?
NO FEAR THERE, CHILD.
HE WILL MOST CERTAINLY FIND YOU...

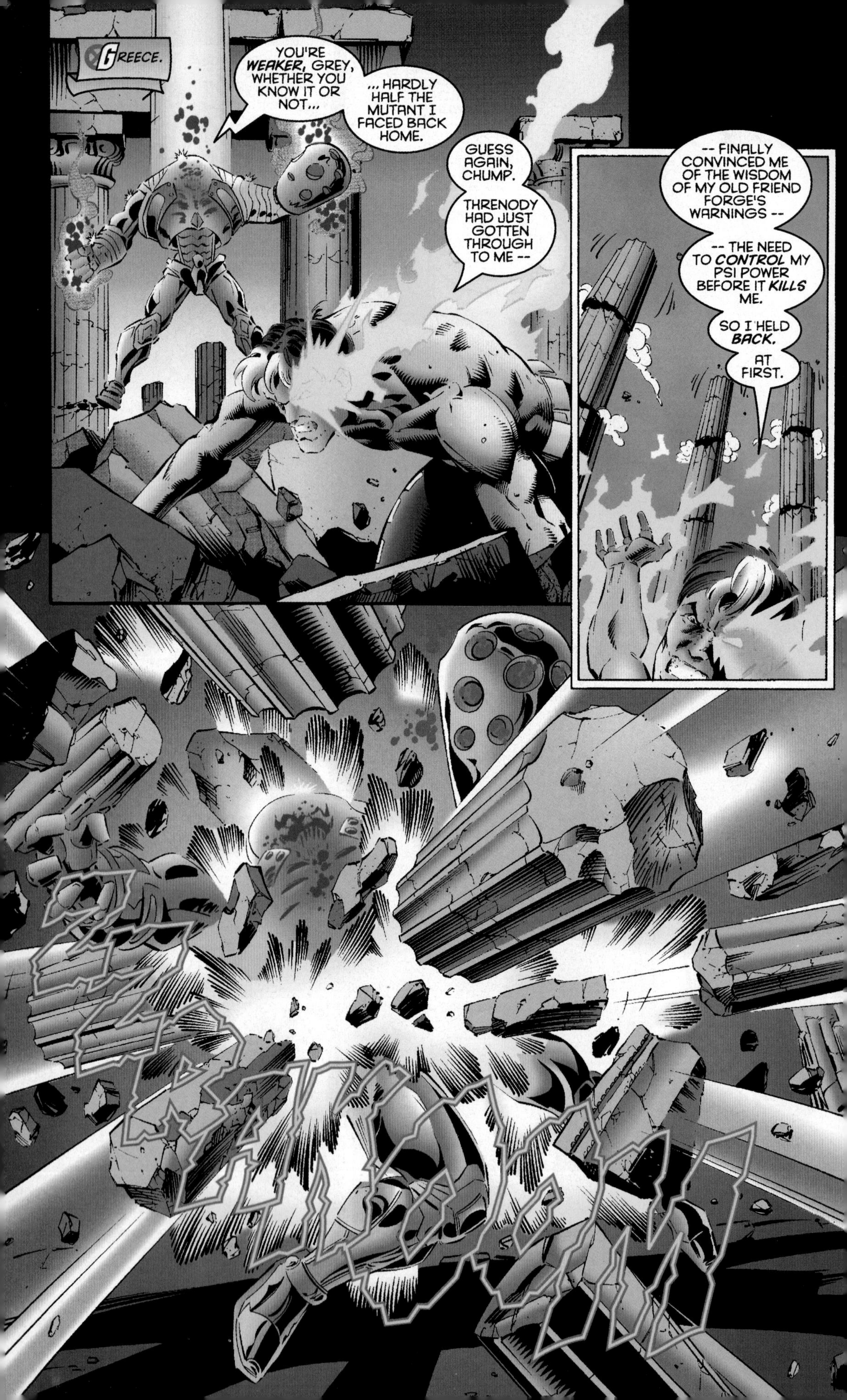
GREECE.
YOU'RE WEAKER, GREY, WHETHER YOU KNOW IT OR NOT...
... HARDLY HALF THE MUTANT I FACED BACK HOME.
GUESS AGAIN, CHUMP.
THRENODY HAD JUST GOTTEN THROUGH TO ME --
-- FINALLY CONVINCED ME OF THE WISDOM OF MY OLD FRIEND FORGE'S WARNINGS --
-- THE NEED TO CONTROL MY PSI POWER BEFORE IT KILLS ME.
SO I HELD BACK.
AT FIRST.

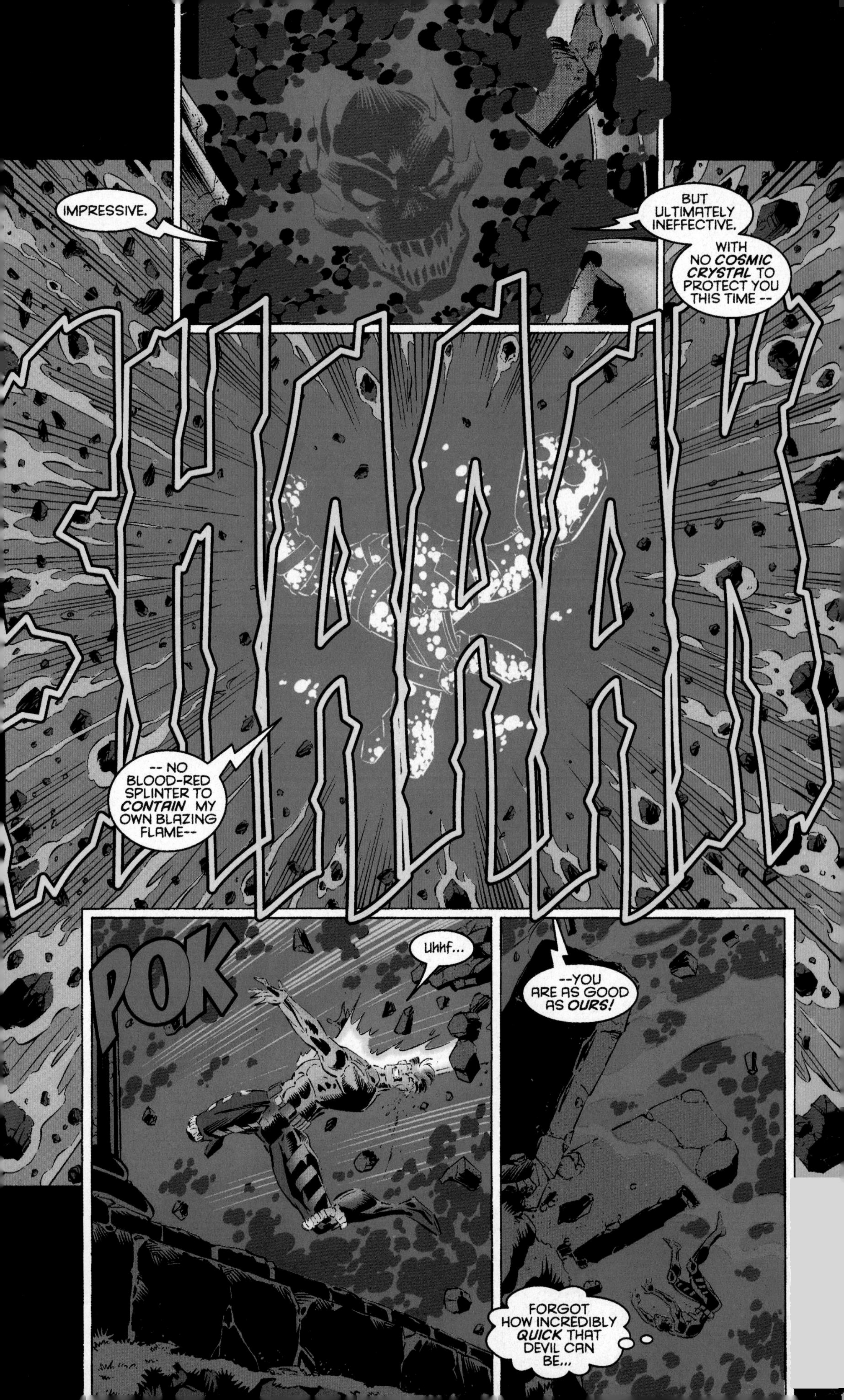
IMPRESSIVE.
BUT ULTIMATELY INEFFECTIVE.
WITH NO COSMIC CRYSTAL TO PROTECT YOU THIS TIME --
-- NO BLOOD-RED SPLINTER TO CONTAIN MY OWN BLAZING FLAME--
POK
Uhhf...
--YOU ARE AS GOOD AS OURS!
FORGOT HOW INCREDIBLY QUICK THAT DEVIL CAN BE...

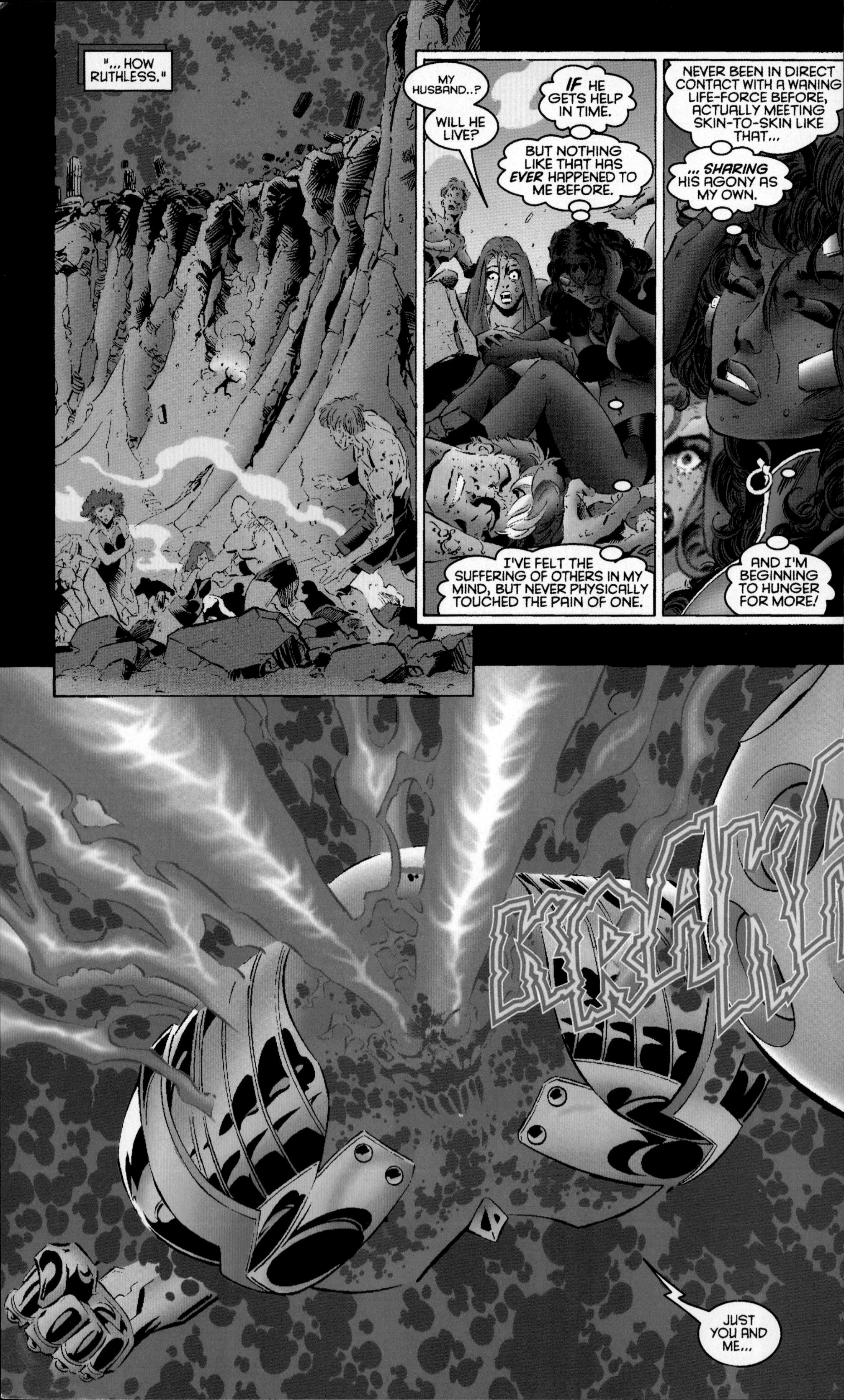
"... HOW RUTHLESS."
MY HUSBAND..?
WILL HE LIVE?
IF HE GETS HELP IN TIME.
BUT NOTHING LIKE THAT HAS EVER HAPPENED TO ME BEFORE.
I'VE FELT THE SUFFERING OF OTHERS IN MY MIND, BUT NEVER PHYSICALLY TOUCHED THE PAIN OF ONE.
NEVER BEEN IN DIRECT CONTACT WITH A WANING LIFE-FORCE BEFORE, ACTUALLY MEETING SKIN-TO-SKIN LIKE THAT...
... SHARING HIS AGONY AS MY OWN.
AND I'M BEGINNING TO HUNGER FOR MORE!
KRAKKA
JUST YOU AND ME...

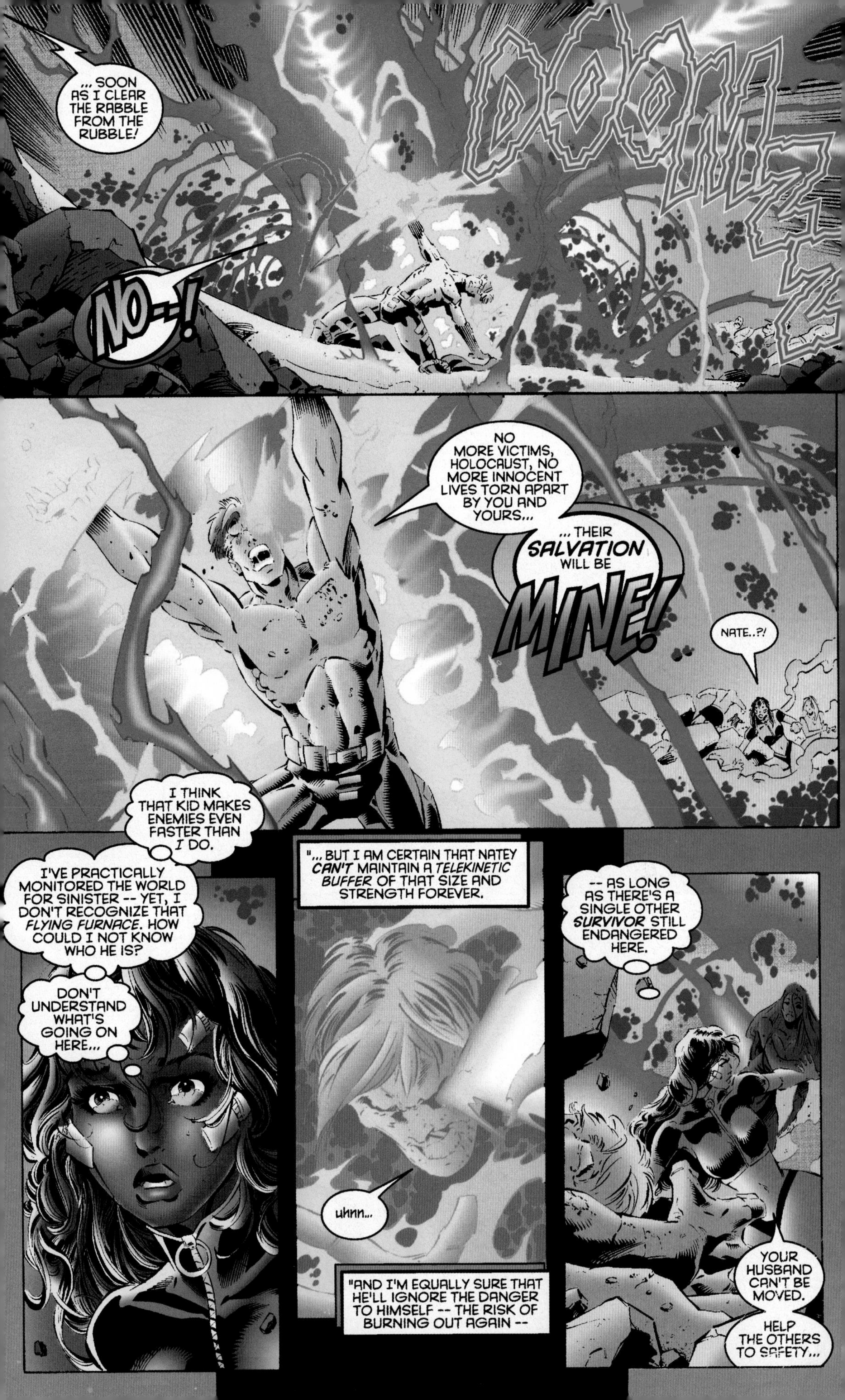

... SOON AS I CLEAR THE RABBLE FROM THE RUBBLE!
DOOOMM
NO--!
NO MORE VICTIMS, HOLOCAUST, NO MORE INNOCENT LIVES TORN APART BY YOU AND YOURS...
... THEIR SALVATION WILL BE
MINE!
NATE..?!
I THINK THAT KID MAKES ENEMIES EVEN FASTER THAN I DO.
I'VE PRACTICALLY MONITORED THE WORLD FOR SINISTER -- YET, I DON'T RECOGNIZE THAT FLYING FURNACE. HOW COULD I NOT KNOW WHO HE IS?
DON'T UNDERSTAND WHAT'S GOING ON HERE...
"... BUT I AM CERTAIN THAT NATEY CAN'T MAINTAIN A TELEKINETIC BUFFER OF THAT SIZE AND STRENGTH FOREVER.
uhnn...
"AND I'M EQUALLY SURE THAT HE'LL IGNORE THE DANGER TO HIMSELF -- THE RISK OF BURNING OUT AGAIN --
-- AS LONG AS THERE'S A SINGLE OTHER SURVIVOR STILL ENDANGERED HERE.
YOUR HUSBAND CAN'T BE MOVED.
HELP THE OTHERS TO SAFETY...

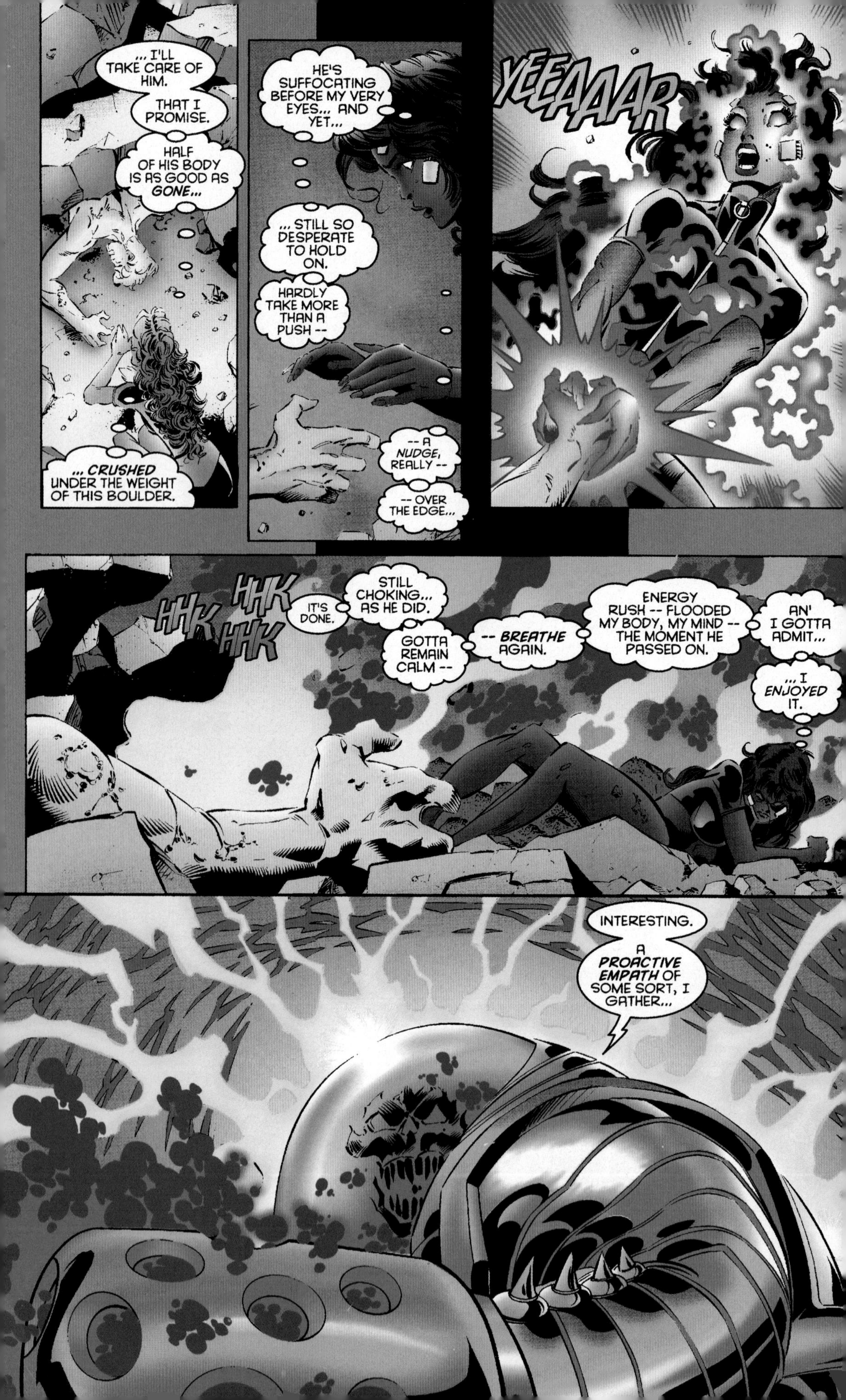
... I'LL TAKE CARE OF HIM.
THAT I PROMISE.
HALF OF HIS BODY IS AS GOOD AS GONE...
... CRUSHED UNDER THE WEIGHT OF THIS BOULDER.
HE'S SUFFOCATING BEFORE MY VERY EYES... AND YET...
... STILL SO DESPERATE TO HOLD ON.
HARDLY TAKE MORE THAN A PUSH --
-- A NUDGE, REALLY --
-- OVER THE EDGE...
YEEAAAAR
HHK HHK HHK HHK
IT'S DONE.
STILL CHOKING... AS HE DID.
GOTTA REMAIN CALM --
-- BREATHE AGAIN.
ENERGY RUSH -- FLOODED MY BODY, MY MIND -- THE MOMENT HE PASSED ON.
AN' I GOTTA ADMIT...
... I ENJOYED IT.
INTERESTING.
A PROACTIVE EMPATH OF SOME SORT, I GATHER...

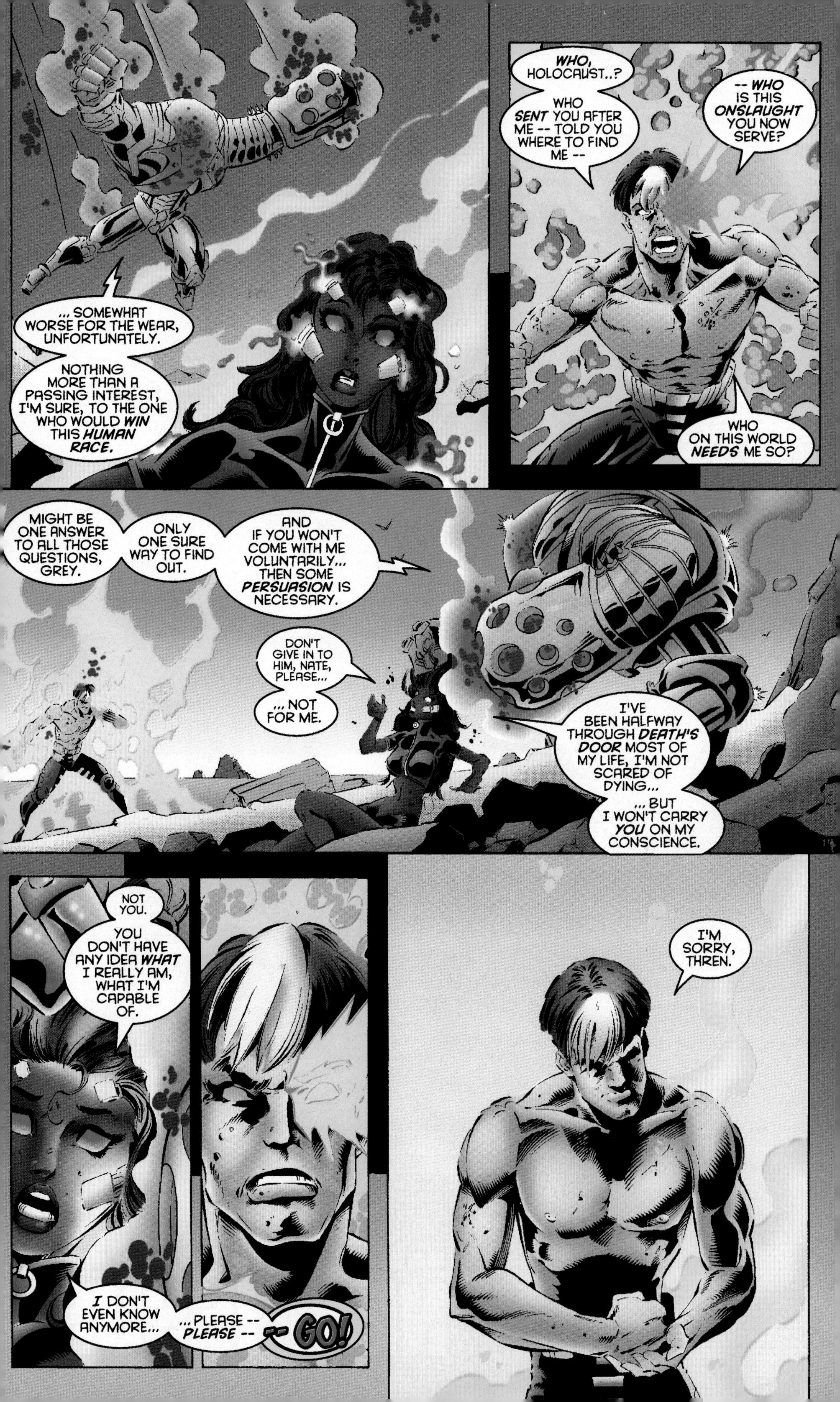

... SOMEWHAT WORSE FOR THE WEAR, UNFORTUNATELY.
NOTHING MORE THAN A PASSING INTEREST, I'M SURE, TO THE ONE WHO WOULD WIN THIS HUMAN RACE.
WHO, HOLOCAUST..?
WHO SENT YOU AFTER ME -- TOLD YOU WHERE TO FIND ME --
-- WHO IS THIS ONSLAUGHT YOU NOW SERVE?
WHO ON THIS WORLD NEEDS ME SO?
MIGHT BE ONE ANSWER TO ALL THOSE QUESTIONS, GREY.
ONLY ONE SURE WAY TO FIND OUT.
AND IF YOU WON'T COME WITH ME VOLUNTARILY... THEN SOME PERSUASION IS NECESSARY.
DON'T GIVE IN TO HIM, NATE, PLEASE...
... NOT FOR ME.
I'VE BEEN HALFWAY THROUGH DEATH'S DOOR MOST OF MY LIFE, I'M NOT SCARED OF DYING...
... BUT I WON'T CARRY YOU ON MY CONSCIENCE.
NOT YOU.
YOU DON'T HAVE ANY IDEA WHAT I REALLY AM, WHAT I'M CAPABLE OF.
I DON'T EVEN KNOW ANYMORE...
... PLEASE -- PLEASE --
-- GO!
I'M SORRY, THREN.

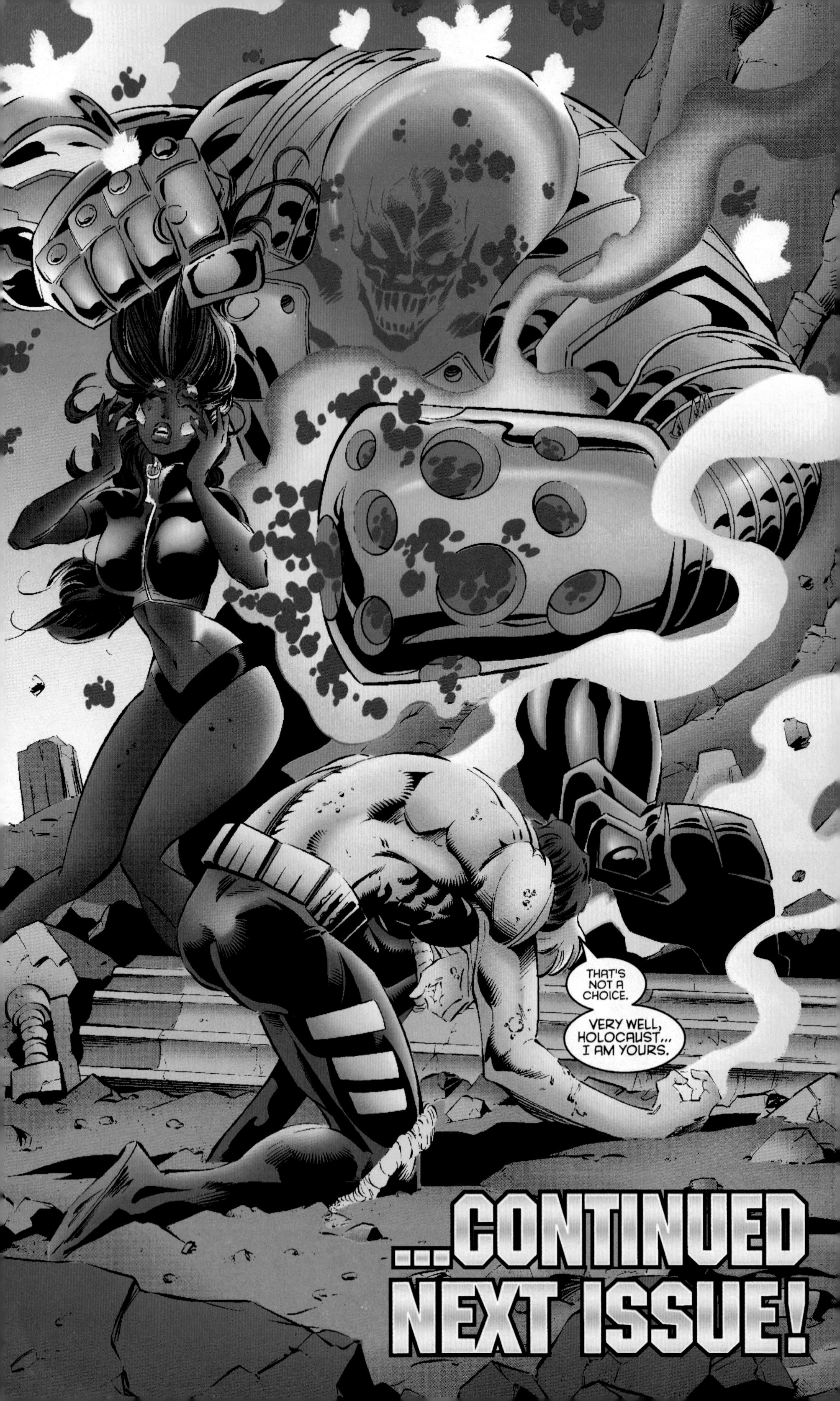
THAT'S NOT A CHOICE.
VERY WELL, HOLOCAUST... I AM YOURS.
...CONTINUED NEXT ISSUE!

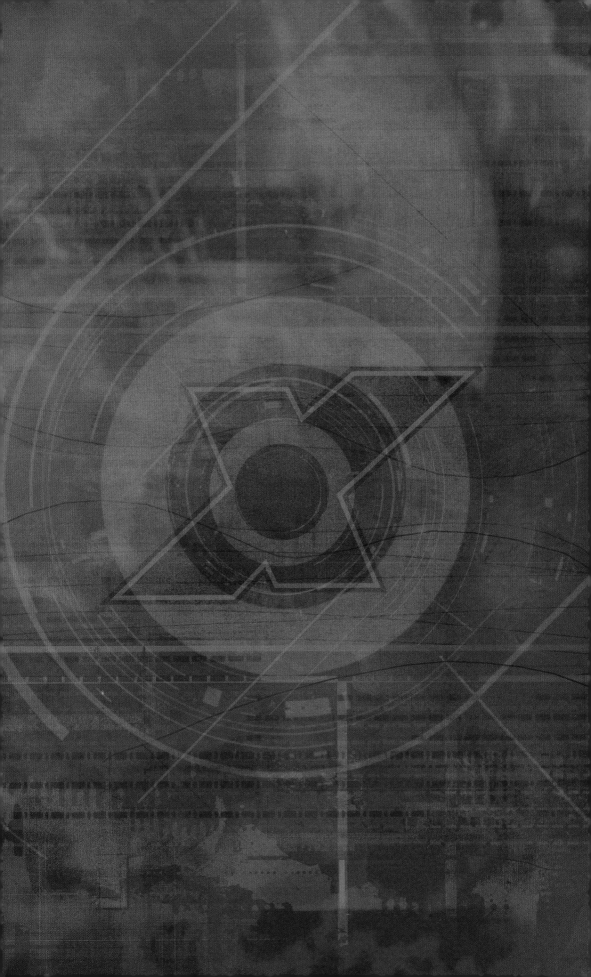

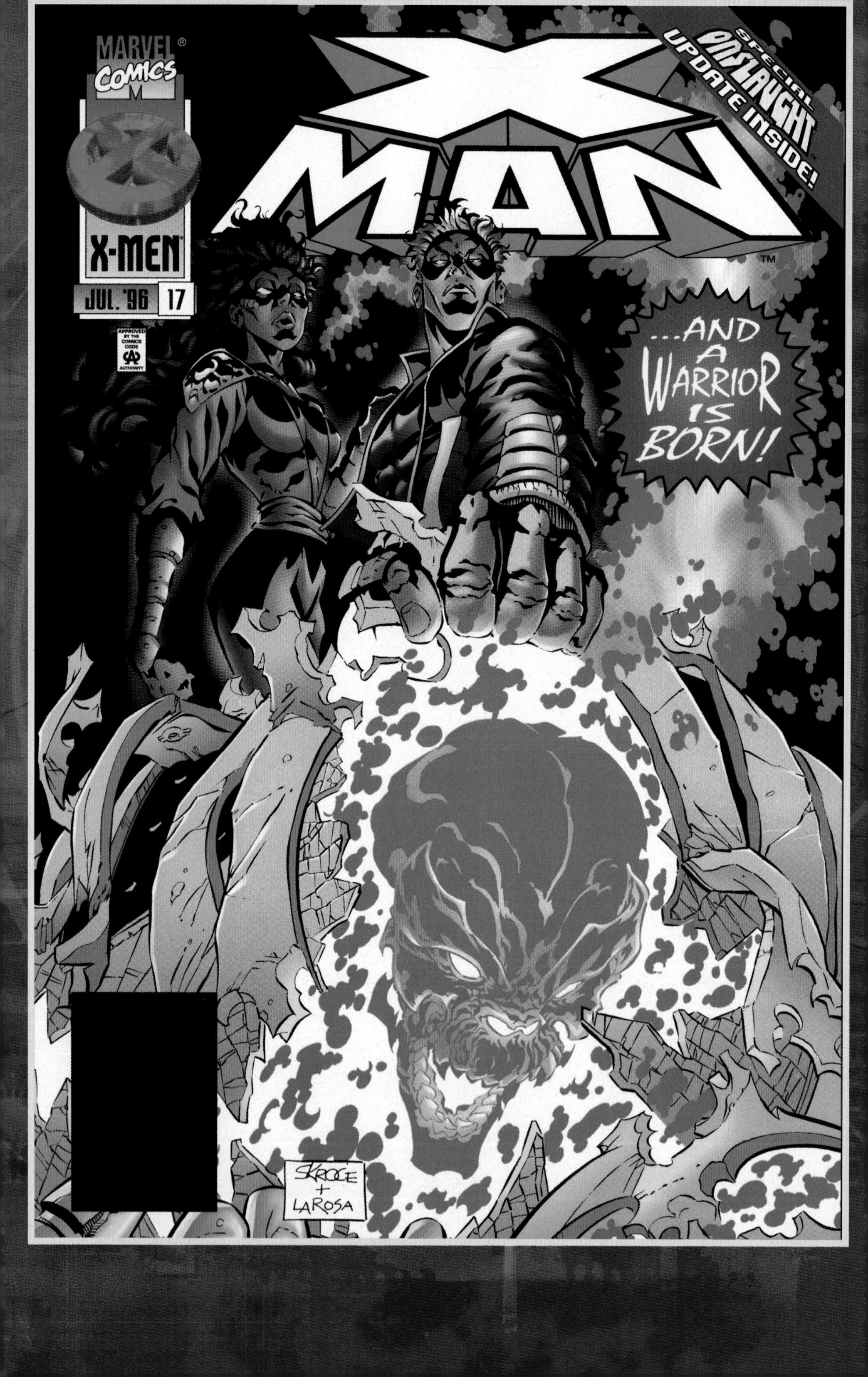
MARVEL COMICS
X-MEN
JUL. '96 17
APPROVED BY THE COMICS CODE AUTHORITY
X-MAN
SPECIAL ONSLAUGHT UPDATE INSIDE!
...AND A WARRIOR IS BORN!
SKROCE + LAROSA

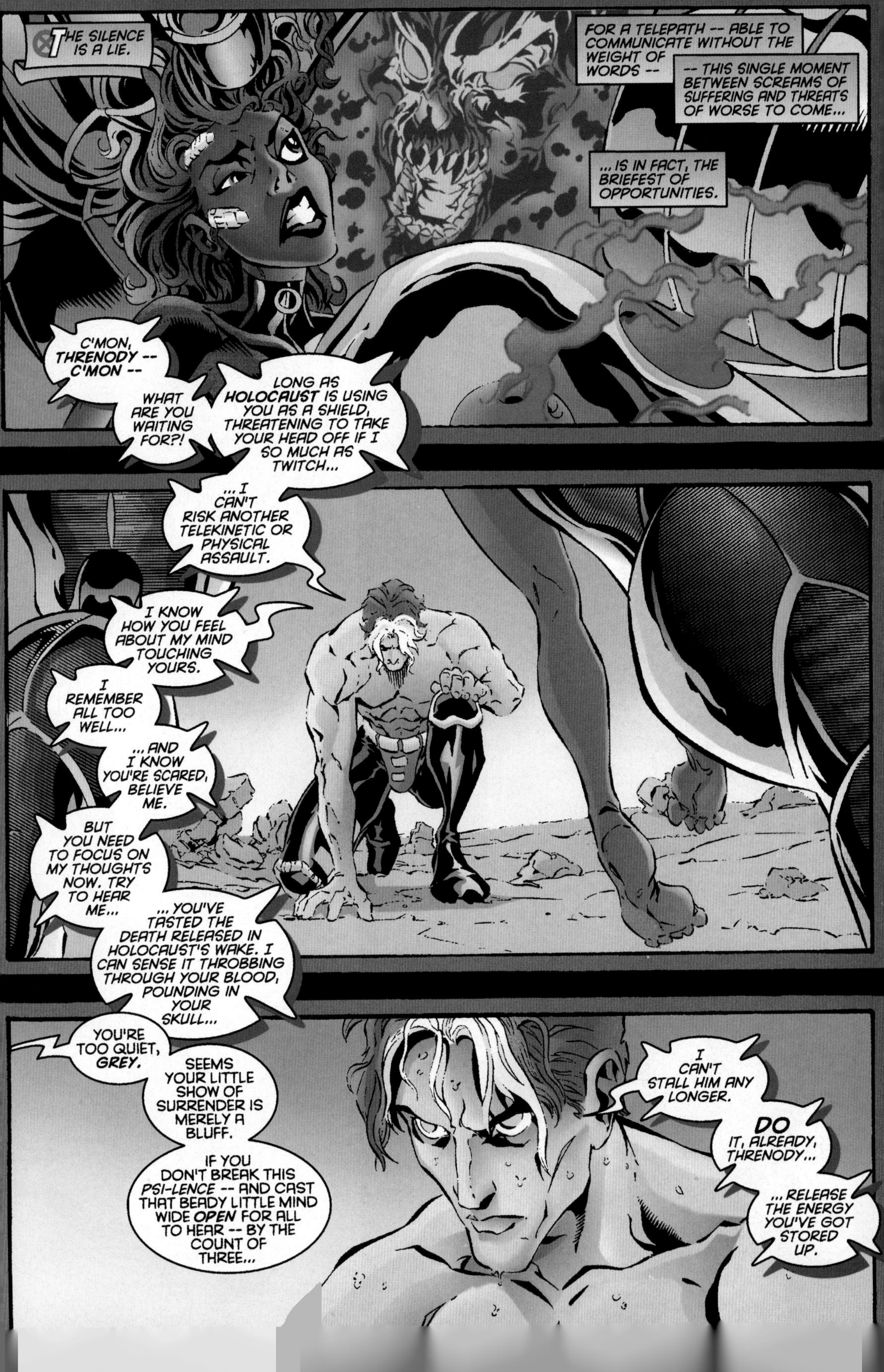
THE SILENCE IS A LIE.
FOR A TELEPATH -- ABLE TO COMMUNICATE WITHOUT THE WEIGHT OF WORDS --
-- THIS SINGLE MOMENT BETWEEN SCREAMS OF SUFFERING AND THREATS OF WORSE TO COME...
...IS IN FACT, THE BRIEFEST OF OPPORTUNITIES.
C'MON, THRENODY -- C'MON --
WHAT ARE YOU WAITING FOR?!
LONG AS HOLOCAUST IS USING YOU AS A SHIELD, THREATENING TO TAKE YOUR HEAD OFF IF I SO MUCH AS TWITCH...
...I CAN'T RISK ANOTHER TELEKINETIC OR PHYSICAL ASSAULT.
I KNOW HOW YOU FEEL ABOUT MY MIND TOUCHING YOURS.
I REMEMBER ALL TOO WELL...
...AND I KNOW YOU'RE SCARED, BELIEVE ME.
BUT YOU NEED TO FOCUS ON MY THOUGHTS NOW. TRY TO HEAR ME...
...YOU'VE TASTED THE DEATH RELEASED IN HOLOCAUST'S WAKE. I CAN SENSE IT THROBBING THROUGH YOUR BLOOD, POUNDING IN YOUR SKULL...
YOU'RE TOO QUIET, GREY.
SEEMS YOUR LITTLE SHOW OF SURRENDER IS MERELY A BLUFF.
IF YOU DON'T BREAK THIS PSI-LENCE -- AND CAST THAT BEADY LITTLE MIND WIDE OPEN FOR ALL TO HEAR -- BY THE COUNT OF THREE...
I CAN'T STALL HIM ANY LONGER.
DO IT, ALREADY, THRENODY...
...RELEASE THE ENERGY YOU'VE GOT STORED UP.

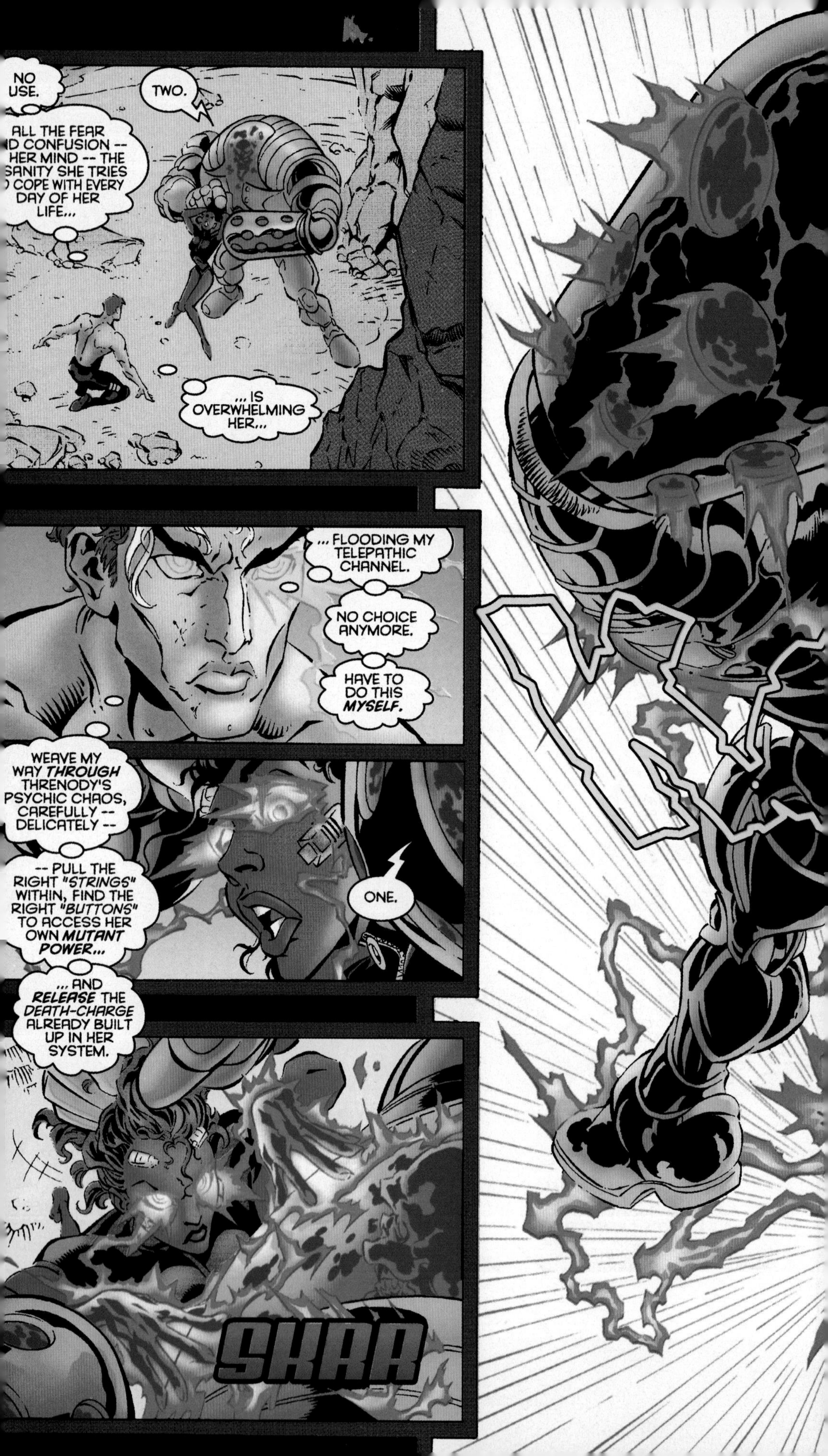
NO USE.
TWO.
ALL THE FEAR ND CONFUSION -- HER MIND -- THE SANITY SHE TRIES D COPE WITH EVERY DAY OF HER LIFE...
...IS OVERWHELMING HER...
...FLOODING MY TELEPATHIC CHANNEL.
NO CHOICE ANYMORE.
HAVE TO DO THIS MYSELF.
WEAVE MY WAY THROUGH THRENODY'S PSYCHIC CHAOS, CAREFULLY -- DELICATELY --
-- PULL THE RIGHT "STRINGS" WITHIN, FIND THE RIGHT "BUTTONS" TO ACCESS HER OWN MUTANT POWER...
ONE.
...AND RELEASE THE DEATH-CHARGE ALREADY BUILT UP IN HER SYSTEM.
SKRA

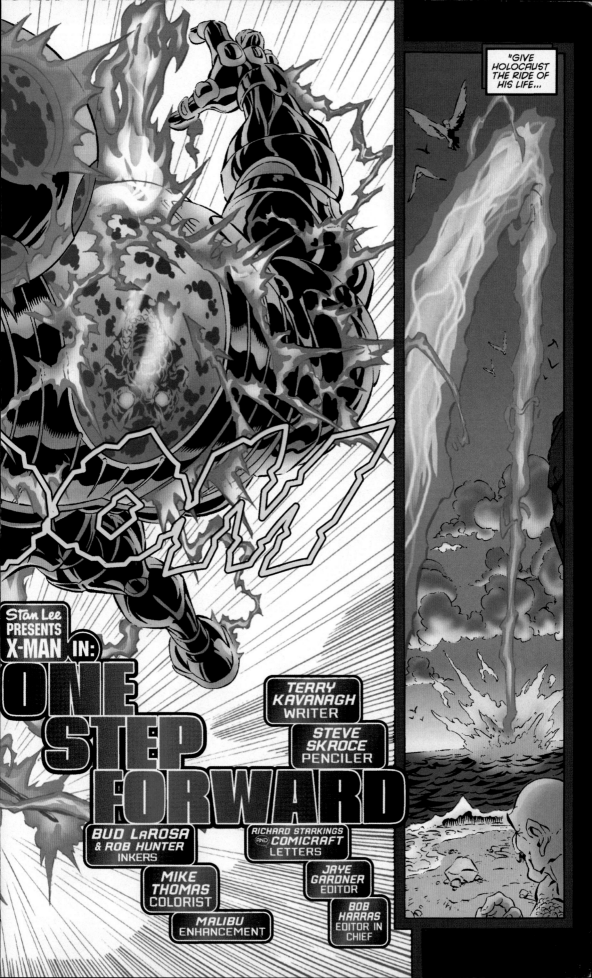

"GIVE HOLOCAUST THE RIDE OF HIS LIFE..."

STAN LEE PRESENTS X-MAN IN:

ONE STEP FORWARD

TERRY KAVANAGH
WRITER

STEVE SKROCE
PENCILER

BUD LaROSA & ROB HUNTER
INKERS

RICHARD STARKINGS AND COMICRAFT
LETTERS

MIKE THOMAS
COLORIST

JAYE GARDNER
EDITOR

MALIBU
ENHANCEMENT

BOB HARRAS
EDITOR IN CHIEF

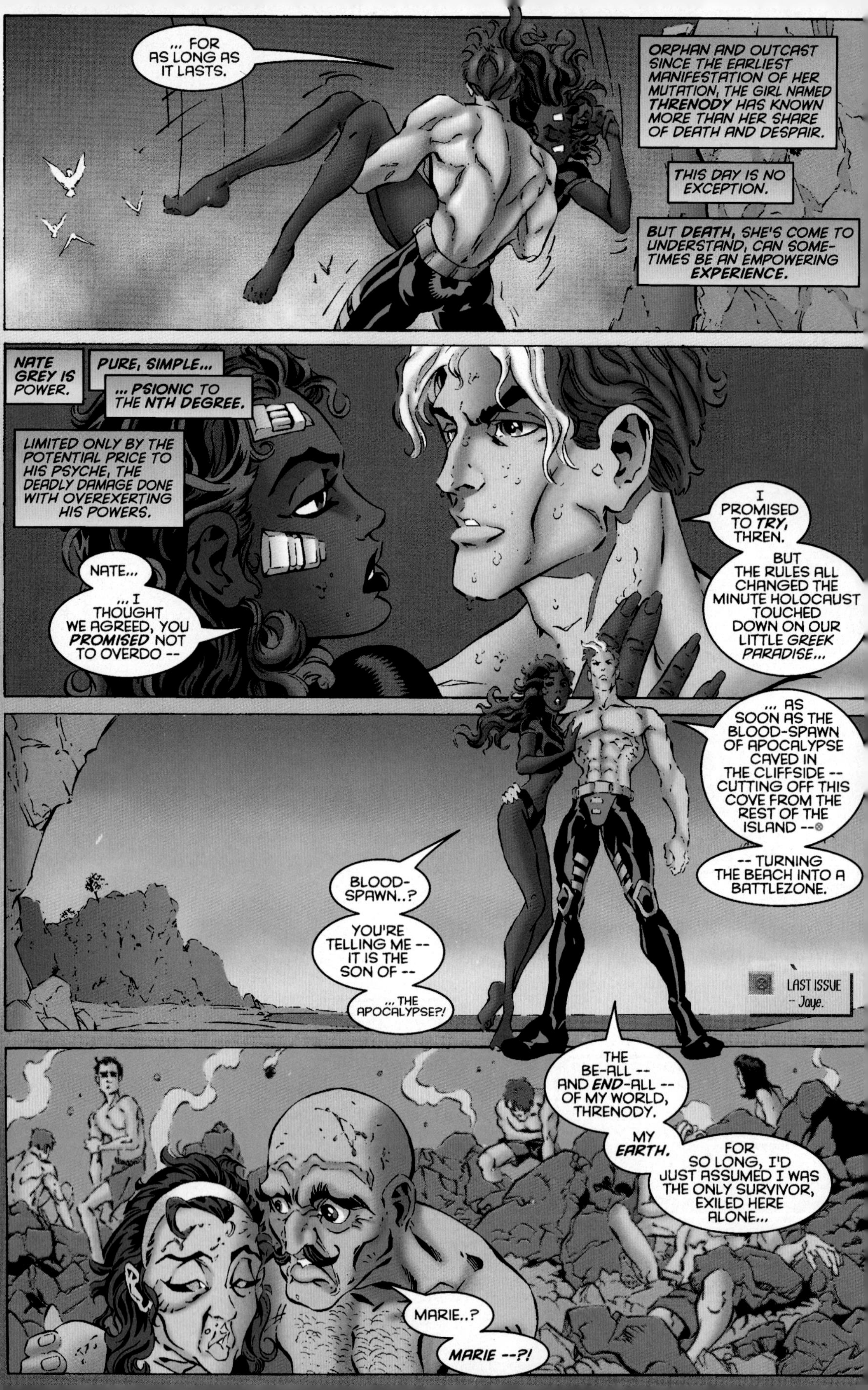

... FOR AS LONG AS IT LASTS.
ORPHAN AND OUTCAST SINCE THE EARLIEST MANIFESTATION OF HER MUTATION, THE GIRL NAMED THRENODY HAS KNOWN MORE THAN HER SHARE OF DEATH AND DESPAIR.
THIS DAY IS NO EXCEPTION.
BUT DEATH, SHE'S COME TO UNDERSTAND, CAN SOMETIMES BE AN EMPOWERING EXPERIENCE.
NATE GREY IS POWER.
PURE, SIMPLE...
... PSIONIC TO THE NTH DEGREE.
LIMITED ONLY BY THE POTENTIAL PRICE TO HIS PSYCHE, THE DEADLY DAMAGE DONE WITH OVEREXERTING HIS POWERS.
NATE... ... I THOUGHT WE AGREED, YOU PROMISED NOT TO OVERDO --
I PROMISED TO TRY, THREN. BUT THE RULES ALL CHANGED THE MINUTE HOLOCAUST TOUCHED DOWN ON OUR LITTLE GREEK PARADISE...
... AS SOON AS THE BLOOD-SPAWN OF APOCALYPSE CAVED IN THE CLIFFSIDE -- CUTTING OFF THIS COVE FROM THE REST OF THE ISLAND --
-- TURNING THE BEACH INTO A BATTLEZONE.
BLOOD-SPAWN..?
YOU'RE TELLING ME -- IT IS THE SON OF --
... THE APOCALYPSE?!
LAST ISSUE -- Jaye.
THE BE-ALL -- AND END-ALL -- OF MY WORLD, THRENODY.
MY EARTH.
FOR SO LONG, I'D JUST ASSUMED I WAS THE ONLY SURVIVOR, EXILED HERE ALONE...
MARIE..?
MARIE --?!

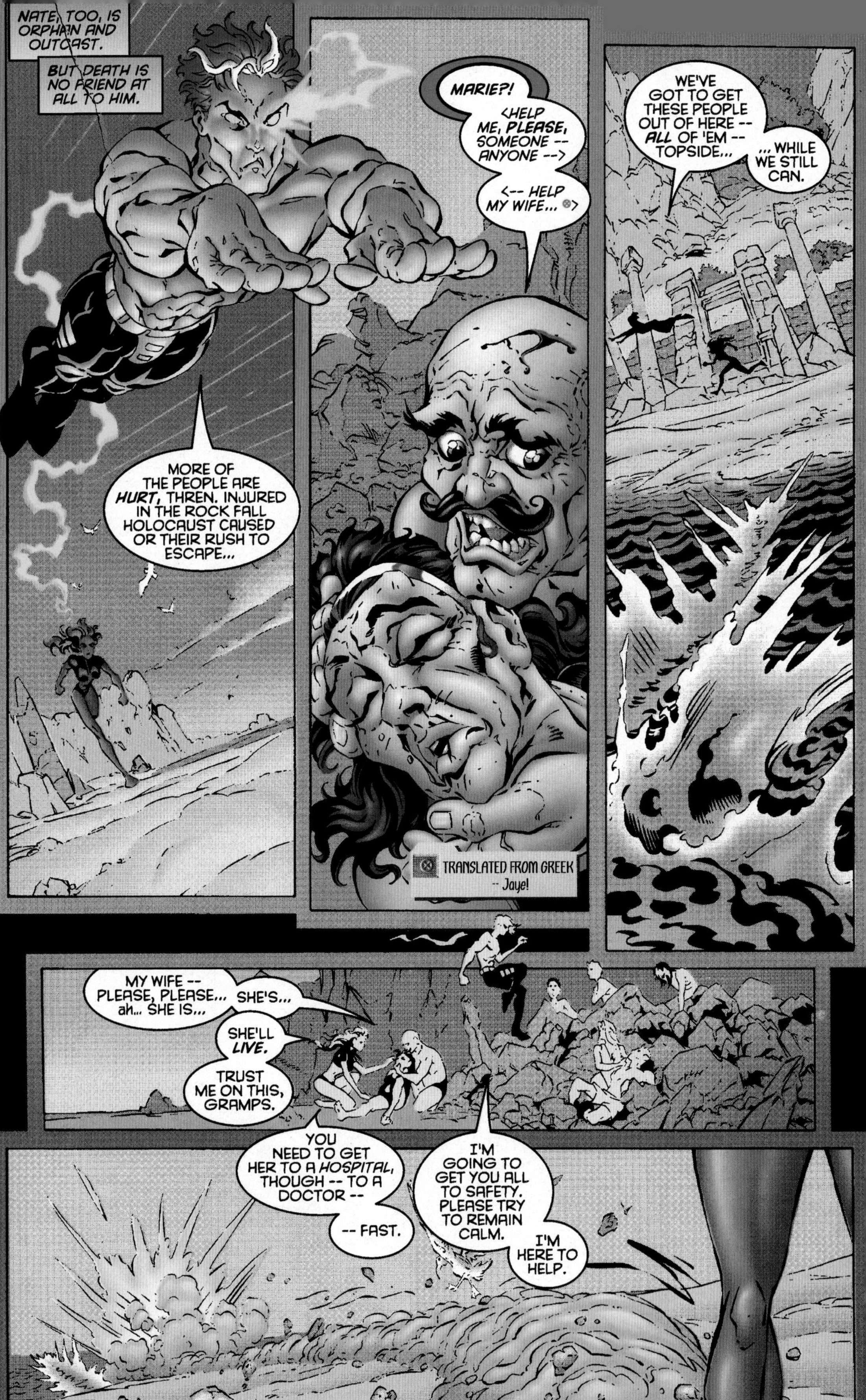
NATE, TOO, IS ORPHAN AND OUTCAST.
BUT DEATH IS NO FRIEND AT ALL TO HIM.
MORE OF THE PEOPLE ARE HURT, THREN. INJURED IN THE ROCK FALL HOLOCAUST CAUSED OR THEIR RUSH TO ESCAPE...
MARIE?!
<HELP ME, PLEASE, SOMEONE -- ANYONE -->
<-- HELP MY WIFE...>
TRANSLATED FROM GREEK -- Jaye!
WE'VE GOT TO GET THESE PEOPLE OUT OF HERE -- ALL OF 'EM -- TOPSIDE...
...WHILE WE STILL CAN.
MY WIFE -- PLEASE, PLEASE... ah... SHE IS...
SHE'S...
SHE'LL LIVE.
TRUST ME ON THIS, GRAMPS.
YOU NEED TO GET HER TO A HOSPITAL, THOUGH -- TO A DOCTOR --
-- FAST.
I'M GOING TO GET YOU ALL TO SAFETY. PLEASE TRY TO REMAIN CALM.
I'M HERE TO HELP.

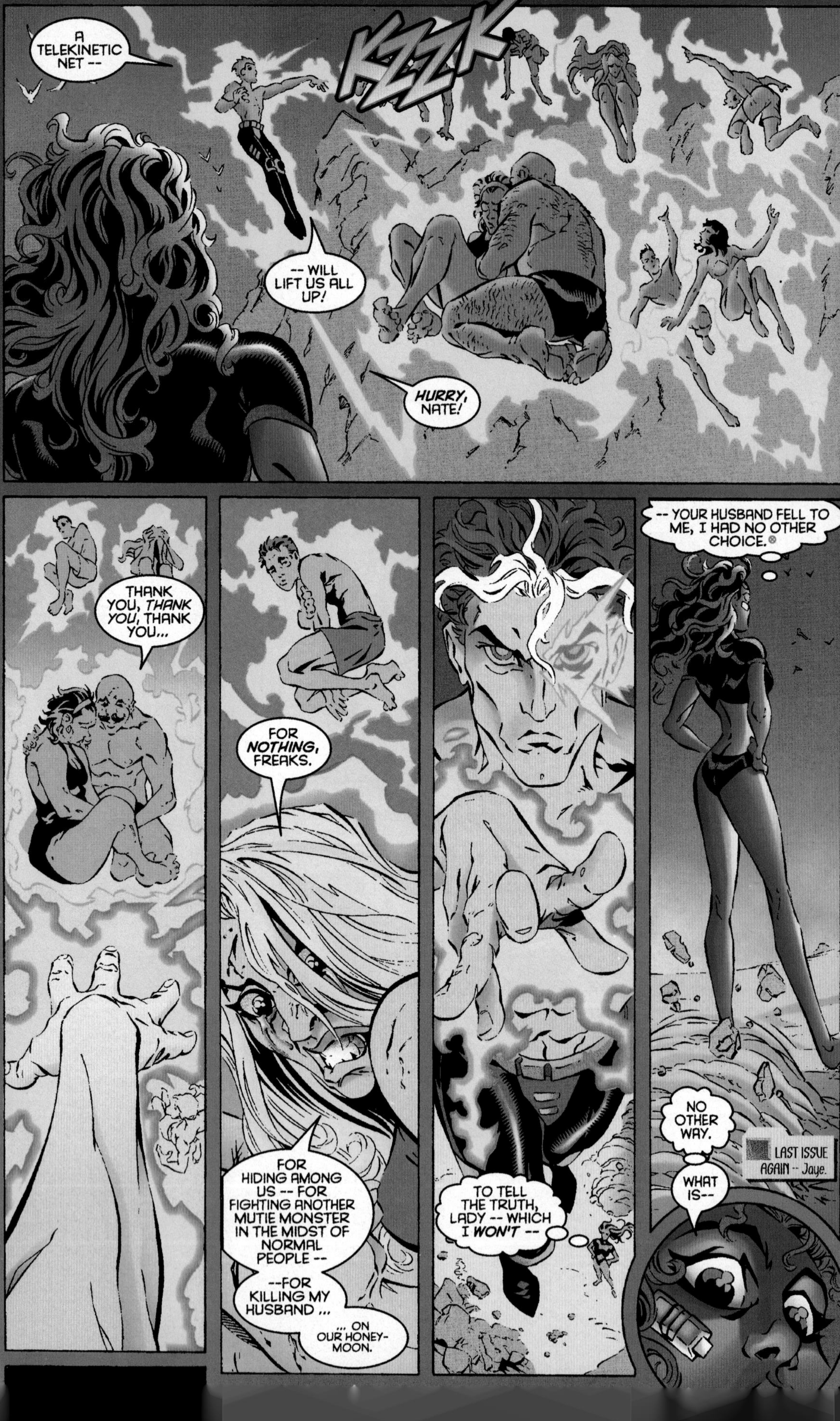
A TELEKINETIC NET --
KZZK
-- WILL LIFT US ALL UP!
HURRY, NATE!
THANK YOU, THANK YOU, THANK YOU...
FOR NOTHING, FREAKS.
FOR HIDING AMONG US -- FOR FIGHTING ANOTHER MUTIE MONSTER IN THE MIDST OF NORMAL PEOPLE --
--FOR KILLING MY HUSBAND ...
... ON OUR HONEY-MOON.
TO TELL THE TRUTH, LADY -- WHICH I WON'T --
-- YOUR HUSBAND FELL TO ME, I HAD NO OTHER CHOICE.
NO OTHER WAY.
LAST ISSUE AGAIN -- Jaye.
WHAT IS--

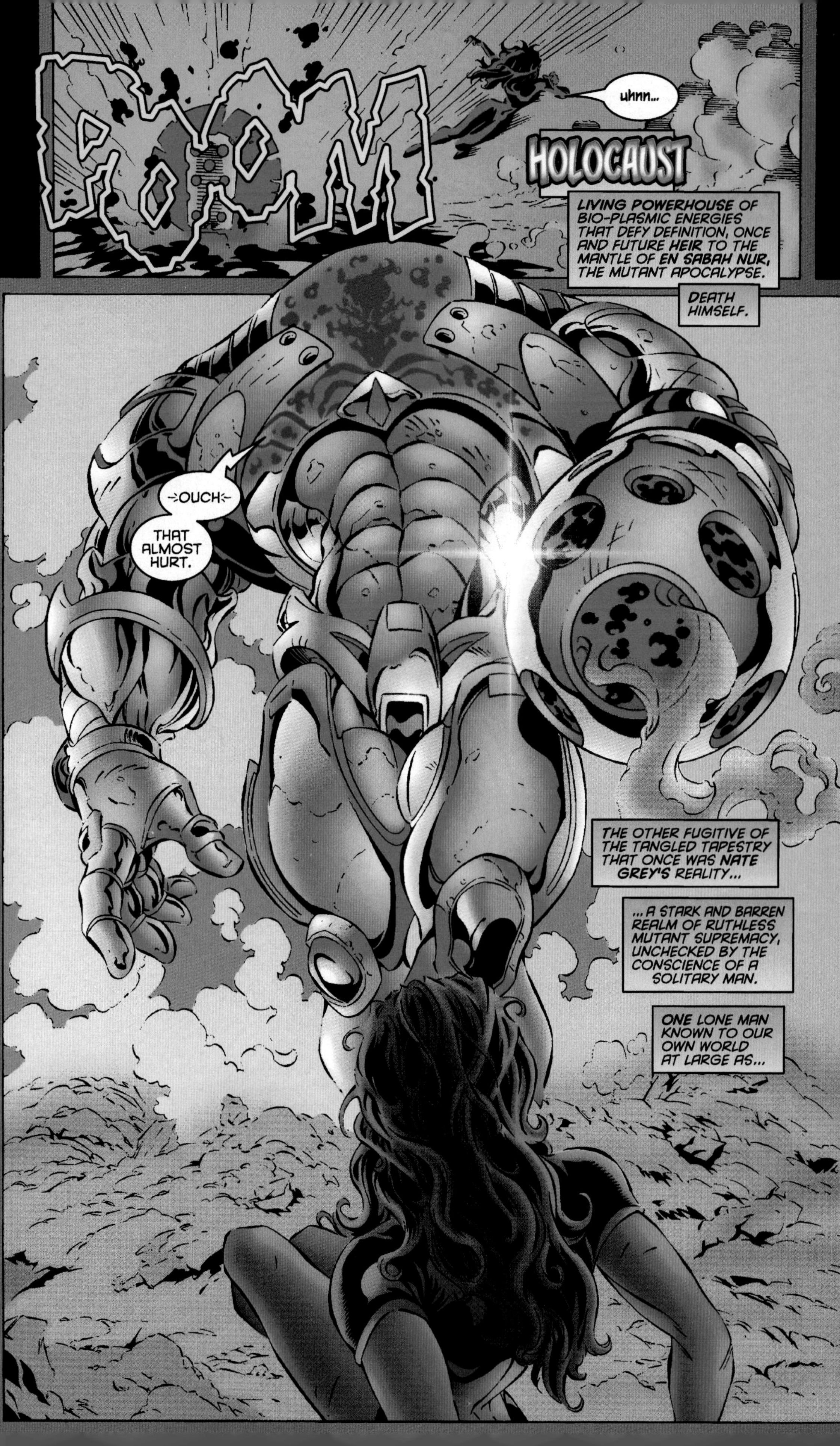
BOOM
uhnn...
HOLOCAUST
LIVING POWERHOUSE OF BIO-PLASMIC ENERGIES THAT DEFY DEFINITION, ONCE AND FUTURE HEIR TO THE MANTLE OF EN SABAH NUR, THE MUTANT APOCALYPSE.
DEATH HIMSELF.
OUCH
THAT ALMOST HURT.
THE OTHER FUGITIVE OF THE TANGLED TAPESTRY THAT ONCE WAS NATE GREY'S REALITY...
...A STARK AND BARREN REALM OF RUTHLESS MUTANT SUPREMACY, UNCHECKED BY THE CONSCIENCE OF A SOLITARY MAN.
ONE LONE MAN KNOWN TO OUR OWN WORLD AT LARGE AS...

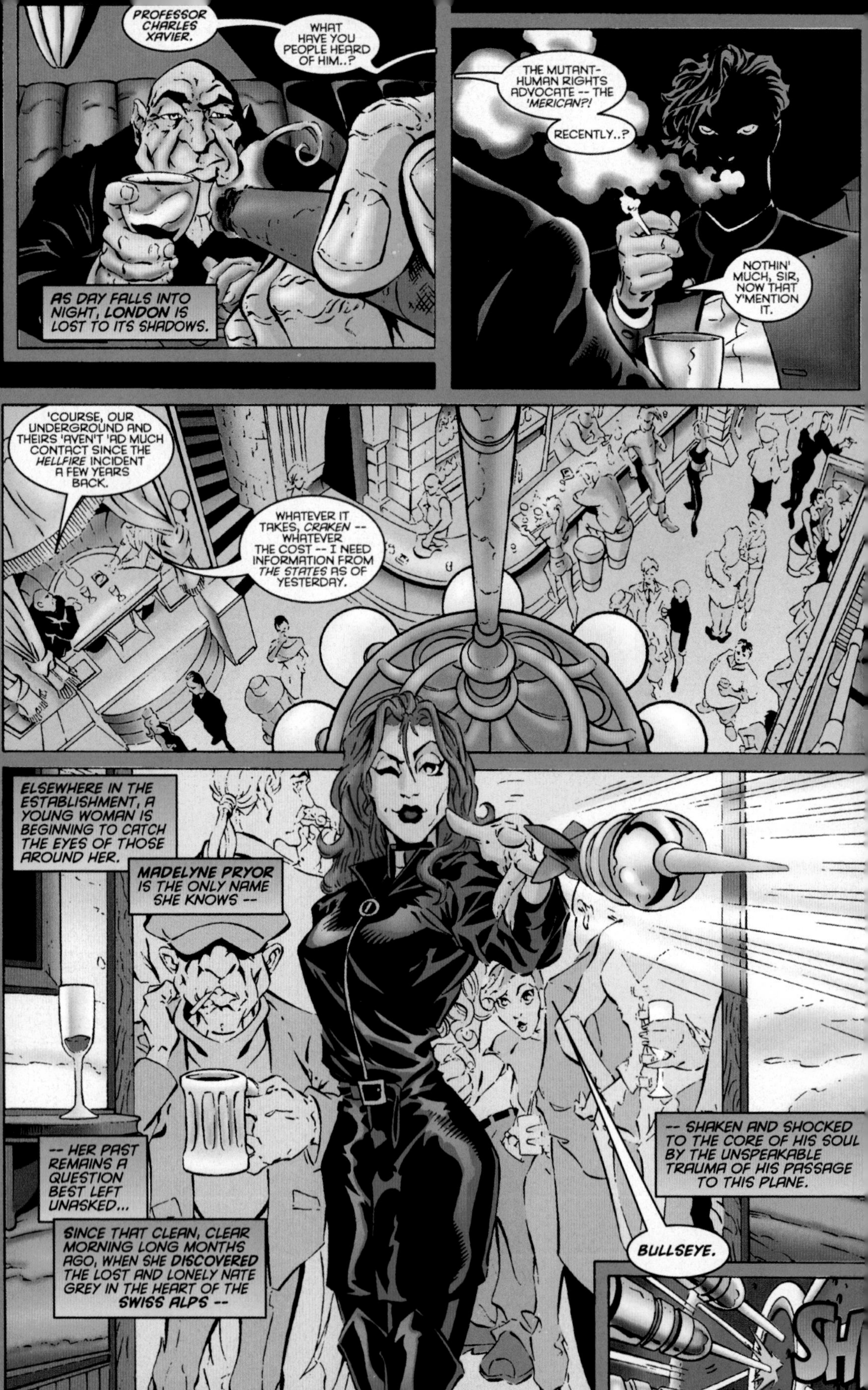
PROFESSOR CHARLES XAVIER.
WHAT HAVE YOU PEOPLE HEARD OF HIM..?
AS DAY FALLS INTO NIGHT, LONDON IS LOST TO ITS SHADOWS.
THE MUTANT-HUMAN RIGHTS ADVOCATE -- THE 'MERICAN?!
RECENTLY..?
NOTHIN' MUCH, SIR, NOW THAT Y'MENTION IT.
'COURSE, OUR UNDERGROUND AND THEIRS 'AVEN'T 'AD MUCH CONTACT SINCE THE HELLFIRE INCIDENT A FEW YEARS BACK.
WHATEVER IT TAKES, CRAKEN -- WHATEVER THE COST -- I NEED INFORMATION FROM THE STATES AS OF YESTERDAY.
ELSEWHERE IN THE ESTABLISHMENT, A YOUNG WOMAN IS BEGINNING TO CATCH THE EYES OF THOSE AROUND HER.
MADELYNE PRYOR IS THE ONLY NAME SHE KNOWS --
-- HER PAST REMAINS A QUESTION BEST LEFT UNASKED...
SINCE THAT CLEAN, CLEAR MORNING LONG MONTHS AGO, WHEN SHE DISCOVERED THE LOST AND LONELY NATE GREY IN THE HEART OF THE SWISS ALPS --
-- SHAKEN AND SHOCKED TO THE CORE OF HIS SOUL BY THE UNSPEAKABLE TRAUMA OF HIS PASSAGE TO THIS PLANE.
BULLSEYE.

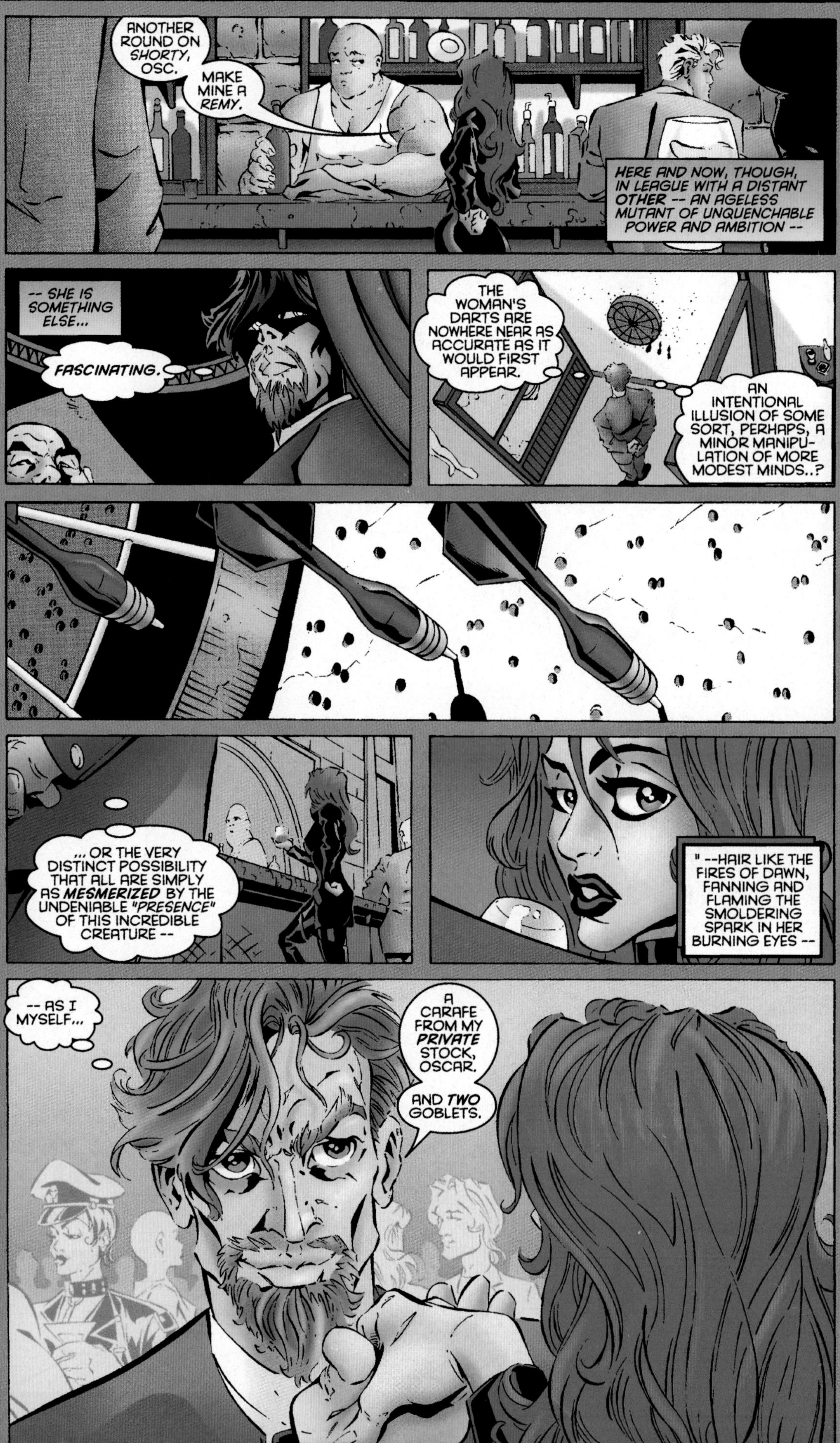
ANOTHER ROUND ON SHORTY, OSC.
MAKE MINE A REMY.
HERE AND NOW, THOUGH, IN LEAGUE WITH A DISTANT OTHER -- AN AGELESS MUTANT OF UNQUENCHABLE POWER AND AMBITION --
-- SHE IS SOMETHING ELSE...
FASCINATING.
THE WOMAN'S DARTS ARE NOWHERE NEAR AS ACCURATE AS IT WOULD FIRST APPEAR.
AN INTENTIONAL ILLUSION OF SOME SORT, PERHAPS, A MINOR MANIPULATION OF MORE MODEST MINDS..?
... OR THE VERY DISTINCT POSSIBILITY THAT ALL ARE SIMPLY AS MESMERIZED BY THE UNDENIABLE "PRESENCE" OF THIS INCREDIBLE CREATURE --
" --HAIR LIKE THE FIRES OF DAWN, FANNING AND FLAMING THE SMOLDERING SPARK IN HER BURNING EYES --
-- AS I MYSELF...
A CARAFE FROM MY PRIVATE STOCK, OSCAR.
AND TWO GOBLETS.

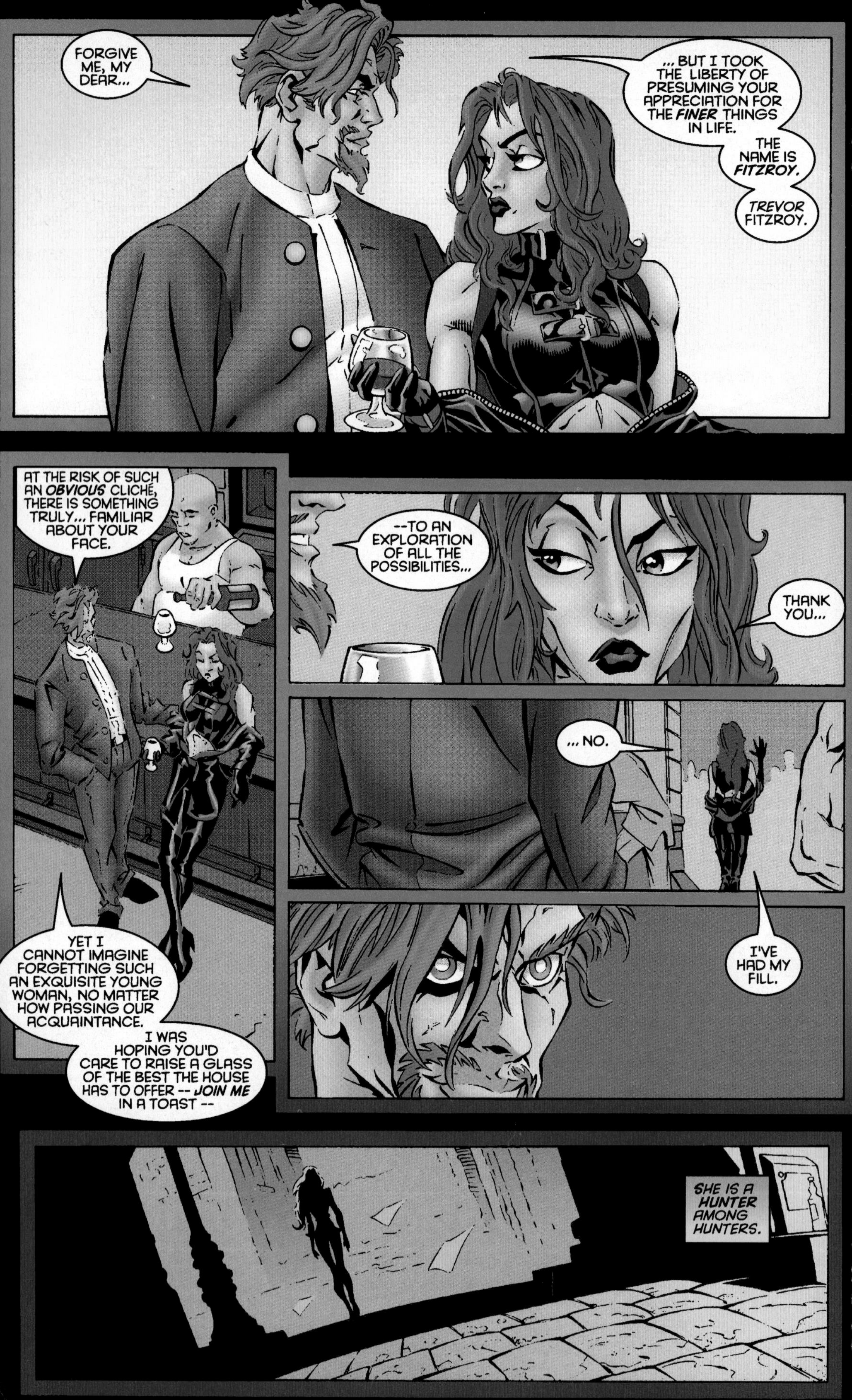
FORGIVE ME, MY DEAR...
... BUT I TOOK THE LIBERTY OF PRESUMING YOUR APPRECIATION FOR THE FINER THINGS IN LIFE.
THE NAME IS FITZROY.
TREVOR FITZROY.
AT THE RISK OF SUCH AN OBVIOUS CLICHE, THERE IS SOMETHING TRULY... FAMILIAR ABOUT YOUR FACE.
YET I CANNOT IMAGINE FORGETTING SUCH AN EXQUISITE YOUNG WOMAN, NO MATTER HOW PASSING OUR ACQUAINTANCE.
I WAS HOPING YOU'D CARE TO RAISE A GLASS OF THE BEST THE HOUSE HAS TO OFFER -- JOIN ME IN A TOAST --
--TO AN EXPLORATION OF ALL THE POSSIBILITIES...
THANK YOU...
... NO.
I'VE HAD MY FILL.
SHE IS A HUNTER AMONG HUNTERS.

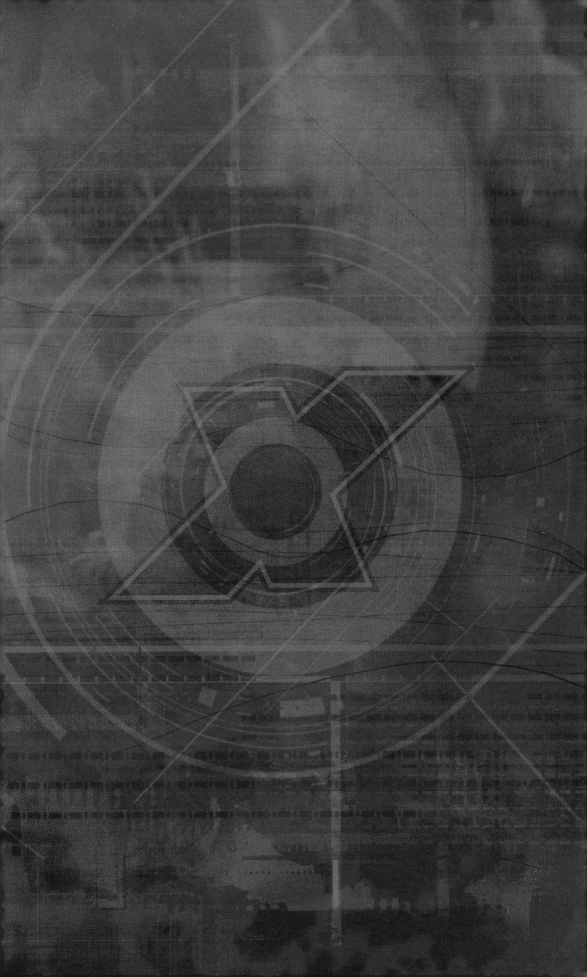

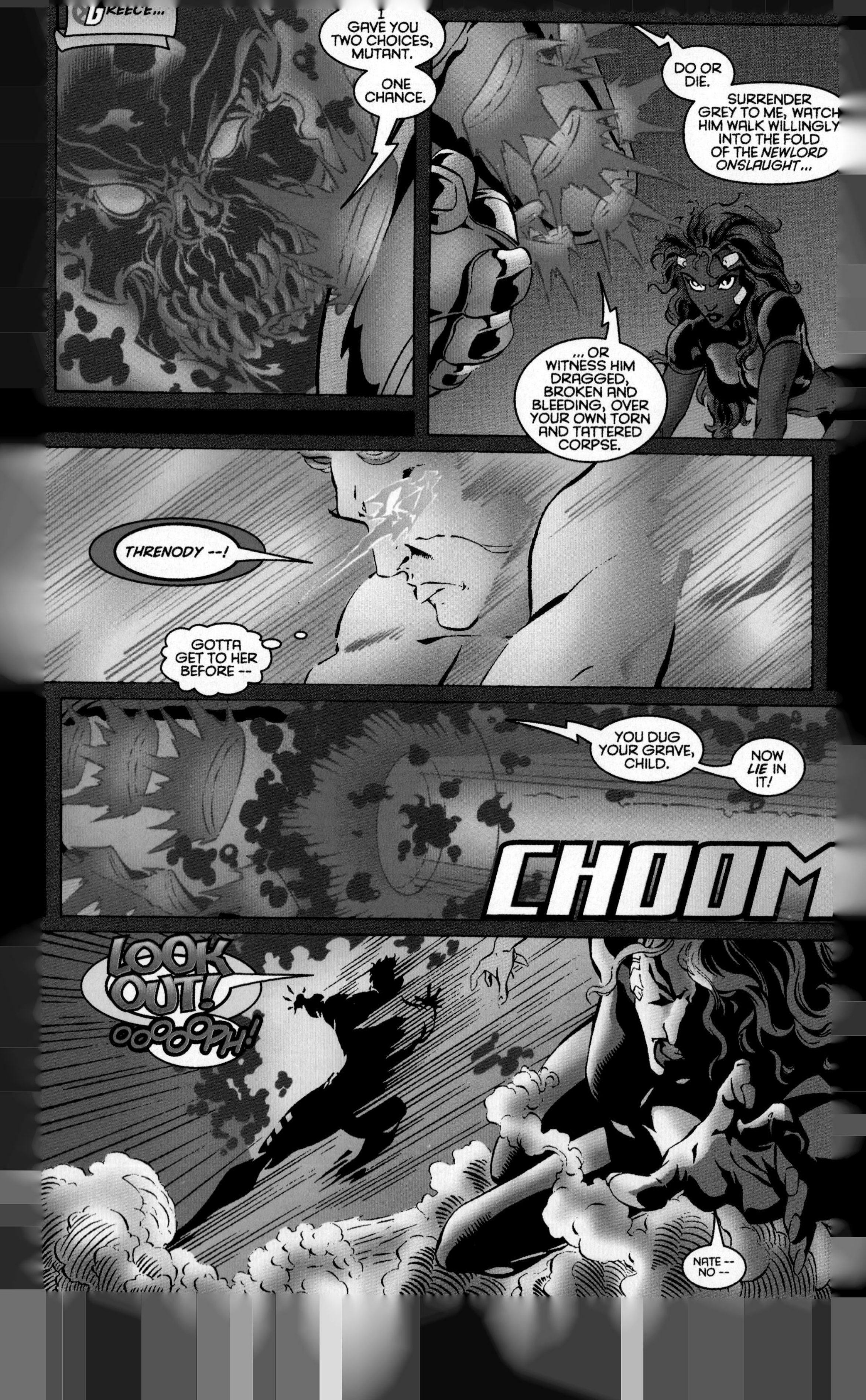
GREECE...
I GAVE YOU TWO CHOICES, MUTANT.
ONE CHANCE.
DO OR DIE.
SURRENDER GREY TO ME, WATCH HIM WALK WILLINGLY INTO THE FOLD OF THE NEWLORD ONSLAUGHT...
...OR WITNESS HIM DRAGGED, BROKEN AND BLEEDING, OVER YOUR OWN TORN AND TATTERED CORPSE.
THRENODY --!
GOTTA GET TO HER BEFORE --
YOU DUG YOUR GRAVE, CHILD.
NOW LIE IN IT!
CHOOM
LOOK OUT!
OOOOOPH!
NATE -- NO --

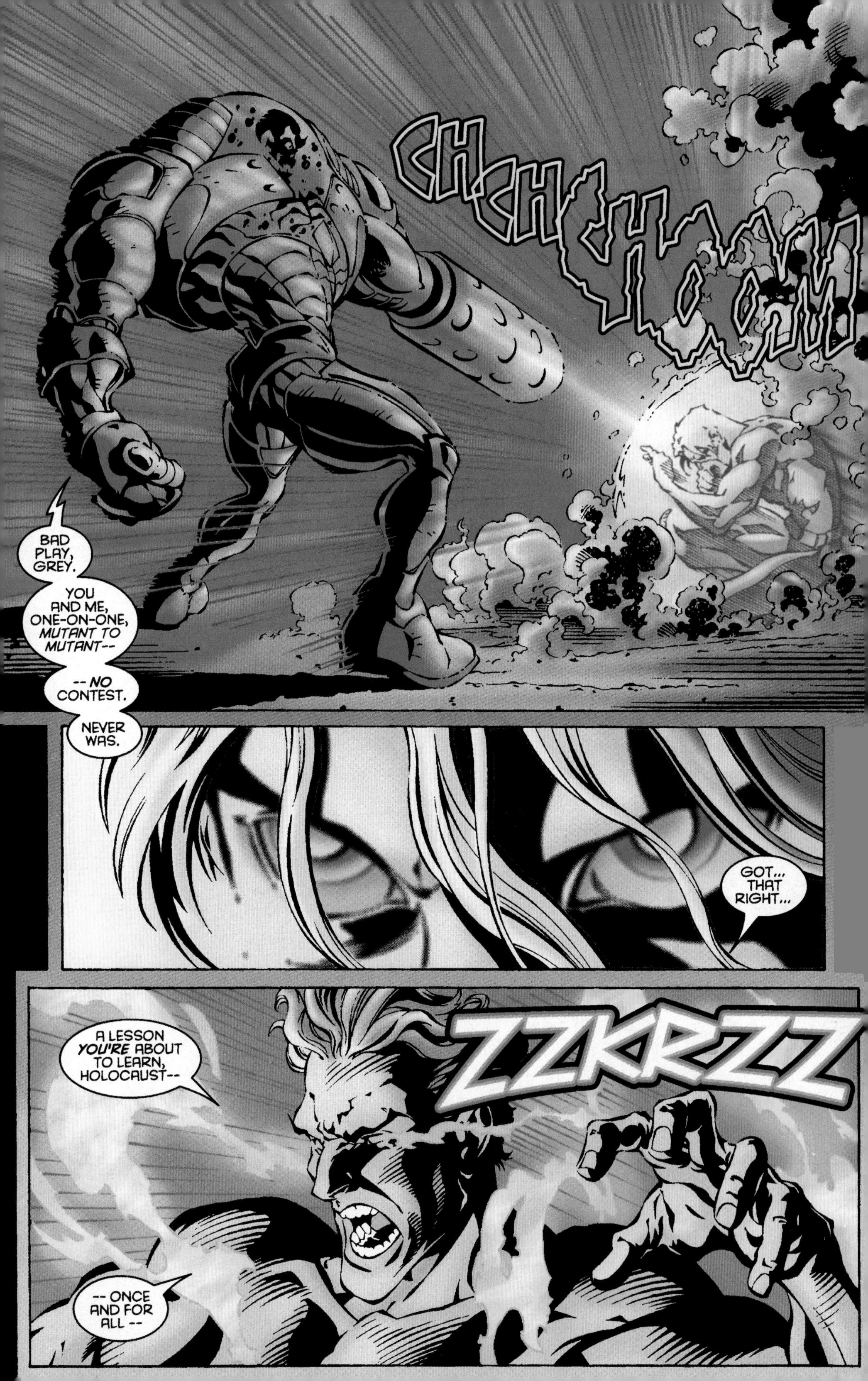
CHCHCHHOOM
BAD PLAY, GREY.
YOU AND ME, ONE-ON-ONE, MUTANT TO MUTANT--
--NO CONTEST.
NEVER WAS.
GOT... THAT RIGHT...
A LESSON YOU'RE ABOUT TO LEARN, HOLOCAUST--
ZZKRZZ
--ONCE AND FOR ALL--

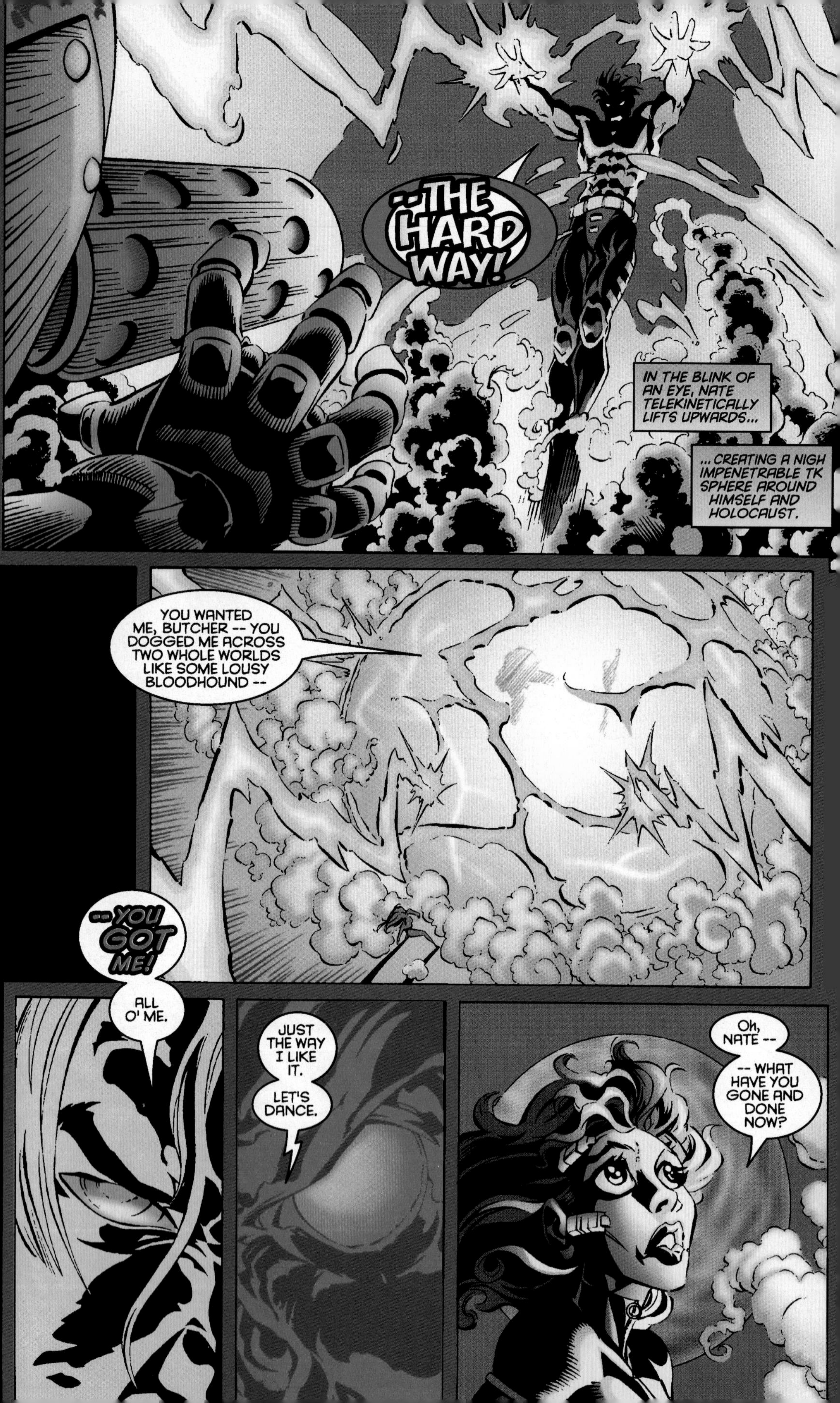

--THE HARD WAY!
IN THE BLINK OF AN EYE, NATE TELEKINETICALLY LIFTS UPWARDS...
...CREATING A NIGH IMPENETRABLE TK SPHERE AROUND HIMSELF AND HOLOCAUST.
YOU WANTED ME, BUTCHER -- YOU DOGGED ME ACROSS TWO WHOLE WORLDS LIKE SOME LOUSY BLOODHOUND --
--YOU GOT ME!
ALL O' ME.
JUST THE WAY I LIKE IT.
LET'S DANCE.
Oh, NATE --
-- WHAT HAVE YOU GONE AND DONE NOW?

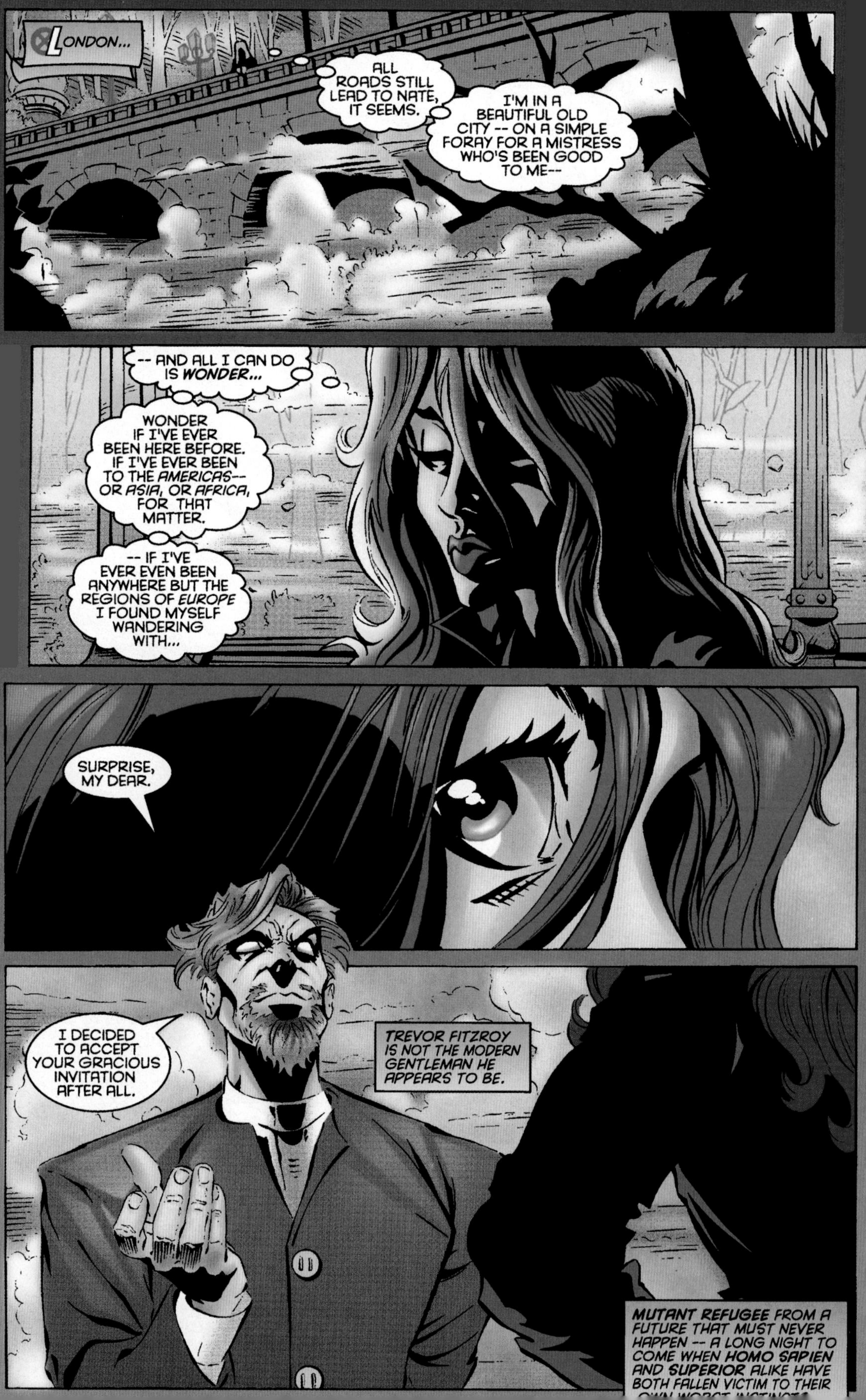
LONDON...
ALL ROADS STILL LEAD TO NATE, IT SEEMS.
I'M IN A BEAUTIFUL OLD CITY -- ON A SIMPLE FORAY FOR A MISTRESS WHO'S BEEN GOOD TO ME--
-- AND ALL I CAN DO IS *WONDER*...
WONDER IF I'VE EVER BEEN HERE BEFORE. IF I'VE EVER BEEN TO THE *AMERICAS*-- OR *ASIA*, OR *AFRICA*, FOR THAT MATTER.
-- IF I'VE EVER EVEN BEEN ANYWHERE BUT THE REGIONS OF *EUROPE* I FOUND MYSELF WANDERING WITH...
SURPRISE, MY DEAR.
I DECIDED TO ACCEPT YOUR GRACIOUS INVITATION AFTER ALL.
TREVOR FITZROY IS NOT THE MODERN GENTLEMAN HE APPEARS TO BE.
MUTANT REFUGEE FROM A FUTURE THAT MUST NEVER HAPPEN -- A LONG NIGHT TO COME WHEN **HOMO SAPIEN** AND **SUPERIOR** ALIKE HAVE BOTH FALLEN VICTIM TO THEIR

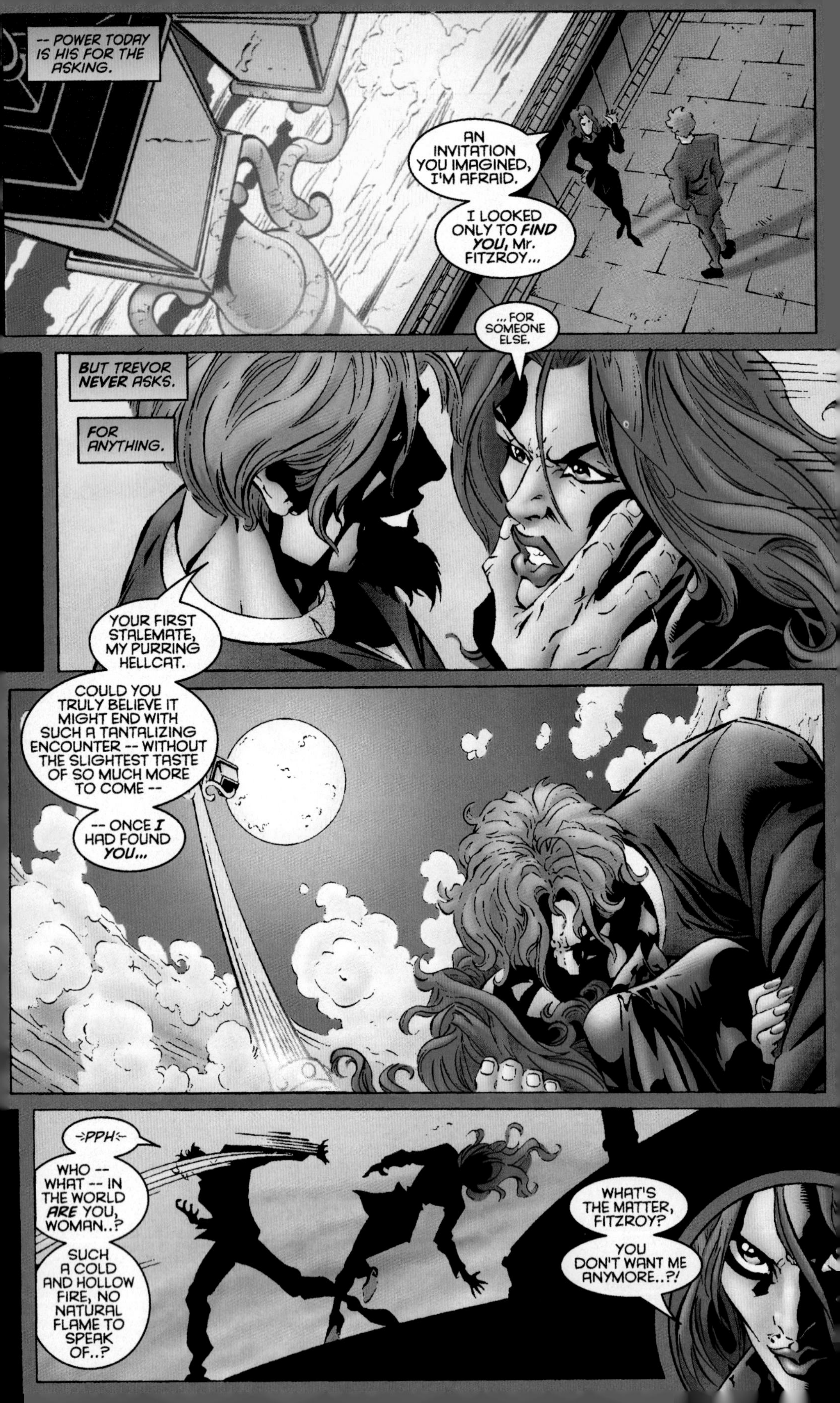

-- POWER TODAY IS HIS FOR THE ASKING.
AN INVITATION YOU IMAGINED, I'M AFRAID.
I LOOKED ONLY TO FIND YOU, Mr. FITZROY...
...FOR SOMEONE ELSE.
BUT TREVOR NEVER ASKS.
FOR ANYTHING.
YOUR FIRST STALEMATE, MY PURRING HELLCAT.
COULD YOU TRULY BELIEVE IT MIGHT END WITH SUCH A TANTALIZING ENCOUNTER -- WITHOUT THE SLIGHTEST TASTE OF SO MUCH MORE TO COME --
-- ONCE I HAD FOUND YOU...
PPH
WHO -- WHAT -- IN THE WORLD ARE YOU, WOMAN..?
SUCH A COLD AND HOLLOW FIRE, NO NATURAL FLAME TO SPEAK OF..?
WHAT'S THE MATTER, FITZROY?
YOU DON'T WANT ME ANYMORE..?!

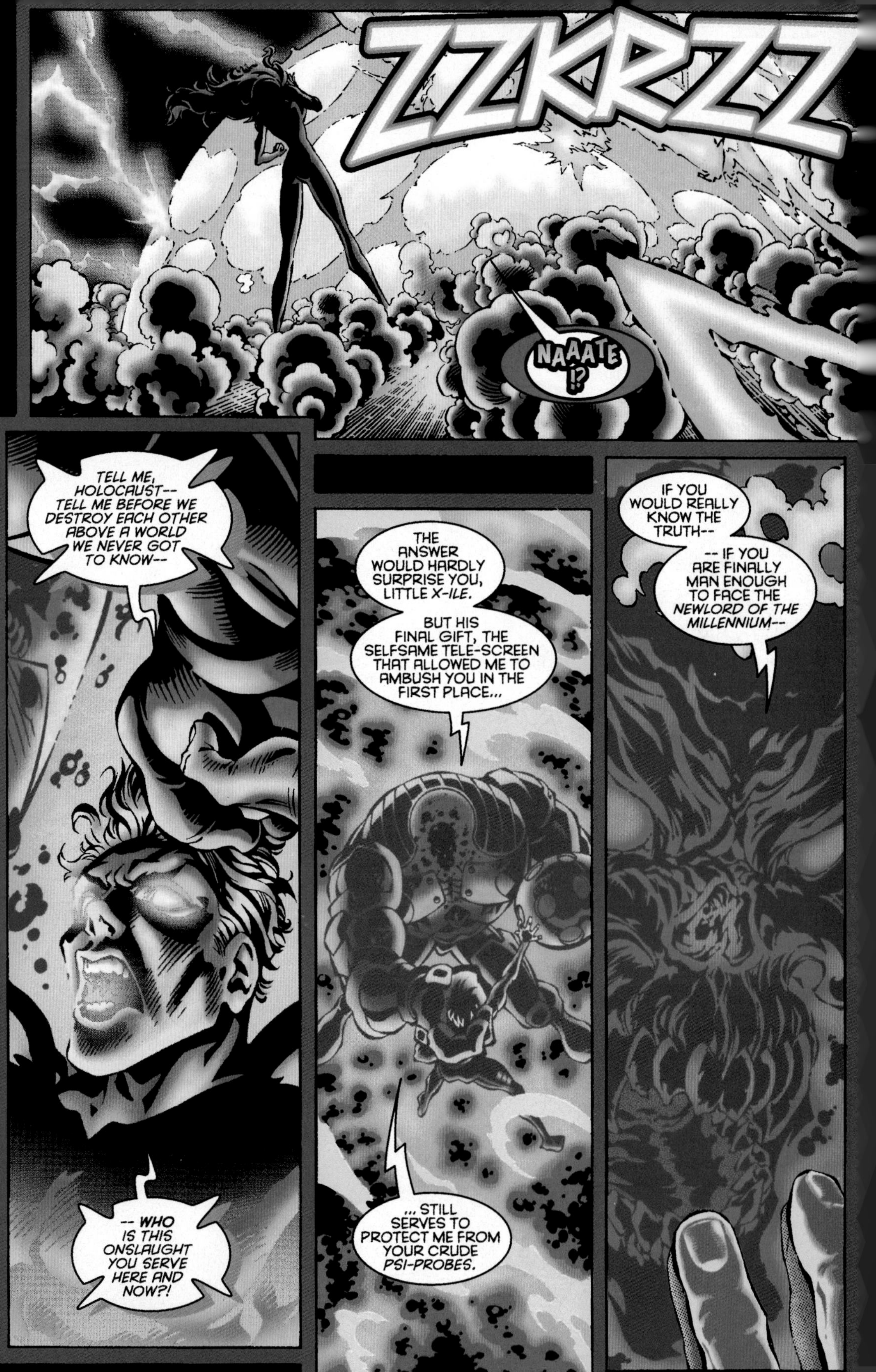
ZZKRZZ
NAAATE !?
TELL ME, HOLOCAUST-- TELL ME BEFORE WE DESTROY EACH OTHER ABOVE A WORLD WE NEVER GOT TO KNOW--
-- WHO IS THIS ONSLAUGHT YOU SERVE HERE AND NOW?!
THE ANSWER WOULD HARDLY SURPRISE YOU, LITTLE *X-ILE.*
BUT HIS FINAL GIFT, THE SELFSAME TELE-SCREEN THAT ALLOWED ME TO AMBUSH YOU IN THE FIRST PLACE...
... STILL SERVES TO PROTECT ME FROM YOUR CRUDE *PSI-PROBES.*
IF YOU WOULD REALLY KNOW THE TRUTH--
-- IF YOU ARE FINALLY MAN ENOUGH TO FACE THE *NEWLORD OF THE MILLENNIUM*--

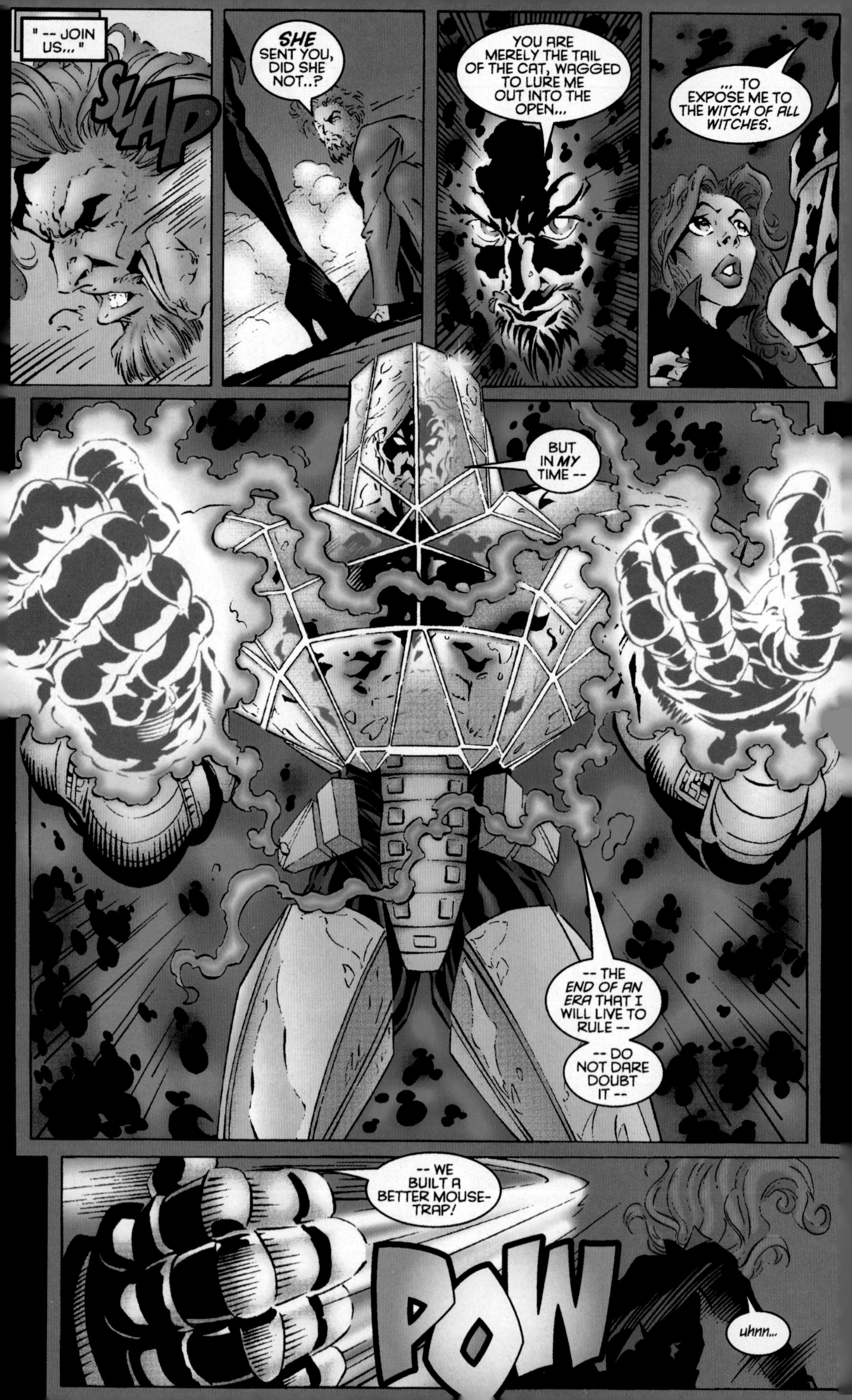
" -- JOIN US... "
SLAP
SHE SENT YOU, DID SHE NOT..?
YOU ARE MERELY THE TAIL OF THE CAT, WAGGED TO LURE ME OUT INTO THE OPEN...
... TO EXPOSE ME TO THE WITCH OF ALL WITCHES.
BUT IN MY TIME --
-- THE END OF AN ERA THAT I WILL LIVE TO RULE --
-- DO NOT DARE DOUBT IT --
-- WE BUILT A BETTER MOUSE-TRAP!
POW
uhnn...

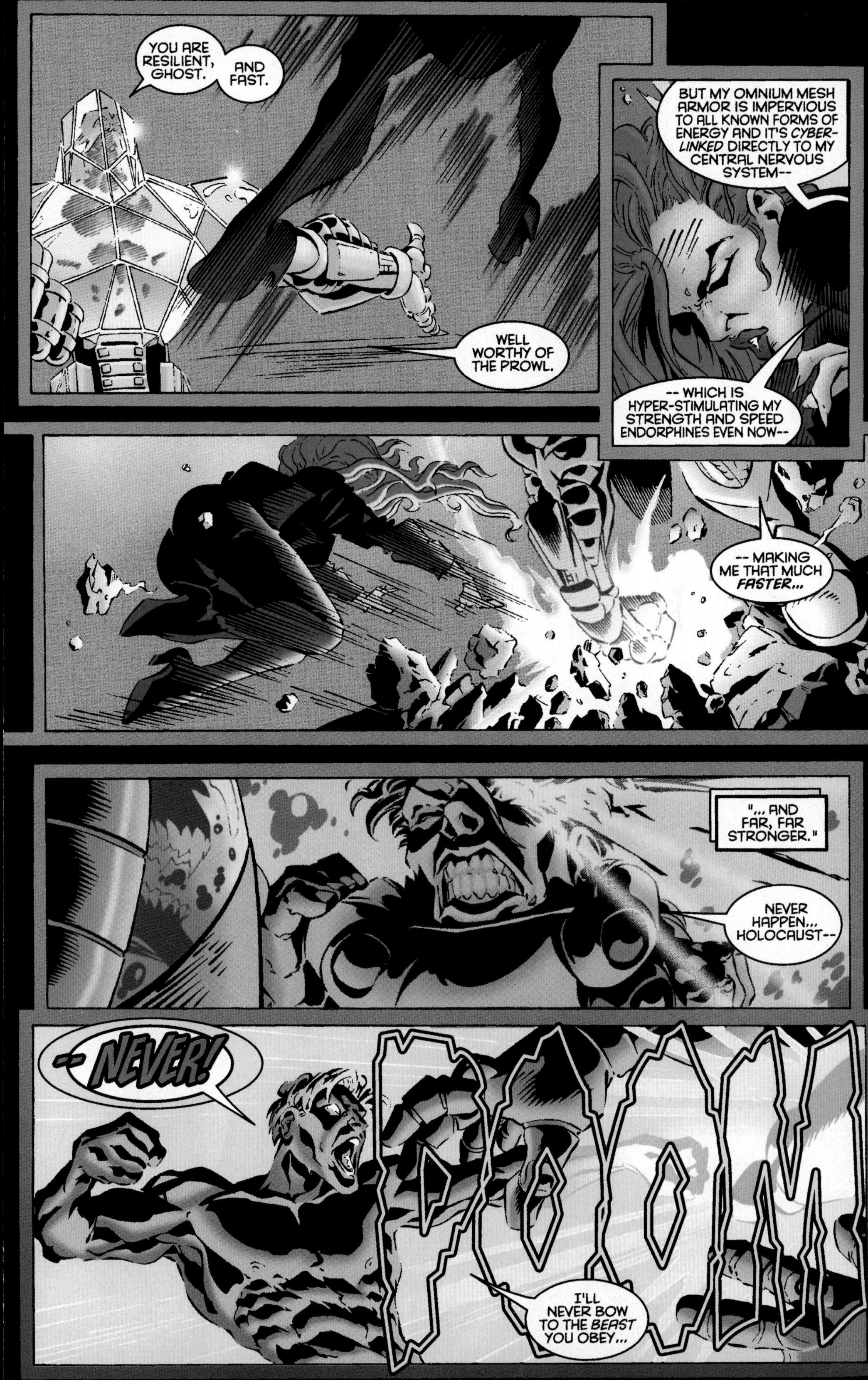
YOU ARE RESILIENT, GHOST.
AND FAST.
BUT MY OMNIUM MESH ARMOR IS IMPERVIOUS TO ALL KNOWN FORMS OF ENERGY AND IT'S *CYBER-LINKED* DIRECTLY TO MY CENTRAL NERVOUS SYSTEM--
WELL WORTHY OF THE PROWL.
-- WHICH IS HYPER-STIMULATING MY STRENGTH AND SPEED ENDORPHINES EVEN NOW--
-- MAKING ME THAT MUCH *FASTER*...
"... AND FAR, FAR STRONGER."
NEVER HAPPEN... HOLOCAUST--
-- NEVER!
POOM
I'LL NEVER BOW TO THE *BEAST* YOU OBEY...

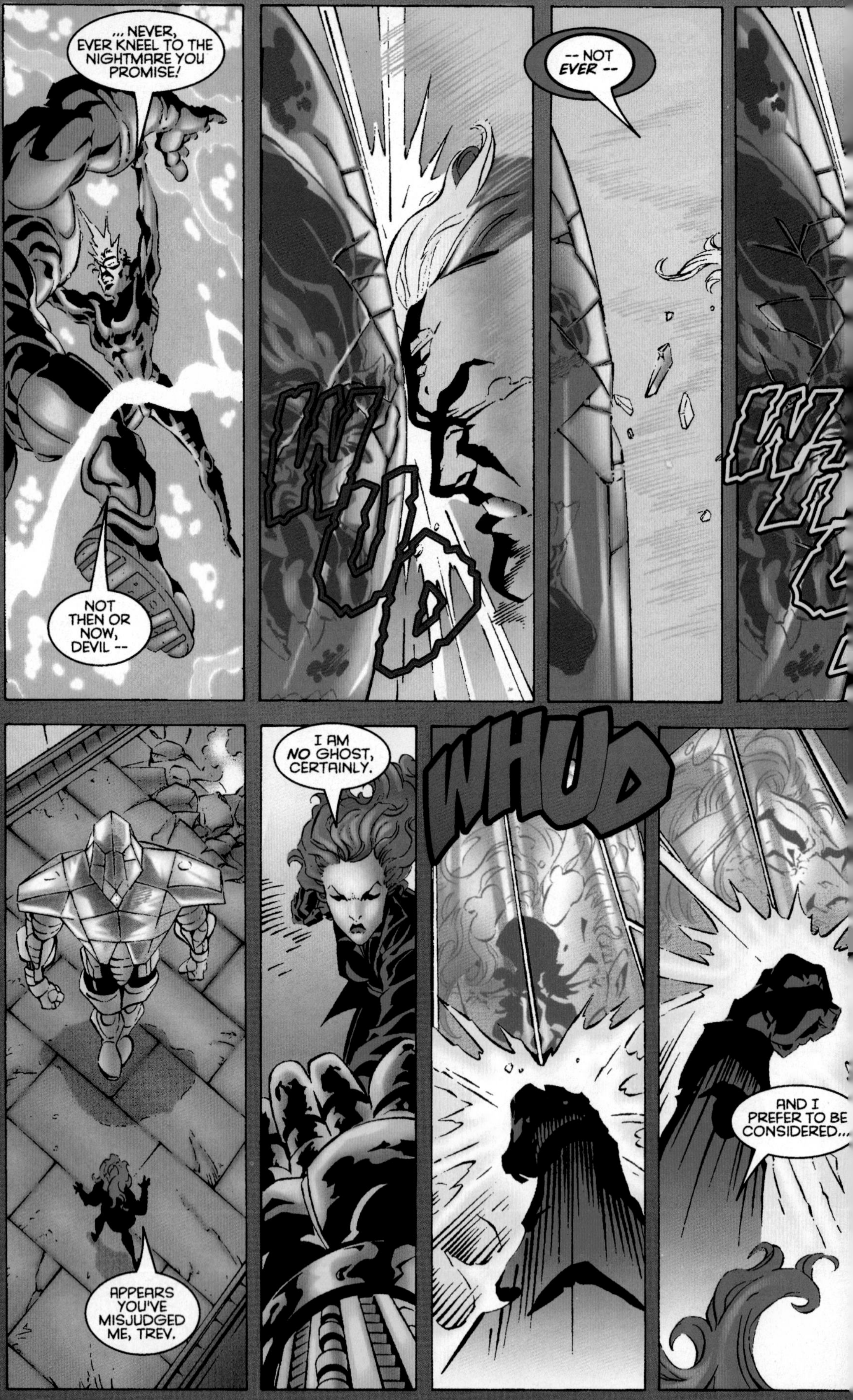

..., NEVER, EVER KNEEL TO THE NIGHTMARE YOU PROMISE!
NOT THEN OR NOW, DEVIL --
WHUD
-- NOT EVER --
APPEARS YOU'VE MISJUDGED ME, TREV.
I AM NO GHOST, CERTAINLY.
WHUD
AND I PREFER TO BE CONSIDERED...

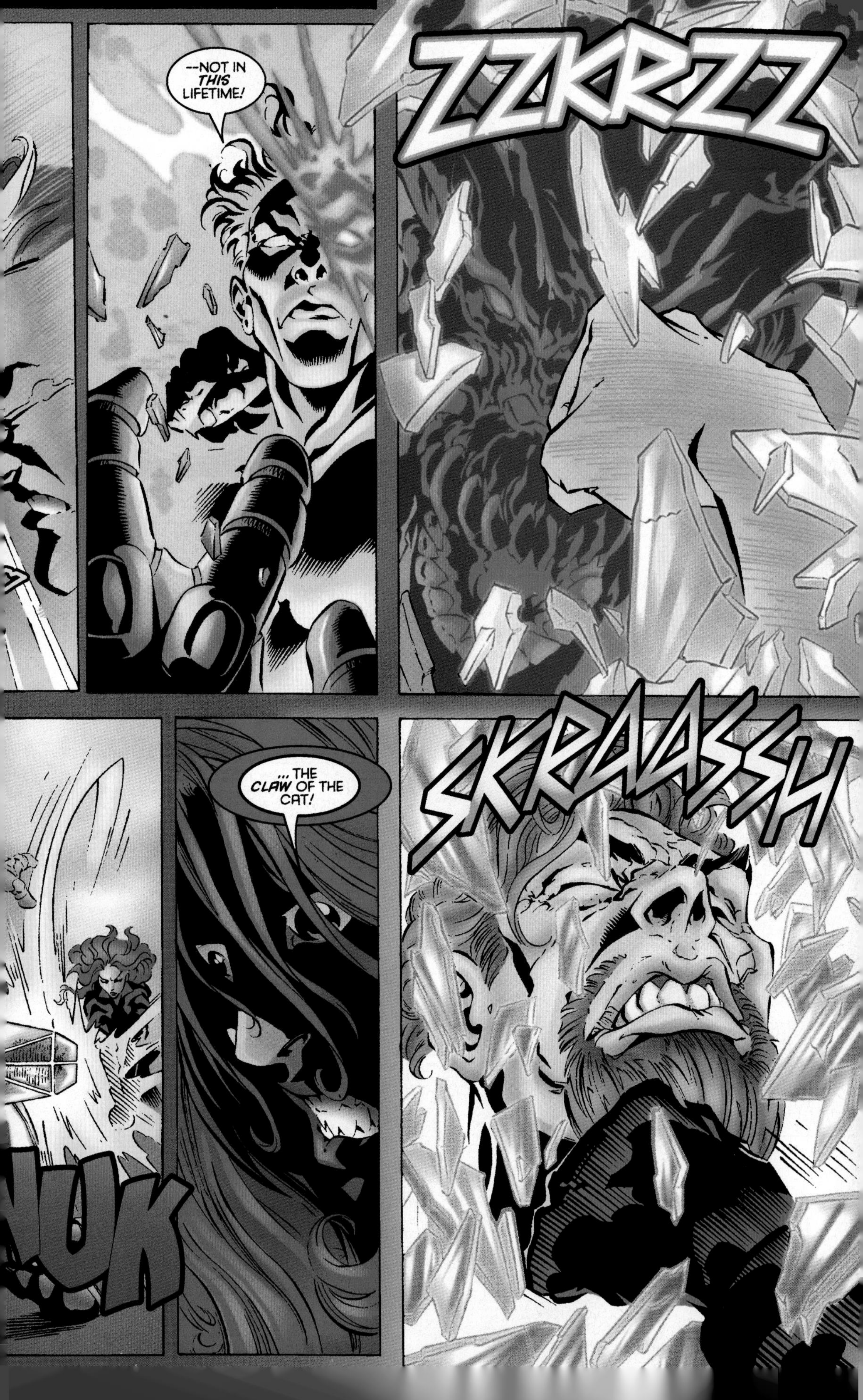
--NOT IN THIS LIFETIME!
ZZKRZZZ
...THE CLAW OF THE CAT!
SKRAASSH

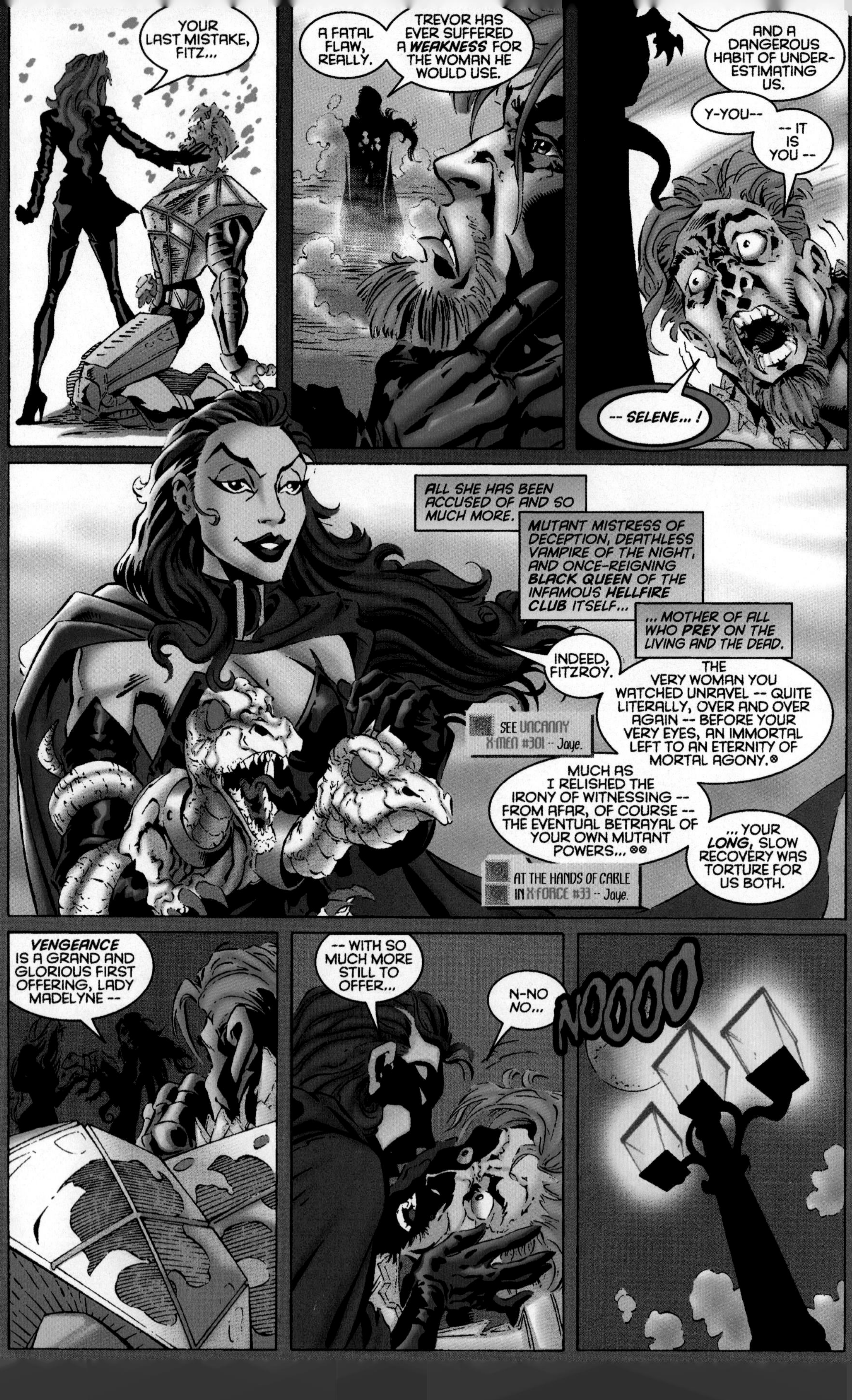

YOUR LAST MISTAKE, FITZ...
A FATAL FLAW, REALLY.
TREVOR HAS EVER SUFFERED A WEAKNESS FOR THE WOMAN HE WOULD USE.
AND A DANGEROUS HABIT OF UNDER-ESTIMATING US.
Y-YOU--
-- IT IS YOU --
-- SELENE... !
ALL SHE HAS BEEN ACCUSED OF AND SO MUCH MORE.
MUTANT MISTRESS OF DECEPTION, DEATHLESS VAMPIRE OF THE NIGHT, AND ONCE-REIGNING BLACK QUEEN OF THE INFAMOUS HELLFIRE CLUB ITSELF...
... MOTHER OF ALL WHO PREY ON THE LIVING AND THE DEAD.
INDEED, FITZROY.
THE VERY WOMAN YOU WATCHED UNRAVEL -- QUITE LITERALLY, OVER AND OVER AGAIN -- BEFORE YOUR VERY EYES, AN IMMORTAL LEFT TO AN ETERNITY OF MORTAL AGONY.⊗
⊗ SEE UNCANNY X-MEN #301 -- Jaye.
MUCH AS I RELISHED THE IRONY OF WITNESSING -- FROM AFAR, OF COURSE -- THE EVENTUAL BETRAYAL OF YOUR OWN MUTANT POWERS... ⊗⊗
... YOUR LONG, SLOW RECOVERY WAS TORTURE FOR US BOTH.
⊗⊗ AT THE HANDS OF CABLE IN X-FORCE #33 -- Jaye.
VENGEANCE IS A GRAND AND GLORIOUS FIRST OFFERING, LADY MADELYNE --
-- WITH SO MUCH MORE STILL TO OFFER...
N-NO NO...
NOOOO

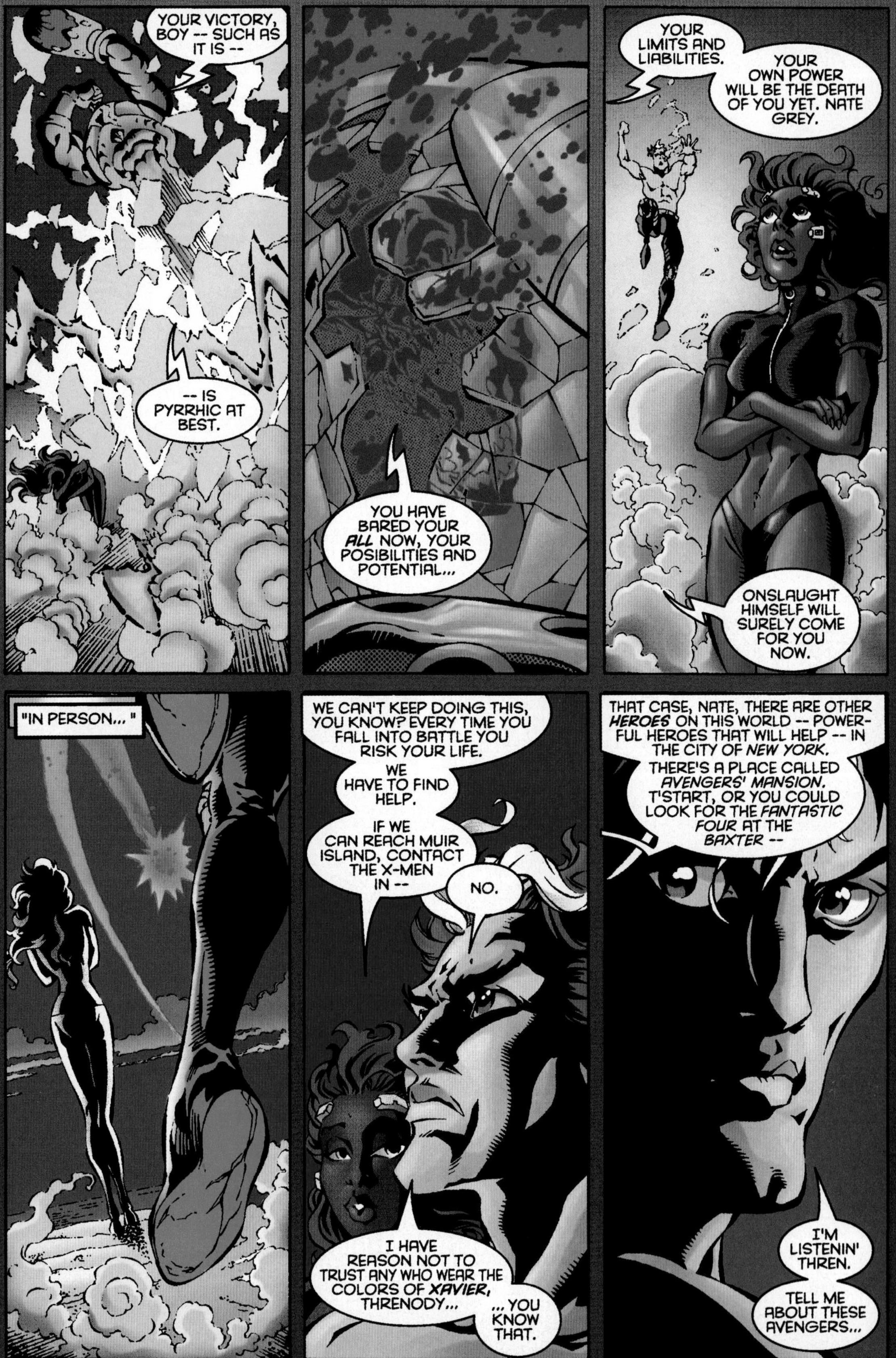
YOUR VICTORY, BOY -- SUCH AS IT IS --
-- IS PYRRHIC AT BEST.
YOU HAVE BARED YOUR ALL NOW, YOUR POSIBILITIES AND POTENTIAL...
YOUR LIMITS AND LIABILITIES.
YOUR OWN POWER WILL BE THE DEATH OF YOU YET. NATE GREY.
ONSLAUGHT HIMSELF WILL SURELY COME FOR YOU NOW.
"IN PERSON... "
WE CAN'T KEEP DOING THIS, YOU KNOW? EVERY TIME YOU FALL INTO BATTLE YOU RISK YOUR LIFE.
WE HAVE TO FIND HELP.
IF WE CAN REACH MUIR ISLAND, CONTACT THE X-MEN IN --
NO.
I HAVE REASON NOT TO TRUST ANY WHO WEAR THE COLORS OF XAVIER, THRENODY...
... YOU KNOW THAT.
THAT CASE, NATE, THERE ARE OTHER HEROES ON THIS WORLD -- POWERFUL HEROES THAT WILL HELP -- IN THE CITY OF NEW YORK.
THERE'S A PLACE CALLED AVENGERS' MANSION. T'START, OR YOU COULD LOOK FOR THE FANTASTIC FOUR AT THE BAXTER --
I'M LISTENIN' THREN.
TELL ME ABOUT THESE AVENGERS...

NEXT MONTH: STRANGE ALLIANCES... GUEST-STARRING X-FORCE

BUT FIRST, BE SURE TO PICK UP AVENGERS #400 ON SALE NEXT WEEK!

MARVEL COMICS
X-MEN
JUN. '96 11
X MEN
MAGNETO AND ROGUE
STARTING OVER

MARVEL COMICS
X-MEN
JULY '96 99
EXCALIBUR
ALAS, POOR DOUGLOCK

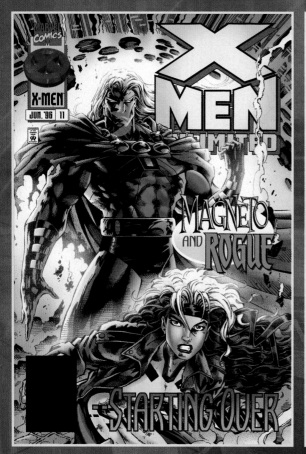

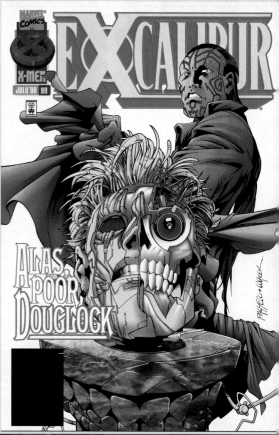

LATER...

As Onslaught prepared to leave the shadows and confront the X-Men, an unexpected variable entered the mix – the seeming return of his "other father," Magneto. Rogue, who had left the X-Men, was captured by Bastion and the mutant-hating Friends of Humanity – but was rescued by an amnesiac, de-aged master of magnetism! Calling himself Joseph, he had no memory of his former life as Magneto – but Rogue found it difficult to trust him, even when they battled side by side against Bastion's armored troops.

By this point, Onslaught had allies everywhere – including the Black Queen of the Hellfire Club's London branch. Now mere hours away from launching his offensive, he ordered them to prepare for his ascension... but before he could sweep the X-Men off the playing field, he had to rid himself of the one man closest to discovering his true identity...

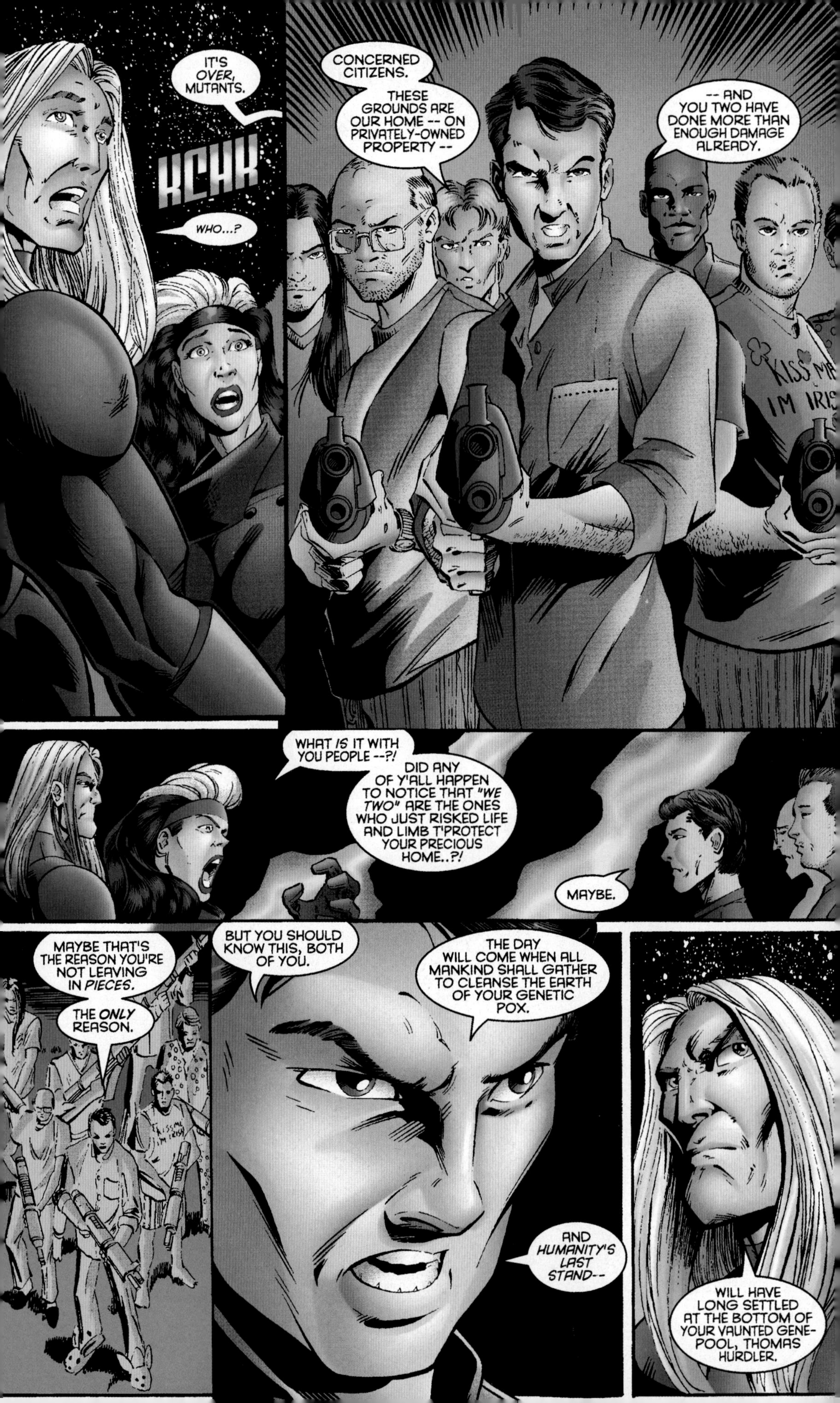
IT'S OVER, MUTANTS.
KCHK
WHO...?
CONCERNED CITIZENS.
THESE GROUNDS ARE OUR HOME -- ON PRIVATELY-OWNED PROPERTY --
-- AND YOU TWO HAVE DONE MORE THAN ENOUGH DAMAGE ALREADY.
WHAT IS IT WITH YOU PEOPLE --?!
DID ANY OF Y'ALL HAPPEN TO NOTICE THAT "WE TWO" ARE THE ONES WHO JUST RISKED LIFE AND LIMB T'PROTECT YOUR PRECIOUS HOME..?!
MAYBE.
MAYBE THAT'S THE REASON YOU'RE NOT LEAVING IN PIECES.
THE ONLY REASON.
BUT YOU SHOULD KNOW THIS, BOTH OF YOU.
THE DAY WILL COME WHEN ALL MANKIND SHALL GATHER TO CLEANSE THE EARTH OF YOUR GENETIC POX.
AND HUMANITY'S LAST STAND--
WILL HAVE LONG SETTLED AT THE BOTTOM OF YOUR VAUNTED GENE-POOL, THOMAS HURDLER.

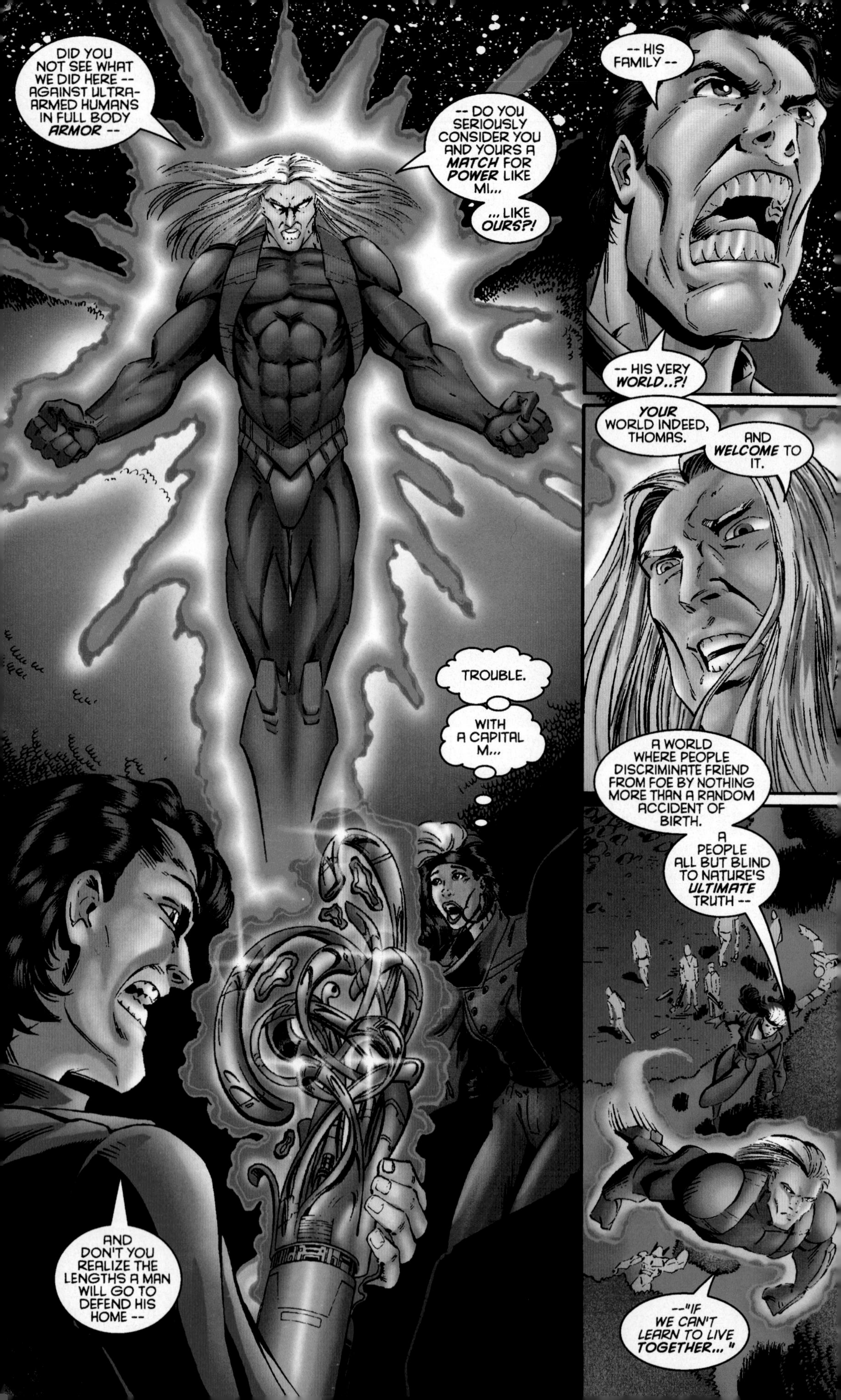
DID YOU NOT SEE WHAT WE DID HERE -- AGAINST ULTRA-ARMED HUMANS IN FULL BODY ARMOR --
-- DO YOU SERIOUSLY CONSIDER YOU AND YOURS A MATCH FOR POWER LIKE MI...
...LIKE OURS?!
TROUBLE.
WITH A CAPITAL M...
AND DON'T YOU REALIZE THE LENGTHS A MAN WILL GO TO DEFEND HIS HOME --
-- HIS FAMILY --
-- HIS VERY WORLD..?!
YOUR WORLD INDEED, THOMAS.
AND WELCOME TO IT.
A WORLD WHERE PEOPLE DISCRIMINATE FRIEND FROM FOE BY NOTHING MORE THAN A RANDOM ACCIDENT OF BIRTH.
A PEOPLE ALL BUT BLIND TO NATURE'S ULTIMATE TRUTH --
--"IF WE CAN'T LEARN TO LIVE TOGETHER..."

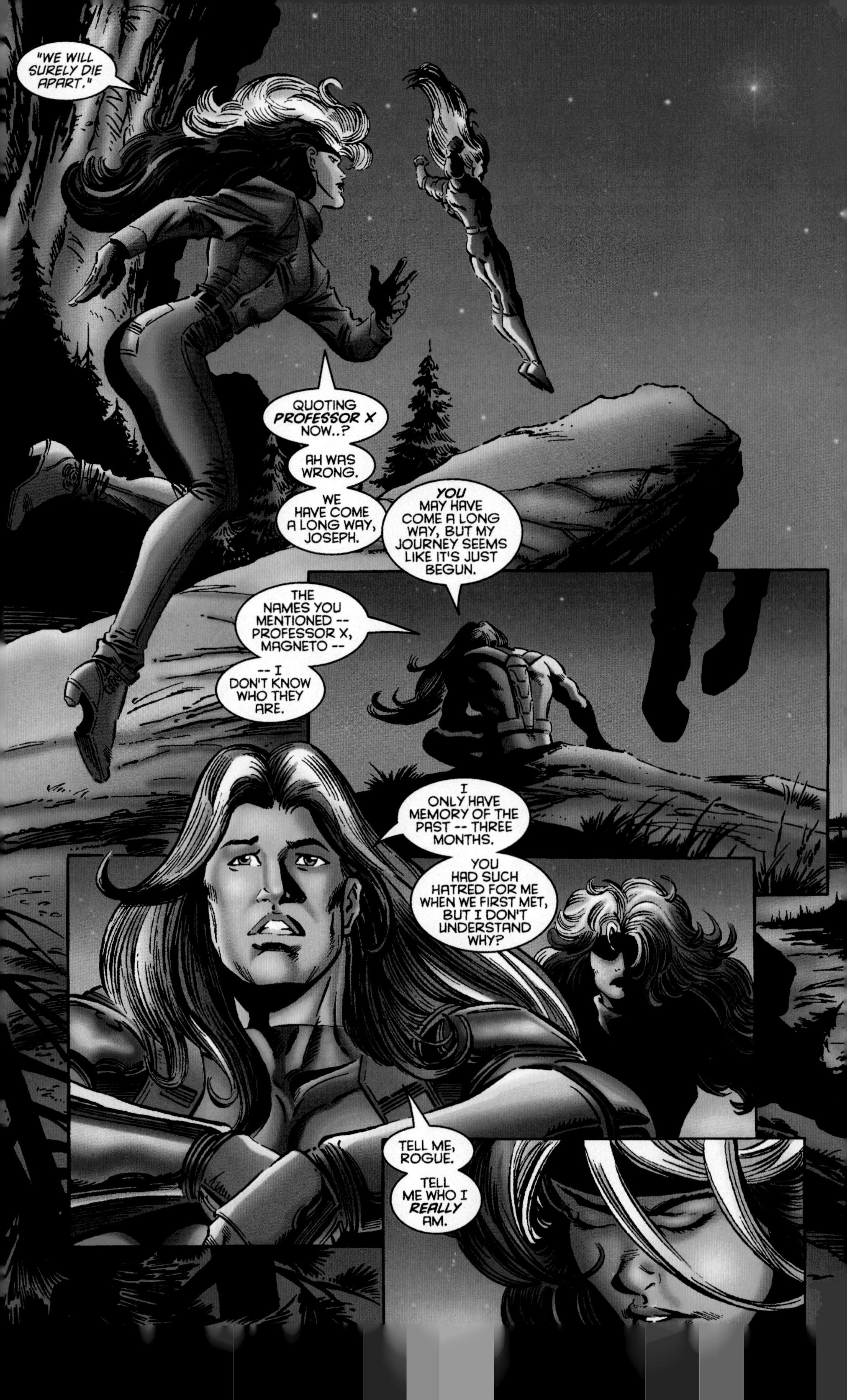
"WE WILL SURELY DIE APART."
QUOTING PROFESSOR X NOW..?
AH WAS WRONG.
WE HAVE COME A LONG WAY, JOSEPH.
YOU MAY HAVE COME A LONG WAY, BUT MY JOURNEY SEEMS LIKE IT'S JUST BEGUN.
THE NAMES YOU MENTIONED -- PROFESSOR X, MAGNETO --
-- I DON'T KNOW WHO THEY ARE.
I ONLY HAVE MEMORY OF THE PAST -- THREE MONTHS.
YOU HAD SUCH HATRED FOR ME WHEN WE FIRST MET, BUT I DON'T UNDERSTAND WHY?
TELL ME, ROGUE.
TELL ME WHO I REALLY AM.

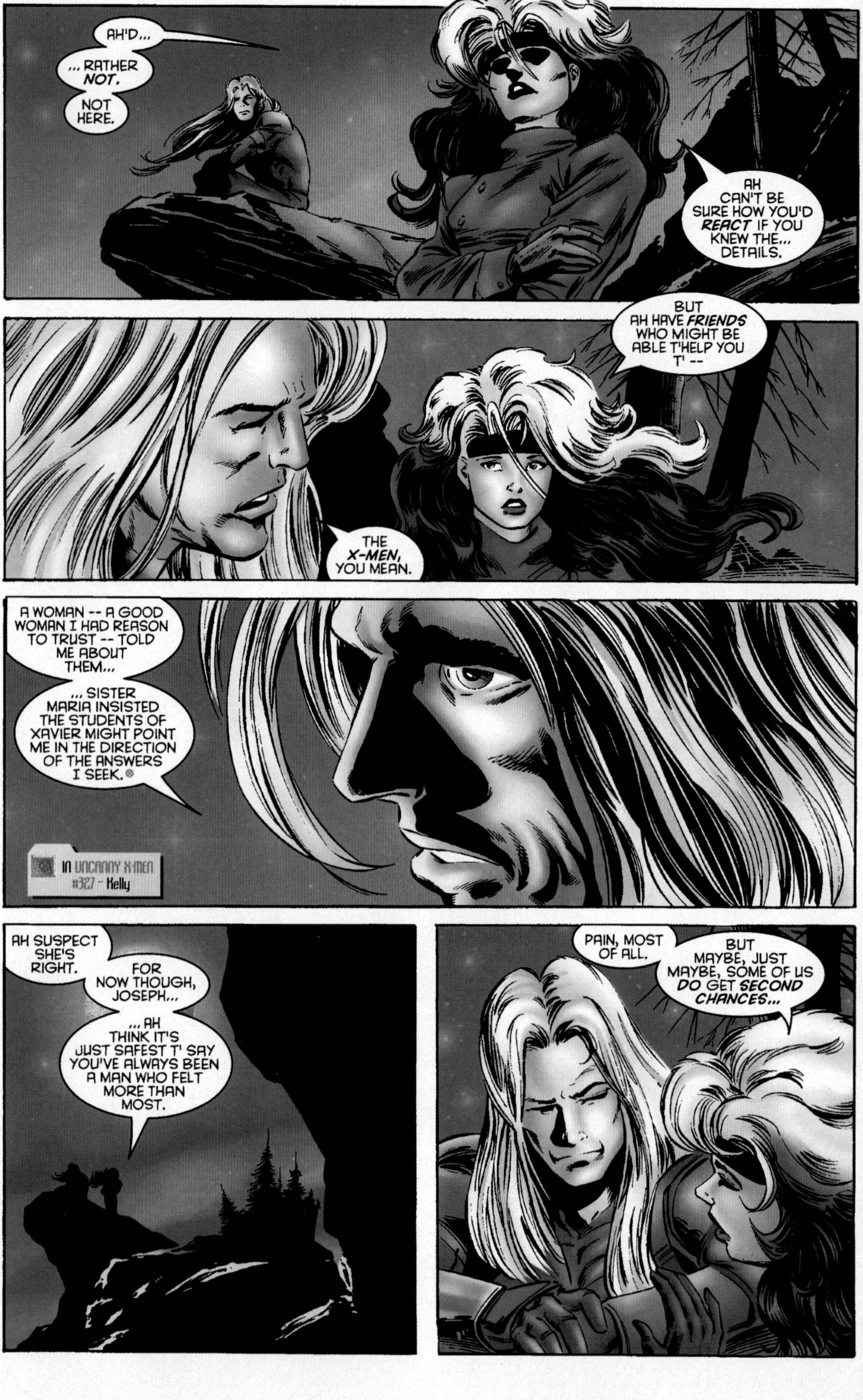
AH'D...
... RATHER NOT.
NOT HERE.
AH CAN'T BE SURE HOW YOU'D REACT IF YOU KNEW THE... DETAILS.
BUT AH HAVE FRIENDS WHO MIGHT BE ABLE T'HELP YOU T' --
THE X-MEN, YOU MEAN.
A WOMAN -- A GOOD WOMAN I HAD REASON TO TRUST -- TOLD ME ABOUT THEM...
... SISTER MARIA INSISTED THE STUDENTS OF XAVIER MIGHT POINT ME IN THE DIRECTION OF THE ANSWERS I SEEK.
IN UNCANNY X-MEN #327 -- Kelly
AH SUSPECT SHE'S RIGHT.
FOR NOW THOUGH, JOSEPH...
... AH THINK IT'S JUST SAFEST T' SAY YOU'VE ALWAYS BEEN A MAN WHO FELT MORE THAN MOST.
PAIN, MOST OF ALL.
BUT MAYBE, JUST MAYBE, SOME OF US DO GET SECOND CHANCES...

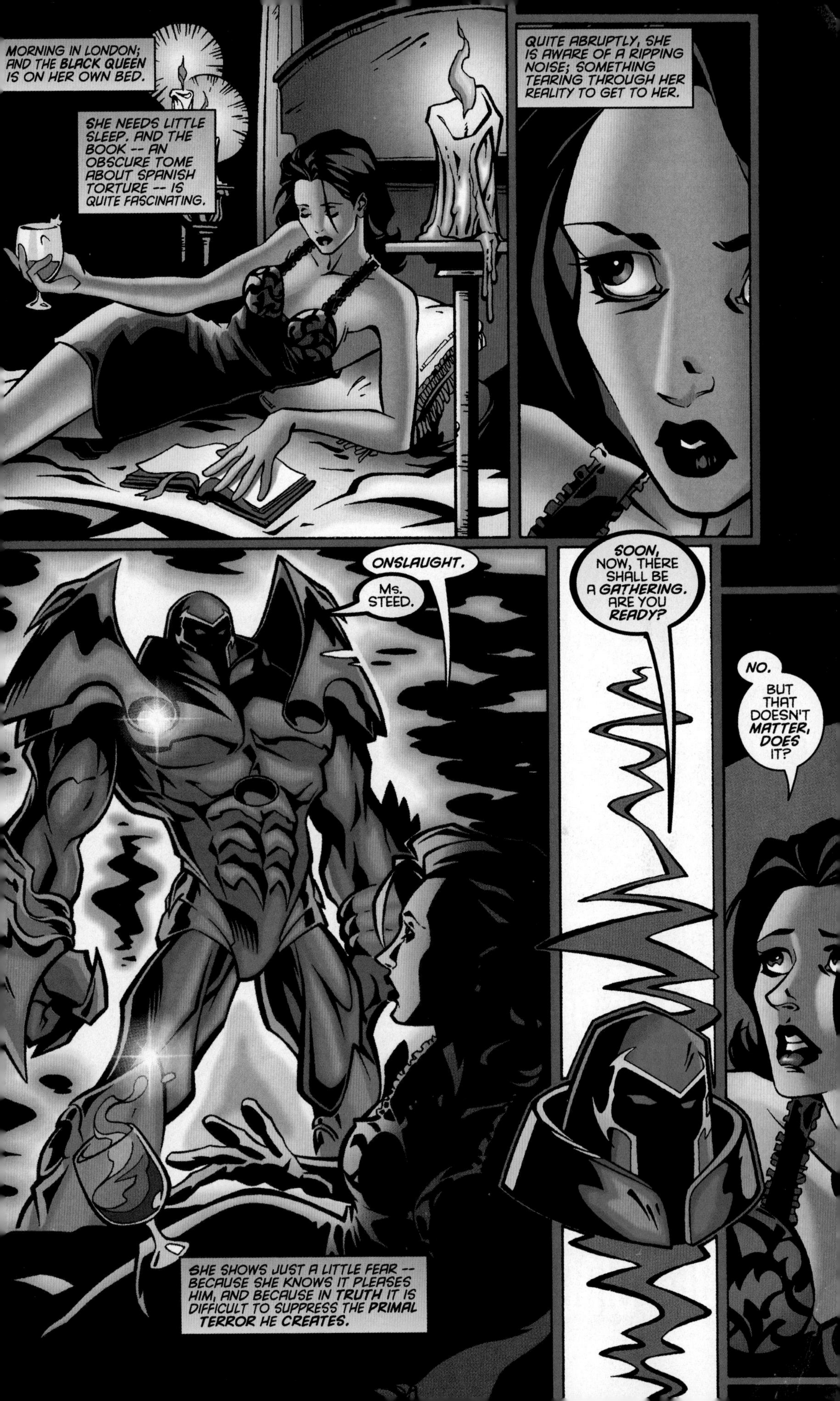
MORNING IN LONDON; AND THE BLACK QUEEN IS ON HER OWN BED.
SHE NEEDS LITTLE SLEEP. AND THE BOOK -- AN OBSCURE TOME ABOUT SPANISH TORTURE -- IS QUITE FASCINATING.
QUITE ABRUPTLY, SHE IS AWARE OF A RIPPING NOISE; SOMETHING TEARING THROUGH HER REALITY TO GET TO HER.
ONSLAUGHT.
Ms. STEED.
SOON, NOW, THERE SHALL BE A GATHERING. ARE YOU READY?
NO.
BUT THAT DOESN'T MATTER, DOES IT?
SHE SHOWS JUST A LITTLE FEAR -- BECAUSE SHE KNOWS IT PLEASES HIM, AND BECAUSE IN TRUTH IT IS DIFFICULT TO SUPPRESS THE PRIMAL TERROR HE CREATES.

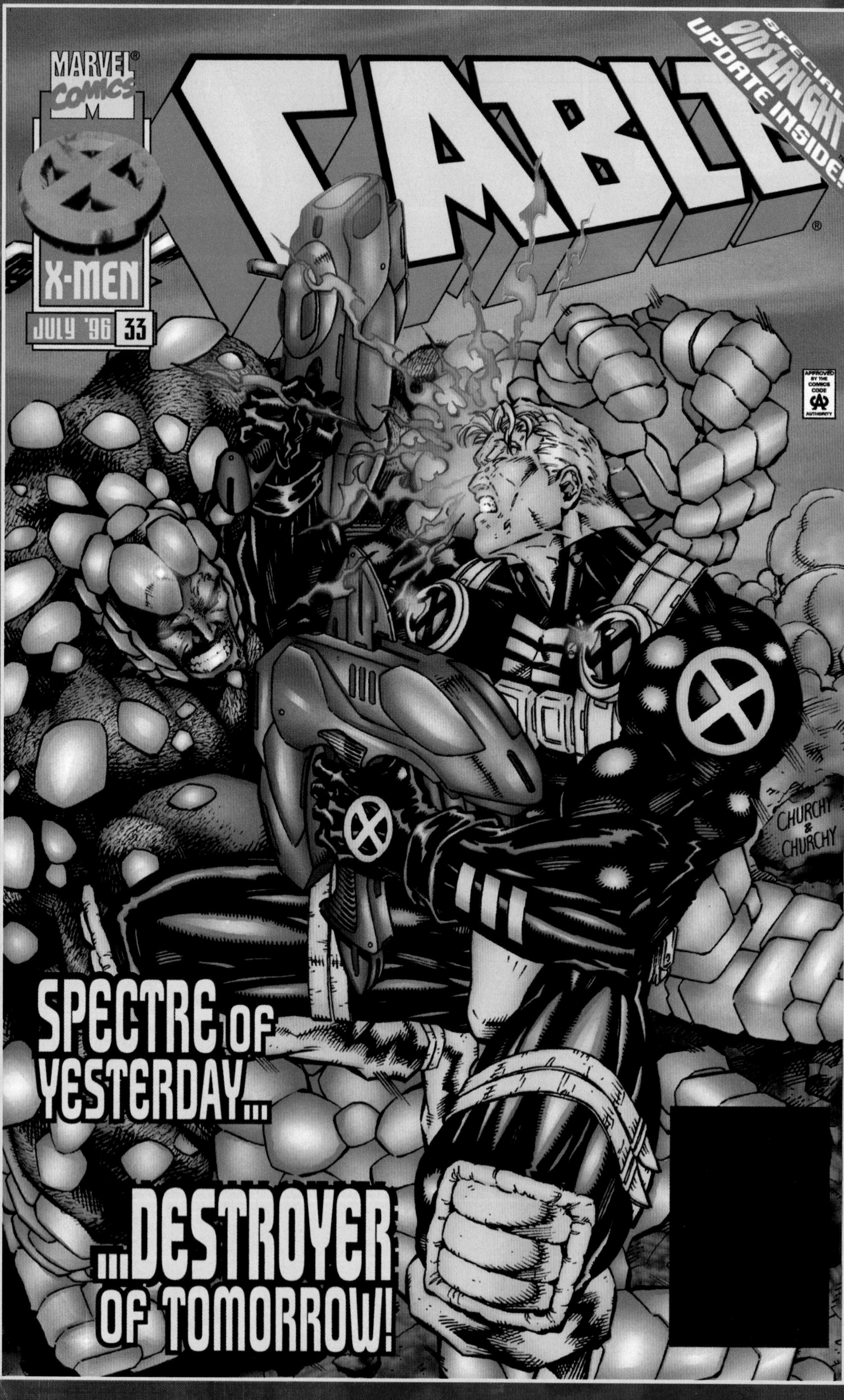
MARVEL® COMICS
X-MEN
JULY '96 33
CABLE®
SPECIAL ONSLAUGHT™ UPDATE INSIDE!
APPROVED BY THE COMICS CODE AUTHORITY
CHURCHY & CHURCHY
SPECTRE OF YESTERDAY...
...DESTROYER OF TOMORROW!

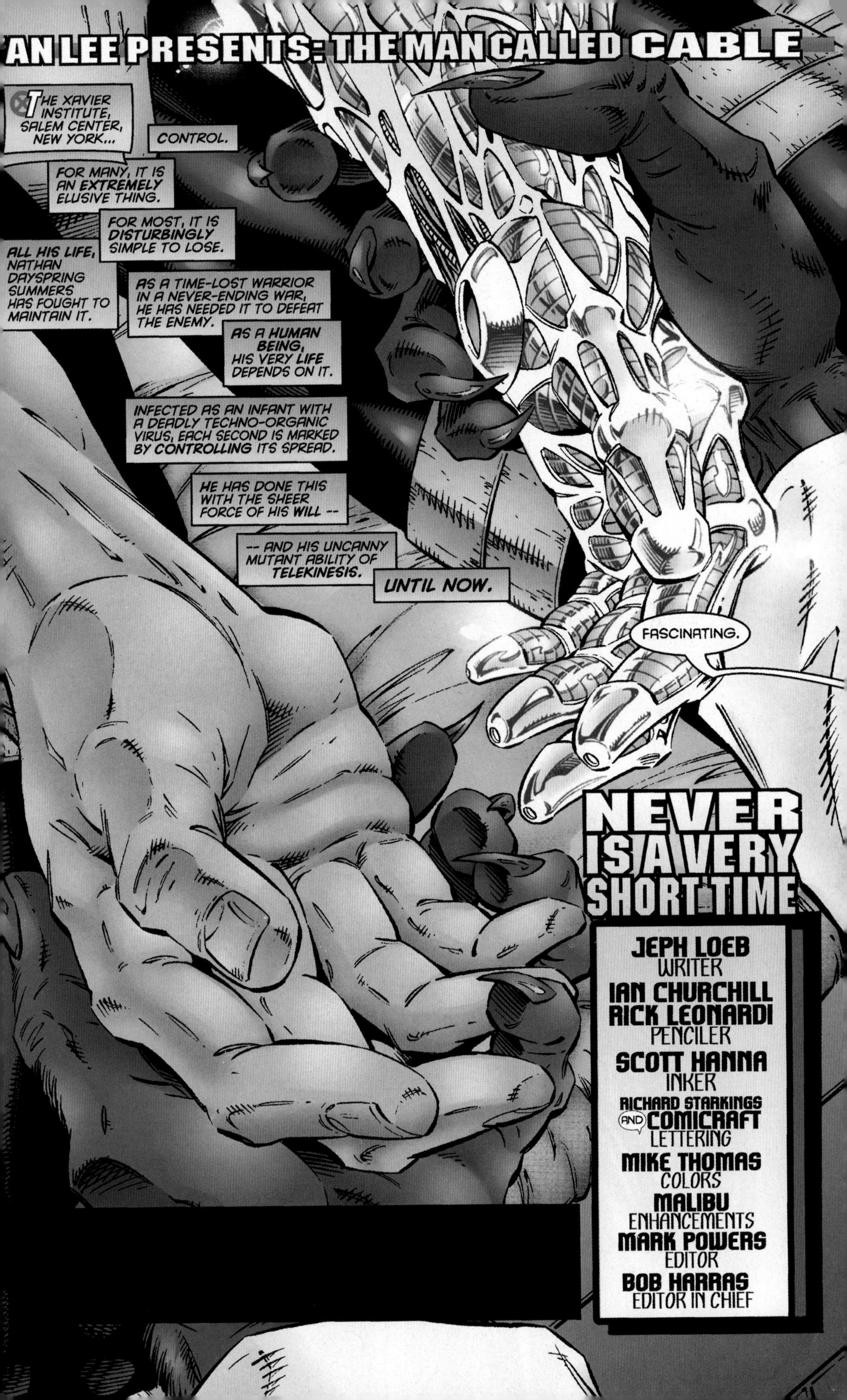
AN LEE PRESENTS: THE MAN CALLED CABLE
THE XAVIER INSTITUTE, SALEM CENTER, NEW YORK...
CONTROL.
FOR MANY, IT IS AN EXTREMELY ELUSIVE THING.
FOR MOST, IT IS DISTURBINGLY SIMPLE TO LOSE.
ALL HIS LIFE, NATHAN DAYSPRING SUMMERS HAS FOUGHT TO MAINTAIN IT.
AS A TIME-LOST WARRIOR IN A NEVER-ENDING WAR, HE HAS NEEDED IT TO DEFEAT THE ENEMY.
AS A HUMAN BEING, HIS VERY LIFE DEPENDS ON IT.
INFECTED AS AN INFANT WITH A DEADLY TECHNO-ORGANIC VIRUS, EACH SECOND IS MARKED BY CONTROLLING ITS SPREAD.
HE HAS DONE THIS WITH THE SHEER FORCE OF HIS WILL --
-- AND HIS UNCANNY MUTANT ABILITY OF TELEKINESIS.
UNTIL NOW.
FASCINATING.
NEVER IS A VERY SHORT TIME
JEPH LOEB WRITER
IAN CHURCHILL RICK LEONARDI PENCILER
SCOTT HANNA INKER
RICHARD STARKINGS AND COMICRAFT LETTERING
MIKE THOMAS COLORS
MALIBU ENHANCEMENTS
MARK POWERS EDITOR
BOB HARRAS EDITOR IN CHIEF

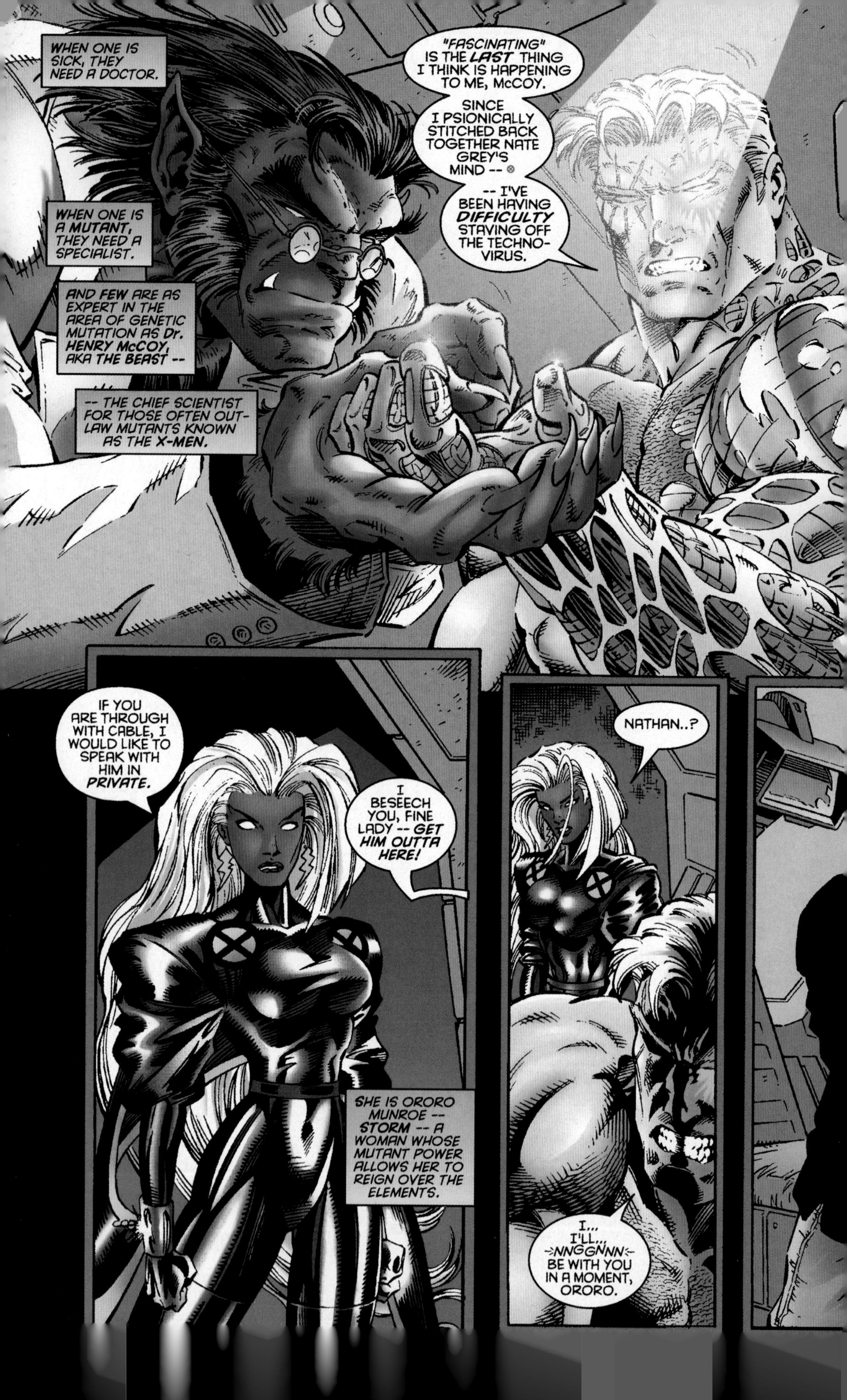
WHEN ONE IS SICK, THEY NEED A DOCTOR.
WHEN ONE IS A MUTANT, THEY NEED A SPECIALIST.
AND FEW ARE AS EXPERT IN THE AREA OF GENETIC MUTATION AS Dr. HENRY McCOY, AKA THE BEAST --
-- THE CHIEF SCIENTIST FOR THOSE OFTEN OUT-LAW MUTANTS KNOWN AS THE X-MEN.
"FASCINATING" IS THE LAST THING I THINK IS HAPPENING TO ME, McCOY.
SINCE I PSIONICALLY STITCHED BACK TOGETHER NATE GREY'S MIND --
-- I'VE BEEN HAVING DIFFICULTY STAVING OFF THE TECHNO-VIRUS.
IF YOU ARE THROUGH WITH CABLE, I WOULD LIKE TO SPEAK WITH HIM IN PRIVATE.
I BESEECH YOU, FINE LADY -- GET HIM OUTTA HERE!
SHE IS ORORO MUNROE -- STORM -- A WOMAN WHOSE MUTANT POWER ALLOWS HER TO REIGN OVER THE ELEMENTS.
NATHAN..?
I... I'LL... -NNGGNNN- BE WITH YOU IN A MOMENT, ORORO.

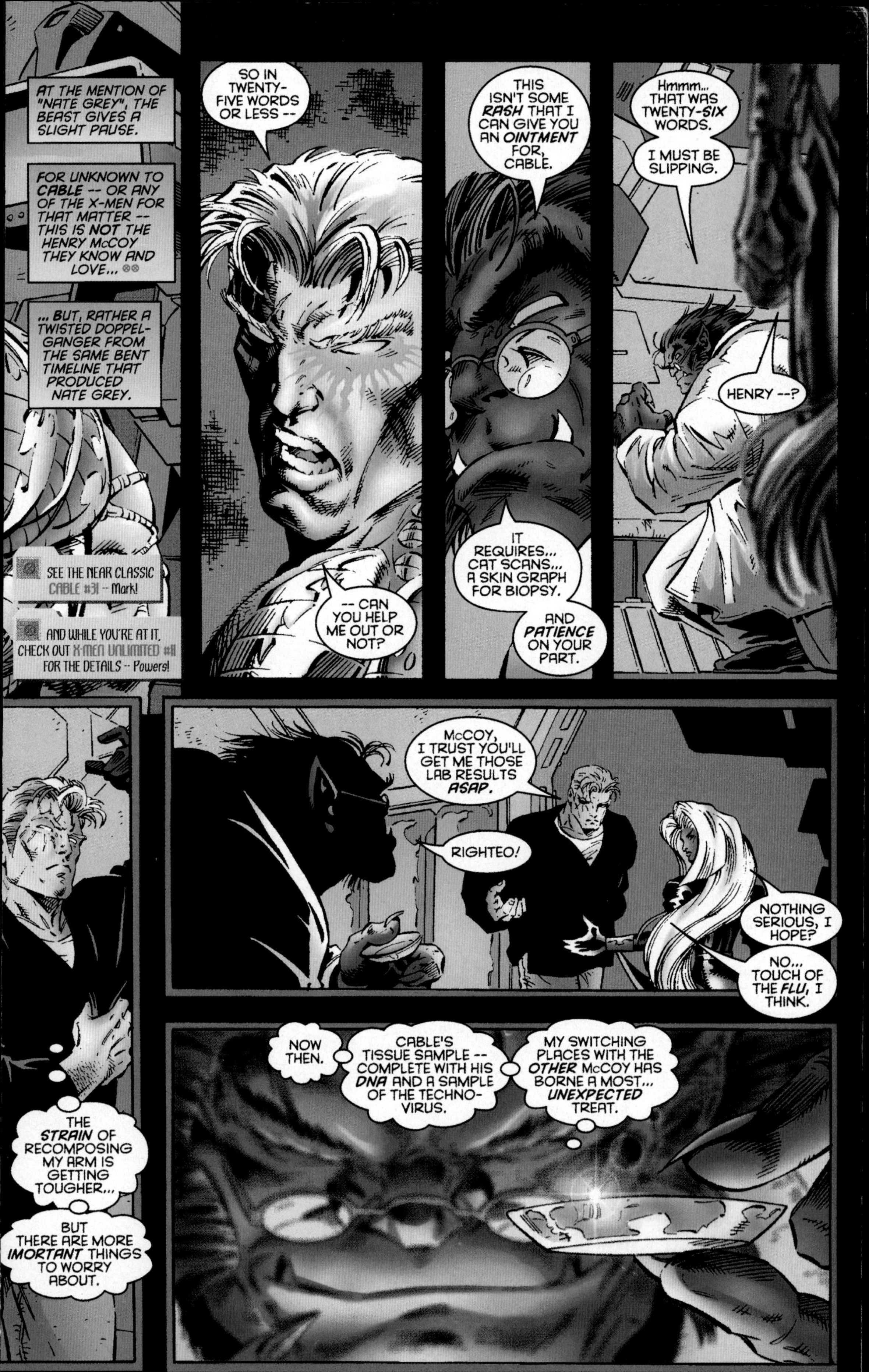
AT THE MENTION OF "NATE GREY", THE BEAST GIVES A SLIGHT PAUSE.
FOR UNKNOWN TO CABLE -- OR ANY OF THE X-MEN FOR THAT MATTER -- THIS IS NOT THE HENRY McCOY THEY KNOW AND LOVE...
... BUT, RATHER A TWISTED DOPPEL-GANGER FROM THE SAME BENT TIMELINE THAT PRODUCED NATE GREY.
SEE THE NEAR CLASSIC CABLE #31 -- Mark!
AND WHILE YOU'RE AT IT, CHECK OUT X-MEN UNLIMITED #11 FOR THE DETAILS -- Powers!
SO IN TWENTY-FIVE WORDS OR LESS --
-- CAN YOU HELP ME OUT OR NOT?
THIS ISN'T SOME RASH THAT I CAN GIVE YOU AN OINTMENT FOR, CABLE.
IT REQUIRES... CAT SCANS... A SKIN GRAPH FOR BIOPSY.
AND PATIENCE ON YOUR PART.
Hmmm... THAT WAS TWENTY-SIX WORDS.
I MUST BE SLIPPING.
HENRY --?
McCOY, I TRUST YOU'LL GET ME THOSE LAB RESULTS ASAP.
RIGHTEO!
NOTHING SERIOUS, I HOPE?
NO... TOUCH OF THE FLU, I THINK.
THE STRAIN OF RECOMPOSING MY ARM IS GETTING TOUGHER...
BUT THERE ARE MORE IMORTANT THINGS TO WORRY ABOUT.
NOW THEN.
CABLE'S TISSUE SAMPLE -- COMPLETE WITH HIS DNA AND A SAMPLE OF THE TECHNO-VIRUS.
MY SWITCHING PLACES WITH THE OTHER McCOY HAS BORNE A MOST... UNEXPECTED TREAT.

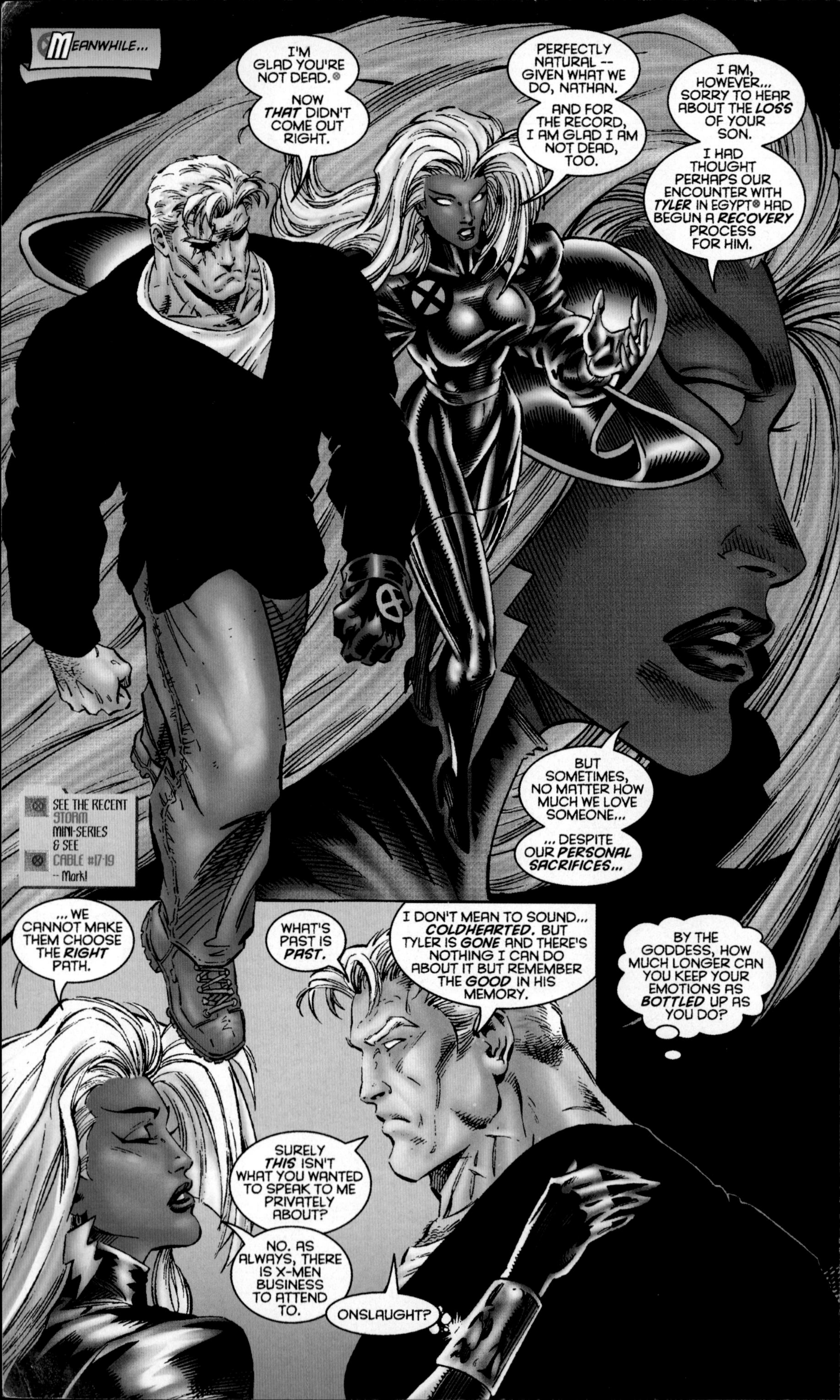
MEANWHILE...
I'M GLAD YOU'RE NOT DEAD.
NOW THAT DIDN'T COME OUT RIGHT.
PERFECTLY NATURAL -- GIVEN WHAT WE DO, NATHAN.
AND FOR THE RECORD, I AM GLAD I AM NOT DEAD, TOO.
I AM, HOWEVER... SORRY TO HEAR ABOUT THE LOSS OF YOUR SON.
I HAD THOUGHT PERHAPS OUR ENCOUNTER WITH TYLER IN EGYPT HAD BEGUN A RECOVERY PROCESS FOR HIM.
BUT SOMETIMES, NO MATTER HOW MUCH WE LOVE SOMEONE...
... DESPITE OUR PERSONAL SACRIFICES...
SEE THE RECENT STORM MINI-SERIES & SEE CABLE #17-19 -- Mark!
... WE CANNOT MAKE THEM CHOOSE THE RIGHT PATH.
WHAT'S PAST IS PAST.
I DON'T MEAN TO SOUND... COLDHEARTED. BUT TYLER IS GONE AND THERE'S NOTHING I CAN DO ABOUT IT BUT REMEMBER THE GOOD IN HIS MEMORY.
BY THE GODDESS, HOW MUCH LONGER CAN YOU KEEP YOUR EMOTIONS AS BOTTLED UP AS YOU DO?
SURELY THIS ISN'T WHAT YOU WANTED TO SPEAK TO ME PRIVATELY ABOUT?
NO. AS ALWAYS, THERE IS X-MEN BUSINESS TO ATTEND TO.
ONSLAUGHT?

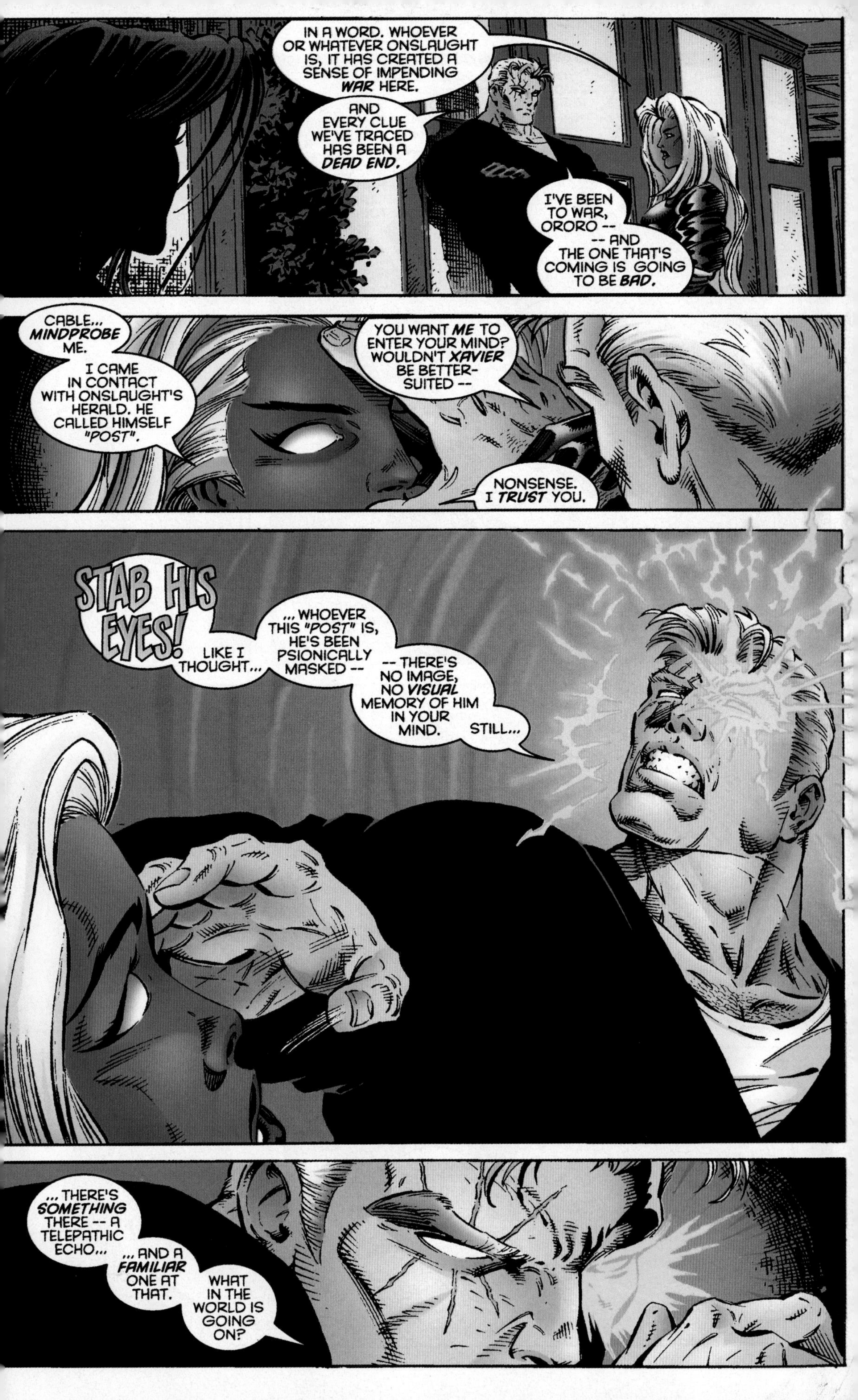
IN A WORD. WHOEVER OR WHATEVER ONSLAUGHT IS, IT HAS CREATED A SENSE OF IMPENDING WAR HERE.
AND EVERY CLUE WE'VE TRACED HAS BEEN A DEAD END.
I'VE BEEN TO WAR, ORORO --
-- AND THE ONE THAT'S COMING IS GOING TO BE BAD.
CABLE... MINDPROBE ME.
I CAME IN CONTACT WITH ONSLAUGHT'S HERALD. HE CALLED HIMSELF "POST".
YOU WANT ME TO ENTER YOUR MIND? WOULDN'T XAVIER BE BETTER-SUITED --
NONSENSE. I TRUST YOU.
STAB HIS EYES!
LIKE I THOUGHT...
...WHOEVER THIS "POST" IS, HE'S BEEN PSIONICALLY MASKED --
-- THERE'S NO IMAGE, NO VISUAL MEMORY OF HIM IN YOUR MIND.
STILL...
...THERE'S SOMETHING THERE -- A TELEPATHIC ECHO...
...AND A FAMILIAR ONE AT THAT.
WHAT IN THE WORLD IS GOING ON?

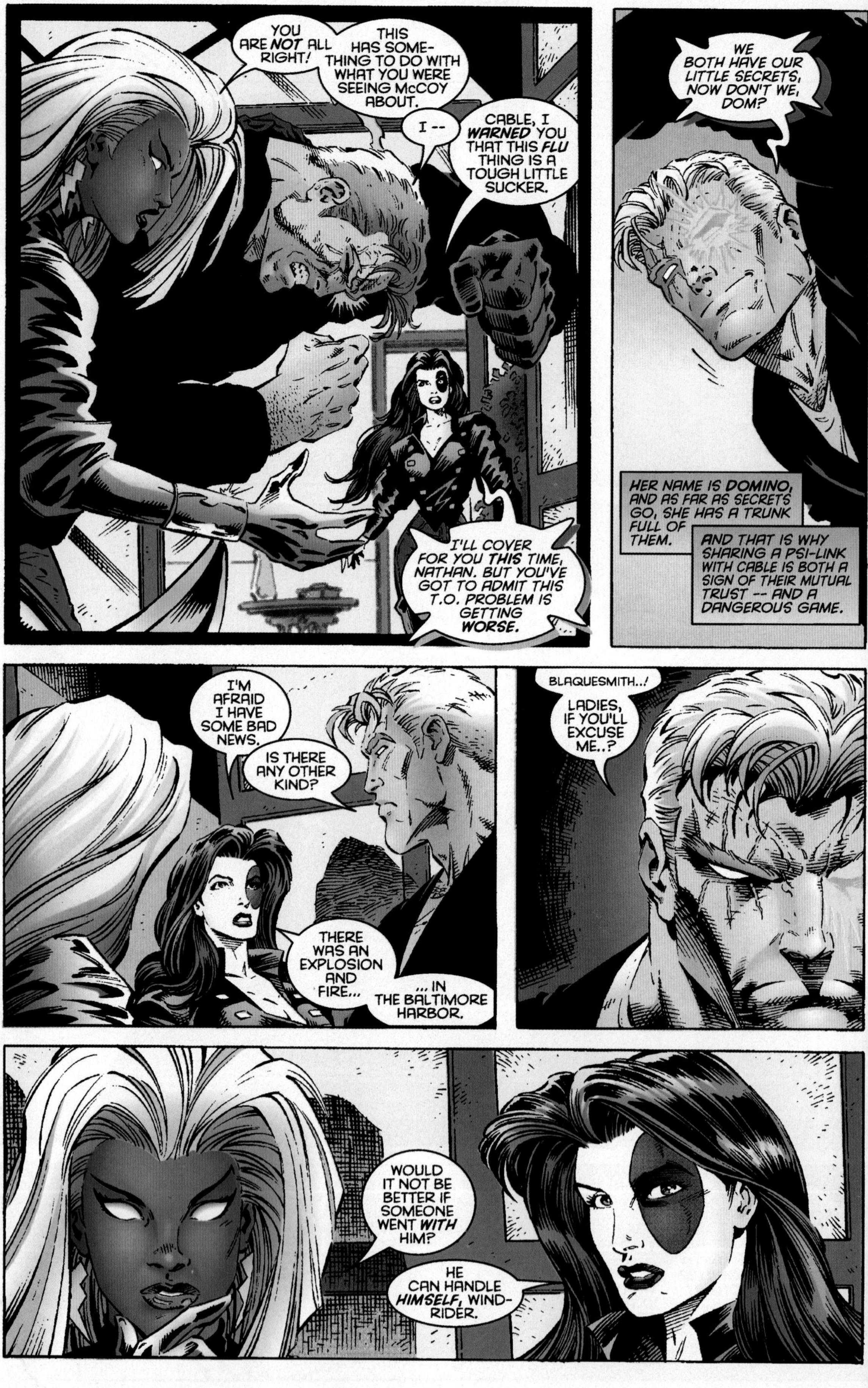

YOU ARE NOT ALL RIGHT!
THIS HAS SOME-THING TO DO WITH WHAT YOU WERE SEEING McCOY ABOUT.
I --
CABLE, I WARNED YOU THAT THIS FLU THING IS A TOUGH LITTLE SUCKER.
I'LL COVER FOR YOU THIS TIME, NATHAN. BUT YOU'VE GOT TO ADMIT THIS T.O. PROBLEM IS GETTING WORSE.
WE BOTH HAVE OUR LITTLE SECRETS, NOW DON'T WE, DOM?
HER NAME IS DOMINO, AND AS FAR AS SECRETS GO, SHE HAS A TRUNK FULL OF THEM.
AND THAT IS WHY SHARING A PSI-LINK WITH CABLE IS BOTH A SIGN OF THEIR MUTUAL TRUST -- AND A DANGEROUS GAME.
I'M AFRAID I HAVE SOME BAD NEWS.
IS THERE ANY OTHER KIND?
THERE WAS AN EXPLOSION AND FIRE...
... IN THE BALTIMORE HARBOR.
BLAQUESMITH..!
LADIES, IF YOU'LL EXCUSE ME..?
WOULD IT NOT BE BETTER IF SOMEONE WENT WITH HIM?
HE CAN HANDLE HIMSELF, WIND-RIDER.

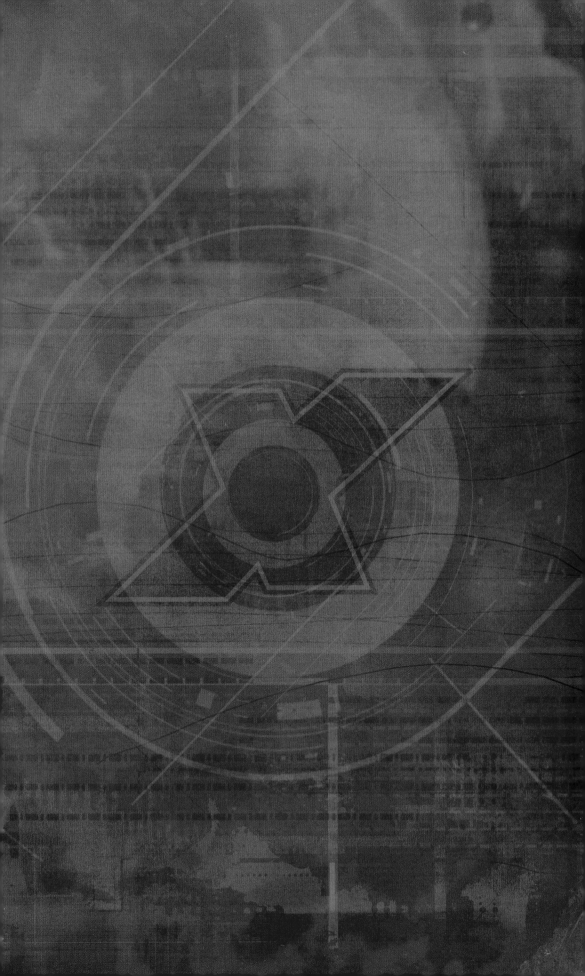

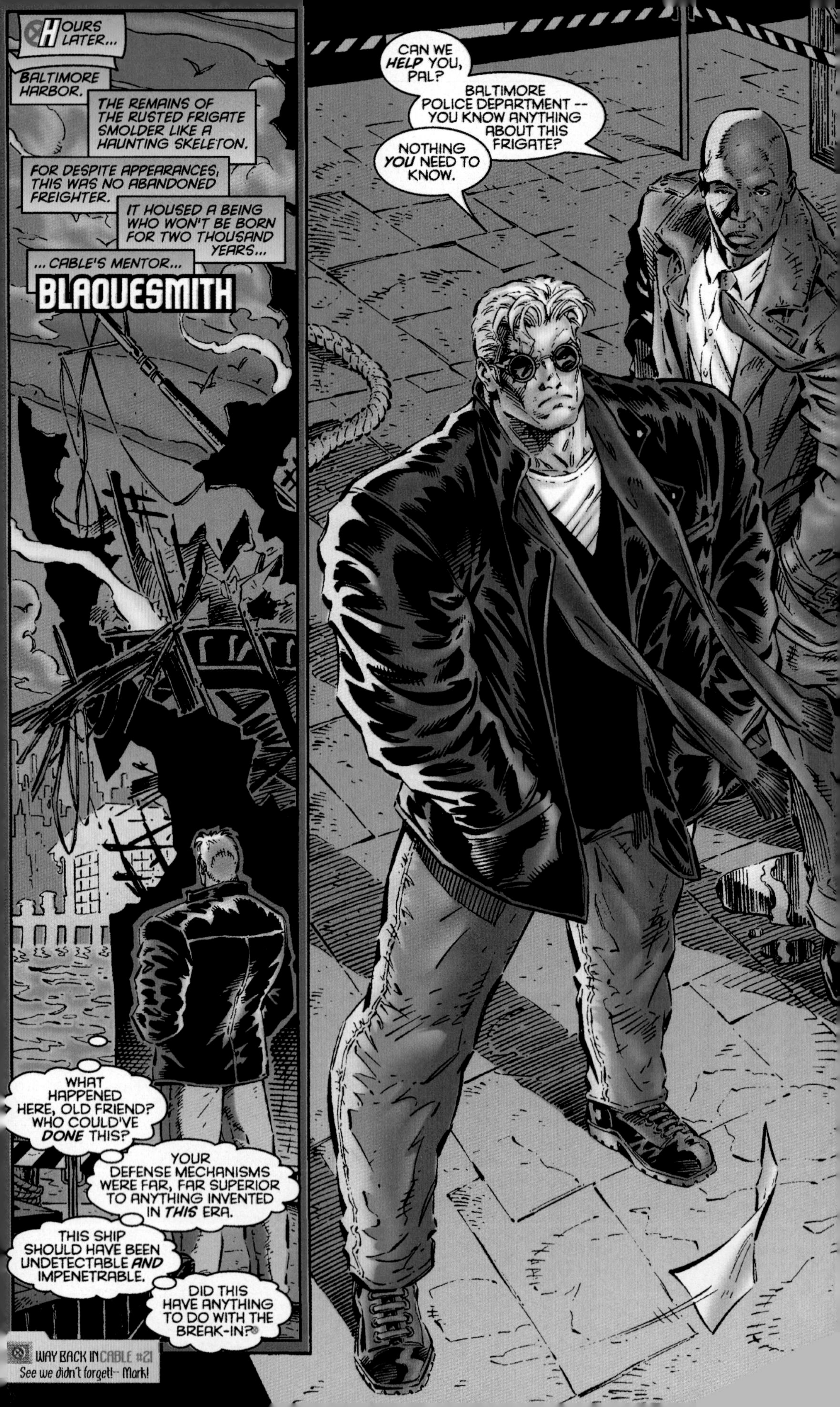

HOURS LATER...
BALTIMORE HARBOR.
THE REMAINS OF THE RUSTED FRIGATE SMOLDER LIKE A HAUNTING SKELETON.
FOR DESPITE APPEARANCES, THIS WAS NO ABANDONED FREIGHTER.
IT HOUSED A BEING WHO WON'T BE BORN FOR TWO THOUSAND YEARS...
...CABLE'S MENTOR...
BLAQUESMITH
WHAT HAPPENED HERE, OLD FRIEND? WHO COULD'VE DONE THIS?
YOUR DEFENSE MECHANISMS WERE FAR, FAR SUPERIOR TO ANYTHING INVENTED IN THIS ERA.
THIS SHIP SHOULD HAVE BEEN UNDETECTABLE AND IMPENETRABLE.
DID THIS HAVE ANYTHING TO DO WITH THE BREAK-IN?
WAY BACK IN CABLE #21
See we didn't forget!-- Mark!
CAN WE HELP YOU, PAL?
BALTIMORE POLICE DEPARTMENT -- YOU KNOW ANYTHING ABOUT THIS FRIGATE?
NOTHING YOU NEED TO KNOW.

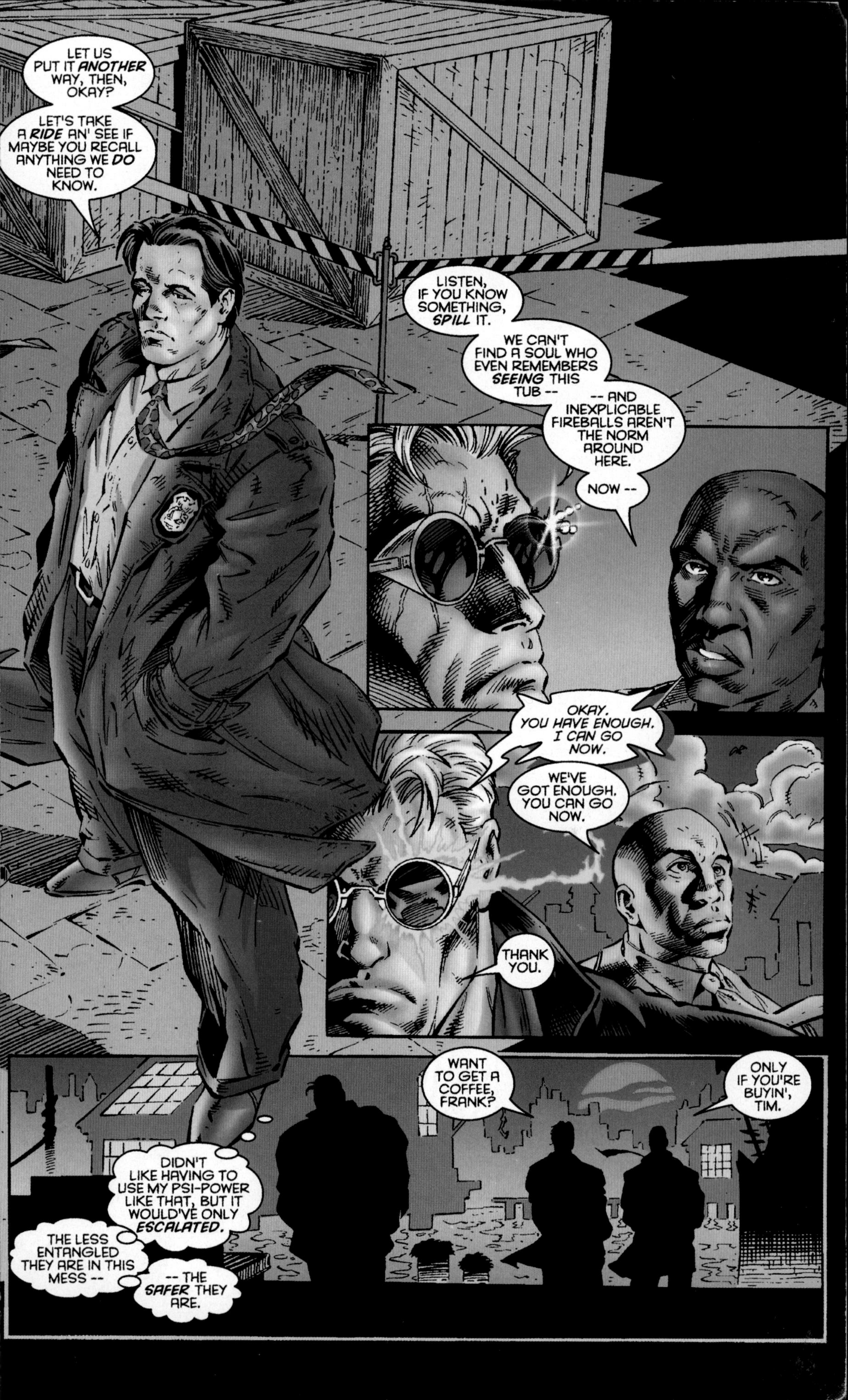
LET US PUT IT ANOTHER WAY, THEN, OKAY?
LET'S TAKE A RIDE AN' SEE IF MAYBE YOU RECALL ANYTHING WE DO NEED TO KNOW.
LISTEN, IF YOU KNOW SOMETHING, SPILL IT.
WE CAN'T FIND A SOUL WHO EVEN REMEMBERS SEEING THIS TUB --
-- AND INEXPLICABLE FIREBALLS AREN'T THE NORM AROUND HERE.
NOW --
OKAY. YOU HAVE ENOUGH. I CAN GO NOW.
WE'VE GOT ENOUGH. YOU CAN GO NOW.
THANK YOU.
WANT TO GET A COFFEE, FRANK?
ONLY IF YOU'RE BUYIN', TIM.
DIDN'T LIKE HAVING TO USE MY PSI-POWER LIKE THAT, BUT IT WOULD'VE ONLY ESCALATED.
THE LESS ENTANGLED THEY ARE IN THIS MESS --
-- THE SAFER THEY ARE.

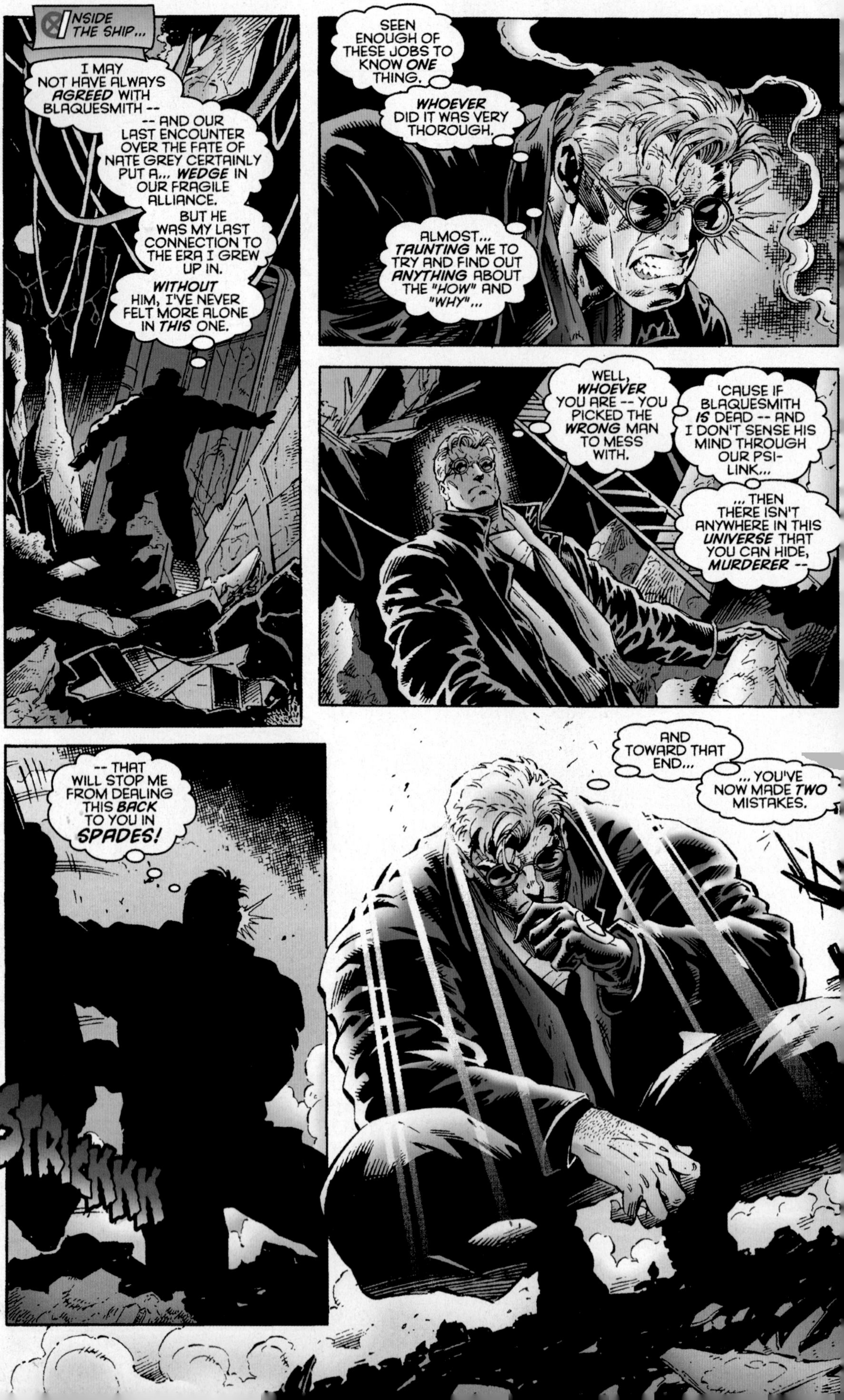
INSIDE THE SHIP...
I MAY NOT HAVE ALWAYS AGREED WITH BLAQUESMITH --
-- AND OUR LAST ENCOUNTER OVER THE FATE OF NATE GREY CERTAINLY PUT A... WEDGE IN OUR FRAGILE ALLIANCE.
BUT HE WAS MY LAST CONNECTION TO THE ERA I GREW UP IN.
WITHOUT HIM, I'VE NEVER FELT MORE ALONE IN THIS ONE.
SEEN ENOUGH OF THESE JOBS TO KNOW ONE THING.
WHOEVER DID IT WAS VERY THOROUGH.
ALMOST... TAUNTING ME TO TRY AND FIND OUT ANYTHING ABOUT THE "HOW" AND "WHY"...
WELL, WHOEVER YOU ARE -- YOU PICKED THE WRONG MAN TO MESS WITH.
'CAUSE IF BLAQUESMITH IS DEAD -- AND I DON'T SENSE HIS MIND THROUGH OUR PSI-LINK...
... THEN THERE ISN'T ANYWHERE IN THIS UNIVERSE THAT YOU CAN HIDE, MURDERER --
-- THAT WILL STOP ME FROM DEALING THIS BACK TO YOU IN SPADES!
STRIKKKK
AND TOWARD THAT END...
... YOU'VE NOW MADE TWO MISTAKES.

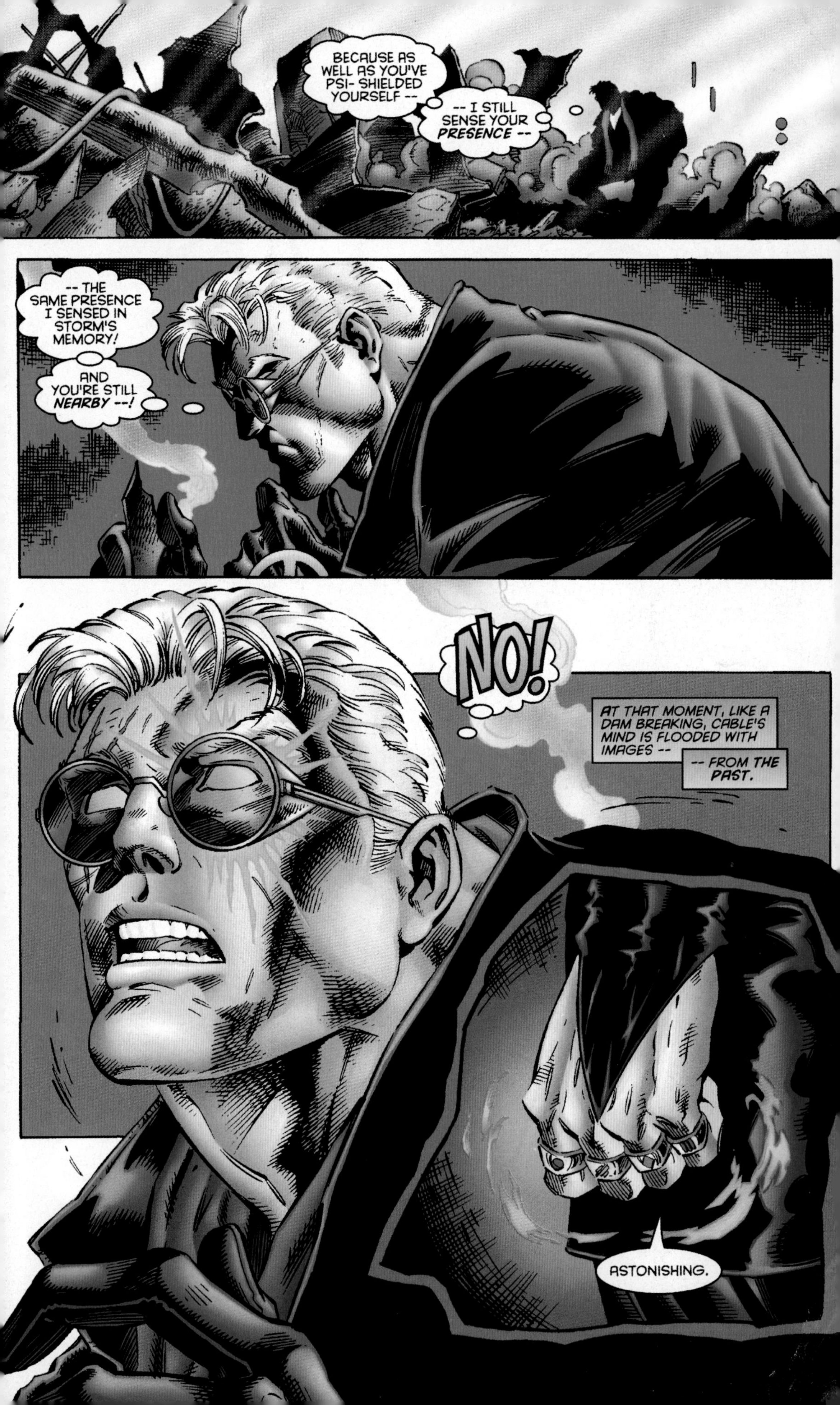

BECAUSE AS WELL AS YOU'VE PSI- SHIELDED YOURSELF --
-- I STILL SENSE YOUR PRESENCE --
-- THE SAME PRESENCE I SENSED IN STORM'S MEMORY!
AND YOU'RE STILL NEARBY --!
NO!
AT THAT MOMENT, LIKE A DAM BREAKING, CABLE'S MIND IS FLOODED WITH IMAGES --
-- FROM THE PAST.
ASTONISHING.

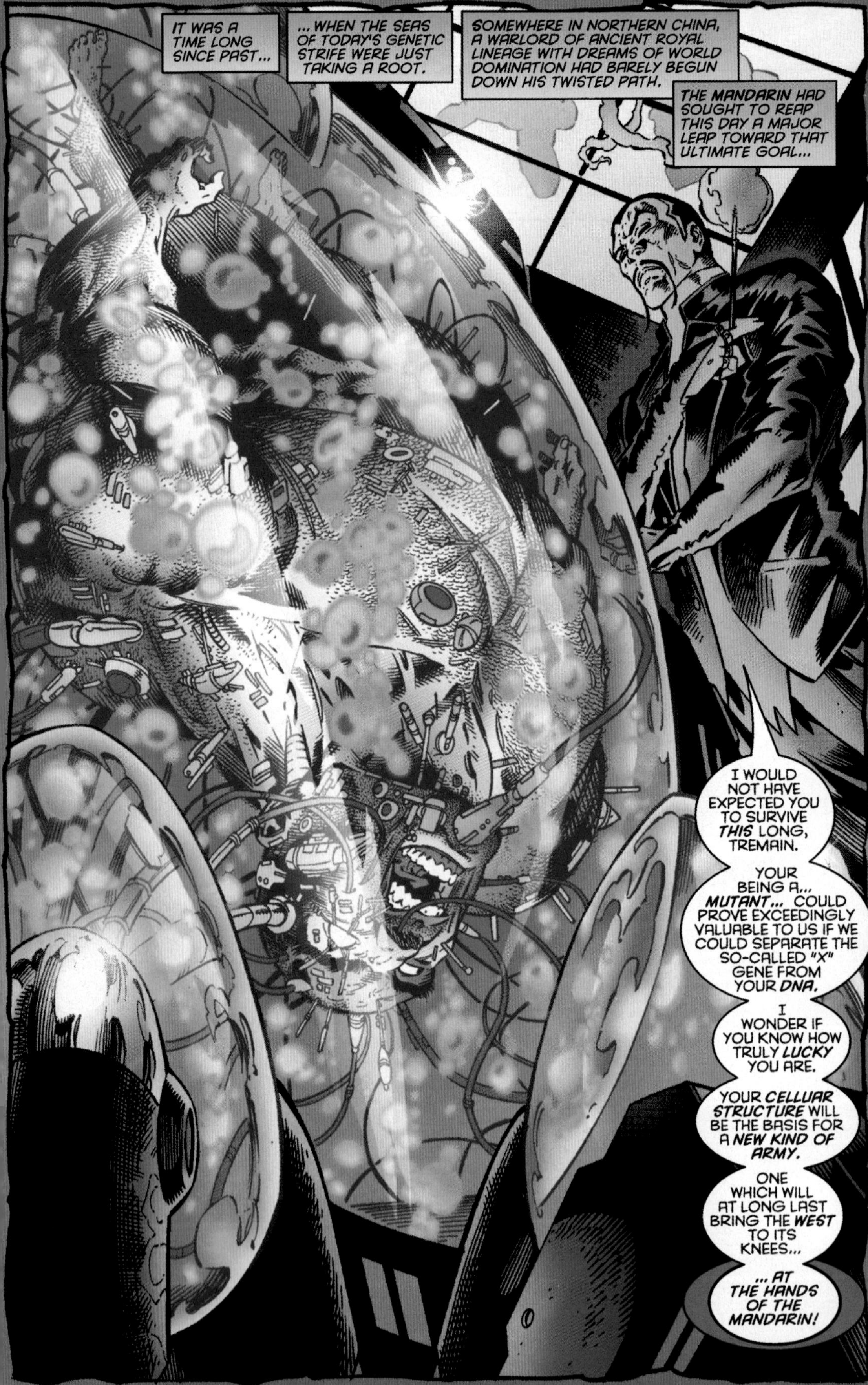
IT WAS A TIME LONG SINCE PAST...
...WHEN THE SEAS OF TODAY'S GENETIC STRIFE WERE JUST TAKING A ROOT.
SOMEWHERE IN NORTHERN CHINA, A WARLORD OF ANCIENT ROYAL LINEAGE WITH DREAMS OF WORLD DOMINATION HAD BARELY BEGUN DOWN HIS TWISTED PATH.
THE MANDARIN HAD SOUGHT TO REAP THIS DAY A MAJOR LEAP TOWARD THAT ULTIMATE GOAL...
I WOULD NOT HAVE EXPECTED YOU TO SURVIVE THIS LONG, TREMAIN.
YOUR BEING A... MUTANT... COULD PROVE EXCEEDINGLY VALUABLE TO US IF WE COULD SEPARATE THE SO-CALLED "X" GENE FROM YOUR DNA.
I WONDER IF YOU KNOW HOW TRULY LUCKY YOU ARE.
YOUR CELLUAR STRUCTURE WILL BE THE BASIS FOR A NEW KIND OF ARMY.
ONE WHICH WILL AT LONG LAST BRING THE WEST TO ITS KNEES...
...AT THE HANDS OF THE MANDARIN!

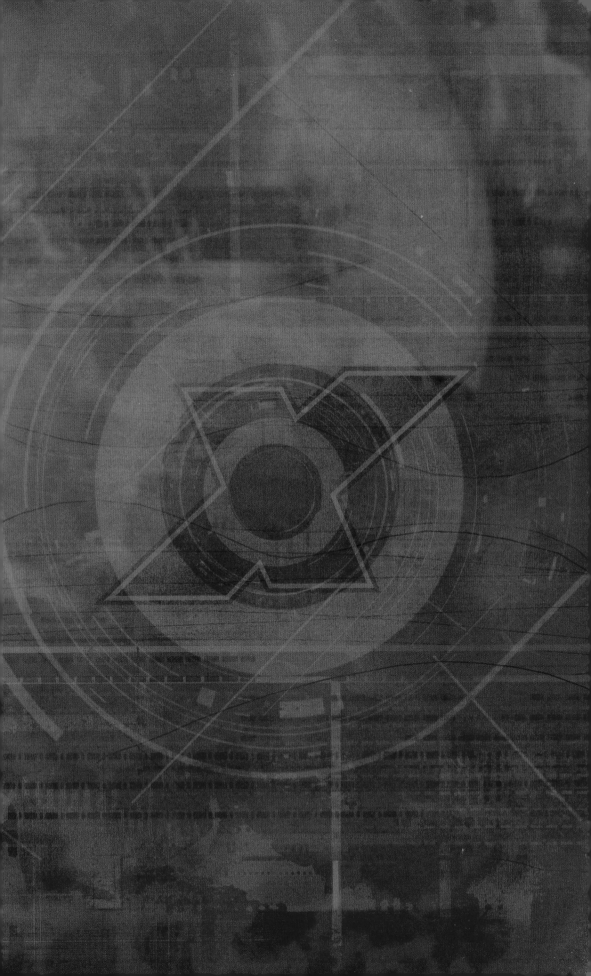

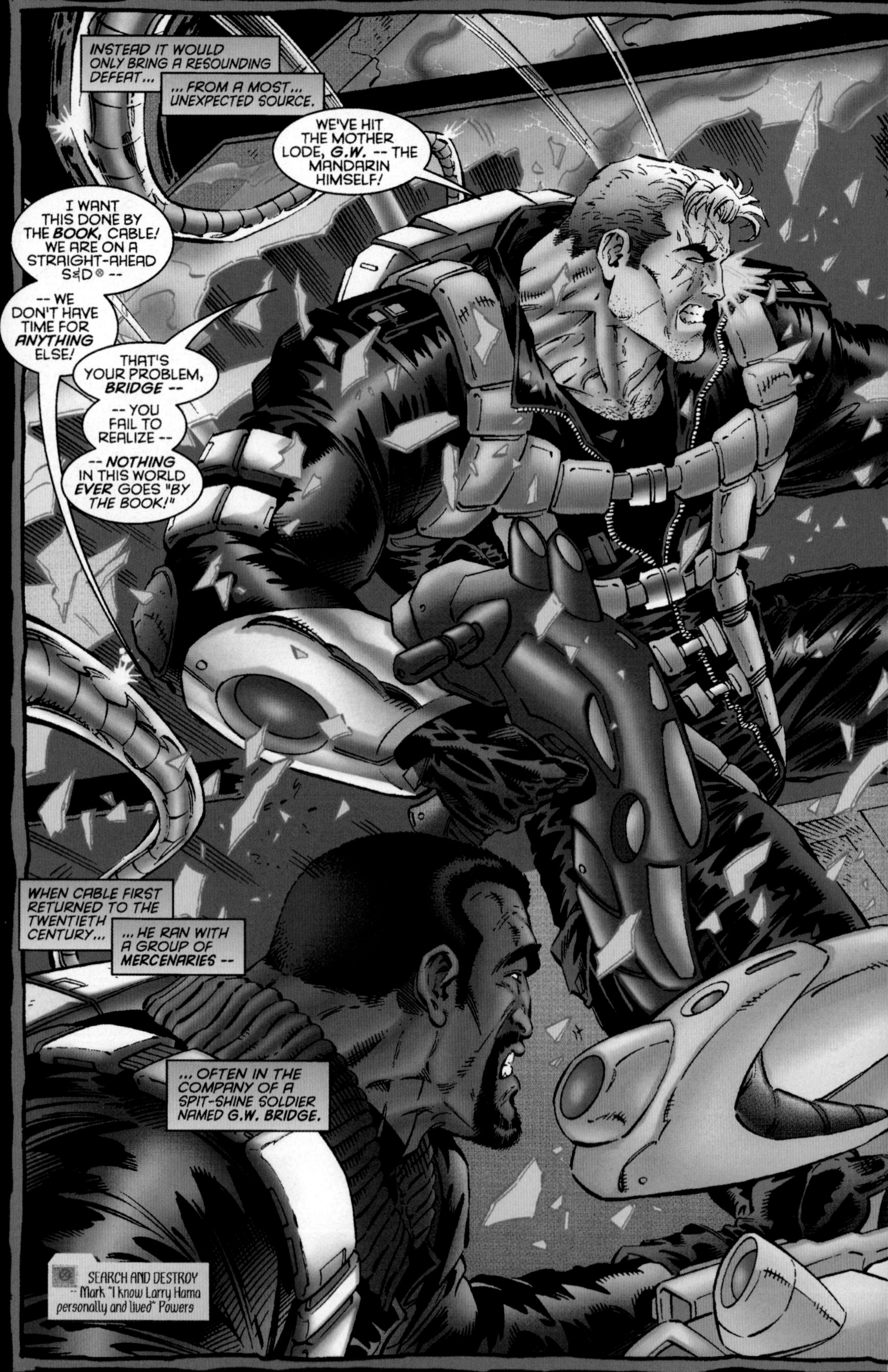
INSTEAD IT WOULD ONLY BRING A RESOUNDING DEFEAT...
...FROM A MOST... UNEXPECTED SOURCE.
WE'VE HIT THE MOTHER LODE, G.W. -- THE MANDARIN HIMSELF!
I WANT THIS DONE BY THE BOOK, CABLE! WE ARE ON A STRAIGHT-AHEAD S&D⊗ --
-- WE DON'T HAVE TIME FOR ANYTHING ELSE!
THAT'S YOUR PROBLEM, BRIDGE --
-- YOU FAIL TO REALIZE --
-- NOTHING IN THIS WORLD EVER GOES "BY THE BOOK!"
WHEN CABLE FIRST RETURNED TO THE TWENTIETH CENTURY...
...HE RAN WITH A GROUP OF MERCENARIES --
...OFTEN IN THE COMPANY OF A SPIT-SHINE SOLDIER NAMED G.W. BRIDGE.
⊗ SEARCH AND DESTROY -- Mark "I know Larry Hama personally and lived" Powers

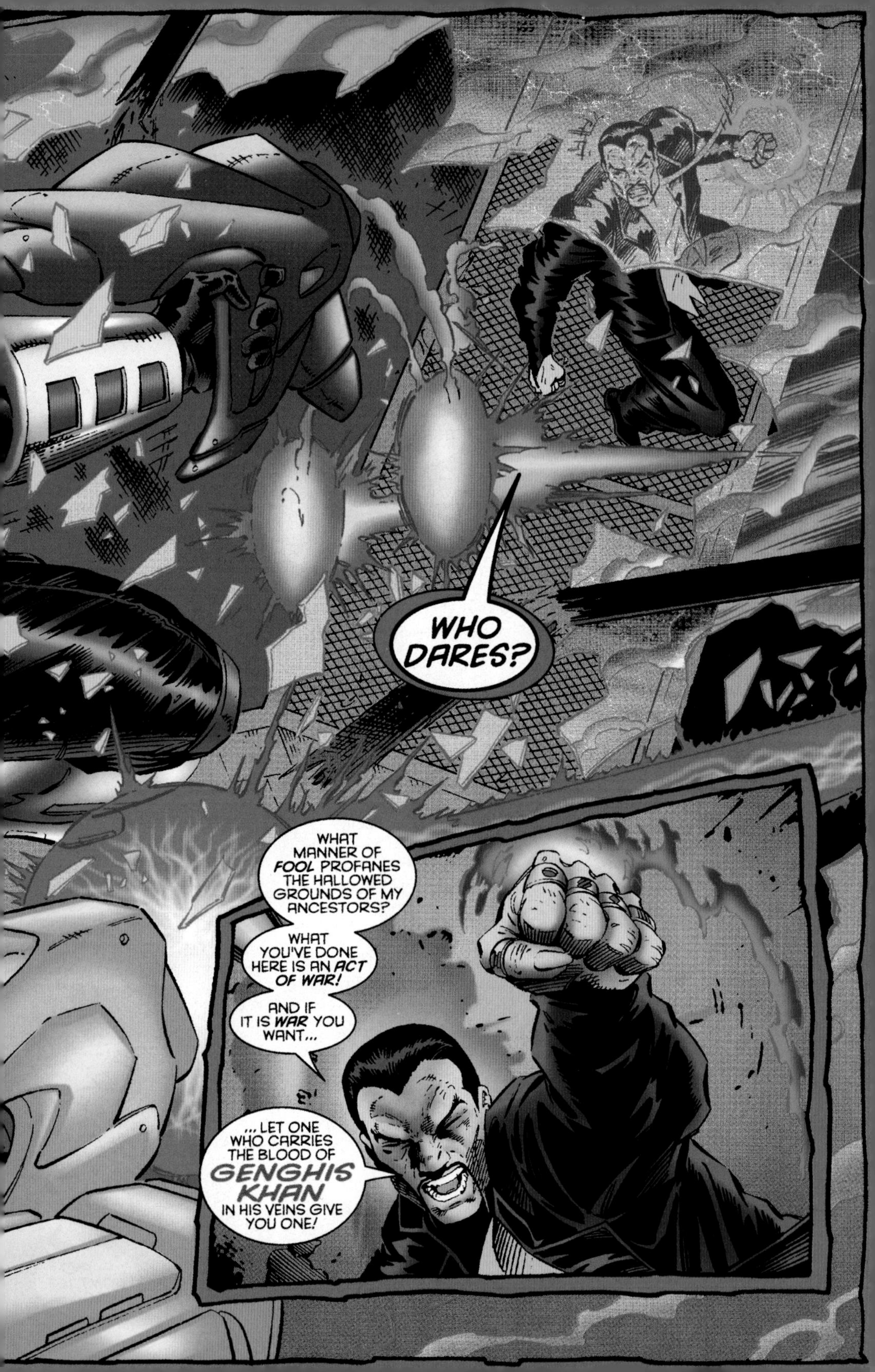
WHO DARES?
WHAT MANNER OF FOOL PROFANES THE HALLOWED GROUNDS OF MY ANCESTORS?
WHAT YOU'VE DONE HERE IS AN ACT OF WAR!
AND IF IT IS WAR YOU WANT...
...LET ONE WHO CARRIES THE BLOOD OF GENGHIS KHAN IN HIS VEINS GIVE YOU ONE!

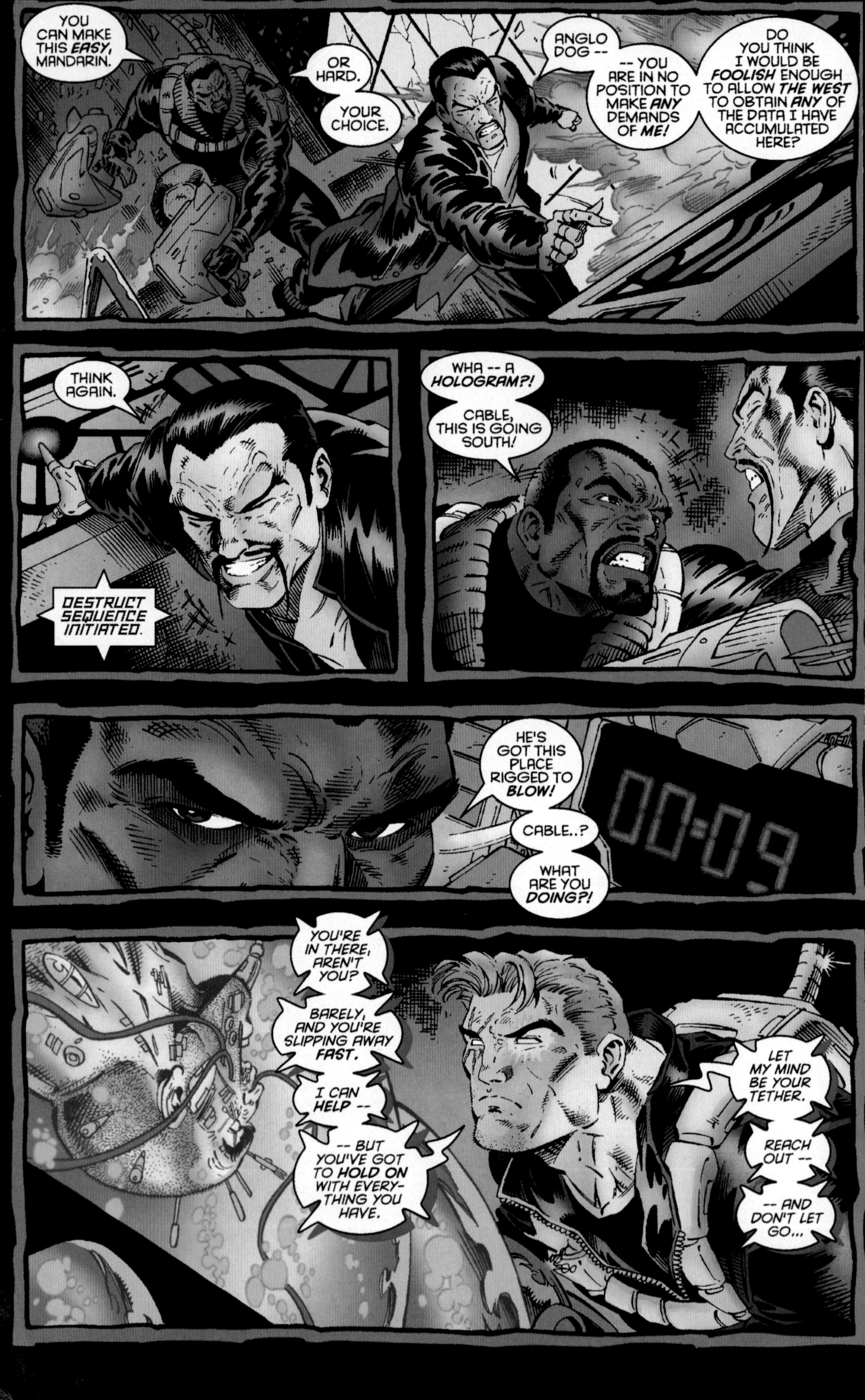

YOU CAN MAKE THIS EASY, MANDARIN.
OR HARD.
YOUR CHOICE.
ANGLO DOG --
-- YOU ARE IN NO POSITION TO MAKE ANY DEMANDS OF ME!
DO YOU THINK I WOULD BE FOOLISH ENOUGH TO ALLOW THE WEST TO OBTAIN ANY OF THE DATA I HAVE ACCUMULATED HERE?
THINK AGAIN.
DESTRUCT SEQUENCE INITIATED.
WHA -- A HOLOGRAM?!
CABLE, THIS IS GOING SOUTH!
HE'S GOT THIS PLACE RIGGED TO BLOW!
00:09
CABLE..?
WHAT ARE YOU DOING?!
YOU'RE IN THERE, AREN'T YOU?
BARELY, AND YOU'RE SLIPPING AWAY FAST.
I CAN HELP --
-- BUT YOU'VE GOT TO HOLD ON WITH EVERY-THING YOU HAVE.
LET MY MIND BE YOUR TETHER.
REACH OUT --
-- AND DON'T LET GO...

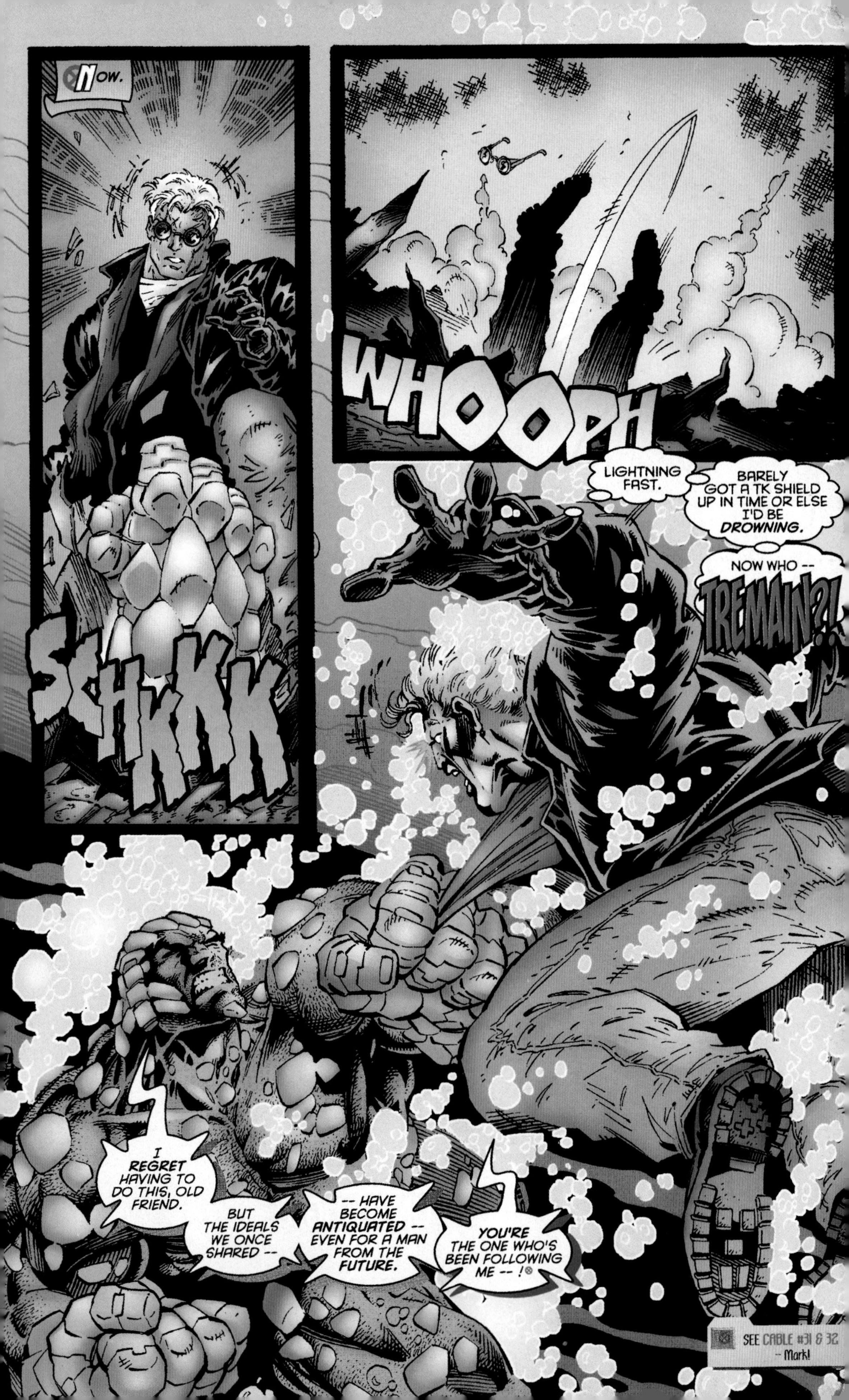
NOW.
SCHKKK
WHOOPH
LIGHTNING FAST.
BARELY GOT A TK SHIELD UP IN TIME OR ELSE I'D BE DROWNING.
NOW WHO --
TREMAIN?!
I REGRET HAVING TO DO THIS, OLD FRIEND.
BUT THE IDEALS WE ONCE SHARED --
-- HAVE BECOME ANTIQUATED -- EVEN FOR A MAN FROM THE FUTURE.
YOU'RE THE ONE WHO'S BEEN FOLLOWING ME -- !
SEE CABLE #31 & 32 -- Mark!

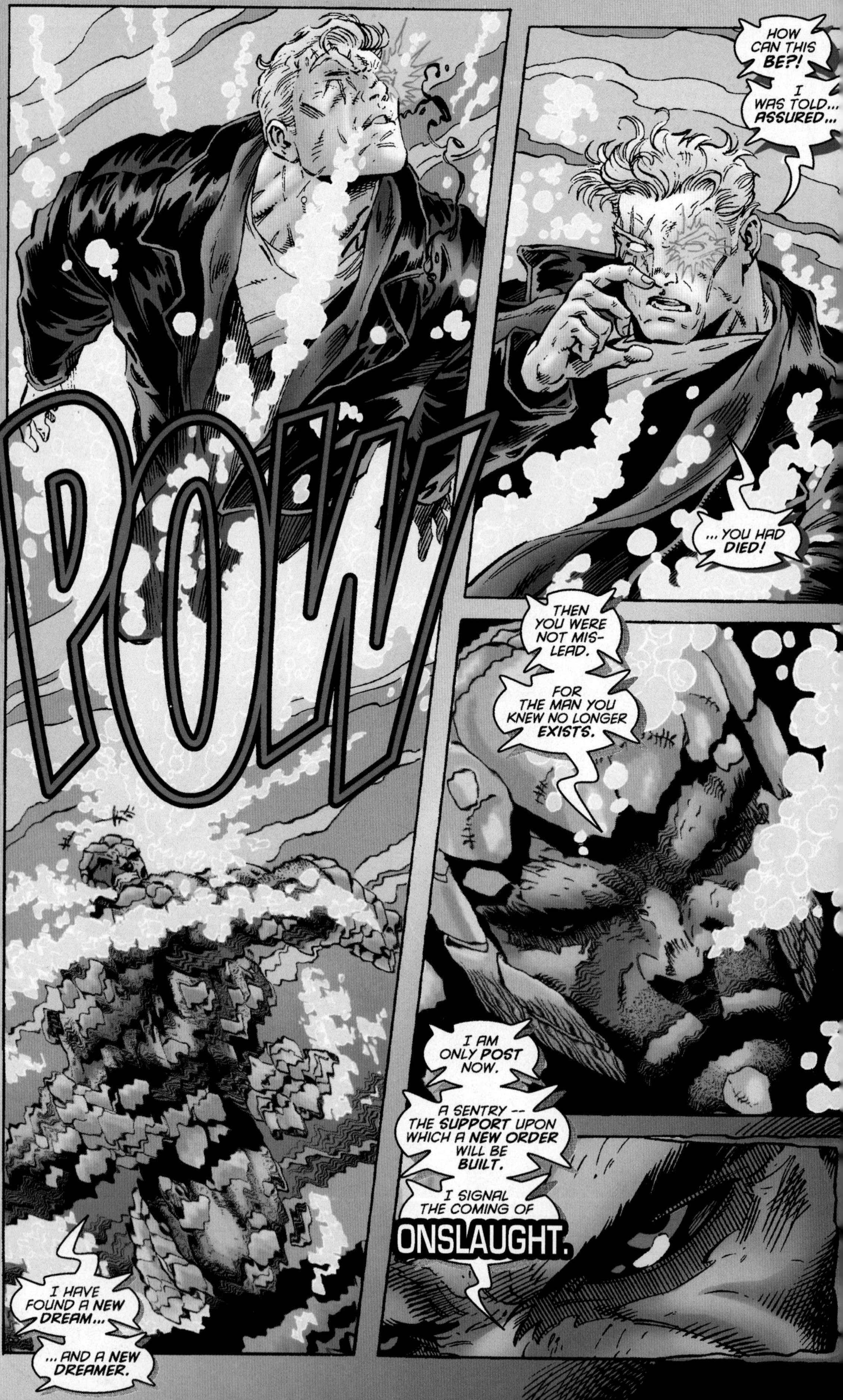
POW
HOW CAN THIS BE?!
I WAS TOLD... ASSURED...
...YOU HAD DIED!
THEN YOU WERE NOT MIS-LEAD.
FOR THE MAN YOU KNEW NO LONGER EXISTS.
I HAVE FOUND A NEW DREAM...
...AND A NEW DREAMER.
I AM ONLY POST NOW.
A SENTRY -- THE SUPPORT UPON WHICH A NEW ORDER WILL BE BUILT.
I SIGNAL THE COMING OF
ONSLAUGHT.

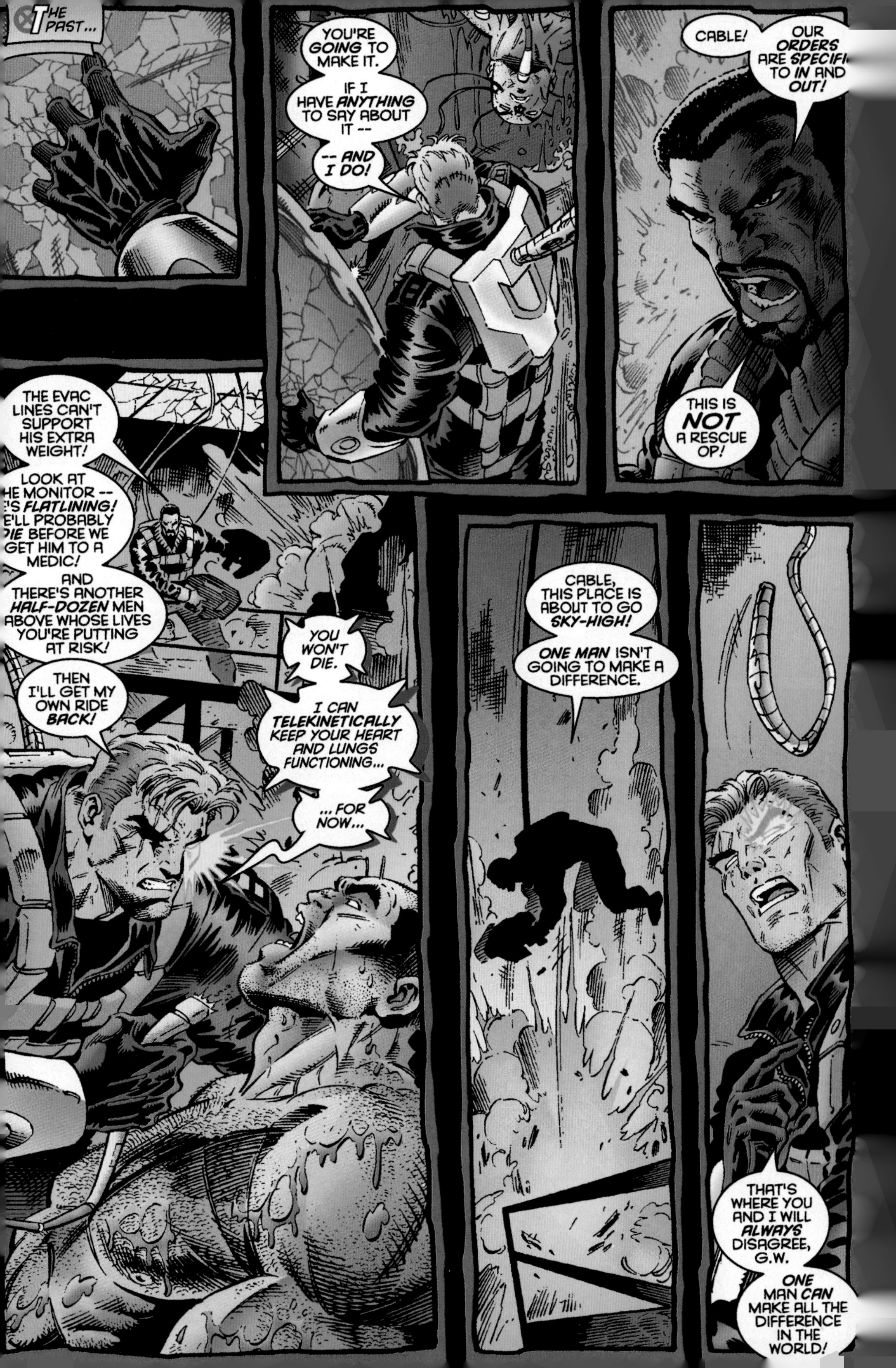

THE PAST...
YOU'RE GOING TO MAKE IT.
IF I HAVE ANYTHING TO SAY ABOUT IT --
-- AND I DO!
CABLE!
OUR ORDERS ARE SPECIFI TO IN AND OUT!
THIS IS NOT A RESCUE OP!
THE EVAC LINES CAN'T SUPPORT HIS EXTRA WEIGHT!
LOOK AT HE MONITOR -- 'S FLATLINING! 'LL PROBABLY DIE BEFORE WE GET HIM TO A MEDIC!
AND THERE'S ANOTHER HALF-DOZEN MEN ABOVE WHOSE LIVES YOU'RE PUTTING AT RISK!
THEN I'LL GET MY OWN RIDE BACK!
YOU WON'T DIE.
I CAN TELEKINETICALLY KEEP YOUR HEART AND LUNGS FUNCTIONING...
...FOR NOW...
CABLE, THIS PLACE IS ABOUT TO GO SKY-HIGH!
ONE MAN ISN'T GOING TO MAKE A DIFFERENCE.
THAT'S WHERE YOU AND I WILL ALWAYS DISAGREE, G.W.
ONE MAN CAN MAKE ALL THE DIFFERENCE IN THE WORLD!

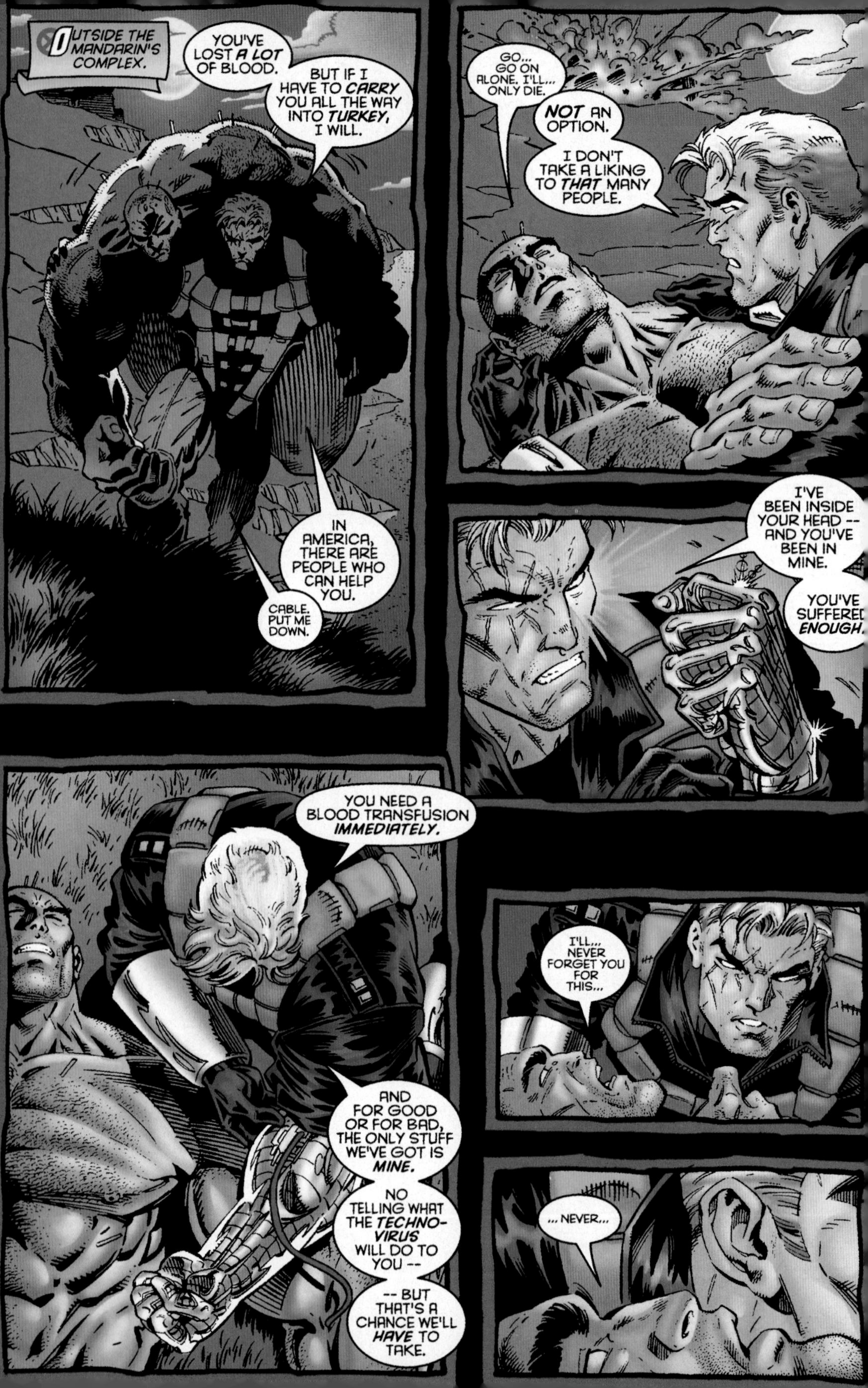
OUTSIDE THE MANDARIN'S COMPLEX.
YOU'VE LOST A LOT OF BLOOD.
BUT IF I HAVE TO CARRY YOU ALL THE WAY INTO TURKEY, I WILL.
IN AMERICA, THERE ARE PEOPLE WHO CAN HELP YOU.
CABLE. PUT ME DOWN.
GO... GO ON ALONE. I'LL... ONLY DIE.
NOT AN OPTION.
I DON'T TAKE A LIKING TO THAT MANY PEOPLE.
I'VE BEEN INSIDE YOUR HEAD -- AND YOU'VE BEEN IN MINE.
YOU'VE SUFFERED ENOUGH.
YOU NEED A BLOOD TRANSFUSION IMMEDIATELY.
AND FOR GOOD OR FOR BAD, THE ONLY STUFF WE'VE GOT IS MINE.
NO TELLING WHAT THE TECHNO-VIRUS WILL DO TO YOU --
-- BUT THAT'S A CHANCE WE'LL HAVE TO TAKE.
I'LL... NEVER FORGET YOU FOR THIS...
... NEVER...

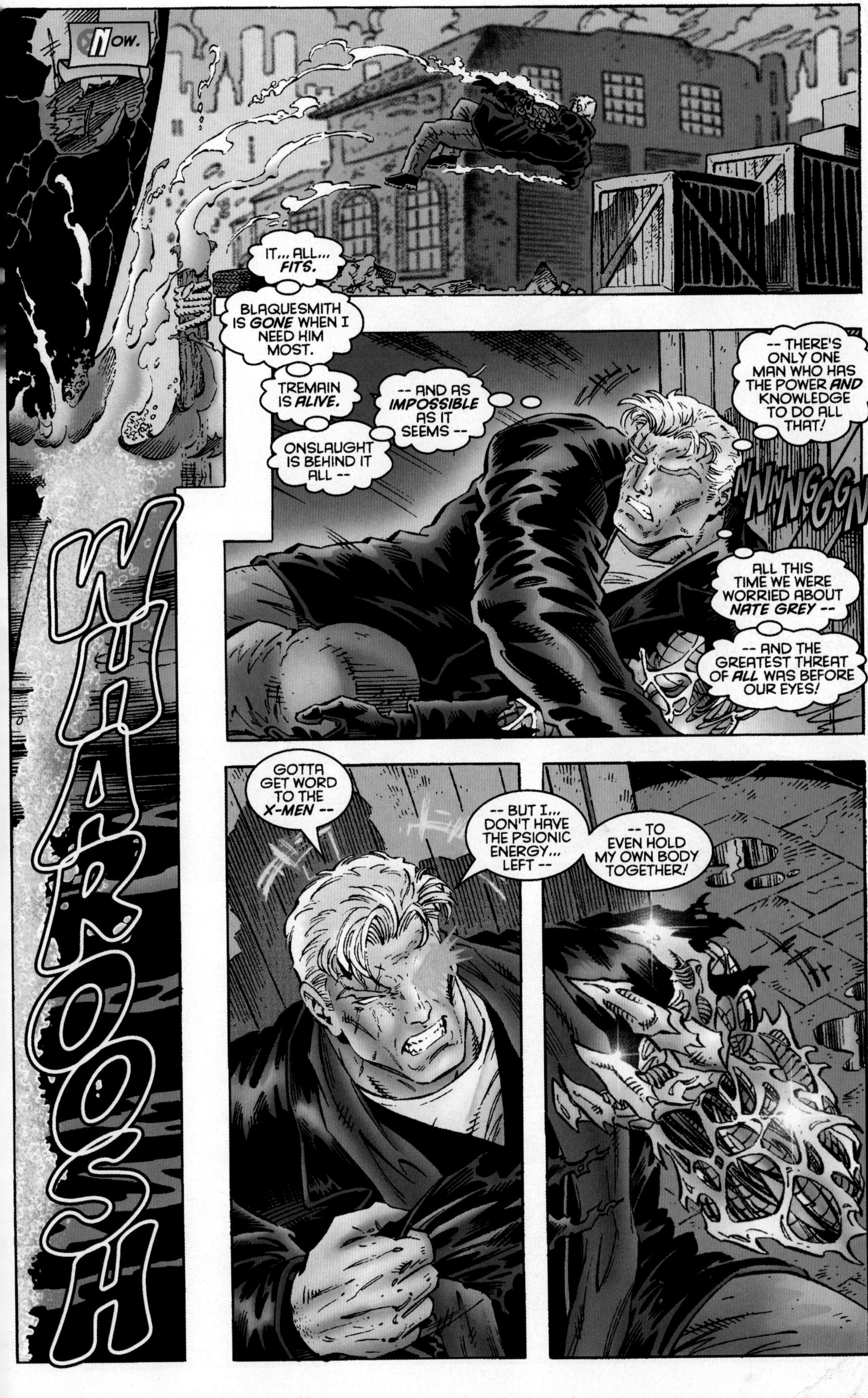
NOW.
IT... ALL... FITS.
BLAQUESMITH IS GONE WHEN I NEED HIM MOST.
TREMAIN IS ALIVE.
ONSLAUGHT IS BEHIND IT ALL --
-- AND AS IMPOSSIBLE AS IT SEEMS --
-- THERE'S ONLY ONE MAN WHO HAS THE POWER AND KNOWLEDGE TO DO ALL THAT!
NNNNGGGN
ALL THIS TIME WE WERE WORRIED ABOUT NATE GREY --
-- AND THE GREATEST THREAT OF ALL WAS BEFORE OUR EYES!
WHAROOSH
GOTTA GET WORD TO THE X-MEN --
-- BUT I... DON'T HAVE THE PSIONIC ENERGY... LEFT --
-- TO EVEN HOLD MY OWN BODY TOGETHER!

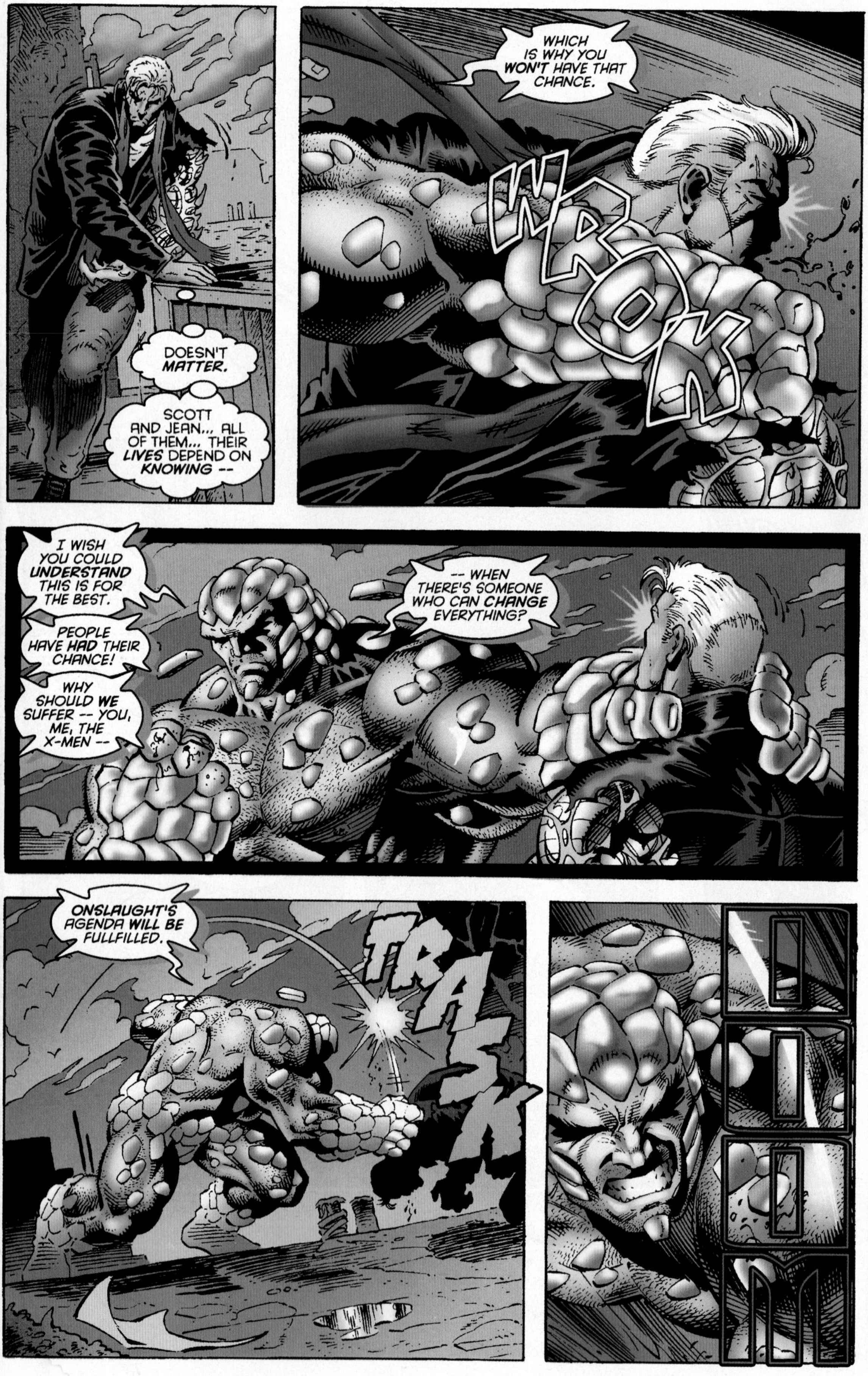
DOESN'T MATTER.
SCOTT AND JEAN... ALL OF THEM... THEIR LIVES DEPEND ON KNOWING --
WHICH IS WHY YOU WON'T HAVE THAT CHANCE.
WRONK
I WISH YOU COULD UNDERSTAND THIS IS FOR THE BEST.
PEOPLE HAVE HAD THEIR CHANCE!
WHY SHOULD WE SUFFER -- YOU, ME, THE X-MEN --
-- WHEN THERE'S SOMEONE WHO CAN CHANGE EVERYTHING?
ONSLAUGHT'S AGENDA WILL BE FULLFILLED.
TRASK

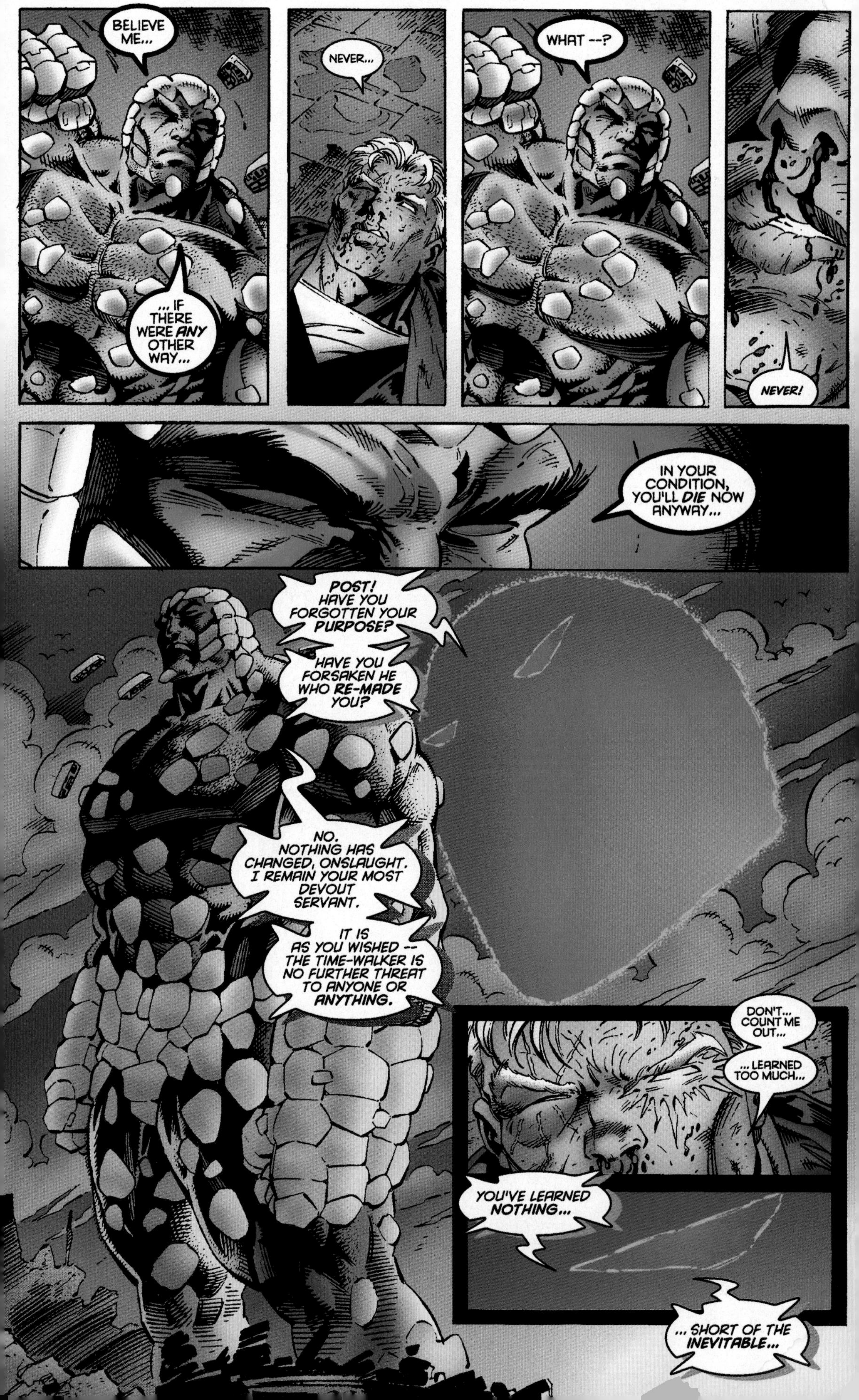
BELIEVE ME...
...IF THERE WERE ANY OTHER WAY...
NEVER...
WHAT --?
NEVER!
IN YOUR CONDITION, YOU'LL DIE NOW ANYWAY...
POST! HAVE YOU FORGOTTEN YOUR PURPOSE?
HAVE YOU FORSAKEN HE WHO RE-MADE YOU?
NO. NOTHING HAS CHANGED, ONSLAUGHT. I REMAIN YOUR MOST DEVOUT SERVANT.
IT IS AS YOU WISHED -- THE TIME-WALKER IS NO FURTHER THREAT TO ANYONE OR ANYTHING.
DON'T... COUNT ME OUT...
...LEARNED TOO MUCH...
YOU'VE LEARNED NOTHING...
...SHORT OF THE INEVITABLE...

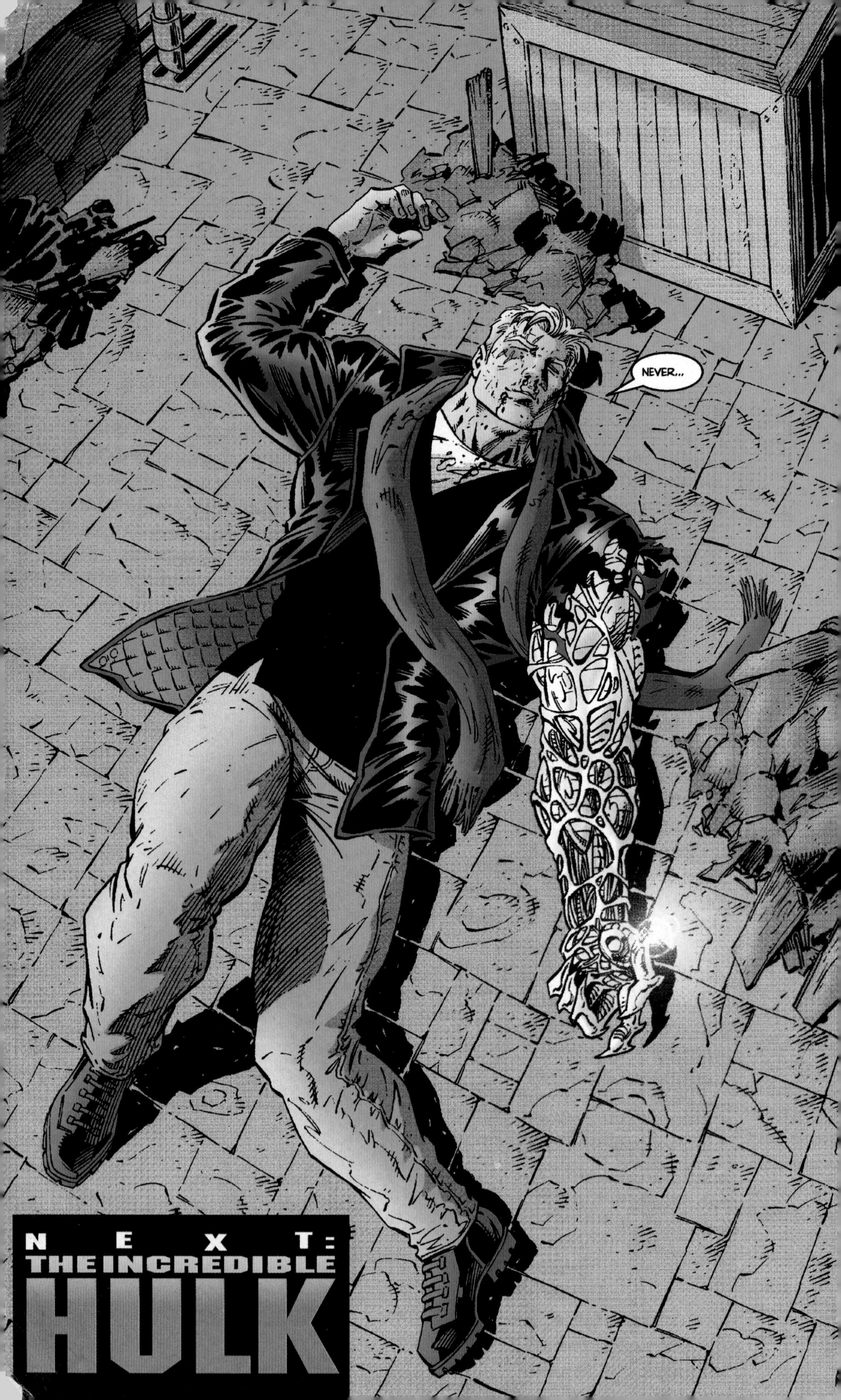
NEVER...
NEXT: THE INCREDIBLE HULK

Will Cable, battered and half-dead, be able to alert the X-Men to his hard-won revelation in time? Can Nate Grey convince the Avengers of the looming threat posed by Onslaught? Will the Juggernaut escape his extradimensional prison and alert Psylocke and Archangel of the coming attack? Does Apocalypse's empty tomb mean what the X-Men fear it does? And how will Joseph's arrival, the Dark Beast's sinister presence, and Wolverine's newly devolved state have on the X-Men as they attempt to stand against Onslaught's carefully laid plans?

The survival of the X-Men, and the entire Marvel Universe, is very much in doubt. Only one thing remains certain: Onslaught is everywhere... and no one is safe.

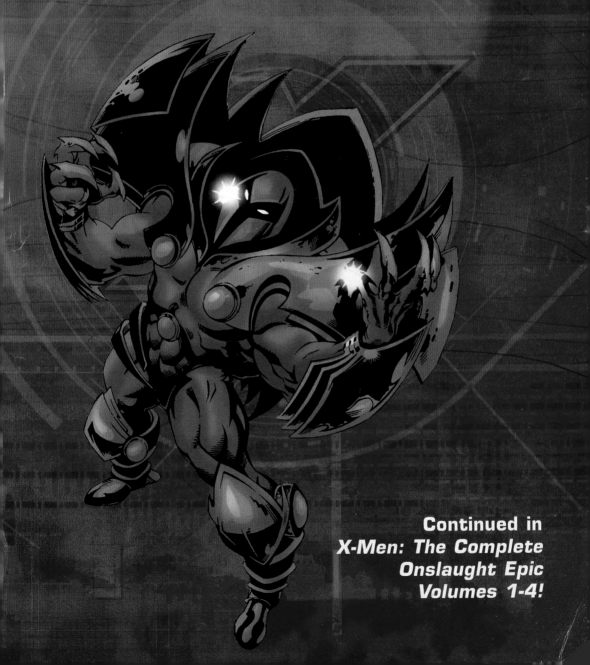

Continued in
*X-Men: The Complete
Onslaught Epic
Volumes 1-4!*

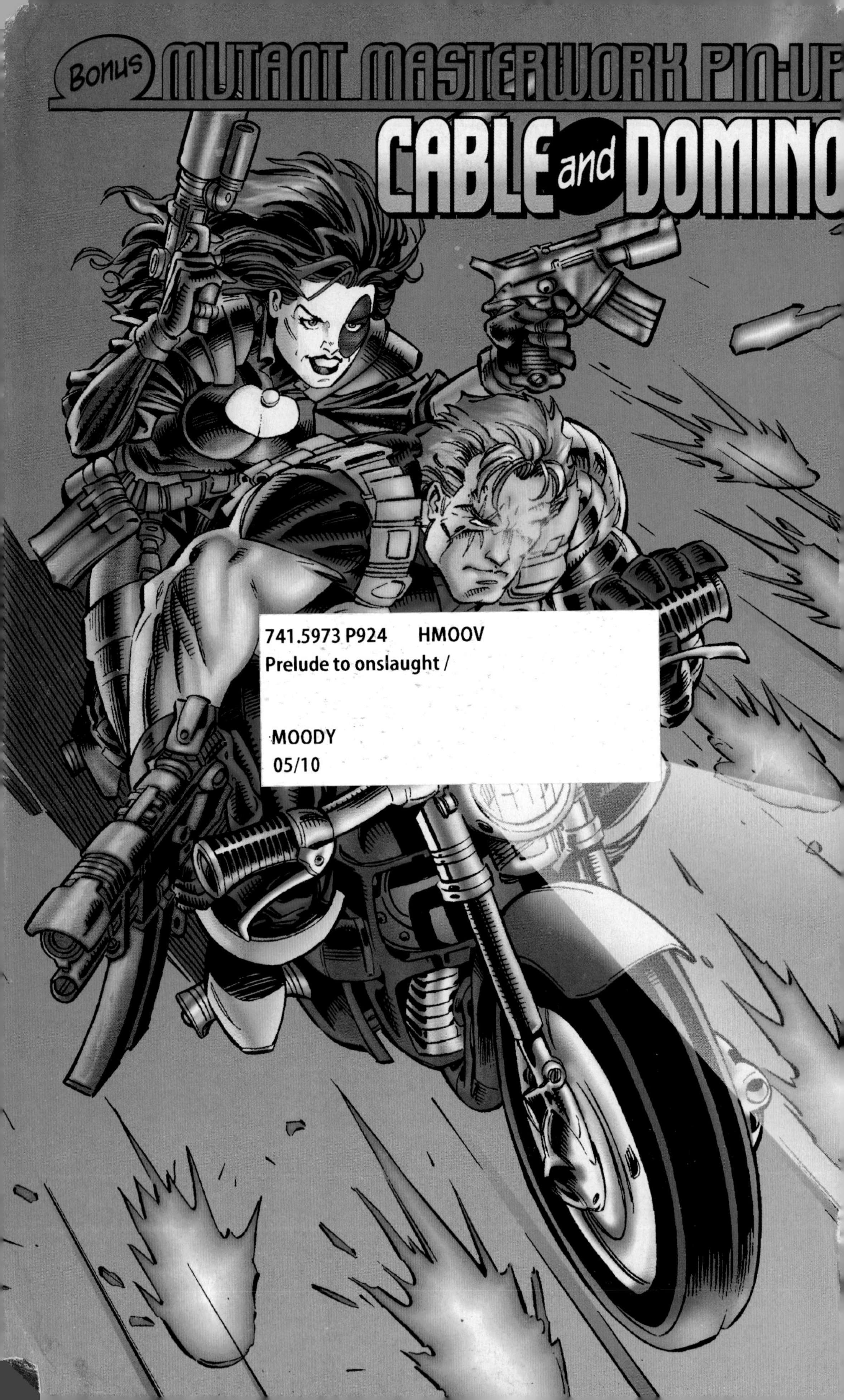
Bonus
MUTANT MASTERWORK PIN-UP
CABLE and DOMINO